AF673361

THE SKANDA-PURĀṆA

Translated and Annotated by

Dr. G.V. TAGARE

PART X

MOTILAL BANARSIDASS PUBLISHERS
PRIVATE LIMITED • DELHI

First Edition: Delhi, 1996

© MOTILAL BANARSIDASS PUBLISHERS PRIVATE LIMITED
All Rights Reserved

ISBN: 81-208-1364-2

Also available at:

MOTILAL BANARSIDASS
41 U.A. Bungalow Road, Jawahar Nagar, Delhi 110 007
8, Mahalaxmi Chamber, Warden Road, Mumbai 400 026
120 Royapettah High Road, Mylapore, Madras 600 004
Sanas Plaza, Subhash Nagar, Pune 411 002
16 St. Mark's Road, Bangalore 560 001
8 Camac Street, Calcutta 700 017
Ashok Rajpath, Patna 800 004
Chowk, Varanasi 221 001

UNESCO COLLECTION OF REPRESENTATIVE WORKS—Indian Series
This book has been accepted in the Indian Translation Series of the UNESCO Collection of Representative Works, jointly sponsored by the United Nations Educational, Scientific and Cultural Organization (UNESCO) and the Government of India.

PRINTED IN INDIA
BY JAINENDRA PRAKASH JAIN AT SHRI JAINENDRA PRESS,
A-45 NARAINA, PHASE I, NEW DELHI 110 028
AND PUBLISHED BY NARENDRA PRAKASH JAIN FOR
MOTILAL BANARSIDASS PUBLISHERS PRIVATE LIMITED,
BUNGALOW ROAD, DELHI 110 007

PUBLISHER'S NOTE

The purest gems lie hidden in the bottom of the ocean or in the depth of rocks. One has to dive into the ocean or delve into the rocks to find them out. Similarly, truth lies concealed in the language which with the passage of time has become obsolete. Man has to learn that language before he discovers that truth.

But he has neither the means nor the leisure to embark on that course. We have, therefore, planned to help him acquire knowledge by an easier course. We have started the series of Ancient Indian Tradition and Mythology in English Translation. Our goal is to universalize knowledge through the most popular international medium of expression. The publication of the Purāṇas in English Translation is a step towards that goal.

Acknowledgements

It is our pleasant duty to put on record our sincere thanks to Dr. R.N. Dandekar and the UNESCO authorities for their kind encouragement and valuable help in the publication of the volumes in this series.

PUBLISHER'S NOTE

The purest gems lie hidden in the bottom of the ocean or in the depth of rocks. One has to dive into the ocean or delve into the rocks to find them out. Similarly, truth lies concealed in the language which with the passage of time has become obsolete. Man has to learn that language before he discovers that truth.

But he has neither the means nor the leisure to embark on that course. We have, therefore, planned to help him acquire knowledge by an easier course. We have started the series of Ancient Indian Tradition and Mythology in English Translation. Our goal is to universalize knowledge through the most popular international medium of expression. The publication of the Purāṇas in English translation is a step towards that goal.

—

Acknowledgement

It is our pleasant duty to put on record our sincere thanks to Dr. R.N. Dandekar and the UNESCO authorities for their kind encouragement and valuable help in the publication of the volume in this series.

CONTENTS

SKANDA PURĀṆA
BOOK IV: KĀŚĪ-KHAṆḌA
SECTION I: PŪRVĀRDHA

ABBREVIATIONS

Common and self-evident abbreviations such as Ch(s)—Chapter(s), p—page, pp—pages, v—verse, vv—verses, Ftn—Footnote, Hist. Ind. Philo.—History of Indian Philosophy are not included in this list.

AGP	S.M. Ali's *The Geography of Purāṇas*, PPH, New Delhi, 1973
AIHT	*Ancient Indian Historical Tradition*, F.E. Pargiter, Motilal Banarsidass (MLBD), Delhi
AITM	*Ancient Indian Tradition and Mythology* Series, MLBD, Delhi
AP	*Agni Purāṇa*, Guru Mandal Edition (GM), Calcutta, 1957
AV	*Atharva Veda*, Svādhyāya Maṇḍal, Aundh
BdP	*Brahmāṇḍa Purāṇa*, MLBD, Delhi, 1973
BG	*Bhagavadgītā*
BhP	*Bhāgavata Purāṇa*, Bhagavat Vidyapeeth, Ahmedabad
Br	*Brāhmaṇa* (preceded by name such as Śatapatha)
BsP	*Bhaviṣya Purāṇa*, Vishnu Shastri Bapat, Wai
BVP	*Brahma Vaivarta Purāṇa*, GM, 1955-57
CC	*Caturvarga Cintāmaṇi* by Hemādri
CVS	*Caraṇa Vyūha Sūtra* by Śaunaka, Com. by Mahīdāsa
DB	*Devī Bhāgavata*, GM, 1960-61
De or GDAMI	*The Geographical Dictionary of Ancient and Mediaeval India*, N.L. De/Dey, Oriental Reprint, Delhi, 1971
DhS	*Dharma Sūtra* (preceded by the author's name such as Gautama)
GP	*Garuḍa Purāṇa*, ed. R.S. Bhattacharya, Chowkhamba, Varanasi, 1964
GS	*Gṛhya Sūtra* (preceded by the name of the author such as Āpastamba)
HD	*History of Dharma Śāstra*, P.V. Kane, G.O.S.
JP	*Purāṇa* (Journal of the Kashiraj Trust), Varanasi
KA	*Kauṭilya Arthaśāstra*
KP	*Kūrma Purāṇa*, Veṅkaṭeśvara Press Edn., Bombay; also Kashiraj Trust Edn., Varanasi, 1971
LP	*Liṅga Purāṇa*, GM, 1960; also MLBD, Delhi, 1981

Manu	*Manusmṛti*
Mbh	*Mahābhārata*, Gītā Press, Gorakhpur, VS 2014
MkP	*Mārkaṇḍeya Purāṇa*
MN	*Mahābhārata Nāmānukramaṇī*, Gītā Press, Gorakhpur, VS 2016
MtP	*Matsya Purāṇa*, GM, 1954
MW	M. Monier-Williams' *Sanskrit-English Dictionary*, MLBD, Delhi, 1976
NP	*Nāradīya* or *Nārada Purāṇa*, Veṅkaṭeśvara Press, Bombay
PdP	*Padma Purāṇa*, GM, 1957-59
PE	*Purāṇic Encyclopaedia,* V. Mani, English Version, MLBD, Delhi, 1975
PR or PRHRC	*Puranic Records on Hindu Rites and Customs*, R.C. Hazra, Calcutta, 1948
ṚV	*Ṛg Veda*, Svādhyāya Maṇḍal, Aundh
Śat Br	*Śatapatha Brāhmaṇa*
SC or SMC	*Smṛti Candrikā* by Devanna Bhaṭṭa
SkP	*Skanda Purāṇa*
SP	*Śiva Purāṇa*
VāP	*Vāyu Purāṇa*
VR	*Vālmīki Rāmāyaṇa*
VdP	*Viṣṇudharmottara Purāṇa*
VmP	*Vāmana Purāṇa*
VP	*Viṣṇu Purāṇa*
VrP	*Varāha Purāṇa*

SKANDA PURĀṆA

BOOK IV: KĀŚĪ-KHAṆḌA

SECTION I: PŪRVĀRDHA

CHAPTER ONE

Increase in the Height of Vindhya[1]

Obeisance to Śrī Gaṇeśa

1. We meditate on that great Lord, the dear son of Maheśāna (Śiva), the Lord of Gaṇas (the attendants Nandin, Bhṛṅgi etc.), whose face resembles that of the leader of a herd of elephants and who is free from ailments.

2. May that Kāśī, the capital city of the enemy of Tripura, protect the universe from ignorance and its consequences—Kāśī which is on the earth yet not on the ground (Kāśī is reputed to be held aloft on the tip of the trident of Śiva), which is far above heaven (in yielding everlasting happiness), though staying below, which is bound to the earth but bestows liberation, wherein the creatures that meet death become immortal and which is always served and attended upon by the Suras on the banks of the river that sanctifies the three worlds (i.e. Gaṅgā).

3. Obeisance to that celebrated Lord of brilliance (the Sun as well as the Absolute Being) around whom the Lords of the three worlds (Brahmā, Viṣṇu and Śiva) move under the pretext of the three joints (dawn, midday and dusk) and carry on their functions (of creation, sustenance and annihilation) for ever.

4. The son of Satyavatī, the composer of the eighteen Purāṇas, recounted to Sūta this holy story that dispels sins.

---

1. Sage Agastya seems to be the first explorer of India to the south of Vindhya. His crossing of the Vindhya mountain is described as the 'subjugation' of Vindhya. The first five chapters of Kāśī Khaṇḍa describe this achievement in mythological terms. This story occurs in Mbh, *Vana*, 104.12-13 and VR 3.11.85.

Śrī Vyāsa said:

5-6. Once, Sage Nārada possessing all Brāhmaṇical powers, took his bath in the sacred waters of Narmadā and worshipped Lord Oṁkāra in the company of Gaurī, who is the bestower of everything on all embodied beings. While proceeding ahead, he saw in front of him Mountain Vindhya washed and sanctified by the waters of Revā, dispelling all possible distresses (in the physical body due to illness, or attack from other living beings or divine intercession) of mundane existence.

Description of Vindhya[1]

7. By means of his two refulgent forms, that of the immobile and that of the mobile (i.e., through precious stones found therein and due to semi-divine beings residing there), he makes Vasumatī (the earth, possessor of treasure of Vasus i.e., gems, fire, rays etc.) true to its name.

8. Through *Rasālas* (mangoes), it is the storehouse of *Rasa* (juice); through *Aśoka* trees it dispels *Śoka* (grief); it is brilliant all round with the trees like *Tāla, Tamāla, Hintāla* and *Sāla.*

9. Due to arecanut trees (*Khapura*), it has (as if) the shape of an ethereal city (*Kha-pura*); with *Śrī-phala* (Bilva) trees it really bestows glory (*Śrī*) as its fruit (that is the mountain appears extremely beautiful with Bilva trees).

Through *Agaru* (fragrant aloewood trees) it has great *Śrī* (brilliance or fragrance); through *Kapitthas* (wood-apple trees) it has the tawny colour of a monkey.

10. It is charming to the mind through *Lakuca* (a kind of bread-fruit tree) that has the shape of the breasts of sylvan deities. It shines with plantain trees laden with nectar-like fruits.

11. It is like the dancing pavilion of Śrī (Lakṣmī) through orange trees of excellent hues. It abounds in *Vānīras* (reeds), *Jambīras* (citrons) and *Bījapūras* (a variety of citron).

12. It appears to be performing *Hallīsaka* (dance in which a single man dances with many women) through the *Kaṁkola*

---

1. VV 7-36 give a beautiful description of the Vindhya mountain. The words used here are pregnant with double meaning and hence it is difficult to comprehend their full implications.

creepers tremulous in the wind. It is, as it were, an abode of gentle, playful dance through the gentle, sportive movements of the creeper *Lavalī*.

13. It appears (as if) to beckon the weary travellers for rest through the gestures of the gently moving leaves of *Karpūrakadalī* (a variety of plantain).

14. It is like an excellent male elephant (or a powerful man) that fondles the breast-like branches of *Mallikā* (jasmine) plant, through the sprouts of *Punnāga* tree that appear like the smooth hands.

15. Through pomegranates burst open, it appears to reveal its heart full of love (red in colour). It appears to embrace the *Mādhavī* creeper in the forest in the form of the husband.

16. It seems that all around it, it holds millions of Cosmic Eggs through the lofty *Udumbaras* shining brilliantly with infinite number of fruits in clusters, like *Ananta* (the infinite one, supreme soul).

17. It is surrounded by *Panasa* (jackfruit) trees that resemble the noses of forest deities and *Palāśa* trees appearing like the nose of a parrot and forsaken by the leaves, because it has (as if) eaten away the flesh of persons in separation.

18. It shines splendidly all around through the group of *Kadambaka* trees that appear to be having the experience of horripilation (due to annoyance) on seeing the *Nīpas* calling themselves *Kadambakas*.

19. It shines with *Nameru* trees having tops as lofty as Meru, as well as *Rājādana* (*Priyāla*) trees and *Madana* (*Dhattūra*) trees resembling abodes of lovers.

20. On every slope there are fascinating *Vaṭa* trees and thus the mountain appears to be surrounded by many lofty tents. With the bunches (of flowers) of *Kuṭaja* tree, it shines as though with cranes perched.

21. With the trees *Karamarda, Karīra, Karañja* and *Karambaka,* it appears like one having a thousand hands, all raised aloft by way of summoning (and receiving) suppliants.

22. With the lustrous *Rājacampaka* buds, it appears to have the waving of lights. With the full-blown *Śālmali* trees, it possesses a lustre that far surpasses the lustre of a lotus lake.

23. It dazzles remarkably with tall *Aśvattha* trees of tremulous

leaves in some places; with golden *Ketaka* trees in some places and with *Kṛtamāla* and *Naktamāla* trees in some places.

24. It remarkably shines with *Karkandhus, Bandhujīvas* and *Putrajīvas* as well as *Tinduka* and *Iṅgudī* trees. With *Karuṇa* trees it is like an abode of pity and sympathy (*Karuṇā*).

25. It appears to always adore Śiva in the form of the Earth-element (one of the eight forms of Śiva) with the pearls dropped from its own hand, through the *Madhūka* flowers that drop down.

26. It appears to be fanned by the trees *Sarja (Śāla), Arjuna, Añjana* and *Bīja*. It has held aloft an umbrella in the sky apparently by means of coconut and date palm trees.

27-28. With lustrous *Picumanda* (Neem tree), *Mandāra, Kovidāra, Pāṭalā, Tintiṇī, Ghoṇṭā, Śākhoṭa* and *Karahāṭaka* too, it appears to be raising aloft an umbrella in the sky.

With the different types of *Śīhuṇḍa, Eraṇḍa, Guḍapuṣpa, Bakula* and *Tilaka*, it looks like one having his forehead marked with *Tilaka* (ritualistic mark).

29. It shines remarkably with *Akṣa, Plakṣa, Śallakī, Devadāru, Haridruma* (and trees, creepers always bearing fruits and flowers such as), *Sadāphala, Sadāpuṣpa* and other trees and creepers.

30. It is covered with the forests of cardamom, cloves, pepper and *Kuluñjana*. It is rendered colourful with *Jambūs, Āmrātakas, Bhallāta, Śelu* and *Śrīparṇī*.

31. It is charming by the forests of *Śāka* (those with leaves rough inside and smooth outside) and *Śaṅkha* and it is embellished by the forests of sandal, red sandal, *Harītakī, Karṇikāra* and *Dhātrī*.

32. It is covered with hundreds of vines of grapes, betel and *Kaṇā*. It is rendered fragrant through *Mallikā, Yūthikā, Kunda* and *Madayantī*.

33. It is embellished with *Mālatī* creepers surrounded by swarms of whirling and hovering bees. Hence, it seems as though Kṛṣṇa has come himself in the guise of the bees in order to have dalliance with the numerous cowherdesses.

34. It is full of different kinds of animals. Many kinds of birds make it noisy. All round there are many rivers, lakes, springs and puddles.

35. It seems occupied by different gods with a desire for complete and all-round enjoyment. They have to come here

after forsaking heavenly regions of insignificant lustre.

36. With leaves and flowers scattered all round, it appears to offer *Arghya* (to the venerable visitor). It seems to welcome (him) from a distance through the cries of peacocks.

37. Then the Mountain too, from a distance, saw Nārada in the firmament. He had the refulgence of hundreds of suns. His garments sparkled. The Mountain advanced forth to greet him.

38. On seeing him arriving, his mental darkness (of ignorance) as well as the darkness of the caves got removed by the brilliance of the body of the son of Brahmā.

39. Though the Mountain was hard, he eschewed the hardness (due to being rocky in nature); he assumed softness because the sense of awe arose in him and due to the spiritual splendour (of Nārada) and because his activities were like those of good people.

40. On seeing the softness (of the mountain) in its two forms (that of the mobile as well as of the immobile) Nārada rejoiced much. The minds of good people can be captivated through humility.

41. On seeing a person coming towards his house, whether he be important or unimportant, if an unimportant person assumes modesty, he must be considered important. (All) important persons are not (necessarily) important.

42. Though standing tall with lofty peaks, he (the Mountain) bent down his head very low touching the ground. The Mountain bowed down to the great sage.

43. (The sage) lifted him up with the tips of his hands and offered his blessings to him. He took the seat offered by him which was on a higher level than even that of his mind.

44. He (the Mountain) adored him (the sage) with *Arghyas* (materials of adoration) having eight constituents, viz. curds, honey, ghee, raw rice grains wet with water, *Dūrvā* grass, gingelly seeds, *Kuśa* grass and flowers.

45. The sage received the *Arghya*. The tired sage was rendered free from fatigue (by the Mountain) by means of rubbing and pressing his feet and other services. On seeing the sage relieved of fatigue, the humble Mountain spoke:

46-48. "The *Rajas* quality in me has been quickly removed

today by the dust particles from your feet. The internal darkness too (of ignorance) in me has been eradicated quickly by the splendour of your physical body.

O sage, my prosperity has become fruitful today. This day has been really a good day. The meritorious actions performed before and the merits earned since long have borne fruit today. My status of being a *Dharādhara* (mountain, the sustainer of the earth) will be respected by mountains today."

On hearing this, the sage heaved a sigh and sat back.

49. With his mind overwhelmed by perturbation, the best among Mountains said:

"O holy Brāhmaṇa well-versed in everything, tell me the cause of your sigh.

50. Whatever is desired in the three worlds has not been unobserved by you. If you have any sympathy for me, let it be mentioned. I bow down to you.

51. My voice has been choked up with excessive delight caused by your arrival. I cannot express myself eloquently. I however would like to say one thing.

52. The ability to sustain the earth is described by earlier persons in regard to Meru and other (mountains) due to their being in a group. As for me, I sustain the earth singly.

53. Himavān is solely honoured by good people because he happens to be the father of Gaurī, the first Lord of mountains and a kinsman of Paśupati (Lord Śiva).

54. Meru is not considered to be worthy of the highest honour anywhere (in any respect) by me, (although) he is full of gold or because his ridges contain precious stones or because he is the abode of Suras.

55. Aren't there hundreds of mountains capable of sportively supporting the earth? They are honoured by good people but they are honoured only in their own regions.

56. The (honour) of the *Udaya* Mountain (Eastern Mountain) is solely dependent on his sympathy for Mandeha demons who have doubts about their bodies[1]. The Niṣadha Mountain does not have medicinal herbs. The *Asta* (Western) Mountain has his lustre bedimmed.

1. They die at night but are revived in the Udaya Mountain the next morning (Viṣṇu Purāṇa).

57. The Nīla Mountain is the abode of blueness (darkness); Mandāra has feeble light and brilliance; the Malaya Mountain is the abode of serpents and Raivata is not aware of wealth.

58. Hemakūṭa, Trikūṭa and others have the word *Kūṭa* (fraud, deception) in the second half (of their names). Kiṣkindha, Krauñca, Sahya and others cannot bear the burden of the earth (because they are insignificant)."

59-61a. On hearing these words of Vindhya, Nārada thought within himself: 'Being puffed up with too much of pride is not conducive to (real) greatness. Are not there mountains here, the chief of whom is Śrīśaila? Are not they spotlessly glorious? The very sight of their peaks leads to the liberation of good people. His intrinsic strength must be seen.'

61b-63. After thinking thus the sage spoke: "While pointing out the capacities of (various) mountains you have spoken the truth.

The leading mountain Meru disparages you much among the mountains. Why I heaved a sigh has been now mentioned to you. Or why should we Mahātmans (those whose souls dwell on the great Absolute) worry about these things? Hail unto you." After saying this, he went along the aerial path.

64. After the departure of the sage, Vindhya became much depressed in mind and censured himself. His desire having become futile, his anxiety increased.

Vindhya said:

65. Fie upon the life of one devoid of the knowledge of scriptures and arts! Fie upon the life of one not exerting himself adequately! Fie upon the life of one defeated by kinsmen! Fie upon the life of one whose desire has become futile!

66. How can he who is surpassed by an enemy eat food in the day-time? How does he get sleep at night? How can he have (sexual) pleasure in privacy?

67. The distress of forest fire does not affect me as much as the continuity of worried thoughts and painful experiences.

68. It has been aptly mentioned by those conversant with the past (or Purāṇas) that the nature of anxiety (anxious thoughts) is extremely terrible. It does not subside through medicines, observance of fasts or other means.

69. The fever of anxiety deprives one of hunger, sleep, strength, beauteous form, enthusiasm, intellect and glory as well as the entire life of men.

70. An ordinary fever is called fever due to indigestion, if six days go by; but this fever of anxiety goes on recurring every day.

71. In regard to this fever of anxiety, the blessed Dhanvantari is verily powerless. Caraka (an ancient physician) does not step in here. Nor are Aśvinī deities competent in any way.

72. What shall I do? Where shall I go? How shall I conquer Meru? Shall I leap on to his head? No, I shan't.

73. I have been rendered wingless by someone belonging to our family, who made Indra furious. Fie upon my endeavour for victory, as I am wingless!

74. Or why does Meru compete with me so much? Usually those who lift the burden of the earth are prone to be erroneous (and ignorant).

75. How can the utterance of falsehood be imputed to Nārada who practises for the realisation of Brahman, who is conversant with the Vedas and is a resident of the Satyaloka (God Brahmā's region)?

76. The consideration of relevance or irrelevance (of the utterance of falsehood) is not proper for persons like me. The mind of only those who are incapable of heroic action takes to (such) thinking.

77. Or, of what avail are futile thoughts like these? I shall seek refuge in the Lord of the universe, the creator of the universe. He will grant me the proper power of judgement.

78. Indeed the Lord of the universe is extolled as the Lord of the helpless, the Lord of all. Meditating on him (even) for a short while, I shall come to a decision.

79. I shall do this only. Procrastination is not desirable. Enemies and ailments getting increasingly powerful, should not be neglected by (really) efficient people.

80. Certainly, the Sun may be circumambulating Meru everyday along with the planets and the groups of stars considering him to be superior in strength.

81. After deciding thus, the Vindhya Mountain began to increase in height with the determination of a tough fighter

by means of his peaks, which would reach and bring about an end to the limitless firmament.

82. No one should, on any account, have hostilities with others at any time. If at all it should be had, then effort should be made to such an extent that people should not laugh at him.

83. After obstructing the path of the Sun, the king of the mountains became calm as though he had achieved his object. The future of all living beings depends upon luck or the will of the Lord.

84-85. 'That person whom the father of Yama (i.e. the Sun) circumambulates is noble, glorious, great and honourable. As long as a powerful man does not display his power, he can be disregarded by everyone like the fire (latent) in the wood.'

86. Thinking thus (the Mountain) shed off the burden of anxious thoughts and remained firmly committed to a steady effort. He eagerly awaited the rise of the Sun like (a true) Brāhmaṇa (for the purpose of the daily adoration).

CHAPTER TWO

Satyaloka

Vyāsa said:

1-2. The Sun who is the soul of mobile as well as immobile beings and who is the enemy of darkness, rose up on the Udaya Mountain. With his widespread pure rays, he encouraged the religious rites of the good (Vedic rituals etc.) and dispelled the *Tāmasa* characteristics (of the bad ones). He also made the clusters of lotuses that are dear to him, but that were closed up during the night, full-blown once again.

3. He inspired people to maintain the regularity in offering *Havyas* (oblations to gods), *Kavyas* (oblations to manes) and *Bhūtabali* (oblations to the spirits, elements etc.) to gods etc. He demarcated the timings of religious rites to be performed at forenoon, midday and after-noon.

4. He allocated the retention of darkness (evil qualities)

to the hearts and faces of the wicked. He resuscitated the universe that was engulfed by (darkness) during night.

5-6a. When the Sun rose Puṇyajanas (righteous persons) rose in prosperity. Thereby the fact that he helped others had its immediate good effect. Had that not been the case, how could the Sun that vanished in the evening come back to life once again in the morning?

6b-13. Prācī (the eastern direction which is likened to be the wife or beloved of the Sun), on the arrival (rise) of the Sun in the morning, is comparable to a woman whose husband spends his night outside with another woman and arrives in the morning (and hence she is naturally smarting from the infidelity of her husband). With a loving touch of his hands (rays) the Sun consoled Prācī and enjoyed her for a short while (i.e. dispelled the darkness and accorded her protection). Similarly he enjoyed Āgneyī (the south-eastern direction) that had been blazing as if with the painful fire of separation.

Thereafter, the Sun proceeded towards the Dakṣiṇā Āśā[1], (the southern direction assumed here to be a heroine or beloved) which was scented with cloves, cardamoms, musk and camphor and smeared with sandalpaste (these bring the products of the southern region). Her lips were rendered red with betel leaves. She possessed splendid breast-nipples in the form of the bunches of grapes. Her arms were like the Lavalī (a very tender creeper) creeper. She had tender, sprout-like fingers like those of the Kaṅkolī (Aśoka) sprouts. Malaya wind represented her breath and sighs. The Milk Ocean served the purpose of her excellent garment. The gold and gems that abound in Trikūṭa were the ornaments on her limbs The Suvela Mountain appeared like her buttocks. The rivers Kāverī and

---

1. The Purāṇa-writer seems to be a Southerner. His affectionate references to important features of South India here (and to flora and fauna of the South) and elsewhere leads one to believe this. The mountains mentioned here: ' Trikūṭa' is in Ceylon and 'Dardura' is the Nilgiri Hills (De 208, 53). Kāñci means 'a girdle' and the city of the same name is in Tamil Nadu. 'Kāñtī' in the text is probably a misreading by the scribe The flattering reference, "Charmingly eloquent", to Māhārāṣṭrī is the unanimous tribute of Alaṅkāra-writers and Gammarians to that Prākrit speech 'Māhārāṣṭrī'. It probably shows that Prākrits were spoken at the time of this Purāṇa.

Gautamī (Godāvarī) represented her calves. The land of Cola served as her silken blouse. The mountains Sahya and Dardura appeared like her fully developed breasts. The city of Kāntī (Kāñcī) adorned her like a girdle. She was charmingly eloquent in the language of Mahārāṣṭra. Even today the deity Mahālakṣmī (of Kolhapur) has not left her. Thus the southern direction is an expert in religious rituals like Śrāddha.

The horses of the Sun who playfully traverse the sky, could not proceed ahead. Then Anūru (Aruṇa, the charioteer of the Sun-god) submitted to the Sun-god.

Anūru[1] *said:*

14. O Sun-god, the Vindhya mountain rising up in his arrogance stands obstructing the pathway of the sky. (Evidently) he competes with Meru and is desirous of getting your circumambulation.

15. On hearing the words of Anūru, the Sun thought within himself with great surprise: 'Oh, even the pathway of the sky is being blocked!'

Vyāsa said:

16. What could even the heroic Sun do, being held up in the desolate pathway? A man may be in great haste, but (if) single-handed, how can he traverse the obstructed path?

17. He does not remain inactive even for a moment, though distressingly held within the arms of Rāhu (during an eclipse). But on being obstructed in the path of the void what can he do? Fate is all-powerful.

18. He who traverses in half the time of the twinkling of the eye two thousand two hundred and two Yojanas according to human calculation, is also held up for a long time!

19. When much time passed, the people in the East and North were extremely distressed, because the fierce rays of the Sun oppressed them with heat.

20. The people in the West and South kept their eyes

1. Aruṇa, the charioteer of the Sun-god. He is 'thigh-less' (an-ūru) as his mother Vinatā, out of jealousy to her co-wife Kadrū, broke the egg before the complete development of the foetus and he was born a permanently disabled thighless bird (Mbh, *Ādi*, 16.16-23).

closed in heavy sleep. They continued to see the star-and-planet-spangled sky, while they continued to lie down.

21. "This is not day because there is no Sun. This is not night because there is no Moon." In the sky with the stars set, it was not possible to decide the time of the day.

22. Will the entire cosmos get dissolved all of a sudden? But how can it happen? The clouds of the time of *Pralaya* (deluge) do not flood the earth with their downpour.

23. The whole space of the earth became bereft of the utterance of Svāhā, Svadhā and Vaṣaṭ (i.e., rituals came to a standstill). Since the five Yajñas (those of the gods, the manes, the spirits, Brahma and human beings) became defunct, all the three worlds began to tremble.

24. Indeed, only when the Sun rises do the performance of Yajñas and all other holy rites commence. By means of those Yajñas gods become pleased. The Sun is the cause thereof.

25. All, beginning with Citragupta, recognize (calculate) the time (of the day) from the Sun. The Sun alone is the cause of creation, sustenance and annihilation (of the world).

26. Since the movement of the Sun was obstructed, all the three worlds became stunned and stuck up. Everything became as though painted in a picture, because it remained where it was originally.

27. On one side it was due to the nocturnal darkness; on the other side it was due to the oppressive heat of the day. Many things got dissolved. The entire universe became terribly frightened (unable to know which way to run).

28. Thus, the entire world consisting of human beings, serpents, Suras and Asuras became agitated. "Alas! What has happened unaccountably and at a wrong time." All the subjects shouted thus and fled here and there.

29. Then all of them saw Brahmā and sought refuge in him. They eulogized him with different hymns and prayers. "Save us! Save us!" They shouted.

The Devas said:
(Eulogy called Abhīṣṭada)

30. Obeisance to Hiranyagarbha (One having the golden Cosmic Egg in the womb). Obeisance to Brahmā in the form

of Virāṭ Brahman. Obeisance to the Absolute, to the incomprehensible Being, of the form of *Kaivalya* (Salvation) and *Amṛta* (Nectar).

31. Obeisance to that Ātman in the form of Consciousness which the Devas do not comprehend, where the mind is impeded and dulled, where speech does not spread (i.e., who is beyond the ken of mind and speech).

32. Obeisance to that glorious Brahman which the steady-minded Yogins perceive in the form of refulgence in the firmament of the heart through meditation.

33. Obeisance to the Being beyond time, who is the ultimate destroyer, who assumes the form of the individual soul by his own will. Obeisance to one whose form constituted the three Guṇas. Obeisance to the being in the form of Prakṛti (Māyā).

34. Obeisance to the Lord, the cause of creation, sustenance and annihilation, who is Viṣṇu in the form of Sattva, Vedhas (Brahmā) in the form of Rajas and Tamas in the form of Rudra (i.e., Rudra, in the form of Tamas).

35. Obeisance to the Being in the form of Buddhi (the principle Mahat, Cosmic Intelligence) who is the egoistic principle of Ahaṁkāra in three ways (*Guṇa*-wise viz. *Vaikārika, Taijasa* and *Tāmasa)*. Obeisance to the Being in the form of *Pañcatanmātras* (the material essences of the five elements). Obeisance to the Being in the form of the five organs of action.

36. Obeisance to the Being in the form of mind, in the five forms of the five senses. Obeisance to the Being identified with the sense-objects.

37. Obeisance to the Being in the form of the Cosmic Egg; to the one immanent therein. Obeisance to thee in the form of the present-day world and that of the past.

38. Obeisance to the Being of the impermanent form; to the Being of permanent form. Obeisance to the Lord of *Sat* and *Asat* (the gross and the subtle). Obeisance to the Being who has revealed his form of his own will, out of compassion for all the devotees (of four types, viz., the distressed, the one eager to know, the one desirous of wealth and the one who has understood everything).

39. The Vedas have come out of your breath; your sweat is the entire universe; all the living beings are your feet; the

firmament originated from your head.[1]

40. The ether came out from your navel; the vegetable kingdom constitutes your hairs; the Moon was born of your mind; O Lord, the Sun was born of your eyes.

41. You are all. O Lord, everything is in you. You alone constitute the eulogizer, eulogy and the one eulogized here. O Lord, all this visible universe is pervaded by you. Obeisance to you again and again; obeisance is made to you.

42. After eulogizing Brahmā thus, the Devas prostrated themselves on the ground like a long straight wood. Brahmā who was pleased then replied to the heaven-dwellers.

Brahmā said:

43. I am delighted at this eulogy conforming to reality. O Suras who bowed to me, get up. I am pleased. Choose an excellent boon.

44. If anyone praises daily by means of this prayer with faith and purity, either me or Hara or Viṣṇu, we all shall always be delighted with him.

45. We shall grant him all his desires, sons, grandsons, cattle and ready cash, all luck, longevity, health, fearlessness and victory in war.

46. (We shall grant him) all pleasures and enjoyments here and hereafter as well as everlasting salvation. Whatever is thought or desired by him shall become fulfilled.

47. This eulogy will be known as *Abhīṣṭada* ('that which gives the desired things'). It will bestow all super-natural powers. This excellent prayer should be read (recited) with all efforts.

48. Again Vedhas spoke to the Suras who prostrated before him and then got up:

"Oh! Ye all be happy and steady. Why are you bewildered even here (in Satyaloka)?"

49. These are all the personified forms of the Vedas, Vidyās (fourteen lores), Yajñas inclusive of the monetary gifts, truth, piety, austerity and self-control.

1. 39b & 40 are echoes of the *Puruṣa-Sūkta* (RV X.90)

50. This is the disciplined life of celibacy; this is the benign Bhāratī (Goddess of Speech); these are the persons of well-accomplished objectives according to the Śrutis, Smṛtis and Itihāsas.

51. None of the following are present here: Anger, rivalry, covetousness, lust, want of fortitude, fear, violence, crookedness, pride, censure and the impure one.

52-53. O Suras[1], see. These are the Brāhmaṇas engrossed in the (study of) the Vedas and austerities; these are ascetics whose sole wealth is their penance; these are the persons who regularly observed various vows such as the monthly fasts, the half-yearly fasts, and the vows of *Cāturmāsya* ('four months'); these are the women wedded to chastity; these others are celibate religious students; and these are the honest fellows behaving like eunuchs towards other men's wives (i.e., who have controlled their passions).

54-55. These are the persons who devoutly served their mothers and fathers. These are the ones who were killed in trying to protect cows. These are the persons who never yearned for the benefits accruing from vows, gifts, Japas, Yajñas, study of the Vedas, propitiating Brāhmaṇas, libations to be offered by Brāhmaṇas, holy spots, austerities, helping others and the regular habits and practices of the dignified and exalted persons.

56. These are the persons who regularly performed the Japa of Gāyatrī-mantra; here are those who regularly performed Agnihotras; these are the persons who gifted away *Dvimukhī Gaus* (cow with two faces, cow at the time of calving before the calf touched the ground); these are the persons fond of gifting *Kapilā* (brown in colour or according to others completely white) cows.

57. These are the persons who cherish no desires; these are those who regularly drink Soma juice; these are the persons who imbibe the water washing the feet of Brāhmaṇas; these are those who died in the holy river Sarasvatī; and these are those who served and attended upon Brāhmaṇas.

58. These are my favourite Brāhmaṇas who could have accepted monetary gifts but did not, who abstained scrupulously

1. VV 52-73 enumerate the acts, vows and observances which lead to Satyaloka (God Brahmā's Region).

from accepting monetary gifts at holy spots and shrines.

59. These are the perfect ones with solar brilliance and pure souls, who took early morning baths for the whole month of Māgha (Jan-Feb) at Prayāga when the Sun is in Capricorn.

60. These are those meritorious persons of pure bodies free from impurities, who have taken their holy dips in Vārāṇasī and Pañcanada (at Pañcagaṅgā Ghāṭ?) for three days in the month of Kārttika.

61. These are those persons who took their holy baths in Maṇikarṇikā and who pleased Brāhmaṇas with monetary gifts. They are sure to enjoy all pleasures and they will stay in my city for the period of a Kalpa.

62. Impelled by that merit, they will reach Kāśī and, undoubtedly, attain salvation, by the grace of Viśveśvara (Lord of the Universe, Śiva).

63. Holy rites performed in Avimukta by men, though they may be very slight, will yield welfare. Its fruit is liberation in the course of other births.

64. Oh, there is no fear of death in the holy spot of Viśveśvara where all await death as a favourite guest!

65. These persons of limbs free from impurities, who stand near me are those by whom unsullied (got by pure means) wealth was distributed among Brāhmaṇas at Kurukṣetra.

66. These are the grandfathers of those persons by whom the grandfathers are propitiated through a Brāhmaṇa whom they approached as a grandfather.

67. O Devas, my region is not attained through holy dip, or monetary gift, by Japa, or by adoration. It is attained through the propitiation of a Brāhmaṇa by means of libations of water.

68. These are the palaces of those persons by whom houses furnished with mortar, pestle and other things along with beds were given as gifts.

69-70. Those persons who make halls for the study of the Vedas, who teach the Vedas, who make a gift of learning, who narrate and expound the Purāṇas, who give away the Purāṇa and other texts, who gift away Dharmaśāstra (scriptural texts) do have their residence here in my city.

71. Those who give unlimited wealth to a Brāhmaṇa for the sake of Yajña, marriage or holy vows shall remain here as brilliant as fire.

72. He who builds a hospital and is interested in patronising a physician, stays here till the end of the Kalpa, enjoying all types of pleasures.

73. Those who make holy spots free from the harassments of the wicked are honoured persons in my inner apartments like my own bosom-born children.

74. Brāhmaṇas are indeed great favourites of Viṣṇu or Śaṁbhu or me. We freely roam about on the earth in their form.

75. Brāhmaṇas and cows constitute one unit divided into two sections, the Mantras remaining on one side (viz. that of Brāhmaṇas) and the *Havis* (ghee-offering) on the other.

76. The Brāhmaṇas are mobile holy spots and sacred rivers created for the sake of the entire earth. Merely by the waters of their wise speech impure persons become pure.

77. Cows are sacred and unparalleled excellent auspiciousness.[1] The dust particles rising from their hoofs are on a par with the waters of Gaṅgā.

78. All the holy spots are at the tip of their horns; all the mountains are at the tip of their hoofs. In between the two horns is Gaurī, the great goddess.

79-80. Great-grandfathers dance on seeing a cow being gifted away. All the sages are delighted. Along with the deities, we become pleased (when a cow is being gifted). The sins continuously cry. So also does poverty along with ailments. Cows are mothers who nurse the entire world in every respect like the real mother.

81. If a man eulogizes, bows to and circumambulates cows, it amounts to the circumambulation of the entire earth consisting of the seven continents.

82. Goddess Lakṣmī in the form of cows, who lives in all living beings and who is stationed in all gods, may be pleased to dispel all my sins.

83. It is she who is Lakṣmī on the chest of Viṣṇu, Svāhā of the Fire-god and Svadhā of the chiefs of the Pitṛs. That cow is always the bestower of boons.

84. Cow-dung is verily Yamunā itself; cow's urine is the

1. VV 77-94 glorify cows and the fruit of serving them and gifting them to Brāhmaṇas.

splendid Narmadā; cow's milk is Gaṅgā. What else can be more sacred than this!

85. 'All the fourteen worlds reside in the limbs of the cows. Hence, may it be auspicious unto me here in this world or hereafter.'

86. Uttering this mantra, a person should gift away one or more cows to an excellent Brāhmaṇa. That person shall become more distinguished than all.

87. The good qualities of a cow have been considered by me and the great sages along with Viṣṇu and Śiva and then this prayer is composed.

88. 'Let there be cows in front of me. Let there be cows behind me. Let the cows be in my heart. I shall stay in the midst of cows.'

89. If any person lustrates his limbs with the touch of the tail of a cow, he shall become rightly fortunate. Ill-luck, quarrel and ailments go away from his limbs.

90. The earth is held aloft and sustained by seven—by cows, Brāhmaṇas, Vedas, chaste women, men of truthful speech, persons with no greed and liberal-minded donors.

91-92. The region above my region is known as Vaikuṇṭha. Above that is the region of Kumāra (i.e. Kārttikeya). Beyond that is the region of Umā. Śiva's region is above it and Goloka ('Region of Cows') is nearby. The cow-mothers Suśīlā and others are there. They are the favourites of Śiva.

93. Those who tend and attend upon cows, and those men who gift away cows, shall stay in one of these worlds with all flourishing prosperity.

94. Those who gift away cows go to that place where rivers flow with milk, where milk pudding forms the sediments and where no old age torments them.

95. Those who are well-versed in Śrutis, Smṛtis and Purāṇas are glorified as (real) Brāhmaṇas. The others simply bear the name (of Brāhmaṇas). They act according to the directions of the former.

96-98. Śruti and Smṛti are the two eyes. Purāṇa is spoken as the heart. One who is devoid of Śruti and Smṛti is blind. If he is devoid of one of them, he is blind of one eye. The blind ones of single eye or both the eyes are better than the heartless one devoid of Purāṇas. The sacred rites and pious practices mentioned in Śruti and Smṛti are elaborated in Purāṇa.

A cow should be given as a gift to that real Brāhmaṇa by anyone desirous of happiness everywhere. It should not be given to a mere bearer of the name Brāhmaṇa. He may lead the donor to downfall.

99-100. If one has an eager desire for knowledge of pious practices and sacred rites, it one is afraid of sins, one should listen to the Purāṇas, which are the roots of pious and scared rites. Purāṇa is the excellent illuminating lamp among the fourteen lores. Due to its brilliance, even the blind shall not fall into the sea of mundane affairs anywhere.

101. By those who desire to attain my region, the Purāṇas should be always listened to. They must live on the banks of Gaṅgā and they must propitiate Brāhmaṇas always.

102. O Suras, thus in general the conventions and arrangements in the Satyaloka have been narrated by me. It accords freedom from fear to those who are distressed with fear. You need not be afraid.

103. Creating obstacles in the path of the Sun, Vindhya competes with Meru. You all have come here in that connection. I shall point out to you the means thereof.

104. There is a great sage of excessive austerities named Agastya. He is the son of Mitra and Varuṇa and he has directed his mind towards Lord Viśveśvara.

105-106. He is now in the great holy shrine of Avimukta that can bring about liberation of everyone and that is presided over by Viśveśa himself, who is about to impart instruction in Tāraka (Praṇava). You go there and request him. He will carry out your task. Once by swallowing Vātāpi, brother of Ilvala, (or by killing both Vātāpi and Ilvala) he saved the entire world.

107. The refulgence of the sage born of Mitra and Varuṇa surpasses the brilliance of the Sun. Ever since that day, there is none in the world who does not fear sage Agastya."

108-109. After saying this Vedhas (God Brahmā) vanished. The delighted Devas with beaming faces spoke to one another: "Oh, we are indeed highly blessed. Incidentally, we shall visit Kāśī and the presiding deities Śiva and Gaurī. How wonderful it is that after many days our desire is about to fructify!"

110-112. After coming to a decision like this, the Suras seeking merit spoke thus: "Only those feet are blessed which walk in the direction of Kāśī. We shall reach Kāśī today due to the merit accruing from our listening to the story narrated by Brahmā. It is only due to the weight of merit that one is able to accomplish a single task serving two purposes."

Speaking thus to one another, the delighted Suras came to Kāśī.

Vyāsa said:

113-114. Those men who listen to this meritorious narration shall be able to shake off all their sins. They will enjoy all pleasures along with their sons and wives. After establishing the lineage here, they will go to Satyaloka and stay there for a long time. Thereafter, they will attain eternity (Mokṣa).

CHAPTER THREE

The Hermitage of Agastya

Sūta said:

1. O holy Sir, O Acyuta (Viṣṇu in the form of Vyāsa), the Lord of the past and the future, O great receptacle of all knowledge and lores, what was done by the Devas after reaching Kāśī. Kindly tell me.

2-4. After learning this divine story, I did not feel fully satisfied. Agastya is the storehouse of austerities. How was he requested by the Devas? How did Vindhya who rose to such a height attain his original form? My mind is eager to take its ablution in the nectarine ocean of your speech.

After hearing this fully, Sage Vyāsa, the son of Parāśara, began to narrate everything to his faithful disciple.

The Son of Parāśara said:

5. O highly intelligent Sūta endowed with devotion and faith, listen. Let these young boys like Śuka, Vaiśaṁpāyana and others too listen.

6-8. *After reaching Vārāṇasī, the Devas accompanied by great sages, at the outset, took without delay their holy bath in Maṇikarṇikā duly along with their garments. Then they performed *Sandhyāvandana* and other holy rites. They then performed the offering of water libation to the primordial Pitṛs with Kuśa grass, sweet scents, gingelly seeds and water. They then delighted and propitiated all the permanent residents of the holy spot severally offering them various things such as jewels, gold, clothes, horses, ornaments and cows.

9. (They gave them) different kinds of vessels made of gold, silver etc., cooked foods tasting like ambrosia, milk puddings with sugar.

10. Food was given with curds and other milk-products. Different kinds of grains were given as gift; sweet scents, sandalpaste, camphor, betel leaves and beautiful *Cāmaras* (chowries) (were given).

11. Soft beds with cotton and bedspreads, lamps, mirrors and seats, palanquins, male servants, female servants, aerial chariots, cattle and houses (were provided).

12. Flags and banners of diverse colours, canopies as charming as the moon were given and arrangements for a regular distribution of food for a year along with all domestic appurtenances (were made).

13-14. The ascetics and saints were given leather and wooden sandals, new befitting silken cloths, different kinds of shawls and blankets of variegated colour, staffs, waterpots, hides of deer, loin cloths, cots sufficiently high and golden pieces intended for the attendants.

15-16. Students' hostels were provided with supply of food, collections of great books. Livelihood was arranged for scribes and clerks and ample funds for guesthouses. Arrangements for providing different kinds of medicines and liberal bequests of all sorts were made. Funds were provided for constructing water-sheds for travellers during summer as well as iron ovens with adequate fuel during winter.

---

* VV 6-27 describe the various ways in which the Devas propitiated those who were present in the holy shrine. It was a part of their performance of the pilgrimage to Kāśī.

17. Umbrellas and protective cloths against rain in rainy season were made abundant. At night facilities for lamps enabling people to read, were provided. There were unguents etc. for massaging feet and many other similar articles.

18. Money provisions were made in every temple to retain expounders of the Purāṇas. Adequate provisions for dance and music in temples were made in different ways.

19. Provisions were made for whitewashing, plastering etc. (of the walls) of the temples and for repairing ruined and dilapidated temples. Costs of painting with pictures and decorating pavilions were met.

20. Waving of lights with many wicks, aromatic fragrant gum-resins, Daśāṅga incense (ten constituents including lac, treacle etc.), camphor, wicks for the adoration of deities were arranged.

21. Bathing of the idols was done with Pañcāmṛta etc. as well as with sweet scents; perfumes were used for sweetening the breath of the deities and provisions for temple gardens were made.

22. (Provision for) big wreaths and garlands for the prominent adorations on the three occasions and conchs, drums, kettle-drums and other musical instruments to be played in the temple of Śiva was made.

23. Vessels facilitating the holy ablution such as water-jars, Bhṛṅgāras (big pitchers) etc., white cloths for wiping and drying, sweet scents such as *Yakṣakardama* etc. (camphor, agallochum, musk etc., mixed together in specific proportions) were provided.

24. Adequate provision for *Japa, Homa,* recitation of hymns and prayers, loud utterances of Śiva's names, Rāsakrīḍās (dance-games) and circumambulations was made.

25. The Suras spent five nights in all these various prescribed sacred rites and rituals and had their holy ablution in the sacred rivers and tanks.

26-27. They made the wretched and helpless destitutes satisfied (by their donations etc.) and then bowed to Lord Viśveśvara. They strictly observed the regulations regarding vow of celibacy etc., and duly concluded all the requisite formalities of visiting holy spots. They frequently visited (the Liṅga of) Viśvanātha, prayed and bowed to him and proceeded to that place where Agastya was present in his eagerness and readiness for helping others.

28. He had installed a Liṅga after his own name and made a Kuṇḍa (a sacred pit) in front of it. Reciting *Śatarudriya*[1] hymn, he sat there with a steady mind.

29. From afar, the Devas saw him blazing like a second Sun. He was brilliant all round with his limbs resembling a blazing fire.

30. Is this the submarine fire itself who performs a penance in personified form? He was quite immovable like a post. He was pure like the mind of a saintly person.

31. Or perhaps, all the fiery refulgences have resorted to this Brāhmaṇical body and practice for the attainment of the greatest abode that is quiescent.

32. Due to the severe penance of this sage, the Sun is able to blaze brilliantly and fire also to burn brightly. *Capalā* (Lightning) has (as if) become *Acapalā* (not fickle, steady).

33. In his hermitage here, these beasts of prey are seen around in perfect *Sattva* (good) form after eschewing their natural enmity.[2]

34. The elephant having become fearless scratches the lion with his trunk. With his manes lifted up, the lion sleeps on the lap of the Aṣṭāpada (*Śarabha*, a fabulous animal of eight legs).

35. The powerful hog with its hairs rigid and stiff has abandoned its herd and roams about in the midst of wild dogs (or jackals or tigers) having its eyes fixed on the *Mustā* grass.

36-38a. *Bhūdāra* ('the hog that digs up the earth') does not dig up the earth here unlike in other places. Because the entire Kāśī is full of Liṅgas, it is afraid of it and so has restrained itself. The hyena has taken up the young one of the hog and is playing with it. The fawn of the deer has pushed out the cubs of the tiger and it is sucking the udder of the tigress with foams coming out of its mouth while the tail continues its wagging.

---

1. A hymn in Yajurveda in praise of Rudra.
2. VV 33-57 show how even birds and beasts forgot their natural animosity and played together, due to the spiritual influence of Agastya. The same influence curbing the instinct of mating is noted in vv 67-71.

38b-41. While the hairy bear goes on sleeping, the monkey carefully examining them with its eyes picks up the lice with its moving fingers and bites them with the tips of its teeth.

The leaders of the herds of various kinds of monkeys, *Golāṅgulas* ('Cow-tailed'), *Raktamukhas* ('Red-faced') and Nīlāṅgas ('Blue-limbed') have abandoned their natural rivalry and are sporting about together in one place.

Rabbits play along with the wolves rolling on their backs frequently.

The mouse scratches the ear of the cat with its mouth moving (all over its body).

The cat nestles itself close to the peacock's tail and takes a pleasant nap.

42-45. The serpent rubs its neck against the neck of the peacock.

The mongoose abandons its hereditary enmity and rolls on the top of the hood of the serpent after sportively jumping and leaping about.

Though distressed and blinded with hunger, the serpent sees the mouse running about in front of its mouth. It does not catch it, nor the other one is afraid of this.

On seeing the hind calving, the tiger is moved with pity reflected in its eyes. He avoids looking at it further and moves away.

The tigress and the hind behave like joyous companions and they communicate to each other the conduct of life of the tiger and the deer (their respective mates).

46. Even after seeing the hunter wielding the powerful bow, the Śambara deer stubbornly sticks to its path (without moving) while he (the hunter) begins to scratch it (lovingly).

47. The Rohita deer fondly touches the wild buffalo unperturbed. The Camarī hind measures its tail against the tresses of hairs of the Śabara woman.

48. Abandoning their acute rivalry and enmity because they have been restrained by the brilliance of the sage, the Gavaya (a species of ox) and the porcupine continue to stay together at one place.

49. The pair of rams, though desirous of victory, do not get ready for a straight head-on fight. The jackal touches the fawn gently with its paw.

50. The beasts of prey here eat only grasses and hedges. Indeed eating meat is the cause of disaster in both the worlds (here and hereafter). Fie upon it!

51. If a person deluded by sins cooks meat for his own sake, he shall remain in hell for as many years as there are hairs on his body.

52. Those evil-minded persons who nourish their own lives through the lives of other living beings suffer the tortures of hells till the end of the Kalpa. Thereafter, they will be preyed upon by them.

53. Even if the vital breaths come upto the throat (i.e. on the point of death) no one should eat flesh. If it becomes essential, then one should eat one's own flesh and not that of others.

54. These beasts of prey that have no inclination towards injuring others because of their service unto Maitrāvaruṇi (i.e. Agastya) are far superior to men prone to violence.

55. In the small puddle here, the crane does not eat the fish though they swim about in front of it. Even the big fishes do not swallow the smaller fry.

56. On one side are all the types of meat, on the other side the meat of fish: Was this Smṛti text remembered by these (cranes) and therefore they avoid fish?

57. Even after seeing the quail, this falcon (a bird of prey) turns away its face.

It is surprising that even here (i.e. in Kāśī) *Madhupas* (bees, those who drink liquor) hover around with dark hearts.

58. Those who are much addicted to imbibing liquor experience the pains of hell for a long time and become Madhupas (bees) once again humming away in their ignorance (hoverings) (*Bhrānti*— ignorance, hovering around).

59. That is why after completely comprehending the truth about the Pināka-bearing Lord those who are conversant with the Purāṇas, thus sing a song pregnant with meaning.

60. Where is flesh and where is the devotion to Śiva! Where is liquor and where is the worship of Śiva! (What a great difference between these!) Śaṅkara stands aloof from those who are addicted to liquor and meat.

61. Without the favour of Śiva, *Bhrānti* (ignorance, wandering) cannot stop. That is why these bees devoid of Śiva (i.e.

comprehension of the truth of Śiva) hover and wander around.

62-63. Seeing thus the lower creatures moving about in the penance-grove like sages, it was understood by the gods that such a miracle had arisen from the holy shrine itself, since, even the lower creatures living here should be liberated by Viśveśvara at the time of their death by imparting the Tāraka Mantra.

64. If after realising the greatness of the holy place anyone resolves to stay here, Viśveśa redeems him, whether he be alive or dead.

65. Men of wisdom who are conversant with the secret of Avimukta (i.e., Kāśī) are liberated. Even the lower creatures without knowledge are liberated because their sins have vanished.

66. This realisation made the Devas wonder when they went within the hermitage. On seeing the flocks of birds, they rejoiced again.

67. The crane (swan) has rested his neck on the neck of the goose. We think, it is not sleeping but meditating on Viśveśvara.

68. The female swan scratches the male swan with the tip of its beak; but when he expresses his desire for mating, she wards him off by means of the fluttering wings.

69. On being held by the male ruddy goose, the female of the species appears to say in its *Kreṅkita* (goose like) utterance: "O foremost one among the lascivious! Why do you exhibit your sexual desire here?"

70. The pigeon from the clusters of hedges chirps sweetly but, it appears, as if it is being warded by the female pigeon saying, "The sage in meditation will hear."

71. The peacock does not utter its *Kekā* sound. It keeps silent perhaps out of fear for him. The Cakora (a kind of Partridge) bird that imbibes moonlight appears silent as if to observe the *Naktavrata* vow (taking food only at night).

72. The Sārikā (female parrot) reciting the truth seems to address the parrot, "Śiva takes one across the sea (of worldly existence) that extends without any limit."

73. By means of its sweet cooing sound the cuckoo seems to utter, "Kali age and Kāla (Death) do not adversely affect the persons staying in Kāśī."

74. After observing these activities of the animals and the birds, the Devas disparaged their heaven that was subject to

unexpected calamities and the sufferings thereof.

75. These birds and animals, the residents of Kāśī, are far superior, because they have no return (to the worldly existence); not so in the case of the Devas who are liable to rebirths.

76. "We the heaven-dwellers are not at all on a par with even the fallen ones residing in Kāśī. There is no fear of downfall in Kāśī but there is a great danger of downfall in heaven.

77. Residence in Kāśī with such observances as monthly fasts etc. is far better. Nowhere else can there be a kingdom free from enemies, with the extensive shade of various kinds of (royal) umbrellas.

78. The position (the final region) that is easily and sportively acquired by rabbits and mosquitoes in Kāśī cannot be acquired even by the Yogins elsewhere even through regular practice of yogic postures etc.

79. Even the beggarly wretch in Vārāṇasī is better since he is free from the fear of Yama. Not so in our case. We the Tridaśas ('gods having only the three states of infancy, teenage and youth') are not so, because our *daśā* (plight) is so miserable on account of a mountain.

80. When the eighth part of a day of Brahmā is over, the region of Indra perishes along with the Guardians of the world, Sun, Moon, Planets and Stars.

81. Even when two Parārdhas (i.e., the entire life of Brahmā) come to an end, no one staying in Kāśī perishes. Hence, one should strive for perfection and welfare in Kāśī.

82. The happiness one derives by residing in Kāśī here cannot be had in the pavilion of the whole Cosmic Egg. If that can be had, how do you account for the fact that all are desirous of residing in Kāśī?

83. The chance to reside in Kāśī here can be obtained by an exchange of all those merits that one has earned in the course of thousands of previous births.

84. Even if the chance can be had, the resident will not acquire *Siddhi* (fulfilment), if the Three-eye Lord were to get angry. Hence, one should always seek refuge in Viśveśvara worthy of being resorted to.

85. The four aims of life named piety, love, wealth and

salvation can be had in Kāśī in their entirety. Not so anywhere else.

86. Even if one proceeds to the temple of Viśveśvara from one's house lazily, one shall acquire more than the benefit of a horse-sacrifice at every step.

87. There is no limit to the welfare and prosperity of one who takes the holy dip in the current of the river flowing towards the north and proceeds to visit Viśveśvara with great faith.

88-93. The devotee shall attain more and more merit by the following pious activities: by visiting, touching, bathing in and drinking the waters of the celestial river (i.e., Gaṅgā); by offering *Sandhyā* prayers, *Japas*, water libations, worship of the Lord; by visiting the Pañcatīrthas (the five holy spots i.e., (i) Kapālmocana, (ii) Pāpamocana, (iii) Ṛṇamocana, (iv) Kulastaṁbha and (v) Vaitaraṇī; by visiting Viśveśvara, faithful touch and adoration, arranging for incense, lights etc., circumambulation, repetition of prayers, prostrations, dances, uttering the names of the Lord such as Devadeva, Mahādeva, Śaṁbhu, Śiva, Dhūrjaṭi, Nīlakaṇṭha, Īśa, Pinākin, Śaśiśekhara, Triśūlapāṇi, Viśveśa and imploring "Save me! Save me!"; by sitting for even half a moment in the Muktimaṇḍapikā (Pavilion of salvation); by narrating the sacred stories, listening to the Purāṇas, practising the daily routine ritualistic activities, receiving and honouring guests and helping others and such other activities.

94. Just as the moon increases digit by digit in the bright half of the month, so also the accumulation of piety of the inhabitants of Kāśī takes place step by step.

95. This *Dharmavṛkṣa* ('the tree of piety') is praiseworthy. Faith is its seed. It is watered by the water (used for) washing the feet of Brāhmaṇas. The fourteen lores are the branches. Riches constitute its flowers. The two fruits are the subtle one of salvation and the gross one of love.

96. Here Bhavānī is the bestower of all riches. Ḍhuṇḍhi (Gaṇeśa) shall get all the desires fulfilled. Here Viśveśa shall liberate all creatures at the time of death, by imparting the Mantra into the ears.

97. *Dharma* (Righteousness) stands on all its four feet (viz., Truth, Penance, Mercy and Religious gifts) here in Kāśī; *Artha* (wealth) in Kāśī is of various kinds; *Kāma* (Love) in Kāśī

is the sole base of all happiness. What is the *Śreyas* (salvation, welfare) elsewhere which is not in Kāśī here?

98. All these are not surprising, because where there is Viśveśvara there is nothing strange. He is the personification of piety, wealth, love and salvation for bestowal. He is of the Cosmic Form. Hence in all the three worlds, there is nothing on a par with Kāśī."

99-101. While saying all these things, the Devas (went ahead and) saw the hut of the sage. It was full of the fragrance of the smoke arising from the Homas. There were many religious students moving around.

It was rendered beautiful by the fawns with piles of Darbha grass in their mouths, following the maidens of the penance-grove seeking handful of Śyāmāka rice.

Many wet bark-garments and loin cloths were seen hanging from the branches of the trees, thereby creating the impression that nets were kept spread all over in order to capture the deer of Vighnas (obstacles, hindrances).

102. On seeing the frontyard of the hut marked by the imprints of the feet of Lopāmudrā, the crest-jewel of chaste women, the Suras devoutly bowed down.

103-104. Agastya, the sage, had concluded his meditation and had worn the rosary around his ears. Then he occupied his *Bṛsī* (i.e., special seat of a sage). On seeing Agastya thus seated in front of them, appearing grand like Brahmā himself, all the Devas including Indra (bowed to him) with delighted beaming faces and uttered loudly "Be victorious! Be victorious!"

105. The sage stood up and made them occupy their seats befittingly. He greeted them with blessings. He then asked them the purpose of their visit.

Vyāsa said:

106-107. One who devoutly listens to this meritorious narrative, or reads or teaches this to those who have faith in these vows, can shake off all sins committed knowingly or unknowingly and certainly proceeds to the city of Śiva by means of a vehicle having the colour of a swan.

CHAPTER FOUR

*The Characteristics of a Chaste Woman**

Sūta said:

1. O great sage, O holy Sir, on being asked by the sage, what did the Devas say? Kindly narrate it for the good of all the worlds.

Śrī Vyāsa said:

2. On hearing the words of Agastya, the Devas respectfully glanced at the face of Bṛhaspati (the preceptor of gods).

Vākpati said:

3. Listen, O illustrious Agastya, to the purpose of the visit of the Devas. You are blessed. You have achieved whatever should be achieved. You are honoured even by great men.

4. Are not there ascetics in every hermitage, on every mountain, in every forest? O excellent sage, but your status is entirely different.

5. You possess the glory of austerities. The Brāhmaṇical refulgence is established in you. The glory of merit of the highest type is in you. There is liberal-mindedness in you. You have a (steady) mind.

6-9. This auspicious and chaste lady Lopāmudrā is your partner in the holy rites. She is more or less like a shadow of your body and a (mere) mention of hers is a giver of merit. It is certain that no one else is considered as excellent as this lady among the chaste ones by Arundhatī, Sāvitrī, Anasūyā, Śāṇḍilyā, Satī, Lakṣmī, Śatarūpā, Menā, Sunīti, Saṁjñā and Svāhā. These chaste ladies are respectively the wives of Vasiṣṭha, God Brahmā, Atri, Kauśika, (Satī, the first consort of) Śiva, Viṣṇu, Svāyaṁbhuva Manu, Himālaya, Uttānapāda (Dhruva's father), Vivasvān (the Sun-god), Agni (Fire-god). O sage, she takes her food after you have had it; when you stand, she also

* The chapter is important from sociological point of view. It portrays the status of women (wives) *vis-a-vis* men (husbands). It is a digest of Smṛti-laws about the duties of married women, especially with relation to the husband.

stands; when you have gone to sleep completely, she goes to bed and she gets up before you.

10. She never comes before you unadorned; when you go elsewhere for some work, she eschews all ornaments.

11. She never utters your name, so that your longevity becomes best assured; she never mentions the names of other men.

12. Though assailed by angry words (by you), she never expresses her displeasure; though beaten (by you), she continues to be pleased with you. If you say "Do this", she replies, "O lord, know that it has been done."

13. When she is called (by you), she leaves off all her other domestic duties and comes near you quickly (and says), "Wherefore, O Lord, have you addressed me; let that pleasure be given to me as favour."

14. She does not stand at the doorway for a long time; nor does she lie near the doorway and block it. She does not give anything to anyone unless asked by you to give.

15. Without being specifically told so, she gets ready all the requisite things for the worship of the deity such as holy water for the observances, Darbha grass, leaves, flowers, raw rice grains etc.

16. She waits for the correct time, fetching the requisite thing at the proper time without being perturbed, nay, taking delight in the same.

17. She takes in the leavings of her husband whether cooked food or fruits and other things. If anything is given to her, she says, "It is your great favour" and then accepts it.

18. She never eats anything without sharing it with gods, manes, guests, servants, cows and mendicants.

19. She soberly dresses and adorns herself; she is efficient (in her job); she is cheerful, she is averse to wastage and over-spending. Without being permitted by you she never takes up holy observances, fasts and vows.[1]

20. She avoids from a distance visiting community festivities; she never goes on pilgrimage or for witnessing marriage celebrations (without you).

1. For the prohibition of non-permitted observance of vows see Manu V.155.

21. If the husband is comfortably seated, sound asleep or in a sportive mood, she never disturbs him by waking him up casually or even for her personal intimate reasons.

22. In the event of the monthly course, she never shows her face (to her husband etc.) for three days. Till she gets purified by her bath thereafter, she never makes her utterance heard by others.

23. After her cleansing bath (on her fourth day), she first looks at the face of her husband and not of anyone else, or after meditating on her husband in her mind, she looks at the Sun.

24-25. A chaste woman sincerely wishing for the long life of her husband shall never be without these: turmeric, saffron, sindūra (red lead), collyrium, blouse, betel leaves, splendidly auspicious ornaments, combing of the hairs and ornaments on the braid of hair, hands, ears etc.

26. A chaste woman never has close companionship with a washerwoman (or a woman in the monthly course), a rationalist, sceptic or heretic, a Buddhist recluse (woman) or a woman of Kāpālika sect or an unfortunate wretched woman.

27. This chaste lady never speaks to a woman who hates her husband. She never remains alone anywhere. She never takes her bath anywhere in the nude.

28. A chaste woman never sits on the mortar or pestle or broom or (grinding) stone or any mechanical contrivance, nor on a raised platform on either side of the front door (or threshold).

29. She never exhibits shameless boldness except at the time of sexual dalliance. She loves whatever her husband is interested in.

30. This is the holy vow for a woman; this alone is the greatest piety; this is the only divine adoration that she never transgresses the words of her husband.

31. She will never disregard her husband whether he be a eunuch, one in a miserable plight, sick, old and senile, affluent or poor.

32. When the husband is delighted, she should be delighted; when he is gloomy and morose, she also should be gloomy and morose. She shall be of meritorious deed if she identifies (herself with her husband) during affluence and in adversity.

33. When ghee, salt, oil etc., are wanting, she should not openly say, "We don't have this and that". A chaste woman never subjects her husband to overstrain.

34. A woman desirous of having holy bath in sacred waters near holy shrines should drink the water with which the feet of her husband are washed. To a woman her husband alone is far superior to even Śaṅkara or Viṣṇu.

35. If a woman disregards the wish of her husband and observes holy vows, fasts etc., she shall reduce the life span of her husband. After death she goes to hell.

36. If a woman resents and retorts, when she is told anything, she is reborn as a bitch in a village or a vixen in a desolate forest.

37. This is cited as the most important and decisive of all rules to be followed by women that they should enjoy everything after worshipping the feet of the husband.

38. A woman should never occupy a high seat. She should never go to other men's houses. She should never utter words that could cause (her or others) to be ashamed.

39. She should never utter slanderous words. She should avoid quarrels. She should never speak aloud or laugh in the presence of elders.

40. An evil-minded woman who forsakes her husband and commits sexual offences (with a paramour) is reborn as a cruel owl residing in the hollow of a tree.

41. If on being beaten, a woman wishes to beat in retaliation, she is born as a tigress or a female cat. A woman leering at another man becomes squint-eyed.

42. If a woman keeps her husband away and herself enjoys sweet dishes, she is born as a sow in a village or a flying fox feeding on its own faeces.

43. If a woman addresses (her husband) disrespectfully and unpleasantly by using 'thou' (instead of respectful 'you'), she becomes dumb. She who is always jealous of her co-wives, becomes wretched again and again.

44. She who glances at others avoiding the sight of her husband is reborn one-eyed, deformed in face or ugly in features.

45-46. On seeing her husband returning from outdoor work, the wife should hasten to give him light meal and water, and betel-leaves; she should fan him, massage his feet, speak pleasing words dispelling his fatigue and worry. Thus, if a woman delights her husband, all the three worlds will be delighted with her.

47. Limited is what a father could give; a brother gives but limited gifts; a son too gives only limited. Hence a woman should always worship her husband who gives unlimited (gifts).[1]

48. Husband is the god; husband is the preceptor; husband alone constitutes piety, holy place and pious vows and observances. Hence a woman should forsake everything and worship her husband alone.

49. Just as a lifeless body becomes impure in a moment, so also a woman bereft of her husband is always impure even though she may bathe scrupulously.

50. A widow devoid of conjugal bliss and weal is the worst of all inauspicious things. There would be no success in a venture, if one sees a widow (at the outset).

51. A sensible man should avoid such a woman bereft of all conjugal bliss and even her blessings, except in the case of his (widowed) mother.[2]

52. At the time of the marriage of a girl, the Brāhmaṇas should pronounce, "Be a constant companion to your husband alive or dead."

53. The husband should always be followed by a woman like a body by its shadow, like the moon by its light or like a cloud by lightning.

54. If a woman joyously follows her (dead) husband from the house to the cremation ground (to immolate herself along with him), she certainly derives the benefit of a horse-sacrifice at every step.

55. Just as a snake-catcher pulls out a serpent from its hollow, so also a chaste woman snatches her husband from the messengers (of god of Death) and takes him to heaven.

56. On seeing a chaste woman from a distance, the messengers of Yama flee after discarding her husband, though he might have been a man of misdeeds.

57. "We, the messengers (of Death), do not fear fire or

---

1. Quoted from Mbh, *Śānti*, 148.6; also echoed in MtP 210.17-18. For Godhood of the husband to wife see Mbh, *Anuśāsana* 146.58.

2. Repetition from SkP III.ii.7.50-51.

lightning as much as seeing a chaste woman coming towards us."

58. On seeing the refulgence of a chaste woman, the Sun blazes more and fire burns brighter and all fiery beings tremble.

59. A chaste woman sportingly enjoys heavenly pleasures along with her husband as many ten thousand crores (of years) as there are hairs on her body.

60. Blessed is that mother in the world, blessed is that father and blessed is that glorious husband in whose house there is a chaste woman.

61. Due to the merit of a chaste woman, all the three, viz. the members of her father's family, those of her mother's family, and those of her husband's family, enjoy the pleasures of heaven.

62. By violation of the chaste and decent behaviour, women of evil conduct cause the downfall of the three families, viz., that of the father, that of the mother and that of the husband. They are miserable too here and hereafter.

63. Wherever a chaste woman sets her foot on the ground, the earth thinks thus: 'I have no burden here. I have become pure.'

64. It is with the apprehension (of committing a sin) that the Sun, the Moon and the Wind touch a chaste woman only for their own purification and not for anything else.

65. Waters always desire the touch of a chaste woman (and say), "Our dampness (ignorance) has perished today. We have become capable of purifying others."

66. Are there no women proud of their charm and beauty in every house? But, only due to devotion to Viśveśa does one get a chaste woman as wife.

67. Wife is the root cause (of everything good) to every householder; wife is the cause of happiness; wife is conducive to the attainment of righteousness; wife is for the increase of progeny.

68. Two worlds, viz., the visible world and the other world, are won over through wife. A man without a wife is not entitled to perform the rites of Yajña pertaining to gods, manes and guests etc.[1]

---

1. Cf. Jaimini, Pūrva Mīmāṁsā VI.1.17ff; also Āpastaṁba Dh. S, II.6.13. 16-17.

69. Only he should be considered a genuine householder, in whose house there is a chaste wife. The other one—the unchaste—is (as if) devoured at every step by old age assuming the form of an ogress (or is as if devoured by a Rākṣasī called Jarā).

70. Just as the body becomes pure through a plunge in Gaṅgā, so also everything becomes pure through the splendid (and benign) glance of a chaste woman.

71. If somehow by chance, a wife does not follow the husband (after death), even then, the chastity should be preserved unviolated. There is downfall through the violation of chastity.

72. A husband falls from heaven due to the misdemeanour of the wife and not for any other reason. Similarly her mother, father and all her brothers (fall).

73. After the death of the husband, if a woman preserves her widowed state (in purity), she goes back to the husband and enjoys heavenly pleasures.[1]

74. The braided tresses of hair of a widow cause disaster to the husband. Hence a woman shall always get her hair shaved off.

75-77. As a rule (a widow) should take only a single meal (per day) and not a second meal. She must observe (fast) for three days, consecutively, or for five days together or for a fortnight. She may observe fast for a whole month. She may perform the expiatory rites of Cāndrāyaṇa, Kṛcchra, Parāka or Taptakṛcchra. Till the life becomes extinct, she must somehow sustain herself with cooked barley, fruit diet, vegetable dishes or mere milk.

78. A widowed woman lying on a couch causes the downfall of her husband. Hence with a desire for the happiness of her husband she must sleep on bare ground.

79. Anointing and smearing of the body should never be

---

1. VV 73-105 describe the duties of widows (*Vidhavā-dharma*). The verses are elaboration of Manu V. 157-160. But later writers on Dharmaśāstra quoted many of these verses from this Chapter of the Skanda as 'authoritative duties of widows', vide *Nirṇaya-Sindhu* (p.626), *Madana-Pārijāta* (pp. 202-6). Kane, however disapproves of Winternitz's criticism of the inhuman attitude of Hindu Dharmaśāstra towards widows (HD II.i.583).

done by a widowed woman. She must not make use of any type of scents or perfumes.

80. Water-libations with gingelly seeds and Kuśa grass should be offered daily to the husband, his father and grandfather mentioning the Gotra and the respective names.

81. Adoration of Viṣṇu should be performed identifying the husband with the Lord and not otherwise. She should always meditate on her husband as the Lord in the form of Viṣṇu.

82. With a desire for propitiating the husband, all those articles which were very dear to him in the world and everything that he had desired should be given as gift to someone of good qualities.

83. She must do special observances in the months of Vaiśākha, Kārttika and Māgha such as holy ablution, gifting of things, pilgrimage and utterances of Viṣṇu's names respectively.

84. Waterpots in Vaiśākha, ghee-lamps in Kārttika and distributing of grains and gingelly seeds in Māgha are of special significance in the heavenly world.

85-87. Sheds where water is offered to travellers should be arranged during Vaiśākha; *Galantikā* (a pot with a hole in the bottom which is filled with water and kept above the image so that there is a continuous flow of water on the top of the idol) should be offered to the deities. Gift of articles like the following should be made to prominent Brāhmaṇas: sandals, fans, umbrella, thin clothes and garments, sandalpaste, camphor, betel-leaves, flowers, many kinds of waterpots and floral houses, various kinds of beverages, grapes, plantains etc. While gifting she should utter, "May my husband be pleased."

88. In the month of Ūrja (Kārttika) she should eat cooked barley or take a meal one time only. Brinjal, *Sūraṇa* and *Śukaśīmbi* (*Mucuna pruritus*) should be avoided.

89. In the month of Kārttika, one shall avoid oil, honey, brass vessel and preserved pickles.

90. If one observes the vow of silence in Kārttika, she should gift a beautiful bell. If she observes the vow of eating in leafy cups and plates, she should give a bell-metal vessel filled with ghee.

91. If lying on bare ground is the vow observed, she

should gift a soft, smooth bed filled with cotton. If the vow is avoidance of fruits, fruits should be given as gifts. In the case of the vow of avoidance of juice, that juice should be offered as a gift.

92. In the case of the vow of avoidance of grains that particular grain should be given as gift or paddy too can be given. With great effort cows should be given well-adorned and accompanied by gifts of gold.

93. (If) all other gifts on one side and the gift of lights on the other (are weighed to compare the merits derived), all other gifts do not deserve even a sixteenth of (the merit accrued from) the gift of lights in Kārttika.

94. The holy ablution in the month of Māgha should be performed when the sun has slightly risen up. A devotee observing the vow of holy ablution in Māgha shall follow the rules and regulations in accordance with his capacity.

95. Brāhmaṇas, ascetics and sages should be fed with sweet cooked foods, sweetmeats, Pheṇikas, Vaṭakas, Iṇḍarika etc. (these are the sweetmeats and snacks specially to be made).

96. They shall be fried or cooked in ghee. Pepper should be added where necessary. They should be flavoured with white camphor. There must be sugar within. The items prepared should be charming to see and of sweet fragrance.

97. Dry fuel should be given in bulk for the purpose of warding off cold. Shirts and blouses filled with cotton should be given along with mattress filled with cotton and with excellent covers.

98-101. Garments red in colour like madder, cotton cloths, nutmegs, cloves, betel-leaves of all sorts, blankets, shawls of various colours, houses affording protection from blowing winds, soft sandals and slippers, sweet-smelling unguents should be offered. She should offer worship as in famous temples with ghee-spread Kambalas (as at Badarikāśrama Temple) after great ablution. Agallochum should be used in the incense in the sanctum sanctorum. Lamps should have thick wicks. There shall be different kinds of food offerings. She should then utter, "May the Lord in the form of my husband be pleased."

102. A widowed lady should spend the months of Vaiśākha, Kārttika and Māgha with such holy vows and observances as these.

103. She should not mount a bullock even when there is danger to life. She should not wear blouses or gaudy garments.

104. A widow who is fond of her husband, should not do anything without asking her sons. A widow who is accustomed to observe all these vows and practices, is considered auspicious.

105. A widow who is chaste and who observes all these pious practices, shall attain the regions of her husband. She shall not be miserable anywhere.

106. If a woman considers her husband as a deity, there is no difference between her and Gaṅgā. She is directly equal to Umā, the consort of Śiva. Hence a sensible man should worship her.

Bṛhaspati said:

107. O Lopāmudrā, O great mother who always fixes her eyes to the lotus-like feet of her husband, it is as good as we have attained the benefit of bathing in Gaṅgā, since we are fortunate enough to see you.

108. After eulogizing the illustrious chaste lady, the princess (Lopāmudrā), Guru (Bṛhaspati) clever in every art and subject, bowed down to the sage and said:

109. "You are Praṇava. She is Śruti. You are Austerity yourself. She is *Kṣamā* (Forgiveness or the Earth). You are the fruit (of a holy rite while), she is the holy rite. Thus, O great sage, you are blessed.

110. This is the refulgence of a Pativratā (chaste wife). You are the great Brāhmaṇical splendour. Still this is the refulgence of penance. What is there impossible to be achieved by you?

111. There is nothing not known to you. I shall, however, tell you why the Devas have come here. O sage, listen to that:

112-114a. This is the glorious Slayer of Vṛtra, who has performed one hundred sacrifices, who wields the thunderbolt, at whose doorway the eight Siddhis eagerly stand awaiting his favourable glance; at the outskirts of his city the herd of Kāmadhenu cows graze; his citizens always lie down in the cool shades of the wish-yielding Kalpa trees; and in his streets the precious and miraculous Cintāmaṇi jewels abound like gravel and pebbles.

114b-116. This is Fire-god, the source of origin of the universe. This one is Dharmarāja. These are Nirṛti, Varuṇa, Vāyu, Śrīda (i.e., Kubera), Rudra and others.

Powerful persons are propitiated by persons of good conduct for (the fulfilment of) all desires. These persons are those who request. You are the one to be begged for the sake of the world. That can be achieved through a mere word from you. It can help the whole world.

117. A certain mountain named Vindhya has blocked the path of the Sun. He has increased in size due to his rivalry with Meru. You will kindly stop his growth in size (height).

118. Those who are hard by nature, those who cause obstruction to the path, those who prosper or increase (in size etc.) out of rivalry, the prosperity of such people, going beyond limits, is inauspicious."

119-120. On hearing these words of Guru, the great sage did not think for a long time. Reflecting for a moment the sage replied, "Let it be so. I shall accomplish your task." After saying thus he dismissed the heaven-dwellers. Agastya then began to think. He engaged himself in meditation.

Vedavyāsa said:

121. After listening to this chapter on chaste women the devotee, whether it is a woman or a man, casts off the bodice in the form of sins and goes to the world of Śakra (Indra).

CHAPTER FIVE

Agastya's Departure

Parāśara said:*

1. Then, O Sūta, after meditating on Viśveśa, the leading sage spoke to that meritorious lady Lopāmudrā these words:

2. "O fair lady, see what has befallen us. Where is that task and where are we, the followers of the path of ascetics (that is, we are not concerned with it.)!

3. Indra has sportingly chopped off the wings of many mountains. How can his power be ineffective in regard to a single mountain?

4. It is he in whose courtyard there is the wish-yielding Kalpa tree. Thunderbolt is his weapon. The eight Siddhis keep waiting at his doorway. And now he requests a Brāhmaṇa for the fulfilment of his desire!

5. O beloved one, mountains are bewildered and perturbed by forest-conflagration. Where has that power of the Fire-god to arrest his growth in size, gone?

6. This Staff-bearing Lord (Yama) is the controller of all living beings. Is he not competent to chastise him (Vindhya), a mere rocky thing?

7-8. Ādityas, Vasus, Rudras, Tuṣitas, the group of Maruts, Viśvedevas, Dasras (Aśvins) and the other heaven-dwellers there are, at a mere glance of whom all the worlds fall. O my beloved, are they not competent enough to prevent the growth of a mountain?

9. Oh! The reason has been comprehended. The wise utterance about Kāśī, sung as a song by sages who know the truth, is remembered.

10. 'Avimukta should not be abandoned at all by those who yearn for liberation. But there shall be obstacles for the good people who dwell in Kāśī'.[1]

---

*This should have been Pārāśarya, as it is Vyāsa, the son of Parāśara who is speaking.

1. Here 'Avimukta' and 'Kāśī' are used as synonyms. But *Tristhalīsetu* limits it (Avimukta) to a circle with Viśveśvara as centre and 200 Dhanus (800 Hastas) as radius (HD IV.628). It is called 'Avimukta' as it is never left by God Śiva.

11. O blissful lady, that obstacle is imminent; it is very great; it cannot be made otherwise because Viśveśa is averse.

12. Indeed Kāśī has been attained through the blessings of Brāhmaṇas. Who will be inclined to leave it? If at all he is inclined to leave it, he is a man of confounded mind who gives away the tasty morsel held in the hand and licks his own elbow.[1]

13. Alas! How do people leave, out of foolishness, this Kāśī which is a solid mass of good merits? (It is difficult to return to Kāśī again.) Is (even an insignificant thing like) the bulbous root of water-lily obtained at every immersion in water? Is (return to Kāśī) so easy? (Hence one should not leave Kāśī and go elsewhere.)

14. People learn from great men that Kāśī is the fruit of a mass of merits acquired in the course of many previous births. They come to it after undergoing various difficulties, still if they are foolish enough to wish to go elsewhere, they are willing to court disaster (or hell) voluntarily.

15. Where is Kāśī, the revealer of the Absolute Being? Where is the activity opposed to staying therein, which cannot but bring about misery all round? Hence a sensible man does not go elsewhere. Can a pumpkin gourd pass through the mouth (throat) of a goat? (Similarly abandoning of Kāśī by a wise man is impossible.)

16. Alas! How can a man who is likely to perish quickly (die at any moment) leave Kāśī, the merit whereof has been revealed (by Scriptures as well as by Lord Śiva)? My mind says that his (such a man's) merit has dwindled certainly (if he were to leave it).

17. If a man is not so sick (as to die), he may leave off Kāśī that helps all types of living beings (in the attainment of all the four aims of life) and which constitutes the mass of merit of a person devoid of lust and try to go elsewhere, and not anyone else (i.e., the sickly one).

18. Those who are liberated souls do not leave Kāśī. Kāśī eradicates all types of sins; it is inaccessible even to gods; it has the excellent perennial supply of water through Gaṅgā; it

1. The lamentation of Agastya at the prospect of leaving Kāśī (vv 12 ff.) shows the importance of stay in Kāśī.

snaps the noose of worldly existence; it is never left by Śiva and Pārvatī; it acts like an oyster shell for the development of the pearl of salvation and it is the very personification of blissful redemption.

19. O ye men, have you been overwhelmed by excess of sins and deceived (by fate or your own ill-luck) that you are endeavouring to go elsewhere after leaving Kāśī that you reached after a great deal of exertion and suffering, the holy city that could be attained only through exchange of profuse wealth of merit.

20. Alas! It is the ignorance of the people that they think (of going) elsewhere, after leaving off Kāśī that is pleasingly brilliant with the sparkling waters of Gaṅgā and that is held aloft[1]—on the tip of the trident of the Foe of the God of Love (Śiva) even during the period of annihilation (besides during that of sustenance of the world).

21. O ye people capable of thinking! How wonderful! Why do you fall into the middle of the ocean of worldly existence filled solely with the waters of grief-causing sins, (after leaving Kāśī) that is capable of routing all the sins that obstruct salvation, that will serve as the raft (of redemption)?

22. Kāśī is not of easy access (solely) through the adoption of the conduct of the good and performance of Vedic rites, yogic practices, making of gifts and severe penances and austerities. It can be easily acquired through the blessings of Brāhmaṇas or through the grace of the Lord of the universe (Śiva).

23. Elsewhere it is possible to acquire righteousness through profuse wealth; so also wealth and love through plenty of gifts and enjoyments. But as far as salvation is concerned, it cannot be had elsewhere in the same manner as it could be had here.

24. No other region is as pure and holy as Avimukta (i.e., Kāśī). Neither by the Vedas nor by scriptures nor by the Purāṇas have the other regions been dealt with so much as Avimukta. So Avimukta has been always the holy spot of refuge.

---

1. The belief that Kāśī is not submerged during Pralaya (annihilation of the world) is probably due to the fact that the site of original ancient Kāśī i.e. Rājaghāṭa plateau was seldom submerged in flood -water. The ancient city of Divodāsa was on this plateau but it was completely destroyed by Qutb-ud-din Aibak, the general of Mohammad Ghori.

25. That (Sage) Jābāli has said: 'O Āruṇi, the river Asi is considered as Iḍā (left tubular vessel of this name); Varaṇā is the tubular vessel (on the right) Piṅgalā. In between these two is Avimukta.[1]

26-28. (Between Iḍā and Piṅgalā) There is the great tubular vessel Suṣumṇā. All the three constitute this Varāṇasī.

At the time of death, Hara expounds the Tāraka Brahman (*Praṇava*) into the right ears of all creatures. Thereby they become Brahman themselves. In this context there is a verse, as the expounders of the Vedas say:

At the time of death here, the Lord, through the instruction in Tāraka Mantra undoubtedly liberates the creatures that reside in Avimukta.

29. There is no other holy spot on a par with Avimukta. There is no other goal than Avimukta. There is no other Liṅga on a par with Avimukta. Again and again it is repeatedly stated that this is the truth.

30. If anyone leaves off Avimukta and takes interest elsewhere, he casts off salvation from his palm and searches for other spiritual powers.' "

31-32. After decidedly concluding through Śrutis and Purāṇas the extraordinary power of the holy place, (since) there is no other Liṅga equal to that of Viśvanātha and there is no city equal to Kāśī in all the three worlds, the noble-souled sage, the leading chief of all the saints, bowed down to Śrī Kālabhairava[2] and submitted: "I have come here to take leave of you, because you are the presiding deity of the city of Śrīkāśī.

33. Alas! O Kālabhairava, did I not propitiate you with fruits, roots and flowers on all Sundays and Tuesdays, on all Aṣṭamīs (eighth day) and Caturdaśīs (fourteenth day) every fortnight? Will you be finding fault with me despite the fact that I am free from sins? (Why are you expelling me from Kāśī?)

34. Ah! O Kālabhairava, you assume a very terrible form that is destructive of heinous sins. Don't you then lift up your

---

1. A Yogic interpretation of the geographical position of Avimukta, vide Jābāla Upa. p. 145 of *Upaniṣat Saṅgraha* (MLBD).

2. He is a Yakṣa regarded as the Police Chief of Kāśī. His stone idol is shown to wield a big cudgel. His temple is about a mile to the north of Viśveśvara temple. (For details vide *infra* ch. 30.)

hand and protect the people residing in Vārāṇasī who gather around extremely terrified by proclaiming to them, 'Do not be afraid?'

35. O Yakṣarāja armed with a staff, O son of Pūrṇabhadra having a form as fascinating as the moon, O excellent one, O protector of the residents of Kāśī, indeed you know the entire misery arising from penance; why do you banish me out (of Kāśī)?

36. You are the giver of food. You are the giver of life. You are the giver of knowledge. You are the bestower of salvation. By means of clusters of matted hair and garlands of leading serpents, you give the final embellishments to the people (after death).

37. Your attendants (named) Saṁbhrama and Udbhrama are experts in the consideration of the biographical details of the people living here. They create great confusion in the minds of evil people and drive them away from this holy place instantly.

38. Listen, O Ḍhuṇḍhi[1] Vināyaka, to my words. I am prattling like a helpless man. All the obstacles are under your control. Do I linger here like a man of evil deeds? (Hence do not drive me away through obstacles.)

39. May these five Vināyakas, i.e., Cintāmaṇi, Kapardin, the two Aśagajas and Siddhivināyaka, listen.

40. I have not made any slanderous reference to anyone. I have not injured the interest of anyone. I had no covetous thought for others' property or wife. Then why this adverse culmination?

41. Gaṅgā was resorted to by me three times (every day). Śrī Viśvanātha is always (regularly) visited by me. Religious processions and pilgrimages have been attended to by me on every festival occasion. Why is then, this culmination causing obstacles?"

---

1. Out of 56 Gaṇeśas in Vārāṇasī, the Ḍhuṇḍhi Vināyaka is the chief. His temple is just near Viśvanātha and as such occupies a central position. His name is derived from√ḍhuṇḍi 'to search' (*Infra* Ch. 57.33). For other Gaṇeśas, see *infra* Ch. 57.59, 113.

42. O mother Viśālākṣī[1], O Bhavānī, O Maṅgalā, O Jyeṣṭhā, O Īśī, O Saubhāgya-Vidhāna-Sundarī (who is a beautiful deity bringing about all conjugal bliss), O Viśve-Vidhe (O multifarious one) and other deities in Kāśī! (Obeisance to you, the swallower of the universe,) O Śrī Citraghaṇṭā, O Vikaṭā, O Durgikā! (These are all the deities in Kāśī.)

43. These deities of Kāśī are my witnesses. May they listen. I am not going away from this place for my own sake. It is because I have been requested by the gods that I am doing this. What of all things is not done for helping others?

44. Formerly did Dadhīci not give his bones? Did Bali not give the three worlds to the suppliant (Vāmana)? Did Madhu and Kaiṭabha not offer their heads (to Viṣṇu)? Tārkṣya (Garuḍa) became the vehicle of Viṣṇu."

45. The eminent sage took leave of all the sages, all the inhabitants of that place including children and old people, the grasses, the creepers and all the trees. He then circumambulated the city and then set out.

46. All the good omens may not be there and he may have to traverse a lowly path even; if a man sets out after visiting the Moon-crested Lord, he will definitely accomplish his intended job.

47. Better is the case of grasses, trees and hedges in Kāśī. They neither commit sin nor move away elsewhere. We are the foremost among the mobile beings, but fie upon us who go away today leaving off Kāśī!

48. (After bath) he rinsed his mouth (with the waters of) Asi again and again. Then the sage said glancing at the rows of mansions (i.e. Temples) all around: "O my eyes, look at Kāśī straight with delight. Where are you and where is this city? Alas! (It is difficult to have a sight of Kāśī again.)

49. May the groups of spirits moving about in the out-

---

1. This is a joint appeal to Goddesses of Vārāṇasī, though they have separate temples as follows:

a. Viśālākṣī - to the south-west of Viśvanātha at Mīrā Ghāṭa

b. Bhavānī - at Rāma Temple near Annapūrṇā

c. Maṅgalā Gaurī - at Rāma Ghāṭa.

d. Jyeṣṭhā - to the west of Jyeṣṭheśvara

e. Saubhāgya-Vidhāna-Sundarī or Saubhāgya Gaurī - in Ādi-Viśveśvara Temple.

skirts, laugh as they please now, clapping their hands and grasping one another's hands. I am going away leaving Kāśī, the sole mass of merits."

50. After lamenting thus very much, though he had his wife to assist him, like those Krauñca birds (in front of Vālmīki formerly), Sage Agastya fell into a great swoon prattling like one in separation: "Alas! Kāśī, O Kāśī, come again and glance at me."

51. He stopped for a short while and said: "O Śiva, O Śiva, O Śiva. Dear wife, we shall go. Indeed those heaven-dwellers are very hard. Don't you remember what they did after sending Madana, who is competent to bestow happiness on the three worlds, to the Three-eyed Lord?"

52. The sage went ahead a few steps with sweat drops appearing on his forehead. By then, it appeared as though the ground shrank below with the fear, 'I will be doomed for not rising up by way of revering him.'

53. Seated as though in the vehicle of his penance, within half the period required for twinkling (of eyes), the sage saw in front of him the lofty Mountain who had blocked the path of the sky.

54-56. On seeing the sage standing before him along with his wife, the Mountain trembled. The sage who had destroyed Vātāpi, the brother of Ilvala, appeared to be blazing like the fire at the time of the final annihilation with three fiery flames, one arising from the separation from Kāśī and the other two from the power of penance and the wrath (of the sage). The Mountain became dwarf-like as though he was desirous of going deep into the earth. He said: "Let me be granted the favour of being commanded. I am your servant."

Agastya said:

57. O wise Vindhya, you are good and you know me factually (i.e. my prowess). Be short in stature till my return.

58. After saying this, the sage, the storehouse of austerities, made the southern quarter duly possessed of a guardian in the form of his footprints in the company of that chaste lady (in that direction).

59-60. When the excellent sage had gone, the trembling Mountain anxiously looked in that direction and thought: 'If he has gone, well it is. I am reborn today as I have not been cursed by Agastya. There is no one blessed like me.'

61. At that time, Aruṇa, conscious of the opportune moment, drove the horses. When the movement of the Sun was revived as before, the whole world derived great relief and normalcy.

62. The Mountain remained as though suppressed by the great burden of the thought, 'Perhaps the sage may return today, tomorrow or the day after.'

63. The sage has not returned till today. Nor has the Mountain increased in size like the tree of wishful thinking of wicked people.

64. There is no doubt about it that if a mean fellow possessing much of jealousy desires to rise up, the very news of his prosperity recedes and this too affects his previous prosperity (It may vanish).

65. The wishes of rogues are not fulfilled. The wishes which are fulfilled are certainly lost. Thereby the whole universe protected by Viśveśa becomes happy.

66. Just as the breasts of widows get plump and absorbed within the bosom, so also the ambitions of the wicked do after soaring up very high.

67. Just as a rivulet becomes over-flooded even when there is a slight shower and begins to erode its banks, so also the affluence of a wicked man based on trivial gains, undermines his own family.

68. If a man tries to demonstrate and display his ability, unaware of that of others, he gets only a derisive laughter. So also this Mountain here had it.

Vyāsa said:

69. Even while roaming about on the charming banks of Godāvarī, the sage could not get rid of the distress due to the separation from Kāśī.

70. The sage used to stretch out his arms and embrace the wind blowing in his direction from the north and enquire about Kāśī and its welfare.

71. (He used to say:) "O Lopāmudrā, nowhere on the

face of this earth can that inexplicable image of Vārāṇasī be seen, because its maker is not Brahmā."

72. The sage wandered here and there prattling like this in some places, standing in certain places, running elsewhere, faltering there and sitting here.

73-75. Proceeding ahead from there, Agastya, the mass of merit, the storehouse of penance, saw in front of him Goddess Mahālakṣmī (of Kolhapur) like a lucky man, the best of glory. She had the lustre of a hundred rising moons. With her own lustre, she appeared to surpass even the Sun, even during the day time. She was brilliantly dazzling, (yet) she appeared to alleviate the distress of his (Agastya's) mind.

76. Lotuses shrink and close during nights. During New-Moon days the Moon goes away somewhere. There is the fear from the Mandara mountain in the Milk Ocean. Hence, it appears as though she has put up her permanent residence here (Kolhapur).[1]

77. Ever since Mādhava retained her with great honour, she had certainly stayed here as though out of spiteful rivalry with her co-wife.

78. A great Asura was frightening the three worlds in the form of a boar. The goddess killed that demon and stayed in the beautiful city of Kolhapur ever since.

79. After reaching the place the excellent sage bowed down to Mahālakṣmī who bestows whatever is desired, through very pleasing words. He was highly delighted in his mind.

Agastya said:

(Prayer to Mahālakṣmī)

80. O mother Kamalā of large eyes resembling lotus, I bow down (to you). O mother of the universe, residing in the lotus-like heart of Śrī Viṣṇu! O Lakṣmī, fair in complexion like the inner kernel of a lotus, be pleased with me. O daughter of the Milk Ocean, you are the sole refuge of those who bow down always.

---

1. This explains why Lakṣmī stayed at Kolhapur. The Purāna-writer is not aware that 'Kola' was the name of the Asura killed by Mahālakṣmī. The assumption of the form of a boar (Kola) by the Asura (v 78) is a conjecture of the Purāṇa-writer as *Kola* means a boar.

81. You are the glorious lustre in the abode of Upendra (Viṣṇu). O sole mother of Madana, you are the moonlight in the Moon, O goddess with a face captivating the mind like the Moon. You are the splendour in the Sun. You shine with all refulgence in all the three worlds. O Lakṣmī, the sole refuge of those who bow down always, be pleased with me.

82. You are the Śakti (the burning power) that always abide in fire; in collaboration with you, Vedhas (Brahmā) creates the different types of worlds. Viśvaṁbhara (Viṣṇu) sustains and supports everything with your (assistance), O Lakṣmī, the sole refuge of these who bow down always; be pleased with me.

83. O deity free from impurities, Hara annihilates only those things forsaken by you; (actually) you create, sustain and annihilate. You are *Parā* (the greatest) and the *Avarā* (the smallest). O pure one, Hari became worthy of being adored by securing you (as his consort). O Lakṣmī, the sole refuge of those who always bow down, be pleased with me.

84. O splendid deity, only he on whom your benign glance falls, becomes heroic with good qualities. He alone is a good scholar; he alone is blessed; he alone is worthy of honour through good ancestry, good conduct and artistic qualities. That man is the only clean one in the entire world.

85. Wherever you happen to stay for even a moment whether in a man, an elephant, a horse, a group of women, grass, lake, temple, house, cooked food, jewel, bird, animal, bed or a plot of land, that alone becomes splendid and glorious, O deity identical with all; none else (can do so).

86. Only the things touched by you get purity. All the things forsaken by you are unclean, O Lakṣmī, O consort of Śrī Viṣṇu. O Kamalā residing in the lotus, wherever your name is (uttered), auspiciousness is there.

87. Where can there be misery unto those who always repeat the names of Lakṣmī, viz., Lakṣmī, Śrī, Kamalā, Kamalālayā, Padmā, Ramā, Nalinayugmakarā, Mā, Kṣīrodajā, Amṛtakuṁbhakarā, Irā and Viṣṇupriyā.

88. After eulogizing Goddess Mahālakṣmī, the beloved of Hari, thus, the sage accompanied by his wife bowed down and lay down like a log of wood with the eight limbs (touching the ground).

Śrī said:

89. O son of Mitra and Varuṇa, get up, get up. Welfare unto you. O chaste lady Lopāmudrā of auspicious holy vows, get up.

90. I am delighted with this eulogy. Let the cherished desire in you heart, whatever it is, be requested for. O highly fortunate princess free of impurities, sit here.

91. I desire to get my body that was scorched by the weapons and missiles of the demon (Kola) alleviated a bit, by these characteristics of your limbs and your sacred vows.

92. After saying this, the beloved wife of Hari embraced that wife of the sage. Out of love, she adorned her with many ornaments indicating conjugal bliss.

93. Again she said: "O sage, I know the cause that torments your heart. The fire of grief caused by the separation from Kāśī indeed scorches all sentient beings.

94. Formerly when that Lord Viśveśa went to Mandara, a condition similar to this befell him too, due to the separation from Kāśī.

95. In order to know the full details of that (Kāśī) the Trident-bearing Lord deputed Brahmā, Keśava, his attendants, Gaṇeśvara and the Devas.

96. Even now all of them are roaming about considering the good qualities of Kāśī. There is no other city like it anywhere. Where is that city?"

97. On hearing this, the highly fortunate sage bowed down and spoke to Goddess Śrī, the following words filled with devotional fervour.

98. "If a boon has to be given to me, if I deserve a boon, let me have an opportunity to return to Vārāṇasī. This is my boon.

99. Never should those people suffer from distress and poverty—the people who always read this prayer composed by me with devotion unto you.

100. Let them not be separated from those whom they love. Let there not be destruction of their assets. Let there be success everywhere. Let there not be any break in the line of their progeny."

Śrī said:

101. O sage, let everything be like the way it has been uttered by you. The recitation of this prayer will bring about my presence.

102. May not Alakṣmī (ill-luck, misfortune) or Kālakarṇī the Ogress, enter their house. For the purpose of quelling (the distresses) of cows, horses and other animals, one should always repeat this prayer.

103. This prayer should be written on a leaf of Bhūrja tree (or the bark) and tied around the neck. It causes the *Śānti* (peaceful alleviation) of children attacked by malignant Planets, Bālagraha etc.

104. This is a greater secret than my own *Bīja.* It should be scrupulously preserved. It should not be imparted to one lacking in faith. It should not be imparted hurriedly.

105. O eminent Brāhmaṇa, listen further to another thing. In the future Dvāpara, the twenty-ninth one, O Brāhmaṇa, you will become Vyāsa. It is true.

106. At that time you will classify the Vedas and teach the Purāṇas and pious practices. Then you will reach Vārāṇasī and attain the fulfilment of all your desires.

107. Now I shall mention something beneficial to you. Act according to it. After proceeding a little ahead, visit Lord Skanda stationed in front.

108. The Six-faced Lord will duly narrate to you the secret of Vārāṇasī in the same manner as has been recounted by Śiva to him. It will cause satisfaction to you, O Brāhmaṇa.

109. After getting the boon thus, Agastya bowed down to Mahālakṣmī and went to the place where the peacock-vehicled Lord Kumāra was present.

CHAPTER SIX

Tīrthādhyāya
(Sacred Places)

Pārāśarya said:

1. O Sūta, O illustrious one, listen to the story comparable (in sanctity) to Śruti which, if retained in the heart, enables a man to attain all his aims in life.

2. Thereafter, the sage accompanied by his wife took a plunge in the holy river with the current of nectarine bliss arising from the vision of Śrī. He derived the highest joy and bliss.

3. O Sūta of pure mind, you are born of the sacred pit of sacrificial fire;[1] listen to a saying uttered by those who know the ancient lore.

4. If a keen sense of helping others is ever wakeful in the heart of the good, all their adversities perish and riches accrue at every step.

5. What is obtained by extending help (to others) cannot be derived through severe austerities; that purity cannot be had through the holy ablution and the sacred waters; that benefit cannot be had through plentiful gifts.

6. The piety resulting from helping others and the piety born of gifts etc., were weighed together in one balance by Brahmā. The former was weightier.

7. After churning through the network of verbal discussions, this is the conclusion arrived at—there is no piety greater than helping others and no heinous sin greater than injuring others.

8. The example is set by Agastya who was keen in helping (the gods). Where is such a misery born (of the separation) from Kāśī? Where is such a benign sight of the face of Śrī?

9. Life and different types of wealth are as fickle as the tips of the ears of an elephant. Hence the only thing to be carried out by a learned man is rendering help to others.

---

1. According to Vāyu Purāṇa I.i.28-33, Sūta was born on the *Sutyā* day in the sacrifice of Pṛthu, from the sacrificial fire, but was regarded as of mixed caste as the oblation meant for Bṛhaspati was mixed with that of Indra.

10. The sage felt to have achieved all his objects by directly seeing that Lakṣmī by uttering whose name a man becomes highly boosted so as not to be contained within anything (i.e. becomes greater still).

11. As he went ahead, he casually espied Śrī Śaila from afar, where Lord Śiva, the slayer of Tripura, was directly present.

12-14. The sage spoke to his wife with a delighted mind: "O my beloved, standing here alone, you look at the extremely brilliant peak of Śrī Śaila. It is glorious and by perceiving it, men will not be reborn here in this world. The extent of this mountain is eighty-four Yojanas. Since it is full of Liṅgas all over, one should circumambulate it."

Lopāmudrā said:

15. I wish to submit something if it is permitted by my lord and master. A woman who speaks before obtaining the permission of her master becomes fallen.

Agastya said:

16. O lady, what is it that you are desirous of saying? Say that unhesitatingly. Indeed no statement of women like you can cause grief to the husbands.

17. Then the pious lady bowed down to the sage and asked for the sake of the welfare of all and for the removal of her own doubts:

Lopāmudrā said:

18. (You say:) By looking at the peak of Śrī Śaila one has no rebirth. If this is the truth, why is Kāśī sought (by you and others)?

Agastya said:

19. O beautiful lady, listen. O pure lady, what you ask is true. This has been decided on many occasions by sages, the seekers of truth.

20. There are many holy spots bringing about salvation. Decision has been arrived at in regard to that also. I shall enumerate them to you. Listen with attention for a short while.

21. The first and the foremost is the well reputed king of Tīrthas (Tīrtharāja) named Prayāga. It is conducive to the realization of the wishes of all the holy spots. (Other holy spots incur the sins of those who resort to them. In order to wipe off those sins, they have to resort to Prayāga.) It accords piety, love, wealth and salvation.

22-25. The others are Naimiṣa, Kurukṣetra, Gaṅgādvāra, Avantikā, Ayodhyā, Mathurā, Dvārakā and Amarāvatī, the place where Sarasvatī and Sindhu join the sea, the meeting place of Gaṅgā and the ocean, Kāntī (Kāñcī), Tryambaka and Saptagodāvarī*, Kālañjara, Prabhāsa, Badarikāśrama, Mahālaya, Oṁkārakṣetra (Amarakaṇṭaka), Jagannāthapurī which is the most excellent of all the shrines of Viṣṇu, Gokarṇa, Bhṛgukaccha (Broach—Gujarat), Bhṛgutuṅga (in Nepal—De), Puṣkara, Śrīparvata and other holy spots and Dhārātīrtha.

26. O my beloved, there are mental holy spots such as Truth etc. These too are the bestowers of salvation. No doubt need be entertained in this regard.

27. The holy spot called Gayātīrtha bestows salvation to the Pitṛs (Manes). Their sons too are liberated from indebtedness to the grandfathers.

Sadharmiṇī (The partner in pious practices, wife i.e., Lopāmudrā) *said:*

28. O highly intelligent one, what are those holy spots called mental holy spots? It behoves you to narrate them.

Agastya said:

29-32. O sinless lady, listen even as I enumerate the mental holy spots. By scrupulously taking the holy dips in them a man attains the greatest goal.

Truth is a Tīrtha (holy place); forbearance is a Tīrtha; control of the organs of sense and action is a Tīrtha; compassion for all living beings is a Tīrtha; straightforwardness is a Tīrtha.

Religious gifting is a Tīrtha; self-restraint is a Tīrtha; contentedness is mentioned as a Tīrtha; celibacy is the greatest Tīrtha; speaking pleasing words is a Tīrtha.

---

* A holy place in Andhra Pradesh, near Solangipur, 16 miles from Pithapur, West Godavari District.

Knowledge is a Tīrtha; courage (fortitude) is a Tīrtha; penance is cited as a Tīrtha; the absolute purity of the mind is the holiest of all holy Tīrthas.

33-35. Holy ablution is not the mere drenching of the body in water. He who has the purificatory bath of mental control, is really the one who has had his holy ablution; he is (really) clean; he has removed all the impurities of the mind.

One who is covetous, slanderous, cruel, a hypocrite and sensualist is sinful and dirty, even if he takes a plunge in all the sacred waters.

A man does not become free from impurities only by doing away with the bodily dirt. If the mental dirt is wiped away, one becomes internally pure.

36. Aquatic beings are born and die in water. But they do not go to heaven because their mental impurities have not been cleansed.

37. Too much of attachment to sensual objects is called mental impurity. Non-attachment to them is cited as freedom from impurities.

38. If the mind within is defiled, it does not become purified by taking a holy dip in sacred waters. It is impure like a pot of toddy washed hundreds of times in water.

39. If the mental predilection is not pure, all these, viz. liberal gifts, sacrifice, penance, cleanliness, pilgrimage and learning, become non-Tīrthas.

40. Wherever a man who has curbed all his organs of sense and action lives, there he has his (holy places like) Kurukṣetra, Naimiṣa, Puṣkara etc.

41. He who takes his holy bath in the mental holy spot that is cleansed with perfect knowledge, that has meditation for its waters and that removes the dirt of attachment and hatred, attains the greatest goal.

42. These characteristics of the mental holy places have been recounted to you, O noble lady. Listen to the cause that brings about sanctity to worldly holy spots.

43. Just as there are certain excellent parts of the body considered very holy and pure, so also some regions of the earth are considered most meritorious.

44. The meritoriousness of holy spots is considered to be a result of the mysterious influence of the ground, of the

water and of the fire thereof as well as of the backing and acceptance (as holy) by sages.

45. Hence he who takes his holy bath in both the holy spots, i.e., the worldly holy spots and the mental holy spots, attains the greatest goal.

46. A man becomes poor by not observing fast for three whole nights, by not resorting to the holy spots and by not giving gold and cows.

47. The benefit that one obtains by undertaking pilgrimages to holy spots is not obtained by performing holy sacrifices including Agniṣṭoma etc., along with liberal monetary gifts.

48. He whose hands, feet and mind are well-controlled, he who possesses learning, penance and reputation enjoys the benefit of a holy spot.

49. One who desists from accepting monetary gifts, one who is contented with whatever accrues to him and one who is devoid of egotistic tendencies enjoys the benefit of pilgrimage to holy spots.

50. One who is free from religious hypocrisy, one who never undertakes (unholy activities), one who eats but very limited quantities, one who has conquered the organs of sense and action and one who is completely free from affectionate attachments enjoys the benefit of the pilgrimage to holy spots.

51. One who is free from anger, one whose intellect is free from impurities, one who is invariably truthful in utterance, one who strictly adheres to holy vows and observances, one who considers all living beings on an equal footing with one's self, enjoys the benefit of pilgrimage to holy spots.

52. If one visits holy spots with an understanding of what is righteous and what is not, if one has sincerity, full faith, mental courage and concentration, he becomes pure even if he perpetrates sins, and still more pure becomes one who regularly performs holy rites.

53. He is not reborn as a brute; he does not take birth in dismal godforsaken places; he never becomes miserable; he attains heaven and gets the means of salvation.

54. A person who has no faith, a sinful soul, an atheist, one who is constantly in doubt and one who is too much a rationalist—these five never attain the benefit of pilgrimage to holy spots.

55. Those men who undertake pilgrimage to holy spots in accordance with the injunctions; those who patiently endure all mutually opposed pairs (of pain, pleasure etc.), attain heaven.

56-57. One who is desirous of undertaking a pilgrimage should at the outset observe fast at home. He should then adore and honour Gaṇeśa, the manes, Brāhmaṇas, holy men in accordance with his ability. After taking food by way of concluding the observance of fast, he should joyously follow the regulations. After returning, he should worship the manes. He will then derive the benefits as mentioned.

58-59. In holy spots, Brāhmaṇas should not be subjected to scrutiny; whoever comes seeking food should be fed. The offering of the balls to the manes shall be in the form of *Saktu* (a preparation from barley flour), *Caru* (rice, barley and pulse boiled) or milk pudding; Śrāddha should be performed, as observed by the sages, through oil-cake and jaggery. *Arghya* and *Āvāhana* (invocation and reception) can be omitted.

60. Whether at the proper time or not, Śrāddha and Tarpaṇa should be performed without delay. There should not be hindrance in the middle.

61. If anyone reaches a holy spot casually (when on some other duty or work) and takes the holy bath, he may very well derive the benefit of the bath but not that of pilgrimage.

62. There will be suppression of the sin of persons committing sins in a holy place. In the case of men having faith, the holy spot shall bestow the benefit as mentioned.

63. He who goes to a holy spot on behalf of others derives one-sixteenth of the merit. He who goes there casually gets half of the merit.

64. A pilgrim should make an effigy (of the persons whom he represents) and take the holy dip in the sacred waters. That person on whose behalf this holy bath is undertaken, obtains one-eighth of the merit.

65. Holy fast should be undertaken in a holy spot. The hairs on the head should be shaved off because thereby the sins of the head vanish.

66. The fast is to be observed on the day prior to the arrival at the holy spot. On the day of arrival he should perform the rite of Śrāddha.

67. While enumerating the holy spots the subsidiary activities too were recounted to you by me. This shall be conducive to the attainment of heaven and a means of salvation too.

68. These seven cities are the bestowers of salvation here itself: Kāśī, Kāntī (Kāñcī), Māyā, Ayodhyā, Dvārāvatī, Mathurā and Avantikā.

69. The entire Śrī Śaila (the area extending over 84 Yojanas) bestows salvation. Kedāra is superior to it. Prayāga is a greater bestower of salvation than Śrī Śaila and Kedāra.

70. Avimukta excels Prayāga, the foremost among holy spots. Undoubtedly nowhere else can salvation be acquired as in Avimukta.

71. The other holy spots of salvation make Kāśī accessible. If one does not get released (from Saṁsāra) even after reaching Kāśī, he cannot get salvation even if he visits millions of other holy spots.

72. In this context, I shall mention an ancient mythological legend as recounted to a Brāhmaṇa Śivaśarman by the attendants of Viṣṇu.

73-74. By listening to this Tīrthādhyāya with a well-controlled mind and by narrating it to Brāhmaṇas endowed with faith and devotion, to Kṣatriyas engrossed in pious practices, to Vaiśyas following the path of the good and to Śūdras devoted to Brāhmaṇas, a Brāhmaṇa becomes rid of sins.

CHAPTER SEVEN

The Seven Holy Cities

Agastya said:

1. There was a certain Brāhmaṇa, the most excellent of all Brāhmaṇas, in Mathurā. His son of great refulgence is well-known by the name Śivaśarman.

2-7. The Brāhmaṇa Śivaśarman duly studied the Vedas and comprehended the meanings of the texts fully. He read Dharmaśāstra texts and understood the Purāṇas. He learnt the

Aṅgas (ancillary subjects), through discussion and pondered over the texts in logic, went through the two (Pūrva and Uttara) Mīmāṁsā systems and mastered Dhanurveda ('science of archery'). He worked hard in the art of dance; he acquired (mastery) in many texts on political economy; he comprehended the behaviour of horses and elephants; he practised the various types of arts; he became an expert in the Science of Mantras (magical and mystical spells); he learnt the languages of the different countries and the scripts of alien lands. Through pious and legitimate means, he earned wealth. He enjoyed pleasures as much as he liked. He begot sons of good qualities and divided his assets among them. He then realised that youth is of fleeting nature. He found that old age reached his ears (in the form of greying hairs). Then the excellent Brāhmaṇa felt great anxiety.

8. He thought: 'My time was spent in reading and learning; then in earning wealth. Lord Maheśāna who is capable of eradicating all karmas was not adored and propitiated.

9. Viṣṇu, Hari, the destroyer of all sins, was not pleased by me; Gaṇeśa, the bestower of all the desires of men, was not adored by me.

10. The Sun-god, the destroyer of masses of darkness, was not worshipped by me anywhere. Mahāmāyā, the creator and sustainer of the universe and the destroyer of worldly bondage, was not meditated upon.

11. The Devas, the bestowers of all prosperity, were not propitiated by all types of Yajñas. Service was not rendered to groves of Tulasī plants for the sake of quelling sins.

12. Brāhmaṇas who are the saviours from adversities here and hereafter, have not been rendered satisfied by me through savoury cooked rice and sweet juices.

13. Trees with plenty of blossoms and fruits, smooth glossy sprouts and ample shade have not been planted by me, an act which could have yielded fruit (viz., happiness) here and hereafter.

14. Noble married women enjoying conjugal bliss, who are capable of providing excellent places of residence here and hereafter have not been adorned (by me) with ornaments for every limb, silk clothes and bodices befitting them.

15. A fertile land (the grant of which) could have warded

off (the necessity to go to) Yama's region has not been gifted to Brāhmaṇas. Gold that utterly removes sins, has not been given to a man of high caste (i.e. Brāhmaṇa)

16. A cow with her calf that removes sins here quickly and accords happiness in the next seven births, has not been bedecked and gifted to a deserving person.

17. No pond, well or lake has been dug in order to wipe off the indebtedness to our mother. No guest, who could have shown the pathway to heaven, has been pleased (by me).

18. No umbrella, pair of sandals, and water pot have been given as gift to a pedestrian, which could have afforded (me) pleasure along the pathway to heaven or while proceeding to Saṁyaminī (i.e. the region of Yama).

19. I have never given monetary help to anyone for celebrating the marriage of (his) daughter, which gift could have increased the happiness here and could have provided one with a celestial virgin (hereafter).

20. Out of covetousness, I did not perform the Vājapeya sacrifice which could have accorded plenty of savoury food and sweet beverages in the course of this birth as well as in the next. Nor did I take the holy valedictory ablution therein.

21. I did not build any splendid temple and install a Liṅga (therein). Had that Liṅga been installed the entire universe would have been stabilized.

22. A holy shrine of Viṣṇu that bestows all prosperities has not been built by me; nor have the idols of the Sun and Gaṇeśa been installed by me.

23. Neither Gaurī nor Mahālakṣmī has been painted even in a picture. If the idols of these are made (the man) never becomes ugly or destitute.

24. For the purpose of obtaining plenty of divine garments, I have not given as gifts fine and glamorous clothes of various colours to Brāhmaṇas.

25. For the cleansing of all sins, gingelly seeds soaked in ghee have not been consigned to the well-kindled holy fire after sanctifying them with Mantras.

26. I have not performed the *Japa* of (Vedic hymns like) Śrīsūkta, Pāvamanī Ṛks, Brāhmaṇas, Maṇḍalas, Puruṣasūkta and Śatarudriya, the remover of sins.

27. Leaving off Sundays and thirteenth lunar days I have

not served (attended upon) the holy fig tree. Indeed it promptly removes sins but not during the night or Fridays.

28. Soft beds with costly cotton have not been gifted along with mirrors and lamps, which are capable of according all prosperities and pleasures.

29-30. None of these things has been given as gifts by me: goat, horse, buffalo, sheep, slave girl, deer's skin, gingelly seeds, water pots along with curd-soaked wheat flour, seat, soft sandals, massage of the feet, lamp as gift, special arrangement for drinking, water-sheds for pedestrians, fans, garments, betel-leaves etc. together with other things rendering the mouth and breath fragrant.

31-32. The daily Śrāddha offering, oblations to the spirits or living beings, worship of guests were not performed and other praiseworthy things were not given. If one gives all these, one does not enter the region of Yama, nor does one see Yama, his messengers or the torturers in the region of Yama. They (such persons) are meritorious. But I have not done any of these things.

33. Kṛcchra, Cāndrāyaṇa and other expiatory rites, the observance of fast by day and a meal at night etc., cause purity of the body. But these were not at all performed by me.

34. The daily mouthfuls of fodder to the cows were not given; I have not scratched the cows for removing the itching sensation; no cow stuck in the mud has been lifted up by me —an act that would have bestowed happiness on me in the Goloka (Region of Cows).

35. Suppliants have not been rendered satisfied by me through the objects requested for by them. Surely, in the next birth, I shall have to roam about saying, 'Give! Give!'

36. Neither the Vedas nor the scriptural texts, neither riches nor the wife nor the son, neither the field nor the mansion can take one to the end of Māyā.'

37-38. Śivaśarman thought thus after racking his brains fully. Ultimately he decided thus in his mind: 'If this is done, it shall be conducive to my welfare. As long as the body is hale and hearty, as long as there is no deficiency in the organs of sense and action, it behoves me to undertake a pilgrimage that can bring about my eternal welfare.'

39-41. The Brāhmaṇa spent five or six days in the house

thus. On an auspicious lunar day, when the week day was good and when the *Lagna* was propitious, the Brāhmaṇa observed fast for the night and performed Śrāddha in the morning. He bowed down to the leaders of the attendants (of Śiva) and the Brāhmaṇas. He came to the decision that pilgrimage is the highest ladder leading to the state of liberation and that it retains all the creatures there. Thereafter the wise Brāhmaṇa took his food and started.

42-43. The Brāhmaṇa went some distance along the way. He then rested on the road for a short while and thought: 'Where shall I go first? There are many holy places on the earth. The span of life is unsteady. The mind is fickle. So I shall go to the seven (holy) cities because all the holy spots and shrines are present there.'[1]

44-45. He went to the city of Ayodhyā and took his holy bath in Sarayū. He propitiated the manes by offering balls of rice in the different holy spots. There he stayed for five nights and fed Brāhmaṇas. Thereafter the delighted Brāhmaṇa went to Prayāga, the king of holy places.

46. That is the place where the two excellent rivers of black and white colours, viz., Yamunā and Gaṅgā are present. They are inaccessible even to Suras. By taking his holy ablution there, (even) a sinner realizes the highest Brahman.

47. That is the holy place of Prajāpati inaccessible to all. Only through merits accumulated, is it obtained and not otherwise or through heaps of wealth.

48. It is the place where the sacred celestial river (Gaṅgā) comes and meets the splendid river (Yamunā) having its source in the Kalinda Mountain, which suppresses (the evils of) the Kali age and the god of Death.

49. The word *Prayāga* means that which is superior to all *Yāgas* (sacrifices). Those who perform sacrifices there and get their bodies made wet by the river are not reborn.

50. The trident and axe wielding Maheśvara is directly

1. The seven cities traditionally regarded as holy and givers of salvation (Mokṣada) are Ayodhyā, Mathurā, Māyā (Haridwar), Kāśī, Kāñcī (Tamil Nadu), Avantikā, Dvārāvatī (Dvārakā). The Brāhmāṇa Śivaśarman, therefore, decides to visit them as a pilgrim. Here Prayāga (Allahabad) is added as it is the 'King of Tīrthas (Tīrtha-rāja). The popular etymology of Prayāga is given in v 49 below. VV 46-69 describe the greatness of Prayāga.

present there himself. It is he who points out the path of salvation to the living beings who take their holy dip there.

51. There is an Akṣayya ('Never-fading') eternal holy banyan tree[1] there, with its roots going deep into the seven nether worlds. At the time of the ultimate annihilation, the son of Mṛkaṇḍu (i.e., Mārkaṇḍeya, the sage) climbed it and stayed (free from annihilation).

52. That should be known as Hiraṇyagarbha himself assuming the form of the banyan tree. The devotee, who feeds Brāhmaṇas with faith and devotion near it, attains eternal merit.

53. The Consort of Lakṣmī directly comes there and takes men to the great region of Viṣṇu in the form of Śrīmādhava.

54. The excellent black and white rivers (Yamunā-Gaṅgā) are mentioned in the Vedas. It is certain that those who get their limbs submerged therein attain immortality.

55-57. Residents from all these worlds, viz., those of Śiva, Brahmā, Umā, Kumāra and Lokas like Vaikuṇṭha, Satyaloka, Tapoloka, Jana, Mahar, Bhuvaḥ, Bhū, all the Nāgalokas, all the heaven-dwellers and the mountains the chief of whom is Himvān as well as the wish-yielding Kalpa and other trees come to Prayāga at dawn in the month of Māgha, in order to take the holy bath.

58. The female deities of the quarters request the winds blowing from Prayāga saying, "Even they (the winds) will sanctify us. What shall we do? We are lame."

59. Formerly horse-sacrifice and other sacrifices were weighed against the dust particles at Prayāga by Brahmā. They (sacrifices) were not equal to the dust particles.

60. The sins embedded in the marrow accumulated over many births become agitated on just hearing the name of Prayāga and get destroyed.

61. This is a perfect Dharmatīrtha. This is a great Arthatīrtha; it is a Kāmikatīrtha; it is certainly a Mokṣatīrtha. (That is, it is conducive to the accomplishment of all the four great human aims.)

62. Brāhmaṇa-slaughter and other sins of embodied beings roar and boast of their powers only so long as they do

1. This is now located in the fort of Allahabad.

not take their bath in the month of Māgha at Prayāga, the annihilator of sins.

63. "Wise men always see the greatest region of Viṣṇu": This is frequently referred to in the Vedas. That is Prayāga itself since it is the giver of salvation.

64. The river Sarasvatī is of the nature of Rajas; the river Yamunā is of the nature of Tamas and the river Gaṅgā here is of the nature of Sattva. All the three together lead (the devotees) to Brahman (the Absolute) which is free from attributes (Rajas etc.)

65. This confluence (of the three rivers) acts as the ladder to the path of Brahman unto a living being whose body is sanctified, whether he takes the holy dip with faith or otherwise or even when he is forcibly dipped into it, and hence proceeds along the path of Brahman.

66. There is a certain noble lady renowned in the worlds as Kāśī.[1] Eager and enthusiastic Arka (Sun-god) and Keśava constitute her tremulous eyes. Varaṇā and Asi are her two arms. This confluence is her Veṇī (unornamented single braid of hair). This Kāśī is proclaimed as the source of everlasting bliss.

Agastya said:

67. O pious lady, who is competent to describe the good qualities of Prayāga, the king of holy places, served and resorted to by the other holy spots?

68. It is resorted to by the other holy Tīrthas in order to get rid of the accumulated sins of the sinners completely washed of (and left behind in it) by them. Hence Prayāga is superior (to them).

69. Having come to know the good qualities of Prayāga, the wise Brāhmaṇa, Śivaśarman, stayed there for the whole of the month of Māgha and then went to the city of Vārāṇasī.

70-71. At the entrance itself he saw Dehalī Vināyaka[2] (Lord

1. Kāśī is regarded as a lady with the Sun-god Lolārka and Ādikeśava (two famous temples at Kāśī) as her eyes. The two rivers Varaṇā and Asi (which form the boundaries of Kāśī) are regarded as her arms. Gaṅgā (which is braided with Yamunā) at Prayāga is her braid of hair.

2. Dehalī Vināyaka (Vināyaka at the threshold) is the guardian of the 'Western Door' of Kāśī. It is on the Pañca-Krośī route.

Gaṇeśa at the threshold) who protects his people (devotees) from great obstacles. With great devotion, he smeared (the idol) with saffron paste mixed with ghee and offered five Modakas (sweetmeats) as Naivedya. Then he entered the inner shrine.

72. After entering, he saw the celestial river that flows towards the north at Maṇikarṇikā, the river that was surrounded by groups of men whose merits as well as sins were washed off and who resembled the attendants of Śiva.

73. That Śivaśarman who knew the details of Karmakāṇḍa (rituals) plunged into the pure waters along with the clothes he wore, O blameless lady, without delay. With his intellect purified he offered libations to gods, sages, human beings, celestial manes and his own manes.

74. He quickly performed the rite of Pañcatīrthikā (five holy waters at Varaṇā, Asi, Pañcanada, Maṇikarṇikā and Daśāśvamedha), propitiated Viśveśvara in accordance with his financial resources and went round the city. On seeing time and again the city of the Enemy of the Three Puras, he wondered, 'Is this seen by me or not?'

75. If scrupulously examined, even that celestial city (Amarāvatī) cannot be on a par with this city, because of the difference in the creation (of the two cities). The said difference is like the difference of a worthless text and the sacred literature written in excellent characters.

76. Even the water here has such divine properties as are incomprehensible. Though the ambrosia in the heavenly city is good, it is worthless in comparison with this. If this is drunk at any time, there shall not be any opportunity to drink the milk from the breasts of one's mother. (One gets *Mokṣa* but Nectar-drinkers have to take birth in Saṁsāra.)

77. By pondering over the Lord of the Vedas, the people here are free from ailments. People performing sacred rites do not do so without referring to Pinākin (i.e. dedicating the fruit thereof to the Lord). They, therefore, imitate the attendants of Śiva in all respects. They attain a status equal to that of the attendants (of Śiva).

78. By whom is this Kāśī not eulogized? At the time of the death, through the fruition of the many merits performed and earned before, the Moon-crested Lord imparts the instruction in Oṁkāra to the embodied beings staying here.

79. The auspicious Lord Śiva, the wish-yielding Cintāmaṇi jewel unto the men of worldly pursuits, whispers the Tāraka Mantra into the (right) ear of good people at the time of death. Hence this holy spot is spoken of as Maṇikarṇikā.[1]

80. This holy spot is a jewel in the great pedestal of Goddess Lakṣmī of salvation, as well as a pericarp of her lotus-like feet. Hence people call this Maṇikarṇikā.

81. The four types of living beings staying here, viz., the womb-born, the egg-born, the germinating ones and the sweat-born ones, are not on the same footing as the gods to whom salvation is unobtainable. They are superior.

82. "My birth was futile till today, because ill-behaved and ignorant (as I was), I did not perceive Kāśikā, the illuminator of liberation."

83. Śivaśarman was not fully satisfied even though he frequently made that holy spot the guest of his eyes, the holy spot that is sacred and wonderful.

84-85. "I know that Kāśī is the chief of all the seven (holy) cities, (since) it is efficient in according excellent salvation. Yet, since the other four cities have not been visited by me, I shall go there and learn their greatness and come back once again."

86. Although he undertook the pilgrimage everyday for a year, he could not visit all the Tīrthas. Indeed, there is a holy spot at every place as small as even a gingelly seed.

Agastya said:

87. O noble lady, though conscious of all the great qualities of this holy spot, the Brāhmaṇa, well-versed in all the means of valid knowledge, did set out (from Kāśī), alas!

88. O fair lady, what can scriptures do though they are authoritative? Who is competent to ward off the inevitable advent of Mahāmāya?

89. Who can cause restraint in the mind which wavers though stationed in an exalted place, or the water though stationed in an elevated place but flows down? The nature of both of them is unsteady.

90. Proceeding from one land to another duly, that

1. Popular etymology of Maṇikarṇikā in vv 79, 80.

Śivaśarman reached the city of Mahākāla (i.e. Ujjayinī) free from the bad effects of Kali and Kāla.

91. He who devours the entire universe in every Kalpa sportingly is Kāla. He who swallows Kāla becomes Mahākāla.

92. The city that saves the universe from sin is called Avantī. In every Yuga, it has a different name. In the Kali age it is called Ujjayinī.

93. A creature in adversity there, even after becoming a corpse, does not emit putrefying smell nor does it become swollen.

94. The messengers of Yama never enter it. There are many millions and millions of Liṅgas there at every step.

95. The self-same fiery Liṅga of refulgence becomes three, viz. Hāṭakeśa, Mahākāla and Tārakeśa and remains pervading the three worlds.

96. The fiery refulgence at Siddhavaṭa is seen by *Dvijas* (men of the first three castes) or those are the meritorious persons who visit Mahākāla.

97. If that Liṅga of Mahākāla is seen by those who suffer from worldly sorrows, they will never be sullied by great sins; they will never be seen by the arrogant soldiers of Yama.

98. When their backs are stroked by the tips of the banners (fluttering on the tops of the mansions) in Mahākāla, the horses of the Sun in the sky get rid of the pain resulting from the lashes of the whip of Aruṇa.

99. The Father of Smara (Viṣṇu) and the Slayer of Smara (Śiva) always remember those who remember and repeat the name Mahākāla constantly.

100. After propitiating thus Mahākāla, the lord of spirits, the Brāhmaṇa went to the city of Kāntī (Kañcī, Tamil Nadu) that is more brilliant than the three worlds.

101. It is definite that Lakṣmīkānta (Lord Viṣṇu) himself directly makes all the creatures staying here Śrīkāntas (possessors of wealth, identical with Viṣṇu) here and hereafter.

102. By visiting Kāntī (Kāñcī) which is refulgent and which is resorted to by those who are brilliant, that Brāhmaṇa also became resplendent. There is no fading of splendour of anyone there.

103. The Brāhmaṇa conversant with all duties, performed everything that should be done there and stayed there for

seven nights. Then he went to the city of Dvārāvatī.

104. There are places and opportunities of entries for all the four aims of life in this city. Hence, it is called Dvārāvatī by learned men who know reality.

105. If the bones of the creatures (dying here) are marked with discus, what wonder is there that they will become Viṣṇus in form, with their hands marked with conch and discus?

106. The god of Death frequently teaches his messengers thus: "They who merely utter the name of Dvārāvatī should be abandoned (by you).

107. Where is that fragrance in sandalwood, where is such a colour in gold, where is that sanctity in (the other) Tīrthas, as is found in the Gopīcandana of Dvārāvatī?

108. O messengers, may all of you hear: He also whose forehead is marked with Gopīcandana, should be kept at a distance like blazing fire.

109. O soldiers, they also should be kept far off and abandoned, those who are adorned with Tulasī, those who repeat the name of Tulasī and those who grow Tulasī plants."

110. For ages together the ocean has been stealing away the jewels of Dvārāvatī all round and so it is being sung about as Ratnākara ('storehouse of jewels').

111. Urged by the god of Death when creatures die at Dvārāvatī, they become Viṣṇu in Vaikuṇṭha endowed with four arms and wearing yellow cloths.

112. There also he (Śivaśarman) offered libations to the manes along with the gods, sages and men. Without lethargy, he took the holy bath in all those Tīrthas.

113. Then he reached Māyāpurī which is inaccessible to sinners and where the Māyā pertaining to Viṣṇu does not fetter the living beings with the nooses of Māyā (those of 'I' and 'mine').

114. Some call this holy spot Haridvāra; others call it Mokṣadvāra. Some call it Gaṅgādvāra and some call it Māyāpura.

115. It is from here that Gaṅgā originated and became well-known all over the world as Bhāgīrathī. By the utterance of its name, the sin of men gets shattered into thousand pieces.

116. People have called Haridvāra as a single flight of steps to Vaikuṇṭha. Those men who take their holy plunge

here go to the greatest region of Viṣṇu.

117-118. He observed the fast customary in a Tīrtha and kept awake at night. In the morning he took his bath in Gaṅgā and offered libations to those who should be offered. When that excellent Brāhmaṇa desired to take food for breaking the fast, he was attacked by cold and fever. Ailing much, he shivered awfully.

119. Alone and a stranger to the place, afflicted with high fever, he was overwhelmed by great anxiety: 'What is this that has befallen me?'

120. He sank in the ocean of anxious thoughts. He abandoned all hopes of life and wealth like a sea-faring merchant whose ship is wrecked in the deep ocean.

121. Where is this holy spot? Where is my wife? Where are my sons? Where are those assets? Where is that wonderful mansion? Where is that collection of books (of mine)?

122. My age is not so ripe now. Hairs have not turned grey. This sickness is awful. God of Death who knows when to strike is also terrible.

123. Death has settled on my head. My residence is far off. When the house is on fire shall one begin to dig a well?

124. Of what avail are these futile thoughts? They but increase my distress. I shall think about Hṛṣīkeśa or Śiva, the bestower of auspicious welfare.

125. Or one good means of salvation has been performed by me. These seven cities of salvation have been directly visited by me.

126. Either heavenly bliss or salvation, one of these two should be invariably achieved by a learned man. If that has not been acquired, one will surely regret with distress.

127. Or, of what avail is this endless series of thoughts? Death is conducive to welfare either in a battle or in a holy spot like mine here.

128. Am I to die somewhere in the street now like an unlucky fellow? I shall die in the river Bhāgīrathī. Why should I worry like a foolish fellow?

129. I shall certainly achieve salvation by dying with this body, a conglomeration of bones and skin.'

130. While he was thinking thus, he experienced a terrible pain. He fell into that condition which one stung by ten

million scorpions falls into.

131. Everything that should have been remembered was forgotten. He did not even know who he was and where he was. After remaining in this condition for fourteen days, he died.

132. By that time, an aerial chariot came there from the region of Vaikuṇṭha. There was a lofty flagstaff therein marked with (the images of) Tārkṣya (Garuḍa).

133. It was very spacious and occupied by a thousand excellent girls with chowries in their hands, wearing golden-coloured silken cloths.

134. It was rendered brilliant by the two attendants Puṇyaśīla ('of meritorious habits') and Suśīla ('of excellent behaviour') endowed with four arms and excellent countenances. The aerial chariot had garlands of tinkling ornaments.

135. Endowed with four arms and clad in yellow garments, he got into that aerial chariot and adorned the path of the firmament.

CHAPTER EIGHT

The World of Yama

Lopāmudrā said:

1. O lord of my life, I have not been fully contented by listening to the meritorious story of the holy cities as narrated by your glorious tongue.

2. Śivaśarman, the excellent Brāhmaṇa, died in Māyāpurī, the city of salvation. Still he did not get salvation. O lord, kindly tell the reason thereof.

Agastya said:

3-4. O pleasant-voiced lady, in these cities one does not attain liberation directly. Formerly an old legend pertaining to this matter was heard by me. O my beloved wife, listen to this story of wonderful implication, destructive of sins, which was narrated by Puṇyaśīla and Suśīla to Śivaśarman.

Śivaśarman said:

5. O meritorious attendants of Viṣṇu, with eyes like the petals of lotus! With palms joined together (in reverence) I wish to submit something.

6. I do not know your names. I have understood something from your features. You are sure to be Puṇyaśīla and Suśīla.

The two attendants said:

7. What is unknown to people like you endowed with devotion to the Lord? These alone are our names as spoken by you, the glorious one.

8. If there is anything else in your mind to be asked, out with it unhesitatingly, O highly intelligent one. With great delight, we shall reply.

9. On hearing these sincere and highly pleasing words uttered by the attendants of the Lord, he replied thereafter:

The divine Brāhmaṇa said:

10. What is this world of very little glory and splendour? It contains the figures of people with very little merit. Who are these persons of ugly features? Speak it to me.

The attendants told:

11-12. This is the world of the *Piśācas* (ghosts). Flesh-eaters live here. Those who give some gifts and then repent, those who say "nay, nay" and then ultimately give something, those who worship Śiva once incidentally and then become impure in mind, those persons of very little merit and much less of prosperity, O friend, they have become these ghosts.

13-14. Proceeding ahead from that place, he saw a world occupied by delighted and well-nourished people. The people residing there had huge bellies, thick mouths (lips) and dark hairy limbs. Their voice is stentorian like that of a thundering cloud. "O attendants, say who are these? What is this world? Is it (acquired) through merit?"

The attendants said:

15-19. This is the world of Guhyakas (Hoarders). These people are remembered as Guhyakas. In the earth (they dig big cavities) and hoard their wealth (of course) earned legitimately. They go their own way. They are rich householders behaving mostly like Śūdras. They share with others what they eat. They are devoid of anger and jealousy. They are easy-going, always fond of happiness and pleasure. They don't observe the different lunar days, the days of the week, the festival days, days of the transit of the Sun, etc. They understand neither impiety nor righteousness. One thing they know perfectly well. They give cows as gifts to that Brāhmaṇa who is regarded worthy of the veneration of the whole family. They clearly abide by his words. Due to these meritorious activities, Guhyakas are prosperous here too. Like Devas, these Guhyakas enjoy heavenly pleasures. They have nothing to fear from anywhere.

20. Thereafter, he espied a world that bestowed happiness unto the eyes. (He asked:) "Who are these people? What is the name of this world? O attendants, please tell (me)."

The attendants said:

21. This world is that of Gandharvas. These persons are the Gandharvas of splendid holy observances, because they sing the praise of the Devas. Those who were Cāraṇas and singers of praises (have now become Gandharvas).

22. Conversant with the science of music, they give much delight to kings and praise wealthy people, because they are fascinated by greed for money.

23-24. They hand over to Brāhmaṇas the excellent garments, wealth, fragrant things like camphor and many other things obtained by them with the favour of the kings. They sing songs day and night. Their mind always dwells on the (Gāndharva) Veda. They persevere in their practice and study of the art of dance.

25. Since Brāhmaṇas were propitiated through the wealth earned by them by means of music, they have become meritorious. Hence their world, the Gandharva world, has special significance.

26. It is due to the power of the science of music, that the great celestial sage Nārada has become worthy of honour in the region of Viṣṇu. He is a great favourite of Śrīśaṁbhu too.

27. Tuṁburu and Nārada both of them are rare (venerable musicians) inaccessible even to the Devas. Śiva is *Nāda* (sound, melody) personified and both of them are conversant with the principles of melody.

28. If a song is sung near the glorious Hari or Hara, the benefit thereof is salvation or a direct visit by them or their presence.

29. If an expert musician does not attain the greatest region (salvation) through his music, he (at least) becomes an attendant of Rudra and rejoices with him.

30. In this world the following Smṛti is always sung about: "Lord Hari and Hara should always be worshipped through the series of their own songs."

31. Even as he heard this, Śivaśarman reached another charming city instantly. He asked, "What is the name of this city?"

The attendants said:

32-35. This is the world of Vidyādharas. They are all experts in various lores. They teach the students different kinds of arts. They are devoid of undue pride and arrogance in their learning. They give the pupil food, sandals, clothes, blankets and medicines for quelling their ailments. They consider the disciples as their own sons. Following pious practices, they give good girls in marriage to them along with clothes, betel leaves and food. They worship the deities of their choice with a keen desire for benefit. These Vidyādharas stay here due to those merits.

36-37. While they were talking thus, Dharmarāja, the lord of Saṁyaminī, came there amidst the sounds of Dundubhis (drums). He had assumed a gentle form. He was seated in an aerial chariot and was surrounded by persons knowing Dharma (pious practices) as well as three or four servants clever in the performance of their services.

Dharmarāja said:

38-40. Well done! Well done, O highly intelligent excellent Brāhmaṇa Śivaśarman! Everything befitting the families of Brāhmaṇas has been adopted by you. The Vedas were studied at the outset; the preceptors were delighted. Pious practices laid down and found in Dharmaśāstras were duly honoured by you. The fleeting body was washed and purified with the waters of the *Muktipurīs* ('Cities of salvation'). You are an expert in matters concerning life and death.

41. The body with putrid odour that is always unclean has been exchanged for the merit accruing from excellent holy spots.

42. It is for this reason that learned people honour and respect learning combined with a sense of discrimination between good and evil. Those scholars do not waste even a single moment of the day.

43. Living beings live for a brief span of five or six moments in their mortal life. There, they should not indulge in vicious and sinful activities.

44. The body is always sure to be destroyed. Monetary assets do not protect at the time of death. Therefore why does a foolish man not exert himself in noble activities like you?

45. Life is fleeting; people of the world are agitated by grief. Hence mind should be directed towards pious practices by righteous men like you.

46. It is due to fruition of your virtuous actions that these two devotees of the Lord, who are worthy of my respect too, have become your friends.

47. Hence let me be commanded. What help can I render? What should have been done by people like me has already been done by you.

48. Today I have become extremely blessed, for the attendants of the Lord have been seen. My readiness to serve always should be conveyed to the divine presence of the Lord.

49. Sent off by those two, Yama entered his city. After Yama had returned, the Brāhmaṇa asked those two attendants:

Śivaśarman said:

50. Directly viewed, this Dharmarāja is indeed of very

gentle features. His words are conducive to righteousness and pleasant to the mind.

51. This city of Saṁyaminī is really extremely splendid in its characteristic features. (But) the mere name thereof, when heard, terrifies the sinners too much.

52. In the mortal world, the people describe the form of Yama otherwise. But what has been seen by me is contrary, just the opposite. O attendants, kindly tell the reason why.

53. Wherefore do people see this world? Who stays here? Is this alone his form, or something else? Let it be narrated.

The attendants said:

54. Listen, O gentle Sir, he is seen very gentle by people like you who are not apprehensive and are meritorious. Naturally, he is the personification of piety.

55-56. This (gentle) Yama is described otherwise in the following manner. He is tawny-eyed. The extremities of his eyes are red due to anger. His mouth is terrible with curved teeth. He looks awful with the tongue lolling like lightning. The hairs on his head stand erect. His limbs are excessively dark in complexion. His voice is loud like that of the thundering cloud at the time of ultimate annihilation. His *Kāladaṇḍa* (fierce staff) is lifted up by his hand. His brows are crooked making the face terrible.

57. (What he is supposed to be ordering is described in the following verses:)[1] "O Durdama, bring him (here); cause him to fall; bind him; beat him soundly. Strike this man of excessive misdeeds with hammers on his head.

58. Hold this wicked man by his feet and dash him against the rocky ground. Place your foot on his neck and pluck out his eyes.

59. Slit open this man's swollen cheeks with the razor quickly. Tie this man's neck with a rope and hang him on a tree.

60. Sever this man's head with a saw as if it were a piece of wood. Kick his face mercilessly and crush it into powder.

61. Chop off this sinner's hand that used to assault and

1. VV 57-89 describe the various kinds of punishments meted out to sinners in different hells.

rape other men's wives. Cut off the feet of this man who used to go to the houses of other men's wives.

62. With needles pierce through the pores of the hairs of the body of this wicked man who used to make nail-marks on the limbs of other men's wives.

63. Spit phlegm into the mouth of this sinner who used to sniff up the scent of the mouths of other men's wives. Thrust a stiff peg into the mouth of this sinner, who used to speak slanderously of other people.

64. O Vikaṭavaktra, roast this man like Bengal gram in a frying pan, along with sand and gravel. He used to harass others.

65. O Krūralocana, immerse the face of this man in the slushy putrid pool of blood. He always used to find fault with blameless persons.

66. O Utkaṭa, this man used to take away other men's articles, not given to him. Catch hold of his palms, sprinkle them with oil and roast them on hot charcoal fire.

67. O Bhīsaṇa, introduce hot iron rods and bars into the mouths of those who had made scandalous remarks about their preceptors and censured Devas.

68. Fix red-hot iron pegs into all the joints of this sinner who used to pierce the vital parts of other people and to reveal their secrets and frailties.

69. O Durmukha, cut off the tongue of this sinner who denies having received the money given by others and who robs others of their means of sustenance.

70. O Kroḍāsya, quickly cut open the belly of this sinner and fill it with faecal worms. He used illegitimately to enjoy temple properties and assets of Brāhmaṇas.

71. O Andhaka, cook this sinner in the vessels of the hell *Kuṁbhīpāka*. He was utterly selfish cooking for himself and not (sharing them with) the deities, Brāhmaṇas and guests.

72. O Ugrāsya, hurry up and take this sinner to the hell of *Mahāraurava* or *Raurava*. He was ungrateful. He used to kill infants. He was guilty of breach of trust.

73-75. O Durdaṁṣṭra, take this Brāhmaṇa-slayer to *Andhatāmisra,* this alcohol-addict to *Pūyaśoṇita,* this gold stealer to *Kālasūtra,* this defiler of the preceptor's bed to *Avīci.* This sinner is in intimate contact with them. Take him to the hell *Asipatra-Vana* till the year is over. Put all these great sinners into the cauldrons filled with hot oil. Let them be constantly afflicted by ferocious ravens with steel-like beaks. Make these sinners stay there permanently till the end of the Kalpa.

76. Hang up for a long time on the Kūṭaśālmali tree the sinners who had killed women, cows and friends, with their feet above and the head down.

77. O Mahābhuja, with a pair of tongs tear off the skin of this sinner who had embraced the wife of his friend. Very soon cut off his hands too.

78. Cause this sinner to fall into the great hell *Jvālākīla*. He had set fire to and burned other men's fields and houses.

79. Cast the sinner who had administered poison to others and who is guilty of perjury into the hell *Kālakūṭa*. Throw the sinner who used to cheat others through false measures and weights into the hell *Kaṇṭhamoṭa* (or push him down after wringing his neck).

80. O Duṣprekṣya, take the sinner who spits into the sacred waters to the hell *Lālāpiba*, the sinner who destroys foetus to the hell *Āmapāka* and that man who distresses others to *Śūlapāka* hell.

81. Torture in the sugarcane-crushing machine that Brāhmaṇa who used to sell juices and beverages (*Ikṣuyantra* may be the name of a hell also). Throw the king harassing his subjects into the hell *Andhakūpa*.

82-84. O Halāyudha, with mortar and pestle thrash constantly the Vaiśya who sells hemp and alcohol, as well as the base Brāhmaṇa who sells cows, gingelly seeds and horses.

O Dīrghagrīva, torture in the hell *Adhomukha* the Śūdra who insults Brāhmaṇas and occupies a cot in the presence of a Brāhmaṇa.

85-87. O Pāśapāṇi, O Kaśāpāṇi, bind the feet of these sinners: the Śūdra who competes with a Brāhmaṇa, the Vaiśya professing to be a Brāhmaṇa, the Kṣatriya who performs Yajñas on behalf of others, the Brāhmaṇa who is bereft of the Vedas, and the base Brāhmaṇa who regularly sells red lac, salt, meat, oil, poison, ghee, weapons and sugarcane products. Hit them hard with whips and take them to *Taptakardama*.

88. Make this woman who had been an unchaste harlot, a stigma on the family, embrace the red hot iron image of her paramour.

89. O Durādharṣa, take into the hell named *Bahubhramaradaṁśaka* ('where there are many black bees and wasps') the sinner who having taken up vows and observances forsakes them, because he could not restrain his sense-organs."

90. Yama is heard uttering these words from far off by men of evil deeds. He is seen as extremely terrible by the sinners who are suspicious of their own activities.

91. Those kings who protect the subjects like their own bosom-born children and punish them as demanded by justice are the members of his assembly.

92. Those kings in whose kingdom the persons belonging to different castes and stages of life invariably perform their respective duties and those who die at the proper time are the members of his assembly.

93. Those kings in whose kingdom neither the impoverished nor the evil-behaved, neither the persons overwhelmed with calamities nor those who are grief-stricken are to be found, are the members of his assembly.

94. The Brāhmaṇas, the Kṣatriyas and the Vaiśyas who are steadfast in their own duties and others who have perfect self-control live in the city Saṁyaminī.

95-97. Uśīnara, Sudhanvan, Vṛṣaparvan, Jayadratha, Rāji, Sahasrajit, Kukṣi, Dṛḍhadhanvan, Ripuñjaya, Yuvanāśva, Dantavaktra, Nābhāga, Ripumaṅgala, Karandhama, Dharmasena, Paramardaka, Parāntaka — these and many other kings abiding by good policies and conversant with the discussion on what is pious and what is not, stay in Sudharmā.[1]

98. We shall mention another thing also to you as to who do not see the son of the Sun (i.e., Yama) or his messengers of fierce faces, wielding staffs and nooses in their raised hands.

99. O Bhaṭas (Yama's officers), those who always repeat the following names are to be let off. (Yama instructs his soldiers thus*:) O Govinda, Mādhava, Mukunda, Hari, Murāri, Dāmodara, Acyuta, Janārdana, Vāsudeva (Viṣṇu's names), O

1. The pious acts of these ancient kings are described in Mbh and Purāṇas, for example Uśīnara's (Śivi's) offer of his own body to a falcon to protect his protégé, a pigeon. Thereby they became the members of Indra's assembly, Sudharmā.

* These verses 99-110 contain 108 names of Viṣṇu and Śiva.

Śaṁbhu, Śiva, Īśa, Śaśiśekhara, Śūlapāṇi (Śiva's names)!

100. O Gaṅgādhara, Andhakaripu, Hara, Nīlakaṇṭha, Bhūteśa, Khaṇḍaparaśu, Mṛḍa, Caṇḍikeśa (Śiva's name)! O Vaikuṇṭha! O Kaiṭabharipu! O Kamaṭha (Divine tortoise)! O Abjapāṇi (lotus-handed) (Viṣṇu's names)!

101. O Viṣṇu, Nṛsiṁha, Madhusūdana, Cakrapāṇi, Nārāyaṇa, Asuranibarhaṇa, Śārṅgapāṇi (Viṣṇu's names)! O Gaurīpati, Girīśa, Śaṅkara, Candracūḍa (Śiva's names)!

102. O Mṛtyuñjaya, Ugra, Viṣamekṣaṇa, Kāmaśatru, Īśāna, Kṛttivasana, Tridaśaikanātha (Śiva's names)! O Śrīkānta, Pītavasana, Aṁbudanīla, Śauri (Viṣṇu's names)!

103. O Lakṣmīpati, Madhuripu, Puruṣottama, Ādya, Ānandakanda, Dharaṇīdhara, Padmanābha (Viṣṇu's names)! O Śrīkaṇṭha, Digvasana, Śānta, Pinākapāṇi (Śiva's names)!

104. O Sarveśvara, Tripurasūdana, Devadeva, Tryakṣa, Uragābharaṇa, Bālamṛgāṅkamauli (Śiva's names)! Brahmaṇya Deva, Garuḍadhvaja, Śaṅkhapāṇi (Viṣṇu's names)!

105. O Śrīrāma, Rāghava, Rāmeśvara, Rāvaṇāri, Cāṇūramardana, Hṛṣīkapati, Murāri (Viṣṇu's names)! O Bhūteśa, Manmatharipu, Pramathādhinātha (Śiva's names)!

106. O Śūlin, Giriśa, Rajanīśakalāvataṁsa, Bharga, Trinetra, Bhava, Bhūtapati, Purāri (Śiva's names)! O Kaṁsaprāṇāśana, Sanātana, Keśināśa (Viṣṇu's names)!

107. O Gopīpati, Yadupati, Vasudevasūnu! O Govardhanoddharaṇa, Dharmadhurīṇa, Gopa (Viṣṇu's names)! O Karpūragaura, Vṛṣabhadhvaja, Bhālanetra (Śiva's names)!

108. O Sthāṇu, Trilocana, Pinākadhara, Smarāri, Viśveśvara, Tripathagārdrajaṭā -kalāpa (Śiva's names)! O Kṛṣṇa, Aniruddha, Kamalākara, Kalmaṣāri (Viṣṇu's names)!

109. O Brāhmaṇas, this series of one hundred and eight excellent names has been wreathed into a garland as though with clusters of excellent jewels. The heroes of these names are exquisite ones (Gods Viṣṇu and Śiva). The string is strong. (It is full of good qualities.) He who wears (commits to memory) this garland will not see Yama.

110. Thus, O excellent Brāhmaṇas, that Dharmarāja always instructs the groups of his servants going to the earth. Others too on the earth, who may be having the marks and characteristics of Hari or Hara, are to be avoided from afar.

Agastya said:

111-112. A bold and intelligent man who always repeats this series of names of the Kaustubha-wearing Viṣṇu and the Moon-adorned Śiva wreathed into a lucid composition by Dharmarāja will never drink the secretion from the breasts of any mother. It destroys the seeds of all sins. Even as he heard this fascinating story that is faultless, O beloved one, Śivaśarman became delighted with a beaming face. He saw in front of him the city of the celestial damsels.

CHAPTER NINE

The Regions of Celestial Damsels and of the Sun

Śivaśarman said:

1. Who are these ladies, the storehouse of beauty, radiance and conjugal bliss, wearing divine ornaments and enjoying divine pleasures?

The attendants said:

2. These are the glamorous courtesans, the beloved ones of the Devas. They are conversant with music, experts in dance and very efficient in the art of playing musical instruments.
3. They are adepts in the art of love making; very clever at the game of dice. They appreciate the beauty of things. They understand the innermost feelings of others. They are very clever in suitable repartees.
4. They are experts in knowing the specialities of different countries and have mastery over the languages spoken in different lands. They are skilful in probing secret news. They move about delightfully at their sweet will in groups, and not alone.
5. They are experts in coquettish gestures exciting amorous feelings and expressions of love and amorous sports. They are adept in continuous light talk. They always delight the minds of the youths through their coquettish gestures and seductive charms.

6. Formerly these celestial ladies emerged from the Milk-Ocean while it was being churned. They are the fascinating weapons of the mind-born god of Love, the conqueror of the three worlds.

7-12. They are: Urvaśī, Menakā, Raṁbhā, Candralekhā, Tilottamā, Vapuṣmatī, Kāntimatī, Lilāvatī, Utpalavatī, Alaṁbuṣā, Guṇavatī, Sthūlakeśī, Kalāvatī, Kalānidhi, Guṇanidhi, Karpūratilakā, Urvarā, Anaṅgalatikā, Madana-mohinī, Cakorākṣī, Candrakalā, Munimanoharā, Grāvadrāvā, Tapodveṣṭrī, Cārunāsā, Sukarṇikā, Dārusañjīvinī, Suśrī, Kratuśulkā of splendid countenance, Tapaḥśulkā, Tīrthamedhikā, Rājasūyārthinī, Aṣṭāgnihomikā, Vājapeya-śatodbhavā.

These celestial damsels number sixty thousand.

13. In this world of celestial damsels other women too live. Their radiance never fades and dims. Their youth never diminishes.

14. Their garments are divine; their garlands are celestial; their scents and unguents are divine; they are richly endowed with heavenly means of enjoyments; they can assume any form they like.

15-16. (Some women[1] in the world) observe the monthly fasts but violate the vow of celibacy once, twice or thrice as ill-luck would have it. It is such women who come to Apsarāloka and stay there enjoying divine pleasures and possessing the rich beauty and refulgence. They realize all their desires.

17. After following the holy vows and observances in accordance with the injunctions along with their ancillaries with a view to obtain their desires, some ladies become adulteresses. Such women come to this world as the objects of enjoyment of the Devas.

18. There are some women of great fidelity but some powerful man might have raped them and they might have enjoyed sexual dalliance with him, wrongly taking him to be their husband. Such women are these, O Brāhmaṇa.

19. When the husbands were away from the homes, some women who had always been observing celibacy, may by chance or due to cruel fate err and fall. These are such ladies of beautiful eyes.

---

1. VV 15-27 state what acts of women result in birth in the world of Apsarās.

20-25. There are various things to be given as gifts such as sweet-smelling flowers; fragrant sandalpaste; exquisitely white camphor; garments of very fine texture; betel leaves that are symmetrical and long, that are ripe and firm, that have golden hue at the tips, that have thick and blue nerve-like lines running through and that are accompanied by sweet-smelling nuts and other ingredients; beds with various kinds of ornaments; all fanciful objects befitting the chamber of love-play and other things too. A lady of excellent complexion should honour a Brāhmaṇa couple and give them the gifts mentioned above. This gift of objects of pleasure is something to be desired. At the time of the monthly transit of the Sun or on the days of *Vyatīpāta* (New Moon in combination with Sunday), these gifts should be made and continued for a year. The lady should repeat the Mantra ("*ko' dāt, kasmā adāt, kāmāyādāt kāmo dātā, kāmaḥ pratigrahītā, kāma etatte*") (of the Vedas[1]) (or any other similar Mantra) and say "May the Lord in the form of god of Love be pleased" and give the things to the Brāhmaṇa couple. She will become the most excellent one among the celestial damsels and stay there for a Kalpa.

26-27. A beautiful virgin was carnally enjoyed somewhere by someone in the form of a Deva. Ever since then that girl continued to be celibate meditating upon the same incident (and not marrying anyone else). That girl attains a divine form and is born here sharing divine pleasures.

28-32. Hearing the origin of the Apsarāloka (the region of Apsarās) in this manner the eminent Brāhmaṇa reached the Solar World in a moment, travelling in an aerial chariot.

Due to the rays of the Sun, the world was shining brilliantly all round like a Kadaṁba flower surrounded by its filaments.

From a distance he saw the Sun sporting two lotuses. He could know that it was the Sun through the wonderful fast chariot of a single wheel drawn by seven horses. It was nine thousand Yojanas in size. It was driven by Anūru who held the reins in front. The celestial damsels, sages, Gandharvas, serpents, Yakṣas and Rākṣasas were there. Then he joined his palms in reverence and bowed down.

---

1. This Mantra is untraced in Lanman's standard *Vedic Concordance*. Probably, it is a Purāṇic Mantra.

33. Lord Sun acknowledged his obeisance with a slight knitting of the eyebrows and traversed a great distance along the path of the sky in a moment.

34-35. When the Sun had gone afar, Śivaśarman joyously spoke to the devotees of the Lord: "How is the region of the Sun to be attained? I wish to hear this. Kindly recount it to me. Friendship among good people is created by a mere exchange of seven words. Urged by friendship for me, you should narrate the same to me."

The attendants said:

36. Listen, O Brāhmaṇa of great intellect. There is nothing that should not be spoken to you. It is through the contact of the good people that a good discourse takes place.

37-39. The Absolute Being is the controller of all living beings. It is the ultimate cause. It is nameless and devoid of a family. It has no form or anything like that. The manifestation and the disappearance (of the universe) takes place when his brows move. That absolute source or originator of the Vedas, the immanent soul of all says thus: "It is clear that I am identical with the *Puruṣa* (Person, Being) who is in the Āditya (Sun). Those who worship another being (deity) enter blinding darkness."

40-41. O excellent Brāhmaṇa, Brāhmaṇas comprehend the meaning of this irrefutable Vedic passage and worship that single Being. He who, having acquired the great deity in the form of the Sun, does not worship it thrice a day, undoubtedly falls in seven days.

42. The devotee should continue (to stand) repeating the Japa while facing the Sun in the morning as long as the disk of the Sun rises up half. In the evening he should perform the Japa silently sitting down till the stars appear (in the sky).

43. The devotee should continue the Japa even as the setting Sun is present in the sky. During midday he should repeat the Japa facing the Sun. The time should not be missed. It should rather be waited for.

44. Plants bear fruit at the proper time. Trees bloom at the proper time. Clouds shower at the proper time. Hence

one should not transgress the proper time (of performing *Sandhyā* prayer).

45. At the time of his rise and setting, the Sun wishes for three handfuls of water inspired by the Mantra and offered by the Brāhmaṇas, for the purpose of the destruction of the demons named Mandehas.

46. Is it not equivalent to the gift of three worlds if three handfuls of water sanctified by the Gāyatrī Mantra are offered to the Sun at the stipulated time?

47-48. Worshipped duly at the proper time, what is it that the Sun does not yield? He bestows long life, good health, prosperity, wealth with cattle, friends, sons, wives, different kinds of fields, the eight types of pleasurable things (viz. sweet scents, women, garments, music, betel-chewing, foodstuff, vehicles and mansions, heavenly pleasures and salvation).

49-50. Among the eighteen esteemed lores, Mīmāṁsā is the greatest; the system of logic is still greater; Purāṇa is greater than it; Dharmaśāstras are still greater, O Brāhmaṇa. The Śruti is greater than they; the Upaniṣad is still greater and Gāyatrī is superior to it.[1]

51. Among all the Mantras, Gāyatrī with Praṇava is the most rare and hence worthy of respect. No Mantra greater than Gāyatrī is sung in the Vedas.

52. It is true. It is true again and again that there is no Mantra on a par with Gāyatrī. There is no city equal to Kāśī. There is no Liṅga on a par with Viśveśa.

53. Gāyatrī is the mother of the Vedas. Gāyatrī gives births to Brāhmaṇas. Since it saves him who sings (performs Japa of) it, it is described as Gāyatrī.

54. The relationship between the two, the Sun and Gāyatrī is that of the word and the object signified by it. Gāyatrī is the great expression and the Sun is the expressed object.

55. It is through the power of Gāyatrī that Kauśika (Viśvāmitra), the Kṣatriya of good control over his sense-organs, discarded his status as a royal sage and attained the status of a Brāhmaṇa sage.

56. He attained another miraculous power of high order, i.e. that of creating a new world. What is it that Gāyatrī served

1. VV 49-58 extol the importance of the Gāyatrī Mantra.

and resorted to very well in this manner, does not bestow?

57. A man becomes a Brāhmaṇa neither by reciting the Vedas nor by learning philosophical texts. One becomes a Brāhmaṇa by repeated utterance of the goddess (i.e., Gāyatrī). Indeed not otherwise.

58. Gāyatrī is the great Viṣṇu; Gāyatrī alone is the great Śiva; Gāyatrī alone is the great Brahmā. Therefore, Gāyatrī alone is the triad of Vedas (which are identical with Brahmā, Viṣṇu and Śiva).

59. That Lord, the creater of the day (i.e. Sun) with rays as a garland, is identical with the triad of the Devas. He is the mass of all lustres. He is Time, the prime mover of time.

60. Residents of our world (i.e., Vaikuṇṭha) who can discriminate between what is essential and what is non-essential, always cite this Śruti with the Sun in view.

61. This refulgent one penetrates all quarters and interior of quarters (sideways, above and below). He is without beginning or end. He is within the womb of the mother. He is the born. He will be the born. O people, he stands pervading every object with faces everywhere (like the Puruṣa of the *Puruṣa Sūkta* —Com.)

62. Those who are active and alert and worship the Sun with the hymns pertaining to the Sun (*Saura hymns*) constantly and those who bow down, are the real Brāhmaṇas and those Brāhmaṇas are on a par with the Sun.

63. Whatever task is undertaken on a Sunday in conjunction with the constellation of Puṣya, Hasta, Mūla or Uttarā does become fruitful and not otherwise.

64-65. The devotee observing holy vows should take his holy bath at sunrise on a Sunday in the month of Pauṣa, and perform the rites of Dāna (gift), Homa and Japa. He should adore the Sun with faith and devotion. He should be free from lust and anger. He shall thereby become brilliant and live here along with the celestial damsels enjoying all pleasures.

66-69. Liberal gifts should be made at the time of the *Ayana* (i.e. during the transit of the Sun to the Tropics of Cancer and Capricorn). Viṣuva days (equinoxes of Meṣa and Tulā), Ṣaḍaśīti etc. (during the transit of the Sun in Dhanus, Mithuna, Kanyā and Mīna Zodiacs) and Viṣṇupadī (i.e. during the transit to Vṛścika, Vṛṣa, Siṁha and Kuṁbha Zodiacs).

Gingelly seeds soaked in ghee should be used for Homa. Brāhmaṇas should be fed. Śrāddha should be performed with the manes in view.

Great Pūjās should be performed and great Mantras should be repeated. Those scholars who do like this attain the world of the Sun and get a lustre on a par with that of the Sun.

Those who perform devotional rites during the transit of the Sun to the various Zodiacs, never become poor, distressed, afflicted with ailments, ugly or unfortunate.

70-71. If gifts are not made, holy bath is not taken in the sacred waters, special Homa is not performed with gingelly seeds soaked in ghee from the milk of a tawny-coloured cow, the men guilty thereof, shall become blind and very poor and will be uttering piteously beseeching "Give, give" at every door wearing rags.

72. A blessed man who makes a gift of a gold piece even as small as a Guñjā berry at the time of solar eclipse in Kurukṣetra shall become meritorious and stay here.

73. When the Sun is swallowed by Rāhu (i.e., during solar eclipse) all waters are on a par with Gaṅgā, all Brāhmaṇas are on a par with Brahmā and everything gifted equal with gold.

74. Whatever holy thing is performed by way of gifts, Japas, Homas, holy baths, Śrāddha etc., at the time of solar eclipse shall be the cause of the presence of the Sun-god.

75. If the transit of the Sun falls on a Sunday or if there is a solar eclipse then, the merit acquired at that time becomes never-ending.

76. If the Sunday coincides with sixth or seventh lunar day and a meritorious holy rite is performed, then that will be enjoyed here itself.

Seventy names of the Sun god
To be Repeated and Arghya offered[1]

77. (1) Haṁsa (the pure Sattva), (2) Bhānu (the refulgent), (3) Sahasrāṁśu (thousand-rayed), (4) Tapana (blazing), (5) Tāpana (scorching), (6) Ravi (protector of the worlds), (7) Vikartana (whetted for more brilliance), (8) Vivasvān (having

1. VV 77-84 give seventy names of the Sun-god. The Com. gives interpretations of each name.

special refulgence), (9) Viśvakarman (of universal activity), (10) Vibhāvasu (of fiery nature),

78. (11) Viśvarūpa (of universal form), (12) Viśvakartā (the procreator of the universe), (13) Mārtaṇḍa (present in the insentient Cosmic Egg in the form of Vairāja), (14) Mihira (destroyer of mist), (15) Aṁśumān (having rays), (16) Āditya (Aditi's son), (19) Aryamān (Triad of Vedas personified), (20) Bradhna (making the universe flourish), (21) Divākara (maker of the day),

79. (22) Dvādaśātmā (having twelve forms), (23) Saptahaya (seven-horsed), (24) Bhāskara (creator of brilliance), (25) Ahaskara (usherer of the day), (26) Khaga (going forth in the firmament), (27) Sūra (one that gives birth to the universe), (28) Prabhākara (illuminator), (29) Śrīmān Lokacakṣuḥ (the glorious one brightening the worlds, the eye of the worlds), (30) Graheśvara (Lord of the Planets),

80. (31) Trilokeśa (the controller of the three worlds), (32) Lokasākṣī (the immanent soul of the world), (33) Tamori (enemy of darkness), (34) Śāśvata (the eternal one), (35) Śuci (sacred), (36) Gabhastihasta (having rays for hands), (37) Tīvrāṁśu (hot-rayed), (38) Taraṇi (redeemer of devotees like a raft across the ocean), (39) Sumahaḥ (of splendid brilliance), (40) Araṇi (the place of maifestation of everything),

81. (41) Dyumaṇi (jewel of the firmament), (42) Haridaśva (green-horsed), (43) Arka (of swift movement, worthy of respect), (44) Bhānumān (possessor of rays), (45) Bhayanāśana (destroyer of fear), (46) Chandośva (having the Metres of the Vedas for horses), (47) Vedavedya (to be realized through the Vedas), (48) Bhāsvān (luminous), (49) Pūṣan (one who nourishes), (50) Vṛṣākapi (showering merit and shaking off sin),

82. (51) Ekacakraratha (having a single-wheeled chariot), (52) Mitra (friendly), (53) Mandehāri (enemy of the demons Mandehas), (54) Tamisrahā (destroyer of pitch darkness), (55) Daityahā (slayer of demons), (56) Pāpahartā (remover of sins), (57) Dharma (sustainer, righteousness personified), (58) Dharmaprakāśaka (illuminator of piety),

83. (59) Helika (moving about in the firmament), (60) Citrabhānu (having variegated rays), (61) Kalighna (destroyer of kali, strife), (62) Tārkṣyavāhana (having Tṛkṣa's i.e., Kaśyapa's son i.e., Anūru as charioteer), (63) Dikpati (lord of the quarters),

(64) Padmininātha (lord of the lotus pond), (65) Kuśeśayakara (having a lotus in the hand), (66) Hari (remover of darkness and sin),

84-89. (67) Gharmaraśmi (hot-rayed), (68) Durnirīkṣya (very painful to look at), (69) Caṇḍāṁśu (hot-rayed), (70) Kaśyapātmaja (son of Kaśyapa).

These seventy names of the Sun-god are meritorious. They are to be used in the dative case with *Om* in the beginning and *namaḥ* (obeisance) added afterwards. (For example '*om mitrāya namaḥ*'). Looking every time at the Sun directly, these names should be uttered holding a copper vessel (free from impurities with both the hands). (The vessel is to be filled with water.) The devotee kneels on the ground and fills the waterpot with Karavīra and other flowers mixed with red sandalpaste. Dūrvā grass and raw rice grains should be put into the waterpot. Meditating on him, the devotee offers Arghya to the most esteemed Savitṛ (Sun) god taking the pot up to the head. The eyes and the mind should not be directed elsewhere.

These seventy names are on a par with great esoteric Mantras. At the end of each name, Mantra, the devotee should bow to the Sun-god. This has to be done both at sunrise and at sunset.

90. Performing the holy rite thus, no man shall ever be poor or miserable. He will be rid of all terrible ailments and (even sins) though acquired in the course of many births.

91. Without medicines, without doctors, without following strict regimen (he will be cured). When he dies in due course, he is honoured in the world of the Sun-god.

92. Thus, O excellent one, an aspect of the Solar world has been recounted. Who can comprehend the special characteristics of this (god), the storehouse of great refulgence.

93. Having attentively listened to this meritorious story, (the Brāhmaṇa) espied the great city of Mahendra soon.

Agastya said:

94. By listening to this story pertaining to the Sun along with that of the world of Apsarās, the devotee will never be afflicted with poverty. He will never engage himself in unrighteous activities.

95-96. This excellent narrative should always be listened to by Brāhmaṇas. It accords the merit that accrues from Vedic study and recitation.

Brāhmaṇas, Kṣatriyas and Vaiśyas listening to this excellent chapter abandon all their sins here, and attain the excellent goal.

CHAPTER TEN

The Worlds of Indra and Agni

Śivaśarman said:

1. What is this excellent city that accords much delight to the eyes and a great deal of pleasure to the mind? Who is the Lord thereof?

The attendants said:

2. O glorious Śivaśarman whose pilgrimage to sacred places (v.l., people whose pilgrimage to holy places) has become a fruitful tree sport about in this world. O Brāhmaṇa, this is the city of the thousand-eyed Indra.

3. It has been built by Viśvakarman through the great power of penance. The places hereof have the splendour of the moonlight even during the day.

4. Whenever during the New-Moon day (and other occasions) the moon becomes invisible, he sends (secretly) his wife Jyotsnā (Moonlight) to move about among these mansions.

5. It is surprising indeed that an immature lady among the celestial women sees her own reflection in the excellent walls of (her house) and begins to suspect that another lady has already come in, and therefore (feeling jealous) she does not enter her own apartment.

6. Even during the day time, darkness stays in this city without fear, after transferring its own blackness on the mansions built of sapphire.

7. People here in this city, collect in their pots the pure

water oozing out of the Candrakānta Crystals (moonstones) and never desire any other type of water.

8. There are neither weavers nor goldsmiths here, because the wish-yielding Kalpa-tree supplies clothes and ornaments.

9. Astrologers clever in the art of calculation are not present here, because the fabulous philosopher's stone (Cintāmaṇi) calculates and understands quickly the innermost thoughts and desires of everyone.

10. There are no cooks here efficient in the art of preparation of beverages and juices, because the cow Kāmadhenu alone yields all types of juices by way of milk.

11. Uccaiśśravas, the jewel among horses, possessing superior power (or which is the *Vibhūti* of Viṣṇu), whose reputation is sung about loudly everywhere in the midst of groups of horses (stays here).

12. Airāvata, the four-tusked excellent elephant, shines here as the second mobile Kailāsa mountain. It is as brilliant as crystal.

13. Pārijāta, the most excellent tree, Urvaśī the jewel among women, Nandana, the most excellent park and Mandākinī (Gaṅgā), the most excellent river (waterway), are here.

14. Thirty-three crores of Suras as mentioned in the Vedas await their turn everyday here for service (unto their Lord).

15. Nothing is more excellent than the status of Indra in the heavenly worlds. Whatever glory and prosperity is in the three worlds, cannot be on a par with his (Indra's) prosperity.

16. What else can be as holy and as great as that which is acquired in exchange for a thousand horse sacrifices?

17. None (of the seven cities of Fire-god and other Guardians of Quarters) viz. Arciṣmatī, Saṁyaminī, Puṇyavatī, Amalavatī, Gandhavatī, Alakā or Aiśī is equal to this in glory and prosperity.

18. He alone is called Sahasrākṣa ('Thousand-eyed'); he alone is Divaspati ('Lord of Heaven'); this lord alone is Śatamanyu ('one with hundred sacrifices'); these are his very famous names.

19. The seven (other) Guardians of the world serve and adore him. He is honoured with blessings by the excellent sages, Nārada and others.

20. The stability of all the worlds is wished for through the stability of this (lord). All the three worlds will be defeated

at the defeat of Mahendra.

21. Dānavas, human beings, Daityas, Gandharvas, Yakṣas, Rākṣasas etc. desirous of Amarāvatī, the city of Mahendra, perform penances with strict self-control.

22. Desirous of seizing the glory and prosperity of Śakra, kings like Sagara, and others, made great effort such as the performance of horse-sacrifices.

23. Whoever keeps all his senses under control and performs a hundred sacrifices without any hindrance on the earth, gets Pulomajā (Śacī) in the city of Amarāvatī.

24. Kings who could not complete a hundred sacrifices reside here; so also do the Brāhmaṇas who perform Jyotiṣṭoma and other sacrifices.

25. Those who offer the sixteen great gifts[1] such as Tulā-Puruṣadāna ('offering things equal in weight to the donor') become purified souls and they attain Amarāvatī.

26. Bold men never uttering timid words, those who never turn back in battles and those who lie down in the battlefield (lit. hero's bed)— those kings stay here.

27. Thus, in general, the situation of the city of Mahendra has been recounted. Those who invariably perform sacrifices, are experts in the science and technique of sacrifices reside here.

28. See this splendid Arciṣmatī, the city of the Fire-god. Those who are devotees of Fire-god and observe excellent vows, reside here.

29. Persons with steadfast Sattva quality and with control over the organs of sense and action entering the blazing fire (for self-immolation), women richly endowed with Sattva quality—all these possess fiery splendour.

30. Brāhmaṇas engaged in Agnihotra, men observing the vow of celibacy, keeping the sacred fire blazing, those who observe the holy vow of Pañcāgni—all these attain the region of Fire and possess fiery splendour.

1. The following are the sixteen great gifts (Mahādānas): Tulāpuruṣa, Hiraṇyagarbha, Brahmāṇḍa, Kalpavṛkṣa, Gosahasra, Kāmadhenu, Hiraṇyāśva, Aśvarathas, Hastiratha, Pañca-lāṅgala, Dharādāna, Viśvacakra, Kalpalatā, Saptasāgara, Ratnadhenu, Mahābhūtaghaṭa. (MtP 274-289; Agni 210)

31. He who makes a gift of bundles of fuel in winter season for the purpose of warding off cold as well as of ovens of fire, shall reside near Fire-god.

32. He who, with great faith, performs cremation and consecration with fire of a helpless person or, if he is incapable himself, urges others to do so, is honoured in the world of Fire-god.

33. A man of meritorious soul who gives a person of chronic indigestion, medicines kindling the gastric fire, shall live in the world of Agni for a long time.

34. He who offers in accordance with his capacity, articles essential for a sacrifice or money for the sake of sacrifice, shall reside in Arciṣmatī.

35. Agni alone is the greatest god bringing about salvation to Brāhmaṇas; he is the preceptor, God, religious vow, holy spot. Nay, Agni is decisively everything.

36. All unholy and unclean things become purified in a moment due to contact with fire. Hence Agni is spoken as Pāvaka ('purifier').

37. Even after studying the Vedas, if one abandons sacrificial fire and cultivates interest elsewhere, he is not a genuine Brāhmaṇa knowing the Vedas.

38. Certainly Fire-god is the immanent soul. It may very well burn (reduce) the external flesh in the belly of women but not the foetus in the womb.

39. The fiery form of Śaṁbhu is of scorching feature. It is the creative, destructive and sustaining force. What is there to be seen without it?

40. This Citrabhānu (Fire) is the eye of the Lord of the three worlds himself. In the world of blinding darkness who else is the illuminator excepting him (Fire)?

41. Incense, lamp, Naivedya (food offerings), milk, curd, ghee and sugarcane juice taken in by this Fire is resorted to by all the heaven-dwellers in the heaven.

Śivaśarman asked:

42. Who is this Kṛśānu (Fire)? Whose son is he? How is this fiery region obtained by him? Recount this to me.

The attendants replied:

43. Listen, O highly intelligent one. We shall describe duly who he is, whose son he is and how the city of Jyotiṣmatī was obtained by him.

44. On the beautiful banks of Narmadā, in the city of Narmapura, formerly there was a sage named Viśvānara, a devotee of Śiva and a meritorious soul.

45. He was in the *Brahmacarya* (celibate) stage of life firmly established therein. He was always engaged in Brahmayajña [the holy Yajña (adoration) of the study of Vedas]. He belonged to Śāṇḍilya Gotra. He was pure, a storehouse of Brāhmaṇical splendour, a man of great self-control.

46. He had understood the meanings of all scriptural texts. He was an expert in social conventions and pious practices. Once he meditated on Maheśvara and thought in his heart thus:

47. 'Which among the four stages of life, is more conducive to the welfare of good people, by properly practising which a man attains happiness here and hereafter?'

48. He pondered over everything carefully and from several points of view: 'This is beneficial', 'This also is beneficial', 'This may be easy to do', and ultimately praised the stage of a householder.

49. To the religious student, the householder, the forest-dweller or the recluse, it is the householder who acts as the supporter and no one else.[1]

50. Devas, human beings, manes and lower animals—all depend upon the householder everyday. Hence the householder is the most excellent one.

51. The householder who partakes of food without bathing, without performing *Homa* or without making any gift becomes indebted to Devas and others and falls into hell.

52. One who eats without bathing, eats dirt; one who takes in without performing *Japa*, drinks putrid blood; one who eats without performing *Homa*, eats worms; and one who eats without making a gift eats special diet of faeces.

---

1. Cf. Manu III. 77-78, Gautama Dh. S. III. 3 for the importance of householder's stage as the support of other Āśramas.

53. Celibacy in the course of a householder's life is free from self-deception. How can such a celibacy be found in a bachelor whose mind is naturally fickle?

54. A bachelor adopts celibacy out of circumstantial compulsion or fear of the public or for some selfish ends. If he indulges in thinking (about wedded bliss), the celibacy adopted by him is no better than non-existent.

55. A householder is considered to be a celibate if he avoids (contact with) other men's wives, is fully satisfied with his wife, carnally enjoying her only on stipulated days after the menstrual bath.

56. A householder who is without undue attachment and hatred, who is devoid of lust and anger, who has a wife and who maintains sacrificial fire, is far better than a forest-dweller.

57. After leaving the house with a feeling of sudden disgust and strong aversion (to householder's life), if a forest-dweller ruminates over the pleasant features of a domestic life, he becomes fallen from both; he is neither a true forest-dweller nor a householder.

58. A householder who maintains (himself and his family) through a means of livelihood that has come to his lot and which does not involve begging, is contented with whatever is received, is far better than a religious mendicant.

59. A recluse who happens to request (beg) at any time for anything even if it be difficult to obtain, if he be discontented with his victuals, he becomes fallen.'

60. After considering the various merits and demerits thus, the Brāhmaṇa Viśvānara married a girl from a good family befitting him, in accordance with the injunctions (in the Śāstras).

61. He was regular in attending to the worship of the sacred fire. He regularly performed the five Yajñas; he engaged himself in all the six duties laid down in the scriptures; he was devoted to gods, manes and guests.

62. The couple had perfect mutual adjustment, free from any apprehension. He thus earned piety, wealth and love in their respective stages of life. He was always in a proper communion with the Supreme Soul.

63. Well-versed in Karmakāṇḍa (Section of Rituals in scriptures), he performed all the rites pertaining to the Devas in forenoon, those connected with human beings in midday and

those with Pitṛs in afternoon.

64-65. Thus a long time passed by. The Brāhmaṇa's wife named Śuciṣmatī continued to observe holy vows like the wife of Kāma (Rati). She could not see (i.e. beget) a son that could have been a means of attaining heaven. She realized that her husband was her sole benefactor. (Once) she bowed down to him and submitted:

Śuciṣmatī said:

66. O son of a noble family, of noble intelligence, O Lord of my vital breath, O my beloved one, fond of holy observances! Due to the worship of your feet, there is nothing inaccessible to me.

67. All the enjoyment which women usually take pleasure in, have been enjoyed by me, with your favour. I had the fullest enjoyment of these and I shall recount them.

68. The enjoyments are of eight varieties: good garments, good houses, good bedsteads, good female attendants, garlands, betel leaves, food and beverages usually enjoyed by persons who perform their duties.

69. But, O lord, one unfulfilled wish has always been within my heart for a long time. It is something in which householders revel. It behoves you to give it to me.

Viśvānara said:

70. O lady of fair hips, O lady desirous of my pleasure and welfare, what is there that cannot be given to you? Hence do request me. O auspicious lady, I shall give it without delay.

71. O auspicious lady, with the favour of Lord Śiva, there is nothing that I cannot get here or hereafter, since I work for the welfare of all.

72-73. On hearing these words of her husband, she who considered her husband as a divine being, became glad. With a beaming face she said: "O lord, if a boon is to be given to me, if I am considered worthy of a boon, I don't wish to choose any other boon. O sinless devotee of Maheśvara, give me a son like Maheśa himself."

74. On hearing these words spoken by Śuciṣmatī that

virtuous one meditated for a moment and thought thus in his heart:

75-76. 'Alas, what is this? A rare thing has been requested for by this lady; it is far away from the path of (i.e., beyond the ken of) even mental wish. Or let it be. He is the creator of everything.

It is by Śaṁbhu himself that these words were uttered by staying in her tongue in the form of Goddess of Speech. Who can make his utterance otherwise. It is bound to happen'.

77. Then that glorious sage Viśvānara who strictly adhered to the vow of having a single wife, told his wife: "O beloved, this will happen."

78. After consoling his wife thus, the sage went (to Kāśī) for performing the penance where Viśveśvara was present as the Lord of Kāśī.

79. Reaching Vārāṇasī quickly and visiting Maṇikarṇikā, he got rid of all the three types of distresses acquired in the course of hundreds of births.

80-85. After taking his holy bath in all the holy sacred pits, tanks, wells and lakes, he visited all the Liṅgas with Viśveśa as the chief among them.

He bowed down to all the Vināyakas and all the Gaurīs; he worshipped Kālarāja and Bhairava, the destroyer of sins.

He earnestly eulogized the Gaṇas (attendants of Śiva) with Daṇḍanāyaka as their chief; he propitiated all the (idols of) Keśavas, the chief of whom is Ādikeśava.

He repeatedly bowed down to all the Suns—the chief of whom was Lolārka; without any lethargy, he offered balls of rice in all the holy spots.

He pleased ascetics and Brāhmaṇas through *Sahasra-bhojana* etc. (feeding a thousand persons, simultaneously) and devoutly he worshipped all the Liṅgas with all the requisite services due to great Pūjās.

Thereafter, he continuously pondered over the question: 'Which Liṅga will accord the accomplishment of desires immediately? Where will the austerities performed with the desire for a son be steady throughout?

[The enumeration of the various Liṅgas[1]:]

1. For their locations *vide Infra* Ch. 73.

86-96. Is it the glorious Oṁkāranātha or is it Kṛttivāseśvara? Kāleśa, Vṛddhakāleśa, Kalaśeśvara, Kedāreśa, Kāmeśa, the three-eyed Lord Candreśa, Jyeṣṭheśa, Jaṁbukeśa, Jaigiṣavyeśvara, Īśāna of Daśāśvamedha, Drumicaṇḍeśa, Dṛkkeśa, Garuḍeśa, Gokarṇeśa, Gaṇeśvara, Ḍhuṇḍhyāśāgajasiddheśa, Dharmeśa, Tārakeśvara, Nandikeśa, Nivāseśa, Patrīśa, Prītikeśvara, Paśupati in the form of Parvateśa, Brahmeśa, Madhyameśvara, Bṛhaspatīśvara or Vibhāṇḍeśvara i.e., Tilabhāṇḍeśvara? Is it Bhārabhūteśvara or Mahālakṣmīśvara? Marutteśa, Mokṣeśa, Gaṅgeśa, Narmadeśvara, Mārkaṇḍa, Maṇikarṇīśa, Ratneśvara or Yoginīpīṭha that bestows good results on the aspirant, Yāmuneśa, Lāṅgalīśa, the glorious lord, Viśveśvara, Avimukteśvara, Viśālākṣīśa, Vyāghreśvara, Varāheśa, the bull-emblemed lord, Vyāseśa, Varuṇeśa, Vidhīśa, Vasiṣṭheśa, Śanīśvara, Someśvara, Indreśa, Svarlīna, Saṅgameśvara, Hariścandreśvara, Harikeśeśvara, Trisandhyeśa, Mahādeva, Upaśāntiśiva, Bhavānīśa, Kapardīśa, Kandukeśa, Makheśvara, or is it Mitrāvaruṇeśa?

97. 'Which among these bestows a son soon?' Thus the wise sage Viśvānara pondered for a moment.

98. 'Oh! I have recollected what was forgotten. My desire is fulfilled. The Liṅga resorted to by Siddhas is the greatest and it causes the fulfilment of all (desires).

99. By visiting it and touching it, the mind becomes exhilarated. Here the portals of heaven are always kept open.

100-105. Goddess Vikaṭā, the manifest personification of all Siddhis, is present in the great pedestal Pañcamudrā which bestows Siddhis on all living beings. She urges the Lord of Devas (Indra) day and night, for the requisite worship.

Siddhivināyaka himself removes all the obstacles of the devotees staying here, and accords all Siddhis. That Siddhikṣetra is the greatest holy spot in Avimukta. It is there that Vīreśvara Liṅga[1] is present, which is considered to be possessing great secrets. There is no ground to the extent of even a gingelly seed in Kāśī, that is without a Liṅga. But there is no other Liṅga on a par with Vīreśa bestowing Siddhi soon. It bestows piety, wealth, love and salvation perfectly. Certainly, there is no other Liṅga

---

1. This is to the south of Saṅkaṭā Devī. It is now known as Ātma-Vīreśvara and is still worshipped for boon of sons.

like Vīreśvara in Kāśī. Formerly, a Gandharva Pañcasvara attained great Siddhi here.

106-112. A Vidyādhara became one with excellent learning. The king of Yakṣas became fully enriched. Formerly, the most excellent one among Apsarās of a sweet voice like a cuckoo, began to dance with great feeling and fervour and got merged in the middle of the Liṅga along with her body.

Formerly a sage named Vedaśiras went on repeating Śatarudriya and (ultimately) merged in the Liṅga of the fiery form of Mantra in his own embodied form.

Candramauli and Bharadvāja, the most excellent ones among the devotees of Paśupati (Śiva), adored Vīreśvara and singing (song of eulogy) became merged (in him).

Śaṅkhacūḍa, a great serpent, offered Nirājana (waving of lights) through the gems in his own hood at night and attained Siddhi within six months.

A Kinnara lady Haṁsapadī, in the company of her husband Veṇupriya, sang sweetly and attained the highest state of salvation.

Numerous Siddhas, thousands of them, have attained Siddhi here. Hence Vīreśvara is stated as the greatest Siddhaliṅga.

113. Jayadratha, born of Videha, had lost his kingdom, but after propitiating Vīreśvara he could kill his enemies. He then got back his kingdom which he maintained uninterruptedly.

114. King Vidūratha, the lord of Magadha, endowed with self-control, had no son. Due to the favour of Vīreśvara, he obtained a son.

115. After adoring Vīreśa here, Vasudatta, a Vaiśya, obtained a daughter comparable to the girls of Vasus (semi-divine beings); so did Ratnadatta as well.

116. I too shall propitiate Vīreśa thrice (a day) and shall soon beget a son as desired by my wife.'

117. After mentally resolving thus, the intelligent Brāhmaṇa Viśvānara became contented. He took his holy bath with the water of Candrakūpa-well and decided to observe a holy vow.

118. For one month, he took only a single meal a day; for (the next) one month he took food only at night; for (the next) one month he never begged anyone for food and for (the next) one month, he completely eschewed intake of food.

119. For one month he observed the milk-vow (took in

only milk); for (the next) one month he had greens and fruits for food; for (the next) one month he took a handful of gingelly seeds everyday as food; and for (the next) one month water alone was his intake.

120. For one month he took in Pañcagavya; for (the next) month he observed the rite of Cāndrāyaṇa; for (the next) one month he drank water through the tips of Kuśa grass; and for (the next) one month he had air alone as his diet.

121-122. Then in the thirteenth month, the Brāhmaṇa took his bath in the waters of Gaṅgā early in the morning. By the time this devotee with austerities as his wealth came to the shrine of Vīreśa, he saw in the middle of the Liṅga an eight year old splendid boy beautified by the application of Bhasma.

123. His eyes were large, extending to the ears. His lips were perfectly red in colour. He had beautiful, tawny, matted hairs on his head. He had a smiling face. He was naked.

124. With some ornaments befitting childhood, he captivated the minds of the onlookers. He was repeating Vedic hymns, even as he sportingly displayed broad smile.

125. On seeing him (the Brāhmaṇa) experienced horripilation (of joy). He gladly eulogized and exclaimed "Obeisance to you" again and again with a choking feeling.

Prayer[1] *(vv 126-133).*

Viśvānara said:

126. The entire universe is Brahman itself, the one having no second. It is true, true; there is no diversity of objects here. Rudra is alone and single. There is no one second to him. Hence, I seek refuge in you, Maheśa, alone.

127. There is only one creator. O Śaṁbhu, you are the sole creator of all. You are devoid of form (really) and you appear to be of one form among the different forms like the same Sun appearing as many in different waters. Hence, I do not resort to any other Īśa except you

1. The prayer regards Śiva as Brahman and is full of Vedāntic concepts like Biṁba-pratibiṁba-vāda (v127), Adhyāsa (v 128) etc.

128. I resort to that Maheśa, on the realization of whom, this apparent universe vanishes even as the (appearance of a) serpent when the rope is known, as silver when oyster shell is known, as watery pool when mirage is known.

129. O Śaṁbhu, I resort to you who are coldness in water, power to burn in fire, warmth in the Sun, delightfulness in the Moon, fragrance in flowers and ghee in milk.

130. Who can perfectly comprehend you? You are without ears yet you perceive sound; you are without a nose yet you smell; you are without foot yet you come from afar[1]; you are without eyes yet you see (everything); you are without tongue yet you (can) taste. Hence I resort to you.

131. The Vedas do not comprehend you directly, O Īśa; nor Viṣṇu, nor the Creator of all, nor the leading Yogins, nor Devas, the chief of whom is Indra; but a devotee comprehends. Hence I resort to you.

132. O Īśa, you have neither a family nor nativity, no name, no form, no habit, no native land. Even though you are of this nature, you are the lord of the three worlds. You will fulfil all my desires. Hence I worship you.

133. Everything originates from you, O enemy of Smara; you are everything. You are the Lord of Gaurī; you are naked and highly quiescent. You are aged, and you are the youth and child. What is it that you are not? Hence I bow down to you.

134. After eulogizing thus the Brāhmaṇa fell down on the ground like a log of wood with great delight. By then the boy, more aged than all the aged ones, spoke to the excellent Brāhmaṇa: "Choose a boon."

135-136. Thereupon the contented sage Viśvānara got up with a delighted mind and replied: "O lord, what is it that is not known to you, the omniscient one? You are the innermost soul, the Lord; you are everything and the bestower of everything. Why does the Lord urge me for a humiliating importunity that causes mental anguish?"

137. On hearing the words of Viśvānara of pure vows and purity, the Lord, the child, smiled pleasantly and said:

1. Cf. Śvetāśvatara Up. 3.19.

The boy said:

138. O pure one, the desire created by you in the heart of Śuciṣmatī will be fulfilled ere long. There is no doubt about it.

139. O highly intelligent one, I shall be your son born of Śuciṣmatī, pure and fond of all immortal ones and well-known as Gṛhapati by name.

140. The prayer uttered by you, called 'Abhilāṣāṣṭaka' ('a prayer in eight verses for the fulfilment of one's desire') is meritorious. By reciting it in the presence of Śiva three times everyday for a year, all desires will be obtained.

141. The recitation of this prayer bestows sons, grandsons and wealth. It causes all peace and quells all calamities.

142-147. There is no doubt about this that it is conducive to the attainment of heaven, liberation and wealth. The devotee should get up early in the morning and take his holy bath. Then he should worship the Liṅga of Śaṁbhu. He should recite this prayer for a year. A man without sons will become a father. In the months of Vaiśākha, Kārttika and Māgha, he should observe special vows and rites and recite this prayer at the time of bath. He shall get all benefits. As a result of propitiation in the month of Kārttika, I, the immutable one, shall become your son. So also, in the case of anyone else who reads this. This Abhilāṣāṣṭaka should not be given to anyone and everyone. It should be strenuously kept a secret. It can cause even a chronic barren woman deliver. Whether a woman or a man, the devotee should recite this for a year invariably in the presence of the Liṅga. Undoubtedly it bestows a son.

After saying this the boy vanished. The Brāhmaṇa too went home.

CHAPTER ELEVEN

The World of Vahni (Fire-God)

Agastya said:

1. O lady of good fortune and excellent lips, listen to the origin of Vaiśvānara (Fire-god) as narrated to Śivaśarman by Puṇyaśīla and Suśīla.

2. When the sacred rite of Garbhādhāna (impregnation) was duly performed by him, his wife became pregnant in due course.

3. Thereafter, for the development (of the power) of the foetus, the rite of Puṁsavana was duly performed by that scholarly Brāhmaṇa before the period of the movement of the foetus, in accordance with the injunctions of the Gṛhya section of the Vedas.

4. In the eighth month, the Sīmanta rite that is conducive to the beauty and full development of embryo was performed by him and also the rite to facilitate easy delivery as he was the knower of all rites.

5-6. Then at an auspicious moment a moon-faced son was born to Śuciṣmatī. With his brilliance, he illuminated the lying-in-chamber destroying all evils. The stars at the time were in excellent positions. Jupiter was in Kendra (i.e., 4th, 7th or 10th house in the horoscope). The Lagna (time of the rising of Zodiac) was auspicious. All the good Planets were in their proper houses (of strong positions).

7. The boy born immediately became the cause of happiness to everyone among the inhabitants of Bhuvar and Svarloka. The winds wafted fragrance according aroma to all the quarters.

8. Great clouds showered heaps of flowers of pleasing smell. The divine Dundubhi drums were sounded. All the quarters became bright.

9. The rivers all around became very clear (of translucent water) along with the minds of all living beings. Darkness became reduced very much. All the dust particles settled down (became free from *Rajas* quality).

10. All animals became endowed with *Sattva* quality. The

earth became splendid. The words everywhere became beneficial and pleasing to all living beings.

11-16. Tilottamā, Urvaśī, Rambhā, the splendid Vidyutprabhā, Sumaṅgalā, Śubhālāpā, Suśīlā and other excellent celestial ladies came there holding vessels joyously in their hands of which the bangles jingled. The vessels contained pearls, Yakṣakardamas (paste of camphor agallochum etc.), blazing diamond and Lapis Lazuli lamps, turmeric and other unguents, emeralds, conchs, oyster shells, curds, ṣaffron, coral and ruby gems, good garlands of Gomeda, Puṣparāga and Indranīla stones. Thousands of Vidyādhara, Kinnara and immortal celestial women came there with auspicious materials in their hands or waving *Cāmaras* (Chowries). A number of beautiful ladies of Gandharvas, serpents and Yakṣas of sweet voice came there singing light musical pieces.

17-23. Many sages came there such as Marīci, Atri, Pulaha, Pulastya, Kratu, Aṅgiras, Vasiṣṭha, Kaśyapa, I (i.e. Agastya), Vibhāṇḍa, Māṇḍavi's son, Lomaśa, Lomacaraṇa, Bharadvāja, Gautama, Bhṛgu, Gālava, Garga, Jātukarṇya, Parāśara, Āpastaṁba, Yājñavalkya, Dakṣa, Vālmīki, Mudgala, Śātātapa, Likhita, Śilāda, Śaṅkha, Uñcchabhuk, Jamadagni, Saṁvarta, Mataṅga, Bharata, Aṁśumān, Vyāsa, Kātyāyana, Kutsa, Śaunaka, Suśruta, Śuka, Ṛṣyaśṛṅga, Durvāsas, Ruci, Nārada, Tuṁburu, Uttaṅka, Vāmadeva, Cyavana, Asita, Devala, Śālaṅkāyana, Hārīta, Viśvāmitra, Bhārgava, Mṛkaṇḍu along with his son (Mārkaṇḍeya), Dālbhya, Uddālaka, Dhaumya, Upamanyu, Vatsa and other sages and their daughters came there for the rite of Śānti (peace and auspiciousness) to the hermitage of Viśvānara.

24-26. Brahmā accompanied by Bṛhaspati, the Garuḍa-vehicled Lord, the Bull-emblemed Lord (Śiva) accompained by Nandi, Bhṛṅgi and Gaurī, Devas, chief of whom was Mahendra, Serpents residing in Pātāla, many great Oceans along with Rivers taking jewels with them, and many immobile ones assuming mobile forms came there in thousands. In that great festival, there was a (continuous) moonlight irrespective of the Moon's presence in the sky.

27-28. Lord Pitāmaha (Brahmā) himself performed the post-natal rites for the child. After pondering over the relevant Vedic passages, he gave the child the name Gṛhapati. "This boy is Gṛhapati by name." The name which should be given on the eleventh day was duly assigned in accordance with the injunctions laid down. He repeated the Vedic passages meant for that purpose.

29-31. The passages are '*ayam agniḥ*'[1] etc. '*agne gṛhapate*' etc. The meaning of the Vedic passages—"This fire named Gārhapatya is the lord of the house. He knows fully well (the means of) wealth of the child (subject). O Agni, O lord of the house, stabilise before us food, fame and strength." Brahmā cited other Vedic passages also. He blessed the child with blessings mentioned in the Mantras of all the four Vedas. After according him the protection special to infants, the Grandfather of all (i.e. Brahmā) set off riding his swan along with Hara and Hari.

32-34. All those who had come there talked to one another in praise of the child: "Oh, what a beauty! Oh, what a brilliance! Oh, all the limbs have exquisite characteristics! Oh, the good luck of Śuciṣmatī, Hara himself has manifested in front. There should be no surprise in the case of the devotees of Śiva. Rudra himself comes among the devotees of Śiva, because the worshippers of Rudra are identical with Rudra." Then all of them went away to different places where they came from, after taking leave of Viśvānara with great delight.

35. Hence persons in householder's stage yearn for a son. The eternal Śruti says, "Through the son (the father) wins all the worlds."

36. The house of a son-less man is void; the acquisition of a sonless man is futile; the family of a son-less man is extinct. A man becomes unholy due to the want of a son.

37. There is no greater gain than a son; there is no greater happiness than (having) a son; there is no greater friend than a son either here or hereafter.

38-39. There are seven kinds of sons: (1) bosom-born, (2) wife's son (through another), (3) a purchased son, (4) son given by others i.e., adopted son, (5) acquired by other means, (6) daughter's son and (7) another one saved from a calamity.

One of these must be kept as a son by a sensible householder. The earlier ones are better than the later ones. The later ones are worse than the earlier ones.

1. Vājasaneyī Saṁ. 3.30a.

The attendants said:

40. The rite of his coming out of the lying-in-chamber was performed by the father in the fourth month. (Formal) *Annaprāśana* (i.e. feeding with cooked rice) was done when half a year elapsed. Cutting of the forelock was performed duly at the end of a year.

41. On the day of Śravaṇa constellation, the ear-piercing ceremony was performed by him who knew the various rituals. In the fifth year (the father) gave him the *Vrata* (i.e., investiture with sacred thread) for increasing Brāhmaṇical splendour.

42. The intelligent Brāhmaṇa then performed the ceremony of *Upākarma* and taught him the Vedas. He (the son) duly learned the Vedas with Padapāṭha and Kramapāṭha along with the Aṅgas (ancillaries) for three years.

43. Exhibiting his qualities of modesty etc., the powerful son grasped all the lores from the mouth of the preceptor who remained only as a witness.

44-45. In this ninth year, Gṛhapati, the son of Viśvānara, began serving his parents. Having come to know of this, the celestial sage Nārada, the intelligent sage who roams about wherever he pleases, reached the hut of Viśvānara. He was offered Arghya and a seat, which he accepted duly and enquired of their welfare.

Nārada said:

46. O illustrious Viśvānara, O virtuous Śuciṣmatī, I hope, this child Gṛhapati acts according to your directions.

47. Indeed, to a son there is no other holy spot (or sacred water), Deva, preceptor, holy rite or pious observance excepting the words of his parents.

48. To a son there is no religious duty other than the directions of the parents in all the worlds. Because of the fact that the mother carried him in the womb and (later) nursed him, the mother is more worthy of respect than the father.[1]

49. After bathing himself with the waters dropping down from the feet of his mother, a son shall attain more purity than from the holy waters of even the celestial river (Gaṅgā).

1. Cf. Manu II. 145.

50. A recluse who has renounced all activities is to be respected more than the father, but his mother should be scrupulously venerated even by an ascetic, who himself is to be venerated by all.

51. This alone is the most intense (fiercest) austerity; this alone is the greatest *Vrata* (vow, observance). This alone is the greatest pious practice, namely the propitiation of the parents.

52. I consider that the parents of other children of lower status are not as much worthy of respect as you two are worthy of the respect of this child Gṛhapati who has been well educated and hence is very polite as is evident from the features of his face.

53. "O Vaiśvānara, come here and sit on my lap. I shall examine the characteristic features (on your palm). Show me your right hand."

54. On being told thus by the sage, the glorious boy took the permission of his parents and sat there humbly after bowing down to Nārada with devotion.

55-56. The sage then examined all the limbs of the boy[1], (particularly) the palate, the tongue and the teeth. He brought a long twine reddened with saffron and twisted it into three threads. He remembered Śiva, Pārvatī and Gaṇādhyakṣa and measured the boy from head to foot as he stood straight facing the north.

57. "A person who is equal in length horizontally and vertically extending to 108 *Aṅgulas* (1 Aṅgula = 1.75cm) (Horizontal measure is the extent with both the hands stretched out) will become a king, O Brāhmaṇa, like your son.

58. Your son has all the thirty-two (auspicious) characteristics. He has five parts exquisite and delicate, five long, seven red, six lifted up, three broad, three short and three deep and majestic.

59. This boy is long-lived, five of his parts are long and praiseworthy, viz., the arms, the eyes, the chin, the knee and the nose of this son of yours.

60. This boy is respectable with three parts short, viz., neck, calf and penis. This child is splendid with three aspects deep and majestic, viz., voice, mind and navel.

1. VV 55ff deal with Purāṇic Chiromancy.

61. So also five parts of his are delicate and exquisitely fine, viz., skin, hair, fingers, teeth and finger-joints. He will gain the status of the Guardian of a Quarter.

62. He has six parts lifted up and raised, viz., chest, belly, curly locks of hair, shoulders, hands and face. It is seen here in this boy. So he will have great fortune and prosperity.

63. Seven parts are red, viz., the palms, the extremities of the eyes, the palate, the tongue, the lower lip, the upper lip and the nails. This bestows the happiness of a kingdom.

64. He has three parts broad, viz., forehead, hips and chest. With all refulgence, he will attain every type of glory and prosperity and not otherwise.

65. His hands as firm as the back of a female turtle are not intended for any hard labour. They indicate that he will get a kingdom. This child's feet are very tender so far as walking along the road is concerned.

66. A line is seen in his (palm) starting from the back of the small finger extending without any break as far as the index finger. This indicates long life.

67. His feet are very strong, red and symmetrical. They are beautiful and exquisitely delicate. The heels are of the same size. The feet are smooth and free from perspiration. Hence they indicate prosperity.

68. The lines on the palm are very few and red. They indicate that he will be happy always. He will become the king of kings, as indicated by the thin and short penis.

69. He has large and conspicuous seat of the body, heels and thighs. His navel is spiral-shaped, moving clockwise. It is reddish in colour. This is the indicator of great prosperity.

70. If when he urinates, a single current flows spiralling clockwise, and if there is the smell of fish and honey in the semen, he will become a king.

71. Broad, strong and smooth, his thighs are indicative of his being habitually happy. The two arms hanging down with beautiful curves are capable of protecting the quarters .

72. The line on his palm is such that he is sure to be the lord of heaven. It has the designs of the scar Śrīvatsa, thunderbolt, discus, lotus, fish, bow and staff.

73. He has thirty-two teeth. His neck is curly like the trunk of an elephant having three folds like a conchshell. His voice

is like the note of a Krauñca bird, Dundubhi drum, swan and thundering cloud. Hence he will surpass even emperors.

74-75. His eyes are tawny-coloured like honey. Royal glory will never desert him. There are five lines on his forehead. He is splendid with leonine belly. The soles of his feet have lines going up. While breathing he gives off the fragrance of a lotus. When the fingers are stretched out, there is no gap between them. His nails are good. Thus he possesses all great characteristics.

76. But fate can pull down a person endowed with all good qualities, one marked by all characteristics and one with all *Kalās* (arts, digits) complete and pure as in the case of a full moon (being eclipsed).

77. Hence this child should be well guarded in every respect with all endeavour. When the fate is crooked, even good qualities turn into defects.

78. I am afraid, some calamity through celestial fire of lightning in this twelfth year (may befall him)"

After saying thus, that intelligent Nārada went away in the manner he had arrived.

79. On hearing the words of Nārada, Viśvānara along with his wife thought of the terrible fall of the thunderbolt then itself.

80. "Alas! I am doomed", uttering these words he beat his chest. Agitated with the grief of his son, he fell into a great swoon.

81. The grief-stricken Śuciṣmatī too cried a lot unbearably with cries of distress and shouts of "Ha!" "Ha!" All her sense-organs became upset.

82. "Alas, my child, a storehouse of great good qualities! Alas! O my child carrying out the words of your father! Wherefore did you come into the womb of me, an unlucky woman?

83. O my son, you are my only child. I have fallen into a great ocean of grief, with all your good qualities for its waves. Excepting you who can save me?

84. Alas, my boy, free from impurities, having long eyes like a lotus! Alas, if the eyes of the general public are Cakora birds, you are the moon (having the sign of a deer)! Alas, my dear one, to the lotus-like eyes of your father, you are like the

Sun! Alas, my child, you are the sole cause for the happiness of a thousand festivals of your mother!

85. O child with a face resembling the full moon! O child, your nails and fingers are exquisite. Your words are sweet like nectar. You are the ocean filled with the waves of nectar. Alas, you have been acquired by me through many sufferings! O Gṛhapati, what all things have not been done by me for obtaining you!

86. Alas, what oblation has not been offered by me to the different deities! O dear child, what holy spots have not been visited by me! What observances have not been practised! What medicines have not been taken in! What Mantras have not been repeated! What Yantras have not been resorted to! Everything for your sake, but you could be obtained only by good merits.

87. O my child, you who are the boat whereby I can cross the ocean of worldly existence, remove the weight of misery. You are the ocean of happiness. Show me your moon-like face, the essence (of everything). The hell named *Put* is extensive like an ocean. From the submarine fire thereof enliven your father through the showers of your nectar-like utterances.

88. The Devas are perfectly delighted on carefully scrutinizing all qualities, habits, full complement of arts, beauty and characteristic signs existing in one place. Perhaps that was why, Alas! they have all assembled simultaneously after coming to know that this would happen at the time of the great festival of his birthday.

89. O Śaṁbhu, O Maheśa, the merciful, O trident-bearing Lord, those who are conversant with the Vedas say that you are Mṛtyuñjaya ('Conquerer of death'). If the god of Death brings about the death of this infant son bestowed by you, say, whose fall will not take place here thus!

90. Alas! O Vidhi (Brahmā), you had created an extensive ocean of good qualities, the depth of which cannot be gauged in the middle and which contains all essential gems. You created everything in the proper manner. If this boy is to be taken away by you, why was he created by you with great endeavour?

91. Alas! O Kāla, is not your queen one with a boy? The moon-like face of your son has not taken away your ability to kill. Therefore, you have (displayed) your ability to kill. Therefore,

you have (displayed) your curved fangs resembling a dagger as sharp and hard as the thunderbolt towards this boy whose sportive play is like that of the excessively tender lotus fibre!"

92. After lamenting thus in various ways, she gave out hot, deep, long breaths, because she was scorched by the heat of the fire originating from the grief for her son. Thereby she dried up the hundreds of rivers with waves lifted up originating from the incessant flow of tears from her eyes.

93. On hearing her piteous lamentations, trees and creepers appeared to shed tears when the flowers dropped down, to cry through the chirping sounds of birds resembling cries of distress, and as though shook their heads moving by the gusts of wind.

94. With cries of distress, she wept bitterly. As though out of sorrow for her, all the quarters too cried along with her under the form of the echoes, with the caves of the mountains for their mouths. The birds, animals and trees were stunned.

95. On hearing the sound of the cries of distress thus, Viśvānara overcame the swoon and got up, loudly uttering "What is this? What? What is this? Where is Gṛhapati, my external vital breath, the lord of all sense-organs, the immanent soul?"

Agastya said:

96. On seeing the parents overwhelmed with grief, he (Gṛhapati) smiled and said: "Dear mother, why such a fear in you both?

97. I have been provided with a good protection for my body through the dust-particles of your feet. Even the god of Death cannot kill me. How can the feeble and insignificant lightning-fire?

98. Listen to my vow, dear parents. If I am your son, I shall do such a thing as would make the lightning afraid of me.

99. (I shall do so) after propitiating the omniscient Mṛtyuñjaya, the giver of everything unto the good, Mahākāla, the slayer of the god of Death, the lord who swallowed the poison Kālakūṭa."

100. On hearing his words, the aged Brāhmaṇa couple had their distress calmed down, as though through an untimely shower of divine nectar. They said then:

101. "Whence does this shower of rain without a cloud,

this outcome of divine nectar without the Milk Ocean, this brilliant moonshine without the Moon, delight us excessively?

102. Say again. Say again. What? What? Again and again 'God of Death cannot kill me. How then can the feeble and insignificant lightning fire?'

103. A great means of remedy has been mentioned by you for removing our distress, namely the propitiation of Lord Mṛtyuñjaya.

104. Hence, O dear one, seek refuge in him. There is no one more beneficial than the Slayer of the god of Death, who can do more than what we wish for.

105. O dear one, is this not heard by you? Formerly the Slayer of Tripura protected Śvetaketu bound by Kālā's noose.

106. Śiva made Nandin, the eight-year old boy, the son of Śilāda, who was grasped by Mṛtyu (Death), his own attendant (after saving him), the delighter of the universe.

107. He saved the three worlds after drinking the terrible Halāhala poison that issued at the time of the churning of the Milk Ocean and which resembled the fire at the time of the ultimate annihilation.

108. With the discus lifted up by the toe of his foot, he killed Jālandhara, the great Daitya of excessive arrogance, when he took away the wealth of the three worlds.

109. After making Viṣṇu his arrow, Dhūrjaṭi burned the three *Puras* formerly through the fire originating from the stroke of a single arrow.

110. Formerly, he kept Andhaka transfixed to the tip of his trident for ten thousand years, when he became deluded on account of the prosperity and glory of the three worlds and made him dried up through the Sun.

111. Even as Brahmā and others were watching, he reduced Kāma to the state of *Anaṅga* (devoid of limbs, body-less) by a mere glance of his eye, though he was powerful enough to conquer all the three worlds.

112. (*Defective text*) Dear son, seek refuge in Śiva the protective jewel of the universe, who is the sole creator of Brahmā, Indra, Acyuta and others."

113. Thus, after getting the permission of his parents and bowing down to their feet, he circumambulated them, consoled them earnestly and set off.

114-118. He reached Kāśī which is inaccessible even to Brahmā, Nārāyaṇa and others: Kāśī which was protected by Viśveśvara from the distress happening at the time of Mahāsaṁvarta (Prākṛtalaya, annihilation); which shone with the celestial river acting like a necklace around its grounds as though around its neck, the river (Gaṅgā) being white like a garland of snow; which warded off through Varaṇā and chopped off through the current of river Asi ('edge of a sword'), the rebirth of the common people distressed on account of many worldly tortures. With his eyes distressed due to worldly affairs and calamities, extending as far as the ears, he, at the outset went to Maṇikarṇikā, which the wise men sang about as Kāśikā, because it made it possible for the devotees to attain Kaivalya (Mokṣa) by merely abandoning their body therein, while that Kaivalya is usually attained by means of steady practice of Yoga with its eight constituents (stages).

119. There he took his holy bath in accordance with injunctions, visited Lord Viśveśvara and bowed down to him, the saviour of all the living beings in the three worlds.

120. He was very glad within his heart, by repeatedly looking at the Liṅga. There is no doubt in this that this is clearly what is called the very bulbous root of the highest bliss.

121. "Oh! There is no one more blessed than I in all the three worlds consisting of mobile and immobile beings, because I have seen today the glorious Lord Viśveśvara.

122-123. The entire essence of the three worlds has become solidified in this (Liṅga) indeed, or is this the divine Ambrosia in a solid lump after coming out of the Milk Ocean? Or is this the first germinating shoot of the brilliant splendour of the realization of the Ātman or is it the excellent bulbous root of the bliss of Brahman (the ultimate goal), the Absolute (elixir-like) bliss of Brahman?

124. What is mentioned as formless and is stationed in the lotus-like heart of Yogins, has that assumed a form in the shape of this Liṅga?

125. Perhaps the entire Cosmic Egg (Brahmāṇḍa) is filled with (a flood of) different kinds of jewels. Or there is no doubt about this that this is the fruit of the tree of salvation.

126. Is this the braid of hair of Nirvāṇalakṣmī ('Glorious Goddess of Salvation') decorated with an excellent flower? Is

this the bunch of flowers of Kaivalya Mallīvallī ('the jasmine creeper of the bliss of liberation') that bestows all the four Puruṣārthas on the eulogizer?

127. Or is it the joyous ball of play of *Niḥśreyasa Śrī* ('the glorious deity of ultimate liberation')? Has the nectar-rayed Moon risen up from the eastern mountain of *Apavarga* (Salvation)?

128. Is this the Sun dispelling the darkness of worldly delusion? Or is it the glamorously beautiful romantic mirror of the beautiful maiden of eternal welfare?

129. Lo! It is known! It cannot be anything else. This is the wonderful citron fruit of many Karma-seeds of all embodied beings.

130. This is Viśvaliṅga, because in this Liṅga that bestows salvation, there is the final absorption of all the seeds of the universe (or all beings)—the seeds called Karma.

131. It is due to the rising of my good fortune that the great sage Nārada came then and said so. I am contented and blessed thereat."

132-135a. Thus with the nectarine juices of the highest bliss, he performed *Pāraṇa* (concluding rite of holy observances).

Then on an auspicious day, he installed the Liṅga that bestows welfare on all and then took up terrible holy observances very difficult to be performed by persons of no control over themselves. Everyday that devotee of pure soul brought Gaṅgā water strained with a cloth and filled it into one hundred and eight pitchers. With this he bathed Śiva everyday. Everyday he used to offer a garland of blue lotuses wreathed with one thousand and eight flowers.

135b-139a. He used to have a diet of bulbous roots, and fruits once in seven and a half days and continued this for six months.

Then taking in withered leaves once in a fortnight, he spent another six months. Then he spent six months taking in only air and spent another six months drinking only drops of water. Thus he spent altogether two years.

On the twelfth year from his birth (Śiva in the guise of) the thunderbolt-armed Indra came near him, as though he would make what is uttered by Nārada a fact. Then he said: "Tell me what boon you want. I shall give you whatever is cherished in your mind. I am Indra, O Brāhmaṇa. I am pleased with your splendid holy vows."

139b-141. On hearing these words of Mahendra, the son of the sage spoke sensibly and sweetly with the sweet voice of a parrot: "O Maghavan, O enemy of Vṛtra, I know you are armed with the thunderbolt. I won't choose a boon from you. Śaṅkara is the giver of boons unto me."

Indra said:

142. Śaṅkara is not someone different from me, O child. I am the lord of Devas. Cast off all your foolishness and request for an excellent boon from me.

The Brāhmaṇa said:

143. O Ahalya's paramour, go away. O unholy enemy of Gotras (families, mountains), O chastiser of Pāka! It is definite that I will not request any other Deva than Paśupati.

144. On hearing his words, Indra became furious with reddened eyes. He lifted up his terrible thunderbolt and terrified the boy.

145. On seeing the *Vajra* (thunderbolt) having hundreds of lightning sparks, the boy remembered Nārada's words and swooned with great fright.

146. Then Śaṁbhu, the consort of Gaurī, appeared in front dispelling the darkness (and said): "Get up, get up; welfare unto you." He appeared to enliven him by gentle touches.

147-152. He opened the lotus-like eyes sleeping as though at the close of the day and got up. He then saw before him Śaṁbhu who had the lustre of more than a hundred Suns. On seeing the eye in the forehead, the Bull-emblemed Lord with a dark throat, he knew the Lord with moon for his crest-jewel, accompanied by the Daughter of the Mountain seated on his left side. He was shining with his matted hair. The trident and Ājagava bow formed his weapons. His limbs were shining like camphor, spotlessly white in colour. He was clad in the elephant's hide. Recognizing him through his preceptor's words and passages from Āgamas, he became excited with tears of joy. His throat became choked. Hairs standing on their ends covered him like a bodice. He stood as if stunned for a moment like the picture of a boy. He somehow steadied himself. Forgetting himself he found it impossible to eulogize or bow down to or submit anything (to Śiva). When the boy was in that predicament, Śaṅkara smiled and said:

Īśvara said:

153. O child Gṛhapati, you are known to be afraid of Śakra with the thunderbolt lifted up in his hand. Do not be afraid. I wanted to know you fully.

154. Neither Śakra, nor his thunderbolt, nor even the god of Death can harm my devotee. It was I who spoke to you in the form of Indra.

155. O gentle boy, I am giving you a boon. You will be the holder of the post of Agni (designated as Agni). You will be the mouth of all the Devas.

156. O Agni, you will be moving among all the living beings. You will get your realm as the Lord of a Quarter in between Dharmarāja and Indra (i.e. between South and East).

157. The Liṅga installed by you will be known after your name. It will be famous as Agnīśvara. It will increase the brilliance of everyone.

158. The devotees of Agnīśvara need not be afraid of the fire arising from lightning. They will never suffer from indigestion. They will never have premature death.

159. One who worships Agnīśvara, the bestower of all prosperities, at Kāśī is honoured in the world of Agni, though he may die by chance elsewhere.

160-162. Then he will come to Kāśī again. At the end of a Kalpa, he shall attain salvation.

A man who propitiates Agnīśvara on the western bank of Gaṅgā to the east of Vīreśvara, shall stay in the world of Agni along with his parents, his own kinsmen, friends and relatives. O Lord of a Quarter, get into this aerial chariot and go.

After saying this he brought his kinsmen, even as the parents were watching; he crowned Agni as the Lord of a Quarter. Śiva then merged into the Liṅga there.

The attendants said:

163. O Śivaśarman, this, the form of Agni—has been explained to you. What else do you wish to hear? We shall narrate. Tell us.

CHAPTER TWELVE

The Worlds of Nirṛti and Varuṇa

Śivaśarman said:

1. O excellent men with the forelocks rendered grey with the dust particles from the lotus-like feet of Puruṣottama (Lord Viṣṇu), describe in due order the worlds of Nirṛti and others.

The attendants said:

2. Listen, O illustrious one, about this city beyond (to the west of) Saṁyaminī. This is the city of Nirṛta, the Lord of the (South-West) Quarter. It is meritorious and is occupied by Puṇyajanas.

3. In this city, Rākṣasas who never hurt others, live. They are Rākṣasas only by birth, but by conduct they are Puṇyajanas (religious-minded).

4-10. Those who live here now were (good people on the earth with the following excellence in behaviour): They follow the path of Vedas approved in the Smṛtis. Even in regard to those born in lower castes, they never encourage the conduct of life not approved in the Smṛtis as regards food and beverages. They are averse to other men's wives and possessions. They never trouble others. Even those born in inferior castes followed meritorious conduct of life. They nourish themselves by means of the wealth and objects acquired through devotion to the twice-born. They shrink their limbs themselves while talking to Brāhmaṇas. When summoned, they approach (Brāhmaṇas) with the ends of their clothes covering their mouths and talk thus in the presence of Brāhmaṇas. They constantly address: 'Be victorious', 'Be long-lived.' 'Bhoganātha'

(O Lord), 'Svāmin' (Master) etc. They are devoted to holy ablutions in sacred spots; they are humble towards Brāhmaṇas, announcing their own names (before talking). All these good qualities contribute to the piety of everyone: self-control, liberal-mindedness, kindness, forbearance, cleanliness, restraint of the organs of sense and actions, non-stealing, truthfulness and non-violence. Wherever these people are born, they are always engaged in essential activities. Here in this world, they enjoy all the luxuries and pleasures in plenty.

11. Those who die in excellent holy spots without committing suicide, enjoy the pleasures here, even if they are Mlecchas (barbarians and uncivilised people). This excludes Kāśī which accords salvation itself.

12. Those people who kill themselves will enter (the world of) blinding darkness. After experiencing the tortures in a thousand hells, they are born as village pigs.

13. Therefore, suicide should never be committed anywhere by a wise one. Nothing auspicious will befall those who kill themselves, here in this world or in the other worlds.

14. Some persons who know the truth lay down permitting death as one pleases at Prayāga that is the king of all holy spots, and that fulfills all desires.

15. Even Śūdras who follow pious and merciful practices and who invariably help others are excellent persons and they live here.

16-17. We shall describe the features of this Lord of the Quarter. Listen for a moment.

Formerly there was a king of hunters' tribe living in the middle of the Vindhya forest. He was the most excellent one among those inhabitants of Pakkaṇas (villages of the hill tribe). This ruler of the Śabara village was very powerful and was well-known as Piṅgākṣa. He lived on the banks of the river Nirvindhyā*. Though strong and heroic, he was averse to cruel practices.

18. Though he might be far away, he used to kill those who were the obstructors (looters) of travellers. With special efforts, he used to hunt down tigers and other wicked (carnivorous) animals.

19-20. He maintained himself as a fowler by profession.

* Modern Newuj, a tributary of Chambal.

Even in that (profession), he was merciful. He never used to kill birds and animals resting confidently, sleeping, engaged in mating, eager to drink water, very young in age or having visible signs of pregnancy. He was very pious and averse to the evil practices of the people of his caste.

21. He gave shelter to the travellers who became weary. He removed the hunger of those who were distressed with hunger. He gave footwears to those who did not have them.

22. He used to distribute among those who had no clothes, very soft deer-hides. He used to accompany and follow travellers along desolate, impassable roads in the forest.

23. He never desired to take any remuneration from them. He used to grant them freedom from fear by saying, "Upto (the boundary of) the Vindhya forest, my name should be taken (uttered) as one who removes the fear from wicked people."

24. Everyday he used to visit pilgrims along with his son. They too blessed him at every holy spot.

25. While Piṅgākṣa remained like this, that forest became a city as it were. No powerful wayfarer attacked weak travellers out of fear of Piṅgākṣa.

26. Once, a long caravan of pilgrims equipped with many articles and making a lot of noise was heard by Piṅgākṣa's uncle who was staying in a nearby village.

27. The fowler was covetous of the wealth of that caravan. The petty fellow attempted to kill them. He went ahead and very secretly blocked the path.

28. Because he was destined to live longer, Piṅgākṣa who had gone ahunting spent that night very near the path in that forest.

29. Let not the evil intentions of those persons who act in hatred of others become fulfilled. It is, therefore, that the universe protected by Viśveśa is happy.

30-31. Hence no wise person should have evil intention at any time. Only what is destined to happen will happen. But by having evil intentions, only sin will result. Hence, one who wants to get the happiness of the soul should not think of good or bad. If he is to think about anything, he should think about the means of salvation and nothing else.

32. When the day dawned, there was a great hue and cry

with chaotic sounds like "Kill; throw him down; make him naked; O soldiers, be quick."

33-35. "O soldiers, do not kill. Save us; we are pilgrims. You can easily rob us. Take away whatever we have. We are travellers without leaders. We depend upon Viśvanātha. We have our saviour in him. But he is far off. Who else can be our protector even if we pray for it? We had faith in Piṅgākṣa. Therefore, we always travel to and fro on this path without any fear from anywhere. But he is far away from this forest."

36. On hearing this utterance of the pilgrims, Piṅgākṣa, the hero, came there from a distance saying: "Do not be afraid. Do not be afraid."

37. The Bhilla (tribal man, here Piṅgākṣa), fond of the pilgrims, hastened to that place in a trice like their own long life.

38. (He said:) "What is this atrocious act? What is this, while I Piṅgākṣa, am alive? Who is desirous of robbing and killing the travellers, who are like the Liṅgas, my vital breath?"

39. On hearing these words, Tārākṣa, his sinful uncle, thought evil of Piṅgākṣa out of avarice for wealth.

40. (He thought thus:) 'This defiler of the family is behaving like this, discarding the traditional practice of the family. I have been thinking about it for a long time. Today, I shall certainly get him killed.'

41. After thinking thus that wicked one angrily commanded his servants, "You should kill this man at the outset, then the pilgrims."

42-44. Thereupon, all those evil-doers fought with him who was alone. (Piṅgākṣa) somehow took those pilgrims near his abode. (By that time) his bows and arrows were broken and his body was wounded with arrows. Then he wished thus in his mind, 'If only I had been powerful, I would have killed these.' Thinking thus he discarded his life for the sake of others. Those pilgrims too (somehow) reached the colony of hunters and became free from fear.

45. The fate (after death) conforms with the thought that is foremost at the time of death. Hence, the lord of the hunters attained the lordship of the quarter in the South-West and became the lord of Nairṛtas (Puṇyajanas).

46. Thus the form and features of this (Nirṛti) have been

narrated to you by us. The world beyond this is the wonderful world of Varuṇa.

47. Those who dig wells, tanks and lakes in this world are honoured in Varuṇa-Loka. They have the same refulgence as that of Varuṇa.

48-56. (The following meritorious persons can attain the region of Varuṇa:) Those who give water during drought (or in a waterless region); those who remove other persons' distress; those who give various kinds of umbrellas and waterpots to the persons who request for them; those who construct free waterstalls (where wayfarers are given water for drinking) with the equipment of all essential utensils and articles (that improve the quality and taste of the water supplied); those who offer free of charge, pots filled with sweet-smelling water; those who regularly water the holy fig tree; those who grow trees along the pathways; those who build rest-houses and waiting halls; those who remove the distress of the weary travellers; those who distribute in the beginning of summer hand-fans of various kinds and colours, embellished with peacock feathers and capable of dispelling the heat of summer; those who, in the summer season, scrupulously give beverages, sweet-smelling, juicy and icy cool, to complete satiety of the travellers; those who perform the Saṁkalpa rite and place at the disposal of Brāhmaṇas, fields of sugarcane as well as many different varieties of sugarcane products; those who give milk products, cows and buffaloes; those who make *Dhārāmaṇḍapas* (water stalls mechanically showering water); those who erect *Chāyāmaṇḍapas* (cool shady groves); those who make arrangements in the temple for many *Dhārāgalantikās* (water-pitchers with holes in the bottom through which water-drops fall down on the image or Liṅga kept below); those who remove dust and sweep holy spots; those who water and clean the pathways in holy spots; those who lift their hands and offer freedom from fear to those who are frightened. All these people stay fearlessly and shine remarkably in Varuṇa Loka.

57. They who remove the ropes around the necks of (innocent people) tied by evil-doers, live in this world of Pāśapāṇi (Varuṇa) as meritorious persons without fear from anywhere.

58. Those who take travellers across the rivers etc., by means of boats and other means of transport, O Brāhmaṇa, became

citizens here, redeeming (people) from the ocean of misery.

59. Those men who make landing places and steps on the banks of holy rivers by means of slabs of stones and bricks to provide convenience to those who want to take water, enjoy here.

60. Those meritorious persons who dispel the thirst of the thirsty (travellers) by means of cool waters, enjoy series of pleasures in Varuṇa Loka.

61. This Pracetā (Varuṇa) is the sole and chief lord of all waterways and receptacles; he is the lord of aquatic beings and the witness of all (our) activities.

62-63. Listen to the origin of the noble-souled Varuṇa, the lord of this world. There was a sage of immeasurable (very large-hearted) soul, well-known as Śuciṣmān. He was the son of Kardama, the Prajāpati. He was very humble and polite by habit. He was enriched by good qualities such as steadfastness, sweetness, courage etc. He was beneficent to all.

64. He went to a lake of pure waters in order to take his bath along with other boys. While he was engaged in aquatic sports an alligator carried him away.

65. When the son of the sage was taken away, the other children came there and recounted to his father the great calamity.

66. His mind did not stray away from Lord Śiva, although he heard about the calamity that befell the son, as he was seated ready for the worship of Hara and kept his mind unmoved in concentration.

67-69. He pondered over the three-eyed, omniscient lord all the more. Near Śaṁbhu, he saw the fourteen worlds, various kinds of living beings within the Cosmic Egg, the Moon, the Sun, the stars, mountains, rivers, trees, promontories, seas, groups of forests, lakes, many kinds of godly beings, many cities of heaven-dwellers.

70-75. (He saw) tanks, wells, lakes, rivulets and many lotus ponds. In a certain lake somewhere there were many sons of sages engaged in playing about in water, sometimes submerging and sometimes emerging, showering one another with water columns splashed by their own hands, as though through mechanical contrivances, the sound of their beating the water reverberating through the quarters and indulging in various other sorts of sports. In their midst, Kardama who was in the state of *Samādhi* (contemplation) saw his child being taken away by an alligator in a greatly excited state. He then saw that the child was forcibly seized from that cruel aquatic being by a certain water nymph and handed over to the Ocean. The Lord of the rivers was rebuked by a certain Trident-bearing Spirit in the form of Rudra, whose face was copper-coloured due to anger in the following words:

76-80. "O lord of *Jala* (water, stupid persons), without knowing the power of Śiva, how is it that the boy of a devotee of Śiva, Kardama, the illustrious, intelligent Prajāpati, was kept by you for a long time?"

On hearing these words, the Ocean was frightened; he found that alligator, adorned that child with jewels, brought him near the lotus-like feet of Śaṁbhu and handed him over. After bowing down to him he submitted: "O Lord, I am not guilty. O Viśveśa, O lord of orphans, O destroyer of the calamities of the devotees, O Śaṁbhu, O wish-yielding Kalpa tree unto the devotees, this child of a devotee of yours was brought by this wicked aquatic being and not by me."

81. Understanding the desire of Śaṁbhu, that Gaṇa (attendant) tied that aquatic being with a rope and handed it over to the child.

82-85. While the Pārṣada (the attendant) was saying at the behest of Śaṅkara, "O dear one, take this son of yours. Go to your house," Kardama, the liberal-minded (sage), heard all this at the time of his contemplation. He gave up his contemplation and opened his eyes. As he looked on, he saw the child in front of him holding the alligator at his side. His ears were adorned. His forelocks were wet with water. The extremities of his eyes were reddish brown in colour. He was a bit less smooth (in his body). The skin was throbbing and the whole mind was perturbed.

86. When the child bowed down, he embraced him and sniffed the lotus-like face. Looking over the child repeatedly, he considered him born again as it were.

87. While Kardama was engaged in contemplation and worship of Śaṁbhu, five hundred years elapsed.

88. Kardama felt that period to be momentary, because Kāla (Time) does not operate in the presence of Mahākāla.

89. Then the son took leave of him and bowed down to his father. Then he hastened to the glorious city of Vārāṇasī for performing penance.

90. There he installed the Liṅga of Śambhu and performed a terrible penance. For five thousand years, he remained motionless like a stone.

91. Mahādeva who was delighted with his penance, appeared before him and said: "O scion of the family of Kardama, say what excellent boon shall I grant to you?"

Kārdama said:

92. O Lord compassionate to devotees, if you are pleased, grant me the overlordship of all waters and aquatic beings.

93. On hearing this, the great Lord, the bestower of all wishes, crowned him there in the great position of Varuṇa.*

94-95. "Be the overlord of all jewels issuing from the ocean, of the rivers, of the lakes, of the puddles, of all water-sources, nay of all those places where water collects and also of the Western quarter. Be the favourite of all gods. You shall be called Pāśapāṇi ('having noose in the hand').

96. I shall grant you another boon beneficial to all. This Liṅga, installed by you, will be known after your name.

97. It will become famous as Varuṇeśa. It will be the bestower of excellent powers in the city of Vārāṇasī. It shall be stationed in the south-west direction of Maṇikarṇeśa Liṅga.

98. When propitiated it shall always be the destroyer of sluggishness of all persons. Those who are devotees of Varuṇeśa, will never have any fear from waters.

99. Never will they have fear from distress and heat, nor premature or accidental death. They need not be afraid of dropsy or acute thirst.

100. Foods and beverages devoid of good taste will become juicy and tasty by remembering Varuṇeśvara. No doubt need be entertained in this regard."

101-102. After saying this Śambhu vanished. Varuṇa adorning this world ever since then, has stayed here, O Brāhmaṇa. Thus

* Mbh, *Ādi* 65.15 differs. There Varuṇa is the son of Kaśyapa and Aditi. He is one of the twelve Ādityas.

the nature of Varuṇaloka has been explained to you, on hearing which no man anywhere is afflicted by evil dangers.

CHAPTER THIRTEEN

Gandhavatī and Alakā

The attendants said:

1. Look at this meritorious city, Gandhavatī of Vāyu, O Brāhmaṇa, the storehouse of great fortune. It is stationed to the north of Vāruṇī (Varuṇa's capital).

2. In this world lives Prabhañjana, the vital breath of the universe, the Lord of the (North-Western) quarter. It was by propitiating Śrīmahādeva that he achieved the guardianship of the quarter.

3-4. Formerly, the son of Kaśyapa, well known as Pūtātmā,[1] performed a profound and elaborate penance in Vārāṇasī, the capital city of Dhūrjaṭi. The illustrious one had installed the great and holy Liṅga named Pavaneśvara and performed penance for ten thousand centuries.

5. Merely by viewing this (Liṅga), a man shall become a purified soul. Eschewing the garment of sins, he shall stay in the city of Pavana.

6. Thereafter, due to his fierce penance, Śiva, the bestower of the benefit of austerities, the great lord in the form of Jyotis (Refulgence), manifested himself from the Liṅga.

7-8. The ocean of the nectarine juice of Karuṇā (mercy) (Śiva), said with delighted mind: "Rise. Get up, O virtuous Pūtātman, choose your boon. As a reward of this severe penance and the propitiation of the Liṅga, O Pūtātman, there is nothing that cannot be granted to you in all the three worlds consisting of mobile and immobile beings."

Pūtātmā said:

9. O Great lord, O Lord of the Devas, O bestower of free-

1. Vāyu was born out of the breath of the Viśvapuruṣa (RV X.90). The Pūtātman legend is the contribution of this Purāṇa.

dom from fear unto the Devas, O bestower of the positions to all the Devas including Brahmā, Nārāyaṇa, Indra and others!

10. O Lord, the Vedas do not know of which nature you are. Though they have attained a hundred pathways (*Śatapatha Brāhmaṇa* of the Vājasaneyins of the *Yajurveda* school), they repeatedly say *'neti neti'* (not this, not this).

11. You are not an object of the words of (i.e. cannot be described by) Brahmā and Viṣṇu or even Vākpati (Bṛhaspati). O Lord, how can a man like me be capable of eulogizing Pramatheśa ('the lord of the Pramathas—spirits').

12. O Lord, my devotion to you compels to eulogize you. What can I do, O Lord of the universe? The sense-organs arc not under my control.

13. There is no difference between you and the universe, because you are one and omnipresent. You alone are the one to be eulogized, the eulogizer and the piece of eulogy. You are both possessed of attributes and attributeless as well.

14. Before creation you were one and single, devoid of form and name. Even Yogins do not comprehend your real nature (which is beyond the ken of words and mind).

15. O Lord moving independently, since you could not by remaining single sport about, therefore your *Icchā* (Divine Will) took its origin, that became your Śakti that is dependent on you.

16. (Though) you are single you became twin-natured as Śiva and Sákti. You are the Lord in the form of knowledge; and your *Icchā* is in the form of Śakti.

17. By both of you, Śiva and Śakti was created *Kriyāśakti* through your own sport; therefrom (arose) this entire universe.

18. O lord, you are the *Jñānaśakti* ('the power of knowledge'); Umā is regarded as *Icchāśakti* ('the power of will'); this universe is *Kriyāśakti* ('the power of activity'); therefore you are the cause thereof.

19. Your right part of the body is Vidhi (Brahmā) and your left part is Acyuta (Viṣṇu); the Moon, the Sun and fire constitute your eyes; the three Vedas are your exhaled breath.

20-21. The storehouses of water (i.e. oceans) originate from your perspiration; the wind is your ear; your arms are the ten quarters; Brāhmaṇas are remembered as your face; the excellent kings are your arms; Vaiśyas are born out of your thighs; O Īśāna, Śūdras are born of your feet; O lord, the clouds are your hairs.

22. You in the form of the Puruṣa and Prakṛti, formerly created the Cosmic Egg. This entire universe consisting of mobile and immobile beings is within the Cosmic Egg.

23. Hence, O Lord in the form of the universe, I don't consider anything different from you. All the living beings are in you. You are in the form of all living beings.

24. Obeisance to you, obeisance to you, obeisance to you, again and again, obeisance, obeisance. O Lord, this alone is the boon. Let my mind be stabilised in you.

25. When Pūtātman said thus, the Lord of Devas, assigned to him the state of being his own form and allotted to him the post of the Guardian of the Quarter.

26. "As a form of mine you will be all-pervader and knower of all principles. You alone will be the main form (or feature) of the life of all.

27. Those men who see this divine Liṅga of yours will become richly endowed with all pleasures; they will enjoy happiness in your world.

28-30. If a man, at least once in the course of his life adores the Pavamāneśvara Liṅga, in accordance with the injunctions, by bathing it with sweet scents etc., and with flowers and sweet-smelling sandalpaste, he is honoured in my world.

The Liṅga is stationed to the west of Jyeṣṭheśa and north of Vāyukuṇḍa. One who propitiates the Pavamāna Liṅga becomes purified instantaneously."

After granting the boons thus, the Lord merged himself into that Liṅga.

The attendants said:

31-32. Thus the characteristic form of the city of Gandhavatī has been explained to you. To the east thereof is this glorious and prosperous city of Alakā of Kubera. The lord of this city has acquired the friendship of Śaṁbhu through loyal devotion. Through the worship of Hara (Śiva) he became the donor and enjoyer of the treasures, the chief of whom is Padma.

Śivaśarman said:

33-34. Who is he? Whose (son) is he? Of what nature is his devotion to Sadāśiva? Whereby did he attain the friendship of Dhūrjaṭi, the Lord of Devas? Thus my mind wishes to hear about the fact that has reached my ears. My mind is steady, because it is satisfied due to the appreciation of your nectar-like words.

The attendants said:

35-36. O very wise Śivaśarman, the master of excessively pure sense-organs, who have washed off all the great sins of all the births in the excellent holy spots and rivers! There is nothing that cannot be said to you, a friend full of love. Conversation with good people is conducive to the increase of all excellences and benefits.

37. In the city of Kāmpilya*, there was a Dīkṣita named Yajñadatta who was an expert in the technique of the performance of Yajñas and he was born in the family of those who had performed Somayāgas.

38. He knew the Vedas, Vedāṅgas and meanings of the Vedic texts. He was an expert in the pious practices mentioned (in the Scriptures). He was honoured even by the kings. He was wealthy and munificent.

39. He was engaged in maintaining sacrificial fire. He was devoted to the study of the Vedas. His son Guṇanidhi[1] had features similar to those of the disc of the moon.

40. After he was invested with the sacred thread, he acquired knowledge of many branches of learning but, unknown to his father he became fond of the game of dice.

41. He regularly took much money from his mother and gave it to gamesters with whom he cultivated friendship.

42. He eschewed all Brāhmaṇical pious practices. He became averse to holy ablutions during the Sandhyās (dawn, noon and dusk). He censured the Vedas and scriptures, Devas and Brāhmaṇas.

43. Devoid of the regular practice of the rites enjoined in

---

* Modern Kampil in Farukkhabad District, U.P. The legend of the precious birth of Kubera recorded here is a contribution of this Purāṇa.

1. The legend of Guṇanidhi is another contribution of the Skanda-writer, who grafts it on the Purāṇic Kubera.

the Smṛtis, he adopted singing and playing musical instruments as a pastime; he had intimate friends among dancers, heretics and cheats.

44-47. Though urged by the mother, he never went near his father. Whenever Dīkṣita who had been busy with the other domestic activities asked his wife, "O dear, Guṇanidhi is never seen by me in the house. Where does he go? What does he do?" she used to reply: "Just now he has gone out after taking his bath and worshipping the Devas so long. After memorising the lessons, he has gone out along with two or three of his friends for further study." Thus the mother who had only one son, used to deceive the Dīkṣita.

48-50. The Dīkṣita was not aware of any of his activities, or his behaviour. He performed the rite of tonsure (of his son) during the sixteenth year and then the marriage ceremony in accordance with the injunctions of the Gṛhya texts. Everyday the mother of great affectionate heart used to admonish the son Guṇanidhi gently. "It is enough if I say that your father is one of bad temper. If he knows your behaviour, he will thrash you and me.

51. I am concealing your vicious activities from your father. Your father commands the respect of all people, not because of wealth, but because of his pious practices.

52. O my son, good learning and association with good people constitute the wealth of Brāhmaṇas. The Dīkṣitas are good Brāhmaṇas well-versed in the Vedas and all lores. They regularly perform Somayāgas.

53. Your grandfather and ancestors have attained celebrity due to this. (Hence) abandon evil practices and association with the vicious. Be engaged in having close contact with the good

54-55. Divert your mind towards good learning. Practise the rites of Brāhmaṇas. This (girl) is worthy of you in all respects, in beauty, age, family and behaviour. You are not yet twenty and she is sixteen years old. Dear Guṇanidhi, your wife is chaste and sweet-voiced.

56. Protect this well-behaved girl. Be affectionate and devoted to your father. Your father-in-law too is worthy of honour and esteem everywhere on account of his good qualities and habits.

57. Therefore, why don't you feel ashamed? O my child,

abandon viciousness. Your maternal uncles, O my son, are unrivalled in learning, habits, descent and such other things.

58. You are thus pure on account of the two families. You are not afraid of them also. Look at the Brāhmaṇa boys of the neighbourhood.

59-61. Even in our house look at these disciples of your father. How humble and polite they are! Dear son, if the king hears about your vicious habits, he will lose confidence in your father and deprive him of his livelihood. Till today the people were saying: 'Oh! Its only childishness.' Later they will laugh at us. Let the status of Dīkṣita be maintained. All of them will disdain and ridicule your Brāhmaṇa father and me.

62-67a. They will rebuke me saying, 'The son adopts the habits of his mother.' Your father is not at all a sinner. Is he not following the paths of Śrutis and Smṛtis? Lord Śiva is witness unto me whose mind is intimately devoted to his feet. No face of a vicious man has been seen by me after the menstrual bath. Indeed the fate that caused your birth is powerful."

Every now and then he used to be admonished by his mother thus. Still that infatuated fellow did not give up his evil habit, because an indulgent fellow cannot be taught sense. Who is not undone and ruined here by vices such as hunting, drinking wine, slander-mongering, whoring, thieving, playing games of dice and chasing other men's wives?

Whatever the wicked fellow saw in the house, even base metals and clothes, he took it away and handed over to the gamesters.

67b-70. Once, while his mother was sleeping, he took away his father's ring set with nine jewels and handed it over to a gamester. Later, once, when the father was returning from the royal palace, the ring was found in the hand of the gamester and recognised by the Dīkṣita who asked him, "From where did your get this ring?" On being repeatedly asked by him he said, "Why do you insult me openly, O Brāhmaṇa? Has this ring been obtained by me stealthily? This has been given to me by your son.

71-73. On the previous day he had won my(?) mother's (embroidered) Saree and taken it away. It is not to me alone that he has given the ring. Much money has been given by him to the other gamesters too. Jewels, base metals, silk cloths, golden vases etc. too have been given away by him. So also vessels of various kinds made of brass and copper. When stripped, the gamesters pledge many things daily.

74-76. In the entire world, O Brāhmaṇa, there has never been such a gamester as he till today. How is it that the fact that your son is a crest-jewel among gamesters, has not been known by you till today? He is proficient in discourteous and immodest behaviour."

On hearing this, the Brāhmaṇa hung down his head due to the weight of shame. He covered his head with a cloth and entered his abode. He made his chaste wife sit down and said to her:

77-78. "O Dīkṣita's wife! Where are you and where is your son Guṇanidhi? Or let him go. Of what use is he? Where is that excellent ring of mine?

At the time of massaging my body with oil, that ring was removed by you from my finger. Fetch me that ring of nine jewels quickly."

79-81. On hearing these words of his, the wife of the Dīkṣita became frightened, but she said: "Kindly conclude your midday rites. I am busily engaged in getting things ready for the adoration of the Lord. You are fond of guests; it is possible that there may be delay in getting things ready for the guests.

Just now I had placed it in some pot somewhere, as I was busy in preparing the sweet-pudding. I don't know where I have forgotten it."

Dīkṣita said:

82-83. O mother of an excellent son, ever speaking the truth, whenever I ask where your son has gone, you invariably reply, "O Lord, he has been memorising lessons; now he has gone out for further study along with two or three friends."

84. O my wife, where is that red petticoat given by me which used to be suspended from the rope holding clothes? Tell me the truth. Do not be afraid.

85. That gold-vase embellished with jewels is not to be seen now. Where is that *Tripaṭī* (special silk robe of distinction with three-folds) presented by the king?

86. Where is that southern brass vessel? Where is that copper

pot from Gauḍa country? Where is that fancy bedstead of ivory?

87. Where is that big statue made of lunar crystals brought from the mountainous region, with a girl holding a lamp?

88. Of what use is too much of talk? O lady born of a noble family, it is futile to be angry with you. I shall take food when I marry again (I won't accept food from you).

89. I have no son in him, that wicked wretch who has defiled the family. Get up, bring water and Darbha grass. I shall offer him libation with gingelly seeds and water.

90. It is better for a man to be issueless rather than have a vicious son defiling the family. This is the eternal good policy: A person shall abandon one for the sake of the family.

91. The Dīkṣita took his bath, concluded his daily rite and on that very day took the hand (in marriage) of the daughter of a Brāhmaṇa well-versed in the Vedas.

92. The son of the Dīkṣita heard what had happened. He cursed his earlier activity and set out (from the house) going towards some direction.

93. He went into deep reflection and became worried: 'Where shall I go? What shall I do? I am not a learned man. Nor do I have ready cash.

94. In an alien land, a man with ready cash and a learned man enjoy happiness. But the man with ready cash has to fear a thief, though the learned man has nothing to fear from anywhere.

95. How incongruous: This is my birth in the family of those who regularly perform Yajñas on one side and this is my indulgence in vices on the other. Alas, the fate is all-powerful! It is what decides one's future.

96. I do not know how to beg. I have no acquaintance here anywhere. Nor do I possess any wealth. What shall be my refuge?

97. My mother used to give me ample good food always even before sunrise. Whom shall I request? That mother of mine is not here.'

98-99. Even as he was reflecting thus, the sun set. In the meantime a certain man, a devotee of Maheśvara came out of the city with a great deal of foodstuffs as presents in order to worship Īśāna after his fast during Śivarātri.

100. Inhaling the sweet scent of puddings and sweetmeat that hungry fellow followed him hopefully thinking, 'This foodstuff should be taken by me after it has been offered to Śiva at night.'

101. With this wishful thought, he sat near the entrance to the temple of Śiva. He witnessed the great adoration performed by that devotee.

102. After concluding the dances and songs, all the devotees went to sleep. Then he entered the sanctum sanctorum in order to take the *Naivedya* (i.e., the foodstuff).

103. When he found the lamp dim, he tore a piece of his cloth, turned it into a wick and lit it brightly in order to see the sweetmeats.

104. He took the sweets and was hurriedly coming out, when hit by the sole of his foot, one of those sleeping persons woke up.

105-106. "Who is this? Who is this man in a hurry? Let this thief be caught." By the time he could say this, the city guards came there and struck him as he was fleeing. In a moment he fell down dead. Because of the power of the future merit, he did not eat the *Naivedya* offering.

107. With nooses and hammers in their hands, the formidable soldiers of Yama bound him and went about to take him to Saṁyaminī.

108. By that time the trident-bearing attendants of Śiva came there with a divine chariot embellished with strings of tinkling bells in order to take him away.

109. On seeing the attendants of Śaṁbhu, the servants of Yama became frightened. After bowing down they said: "Oh Gaṇas, this Brāhmaṇa is vicious in his habits.

110. He violated the noble practices of the family. He was averse to the words of advice of his parents. He swerved from the path of truth and purity. He remained without holy ablution during the Sandhyās.

111. Let his activities be kept apart. He took away the *Nirmālya* (remnants of adoration) of Śiva which you have seen directly. He is not worthy of being touched by people like you.

112. The very touch of these persons causes loss of merit: those who enjoy Śiva's Nirmālyas, those who transgress Śiva's Nirmālya and those who give away Śiva's Nirmālya.

113. One can stir and drink poison; observing fast is more conducive to welfare, but Śiva's possession should not be resorted to even when the very vital breaths are near the throat (i.e. about to die).

114. You are the ultimate authority regarding piety. We are not so. O Gaṇas, if there is a vestige of piety in this man let us hear about it."

115-116. On hearing these words, the attendants of Śiva said: "O servants (of Yama), the pious practices of (a devotee of) Śiva are very subtle. How can they be viewed by you of gross vision? They can be viewed (and realised) by only men of subtle vision. Listen to what has been done by this sinless one.

117. The shadow of the lamp falling on the top of the Liṅga was prevented by him, for he added a wick to the lamp at night from the corner piece of his own cloth.

118. O servants (of Yama), another great act of piety has been added to his credit by him, as he listened to the names of Śiva repeated casually by someone.

119. The worship that was being performed duly by a devotee was witnessed by this man with steady mind, who had observed fast on the fourteenth lunar day.

120. This excellent Brāhmaṇa whose sins have been dispelled shall now become the king of Kaliṅga. O messengers (of Yama), you all may go in the manner you have come."

121-125. Thus that Brāhmaṇa was released from the messengers of Yama by the attendants (of Śiva). He became Dama, the son of Arindama, the lord of Kaliṅga.

In due succession, when the father passed away, the young prince acquired the kingdom. King Dama who could not be suppressed, does not know any other pious practice than the lighting of lamps in all the temples of Śiva, O Brāhmaṇa.

He called together all the leaders of the villages within his kingdom. He gave an order thus: "He who does not carry out my behest, will be duly punished by me. In all the temples around in the village concerned, lamps should be lighted always unhesitatingly. If anyone is guilty of disobeying my order, I shall undoubtedly cut off his head."

126-128. Thus for fear of his punishment the lamps were lighted in every Śiva temple. By means of this pious practice throughout his life, King Dama obtained great legitimate prosperity and ultimately died. This practice of lighting lamps having been steadily continued by him, he became the lord of Alakā possessing many lamps of jewelled flames. Thus even very little that is done for the sake of Śiva bears fruit at the proper time.

129-131. After knowing this, the worship of Śiva should be performed by those who seek their own happiness. Where is that son of a Dīkṣita who was averse to all pious practices? Where is this status of the Guardian of a Quarter? Look O Śivaśarman.

He illuminated the wick of the lamp for his own selfish purpose, but thereby he dispelled the darkness on the top of the Liṅga. He acquired the kingdom in the Kaliṅga country and was always interested in pious practices. As a result of his earlier (of the previous birth) practice, he caused lamps to be lighted in Śiva temples. Now he, who had been a mere human being, enjoys great status as the Guardian of a Quarter.

The Gaṇas said:

132. Please listen to the story how he attained the constant companionship of Śiva with concentration of mind. We shall narrate.

133. In the Padma Kalpa formerly, O Brāhmaṇa, Viśravas was born of Pulastya, a mental son of Brahmā. His son was Vaiśravaṇa.

134. This city of Alakā created by Viśvakṛt was enjoyed by him by propitiating Lord Tryaṁbaka (three-eyed) formerly, by means of severe austerities.

135. When that Kalpa had passed by and Meghavāhana Kalpa began, this son of Yajñadatta (i.e., Guṇanidhi), the donor of wealth, performed a severe penance.

136-140. After understanding perfectly the power of the devotion to Śaṁbhu through the lighting of the lamps alone, he went to Kāśikā, the city of Purāri that illuminates *cit* (full consciousness). There he brightened the lamp of *Cittaratna* ('the jewel of the mind') having Śiva for its sole wick. It has devotion that never turns elsewhere for its oil supply. It was motionless due to the meditation on his splendour. The great vessel was the union with Śiva. It was enhanced through the fire of penance. It was free from the attack of fire-flies in the form of lust, anger and other obstacles. It was windless, because the vital breath has been stopped and it was free from impurities, because of pure vision. Then he installed Śaṁbhu's Liṅga adored with the flowers of the feelings of devotional fervour.

He thus performed the penance for ten thousand centuries until his body was reduced to mere skin and bones.

141-142. Thereupon, Lord Viśveśvara himself accompained by Goddess Viśālākṣī manifested with a delighted mind. He glanced in the direction of the lord of Alakā, who was standing motionless like a post directing the mind towards the Liṅga. The Lord said, "I am the bestower of boons. Enough of your penance, O lord of Alakā."

143-145a. The ascetic opened his eyes and when he looked ahead, he saw in front of him the Moon-crested Consort of Umā, Śrīkaṇṭha whose lustre was more than that of a thousand Suns. This bright splendour dazzled his eyes and he closed them. Then he spoke to the Lord of the chiefs of Devas, who was beyond the comprehension of the mind:

145b-147. "O Lord, give unto me the capacity of the eyes to see your feet. O Lord, this alone is the boon that you are being seen directly. O Lord, of what use is any other boon? Obeisance to you, O Moon-crested One."

On hearing his words, Umāpati, the Lord of Devas, granted him the ability to see by touching him with his palm.

148-152. After opening his eyes, he looked at Umā at the outset. "Who is this woman near Śaṁbhu, beautiful in every limb? Has any penance been performed by her even greater than my penance? Ha! What a beauty! Ha! What love and conjugal bliss! Everything is at its height!"

While he espied with a ruthless eye, saying this repeatedly, his left eye burst asunder, because he was looking at a woman.

Then the Goddess spoke to the Lord, "Why does this wicked sage look at me frequently disrespecting the lustre of my penance? He looks at me repeatedly with his right eye. He seems to me jealous of my beauty, love and assets of conjugal bliss."

153-154. On hearing the words of the Goddess, the Lord laughed and said to her: "Oh! Umā, this is your son. He does not see with cruel eyes. But he over-describes your glorious penance."

After telling this to the Goddess, the Lord spoke to him again:

155-158. "O dear one, I shall grant you boons, because I have been propitiated by this penance. Be the lord of the *Nidhis* (Treasures) and the overload of Guhyakas. O virtuous one, you shall be the king of Yakṣas, Kinnaras and kings too. You shall be the lord of the Puṇyajanas, and the bestower of wealth on all. Your friendship with me shall be constant. I shall stay near you, O friend, and very near Alakā for the purpose of increasing your pleasures. Come, fall at the feet of this lady. She is your mother."

After granting the boons thus, Lord Śiva spoke to Umā once again, "O goddess of the Devas, grant your favour to this sage, your son here."

The Goddess said:

159. O dear one, let your devotion to Śiva be steady always. Be one with a brownish eye with your left eye lost.

160. Let those boons granted by the Lord to you be so. Be Kubera ('one with ugly body') by name, O son, because you were jealous of my beauty.

161. The Liṅga installed by you, shall be (known) after your own name. It will bestow Siddhis on all aspirants and it will be destructive of all sins.

162. A man who visits Kubera Liṅga (Kubereśvara Liṅga) shall never be without wealth, friends or kinsmen.

163. The devotee should worship Kubereśa in the southern side of Viśveśa. That man shall never be touched by sins, poverty or unhappiness.

164. After granting boons thus to Dhanada, Lord Maheśvara entered the great abode of brilliance of Viśveśvara along with the Goddess.

The attendants said:

165-166. Thus Dhanada attained the close friendship of Śrīśaṁbhu. Kailāsa, the abode of Śaṅkara, is very near Alakā. Thus the features of the city of the lord of Yakṣas have been explained to you, on hearing which a man shall become released from all sins.

CHAPTER FOURTEEN

Somaloka

The attendants said :

1. In front of Alakā is the prosperous city of Īśāna. Sages who are devotees of Rudra always dwell there.

2. They are deeply engrossed in remembering Śiva; they are interested in the holy vows and observances pertaining to Śiva; they are always engaged in the worship of Śiva.

3. Those who perform penances with a desire for the enjoyment of heavenly pleasures, assume the form of Rudra here, in the beautiful city of Rudra.

4 Eleven Rudras, the chiefs of whom are Ajaikapāt and Ahirbudhnya, are the leaders here; they have tridents in their raised hands.

5. They protect the eight cities from the wicked enemies of Devas. They are the excellent ones who always grant boons to the devotees of Śiva.

6. After reaching the city of Vārāṇasī and installing the great Liṅga named Īśāneśa that accords splendid things and auspiciousness, they too have performed penance.

7. With the favour of Īśāneśa, they became the Lords of the Quarter in the North-East. All these eleven move about together. They are adorned with crown-like mass of hair (on the head).

8. They have an eye in the forehead. Their throat is blue in colour. Their limbs are fair and pure. They are bull-emblemed. The Rudras on the surface of the earth are thousands in number, (nay) they are innumerable.

9-14. They stay in this city of Īśa endowed with all sorts of pleasures.

After worshipping Īśāneśa in Kāśī as well as in other places, those who die are born as priests here due to that merit.

Those who worship Īśāneśa on the eighth or the fourteenth lunar day, should be known as Rudras undoubtedly here and hereafter.

A man who keeps awake at night in the presence of Īśāneśvara, after observing fast on any fourteenth day never enters any womb again (i.e., gets liberated from Saṁsāra).

Hearing the story narrated by the attendants of Viṣṇu on the path to heaven, Śivaśarman saw moonlight even during the day. It delighted the mind much along with all the sense-organs causing great surprise.

Śivaśarman asked them: "O attendants of Hari, what is this world? It gives delight and inspires admiration".

They replied to the Brāhmaṇa.:

The attendants said:

15. O blessed Śivaśarman, this is the world of the Moon whose nectar-showering rays enliven the world.

16. O Brāhmaṇa, Atri, the father of Soma (Moon), a pious and magnanimous sage, was born of Brahmā as his mental son, when he (Brahmā) was desirous of creating the subjects.

17. We have heard that he formerly performed a penance named *Anuttara* ('than which there is nothing greater') for three thousand divine years.

18. His semen virile flowed upwards and became the Moon (or *Somarasa*). It oozed out through the eyes in ten directions brightening the quarters.

19. On being commanded by Brahmā, the ten deities (of the ten directions) tried to hold that in their womb. They wished to conceive collectively but could not.

20. When those directions were incapable of conceiving the foetus, Soma fell on the earth along with them.

21. On seeing Soma fallen, Brahmā, the grandfather of the world, placed him on a chariot with a desire for the welfare of all the worlds.

22. Druhiṇa (Brahmā) made him circumambulate the ocean-girt earth twenty-one times, along with that excellent chariot.

23. His overflowing refulgence reached the earth when herbs took their origin, through which the universe is sustained.

24. O blessed one, that venerably glorious (Moon) caused to flourish by Brahmā himself, obtained brilliance and performed penance for a hundred *Padma* years (*Padma* is one thousand billion).

25-26. He went to Avimukta, the highly sacred holy spot, and installed an Amṛta Liṅga called Candreśa,[1] after his own name. With the favour of the Pināka-wielding Viśveśa, the Lord of Devas, he became the king of seeds, herbs, waters and the *Agrajanmans* (Brāhmaṇas).

27. He made a well there, remembered as Amṛtoda, by drinking the waters of which or bathing wherein a man is released from ignorance.

28-30. He was held by the delighted Lord of Devas on his own head. Later even when he was cursed by Dakṣa and he became reduced in size at the end of the month, he took up the single Kalā (the digit) that is highly enlivening in power. The Moon becomes bigger through that digit alone.

After acquiring the great kingdom, Soma, the most excellent one among the possessors of nectar, performed a Rājasūya sacrifice in which a hundred thousand was given as Dakṣiṇā.

31. We have heard that Soma gave the three worlds as Dakṣiṇā to those members of the assembly, the chiefs of whom were many Brāhmaṇa-sages, O Brāhmaṇa.

32. Hiraṇyagarbha, Brahmā, Atri and Bhṛgu were Ṛtviks there and Hari along with many sages became the member of the assembly.

33. Nine goddesses, viz., Sinī, Kuhū, Dyuti, Puṣṭi, Prabhā, Vasu, Kīrti, Dhṛti and Lakṣmī, served him.

34. He propitiated Rudra accompanied by Umā through the sacrificial rite and became well-known as 'Soma',[2] the title given by Śaṁbhu accompanied by Umā.

35. It was there alone, in front of Candreśvara, that Soma performed the excessively difficult penance and Rājasūya sacrifice as well.

36. There alone he was told thus by the Brāhmaṇas pleased with him: "This *Kalānidhi* ('storehouse of refulgent digits') Soma, who gave the three worlds as Dakṣiṇā, is the king for all of us, the Brāhmaṇas.

37. There alone he attained the status of the eye of the

1. Candreśvara is now better known for its shrine of Siddheśvarī Devī. It contains Candrakūpa called Amṛtoda here.

2. Soma derived as Sauma ('along with Umā'). The Moon-god propitiated Rudra along with Umā. Hence the designation.

Lord of Devas. The Lord who was pleased in his mind, thus gave delight to all the three worlds.

38-39. He was told thus, due to the power of his penance: "You are my *Aparā* (lesser) *Mūrti* (form). On your rise the world will find its happiness rising. The world including mobile and immobile beings, pervaded by the heat of the Sun, will suffer distress, which it will get rid of when touched by your rays full of nectar."

40-44. After saying this, Maheśāna joyously granted other boons too: "O Dvijarāja, since a severe penance has been performed by you here, since the ultimate offer of (the benefits of) the sacrifice has been made in favour of me and since this Liṅga of mine named Candreśvara has been installed by you, O Soma, I shall assume the form of having Umā in half of the body and reside in this Liṅga named after you. Though I am omnipresent, I shall reside here on the fifteenth day in the bright half of every month for the whole of the day and night with all the prosperity of the three worlds."

Hence even the least of the holy rites performed here on a full-moon day, viz. Japa, Homa, Arcanā, Dhyāna, Dāna and the feeding of the Brāhmaṇas shall be in fact, a great adoration and it will be for my pleasure.

45-46. Repairing of the ruins etc., offering of dance, instrumental music etc., the rites like hoisting the holy flag etc., the propitiation of ascetics and sages, performed at Candreśvara at that time shall be capable of yielding never-ending benefit.

I shall tell you, O storehouse of digits, another great secret. Listen.

47-51. This should not be mentioned to one who is not a devotee, one who is an atheist, one who hates the Vedas.

O Soma, when a new-moon (day) occurs on a Monday, good men should observe fast on the fourteenth day with great respect.

If the Pradoṣa happens on a Saturday, O Soma, listen, the devotee should finish his daily rite on the thirteenth day, worship the Candreśvara Liṅga, observe all the regulations on the thirteenth day at night, observe a fast on the fourteenth day and keep vigilance at night and in the morning, when there is the combination of Soma and Kuhū, he should take his holy bath in the waters of Candroda lake.

He should then duly perform Sandhyā rites and offer all libations and perform similar rites. He should then perform Śrāddha duly near the holy spot Candroda.

52-56a. He should scrupulously offer balls of rice without *Āvāhana* (invoking) and *Arghya* to the three generations in the form of Vasu (father), Rudra (grandfather), Aditisuta (great-grandfather), maternal grandfather and others of the Gotra in view. He should utter the names of his preceptor, father-in-law and other kinsmen and offer balls of rice.

One who performs Śrāddha at this holy spot with faith redeems all (ancestors).

Through the Śrāddhas in the holy pit Candroda here, the ancestors are as much pleased as they are by means of the offer of balls of rice at Gayā.

Just as a man is released from all indebtedness to the Pitṛs at Gayā, so also he is released from that indebtedness by offering balls of rice at Candroda.

56b-60. When an excellent man sets out to visit Candreśvara, all his previous ancestors become joyous and they dance: "This scion (of our family) will perform Tarpaṇa unto us in the holy waters of Candroda. If due to our deficiency in fortune, he does not do so, at least he will touch the holy waters and we shall be satisfied thereby. If the stupid fellow does not even touch, he will surely see and that is conducive to our satisfaction."

Thus the devotee having the holy vow shall perform Śrāddha, touch Candreśvara, propitiate the Brāhmaṇas and ascetics and then perform the Pāraṇa (breaking the fast) rite.

Thus, O deer-stained one, with my favour one shall become released from the three types of indebtedness by performing this holy rite in Kāśī on a new-moon day falling on a Monday.

61. Here on the *Mahācaitrī* (full-moon day in the month of Caitra) residents of this holy spot should perform the rite of *Yātrā* (procession) for the purpose of acquiring knowledge of Tāraka Mantra. It shall prevent all obstacles in the holy spot.

62. One who worships Candreśvara, but dies elsewhere shall pierce clusters of sins and attain Somaloka.

63. In the age of Kali, the greatness of Candreśa is not

understood by unlucky ones. O lord of the night, I shall mention to you another great secret.

64-67. This Pīṭha called Siddhayogīśvara bestows Siddhi on *Sādhakas* (aspirants).

Here, in front of me, are seven crores of Siddhas belonging to Suras, Asuras, Gandharvas, Nāgas, Vidyādharas, Rākṣasas, Guhyakas, Yakṣas, Kinnaras and human beings.

One who meditates on Viśveśvarī here after being strictly regular in diet for six months, sees the Siddhas who come for worshipping Candreśvara. Siddhayogīśvarī shall be the granter of boons to him directly. You too will have great Siddhi by visiting Siddhayogīśvarī.

68. There are many Pīṭhas on the earth for the achievement of Siddhi by an aspirant. But there is nothing else that bestows Siddhi quickly all over the earth except Yogīśvarī Pīṭha.

69. O Śaśin, this alone is that Pīṭha, where the Liṅga Candreśvara has been installed by you. It is invisible to persons of no self-control.

70. Persons who have won over lust, anger, covetousness, desire, egotism and arrogance, see Yogīśvarī, my Śakti, who is excessively beneficent.

71-72. Those people who are endowed with devotion and worship the goddess whose form is invisible, but who is glorious and tawny-coloured and who bestows all Siddhis, with incense, food offerings, lamps etc., in the Siddhayogīśvarī Pīṭha every eighth and fourteenth lunar day (shall be blessed). The goddess shall appear in front of them."

73. Thus, O Brāhmaṇas, Śaṁbhu, the great Īśāna granted boons to the Moon-god and thereafter vanished behind Viśveśvarapura.

74. Ever since then, Dvijarāja became the lord of this world, making the directions devoid of darkness by means of his rays spreading everywhere.

75. Indeed, men who observe Somavāra (Monday) vow, who invariably imbibe Somarasa, go to Somaloka by means of a vehicle having the lustre of the Moon.

76. A man who listens devoutly to the origin of Candreśvara as well as to the penance of Candramas (Moon-god) is honoured in the world of Candra.

Agastya said:

77. Narrating this story which bestows welfare on Śivaśarman and dispels fatigue in the divine journey, the attendants thereafter went to the excellent *Uḍuloka* (Stellar world).

CHAPTER FIFTEEN

Description of the Stellar World

Agastya said:

1. Listen, O my wife Lopāmudrā of great excellence, O my partner in religious rites, to the story narrated by the two attendants of Viṣṇu to Śivaśarman.

Śivaśarman said:

2. O dear Gaṇas, skilful in narrating everything, this wonderful story of Candra (Region of Candra) has been heard. Now, tell me the story of the world of stars.

The attendants said:

3. Formerly, Dakṣa the patriarch, an expert in the creation of subjects, was born of the back of the thumb of the Creator (Brahmā) who was desirous of carrying on the activity of creation.

4. He had sixty daughters, the chief of whom was Rohiṇī. They were expert in performing austerities and had increasing skill and excellence in everything.

5. After reaching the city of Viśveśvara, a severe penance was performed by them. The moon-embellished great Lord accompanied by Umā was propitiated by them.

6. When Īśāna was pleased, he came there in order to grant the boon. With a satisfied mind he said, "Request for an excellent boon."

7-8. On hearing the words of Śambhu, those girls replied: "O Śaṅkara, if we deserve a boon and if a boon can be given to us, let him be our husband—he who is equal to you in beauty, O great lord, and who can dispel the distress due to worldly existence, even better than you."

9-10. A great Liṅga named Nakṣatreśvara was installed by them on the beautiful banks of Varaṇā near Saṅgameśvara. A great penance named Puruṣāyita,[1] which cannot be performed even by men, was performed by them for a thousand divine years.

11. Then Viśveśvara who was pleased, granted an excellent boon to all those (girls) of being wives of a single person and mental steadiness.

Śrī Viśveśvara said:

12. Such an excessively severe penance as this has never been endured formerly by women. Hence your name will be Nakṣatra here.

13. Since the penance named Puruṣāyita has been performed by you now, you will have the state of males if and when you please.

14. You will become foremost in the entire system of luminaries. You will be the excellent source of origin of all the Zodiacs beginning with Meṣa (Aries).

15. O splendid-countenanced ones, all of you will have (the Moon) as husband, who is the lord of herbs, nectar and Brāhmaṇas.

16. By worshipping your Liṅga named Nakṣatreśvara, a man will go to your excellent world.

17. Your world shall be above the Moon. You will be the most esteemed among all the Tārakas (Constellations).

18. Those who worship Stars, those who regularly observe the vows of Stars, will stay in your world with a lustre similar to that of the Stars.

19. Those who visit and have a vision of Nakṣatreśvara at Kāśī will never be adversely affected by Stars, Planets and Zodiacs.

Agastya said:

20. Even as the two attendants, of minds engrossed in Viṣṇu, were narrating the excellent story of the Stars, the world of

---

1. "As is practised by men" (Com).

Budha (Mercury) became the guest (object) of the eyes of Śivaśarman.

Śivaśarman said:

21. O attendants of the glorious Lord, whose unparalleled world is this? Tell me. It delights me much like that of the Moon.

The attendants said:

22. For (your) diversion during the travel through the heavenly path, O Śivaśarman, listen to this story that dispels sins and destroys the three types of distress.

23. He has been described to you by us as possessing excessive lustre; he is the king of Brāhmaṇas, and has acceded to the position of an emperor.

24. By him the three worlds were given as Dakṣiṇā (gift) in the course of a Rājasūya sacrifice. He performed a very severe penance for one thousand billion centuries.

25. He was born of the eyes of Atri; is the grandson of Brahmā; is the lord of herbs and the luminaries.

26. He is praised as the storehouse of pure Kalās (digits); he while rising, destroys others' distresses.

27. He increases the delight of the night-blooming lilies along with that of all the worlds; his disc acts as a mirror when the maidens in the form of different quarters have their makeups.

28. Of what avail are other qualities of the Moon? The following alone indicate that there is nothing equal to the Moon whose digit the omniscient Lord Śiva uses as his crest jewel.

29-30. He became deluded due to the arrogance born of glorious possessions. He hurriedly abducted the beautiful wife Tārā of Bṛhaspatī,[1] the preceptor and Guru, the son of his paternal uncle Aṅgiras. He was proud of his handsome features, though he was prevented by the Devas and many celestial sages (he did so).

31. This is not the fault of the king of Brāhmaṇas, the stroehouse of digits. Excepting the three-eyed Lord Śiva, who

1. For the abduction of Tārā and Budha's birth cf. VaP II 28.28.ff.

has not had his mind afflicted by Kāma (the lord of lust)?

32. There is this darkness spreading everywhere and the means to suppress it has been created by Brahmā such as lamps, sun's rays etc.; but no great remedy for the darkness due to the delusion born of lordship (is available).

33. Words of advice regarding Viṣṇu's devotion etc., though expressed clearly, do not touch one deluded by the haughtiness of lordship, like a man of pure mind, sanctified by holy ablutions performed by him, who does not touch a wicked man of adverse mentality.

34. Fie! Fie upon the (sinful) activities of a man of surplus wealth by whom everything is seen as though twirling round! He always sees through the eye of indiscretion that has instantly become destructive and a source of calamity.

35. In all the three worlds, who is he who has not been overpowered by Kāma who has only the flowers for his arrows? Who has not been overcome by anger? Who has not been deluded by covetousness? Who has not suffered disaster with his heart pierced by the dartlike eyes of young maidens? Which man, though endowed with excellent vision, has not been led along blind paths after acquiring the glory of a kingdom?

36. The glory of lordship is very fickle. By acquiring it, if anything is earned, it can certainly be good or bad. Men of noble conduct should always do what is highly beneficial.

37. When he became aggressive and did not give up Tārā to Bṛhaspati, Rudra took up his *Ājagava* ('made of goat's and cow's horn') bow and came to his succour.

38. The noble-souled Moon discharged the great missile named Brahmaśiras towards the Lord of Devas. That was destroyed by him (Rudra).

39. The battle between them caused by Tārā became very terrific. Thereupon Brahmā became afraid of an untimely annihilation of the cosmos.

40. Preventing Rudra whose brilliance was like that of the fire at the time of ultimate annihilation, from continuing the battle, Brahmā himself gave Tārā to the son of Aṅgiras (i.e., Bṛhaspatī).

41. On seeing Tārā pregnant, Bṛhaspatī said, "No foetus at all can be carried by you in your womb that belongs to me".

42. She then went near a cluster of Iṣīka grass and dis-

charged the foetus. As soon as that divine being was born, he eclipsed the body of the Devas (surpassed them in excellence and brilliance).

43. The excellent Suras whose suspicion was aroused said, "Tell us the truth, whose son is this, Bṛhaspatī's or the Moon's?"

44. Even after being asked by the Devas, the excessively bashful Tārā did not say anything. Then the highly brilliant son was about to curse her.

45. Brahmā prevented him and asked Tārā regarding his doubt. With palms joined together to Brahmā, she said to him, "It is of Soma".

46. Then that king (of herbs), the lord of the subjects, sniffed the head of the child. He named that intelligent boy "Budha".

47-49. Budha who was superior to all the Devas in refulgence, beauty and strength, decided to perform a penance. He took leave of Soma and went to Kāśī, the mass of salvation, guarded by Viśveśa. There he installed a Liṅga named Budheśvara after him. Meditating upon the extremely terrific Ugra (Śiva) in his mind, in the form of the moon-crested Lord Śiva, the boy performed the penance for ten thousand years.

50. Then the glorious Viśveśa, the creator of the universe, the lord of the universe of great productivity, manifested himself from the Liṅga Budheśvara.

51-52. The delighted great lord in the from of great brilliance said: "O highly intelligent Budha, the foremost among other suras and scholars, seek a boon (you would like to have). I am pleased with your excellent penance and the meditation through the Liṅga. O great son of Soma (O excessively polite one), there is nothing that cannot be given to you."

53-54. On hearing these words like the deep sound of thunder, appearing as though enlivening the vegetation faded due to drought, the boy opened his eyes and saw in front of him the Three-eyed, Moon-crested Lord in the Liṅga.

Budha's Prayer

Budha said:

55. Obeisance to you of sanctified soul. Obeisance to you, O lord in the form of brilliant refulgence! Hail to you of

cosmic form. Obeisance to you who have transcended all forms.

56. Obeisance to the auspicious-souled one, the destroyer of all the distress of those who bow down. Obeisance to you, the omniscient one. Obeisance to you, the creator of all.

57. Obeisance to you, the merciful one. Bow to you who can be realised (only) through devotion. Obeisance to the bestower of the beneficial fruits of penance. Obeisance to you, the lord in the form of penance.

58. O Śaṁbhu, O Śiva, O consort of Śivā, O quiescent lord! O Śrīkaṇṭha, O trident-bearing one, O moon-crested lord, O Śarva, O Īśa, O Lord Śaṅkara, O Dhūrjati!

59. O Giriśa with Pināka in the hand, O Śitikaṇṭha, O Sadāśiva! Obeisance to you, O great Lord; obeisance to you, the Lord of Devas.

60. O Maheśvara fond of prayer, I do not know how to eulogize. Let there be my unparalleled devotion to the pair of your lotus-like feet.

61. O lord, this alone is the boon (I wish to have), if you are pleased. O Īśvara, the ocean of the nectar of mercy, I do not choose any other boon.

62-64 Then Maheśāna who was propitiated by his eulogy said: "O (adopted) son of Rohiṇī, O highly fortunate son of the Moon-god, O Storehouse of polite words, your world will be above the world of the Stars. You will have great honour amongst all the Planets. This Liṅga installed by you will bestow wisdom on all. It will remove evil intentions. O gentle one, it will accord a residence in your world."

65. After saying this, Lord Śaṁbhu vanished from there itself. Budha went to the heavenly world, with the favour of the Lord of Devas.

The attendants said:

66. A man who has gained wisdom by worshipping Budheśvara at Kāśī will not get submerged in the deep ocean of worldly existence even after falling into it. He will be like moonshine unto the eyes of good people. With beaming countenance, he will reside there in the world of Budha.

67. Even at the time of death, no living being will be

deficient in intellect, if he has visited Budheśvara Liṅga to the east of Candreśvara.

68. By the time, the attendants concluded the narrative of Budha's world, the aerial chariot reached the excellent world of Śukra.

CHAPTER SIXTEEN

The World of Śukra (Venus)

The attendants said:

1. O Śivaśarman of great intellect, this is the wonderful world of Śukra. Kavi, the preceptor of Dānavas and Daityas stays here.

2-3. He inhaled the smoke of burning rice-husks for a thousand years though it was unbearable (and performed a great penance). Thereby he acquired the great Vidyā called Mṛtyusañjīvinī (i.e. that which enables one to resuscitate dead ones to life) from Lord Śiva.[1] Even the preceptor of Devas does not know this difficult Vidyā. (None) except Mṛtyuñjaya (Śiva), Skanda, Gaṇeśa and Pārvatī knows this.

Śivaśarman said:

4-6. Who is this one well known as Śukra and whose excellent world is this? How did he acquire Mṛtyusañjīvinī Vidyā from Lord Śiva? Narrate this to me, O Lords and Devas, if you have any love for me.

Then those two Devas recounted to him the great story of Śukra on hearing which, those who have faith, will not have premature death. Nor will they have any fear from spirits, ghosts and vampires.

7-8 When there was a great battle between Andhaka and Andhakavairin (i.e., Lord Śiva) the lords of impregnable Girivyūha ('Array of the army in the form of mountain') and Vajravyūha

1. Mentioned below in vv 21, 22, and 95-96, 116-119. For such penance by Śukra see VaP. II.35. 116-118; also PE p.761 where Vāmana Purāṇa, Ch. 62 is mentioned.

('Array in the form of a thunderbolt'), Andhaka left the battlefield and approached Śukra. Getting down from the chariot, he spoke thus:

9. "O holy lord, depending upon you, we consider the Devas beginning with Rudra and Upendra (Viṣṇu) along with their followers on a par with (insignificant things like) blades of grass.

10. O Preceptor, with your favour the Suras are afraid of us like elephants are of lions and serpents of Garuḍas.

11. The Daityas and Dānavas entered the unbreakable (i.e., impregnable) Vajravyūha after scattering the Pramatha forces like those who, distressed with heat, would enter a whirlpool.

12. O Brāhmaṇa, after resorting to you for refuge we are steady like mountains and move about fearlessly in this great battle against Indra.

13. Along with our wives and sons, we serve day and night your pleasing feet with great trust and close intimacy.

14-16. O Brāhmaṇa, be pleased to protect all of us who have resorted to you. See these warriors attacked by the Pramathas of terrific exploits, who pound like the god of Death (our warriors like) Huṇḍa, Tuhuṇḍa, Jaṁbha, Kujaṁbha, Pāka, Kārtasvana, Vipāka, Pākahārin and the heroic Candradamana, who tore up the brave Devas. They are all killed and felled down like sandal trees by Drāviḍas.

17. The time of the utility test has come now for the excellent Vidyā that was acquired by you formerly after inhaling the smoke of rice husks for a thousand years.

18. The benefit of your Vidyā is when you can revive the Daityas. Let all the Pramathas see these resuscitated to life by you."

19. On hearing these words of Andhaka the descendant of Bhṛgu, the sage of steady mind, smiled a little and spoke to the leader of Dānavas:

20-23. "O lord of Dānavas, everything that has been spoken by you is true. Indeed it is for the sake of the Dānavas that I have acquired this Vidyā. After inhaling for a thousand years the offensive smoke of rice husks, this Vidyā that is conducive to the pleasure of all kinsmen, has been acquired from Īśvara. By means of this Vidyā, I shall revive those who have been shattered (killed) by the Pramathas in the battle, like the cloud that enlivens dried-up crops. In this Muhūrta itself, O king, you will see the Dānavas rising up free from ailments and free from wounds, getting up as though after sleeping."

24. After saying this to the Lord of the Dānavas, Kavi (i.e. Śukra) recited the Vidyā (Mantra) with respect to everyone (of the Dānavas) and they rose up lifting up their weapons.

25. They rose up like the Vedas practised by good people, or like the timely clouds or like the monetary gifts made over to the Brāhmaṇas with great faith, at the time of great danger.

26. On seeing those great Asuras, Tuhuṇḍa and others revived again, the demons shouted (gladly) like clouds full of water.

27. On seeing the Dānavas resuscitated to life by Śukra, the leaders of the Gaṇas spoke to one another that the matter should be conveyed to the Lord of the Devas.

28. While that Yuddhayajña ('sacrifice in the form of battle') was going on causing a great deal of surprise to the leaders of Pramathas, the son of Śilāda (i.e., Nandin) who became furious on seeing the work of Śukra, approached Maheśa.

29-32. After hailing "Be victorious" to Ugra (Śiva), the cause of all success and bright like gold, Nandin said: "O Lord, the manner of fighting of the leading Gaṇas is very difficult even for the Devas including Indra. That has been rendered ineffective by Bhārgava (Śukra) after easily enlivening these enemies who had died in the battle, by reciting the Vidyā that accords life unto the dead. O Īśa, Tuhuṇḍa, Kujaṁbha, Jaṁbha, Vipāka, Pāka and other great leading Asuras have returned from the abode of Yama. They are moving about routing the Pramathas. O Maheśa, if he were to enliven all those excellent Daityas again and again after being killed, when can we have victory? Whence can there be peace for the leading Gaṇas?"

33. On being reported thus by Nandin, the Lord of the Pramathas, Lord Śiva, the lord of the chiefs of the Pramathas laughingly told Nandin, the king of the chiefs of all Gaṇas:

34. "O Nandin, go quickly and lift up the excellent Brāhmaṇa from the midst of the demons like a vulture seizing a quail and bring him here."

35. On being told thus by the Bull-emblemed Lord, Nandin shouted loudly in a stentorian and leonine voice. He penetrated

the (enemy's) army quickly and reached the place where the brilliant lamp of the family of Bhṛgu was present.

36. The powerful Nandin caused great agitation among the Daityas and like a Śarabha (fabulous animal with eight feet) that seizes an elephant, he carried away Kāvya (Śukra) who was being protected by all the Daityas with nooses, swords, trees, boulders and rocks in their hands.

37. The Asuras shouting with leonine roar followed him as though they would secure his release, even as he was caught by that powerful (Nandin) with the hairs dishevelled, ornaments dropped down and clothes slipping off.

38. Like clouds showering water, the leading Dānavas sent forth volleys of missiles like thunderbolt, tridents, swords, axes, fierce discus, stones etc. on Nandīśvara.

39. After seizing Bhārgava, the lord of the Gaṇas burned through the fire from his mouth, the hundreds of missiles. When the battle between the Asuras and the Devas became excessively fierce, he tormented the army of the enemies and came near Bhava.

40. "Here is that Śukra, O Lord". Saying this he handed him immediately over to Bhava. The Lord of the Devas accepted Śukra like an oblation offered by a pure devotee.

41. The protector of the spirits did not say anything. He put Kavīndra (Śukra) into his mouth as though he was a mere fruit. Loud sounds "Hā! Hā!" (expressing grief) were made by all the Asuras.

42-45. When Śukra was swallowed by the Lord of Girijā, the Daityas lost all hopes of victory, like lordly elephants with severed trunks or cows and bulls shorn of their horns, like groups of living beings without bodies, like Brāhmaṇas without (the Vedic) study, like the Sattvaguṇas devoid of efforts, like efforts lacking luck, like women bereft of their husbands, like volleys of arrows devoid of their feathers, like lives devoid of merits, like learning unattended with good character, all the (religious) activities become devoid of their benefits without the Śakti of Bhava. So without that excellent Brāhmaṇa, the Daityas became devoid of hopes of victory.

46. When Śukra who was carried away by Nandin was swallowed by Śiva, the Daityas became distressed, with their enthusiasm for battle getting diminished.

47. On seeing them losing their morale, Andhaka said to them: "We have been deceived by Nandin who carried away Śukra by force."

48-49. Without (affecting) the bodies, he has taken away the lives of all of us. All our fortitude, heroism, wisdom, fame, zeal, manliness and exploit have been simultaneously taken away when Śukra alone was abducted. Fie upon us by whom this sole excellent representative of our family, the most venerable one of our race, the preceptor, the protector and one who is capable of everything, has not been protected by us at the time of danger!

50. Hence be bold and fight with the enemies. I will kill all of the Pramathas along with Nandin.

51. Today I shall kill these helpless ones along with the Devas including Indra and release Bhārgava like a Yogin who releases the individual soul from the bondage of karmas.

52. If that Yogin (i.e. Bhārgava), our lord, comes out of his (i.e. Śiva's) body by means of his Yogic power, he shall protect the others left among us."

53. On hearing these words of Andhaka, the Dānavas shouted like thunder and harassed the Pramathas, resolving to fight unto death.

54. "If we have the life-span (destined), the Pramathas will not be able to overpower us. If we have no life-span, of what avail is our departure from the battle after leaving our master?

55. If the people who consider honour as wealth, forsake the master in the battle, they are sure to go to the hell Andhatāmisra.

56. Those who forsake battlefield tarnish their reputation through the darkness of ignominy. They can never be happy here or hereafter.

57. If one has taken the holy ablution in the Tīrtha of the battlefield which dispels the dirt of rebirth, of what avail are monetary gifts, austerities and taking plunges in the sacred Tīrthas?"

58. After thinking and deciding thus by talking to one another, those Danujas sounded the war drums and pounded the Pramathas in the battlefield.

59-60. There they created a great deal of havoc by striking one another with various weapons and missiles like arrows, swords, thunderbolts, machine-hurled stones, Bhuśuṇḍīs, Bhindipālas, tridents, javelins, axes, Khaṭvāṅgas, Paṭṭiśas, batons and mallets.

61. There was the din and noise of arrows flying about, bows drawn with twangs, the hissing noise of Bhindipālas and Bhuśuṇḍīs and the battle cries (of the soldiers).

62. There was a great tumult of beating of war-drums and the blare of horns, the trumpeting sounds of elephants and the neighing of horses.

63. The entire space between heaven and earth was filled as it were with echoes and reverberations. Hairs stood on ends in the case of both the cowards as well as the courageous ones.

64-65. The armies on both the sides fell into a swoon utterly thirsty, their ears becoming rent and split due to the loud trumpets and neighing of elephants and horses, the flags and flagstaffs torn and broken, the missiles and weapons becoming powerless. They appeared variegated with the vomitted blood and they were deprived of their horses and elephants.

66. On seeing his army hit and shattered here and there by the Pramathas, Andhaka himself came to the battlefield and routed the Gaṇas.

67. The Pramathas perished when hit and struck with thunderbolt-like arrows like mountains struck with Indra's thunderbolt or as waterless clouds scattered by the wind.

68. On seeing the soldiers going nearby or the soldiers approaching from far off, Andhaka hit every one of them with numerous arrows like the hairs (over the body).

69-70. Andhaka was blinded through the incessant volleys of arrows, tridents and javelins thrown by the ferocious Gaṇas like Vināyaka, Skanda, Nandin, Somanandin, Naigameya, Śākha and the powerful Viśakha.

71-74. A great tumultuous din was produced by the armies of the Pramathas and the Asuras. By that great sound, Śukra who was within the belly of Śaṁbhu searched for an exit like the wind trying to escape, through some hole. He wandered about in the body of Rudra. He saw the seven worlds and their guardians. He saw the mysterious worlds of Brāhmā, Nārāyana, Indra, Ādityas and celestial damsels. He saw the battle between the Pramathas and the Asuras. He thus wandered around in the belly of Bhava for a hundred years. He could not see any hole to escape through, like a rogue who cannot see any weak spot in a pure man.

75. By the power of Yoga acquired from Śaṁbhu, Bhārgava dropped out (from the body of Śiva) in the form of semen virile. When he bowed down to the Lord, he (Śiva) spoke to him thus:

76. "Since you dropped out like the Śukra (Semen), O scion of the family of Bhṛgu, you are Śukra on account of this act; you are my son. You can go."

77. When Śukra came out of his body, the Lord rejoiced much. It is good for me that while moving about in my belly, the Brāhmaṇa did not die.

78. On being addressed by the Lord thus, Śukra with brilliance like the Sun entered the army of the Dānavas, like the Moon that enters the cluster of clouds.

79. Just as the great ocean surges with waves gleefully at the rise of the Moon, so also the vast ocean of the Dānava army became delighted at the appearance of Śukra.

80. It was thus that the delighter of the family of Bhṛgu became Śukra by name, while the great battle between Andhaka and the slayer of Andhaka was going on.

81. How Kāvya (Śukra) got the Vidyā, the great Mṛtasañjīvanī with the favour of Śaṁbhu, listen to that, O Brāhmaṇa of good holy rites.

The Gaṇas said:

82-83. Formerly this scion of the family of Bhṛgu went to the city of Vārāṇasī that accords salvation to the four types of living beings viz., oviparous, sweat-born, germinating from seeds and viviparous. He installed the Liṅga of Śrī Śaṁbhu and dug a well before it. Meditating upon Lord Viśveśvara, he performed penance for a long time.

84-93. He showered the Lord with different kinds of flowers such as Rājacaṁpaka, Dhattūra, Karavīra, Kuśeśaya, Mālatī, Karṇikāra, Kadaṁba, Bakula, Utpala, Mallikā, Śatapatrī, Sinduvāra, Kiṁśuka, Aśoka, Karuṇa flowers, Punnāga, Nāgakesaras, the small Mādhavī flowers, Pāṭalas, Caṁpakas, Bilva, Navamallī, Vicikila, Kunda Mucukundaka, Mandāra, leaves of Bilva, Droṇa, Marubaka, Baka, Granthiparṇa, Damanaka, Surabhū, Cūta sprouts, Tulasī, Devagāndhārī, Bṛhatpatrī, Kuśa shoots, Nandyāvarta,

Agastya, Śāla, Devadāru, Kāñcanāra, Kurabaka, Dūrvāṁkura, Kuraṇṭaka flowers. He adored with each of these flowers separately and with other foliages, also with hundred thousands of leaves he worshipped Śaṅkara.

Strenuously he bathed the Lord a hundred thousand times with Pañcāmṛta measuring a Droṇa and with many kinds of sweet-smelling bathing materials. With sandalpaste and Yakṣakardama, he smeared the Lord a thousand times. He applied the Lord of the Devas with sweet-smelling unguents. He offered songs and dances to the Lord. He eulogized Lord Śaṅkara with many prayers from the Śruti, the Thousand Names and other prayers and hymns. Thus Śukra performed the austerities for five thousand years.

94. When he did not see the Lord even a bit inclined to bestow boons, he adopted other terrible and unbearable vows.

95-96. Kavi (Śukra) washed the great dirt of the mind in the form of fickleness by means of the waters of deep meditation and absorption. He cleansed the mind along with the sense-organs many times. After making that gem of mind free from dirt, he offered it to the Pināka-wielding Lord. Then he inhaled the smoke of rice husk for a thousand years.

97. Then the Lord became pleased with the noble-souled Bhārgava. With a lustre brighter than that of a thousand Suns, he came out of the Liṅga.

98. Virūpākṣa, the consort of Dākṣāyaṇī, directly spoke to him, "O Bhārgava, the storehouse of austerities, I am pleased; choose a boon."

99-100. On hearing these words of Śaṁbhu the lotus-eyed Brāhmaṇa became excessively delighted. Hairs stood on their ends all over his body. With eyes beaming with pleasure, he eulogized the Eight-formed Lord. Keeping his joined palms over his head, he uttered: "Be victorious; be victorious."

Bhārgava said:

(VV 101-109: Prayer by Śukra*)

101. (*Śiva as the Sun-god praised*) With these brilliant lustres,

* God Śiva is eight-formed (Aṣṭamūrti). Each form of Śiva is here eulogized by Śukra or Bhārgava.

you assail the entire darkness and make the desires of the night-stalkers set and disappear. O jewel of the day, for the welfare of the three worlds you shine in the firmament. O Lord of the universe, obeisance to you.

102. (*Śiva-as the Moon-god praised*) In this world, every moment, with your great lustre extending beyond the billowy shore, you increase the pleasure of the night-blooming lilies and the seas. You have routed the entire host of darkness and are excessively splendid. O Moon with cool rays, filled with the flood of nectar, obeisance to you.

103. (*Śiva-as the Wind-god*) O breaker of the stubborn ones, O wind that makes all creatures flourish, who makes the clan of serpents delighted, O omnipresent one, obeisance to you. On the sacred path you always move about (or you are adorable in the Vedic path). You are worthy of being attended upon. O enlivener of the universe, who is able to live without you?

104. (*Śiva as the Fire-god*) O immortal one, O Pāvaka (Fire), O immanent soul of the universe, O sole sanctifier of the universe, without your sanctifying sole power, the universe, consisting of the divine, corporeal and animal activities, does not live and function. Hence obeisance to you who bestow peace at every step.

105. (*Śiva as Water*) O great Lord in the form of water, O sanctifier of the universe, O Lord of diverse excellent conduct, since you make this diverse-featured world pure and free from impurities through imbibing and plunging, O Lord of the universe, I bow down to you.

106. (*Śiva as Ākāśa—the Ether*) O lord in the form of the firmament, this universe becomes full-fledged and developed because you give it the space externally and internally. O merciful one, it breathes by your grace. It becomes shrunk through its own nature and merges in you. Hence I bow down to you.

107. (*Śiva as the Earth*) O Lord in the form of the Earth, O Lord of the universe, O dispeller of darkness, who else than you sustains the universe? O Lord, greater than the greatest, O Lord embellished by the Daughter of Himālaya and by the serpents! Among those who maintain control of mind there is no person worthy of being eulogized other than you. Hence I bow down to you.

108. (*Śiva as the Supreme Soul*) O Hara in the form of the Ātman, this universe, consisting of the mobile and immobile beings, is pervaded by this series of your forms. O Lord in the form of the Supreme Absolute, O Lord with eight divine forms, O immanent being having the inner soul as abode, O Lord existing in every form, I bow down to you always.

109. O Lord adorable to Umā. O Bhava, the most venerable among all venerable ones, O Lord with forms spread over the universe, O Lord accessible to those who bow down, O Lord, the true one among all objects, hence, I bow down to you.

110. After eulogizing his dear Lord Bharga with the octave of the eight forms, Bhārgava bowed down again and again, placing his head on the ground.

111-114. On being eulogized thus by the excessively brilliant Bhārgava, the great Lord lifted him up from the ground with his hands. Holding the Brāhmaṇa who had bowed down, the Lord said, illuminating the quarters through the moonshine-like lustre of his teeth: "I consider you on a par with my two sons because of this excessively fierce penance hitherto not performed by anyone else, the meritorious activity of installing the Liṅga, its propitiation, the offering of the gem of the mind which is pure and steady and the holy activity in the great holy spot of Avimukta.

115. You get into the cavity of my belly with this body itself. Coming out through my organ of generation, you have the status of being my son.

116-118. I shall grant you another boon difficult to be acquired even by my attendants. I have a pure Vidyā named Mṛtasañjīvanī which I have kept concealed from Viṣṇu and Brahmā. It has been evolved by me by the power of my penance. O extremely pure one, it is in the form of a Mantra which I shall pass on to you today. O storehouse of pure penance, you deserve that Vidyā.

119. O most excellent one among the masters of Vidyā, if you recite this Vidyā (i.e., Mantra) in respect of any particular person, he will certainly come back to life.

120. Your brilliance shall be one surpassing the sun, fire and stars in the sky. It shall be dazzling. Be the foremost one among the Planets.

121. If men or women were to undertake any journey facing you, all their undertakings will perish by your glance.

122. O noble one of excellent holy rites, marriage and other rites, all pious activities, taking place after your rise shall become fruitful unto men.

123. All inauspicious lunar days shall become auspicious due to your association. Your devotees will have plenty of semen and hence of prolific progeny.

124. If people worship the Liṅga installed by you under the name Śukreśa, they will achieve success.

125-127. Listen to the benefit acquired by those men, who observe *Naktavrata* (taking food only at night) every Friday for a whole year, those who perform libation rites in the Śukrakūpa on your day (i.e., Friday) and worship Śukreśa. Those men will have never failing semen. They will have sons and plenty of semen. There is no doubt about this that they will be endowed with manliness and conjugal bliss. They will have no hindrance of any sort. All those people shall be happy."

After granting these boons, the Lord vanished in the Liṅga.

The Gaṇas said:

128. O scorcher of foes, Śukreśa is to the south of Viśveśvara. Those who are devotees of Śukreśvara live in the world of Śukra.

129. Merely by visiting it, one is honoured in the world of Śukra. Thus, O highly intelligent one, the situation of the world of Śukra has been recounted.

Agastya said:

130. O dear wife of excellent holy rites, listening to this story of Śukraloka thus that Brāhmaṇa saw the world of Aṅgāraka (Mars).

CHAPTER SEVENTEEN

The Worlds of Mars, Jupiter and Saturn

Śivaśarman said:

1-3. O divine ones, the splendid story relating to Śukra has been heard by me. My ears are extremely pleased merely by hearing it. Who is that storehouse of merit, who has this pure and grief-dispelling world? Kindly endeavour to recount this to me. I am not satisfied by imbibing the nectar-like speech issuing out of your mouth, by taking it in the vessel in the form of my ears.

The Gaṇas said:

4. O Śivaśarman, know that this is the world of Lohitāṅga (Mars). We shall tell you his origin, how he became the son of the Earth.

5. Formerly, Śaṁbhu was performing a penance due to the separation from Dākṣāyaṇī. At that time, a drop of sweat fell on the ground from his forehead.

6. A boy, reddish in limbs, was born from the surface of the Earth. He was lovingly nourished and brought up by the Earth in the capacity of a nurse.

7. He has acquired a great celebrity as Māheya (=son of the Earth). O sinless one, he performed a very severe penance in the city of Śaṁbhu.

8. It is the place where there are the two splendid rivers Asi and Varaṇā. For the sake of the welfare of all the worlds they join with the celestial river (Gaṅgā) flowing northwards.

9. Although he is omnipresent, Viśveśa shines there always for the sake of (granting) salvation to all the creatures who cast off their bodies here at the proper time.

10. The embodied beings, who die here, attain immortality i.e., salvation (Mokṣa) by obtaining the blessings of Viśveśvara.

11. Those who cast off their bodies in Avimukta do not adopt bodies again. (They get salvation) without Sāṅkhya (knowledge discriminating the soul from the non-soul) and Yoga (the eight-limbed practice of restraint) and without the observance of various kinds of vows and pious practices.

12-13. In the great holy spot named Pāñcamudra to the north of Kaṁbala and Aśvatara (two prominent serpents in the form of deities), he duly installed the Liṅga Aṅgārakeśvara named after him. A severe penance was performed by that noble soul until a brilliance issued out of his body like a blazing coal.

14. Hence he is praised in all the worlds by the name Aṅgāraka. The delighted Mahādeva granted him the great status of a Planet.

15-21. Those excellent men who worship Aṅgārakeśāna after taking the holy ablution in Gaṅgā with its current flowing northwards on an Aṅgārakacaturthī day (i.e. Tuesday in combination with the fourth lunar day) will never experience the oppression caused by malignant Planets.

The fourth lunar day in combination with Tuesday is considered to be a holy day on a par with eclipse by those who know (auspicious) times. Whatever holy rite is performed on that day, such as monetary gift, Homa, Japa etc. will have never-ending benefit. The ancestors of those who perform Śrāddha rite with full faith on the day when the Caturthī coincides with Tuesday will have satisfaction lasting twelve years.

Formerly Gaṇeśvara was born on an Aṅgāraka Caturthī day. Hence that is mentioned as a festival day for the purpose of increasing merit.

A devotee who observes the holy vow of taking a single meal a day on that occasion, worships Gaṇanāyaka and makes some gift dedicating it to that Lord is never afflicted by obstacles.

Those excellent men who were devotees of Aṅgāreśvara in Vārāṇasī stay in this world of Aṅgāraka with the utmost prosperity.

Agastya said:

22. Even as the attendants of the Lord were recounting the sweet and meritorious story, the city of Guru (Jupiter) appeared before their eyes.

23. On seeing that city of the excellent one among Ācāryas (i.e., Guru), delighting the eyes, Śivaśarman asked: "Whose is this excellent city?"

The Gaṇas said:

24. O friend, there is nothing which cannot be described to you. We shall narrate with pleasure the story of this city for dispelling the fatigue of the journey.

25. Even as Brahmā was joyously desirous of creating the three worlds formerly, his seven mental sons appeared before him, all of them being on a par with him.

26-27. Marīci, Atri and Aṅgiras were the chief ones among them. All of them were engaged in creation. A son named Āṅgirasa was born of Aṅgiras, a patriarch among them. He was the most excellent among the brilliant ones. He was the foremost among scholars with high intelligence. He was calm with perfect control over the sense-organs. He had conquered anger. He was gentle in speech and pure in mind.

28-30. He was conversant with the Vedas and fully understood their meanings. He was free from impurities and was an expert in all arts. He had mastered all sacred lores. He was the most excellent one among those who knew excellent policies. He was an advisor of what is wholesome. He did everything beneficial (to others). He was always against those who acted prejudiciously to others welfare. He was handsome and endowed with good habits and conduct. He had good qualities. He knew the correct time and place (of action). He was a darling of his elders. He had all the good characteristics. Adopting the practice of great ascetics, he performed penance at Kāśī.

31. He installed a great Liṅga of Śaṁbhu and meditating a lot, performed great austerities for ten thousand divine years. With great penance he acquired divine brilliance.

32. Thereupon, Lord Viśveśa, the creator of the universe, became pleased. Manifesting himself from the Liṅga, the Lord, a mass of brilliance, spoke:

33. "I am pleased; speak out the boon you have mentally thought of." On being told thus he was highly delighted and looking at Śaṁbhu he eulogized:

Prayer of Bṛhaspati: VV 34-41

Āṅgirasa said:

34. Be victorious, O Śaṅkara, O quiescent one, O Lord having the lustre of the moon, the bestower of beautiful objects

(the four Puruṣārthas), destroyer of all, the purest of all. O Lord accepting the great adoration offered by the pure ones, O Lord dispelling the great distress of all the devotees.

35. O Lord pervading the firmament of the heart of everyone, O bestower of boons, O Lord humble to the humble ones, O Lord who act to burn the great forest of sins! O Lord, one with the body having diverse activities, O Lord with a handsome body, O storehouse of courage in the act of drying up (i.e., destroying) the Lord of Love having tender flowers for arrows!

36. O Lord, bowed down to by those devoid of death etc., O Lord fulfilling the desire of those who do their duty! O Lord, the wearer of serpents, O Lord with the Daughter of the Lord of Mountains stationed on the left side of the body, O Lord pervading the entire universe by means of your own body!

37. O Lord identical with the three worlds, O Lord without form, O perfect-visioned Lord, O Lord creating fire by means of opening and closing of the eyes, O Bhava, O Lord of Bhūtas, O sole Lord of Pramathas, O Lord lending a hand even unto the fallen ones!

38. O pervader of the entire extensive world, O abode of the sound of Praṇava, O holder of the Moon, O Lord gladdened all around by the great goddess, the Daughter of the Lord of the Mountains, O Śiva, I bow down.

39. O Lord Śiva, O great Lord Giriśa, O bestower of riches, O Īśa, Giriśa, O Śiva, O Mṛḍa, O supporter of the Lord of Constellations, protect the three worlds. O restrainer of those who cause obstruction to devotion!

40. O Hara, here I do not fear even the god of Death. O Lord with unfailing intelligence, strike (destroy) the great sin quickly. I do not know any other thing than bowing down to Śiva's feet to bring about welfare. Hence I bow down.

41. In this entire extensive world, the propitiation of Hara alone is highly meritorious and destructive of sins. Hence, O Īśa, I bow down to the Lord of annihilation, devoid of attributes, having the lord of serpents for his great bracelat.

42. After eulogizing the great Lord, the son of Aṅgiras ceased. Delighted with the eulogy, the great Īśāna granted many boons.

Śrī Mahādeva said:

43. O Brāhmaṇa, become the preceptor of Devas, as a result of this elaborate penance. With the name of Bṛhaspatī be an adorable one among the Planets.

44. By the adoration of this Liṅga you have become my very vital life. So you will be known by the designation 'Jīva' in all the three worlds.

45. Since the Lord who is beyond phenomenal world had been eulogized by means of clever display of words, become Vācaspati, the lord of the world of words.

46. By recitation of this eulogy, the Goddess of Speech becomes manifest to the eulogizer. If he recites thrice (daily) for three years, his speech will be polished and cultured (even by listening to the recitation of the eulogy).

47. He who reads this prayer called Vāyavya[1] everyday (does not) lose his presence of mind when a great task appears before him.

48. By reciting this eulogy regularly in my presence, even men of no discrimination will not become engaged in evil action.

49. Any living being reciting this hymn can ward off the affliction arising from (evil) Planets. Hence this eulogy must be recited in front of me.

50. If a man gets up early in the morning everyday and reads this prayer, I shall remove all his terrible obstacles.

51. One who recites this eulogy after scrupulously performing the adoration of the Liṅga installed by you, shall acquire whatever he mentally desires.

52. After granting the boons thus, Śaṁbhu summoned Brahmā again along with all the groups of Devas including Indra, Yakṣas, serpents and Kinnaras.

53-54. On seeing them arrived, Śiva told Brahmā: "O Brahmā, at my instance make this sage Bṛhaspatī, weighty with his good qualities, the preceptor of all leading Suras for the pleasure (of all). Crown him in the office of the preceptor of Devas in accordance with the injunctions.

---

1. The commentary gives various far-fetched interpretations of the word. Two are accepted here: (1) which is able to bestow the position of Hiraṇyagarbha and (ii) which gives immediate benefit.

55-59. This lord of intellect will become a great favourite of mine."

"It is your great favour", saying thus and receiving the behest by (bent) head, instantly Brahmā made Āṅgirasa, the preceptor of Suras. The divine drums were struck. The groups of celestial damsels danced. All the Devas with their faces beaming with delight performed the adoration of Guru. He was sprinkled with water sanctified with Mantras by Vasiṣṭha and others.

Then Giriśa granted another boon to the Lord of Speech (i.e., Bṛhaspatī): "Listen, O pious-souled son of Aṅgiras, the teacher of Devas, the delighter of (all the members of) the family. This Liṅga installed by you will cause the increase of excellent intellect. It will become well-known as Bṛhaspatīśvara at Kāśī.

60. Whatever men do after worshipping this Liṅga when Guru and Puṣya are in conjunction, will attain great fulfilment.

61. The Liṅga Bṛhaspatīśvara should be guarded very well by me in Kali age. Merely by the sight of this, great intellect is obtained.

62. By worshipping Dhiṣaṇeśa situated to the south of Candreśvara and to the south-west of Vīreśa, one is honoured in the world of Guru.

63. The sin incurred by the carnal intimacy with the wife of the preceptor shall certainly be dispelled by resorting (to the Liṅga) for six months, like the darkness at sunrise.

64. For the same reason, the Bṛhaspatīśvara Liṅga that destroys great sins should be well guarded. It should not be mentioned to anyone and everyone."

65-66. After saying this and granting boons thus, the Lord vanished there itself. Accompanied by the elders and Indra and Upendra too, Brahmā crowned Bṛhaspatī in this city. Then he sent off Indra and other Suras. After that, on being permitted by Viṣṇu, O Brāhmaṇa, he adorned his own world.

Agastya said:

67. O Lopāmudrā, after passing beyond the world of Guru, Śivaśarman saw the city of Śani (Saturn) embellished with a circle of brilliant splendour.

68. On being asked by that Brāhmaṇa, O lady of pure smiles,

those two excellent Gaṇas pointed out that city to the excellent Brāhmaṇa.

The Gaṇas said:

69. O Brāhmaṇa, the hot-rayed Sun was born as the son of Kaśyapa (son of Marīci) and Dākṣāyaṇī (daughter of Dakṣa i.e., Aditi). Saṁjñā, the daughter of Tvaṣṭṛ, the patriarch, became his wife.[1]

70. Hence she was a great favourite of her husband. She was endowed with beauty and youth. Due to a very brilliant penance, Saṁjñā became endowed with brilliance.

71. The form of the disc of the Sun along with the splendour, (Saṁjñā) retained in her limbs, but her complexion was not as refulgent as it was. [v.l. Though her body was scorched by his refulgence, her mind remained attached to him.]

72. Out of love (Kaśyapa) spoke: "Stationed in the egg, he did not die." Ever since then he is called Mārtaṇḍa in the world.

73. She was unable to bear that super-abundance of refulgence of Vivasvān (Sun), whereby he blazed the three worlds with hot rays.

74. The storehouse of refulgence, Āditya, begot of her three children, O Brāhmaṇa: a daughter and two partriarchs (i.e., sons).

75-77a. They were Manu Vaivasvata, who was the eldest and then Yama and Yamunā. She was not capable of enduring the highly refulgent form of Vivasvān. Therefore, she created her own shadow with the same colour by means of her magical power. Then the shadow (Chāyā) bowed down to Saṁjñā with joined palms and said: "O goddess, command me who will carry out your behest. What shall I do?"

77b-81. Then Saṁjñā spoke to Chāyā: "O beautiful lady of the same complexion (as mine), listen. I will go to the abode of Tvaṣṭṛ. O fair lady, at my behest, you stay here in my abode without any hesitation. This Manu and the twins named Yamunā and Yama—these three children should be viewed by you as

1. The story of the Sun-god and Saṁjñā and the birth of Aśvins and Śani is given in Mbh, *Ādi* 66.35, *Anuśāsna* 150. 17-18. VāP. II.22.30-85 confirms the details of this story.

though they were your own children. This fact should not be mentioned to your (i.e., my) husband, O lady of pure smiles."

On hearing this, Chāyā said to the noble lady, the daughter of Tvaṣṭṛ: "Until and unless my tresses of hairs are pulled, or I am threatened with a curse, I will not mention this conduct of yours. O fair lady, go away happily."

82. Thus, after commanding Savarṇā (i.e., Chāyā) and after being told, "Let it be so" by Savarṇā, she approached her father. After bowing down to him, she spoke to Tvaṣṭṛ:

83. "O father, I am unable to endure the refulgence of the storehouse of refulgence, the bright splendour of the son of the noble-souled Kaśyapa, O noble Sir."

84. After hearing what was spoken by her, she was rebuked by the father very much. She was again and again urged, "Go to your husband."

85. She was worried very much. "Fie upon the activity (life) of women!" She thus cursed and censured herself. She very much blamed her womanhood too.

86. 'There is no freedom to women at any time anywhere. Fie upon a freedom-less life! She has to fear her father, husband and son in childhood, youth and ultimately in old age.

87-90. Alas! Out of foolishness the house of the husband has been abandoned by me, doing everything without proper reflection. If without being found out I were to go back to my husband's abode, that Savarṇā whose desire has been fulfilled is present there. If after being rebuked by my father, I were to stay here itself, the hot-rayed Sun will become more fierce than my parents. He will become terrible. Alas! This is the same story as is mentioned by the common people, that is handling a burning coal with one's own hands. This has been clearly seen by me today. Husband's abode is lost due to foolishness. There is no welfare in the abode of father (the abode of father is no better).

91-92. My stage of life is youth; the beauty is splendid, worthy of being desired by the three worlds. My womanhood and the pure family surpasses all. My husband is such (a splendid person). He is omniscient. He is the eye of the world. He dispels darkness. He is the witness of all activities. He is identical with all (because he is a form of Lord Aṣṭamūrti). He is capable of moving about everywhere.

93-94. 'What shall be conducive to my welfare?' Thinking thus she, not censured anywhere around, assumed the form of a mare and went to the Northern Kurus for performing penance. She grazed dry grass. 'By the power of penance, I will be sufficiently able to bear that excessive brilliance of my husband.' Deciding thus she performed a severe penance keeping her husband in the mind.

95-99. The Sun-god considered Savarṇā to be the real Saṁjñā. He begot of her the eighth excellent Manu i.e., Sāvarṇi, the second, a son Śanaiścara (Saturn) and the third child, a girl named Bhadrā (i.e., Tapatī). Due to co-wifely feeling and natural feelings of women (for their own children) Savarṇā loved her own children more than the earlier ones. Manu, the eldest, endured, though he saw the feeding, embellishing and fondling more directed towards Sāvarṇi and others; but Yama did not (brook it).

Once due to anger, born out of childishness or the gravity of the inevitable future, Yama threatened with his (raised) foot the lady in the guise of Saṁjñā. Then the mother of Sāvarṇi angrily cursed him:

100. "O sinful one, you were desirous of killing me. Since the foot was raised by you, let it fall ere long." After cursing, she became excessively grief-stricken.

101. Afraid of his mother's curse, Yama narrated the whole incident to his father and said, "Save me, save me."

102. "Equal treatment should be meted out to all the children by a mother. Though the foot was raised by me it was not caused to fall on (did not touch) her body.

103. Whether this is due to my childishness or delusion, you will please forgive me, O lord of rays. Save me from the curse of my mother. Let not my foot fall down."

Vivasvān said:

104-105. Though a thousand crimes might have been committed, a mother shall not curse her son. Hence, O my boy, there will be some (real) reason wherefor she cursed you agrily, though you are conversant with piety and truthful in speech. A mother's curse cannot be altered (or nullified) by anyone anywhere.

106. Worms will take away some flesh from this foot and pass on to the ground. Thus the curse can be fulfilled. You will also be saved.

107. After consoling his son thus, the Sun-god went to the inner apartment. After staring at her for a long time, Savitṛ spoke these words to his wife:

108. "O wrathful lady, when all the children are equal to you why is more affection shown towards Sāvarṇi and others who are not the elders?"

109. When she did not say anything to the Sun-god though he insisted on the question, he concentrated his mind and came to know everything.

110. Then she confessed everything to the lord who was about to curse. She told him the truth as it had happened. The lord became pleased.

111. From the utterance of the truth, Ravi knew her to be sinless. Though he was angry, he did not curse her. He went to Tvaṣṭṛ.

112. Tvaṣṭṛ at the outset worshipped the hot-splendoured Sun who was about to curse. He consoled him befittingly and joyously. After knowing his intention Tvaṣṭṛ spoke to Ravi:

Tvaṣṭṛ said:

113. O Ravi, she was afraid of your excessive brilliance. Assuming the form of a mare, she has gone to Northern Kurus. She is roaming about in the grassy tract.

114. You will see her today. Your wife is of noble conduct. She is unassailable to all living beings due to the restraint of the refulgence.

115. With the permission of the Sun, Tvaṣṭṛ pared him carefully after placing him on the lathe. Then he became more pleasingly brilliant.

116-117. After getting the permission, Savitṛ went to the Northern Kurus hurriedly. He saw her performing great penance. She was as if the personified glory of penance. She had the splendour of the submarine fire. In the form of a mare, she was grazing only the dry grass by means of her Yogic Māyā.

118-120. Coming to know that she was the daughter of Tvaṣṭṛ and free from sins, moving about in the form of a mare, the Sun-god assumed the form of a horse and cohabited with her in the mouth. Suspecting him to be another male, she hurriedly whirled round and hurled out the semen of Vivasvān through her nostrils. The divine beings, Aśvins, the foremost among physicians were born of that. The jewel of the firmament (the Sun-god) revealed his befitting form to her.

121-122. On seeing the Sun giving delight to her eyes, she became pleased. The chaste lady saw her husband with gentle brilliance, dispelling the distress in her mind. She attained great delight. What is it that is difficult to obtain through penance? Penance is the greatest welfare. Penance is the greatest wealth.

123-124. Penance alone is considered the great cause of divinity.

O Śivaśarman what is seen here as highly dazzling in the form of a circular refulgence above and below in the sky, know it to be the great refulgence of penance.

125-126. It was thus that Śanaiścara was born of Savarṇā and Vivasvān. Śani went to Vārāṇasī, respected by all the Devas, performed an extensive penance after installing the Liṅga of Śaṅkara, and obtained this world and the lofty status of a Planet by worshipping Hara.

127. By visiting the highly splendid Śanaiścareśvara in Vārāṇasī and worshipping him on a Saturday, one can ward off the oppression caused by Saturn.

128. By worshipping Śanaiścareśvara lying to the south of Viśveśa and north of Śukreśa, one rejoices in this world.

129. On listening to this chapter of great merit, one can ward off the affliction caused by (malignant) Planets. To him who lives in Kāśī, there is no fear from evil portentous phenomena.

CHAPTER EIGHTEEN

The World of Seven Sages

Agastya said:

1-2. Listening thus to the beautiful story, Śivaśarman belonging to Mathurā, who had his holy ablution in Muktipurī, who died in Māyāpurī and who was going ultimately to Vaiṣṇava world because he had visited Viṣṇupurī, saw the region of the Seven Sages.

3-5. He was eulogized by the Cāraṇas and the Māgadhas and requested by the celestial girls: "Stop. Please stop for a while." Then they stood by heaving sighs, "We are deficient in fortune. Since he is extremely meritorious, he has gone to the meritorious worlds." While going on in the aerial chariot, he heard these words uttered by them. He was delighted and spoke (to the Gaṇas): "O divine ones, whose is this unrivalled, brilliant and splendid world?"

6-8. On hearing these words of the Brāhmaṇa the excellent Gaṇas said: "O Śivaśarman of auspicious intellect, the Seven Sages devoid of impurities, who were directed by Brahmā to create subjects, live here. They are Marīci, Atri, Pulaha, Pulastya, Kratu, Aṅgīras and the illustrious Vasiṣṭha. They are the mental sons of Brahmā. They have been termed Seven Brahmās in the Purāṇas.

9. Sambhūti, Anasūyā, Kṣamā, Prīti, Sannati, Smṛti and Ūrjā (i.e. Arundhatī) are their wives respectively. They are the mothers of the world.

10. The entire region of the three worlds is held aloft by the power of penance of these. After creating them formerly, Brahmā said to these great sages:

11-13. "O my sons, create subjects of different forms with due effort."

They resolved to perform penance. After performing obeisance to Brahmā, they went to Avimukta, the holy spot presided over by Kṣetrajña (Śiva in the form of the individual soul) and never forsaken by Śiva for the purpose of securing the liberation of all living beings. They then installed Liṅgas named after them. With great devotion to Śiva, they performed severe austerities.

14-16. Pleased with their penance, Śambhu bestowed on them the region *Prājāpatya.*

Those who visit the Liṅga Atriśvara etc., in Kāśī scrupulously, stay in this Prājāpatya world with dazzling brilliance.

By visiting Atriśvara Liṅga that has been installed on the western banks of the lake of Gokarṇeśa, one can get one's Brāhmaṇical brilliance enhanced.

The excellent Kuṇḍa (deep pit) of Marīci is in the north-east of Karkoṭavāpī (well or tank called Karkoṭa).

17. By taking his bath there devoutly, a man shines like the Sun.

The Liṅga named Marīcīśvara has been installed there.

18. By visiting that Liṅga, O Brāhmaṇa, one shall attain the world of Marīci. He becomes the foremost among all men and shines like the Sun of brilliant rays.

19. (The Liṅga) Pulaheśa and Pulastyeśa are on the west of Svargadvāra[1] ('Doorway to Heaven'). By visiting them a man is honoured in the Prājāpatya world.

20. By visiting Aṅgiraseśvara in the beautiful Harikeśavana the man shall stay here in this world, O Brāhmaṇa, with fully developed brilliance.

21. By visiting Vasiṣṭheśvara on the beautiful banks of Varaṇā, and Kratvīśvara too there itself one attains residence here.

22. These Liṅgas resorted to by those who wish for splendour and auspiciousness at Kāśī, bestow everything desired in this world and in the other world.

The Gaṇas said:

23. O Śivaśarman of great fortune, that beautiful lady Arundhatī of great merit engaged in conjugal fidelity, stays here.

24-25. Merely by remembering her, one shall get the benefit of the holy ablution in Gaṅgā.

Lord Nārāyaṇa, accompanied by two or three holy persons

1. Svargadvāra is now a temple set into the city several hundred yards uphill from the river Gaṅgā along the lane called Brahma Nālā, which itself was a former rivulet.

of the Antaḥpura, joyously describes her and discusses her story in front of Lakṣmī. He is highly pleased with her chastity.

26-30. "O beautiful Kamalā, no other woman anywhere in the world has such a pure mind as that of Arundhatī. Neither the beauty nor the blameless conduct, neither the nobility nor the skill in arts, nor the eagerness to serve her lord, nor the sweetness, nor the majesty, nor the ability to delight noble persons, any other lady anywhere possesses, O beloved one, as in the case of Arundhatī. Blessed are those women who mention the name of Arundhatī in any context. They are fortunate. They have the purest of intellects.

Whenever there is any discussion on chaste women in our houses, it is she who adorns the first row."

31. While those Gaṇas of Viṣṇu were recounting the delightful story, the world of Dhruva (Pole Star) that is devoid of annihilation, came into their view.

CHAPTER NINETEEN

The Story of Dhruva[1]

Śivaśarman said:

1. O excellent ones, who is this whirling about with the tips of fingers holding many strings, standing on a single foot and keenly observing everything?

2. He resembles the pillar of the pavilion of the three worlds. He is surrounded by radiant rays. He appears to weigh and measure the limitless expanse of luminaries.

3. He holding strings appears to measure the expanse of the firmament. It seems that the beam-like great foot of Trivikrama has been lifted up in the courtyard of the sky.

4. Or he has assumed the form of a powerful sacrificial post in the vast lake of the firmament. Who is this? O divine ones, recount this to me with great mercy.

* * *

1. The story of Dhruva, his insult in his father's Durbar, his penance and attainment of a permanent post as the pivot of the universe is given in details in BhP IV. Chs. 8 & 9; V. 23.1-9 and Vāyu P.II.1.75-79.

5. On hearing the words of their friend, thus the Gaṇas proceeding ahead in the aerial chariot narrated to him lovingly the eternal story of Dhruva.

The Gaṇas said:

6. Uttānapāda was the son of Svāyaṁbhuva Manu. O Brāhamaṇa, that king had two sons.

7-10. The eldest was Uttama born of Suruci and the younger one Dhruva born of Sunīti. That boy was once adorned by Sunīti and directed to serve the king as he was seated in the middle of the royal court. Dhruva, a polite and humble boy, accompanied by the sons of other co-wives went near King Uttānapāda and bowed down. On seeing Uttama sitting in the lap of his father, the king seated on a lofty throne, Dhruva, the son of Sunīti, became desirous of climbing on to his lap due to childish fickleness.

11-16. On seeing him desirous of climbing on to the lap, Suruci said to Dhruva, "O son of an unlucky woman, why do you wish to climb on to the lap of a king?

O boy, born of the womb of an unfortunate woman, why do you aspire to this out of childish desire? No merit has been practised by you to sit on this throne.

If there had been any merit, how did it happen that you got into the womb of an unlucky woman? By imlication know the meagreness of your merit.

Though born as a prince, you had not adorned my womb. See this Uttama who has no one to excell him because he was born of an excellent womb.

He is fondled proudly by the king upon his knees. If you have any desire to get on to this lofty throne, why did you remain elsewhere leaving off the brilliant womb of Suruci?"

The boy was thus rebuked by her in the middle of the royal court.

17-23. While going out, the boy courageously drank the tears (i.e., controlled the tears). He did not say anything. The king also did not say anything approving or disapproving, because he was restrained by excessive conjugal bliss of the crowned queen.

The boy left the assembly-hall after dispelling his grief

(again) with childish activites. He bowed down to the king and went to his own abode.

On seeing the boy, the abode of good discipline and practices, Sunīti came to know through the (peculiar) glow of his face that Dhruva had been extremely insulted.

She approached the boy who appeared to be languishing slightly, and sniffed at his head many times. She embraced him by way of consoling him.

On seeing Sunīti who always stayed hidden in the inner apartment, he sighed deeply many times before his mother and cried.

With tears in her eyes, she consoled him and wiped off his face with the border of her silken garment, with a gentle touch of her hand. The mother asked him to speak out the reason for his cry. "By whom were you insulted in the very presence of the king?"

24. After drinking water and chewing the betel, when his mother pressed her question further Dhruva spoke to her:

25-28. "Oh mother, I am asking you. Tell me clearly. Though the status of being the wife of the king is common (to you both), how is it that Suruci is a greater favourite? How is it that you, dear mother, are not a favourite of the king? In what way did Uttama, the son of Suruci, become superior? Though the status of being a prince is common, how am I not better? How is it that you are unlucky? How does Suruci have a better womb? How is it that the royal throne is proper for Uttama and not for me? How is my merit insignificant and that of Uttama excellent?"

29-30. On hearing these well-reasoned words of her child who was conversant with the royal usage, Sunīti sighed a little. Sunīti who was well-versed in politics set aside her co-wifely enmity. In order to pacify the anger of the child, she began to speak in her naturally sweet voice:

Sunīti said:

31. O dear boy of great intellect, I shall narrate everything to you with a clear conscience. Do not take to heart the insult (you have suffered now).

32. Whatever has been spoken by her is true and not otherwise.

She is the crowned queen of the king, her husband. She is the greatest favourite among all queens.

33. O dear boy, she had acquired great merit in her previous birth. It is due to that store of ample merit that the king loves Suruci very much.

34. There is only nominal queenhood vested in those young women who are unlucky like me. The king has no interest in them.

35. With the abundance of great merits, Uttama lay in the most excellent womb of that highly meritorious lady and hence deserves the throne.

36-48. (Fruits of good merits)

Royal umbrella resembling the moon, excellent chowries, high throne, elephants in their rut, horses of swift gaits, life without worry and sickness, splendid kingdom without enemies, excellent worship of Hari and Hara, wide knowledge of arts, never failing success in studies, conquest of the six inherent enemies (anger, etc.), naturally Sāttvic mentality, merciful vision, sweet voice, absence of lethargy in one's work, obeisance (humility) to the elders, cleanliness everywhere, readiness to help others always, liberal-mindedness, perpetual ability to speak courageously, scholarship in the assembly, masterliness in the battlefield, straightforwardness with kinsmen, firmness in buying and selling, softness in dealing with women, fondness towards progeny (or subjects), fear of Brāhmaṇas, livelihood according to the excellent conduct of mature people, residence on the banks of Gaṅgā or in a holy spot, death in a holy spot or in battle, aversion to turning the face away from suppliants and especially from enemies, enjoyment in particular with all followers, donating liberal gifts everyday, uninterrupted pursuit of learning, service to the parents everyday, daily accumulation of fame and piety, acquisition of heavenly benefits and salvation, embellishment of permanent good conduct, perpetual contact with good people, friendship with the friends of parents, eagerness to always listen to Itihāsas and Purāṇas, fortitude even in danger, steadfastness during affluence, majesty in the use of words, liberal attitudes toward those who come with bowls in their hands, leanness only in the body due to austerities, holy observances and vows: It is through these fruits that the trees of austerities fructify.

49. Hence, due to the paucity of austerities you and I, O highly intelligent one, have been denied royal glory though we are very near the king.

50. Hence what has been done by oneself is the greatest cause of honour and dishonour. Even the Creator is not powerful enough to eradicate what has been committed by one. So do not feel sorry for anything, dear son. Good fortune will usher in what is desired.

51. On hearing these great words of excellent purport of Sunīti, Dhruva, the son of Sunīti, uttered these words in reply:

Dhruva said:

52. O mother Sunīti, listen to my words without any excitement. Do not slight me thinking that I am only a boy, O lady of great penance.

53-54. If I am born in the highly sacred race of Manu as the son of Uttānapāda out of your womb, and if, O mother, austerity alone is the cause of all riches, then know that what is inaccessible to others has been achieved by me.

55. Render only one help to me without hesitation, O dear mother: I only want your permission (to perform penance) and bless me duly.

56. Realising that the boy born of her womb possesses great vigour and shines with great wealth of energetic enthusiasm, she spoke to him:

57. "O son of Uttānapāda, you have just completed your eight years. Hence I am not able ot give (free) permission to you. Still I say this:

58. My heart is deeply pierced by the arrow-like words of my co-wife. The waters of the tears of yours are not controlled. What shall I do?

59. O child, those tears flow through my eyes and cause rivers to flow through waters of sorrow.

60-64. My eyes are eagerly attached to your face. You are a stick to support me (my person). You have been obtained by me after a great deal of suffering and after praying to desired deities (liked by me). O my dear one, when the moon-like face of yours beams, the milky ocean of my mind, becomes swollen with tides rising after filling my breasts with the milk of delight. When I touch your body, a cool wave of happiness passes through me and covers my body with rising hairs. I lie in the cozy bed of happiness.

O dear son of moon-like face, after drinking water and chewing betel leaves, and imbibing the nectar caused to be flooded by the milky ocean of the lips in your face, I am not fully satiated.

65. Whenever the sweet, cool words of yours reach my ears, the agitation due to the wounding words of the co-wife becomes nullified.

66. When, O son, you sleep for a long time, I continue to meditate like, 'when will this sleep come to an end and your face will beam like a lotus at sunrise?'

67. When you return home, O dear child, after your child-like sports and pastimes, my breasts appear to be eager to shower the most esteemed *Arghyas*.

68. Whenever you go out of the palace, the imprints of your feet with the lotus-like lines constitute the sole support to my vital airs wishing to depart.

69. Whenever, O dear son, you go out even three or four steps, my vital air becomes the guest of the throat (out of eagerness).

70. O wonderful (child), whenever you delay outside, my mind like a (Cakora) bird hastens to go out towards you who resemble a massive store of nectar.

71. When you go out for the purpose of penance, let the vital airs of hard calibre stay in the fridge of the forest of the throat, performing austerities."

72. After getting the permission, Dhruva bowed down to the lotus-like feet of his mother covering them with his hairs and went out.

73. A garland consisting of the blue lotuses of her eyes was given by Sunīti as present to Dhruva after wreathing it and tying it with the string of fortitude.

74. Then hundreds of blessings that could not be obstructed by others, were sent as his followers by the mother, for the sake of his protection on the way.

75. Coming out of his mansion that boy of great provers

uncommon to children entered the forest as his way was pointed out by a favourable mind.

76. Dhuva entered the forest as though he was called by the forest under the pretext of moving the tips of the branches of the trees by the wind.

77. Considering his mother as his deity and accustomed only to the royal roads, the prince could not comprehend the forest pathways. He (closed his eyes and) meditated for a short while.

78. When Dhruva opened his eyes and looked before him, he saw the Seven Sages of unexpected movememt in the forest.

79. When people of childlike helplessness do not get any other assistance, fortune alone comes in handy in great forests, or battles or in the house itself. Therefore fortune alone is the cause (of happiness).

80. Where is the son of the king, a mere boy? Where is that dense forest? Obeisance to you, O inevitable fate, who bring forcibly everyone under your control.

81. If anything is to happen to anyone, good or evil, the rope of the inevitable does drag it from somewhere and hand it over to him.

82. Out of the power of his intellect a man does something in some manner but fate disposes of it through the power of the inevitable.

83. Neither the age nor the varieties of activities, neither the wonderful strength nor the exertion of men cause benefit. What has been done before is the real cause.

84. On seeing the Seven Sages whose splendour exceeded that of the Sun and who were, as it were, dragged by means of the strings of luck and brought there, he rejoiced.

85-87. Their foreheads were marked with *Tilaka* (ritualistic mark on the forehead). They held Kusa grass with their fingers. They were seated on deer hides. They were embellished with sacred threads. They had rosaries in their hands. They had kept their eyes closed a little. They had covered themselves with well-washed silken garments dyed red. They appeared to be like the seven oceans of great fortune assembled together unexpectedly in order to raise up the subjects sunk in adversity.

88. With palms joined in reverence, Dhruva approached

them humbly. After bowing down to them he spoke these gentle words:

Dhruva said:

89. O excellent sages, know me as the son of Uttānapāda, born of the womb of Sunīti. I am Dhruva, whose mind has become dejected.

90. I have reached this forest traversed by my feet. I am almost ignorant in respect to everything but my mind dwells upon great achievements.

91-94. On seeing the brilliant boy of naturally sweet form and features, possessing excellent dress and speaking gently but majestically, they made the boy sit near them. They were highly surprised and said: "O boy of large eyes, O son of a great king! Even after pondering over it, we cannot understand what might have caused you dejection; tell us. Today you have no worries over wealth. How can there be insult in your mother's house? You are free from ailments. You are endowed with good physique? What is then the cause of your dejected state of mind? Usually disgust over worldly affairs happens in the case of men of unfulfilled desires.

95-100. You are the prince of the king, the overlord of the seven continents. So how is this? In this world, people are of different tastes naturally. It is not possible to know the mental predilection of a young man, old man or even a child."

On hearing these words of them, full of natural affection that boy of lofty ambition spoke thus:

Dhruva said:

O great Sages, I was sent by my mother to be of service to the king. When I was desirous of getting on to the lap of the king, I was rebuked by Suruci. She contemptuously reproached me and my mother and praised Uttama making him seem to be the superior. This is the cause of my dejection.

On hearing these words of the boy, they looked at one another. Incapable of understanding even a boy, they said that it was due to his Kṣatriya nature.

The Sages said:

101. What should be done by us? What is your wish? Let it be known. Let us hear it.

Dhruva said:

102. O Sages, Uttama who is my (step) brother is the best among all good people. Let him occupy that excellent throne bequeathed by his father.

103. O Sages of excellent vows, I wish that this help be rendered by you, venerable ones. Being a child, I almost do not know. May your instruction be in that respect.

104. How that inaccessible thing is to be acquired? That which no other king has enjoyed, that which is loftier than everything else, that which Indra and others cannot achieve.

105. I do not desire what is passed on to me by my father. I wish that which is earned and acquired by my own arms, which, wonderfully enough, will be beyond the ken of the wishful thinking of even my father.

106. Those who enjoy the legacy of their fathers are generally not those who consider fame as their sole possession. They are to be known as excellent men, those who demonstrate their excellence over their fathers.

107. Let there be death unto those people of evil intentions and activities who destroy and defile what is acquired by their father's fame, learning and wealth.

108. On hearing his words powerfully depicting his prudence, Marīci and other Sages said to Dhruva what was relevant to his request:

Marīci said:

109. How can one who has not worshipped the feet of Acyuta secure that position which you speak of? O dear one, I am not speaking what is not true.

Atri said:

110. One who has not tasted the juice of the dust-particles of the lotus-like feet of Govinda cannot gain that prosperous

position beyond the reach of wishful thinking.

Aṅgīras said:

111. That position of the acquisition of all riches is not far from a person who regularly meditates on the lotus-like shining feet of the lover of Kamalā.

Pulastya said:

112. O Dhruva, bestower of everthing is that Viṣṇu, merely by remembering whom the mass of great sins becomes ultimately destroyed.

Pulaha said:

113. That Acyuta will bestow everything, Acyuta whom they call the greatest Brāhmaṇa, who is beyond Pradhāna and Puruṣa, and by whose Māyā everything in this visible world is pervaded.

Kratu said:

114. Viṣṇu is the Puruṣa of Yajñas; he is to be known only through the Vedas; he is Janārdana; he is the immanent soul of this universe. Once satisfied what is it that he does not bestow?

Vasiṣṭha said:

115. Even salvation cannot be far, if one propitiates Hṛṣīkeśa to the bidding of whose dancing eyebrows the eight Siddhis are subject, O prince.

Dhruva said:

116. O eminent Sages, what is said regarding the propitiation of Viṣṇu is true. How should that Lord be propitiated? Let that procedure be imparted.

The Sages said:

117. The Japa of Nārāyaṇa should be performed regularly whether one stands or walks, sleeps or keeps awake, lies down or sits.

118. Who has not achieved Siddhi by meditating on the four-armed Viṣṇu and performing the *Japa* of the twelve-syllabled Mantra consisting of the name Vāsudeva (i.e., *om namo bhagavate vāsudevāya*).

119. Who does not get everything fulfilled in this world by seeing even for a moment Lord Acyuta identical with all, resembling an Atasī flower, wearing yellow garment?

120. A man performing the Japa of Vāsudeva undoubtedly attains everything, namely sons, wives, friends, kingdom, heaven and salvation.

121. Neither the terrible messengers of Yama nor obstacles touch those who are engrossed in the Japa of Vāsudeva even if they are sinners.

122. This great Mantra was resorted to by Manu, your grandfather, who was a devotee of Viṣṇu, who had great prosperity and who was desirous of the kingdom.

123. O excellent one, you too be devoted to Vāsudeva through this Mantra. Successfully achieve quickly the prosperity as has been desired.

124. After saying this all, those noble-souled great Sages vanished. Dhruva too turned his mind towards Vāsudeva and went away for the performance of the penance.

CHAPTER TWENTY

The Story of Dhruva: The Vision of the Lord

The Gaṇas said:

1-2. Coming out of that forest, O Brāhmaṇa, the son of Uttānapāda reached the beautiful forest Madhuvana on the banks of Yamunā. It is the first great holy spot of Lord Harimedhas. Even a sinful creature shall certainly become sinless after reaching that spot.

3. Performing the Japa of the holy name of Vāsudeva, the great Brahman, free from all ailments, he with his eyes fixed in meditation, saw the entire universe full of that Lord.

4. (He saw) Hari in all the quarters—Hari in the rays of

the Sun, Hari going about in the forests in the form of jackals, deer and lion and other animals.

5. (He visualised) Lord Hari in the form of frogs, tortoises etc. in the water, Hari in the form of horse etc. in the stables of kings.

6. He was in the form of Ananta (Śeṣa) in the nether worlds. In the firmament, he is termed Ananta (Infinite). Though he is single and undifferentiated, he has infinite number of forms.

7. He who resides always in the Devas, he who is the abode of Devas is Vāsudeva. Due to his Vāsanā (Avidyā) he shines eveywhere.

8. The root √*Viṣ* means to pervade. It becomes meaningful in the name of Viṣṇu alone who pervades everything.

9. The supreme lord has all-powerful control over all the sense-organs. Hence he is well known as Hṛṣīkeśa. He is present everywhere.

10. Even in the great Pralaya (ultimate annihilation) his devotees never perish. Hence he is Acyuta. He alone is all-pervasive in the entire world. He is immutable.

11. He bears and sustains sportingly the entire universe including the mobile and immobile beings, by direct administration as well as by richly endowing the devotee with his own identity (salvation). Hence, he is Viśvaṁbhara.

12. His (Dhruva's) eyes never saw anything other than the feet of Viṣṇu, because invariably Puṇḍarīkākṣa and no one else is worthy of being seen.

13. His ears never heard any other words except Mukunda, Govinda, Dāmodara, Caturbhuja (and other names of Viṣṇu).

14. His hands marked by the lines of conch and discus did no other work, except the adoration seeking the feet of Govinda and such work as is loved and approved by him.

15. His mind dwelt upon the pair of feet of Hari free from the pairs of opposites afflicting the world. Eschewing the thought of everything else, it became perfectly steady.

16. As he performed the elaborate penance, his feet taking refuge only in Viṣṇu, never stirred out anywhere leaving the precincts of Nārāyaṇa's abode.

17. The organ of speech was authorised solely in the extolling of the good qualities of Govinda by him, taking delight

therein and performing the penance with a lofty purpose.

18. Tasting solely the nectarine juice of the names of the Consort of Kamalā, his tongue was not desirous of any other juice.

19. Delighted and rendered fragrant by the sweet scent of the lotus-like feet of Śrīmukunda, his organ of smell steadfastly avoided other scents.

20. After touching the pair of feet of the Enemy of Madhu, the organ of touch of that prince attained the pleasure of all types of tactile pleasures.

21. After having attained the greatest Lord Dāmodara, the essential basis of all sorts of objects of sense, the sense-organs of Dhruva became perfectly contented.

22. At the rise of the Sun of his penance that illuminated (scorched) the three worlds all the splendour of the Moon, Sun, fire and the stars became extinguished.

23. (Due to Dhruva's penance) Indra, Candra, Agni, Varuṇa, Vāyu, Kubera, Yama, Nairṛta and other important (heavenly beings) became doubtful of their positions.

24. The other heaven-dwellers too, who move about in aerial chariots and the chief of whom were the Vasus, became afraid of Dhruva, feeling increasing anxiety about their official rights.

25. Wherever Dhruva set his feet on the ground, the earth bent down overwhelmed by his weight.

26. It is wonderful that the waters that come into contact with his limbs eschew their sluggishness (liquidity) due to their fear for him and retain their position even elsewhere and remain tasty.

27. Due to the splendour of his penance, all the radiant refulgences present everywhere with the forms and qualities of Siddhas displayed, came within his vision.

28. His own quality of touch though stationed elsewhere in a far-off place was brought as the object of his (Dhruva's) organ of touch by the wind for ever.

29. The entire range of sounds (words) was placed under the disposal of his (Dhruva's) ears by the firmament too, the quality whereof is sound, because he was bent upon propitiating Dhruva.

30. Propitiated day by day by the five elements too, he

considered penance alone greater than everything else with his mind dedicated unto Govinda.

31. Due to the meditation on (Lord Viṣṇu) having the chest embellished with the jewel Kaustubha and clad in yellow silk garments, the universe was seen by the prince fully radiant and resplendent.

32-36. Afraid of his penance, Indra became excessively worried. 'If Dhruva were to desire my position, he would have certainly seized it. The group of the celestial damsels is capable of nullifying the practice of restraint by (grown up) recluses. They are not powerful in regard to a boy, though they are so in regard to youth. What shall I do? There are two assistants of mine in destroying the austerities of saints, viz., lust and anger. They are not powerful in regard to the child Dhruva. Only one means of mine will be effective on this child. I shall send terrible hosts of evil spirits to frighten him. In his childish weakness, he will be frightened by the evil spirits and will abandon austerities surely.'

Deciding thus, Vāsava sent the host of evil spirits.

37. A certain evil spirit of awful teeth resembling a bear in every limb, with a long neck like that of a camel rushed at that child.

38. A certain evil spirit with the face of a tiger perched itself on the lofty body of an elephant. It opened its gruesome mouth widely and rushed at him roaring frequently.

39. Hurriedly chewing a piece of flesh, a certain spirit of hideous fangs, angrily rushed at him as though looking at him and threatening him.

40. Tearing up the high banks with the sharp tips of his horns and rending the ground with his hoofs, a great bull bellowed at him.

41. Assuming the form of a serpent, a certain spirit of terrible hood spreading out, and dangling and rolling a pair of tongues hissed very near him.

42. A certain spirit in the form of a buffalo hurled boulders with the tips of his horns and lashed the ground with his tail. Breathing furiously, he approached Dhruva.

43. Having a pair of thighs resembling palm trees partially burned by forest fire, a certain spirit tried to frighten him opening his mouth widely.

44. With his hairs struggling against the clouds, a spirit with a long, lean belly and sunken tawny eyes theatened him.

45. Holding a dagger in his (right hand) and a skull in his left, a certain spirit with his face cut, rushed at the child, roaring and whistling fiercely.

46. Holding a huge *Sāla* tree and making hideous din, a certain spirit rushed at him like the god of Death holding a stout staff.

47. Possessing the huge mouth of a tiger, a place of meeting of pitch darkness, resembling the cave of the god of Death, a certain spirit rushed at him.

48. Assuming the form of an owl, a spirit tried to frighten Dhruva with awful hissing noises making the heart quiver.

49. A female ogress brought someone's crying child and drank the blood from its bowels and chewed the bone, as though it was a lotus stalk.

50. She continued the chewing saying "O Dhruva, I am thirsty. I will drink your blood too after chewing your bones like those of this boy."

51. A certain female evil spirit brought grass and wood and scattered them all around; she then kindled a forest fire rendered more fierce by a violent gust of wind.

52. Assuming the form of a vampire, a certain ogress split trees and rocks and blocked the path of the firmament causing it to quake very much.

53. Another one took the form of Sunīti. Glancing in the direction of the boy from far off, she lamented a lot in great misery beating her breasts frequently.

54. Deceitfully she expressed cajoling words of sympathy and affection.

55. "O dear one, you are my sole refuge. But the god of Death wants to kill me. Oh, you are indeed endearing to those who seek refuge in you! My life is almost gone. Save me. Save me.

56. I am tired wandering over every village, every city, every pathway in every forest and mountain, in every hermitage eager to see you.

57. O boy, ever since you set out for the sake of the penance, from that very day I too have come out in your quest.

58. O my child, I am also distressed in the same way as

you were at the mischievous words of my co-wife. Her words scorch me like a fire.

59. I never sleep nor keep alert and awake. I never eat or drink. I simply meditate upon you like a Yoginī in my grief of separation from you.

60. With my eyes bereft of sleep, I, the most unfortunate one, do not see even in dream your face that is delightful to me in every respect.

61. I am too eager to dispel the distress in my separation, yet I do not even see the rising moon, the representative of your face.

62. The unarranged forelocks of my hairs have spread over my ears. Hence the cuckoo chirping sweetly like your lisping words has not been heard by me.

63. Nor has the wind, exquisitely sweet, due to the contact with your body, been embraced by me with adequate rest, O Dhruva, as I am excessively agitated (due to motherly affection).

64. What countries, what rivers, what mountains, O Dhruva, have not been traversed by me walking all the way, despite the fact that I am the wife of a king?

65. Seeing all these without Dhruva I have been rendered blind. Dear son, assume the status of the supporting staff of a blind one and save me, your nursing mother.

66. O dear one, foremost among human beings, where are those tender limbs of yours? Where is this austere penance that can be achieved only by hardy men?

67. O dear one, you are free from sins. What else, more than the status of the prince of an emperor, is sought to be achieved through this penance?

68. O boy, at this age of yours, you ought to play with toys befitting young children along with the other children of your own age.

69. Having reached youth thereafter you ought to be contemplative and become the master of all lores.

70. Thereafter, attaining the maturity of youth, you will enjoy many pleasures through women, garlands, sandalpaste etc. fulfilling the obligations of the senses and sensual objects.

71. Beget many virtuous sons of very excellent conduct, transfer your royal glory and assets to them and then you do

carry on your austerities and penance.

72. Why this extraordinary effort in respect of penance now itself in your boyhood? When can the fire on the dry cowdung sticking to the toe reach the top of the head?

73. Distress of austerity should be undergone by one assailed by an enemy, or by one whose honour has been slighted by someone or by one who has lost all prosperity. Are you one of these? If so, which?"

74. On hearing the words "Distress of austerity should be undergone by one whose honour has been slighted," Dhruva heaved a deep sigh breathing hot air out and then meditated on Hari in his heart.

75. He did not speak to his mother. He did not have any fear from the evil spirits. Once again Dhruva engaged himself in meditating on Acyuta.

76. The host of other evil spirits with many hideous things worn as ornaments showed many gestures to terrify him but saw the discus Sudarśana all round.

77. (Evidently) it had been sent there for protecting him from the demons and ogresses. It had the refulgence of a halo all round. Its lustre was exalted like that of the Sun.

78-80. The host of evil spirits saw the dazzling discus Sudarśana, excessively brilliant, according protection to Dhruva from all sides even as he sat there with a steady heart with his mind dedicated to Govinda. He appeared to be like the seedling of austerities that burst open the ground and grew up. The host of evil spirits themselves became frightened. They were disappointed in their evil intentions. They bowed down to Dhruva of fixed resolution and went away along the path they had come.

81. Just as a thundering cloud becomes scattered and ineffective after being shaken by wind (so also the host of evil spirits dispersed).

82. Then, O Brāhmaṇa, all the terrified heaven-dwellers held discussion with Indra and hurriedly sought refuge in Brahmā.

83. They bowed down to and eulogized him, the Grandfather (of the worlds). On being asked for the reason of their visit and finding a suitable opportunity for their submission they did so.

The Devas said:

84. O Dhātṛ (Creator), all the residents of the three worlds have been distressed by the extremely brilliant son of Uttanāpāda, who is performing a penance.

85. O dear one, we do not perfectly comprehend the intention and desire of Dhruva. From among us whose office he is eager to capture by performing the great penance. (We have not understood.)

86. On being informed thus by the Devas, the Four-faced Lord laughed and replied to them who were gripped with fear in their minds from Dhruva.

Brahmā said:

87. O Suras, there is no need to fear Dhruva who is desirous of a firm and fixed position. All of you may go without needless excitement and mental anguish. He is not desirous of your offices.

88. No one need be afraid of that devotee of the Supreme Lord. Those who are the devotees of the Supreme Lord will not certainly be the tormentors of others.

89. After propitiating Viṣṇu, the Lord of Devas, and obtaining his cherished desire he will make your own positions still more secure.

90. On hearing these words uttered by Brahmā, the Devas bowed down to him and departed in great delight.

91. Seeing him to be fully resolved in his mind and realizing that the boy had no other refuge, Lord Nārāyaṇa approached him seated on his vehicle Tārkṣya (Garuḍa) and said:

Śrī Viṣṇu said:

92. O boy of great dignity and fortune, I am delighted. O child of good holy vows, choose your boons. Desist from proceeding ahead in this penance. You are already distressed with a long drawn (austerity).

93. On hearing the nectarlike words, he opened his eyes

and saw a massive column of the brilliant splendour of sapphire gems.

94. It appeared like a lake expanding over heaven and earth with full-blown clusters of blue lotuses.

95. Dhruva then saw the entire space between heaven and earth blessed with the benign glances of Goddess Lakṣmī.

96. There in front of him, Lord Kṛṣṇa clad in yellow garments was visualized by him; he had the splendour of the lightning streak in the midst of rising clouds.

97. The Garuḍa-vehicled Lord was seen by Dhruva like the sky resembling a whet-stone having the golden Meru for the testing.

98. He saw Hari clad in yellow garments like the dark blue sky embellished with the moon.

99. He prostrated before the Lord stretching himself like a long staff. He rolled and cried like a sad child seeing its father after a long time.

100-102. The Lord who had been continuously eulogized by Nārada, Sananda, Sanaka, Sanatkumāra and other Yogins, who is the most excellent one among Yogins and whose eyes resembled a wet lotus, being full of tears of kindness, raised Dhruva with his hand. The discus-bearing Hari touched his soiled limbs with his hands rendered firm by wielding the arms incessantly.

103. At the touch of the Lord of Devas, splendid flow of words issued from his mouth. Dhruva eulogized Hari thus:

CHAPTER TWENTYONE

The Story of Dhruva: Dhruva's Eulogy of Viṣṇu

Dhruva said:

1. Hail to you, O Hiraṇyagarbha ('the support of the Golden Egg'—Comm.), the performer of the function of all (sorts, e.g. ādhyātmika, ādhibhautika) creation, one who has gold as his semen virile, the bestower of gold!

2. Obeisance to you, the Lord in the form of Hara, the

cause of the annihilation of all living beings. Obeisance to the controller of all living beings, the soul of all great living beings.

3. Obeisance to you, the cause of sustenance, Viṣṇu (the all-pervader), the powerful one. Obeisance to Kṛṣṇa, the destroyer of thirst (for worldly affairs), the endurer of the great burden (of the earth as the Divine Boar),

4. Obeisance to you in the form of the forest conflagration for the great forest of Daityas, the axe that fells down the trees in the form of Daityas. Obeisance to you holding the Śārṅga bow in your hand.

5. O holder of the mace, obeisance to you whose fingers are firmly engrossed in holding the Kaumodakī mace; obeisance to the holder of (the sword) Nandaka, for the destruction of the great Danujas.

6. Obeisance to you, the Consort of Śrī (Goddess of Fortune); obeisance to the wielder of the discus. Obeisance to the great soul in the form of the Divine Boar supporting the Earth.

7. Obeisance to you, to the holder of the lotus in the hand, the lover of Goddess Lakṣmī; obeisance to the Lord in the form of Fish etc. Hail to you wearing the gem Kaustubha on the chest!

8. Obeisance to the Lord who can be comprehended only through the Vedānta; obeisance to the Lord having Śrīvatsa; obeisance to the Lord in the form of the Guṇas; to one who is with and without attributes.

9. Obeisance to you having the lotus in the navel; obeisance to the holder of Pāñcajanya conch. O Vāsudeva, obeisance to you, the delighter of Devakī.

10. Obeisance to Pradyumna, to you Aniruddha; obeisance to the killer of Cāṇūra.

11. O Dāmodara, O Hṛṣīkeśa , O Govinda, Acyuta, Mādhava, Upendra, O enemy of Kaiṭabha, O slayer of Madhu, O Adhokṣaja!

12. Obeisance to you, Nārāyaṇa, the destroyer of (the demon) Naraka, the destroyer of sins; obeisance to you, Vāmana; bow to Hari, Śauri.

13. Obeisance to you, the infinite one; obeisance to the Lord with Ananta (Serpent Śeṣa) for your couch; obeisance to you the Consort of Rukmiṇī, to the suppressor of Rukmi.

14. Obeisance to you, the slayer of Caidya (Śiśupāla); obeisance to the enemy of Asuras, the enemy of the enemies of Suras,

O Mukunda of great bliss; obeisance to the favourite darling of the cowherd Nanda.

15. Obeisance to you the lotus-eyed one, the destroyer of leading Danujas. Bow to the Lord in the form of the cowherd, to the player on the flute.

16. Repeated obeisance to the lover of the cowherdesses. Obeisance to Rāma Rāghava, the leading member of the family of Raghu, to the slayer of Keśin.

17. Bow to you, the enemy of Rāvaṇa, to the bestower of refuge to Bibhīṣaṇa, to the unborn one, to the victory incarnate, the expert in fighting.

18. Obeisance to the form of Kāla (Time) such as Kṣaṇa (moment) etc., the assumer of various forms, the wielder of the Śārṅga bow, the mace and the discus, the suppressor of multitudes of Daityas.

19. Obeisance to the powerful one, to Balabhadra, to the Lord dear to the enemy of the demon Bala. O destroyer of the sacrifice of Bali, obeisance to you, the bestower of boons on your devotees.

20. O Lord who tore the chest of Hiraṇyakaśipu; O Lord fond of battles; O Lord benevolent to Brāhmaṇas; O Lord causing the welfare of cows and Brāhmaṇas!

21. Obeisance to you, righteousness personified. Bow to one possessing the Sattva quality. Obeisance to the thousand-headed one, to the Supreme Puruṣa.

22. O thousand (i.e., innumerable)-eyed one; O thousand-footed one, obeisance to the thousand rayed one. O thousand-formed one, O Consort of Śrī, O deity of sacrifice, obeisance to you.

23. O Lord whose form can be comprehended only through the Vedas, O lord to whom Vedas are dear, O lord of the form of knowledge (and consciousness), obeisance to you, the propounder of the Vedas, to the Lord treading the path of those of good conduct.

24. Obeisance to you, the son of Vikuṇṭhā; obeisance to the Lord residing in Vaikuṇṭha; obeisance to the Lord moving about on Garuḍa; obeisance to the Lord heard (and sung about) in the Vedas.

25. Obeisance to you, O Viṣvaksena, O Janārdana, identified with the universe; obeisance to Trivikrama, to the truthful

one, to the Lord fond of truth.

26. Obeisance to Keśava; obeisance to you, to the controller of Māyā, to the singer of the Vedas. Obeisance to you, austerity personified, to the bestower of the benefit of austerity.

27. Obeisance to the Lord worthy of eulogy, eulogy personified; to the Lord interested in the eulogy of devotees. Obeisance to you in the form of the Vedas, to the Lord pleased with the conduct of life in accordance with the Vedas.

28. Obeisance to you, identified with the egg-born beings (birds); obeisance to you born of the sweat (lice etc.); obeisance to you in the form of the uterus-born; obeisance to you in the form of the *Udbhijja* (germinating plants).

29. Among the Devas you are in the form of Indra*; among the Planets you are the Sun; among the worlds you are Satyaloka; among the oceans you are the Milky Ocean.

30. Among rivers you are the heavenly Gaṅgā; among lakes you are the Mānasa lake; among mountains you are Himavān; among cows you are the wish-yielding divine cow.

31. Among metals you are gold; among precious stones you are crystal; among flowers you are blue lotus; among trees and plants you are Tulasī (Basil) Plant.

32. Among the stones worthy of the worship of everyone, you are the Sālagrāma stone; among the holy salvation-giving places you are Kāśī and among the sacred regions you are Prayāga.

33. Among colours you are the white; among bipeds you are the Brāhmaṇa; O Lord, you are Garuḍa among birds; of all activities you are speech.

34. Among the Vedas you are of the form of the Upaniṣads; among Mantras you are Praṇava (Om); among the letters you are the letter A and among sacrificial beings you are one of the form of Soma.

35. Among the blazing ones you are fire; you are forgiveness (of Earth) among those who have forbearance; among donors you are the presiding deity of Parjanya (rain-bearing cloud); among the sacred ones you are the greatest.

36. Among all weapons you are the bow; you are wind

---

* Cf. Bhagavad Gītā, Ch. X, for the Vibhūtis described here in vv 29-43.

among those moving with velocity; among sense-organs you are the mind; among the fearless ones you are hand (since at the time of physical danger, all raise their hands in resistance).

37. Among those who pervade you are the firmament; among the souls, you are the Supreme Soul. O Lord, among all daily rites you are the Sandhyā Prayer (performed at dawn and dusk).

38. Among holy sacrifices you are the horse sacrifice; among gifts you are the gift of freedom from fear; among acquisitions you are the birth of a son; O Lord, among seasons you are the spring.

39. Amog the Ages you are the first one (Kṛta); among the lunar days you are the New Moon (Kuhū); among constellations you are Puṣya and among all holy days you are the transit of the Planets (from one zodiac to another).

40. Among Yogas (combinations of Planets, stars etc.) you are Vyatīpāta; among the grasses you are the Kuśa grass; among all the efforts or human interests (Puruṣārthas) you are salvation, O Lord.

41. O unborn Lord, among all purposeful activities you are the intention to be righteous; among all trees you are Aśvattha and among the creepers you are the Soma creeper.

42. Among all purifying expedients you are Prāṇāyāma; among all Liṅgas you are the glorious Viśveśvara Liṅga, the bestower of everything.

43. Among all friendly ones you are the spouse; among all kinsmen you are Dharma (pious activity). O Nārāyaṇa, there is nothing other than you in the whole world including the mobile and immobile beings.

44. You alone are the mother; you are the father; you are the son; you are a great asset; you alone are the achievement of all happiness; you are the life span; you are the lord of life.

45. That is the holy discourse where your name (is sung); that is the genuine mind which is dedicated to you; that is the real activity which is offered unto you; that is the penance wherein you are remembered.

46. That wealth of the rich which is spent for your sake is the pure one; that alone is the time fruitfully spent when you are adored, O Jiṣṇu.

47. Life is beneficial as long as you are present in the heart; illnesses perish by taking in the holy water (of the worship) of your feet.

48. O Govinda, all great sins (such as Brāhmaṇa killing) incurred in the course of many births become annihilated immediately by uttering (your name) Vāsudeva.

49. Alas, the great delusion of men! Ah! Pity! The blunder of men whereby they slight Vāsudeva and put in effort elsewhere!

50. This alone is conducive to happiness and auspiciousness; this alone is acquisition of wealth; this is the fruit of life viz. the glorification of Dāmodara.

51. There is no greater pious activity apart from Adhokṣaja; there is no wealth greater than Nārāyaṇa; there is no (true) desire apart from Keśava; there is no salvation without Hari.

52. This is the greatest loss, this alone is the greatest harassment, this is the height of bad luck, whereby one does not remember Vāsudeva.

53. What is it that the propitiation of Hari does not achieve? It accords sons, friends, spouses, riches, kingdom, heavenly pleasures and ultimate salvation.

54. It dispels sin, destroys ailments, and controls mental anguishes. It quickly increases piety and accords what is desired.

55. The unwavering meditation on the pair of feet of the Lord is the most excellent thing. Even if it is performed by a sinner and that too casually, it accords the greatest benefit to oneself.

56. The utterance of the name of Hari during very deep meditation will remove even the sins designated as the greatest ones of sinners.

57. Just as a particle of fire when touched even by mistake, causes a burn, so also the name of Hari that slightly touches the lips, dispels sin.

58. If anyone makes his mind quiescent and directs it steadily towards the Consort of Kamalā and practises (meditation) even for a moment, indeed the Goddess of Wealth is steady and firm there (with him).

59. This is the greatest pious practice; this is the greatest austerity; this is the most excellent of all holy spots whereby

one imbibes the water that washes Viṣṇu's feet.

60. O Yajñapuruṣa, he who devoutly takes in the Naivedya offered to you, has become a man of great intellect. It is as good as Puroḍāśa has been regularly taken in by him.

61. If a man takes the water with which the feet of Viṣṇu have been washed in a conchshell and performs the holy ablution with that (it is as good as) he has actually performed the Avabhṛthasnāna (valedictory bath after a holy sacrifice) and he has taken the holy bath in the waters of Gaṅgā.

62. He, by whom a Śālagrāma stone has been worshipped with Tulasī leaves, will be worshipped in the heavenly world with the garlands of divine Pārijāta flowers.

63. Whether he is a Brāhmaṇa, a Kṣatriya, a Vaiśya, a Śūdra or anyone else, one endowed with devotion to Viṣṇu, should be known as the most excellent one among all.

64. If a man sees a devotee with sandalpaste marks[1] of conchshell and discus, wearing a bunch of Tulasī flowers on the head and having marks of Gopīcandana paste over the body, he will be free from all sins. No other sin shall defile him.

65. He who worships everyday twelve stones of Śālagrāma and Dvārāvatīcakra[2] stones(?) is honoured in Vaikuṇṭha.

66. The servants of Yama never approach that house where Tulasī is worshipped everyday.

67. The followers of Yama will never touch one in whose mouth the letters constituting the name of Hari (dwell for ever), whose forehead is marked with Gopīcandana and whose chest is garlanded with Tulasī leaves.

68. If these five things: Gopīcandana clay, Tulasī leaf (plant), conchshell, Śālagrāma and Cakra (discus) are present in any one's house, whence need he be afraid of sins?

69. A person is plundered by Yama in all those Muhūrtas, Kṣaṇas, Kāṣṭhās and Nimeṣas that have been spent without remembering Viṣṇu.

1. The commentator, on the authority of *Bṛhannāradīya Purāṇa*, strongly condemns the branding with red-hot metal pieces the mark of Viṣṇu's arms (conch, discus etc.) on one's body (as is the practice among the followers of Madhva). He emphatically states that marks with sandal or Gopīcandana are prescribed in this Purāṇa.

2. Special types of pebbles from Dvārakā (Comm.)

70. What a great disparity there is between the name of Hari consisting of two syllables and blazing like sparks of fire and the great mass of sins comparable to a heap of cotton!

71. I neither know, nor resort to, nor even remember anyone else leaving Govinda, the highest bliss, Mukunda, the slayer of Madhu.

72. I never bow down to, neither eulogize nor even see with my eyes, neither touch nor approach nor sing about anyone except Hari.

73-74. I see everywhere the dark-complexioned Lord with Śrīvatsa mark on the chest, in waters, on the earth, in nether regions, in wind, in fire and on mountains, among Vidyādharas, Asuras, Suras, Kinnaras, monkeys, human beings, in grass, groups of women, stones, trees, and creepers.

75. You have your residence in the heart of everyone. You alone are the direct witness. Whether without or within, I do not know any other omnipresent being except you.

76. After saying this, O Śivaśarman. Dhruva stopped. With delight evident in his eyes, Lord Viṣṇu spoke to him:

The Lord said:

77. O child Dhruva of wide large eyes, free from sins and having fixed resolve, the desire cherished in your heart has been clearly understood by me.

78. The living beings originate from food; food grows through rain; the Sun is the cause of that rain. O Dhruva, you be the support of the Sun.

79. You will become the pivot of the entire group of Planets, Stars etc., of the system of luminaries that moves about in the firmament for ever.

80. Like a pivotal pillar unto them, controlling them by holding them together with aerial strings, you stay there till the end of the Kalpa and make the luminaries revolve.

81. By propitiating Lord Mahādeva formerly this position was acquired by me. Due to your penance it (the position of Dhruva) has now been given over to you.

82. Some of them remain for a period of four Yugas, O Dhruva, and some for a period of a Manvantara. You will be holding this position for a Kalpa.

83. O Dhruva, can what was not obtained by even Manu, be obtained by other men? That position which is inaccessible to Śakra and others, has been entrusted to you.

84. I have been rendered delighted by this prayer. I shall grant you other boons too; your mother Sunīti too will be near you.

85. If a man recites this excellent prayer with concentration and mental purity during the three Sandhyās, his sin will perish.

86. Undoubtedly Lakṣmī will never leave his house. He will never be separated from his mother, nor will he have any quarrel with any of his kinsmen.

87. This prayer of Dhruva is meritorious and destructive of great sins. Even a Brāhmaṇa-slayer will be freed therefrom. What to speak of other sinners?

88. It will produce great merit. It will accord great riches. It suppresses all harassments and tortures. It destroys great ailments.

89. He who is pure in mind and has great devotion to me, should perform the Japa of this Dhruva prayer which delights me much.

90. He who joyously repeats this prayer attains that benefit which a man usually gets by taking the holy dip in all holy rivers.

91. There are many other eulogies and they do delight me. But they do not merit even a fraction of a sixteenth part of Dhruva's prayer.

92. By listening to this prayer with great faith and joy, a man gets liberated from sins immediately and he shall attain great merit.

93. By reciting Dhruva's prayer a sonless man acquires (begets) a son, a poor man gets wealth and a man without devotion shall become devout.

94. Through this prayer, a man get those benefits which one gets by making many religious gifts and by observing different holy vows.

95. Abandoning all activites, setting aside many of the other Japas, this Dhruva-prayer which accords all desires should be repeated regularly.

Śrībhagavān said:

96. O Dhruva, be attentive. O highly intelligent one, I shall mention what is beneficial to you and whereby this position of yours will become unchangeable.

97. Formerly, I was desirous of going to the splendid Vārāṇasī where Viśveśvara himself, the cause of salvation, is ever present.

98. It is there that Viśveśvara whispers into the ears of dying beings that Mantra which is capable of uprooting all (binding) Karmas.

99. There is only one means of remedy for the misery of the mundane world that accords all sorts of troubles and that is Kāśikā, the Ānandabhūmikā ('the blissful holy spot').

100. The (discriminatory) feeling "this is beautiful, this is not", is the seed of the great tree of misery. When that is burnt down by means of the fire of Kāśī, where is the occasion for misery?

101. That Ānandakānana (Kāśī) is the spot of the greatest bliss; it is through it that everything worth attaining is attained and there remains no cause of regret thereafter.

102. If a man resides elseswhere after forsaking the Ānandakānana of Śaṁbhu, the site of divine nectar, whence can he hope to have the rise (outcome) of happiness?

103. It is better to go a-begging in Kāśī in the streets abounding in Cāṇḍāla houses with a bowl in the hands, rather than reign over a kingdom elsewhere without any enemy.

104. From the city of Vaikuṇṭha, I regularly go to Kāśī worshipped by the entire universe, in order to adore Viśveśa worthy of being worshipped by the universe.

105. That supreme Maheśāna who gave (me) Discus Sudarśana is the cause of the great power in me, capable of protecting the three worlds.

106. Formerly, Hara created a Cakra arising out of the lines at the tip of the big toe and slew the Daitya Jālandhara who made even me tremble.

107. That Cakra has been obtained by me by adoring the Lord with the lotus-like eye. This Cakra named Sudarśana suppresses hosts of Daityas.

108. In order to protect you by driving away the evil spirits, that Cakra was sent by me ahead and then only have I come here.

109. Just now, I will go to Kāśī for visiting Viśveśvara. Today there is a great pilgrimage held in the month of Kārttika. It accords great merit.

110. If a man takes his holy bath in the north-flowing (Gaṅgā) and visits Viśveśa on the fourteenth day in the month of Kārttika, he never comes back (to the human world of misery).

111. After saying this and making the extremely delighted Dhruva ride on Garuḍa, Hari reached immediately Vārāṇasī where Smarahara (Lord Śiva) is present.

112-113. After reaching the outskirts of Pañcakrośī (limit of ten miles perimeter), Lord Janārdana got down from Garuḍa. Holding Dhruva by the hand, he had the ablution at Maṇikarṇī and worshipped Viśveśa. Then desirous of doing something beneficial to Dhruva, the Lord said to him:

114. "Scrupulously instal a Liṅga here itself in the holy spot of Avimukta, so that you will have the never-ending merit establishing you in the three worlds.

115. The benefit that is acquired by installing a million Liṅgas elsewhere, is obtained by installing a single Liṅga here.

116. If anyone repairs the ruins here due to lapse of time, that benefit does not come to an end even at the time of Pralaya.

117. He who does not grudge in spending money here and building a palace (to Śiva), has actually made a gift of the entire Meru extending to a million Yojanas.

118. If anyone digs wells, tanks or lakes in accordance with his capacity in this holy spot, his merit becomes a hundred million times more than what is obtained by doing it elsewhere.

119. If a man grows a beautiful flower-garden here for the purpose of worship, the benefit acquired by him for each flower is more than that of a golden flower.

120. If anyone makes a Brahmapurī (a colony of Brāhmaṇas) here and hands it over to Brāhmaṇas along with the arrangement for fooding for a year, listen to the benefit he will get.

121. The waters of the ocean may be dried up. The *Trasareṇus* (dust particles) of the earth may perish, but there is no destruction of the merit of that devotee staying in Śivaloka.

122. If anyone builds monasteries and hands them over to saints along with sustenance of life, he too will have the benefit said before.

123. After performing great and meritorious rites, a man must dedicate the fruit thereof to Viśveśvara. He never returns to the terrible ocean of worldly existence.

124. It is sung about here in this world that I am Ananta, but the end of the good qualities of Kāśī is not obtained even by me.

125. Hence, O Dhruva, one should scrupulously resort to permanent weal at Kāśī. The benefit of weal acquired by man from Kāśī is everlasting.

The Gaṇas said:

126-127. After advising Dhruva thus, the Garuḍa-emblemed Lord went away. Dhruva then installed a Liṅga near Vaidyanātha. He built a great palace and made a holy pit in front of it. After worshipping Viśveśvara, he became contented and went home.

128. By worshipping Dhruveśvara and offering water libations in Dhruvakuṇḍa, a man attains Dhruva's world endowed with all pleasures and enjoyments.

129. He who reads, narrates and makes others read the great narrative of Dhruva, reaches Viṣṇu's world and becomes a favourite of Viṣṇu.

130. Remembering even casually the story of Dhruva, a man shall attain great merit. He will never be assailed by sins.

CHAPTER TWENTYTWO

Brahmā Praises Kāśī

Śivaśarmā said:

1. O Gaṇas, I have become contented and pleased on listening to this story of Dhruva. It is very charming and destructive of great sins. It causes one to wonder and produces merit.

Agastya said:

2. Even as the Brāhmaṇa said this, the aerial chariot of

a speed rivalling that of the wind, reached Maharloka, more miraculous than the heavenly world.

3. Then on seeing that region enveloped in refulgence all round, the Brāhmaṇa said to the Gaṇas again, "What a charming world is this!"

4-6. Then they said to the Brāhmaṇa: "O highly intelligent one, listen. This is that Maharloka which is more wonderful and mysterious than the heavenly world. People who have dispelled their sins by their austerities live here for one Kalpa. By meditating on Viṣṇu, all their miseries have subsided. Excellent Suras practising the great Yoga (of the identity of the Supreme Soul with the individual soul) see this region full of refulgence by means of genuine meditation and they stay here."

Agastya said:

7. O dear one, even as the attendants of the Lord said this, the aerial chariot took them to Janaloka within half a moment.

8. It is there that the sinless mental sons of Brahmā, leading Yogins (like) Sanandana and others, who have sublimated their sex-instinct (*ūrdhvaretasaḥ*) dwell.

9. There are other Yogins too residing here. They are extremely pure. They never waver from celibacy. They are free from all Dvandvas (opposing pairs) like heat and cold.

10. Tapoloka which is beyond Janaloka was brought within their view by that aerial chariot that was proceeding at a speed equalling that of the mind.

11. Vairajas (created by Hiraṇyagarbha) (a class of Devas) free from thirst (or fire ending the world), reside there. They have their minds directed and their actions dedicated to Vāsudeva.

12. Those who have conquered their sense-organs and have propitiated Govinda through their penance, attain this Tapoloka and stay there free from all ambitions and desires.

13-21. Those who have pursued the following kinds of austerities in the world, live in Tapoloka and have the same span of life as Brahmā: those who sustain themselves by means of pieces of grains lying scattered on the ground; those who use their teeth alone as the mortar for cleansing husks; sages and devotees using stone for breaking the grains; those who eat only decaying leaves scattered on the ground; those who perfom penance in the midst of five fires during summer; those who lie on bare rough ground during rainy season; those who spend half of Hemanta and Śiśira (i.e., winter) staying in water during the nights; those ascetics who drink only the drops of water from the tips of Kuśa grass when thirsty; those who when very hungry take in only wind; those who touch the ground with the tips of their toes while performing penance; those who keep their hands lifted up; those who keep looking at the Sun; those who stand motionlessly on a single foot; those who never breathe during the day (i.e., practice Kumbhaka type of breath control—Comm.); who exhale (breath) throughout the month (Comm.); those who have taken the vow of fasting for a whole month; those who have similar vows for four months altogether; those who drink water at the end of every season (i.e., two months); those who observe fast for a period of six months; those who wink their eyes once in a year; those who quench their thirst with rain water; those who resemble posts and give the deer the pleasure of scratching when their bodies itch; those who have nests of birds within the forest-like growth of matted hairs; those round whose limbs anthill has grown; those who are mere skeletons with sinews tying the bones together; those whose bodies are entwined all round by spreading creepers; those round whose limbs even plants grow and remain there for a long period. Those ascetics who have subjected their bodies to various sorts of torture stay here without any fear from anywhere.

22. Even as that meritorious soul (i.e., Śivaśarmā) was listening to these words issuing from the mouths of those two attendants, the excessively refulgent Satyaloka came within his view.

23. Those two attendants then hurriedly got down from the aerial chariot and, along with Śivaśarmā, bowed down to the Creator of all the worlds.

Brahmā said:

24. O attendants, this Brāhmaṇa is intelligent and a master of Vedas and Vedāṅgas. He is proficient in the practice of the code of conduct laid down in Smṛtis. He is averse to sinful activities.

25. O Brāhmaṇa of great intellect, I know you, O Śivaśarman, O dear one, you have done well in abandoning your life in a holy spot.

26. Whatever is seen by you will quickly pass off. I am creating them again and again after *Pralaya* (annihilation).

27. I am creating everything upto Vairāja and Hara annihilates them at every step. Nothing need be said about men who are insignificant like mosquitos and mortal by nature.

28. Out of the four categories of living beings (e.g. the egg-born, the sweat-born etc.) for men there is one good advantage in Bhāratavarṣa, a great land of religious rituals (the advantage is mentioned in v 35).

29-35. After conquering the fickle sense-organs along with the mind, after eschewing greed which pervades all inherent qualities; after dispelling thoughtfully lust that destroys the whole of righteousness, that removes collection of wealth and that brings about greying of hairs and old age; after courageously overcoming the enemy in the form of anger that removes power of penance, reputation, glory and even the body and that leads one along the path of darkness; after abandoning forever arrogance that accords the sole basis for erring, that is the sole refuge of all faults and that turns back all riches; after eschewing egotism that causes dishonour everywhere and that makes one endeavour to defame and blame even good persons; after giving up delusion that causes the growth of excessive hatred, that benumbs intellect and renders it powerless, that utterly blinds the people and that guides one to 'eternal darkness' (a hell of that name viz., Andhatāmisra) people can climb the steps of Dharma (righteousness) that is laid down by Śrutis, Smṛtis and Purāṇās and that is followed by great men and then they come here with care. (This is the advantage mentioned in v 28 above, that human beings can get.)

36. O Brāhmaṇa, all the heaven-dwellers desire and seek the land of pious rites (*Karmabhūmi*), because therein all these people enjoy what is earned by them at different lower and higher levels.

37. Nowhere in the entire 'Cosmic Egg' is there a land on a par with Āryāvarta, a city similar to Kāśī and a Liṅga equal to Viśveśvara.

38. There are many types of Svargas free from non-hap-

piness (i.e., are full of happiness). All of them are the sole outcome of merits (achieved). They are endowed with all kinds of riches and prosperities.

39. (It is the belief) that there is nothing in the entire 'Cosmic Egg' more charming than the heavenly world. All people endeavour to attain Svarga through penance, gifts, holy vows and other things.

40. "The nether regions are better and more charming than even Svarloka." So said Nārada in the open assembly of heaven-dwellers, when he returned from Pātālas.

41. With which can Pātāla be compared, where the jewels set in the ornaments on the limbs of Nāgas are highly refulgent, splendid and very pleasing?

42. Pātāla that is resplendent with the damsels of Daityas and Dānavas, delights everyone. Who is not delighted with it, even if he be a man devoid of attachment?

43. During day-time rays of the Sun merely spread lustre there and not fierce heat. During night rays of the moon spread only light and do not increase chillness.

44. (Hence) the time that passess off is not known by Danujas and others (i.e., they are not aware of it).

The forests and rivers are very charming. The lakes contain excellent waters.

45-47. The following things are enjoyed by the denizens of the nether regions: sweet chirping sounds of the male cuckoo, good garments, clean clothes, very charming ornaments, sweet scents and unguents, the sounds of flute, lute etc. that captivate the ears. These and other excellent things worthy of being enjoyed are duly enjoyed by the Dānavas, Daityas and Serpents residing in the interior of Pātāla. The great Liṅga called Hāṭakeśa bestows all cherished desires.

48. O Brāhmaṇa, the continent called Ilāvṛta that is stationed nestling within the ridges of Meru (surrounded by its peaks) is more charming than Pātāla.

49. O Brāhmaṇa, there meritorious persons are always enjoying all pleasures. Fawn-eyed damsels are ever youthful there.

50. This is called Bhogabhūmi ('Place of enjoyment') acquired and enjoyed by people like you by exchanging their merits in view of their having abandoned their bodies in the holy spots on the earth.

51. They are no speakers of falsehood. They are not devoid of sons, wives etc. They used to spend their happiness, span of life and hoarded wealth for the sake of helping others.

52. There are many islands and continents stationed within oceans. But nowhere on the whole surface of the earth is there a continent like Jaṁbūdvīpa.

53. There are the nine Varṣas and among them Bhārata is the most excellent. This is called *Karmabhūmi* ('Land of righteous acts'). It is inaccessible even to Devas.

54. The eight (*Varṣas*) including Kiṁpuruṣa and others are the places worthy of being enjoyed by Devas. The heaven-dwellers arrive there from Svargaloka and sport about.

55. The chief of them, Bhāratavarṣa, is nine thousand Yojanas (Yojan = 12 Kms.) in extent. It is situated to the south of Meru.

56. There too the region between Himālaya and Vindhya is the greatest bestower of merit. The region called Antarvedī between the Gaṅgā and the Yamunā is the most excellent of all.

57. Kurukṣetra is superior to all the other holy spots. There too the Naimiṣa forest is the most excellent means of achieving heaven.

58. On the entire earth Tīrtharāja Prāyāga is the most excellent one among all the holy places, even greater than Naimiṣāraṇya.

59. It is the bestower of heaven. It is the bestower of salvation. It is the bestower of all the cherished desires. That great holy place Prayāga is called Tīrtharāja.

60-61. O Brāhmaṇa, all the Yāgas were held in the balance by me for weighing. That holy place is the most excellent one among all holy places. It is the most charming and desirable because it fulfils all desires. That holy place too is held in the balance. On finding the holy place better and more excellent than all the Yāgas well endowed with Dakṣiṇās etc., it was named Prayāga by Hari, Hara and others.

62. By remembering merely the name of Prayāga thrice (a day), no sin can stay anywhere in the body of the person remembering.

63. There are many Tīrthas saving people from sins. They are not capable of giving anything more than redemption from the sins committed.

64. The heap of sins committed in the course of the numerous

previous births cannot be removed adequately by holy vows, Dānas, Japas and penances.

65. Like a tree assailed by wind that mass of sins begins to tremble in the limbs of that man of auspicious nativity, who has intended to go to Tīrtharāja.

66. Then it begins to set out and go to another place from the body of the man who has traversed half the distance and who has resolved firmly in the mind to go to Prayāga.

67. If fortunately the Tīrtharāja comes within the vision of that noble soul, that collection of sins begins to flee like darkness at sunrise.

68. In the body consisting of the seven *Dhātus* (constituent elements) the sins collect together in the hairs. On being shaved they clear out.

69. After becoming free of sins thus, the devotee should take his holy bath in the *Sitāsita* (i.e. the confluence of the white Gaṅgā and the black Yamunā.) Thus he achieves whatever he desires and not otherwise.

70. He attains enormous quantity of merits and meritorious enjoyment of pleasures as desired. Due to that merit he attains heaven. If he is devoid of desires, be attains salvation.

71. If anyone takes the holy dip eschewing other desires but desiring salvation, he too attains salvation from the Tīrtharāja, the bestower of all desires.

72. It is certain that in the great Varṣa named Bhārata, if anyone leaves off the Tīrtharāja and desires anything from elsewhere, he shall not attain his desire.

73. O Brāhmaṇa, I do not know of any distinction between Satyaloka and Prayāga. Those who perform excellent rites there become the residents of my world.

74-75. No other holy place should be resorted to by men desirous of (visiting) holy places.

O excellent Brāhmaṇa, the difference between Prayāga, the Tīrtharāja, and other places in the world is like the difference between a king and a servant of another man. Only an example (of comparison) is cited between Prayāga and other holy spots.

76. If anyone casts off his life here in this holy spot somehow, he does not incur the sin of suicide. He shall achieve everything desired.

77. If, O Brāhmaṇa, the bones of any fortunate man re-

main here, he will never have even an iota of sorrow in any of his births.

78. Prayāga should be duly resorted to, certainly in accordance with the injunctions of a Brāhmaṇa, by a person desirous of performing expiatory rites for the sins of Brāhmaṇa-slaughter etc.

79. O eminent Brāhmaṇa, why say more? The holy spot *Sitāsita* (Prayāga), the most excellent one in the entire world, should be resorted to by one desirous of acquiring great rise in prosperity.

80. By terminating the mortal body at Kāśī, one gets salvation without effort more than from even Prayāga, the lord of all Tīrthas, in all the world.

81. Undoubtedly Avimukta is more charming than even Prayāga, because Viśveśvara is directly presiding over it.

82. Nothing anywhere in the entire Cosmic Sphere is more charming than Avimukta, the great holy spot presided over by Viśveśa.

83. This holy spot Avimukta is away from the middle of the Cosmic Egg to the extent of five Krośas (1 Krośa = 3 Kms.), though it is in the centre of the Cosmic Egg.

84. As and when the water of the vast ocean rises up (at the time of Pralaya), the Lord lifts up the holy spot from the Pralaya water-level.

85. O Brāhmaṇa, this holy spot rests on the tip of the trident of Lord Śiva in the intermediate region without touching the ground. Men of deluded intellect do not perceive it.

86. There is perpetual Kṛtayuga here. There is great festivity here forever. There is no defect or adverse condition in the hermitage of Viśveśvara, caused by the rise or setting of the Planets.

87. There is perpetual Saumyāyana (the gentle transit i.e. the northern transit of the Sun) there; there is auspiciousness forever, where Viśveśvara is stationed.

88. O Brāhmaṇa, Kāśī should not be considered on a par with the thousands of cities that exist on the surface of the earth. It is superior to (higher than) the fourteen worlds.

89. O eminent Brāhmaṇa, fourteen worlds have been created by me. But the creator of this city is Lord Viśveśvara himself.

90. Formerly Yama performed a very severe penance for

a long time. He acquired authority over all the three worlds, excepting the city of Vārāṇasī.

91. All the activities of the entire world consisting of mobile and immobile beings are within the ambit of the knowledge (i.e., record) of Citragupta and not so in the case of the residents of Kāśī.

92. O excellent Brāhmaṇa, the messengers of Yama have no right of entry anywhere within the city of Kāśī. The Gaṇas of Rudra stand guard there.

93. Viśveśa himself is the controller of those who give up their bodies at Kāśī. Kālabhairava is the chastiser of those who commit sins there.

94. No sin should be committed there. Torture from Rudras is highly terrible. Oh, the state of being a Rudrapiśāca is extremely unbearable, more than the sufferings in hell.

95. If the mind is bent upon committing a sin, may it be comfortably perpetrated elsewhere. The earth is very vast.

96. Even a lustful creature avoids its mother. Kāśī alone is to be avoided by a committer of sin if he seeks salvation.

97. Kāśī should not be resorted to by a person habituated to scandalise others, and by one who desires adultery with another man's wife. Where is Kāśī and where is that hell? (What a great difference between the two!)

98. Those who always seek wealth here through *Pratigraha* (accepting monetary gifts), or others' wealth through fraudulent means, should keep away from Kāśī. Kāśī should not be resorted to by those men.

99. All activities causing affliction to others should always be avoided at Kāśī. If that is persisted in, of what avail is the residence at Kāśī of the evil-minded one?

100. If the people adore other deities abandoning devotion to Viśveśvara, they should not at all reside here. It is the capital city of the Lord wielding Pināka.

101. Avimukta should not be resorted to, O Brāhmaṇa, by those men who seek wealth and those who seek sexual enjoyment, because this is the holy spot of salvation.

102. Vārāṇasī should not be resorted to by those who are engaged in censuring Śiva, those who ridicule the Vedas and those who are against the conduct of life laid down in the Vedas.

103. Kāśī is not conducive to the spiritual achievement of

those who think of harassing others, those who are jealous of others and those who torment others.

104. Even the talk of salvation is irrelevant in the case of those of evil action and mentality who do not praise Kāśī (even) in their minds.

105. Without knowledge there is no salvation anywhere in the world, and that knowledge cannot be got through vows and rites including Cāndrāyaṇa.

106-109. Knowledge is not properly gained by any of these means: through gifts, of which *Tulāpuruṣa* (that is making gifts of things equal in weight to the donor) is the chief one even if they are done with faith, even if they are made in accordance with the injunctions, even if they are made over to the deserving persons at the proper place and time. (Knowledge is not obtained) through activities of restraint such as vow of celibacy etc., through worships etc., through severe austerities causing emaciation of the body, O excellent Brāhmaṇa.

(It cannot be gained) through the Japas of great Mantras imparted by preceptors, through study of the Vedas as laid down, nor through scrupulous maintenance of the holy fire.

Knowledge is not obtained through service done to preceptors, through Śrāddhas or through the adoration of the deities, nor through different kinds of pilgrimages.

110. Without Yoga there is no knowledge and Yoga is meditation on *Tattvārtha* i.e., the nature of reality, in accordance with the teachings of the preceptor and repeated practice.

111. There are many obstacles such as Siddhis like Sudūraśravaṇa etc. (ability to hear what is far off — Yogic Siddhis obstruct the ultimate knowledge). Hence knowledge is not acquired in a single birth through Yoga.

112. (But) O righteous one, without penance, Japa and other things, without Yoga, salvation is obtained at Kāśī here itself in a single birth.

113. Merit has been acquired by you of pure mind and intellect at Kāśī. O excellent Brāhmaṇa, the ultimate benefit of that merit is indeed very great.

114. After saying this Brahmā stopped even as the attendants were listening. That Śivaśarman of a noble mind also became very glad.

CHAPTER TWENTYTHREE

Caturbhujābhiṣeka

Śivaśarman said:

1. O Vidhi, O Lord of Satyaloka, O grandfather of all, I am desirous of submitting something but I do not dare to speak out due to fear.

Brahmā said:

2. What you are about to ask, what is lurking in your mind is known to me. You are desirous of asking me about salvation. These two Gaṇas will describe it to you.

3. There is nothing that is not known to these two attendants. They know everything whatever there is in the Cosmic Sphere.

4. After saying this, Brahmā honoured the attendants (and the Brāhmaṇa). After bowing down to the creator of the world, they too started joyfully.

5. Again they got into their vehicle and went towards Vaikuṇṭha. The Gaṇas were asked by that Brāhmaṇa while going ahead:

Śivaśarman said:

6. How far have we come? How much are we yet to go? O fair ones, I am asking another thing too. Be pleased to answer that too.

7. There are seven cities granting salvation, viz., Kāñcī, Avantī, Dvārāvatī, Kāśī, Ayodhyā—the fifth one, Māyāpuri and Mathurā.

8. Leaving off the other six cities, salvation has been stabilized only in Kāśī by the Creator. Then how is it that I have no salvation as yet?

9. I shall be grateful if you please clarify it to me.

On hearing these words of his, the Gaṇas spoke with due respect:

The Gaṇas said:

10. O sinless one, we shall tell you truthfully what you have asked. By Viṣṇu's grace, we two know the past, the present and the future.

11. O Brāhmaṇa, that extent of space which is illuminated by the rays of the Sun and the Moon is called the earth having oceans, mountains and forests.

12. Above those is the sky, extensive and circular. The Sun is two hundred thousand Yojanas above the earth.

13. The Moon is seen a hundred thousand (Yojanas) above the Sun. The region of the stars is a hundred thousand Yojanas above the Moon.

14. Budha (Mercury) is two hundred thousand (Yojanas) above the stellar region. Śukra (Venus) is two hundred thousand Yojanas away from Budha and Bhauma (Mars) is two hundred thousand (Yojanas) away from Venus.

15. Bṛhaspati (Jupiter) is two hundred thousand Yojanas above Bhauma (Mars). Śauri (Saturn) is two hundred thousand Yojanas above Bṛahaspati, the priest of gods.

16. The region of the Seven Sages (Great Bear) is a hundred thousand Yojanas away from Śani. Dhruva (the Pole Star) is stationed a hundred thousand Yojanas away from the Seven Sages.

17. Whatever object there may be which could be reached by walking on foot is known as (included in) Bhūrloka containing oceans, continents, mountains and forests.

18. The space extending from Bhūrloka to the Sun is known as Bhuvarloka. The space from the Sun extending up to Dhruva is known as Svarloka, O Brāhmaṇa.

19. Maharloka is ten million Yojanas above the earth. Janaloka is calculated to be twenty million Yojanas above Bhūrloka by the people.

20. Tapoloka is forty million Yojanas from the earth. Satyaloka is spoken as eighty million Yojanas above the earth.

21. Vaikuṇṭha is above Satya. It is calculated as one hundred and sixty million Yojanas above the earth.

22. It is there that Śrīpati dwells in person. He is the bestower of freedom from fear on all. Kailāsa is sixteen times more than that. It is the abode of Śiva.

23. It is there that Śambhu, the Lord of the universe, dwells

with Pārvatī, Gajāsya (Ganeśa), Skanda and others. He is regarded as *Sakala* (accompanied with Kalā i.e., Pārvatī or in his entire form) and the supreme one.

24. He assumes forms sportingly. The entire universe is a sport of that Lord. He is well-known as Viśveśa (Lord of the universe). This universe obeys his command.

25. He is the controller and chastiser of all. There is no one else to control him. He himself creates living beings. He himself protects them and eats them up (i.e., annihilates them).

26. He is spoken as *Sarvajña* (omniscient) and single. His activities depend upon his will. There is no one to make him act or desist from any activity.

27. He is *Amūrta* (having no visible form) and the supreme Brahman. He is described by Śrutis as *Mūrta* (having visible forms). He is omnipresent. He is eternal. He is the truth. He is devoid of Dvaita (duality).

28. He is far beyond Pradhāna which is beyond Mahat and other (causal) categories. As stated by the Śrutis, he is the blissful form of Brahman.

29. Even the Vedas do not comprehend him; neither Viṣṇu nor Vidhi know him fully. Words recede from him along with the mind after failing to reach him.

30. He is self-known. He is the great brilliant splendour stationed in the heart of everyone, comprehended by Yogins. He cannot be narrated and described. Means of valid knowledge do not comprehend him. Vedas alone know him.

31. Though he appears in many forms, he is formless. Though present everywhere, he is imperceptible. Though he is infinite, he has the form of the annihilator. Knower of all, he is devoid of activities.

32. This is the divine form of that Lord having the crescent moon for embellishment, a throat dark like Tamāla and a sparkling eye in the forehead.

33. The left half dazzles with the form of a woman, Serpent Śeṣa constitutes his splendid armlet and the matted hairs are perpetually washed by the excellent contact with the waves of Gaṅgā.

34. He is refulgent with the limbs smeared with the ashes of the body of Smara (god of Love) and great serpents for ornaments worn round the wonderful body.

35. He moves about in a vehicle in the form of the great Bull; he has the humming and twanging bow Ājagava; he has the upper garment made of elephant hide and five faces.

36. He is surrounded by extremely powerful Gaṇas who can frighten Mahāmṛtyu (the great god of Death); he accords protection to those who seek refuge; he is the cause of salvation unto those who bow down; he is beyond the ken of even mental powers; he is eager to bestow boons.

37. O Brāhmaṇa, his greater and lesser Rudra Forms pervade everything. Actually he is of the form of the Truth and is beyond all forms.

38. Though without shape and form, he has forms. Śiva alone is the cause of enjoyment of pleasures, and attainment of salvation. There is no one other than Śiva who bestows salvation.

39-40. Just as this visible and invisible world consisting of mobile and immobile beings has been handed over to the Consort of Pārvatī by that formless Being, so also the entire universe has been handed over to Viṣṇu by the Consort of Mṛḍānī, O Brāhmaṇa, and he sports about in his unfettered playful activities.

41. What is Śiva, so is Viṣṇu; what as Viṣṇu, so is Śiva; there is no difference at all between Śiva and Viṣṇu.

[Preparation for the Coronation of Viṣṇu (VV 42-52)]

42. At the outset, he summoned all the gods including Brahmā, Vidyādharas, serpents and others, Siddhas, Gandharvas and Cāraṇas.

43. He made a splendid throne on a par with his own throne and made Hari sit thereon. Then he made a charming umbrella.

44. It was beautiful with ten million ribs and designed by Viśvakarman. It was white in colour. The handle was embellished with jewels. Big pearls were suspended from it.

45. A wonderful pot shone above it. It extended to a thousand Yojanas. It was very splendid with all kinds of gems embedded therein.

46. It was embellished with chowries consisting of silken cords. There were all articles essential for the coronation of a king. There were all medicinal herbs.

47. There were five beautiful pots filled with holy waters from all visible holy spots and white mustard, raw rice grains and Dūrvā grass. They had come there themselves with the Mantras which inspired them.

48. Sixteen virgins were brought from each of the families of the Devas, Sages, Siddhas and Serpents. These virgins had auspicious articles in their hands.

49. There were musical instruments like Lute, Mṛdangas, Conches, Wardrums (Bherī), Marus, Ḍiṇḍimas, Jharjharas, Ānaka drums, brass cymbals etc. and also light music.

50. With these sounds and chanting of the Vedic Mantras, the entire sky was filled. The lunar day was auspicious, the Lagna was splendid possessing the power of the Moon and the Stars.

51-53. A beautiful crown was placed on the head of Viṣṇu. He shone beautifully with the requisite auspicious threads etc. essential for the solemn ceremony. Mṛḍānī herself did the make-up and embellishment. The glorious goddess Śri accompanied him. Maheśa himself crowned him pouring the auspicious sacred waters. There in the Brahmāṇḍa Pavilion, all his riches and prosperity were passed on to Viṣṇu, everything that was Śiva's and hitherto not gone to anyone else.

Then the Lord of Devas accompanied by his Pramathas eulogized Śārṅgin. Then he spoke the following words to Brahmā, the creator of the worlds.

54. "This Viṣṇu is worthy of my adoration. You too bow down to this Hari." After saying this, Rudra himself bowed down to the Garuḍa-emblemed Lord.

55-58. Thereafter, Lord Viṣṇu, the excessively refulgent one was adored by all the Gaṇeśvaras, Brahmā accompanied by Devas, Sanaka and other Yogins, Siddhas, divine sages, Vidyādharas, Gandharvas, Yakṣas, Rākṣasas, groups of celestial damsels, Guhyakas, Cāraṇas, Bhūtas, Śeṣa, Vāsuki and Takṣaka, birds, all the Kinnaras, and all mobile and immobile beings. They uttered, "Be victorious, be victorious" and "Obeisance to you, obeisance to you."

Then in the assembly of the heaven-dwellers Hari was adored by Maheśa of great splendour, and all these who made loud sounds.

[Eulogy of Viṣṇu:]

59. "You are the creator of all living beings; you are the protector. You alone are the annihilator; you alone are worthy of being worshipped by all the worlds. You alone are the Lord of the universe.

60. You will be the giver of Dharma (Virtue), Wealth and Love. You will be the chastiser of persons of evil deeds. You will be invincible in battle even unto me.

61. O Viṣṇu, accept these three Śaktis handed over by me, i.e. *Icchāśakti* (power of will), *Kriyāśakti* (power of action) and the excellent *Jñānaśakti* (power of knowledge).

62. Indeed, O Hari, those who hate you should be scrupulously admonished by me. O Viṣṇu, excellent salvation should be granted by me to your devotees.

63. Accept this Māyā too. It cannot be dispelled by Suras and Asuras. Deluded by it, the entire universe will become bereft of knowledge. They will not have the least vestige of knowledge.

64. You are my left arm. This Pitāmaha shall be the right arm. You will be the progenitor and protector of this Vidhi too."

65. Granting thus Vaikuṇṭha and entire *Aiśvarya* to Hari, Hara, the Consort of Umā, freely sports about in Kailāsa along with Pramathas.

66. Ever since then, Hari, the destroyer of the Dānavas, administers the three worlds wielding his mace and the bow Śārṅga.

67. Thus, O Brāhmaṇa, the situation of all the worlds has been recounted to you. Now we shall tell you the cause of salvation.

68. He who listens attentively to this great narrative, will go to heaven and shall attain salvation in Kāśī.

69-70. This narrative should be read scrupulously on the following occasions for the success of those activities: festivals, Yajñas, marriage celebration, all auspicious occasions, at the time of coronation, while installing deities, while relinquishing authority and while entering a new house.

71. One without sons shall get a son; one without wealth shall become rich; the sick becomes rid of the ailments and

a man in bondage gets release.

72. This is to be used for Japa by those who seek welfare strenuously. It subdues all inauspiciousness. It is liked by Hara and Nārāyaṇa.

CHAPTER TWENTYFOUR

Śivaśarman Attains Salvation

The Gaṇas said:

1-4. O Śivaśarman, we shall speak what you are destined to have in future. Listen. Here in the world of Viṣṇu you will enjoy all pleasures in plenty. For the period of a year of Brahmā you will be sporting about with groups of celestial damsels. Due to the residue of the merit acquired by dying in an excellent holy place, you will become a king in the city of Nandivardhana. You will acquire a kingdom without any rivals or enemies. You will have plenty of vehicles and divisions of the army. In the kingdom, all the learned men will be hale and hearty. They will be having charming golden ornaments. The people there will perform regularly virtuous rites of *Iṣṭa* and *Pūrta*.

5. There will be perpetual growth of vegetation. The fields will be very fertile. All the region will be excellent, the subjects noble and healthy. There will be plenty of cattle and pasture-lands.

6. It will have many rows of shining temples for the deities. Excellent sacrificial posts will be found in all the villages, prosperous and remarkable in every way.

7. There will be excellent man-made parks with plenty of flowers and perpetually fruit-bearing trees. All the plots of lands will have lakes and lotus-ponds in plenty.

8.* There the rivers are Sadāmbhāḥ (*Sad-ambhaḥ:* having excellent, translucent water) but seldom are the people *Sadaṁbha*

* The play on words (puns) in vv 8-21 is very interesting.

(*Sa-daṁbha* - having hypocrisy). The families (thereof) are of noble descent (*Kūlināni*) and not possessors of ill-gotten wealth concealed in the earth (*Ku-līnāni*).

9. There is *Vibhrama* (coquettishness) in women. There is no *Vibhrama* (ignorance, delusion) in learned men. Only rivers are *Kuṭilagāminyaḥ* (going along zigzag paths) and not the subjects in that land.

10. In that land the nights in the dark half of the month are full of darkness. The men are not *Tamoyukta* (possessed of Tamas quality). Only the women are *Rajoyujaḥ* (having menstrual flow of blood) and not men full of righteousness (i.e. they do not have the quality of Rajas.)

11. The people are *Anandha* (not blind) due to wealth and not food (not having rice). The chariot is *Anayaḥ* (*an-ayas*) (having no iron but gold-plated) but the king's office is not *Anayaḥ* (*a-nayaḥ:* devoid of good policies).

12. There is *Daṇḍa* (staff, wooden handle) in axes, spades, chowries, umbrellas etc. but there is seldom *Daṇḍa* (punishment) due to anger or guilt.

13. Except in the case of gamesters nowhere else there is *Paridevanam* (playing with dice; lamenting). Only gamesters are seen *Pāśakapāṇis* (having dice in the hands/hands bound with ropes).

14. The talk of *Jāḍya* (chillness, sluggishness) is only in regard to water; only the middle part of women is *Durbala* (slender) and not men (weak). There, only the ladies are having hard breasts (*Kaṭhorahṛdayāḥ*) and not men (cruel in the heart).

15. There is *Kuṣṭhayoga* (medicinal preparation from the drug Kuṣṭha) in medicines alone but (attack of leprosy) not in men. There is *Vedha* (one hole) in excellent jewels and (*Vedha*—beating) not elsewhere. There is *Śūla* (trident) in the hands of idols but no *Śūla* (pain) in men.

16. There is *Kaṁpa* (trembling) due to Sāttvika Bhāva (affection and fidelity) and not due to fear in regard to anyone at any place. *Saṁjvara* (fever) in that city is due to love but *Saṁjvara* (distress for want of money) is not there. There is poverty but that of sinfulness.

17. There is scarcity of sin and not in regard to merit or commodities. Only elephants are *Pramattas* (in rut, mad) but

not others. There is war only in lakes between waveș

18. There is cessation of the flow of ichor (*Dāna*) among elephants and not stopping of the flow in religious gifts (*Dāna*) among the people. There are *Kaṇṭakas* (thorns) on the trees and no *Kaṇṭakas* (troublesome persons) among the public. There are *Vihāras* (sports) among the people but nobody's chest was without a necklace (*Vi-hāra*: necklessness).

19. There is *Guṇaviśleṣa* (separation from the string) only in regard to the arrows. There is a firm mention of binding (*Bandhoktiḥ*) only in regard to books (which require strong binding). *Snehatyāga* (eschewing oily and fatty substance, abandoning affection) is only in regard to Pāśupatas (and not in regard to others).

20. The usual talk about *Daṇḍa* (sacred staff) is among *Sannyāsins* (and not of *Daṇḍa*—punishment). *Mārgaṇas* (arrows) are only on the bows but there was no *Mārgaṇa* (begging) anywhere else. And only religious students beg as a ritual and hence are beggars (*Sannyāsins* are cordially invited for meals and need not beg).

21. There, only *Kṣapaṇakas* (Jaina recluses) have the impurities of the body (due to non-bath) and are seen so; generally the bees alone are fickle in their activities (wandering from flower to flower).

22-27. You will be ruling a kingdom consisting of all the virtues mentioned before. You will be righteous and conversant with the duties of a king. You will be heroic too.

You will possess all good fortunes and handsome features. You will be endowed with such virtues as heroism, liberal-mindedness etc. You will have ten thousand queens, all beautiful women, who will have earned good reputation through their beauty. You will beget three hundred sons.

You will be famous by the name Vṛddhakāla. You will be awe-inspiring and capable of conquering the cities of foes. You will be victorious in many battles. You will propitiate suppliants with your wealth. You will be full of many good qualities. Your lustre will be like that of the full Moon. You will be a leading king with your tresses of hairs kept wet due to the incessant performance of *Avabhṛtha Snāna* (holy ablution as a valedictory rite after concluding sacrifices). You will be richly endowed with the quality of ably protecting the subjects. You will be making Brāhmaṇas delighted through your treasury. You will be meditating on the lotus-like feet of Govinda in your heart with care. You will be spending days and nights in discoursing on the exploits of Vāsudeva.

28. Once you are seated in the assembly of the kings, O Brāhmaṇa, you are seen from a distance by Karpaṭikas (saints in red garments) who arrive from Vārāṇasī.

29. Then you are congratulated and blessed in a manner befitting your merits by all of them, through their words of benediction addressing you "O tiger among kings."

30. "May the glorious Lord Viśveśvara, the preceptor of all the worlds, Lord of Kāśī, wipe off all your evil intentions and ignorance.

31. The Lord of Kāśī is the bestower of riches in the form of salvation even when you only remember him. May he grant you knowledge free from all impurities.

32. The excellent kingdom free from foes has been acquired by you through merit. May the balance of the same merit bring about your inclination towards Viśvanātha.

33. May that Viśveśa be pleased with you—Viśveśa with whose favour long life, sons, garments and women, all prosperities, heavenly pleasures and salvation are easily available.

34. May that Viśveśa be present in your heart—Viśveśa, merely by listening to whose name all great sins will be split and dispelled."

35. On hearing this continuous series of benediction you, king Vṛddhakāla, will remember this present incident with hairs standing on their ends.

36-37. Concealing your reactions and features, you will be giving them much wealth. At an auspicious hour, you will be entrusting the kingdom to your son. Accompanied by Anaṅgalekhā, the (chief) queen, you will go to Kāśī. You will be making many gifts and propitiating many people seeking various things.

38. You will instal a Liṅga named after you. It will be the cause of salvation. You will erect a big palace-like mansion there and dig an excellent well there.

39-40. You will duly perform the rites of establishing the sacred pot (Kalaśa) etc. and will make gifts of jewels, rubies, yellow silk garments, elephants, horses, cows, money, great banners and flags, umbrellas, chowries, mirrors and many other things essential for the Lord. You will then relax.

41. With the entire body emaciated and fatigued through holy vows, fasts and other restraints and observances, you will see a sage at midday in an isolated place.

42-43. His body will be extremely feeble. He may be having tawny matted hairs. He will appear as though the personified form of excellent piety. He will be captivating the minds of the people with the burden of his slender body placed on a firm staff. He will be seen coming out of the sanctum sanctorum and proceeding towards the main pavilion.

44-45. He will sit near you and will ask thus (questions) one after another: "Who are you ? Why are you here? (Referring to Anaṅgalekhā) Who is this like a second person unto you? By whom was this palace (mansion) built? If you know, tell me. What is the name of this Liṅga? I almost do not know anything due to old age."

46-48. On being asked thus by that old sage, then, you will say: "I am the well-known king Vṛddhakāla. I am a Southerner who have come with this my wife. I meditate on this Liṅga. But I do not pray for anything. O sage with matted hairs, Śiva has caused the erection of this palace. I do not certainly know the special name of this Liṅga."

49-51. On hearing these words of the king, the old man with matted hairs said (will say): "Indeed one truthful statement has been made by you that you do not know the name of the Liṅga. I see you everyday sitting motionless. Certainly it must have been heard by you by whom the palace was constructed. Speak that to me, if you do know it for certain."

On hearing these words you said (will say) thus:

52. "It is Śambhu who does things and makes others do. Do I utter a lie? Or, O sage, what do I gain with thinking like this (as to who built etc.)?"

53. After uttering this when you kept (will keep) quiet, that aged sage said (will say): "I am thirsty. Fetch some water quickly and give it to me."

54-55. On being urged by him, you will bring water from the well and make him drink. Instantly, that aged sage becomes one shining with the lustre of the Full Moon, due to the fact that he drank that water. He turned (will turn) into a young man endowed with comely features like a serpent that has cast off its slough.

56-57. He was (will be) asked then by you who become surprised: "O honoured Sir, what is that power whereby you cast off your old age and shine now (as a youth)? O sage, if you have time, please tell me."

The sage said (will say):

58. O king Vṛddhakāla, O highly intelligent one, I know you. I know this chaste wife of yours too.

59. O king, being born of this Turvasu who was the embodied form of the Vedas, she was a Brāhmaṇa's daughter of excellent countenance and splendid conduct.

60. She was given in marriage by him to the noble-souled Naidhruva. That Naidhruva passed away even before reaching the age of youth.

61. Suffering widowhood courageously and observing holy vows, she ultimately died at Avantī. Due to that merit, she was born as the daughter of the Pāṇḍya king.

62. She was married to you, O king. She is always devoted to her husband. She came here along with you. She will attain the excellent salvation.

63-64. Even if sinners die in due course at Ayodhyā, Avantī, Mathurā, Dvārāvatī, Kāñcī or Māyāpurī, O king, they will come here at Kāśī and attain salvation.

65. I know you too, O king. You were a Brāhmaṇa in your previous birth. A citizen of Mathurā, named Śivaśarman, you died at Māyāpurī.

66. Due to that merit, you attained Vaikuṇṭha and enjoyed all charming pleasures. Due to the residue of that merit, you became a king at Nandivardhana.

67. O King Vṛddhakāla, due to that very merit, you reached this holy spot of salvation. You will attain excellent salvation.

68. Listen to another point, O eminent king. Your statement that "It is Śambhu who does things and causes others do" is clear (and relevant).

69. A meritorious act (performed by oneself) should never be frequently boasted of. By saying "It has been done by me", merit diminishes instantly.

70. Hence with all effort, a meritorious act should be concealed and guarded like a treasure. By boasting about it, it becomes futile like the Homa preformed on *Bhasma* (ash).

71. Certainly, O sinless one, you have been directed by Viśvanātha and the palace etc. has been built by you. I know it.

72. Know that this Liṅga, named Vṛddhakāleśvara, O king, already existed since time immemorial. But you were the instrumental cause.

73. By seeing, touching, worshipping, hearing about and bowing down to the Liṅga Vṛddhakāleśvara one gets whatever is desired.

74. This well named Kālodaka dispels old age and sickness. By drinking its waters one ceases to drink the breast-milk of a mother (i.e. becomes liberated from Saṁsāra).

75. A man who takes his bath with the water of this well and who worships this Liṅga acquires fulfilment of whatever is desired by him in one year.

76. If Kālatamodaka water is drunk or touched, leprosy, swelling, itch, scab and phlegmatic attack are dispelled.

77. By resorting to it and drinking it many diseases are cured, such as indigestion, colic pain, diabetes, diarrhoea, difficulty in urinating, itches etc.

78. Fever due to the attack of evil spirits, recurring fever etc. quickly get subdued by resorting to the water of this well.

79. Before you, my old age and grey hairs became dispelled in a moment by drinking the water of this well duly. I have become a new man.

80. If Vṛddhakāleśvara Liṅga is served, one does not incur poverty; neither calamities nor ailments, no sin and no evil consequences of the sins occur.

81. At Vārāṇasī, the Liṅga Vṛddhakāleśvara to the north of Kṛttivāsa should be visited carefully by those who desire emancipation and fulfilment.

82. After saying this, the sage took that king by the hand along with the queen Anaṅgalekhā and became merged into the Liṅga.

83. By repeating 'Mahākāla', 'Mahākāla' a hundred times, one gets released from sins. No doubt need be entertained in this connection.

84. After enjoying many kinds of pleasures in the splendid city of Vaikuṇṭha, your ultimate liberation shall take place thus by seeing the enemy of Kaiṭabha (i.e. Viṣṇu).

85. Thus after hearing his own future from those attendants of the Lord, the Brāhmaṇa experienced horripilation due to exhilaration and saw Hariloka, beautiful and resplendent with ten million Suns.

Maitrāvaruṇi (Agastya) said:

86-88. O dear Lopāmudrā, that eminent Brāhmaṇa enjoyed charming pleasures. Casting off his life at Māyāpurī, and due to the power of that merit, he returned from Vaikuṇṭha and was born in the city of Nandivardhana. He enjoyed all worldly pleasures, begot handsome sons and entrusted the kingdom to them. He reached the city of Vārāṇasī and propitiated Viśveśvara. He then attained salvation.

89. By listening to this meritorious narrative of the Brāhmaṇa Śivaśarman one gets rid of one's sins and attains the highest wisdom.

CHAPTER TWENTYFIVE

Agastya Visits Skanda

Vyāsa said:

1. Listen, O Sūta, I shall recount the story of the Pitcher-born Sage (Agastya), on hearing which a man becomes free from Rajoguṇa and possessor of knowledge.

2. After circumambulating the Śrīgiri mountain, Agastya, accompanied by his wife, saw the great beautiful forest of Skanda.

3. It was rich in the flowers of all the seasons. The trees were laden with juicy fruits. It abounded in roots (*Mūla*), bulbous roots (*Kanda*) that could be easily had. The trees had excellent barks.

4. The hosts of beasts of prey there were tamed. There were many rivers and puddles all round. There was a deep lake of clear water. It appeared to be the great essence of the entire earth.

5. It was teeming with different kinds of birds. Many sages stayed there. It appeared to be the secret meeting place of all types of austerities. It was the chief place of riches.

6. There is a mountain named Lohita there. It has the lustre of Meru with excellent caverns and rivulets; it shone well shedding lustre from its peaks and ridges.

7. It was as though a bit of Kailāsa had come to the land of holy rites (Bhārata) for performing lofty penance. It was full of mysteries and miracles.

8-9. There the excellent sage Agastya saw the Six-faced God directly. Accompanied by his wife, the sage of great penance prostrated before him like a log of wood. Joining the palms together in reverence, he eulogized the Son of the Daughter of the Mountain with the Sūktas of the Vedas and prayers composed by himself.

Agastya said:

(Agastya's Prayer)

10. Obeisance to the Six-faced Lord whose lotus-like feet are worthy of being revered by groups of Devas. You are the sea of nectar (Supreme Bliss), whose exploits are endless and who are the cause of mental delight to Gaurī.

11. Salutations to you, the destroyer of the distresses of those who bow down (to you), the bestower of the cherished desires of all, the destoyer of the designs of cheaters of others, the slayer of the fierce Asura (called) Tāraka.

12. Obeisance to you, the peacock-vehicled one, to you who are both unembodied and embodied, thousand-formed, attributeless, greater than the greatest; you who are endowed with good qualities and are virtue (incarnate), one whose expanse cannot be comprehended and the supreme one.

13. Obeisance to you, the most excellent one among those who have realized Brahman, the supreme Being, one with the directions for the garments (Digambara), one who is stationed

in the firmament, one with golden complexion, one with golden arms (or firmament-bodied one). Obeisance to the golden one (*Sāttvika* in form) and one with gold as semen virile (i.e., Rudra).

14. Obeisance to the Lord who is austerity incarnate, one who has austerity as asset, to the Lord bestowing the fruits of penance, one who is perpetually child-like in form, to the Lord who has conquered Māra (god of Love), one who has considered all prosperity and riches as (worthless as) grass. Obeisance to the detached one.

15. Hail to you, the reed-born Lord, to the Lord with a row of teeth having the colour (brightness) of the morning Sun, to you, a child of great heroism uncommon to children, to the Lord nurtured by six mothers, to the Lord completely unafflicted and unperturbed.

16. Obeisance to *Mīḍhuṣṭama* ('the most excellent one among those who bestow desired fruits'), to *Uttaramīḍhus* ('bountiful bestower of future benefits'); obeisance to the Lord of the Gaṇas. Obeisance to the Lord who himself is a Gaṇa (of Rudra); obeisance to you who have transcended birth and old age; obeisance to Viśākha with an excellent Śakti in the hand.

17. Permanent obeisance to you, to the son of the Lord of everything, to the enemy of Krauñca mountain, to the slayer of Tāraka. Obeisance to you, O son of Svāhā, Gaṅgā, Kṛttikās and Śiva.

18. After eulogizing Kārttikeya thus saying "Obeisance, obeisance to you", he circumambulated him twice and thrice (i.e.five times) and stood in front of him. Then he was told, "O eminent sage, be seated."

Kārttikeya said:

19. O Pitcher-born Sage, the support and assistance to gods, I know that you have come here and also about the increase in the size of the Vindhya mountain.

20. Everything is well in the great holy spot Avimukta protected by the Three-eyed Lord. Virūpākṣa is there bestowing salvation directly to those who die there.

21. O sage, such a sanctifying holy spot has nowhere been

seen by me on the earth, Bhuvarloka, Svarloka, Pātāla region or in the higher worlds.

22. Though I move about alone, O Sage, I perform penace here to attain that holy spot. Till today, my ambitions have not become fruitful.

23. It cannot be attained by merits alone, by making gifts, by performing penance or by means of Japas. It cannot be attained through different kinds of Yajñas. It can be obtained only through the blessings of Īśa.

24. Residence in inaccessible Kāśī can become easily achievable, O Sage, only through the blessings of Īśvara, certainly not by millions of merits.

25. It is a separate creation excelling that of the creator (Brahmā), because even Īśvara is not capable of enumerating the merits of that holy place.

26. It is the height of the weakness of intellect, Alas! it is the outrageous adverseness of fortune, Alas! it is the grand power of delusion, if Kāśī is not resorted to.

27. The body grows old and emaciated incessantly, the sense-organs continuously become weak. Alas! the god of Death has made life, his target like a deer by a hunter.

28. One should resort to Kāśī after realizing that riches are fraught with dangers, that the body is excessively subject to adversity and that life is as fickle as lightning.

29. As long as the end of the life does not approach, Kāśī is not abandoned. Kāla (Time, god of Death) shall not forget to count even the least bit of a second.

30. Ailments thrown in very near to old age do harass very much. Still the body vexed with different kinds of ambitions and aspirations does not yearn for Kāśī.

31. Without (spending) money, Dharma (piety) can be achieved through ablutions in holy places, performance of Japas, helping others and utterances (of good words, prayers etc.). From Dharma wealth issues spontaneously.

32. Even without a specific means of earning money, wealth certainly comes out of Dharma. Hence, giving up the worry for wealth, one should resort to Dharma alone.

33. Wealth is obtained through Dharma; from wealth Kāma can be obtained; all happiness comes from Kāma. Even heavenly pleasure is easily obtained through Dharma; but Kāśī

alone is very difficult to attain.

34. After clearly scrutinizing everything, Sthāṇu spoke to Śarvāṇī only about three means of salvation.

35. First comes Pāśupatayoga (consisting of use of Bhasma etc.), then *Sitāsita* (i.e., Prayāga), then the effrotless means of salvation namely Avimukta (i.e., Kāśī).

36-41. There are many reputed means of salvation as mentioned in scriptures. These are: Śriśaila,[1] Himālaya and other mountains; many *Āyatanas* (holy spots and shrines); holding of the three *Daṇḍas* (Staffs) (i.e. entrance into Sannyāsa); renunciation of all rites; different kinds of austerities, holy vows, observances and (self-) restraints; confluences of many rivers; many holy forests;[2] mental activities (fortitude etc.); physical *Dhārātīrtha* etc.; *Ūṣaras*[3] (saline lands such as Reṇukā, etc., nine in number); Pīṭhas (seats of knowledge established by Ācāryas); unbroken teaching (and reciting) of the Vedas; Japa of Mantras; *Havanas* (oblatinos) performed in fire; various kinds of gifts; sacrifices; *Upāsanās* (adoratinos) of the deities; Trirātra, Pañcarātra; Sāṅkhya, Yoga etc., and the propitiation of Viṣṇu. All these have been mentioned as good means of attaining salvation. Cities[4] too have been mentioned as the bestowers of salvation on those who die there. It is certain that all these are the means unto salvation.

42. It is true that all the means mentioned before are real but so only through their ability to bring a devotee to Kāśī. A living being becomes liberated ultimately after reaching Kāśī and not elsewhere.

43. That is why that holy spot is very sacred and extremely wonderful. It is a favourite of Viśveśvara in the entire Cosmic Sphere.

---

1. Śriśaila: In Karnool district of Andhra Pradesh, famous for its Jyotirliṅga Mallikārjuna. But here as the Comm. notes, the word *ādi* includes Mandara and other holy mountains.

2. The Comm. states the following as 'holy forests' : Saindhava, Daṇḍakāraṇya, Jaṁbūmārga, Puṣkara, Utpalāraṇya, Naimiṣa and Kuru-Jāṅgala, Hemada and Arbuda.

3. *Ūṣara* though translated as 'saline' or salty land as per MW Dictionary, the *Ūṣaras* listed by the Commentator, viz., Reṇukā, Badarikā, Sūkara, Kāśī, Kālañjara are not 'saline' or 'salty' as there is no seashore near them.

4. The seven cities like Ayodhyā, Mathurā etc., believed to be Mokṣa-giving.

44. It is the same holy spot that made me enquire about your welfare. Come on. Come on. Give unto me the contact with your body, O noble sage of holy vows.

45. Even the contact with the wind blowing from Kāśī is desired (and welcomed) by me who stay here. But you yourself have come from there.

46. The dust particles from the feet of those who stay at Kāśī even for three nights with the senses under control, can purify invariably when touched.

47. But you have stayed there for a very long period; you have performed many meritorious rites there and your hairs have become tawny-coloured through (continuous) ablutions in the current flowing northwards.

48-49. In the vicinity of Agastīśvara there is your Kuṇḍa (holy pit). One who takes holy ablution there, drinks the water and performs all the libation rites and propitiates the Pitṛs through balls of rice in the course of the performance of Śrāddha with faith, shall become blessed. The devotee shall obtain the benefit of (pilgrimage to) Vārāṇasī.

50. After saying this and touching all the limbs of (i.e., embracing) the Pitcher-born Sage, Skanda obtained the pleasure of taking a plunge in the waters of a nectarine lake.

51. Closing his eyes, saying "Be victorious, O Viśveśa", Guha remained motionless like a post and meditated for a short while on something (i.e., the Supreme Being that cannot be perceived through the sense-organs).

52. When Skanda stopped his meditation with excessive delight in his mind and countenance, the sage who was waiting for an opportunity to speak some words, asked Guha:

Agastya said:

53-54. O Lord, the greatness of Vārāṇasī was spoken to the goddess born of Himālaya Mountain by the holy Lord formerly. Seated on her lap, you had heard everything as spoken by the Lord. O Six-faced Lord, be pleased to narrate it in the same manner as you have heard. That holy spot extremely appeals to me.

Skanda said:

55-56. Listen, O sinless sage Maitrāvaruṇi (Agastya), to the greatness of that holy spot Avimukta, being narrated by me in the same manner as it was narrated by the Lord to my mother formerly and heard by me with steady mind, as I lay on her lap.

57. Avimukta has been mentioned as the most esoteric of all esoteric things here. There achievement (of objects or Mokṣa) is always spontaneous as the Lord is stationed forever there.

58. That holy place has no contact with the earth but (is situated in the intermediate region (Antarikṣa). Non-yogins do not see it; Yogins do see it.

59. O Brāhmaṇa, he who stays there with mental purity and self under control, shall be on a par with one who subsists on air only, though he may be taking food thrice a day.

60. Though one may remain in Avimukta only for a moment, yet if he has excessive devotion, it shall be as though a great penance has been performed by him with strict adherence to celibacy.

61. If a wise one were to stay there for a month, taking only light food and keeping the sense-organs under control, it is as good as the divine Pāśupata Vrata (vow) performed by him.

62-63. If someone stays there for a year after conquering anger and the sense-organs, if he does not depend on another man's money for his nourishment (food), if he avoids cooked food doled out by others, if he does not scandalise others and engages himself in making some gifts, it is as good as a great penance preformed by him over a thousand years.

64. If a man conversant with the greatness of the holy spot stays there for the whole life, he attains the greatest goal casting off the fear of birth and death.

65. The goal that cannot be obtained elsewhere in the course of hundreds of births through Yogic practices, can be sportingly obtained here with the favour of Īśa.

66. If any Brāhmaṇa-slayer were to go to the city of Vārāṇasī by chance, his sin of Brāhmaṇa-slaughter recedes, due to the greatness of the holy spot.

67. If anyone does not leave Avimukta till his death, not

only the sin of Brāhmaṇa-slaughter but even the Prakṛti (Avidyā or Nescience) recedes.

68. With his mind not turned elsewhere, if a man sticks to that holy spot and does not leave it off, he becomes free from birth and death and the unbearable sufferings of staying in the womb.

69. If an intelligent man does not wish rebirth on the earth, he should resort to Avimukta resorted to by divine sages.

70. One should not leave off Avimukta that releases one from the fear of worldly existence. After coming to Lord Viśveśvara, one is not born again.

71. Better to become a Piśāca (vampire) after committing thousands of sins here, rather than attain Svarga that can be achieved through a hundred sacrifices without Kāśī.

72. At the time of death, when the sensitive weak spots get pierced and they are afflicted with rheumatism, men will lose the power of memory.

73. There, at the time when the soul comes out, Lord Viśveśvara himself imparts the Tāraka Brahman (Rāma Mantra of six syllables) Mantra, whereby the individual identifies himself with it (Supreme Being).

74. Realizing that human life is not permanent and it involves much of sin, one should resort to Avimukta that is destructive of the fear of worldly existence.

75. He who does not leave off Avimukta though shaken by obstacles, attains the glory of salvation and meets the termination of misery.

76. Which sensible man does not resort to Kāśī in the end, that suppresses multitudes of great sins, that causes the increase of merits and bestows worldly pleasures and salvation?

77. After comprehending this, a wise man should not leave off Avimukta, because he becomes Mukta (liberated), due to the grace of Avimukta.

78. How can the greatness of Avimukta be described by me through the six months which even (Śeṣa) of a thousand mouths cannot?

CHAPTER TWENTYSIX

Description of Maṇikarṇikā[1]

Agastya said:

1. O Skanda, if you are pleased and if your affection for me is excellent, O holy Sir, narrate to me what has been long cherished in my heart.

2. Since when has this holy place Avimukta attained the greatest reputation? How has it become the bestower of salvation?

3-5. Wherefore is this Maṇikarṇikā reputed as worthy of being eulogized by the three worlds? O master, what was there formerly when there was no celestial river here? O Lord, how did this city get the names Vārāṇasī, Kāśī, Rudravāsa ('Abode of Rudra')? O Peacock-emblemed One, how did this beautiful Avimukta, Ānandakānana ('forest of pleasure') later come to be reputed as Mahāśmaśāna ('Great Cremation Ground')? I wish to hear about this. Dispel my doubt.

Skanda said:

6. What has been asked by you is a great unprecedented burden of questions. O Pot-born Sage, Aṁbikā asked Hara this very thing.

7. I shall narrate to you in the manner in which it has been recounted to the Mother of the universe, by the omniscient Lord of the Devas.

8. At the time of the ultimate annihilation, when all mobile and immobile beings had perished, everything was in great darkness without the sun, stars and planets.

9. It was without the moon, without day or night, without fire, wind and earth, without Pradhāna, devoid of firmament, devoid of all other luminaries.

10. There was no seer etc. It was without sound and touch, devoid of smell and colour, without taste and having no quarters.

11-17. While the situation was like this with thick darkness that could (as if) be pierced with a needle, the Supreme Absolute alone existed. It is what the Śruti always refers to as *Sat, Brahman* and *Ekam* (Single). It is beyond the reach of the mind; it is not an object of expression in any manner whatsoever. It has neither name nor form nor colour. It is neither stout nor lean. It is neither short nor long. It is neither light nor heavy. There is neither increase in size or decrease in size therein. The Śruti says hesitatingly about it that it exists. It is truth, infinite and consciousness. It is the great splendour of bliss. It cannot be gauged. It has no other basis or support. It has no modification. It can be perceived by Yogins alone. It is omnipresent and the sole cause of all. It is *Nirvikalpa* ('having no difference of any sort'); *Nirāraṁbha* ('having no beginning'), *Nirmāya* ('free of Māyā') and *Nirupadrava* ('free from troubles'). This being whose names are being considered variously and who was moving about alone had a desire for a second one (entity). Hence a form was evolved sportingly by that formless Being.

18-20. That form was endowed with all qualities and *Aiśvaryas* (glories); it was splendid and full of all consciousness and knowledge; it was omnipresent and omniformed, omnieyed and omnipotent. It was the sole object of veneration for all; it was the first of all things; it was the being potentially capable of perfectly creating everything always.

After evolving that pure divine form, the supreme being called Brahman that is immutable and all-reaching vanished.

21. O my beloved, I am the form of that formless one which is called the Supreme Absolute. Both moderns, and ancients among scholars call me Īśvara.

22. Thereafter from my own body, a being that does not swerve away from my person, was created by myself, moving about as I pleased, though alone.

23. It is you that I created. They call you Prakṛti and Pradhāna; the greatest Māyā, possessor of all attributes; the mother of the Buddhitattva (the great Hiraṇyagarbha); one without Vikṛti or modification (the basis of *Vivarta*, transformation).

24. Simultaneously, this holy spot too was created by me, the primordial Puruṣa, one in the form of eternal Time; in the company of you, the Śakti.

Skanda said:

25-27. That Śakti is called Prakṛti. That Puruṣa is the great Īśvara. O Pitcher-born Sage, that holy spot is never left by Śiva and Śivā who has the form of Supreme Bliss and who sports about in that holy place. It extends to five Krośas (1 Krośa = 3 Kms). It was created from the soles of their own feet and that is blissful in form. They never leave that holy place, even at the time of the great annihilation. Hence, they know that it is 'Avimukta.'

28. This holy spot was created by Īśa for the purpose of his holy sport, when there was neither the sphere of the earth nor the creation of water.

29. This is the secret of the holy spot. O Pot-born Sage, no one knows. It should never be mentioned to an atheist endowed with only a mortal eye.

30. It should be revealed to one having faith, to the humble one; to one with an eye to know the three aspects of time; to a devotee of Śiva; to a quiescent one who has a keen desire to get liberated.

31. Ever since then this holy place is called Avimukta; this has served as couch for Śiva and Śivā, a place for incessant bliss.

32. The non-existence of this holy place that brings about salvation can be imagined by foolish ones by whom the non-existence of Śiva and Śivā is accepted.

33. Even a person well-conversant with Yoga and other means will not attain salvation without propitiating Maheśa and visiting Kāśī.

34-35. This holy place was at first named Ānandavana by the Pināka-bearing Lord, because it was the cause of bliss. Later on it was named Avimukta. All the Liṅgas in that Ānandakānana should be known as the shoots of the bulbous root in the form of bliss.

36. It was thus, O Pot-born One, that this became famous as Avimukta. Similarly I shall tell you how Maṇikarṇikā came into being.

37-38. Formerly while Śiva and Śivā were sporting about in this Ānandavana, O Pot-born Sage, they had this desire that another (being) should be created. 'When the great burden is vested in that being, we shall be moving about as we please. We shall grant salvation only to the regular residents of Kāśī.

39. He creates everything, he alone protects and he alone withdraws it in the end. And he is the storehouse of all glory

and prosperity.

40-41. With his grace, we shall stay happily behind in the Ānandakānana after stabilizing the vast ocean-like mind which becomes stirred up due to the billows of worried thoughts. It has Sattva quality for its jewels, the Tamas quality for its alligators and the Rajas quality for its coral reefs. Where is happiness in one who is worried with thoughts and whose mental activity is scattered and diffused?'

42-43. After resolving thus in the company of that Mother of the universe, the nature of consciousness, Dhūrjaṭi, the creator of the universe, let his nectar-exuding eye pass over his left limb. Therefrom a person of the most handsome features in all the three worlds manifested himself.

44. O sage, he was calm and endowed with Sattva quality. In majestic depth, he excelled the mighty ocean. Unrivalled as he was, he was endowed with forbearance too.

45. He had the splendour of sapphire. He was gloriously resplendent with excellent eyes resembling lotus. He was clad in good-coloured brilliant silk garments.

46. His powerfully ferocious pair of arms made him brilliant. An excellent lotus of exquisite scent beautifully issued from his deep navel.

47. He was the sole abode of all good qualities; he was the chief storehouse of all arts; he was the most excellent of all. Hence he is known as Puruṣottama.

48-49. On seeing that great Being embellished with supreme greatness, Mahādeva said, "O Acyuta, be Mahāviṣṇu. The Vedas shall be your exhalation; you will understand everything through them. Do everything in a befitting manner in the way laid down in the Vedas."

50. After saying this to Viṣṇu of the nature of Cosmic Intelligence, Rudra, the great Īśāna, entered Ānandakānana accompanied by Śivā.

51. Thereafter, Lord Viṣṇu received that behest with (bowing) his head, meditated for a short while and resolved on performing penance.

52. Digging by means of his discus, a beautiful lotus-pond, Hari filled it with sweat drops issuing from his limbs.

53. There, on the banks of Cakrapuṣkariṇī (i.e., the lotus-pond dug by means of the dicus), he remained motionless like

a post and performed a severe penance for fifty thousand years.

54-56. On seeing him motionless with eyes closed and blazing through the penance, Lord Īśa, Mṛḍa accompanied by Mṛḍāni spoke to Hṛṣīkeśa, shaking his head frequently (in approval): "Oh, the wonderful greatness of the penance! Oh, how wonderful is the patience of the mind! Oh, this wonderful fire is blazing continuously without fuel! O Mahāviṣṇu, enough of your penance. O most excellent one among the great, choose your boon."

57. After recognizing this repeated utterance of Mṛḍa the Four-armed Lord opened his lotus-like eyes and stood up.

Śrīviṣṇu said:

58. O Lord of Devas, O great Lord and chief among the divine beings, if you are pleased, I wish to see you always in the company of Bhavānī.

59. The boon to be granted to me, O Moon-crested Lord, is such as should enable me to see you going ahead everywhere at the time of all my activities.

60. Let my mind that resembles a black-bee cease to wander (aimlessly) and be enthusiastic for the honey issuing from the lotus-like feet of yours. Let it be extremely steady.

Śrīśiva said:

61. O Hṛṣīkeśa, O Janārdana, let everything turn out as said by you. I shall grant you another boon. Listen to it, O excellent one of noble vows.

62-63. On seeing the steady increase of this penance of yours, I shook my head having serpents. As a result of that movement, my gemset earring fell down. It was set with jewels and was beautiful in appearance. Let this (sacred expanse of water) be named Maṇikarṇikā.

64-65. This splendid sacred place had become well known as Cakrapuṣkariṇī Tīrtha formerly, because it was dug out by means of your discus, O Lord holding the conch, discus and mace. Let it become famous by the name Maṇikarṇikā here in this world, ever since the time when the gemset earring fell into it from my ear.

Śrīviṣṇu said:

66. O Lord, O beloved of the Daughter of the Mountain, by virtue of the dropping of your pearl earring here, let this holy spot become the greatest of all holy spots that are salvation- granting holy places.

67. O mighty Lord, since that brilliance which cannot be adequately described, shines here, let another name 'Kāśī' be well-known for it.

68. O Lord, I choose another boon as well. It should be granted unhesitatingly. O Śiva, O jewel protecting the universe, it is intended to further your benefaction to others.

69. Beginning with Brahmā and ending with a blade of grass, there are numerous living creatures in the four species of living organisms. Let all those attain salvation in Kāśī.

70-73. O Śambhu, in this sacred Tīrtha of the gemset earring, those who perform the following religious rites are to be benefited by the same performance. The rites are: *Sandhyā* prayers, holy ablution, *Japa*, *Homa*, the excellent study of the Vedas, *Tarpaṇa* (rite of libation), offerings of balls of rice, the worship of the deities, many *Saptatantu* sacrifices, the gifts of cows, plots of land, gingelly seeds, gold, horse, light, cooked rice, garments and ornaments, giving a virgin in marriage, *Vratotsarga* rite, *Vṛṣotsarga* (leting off a bull-calf) rite, installation of Liṅgas etc. The devotee realizes that life is transient. (Being) highly intelligent, he is conscious that dangers are extensive and riches are momentary. Let those who perform all these rites attain everlasting liberation as the fruit of those holy rites.

74-76. Let those other rites too, performed excellently and with faith, be the bestower of salvation. Barring *Prāyopaveśa* (fasting unto death), no one shall indulge in self-killing. O Īśāna, let those rites be the cause of ultimate salvation. After performing a noble rite even on some other occasions, the devotee should neither boast about nor regret it. O Īśa, with your blessings let all those holy rites bear everlasting fruits here. O Īśa, with your grace let everything concerning him be of never-ending benefit.

77. O Sadāśiva, let this holy place be more splendid in its outcome than whatever exists, had existed and will exist later.

78. Just as, O Sadāśiva, there is nothing superior to you,

so also let there not be anything greater and better than this Ānandavana.

79. Let there be salvation to all living beings without Sāṅkhya (knowledge), Yoga, without dwelling on the identity of Jīva and Brahman, without Vratas, Dānas etc.

80. Let those who die at Kāśī be initiated into Nirvāṇa (salvation); let even rabbits, mosquitoes, worms, locusts, horses or serpents dying within the five Krośa limits of Kāśī attain salvation.

81-82. Let there be the destruction of the sins of those excellent men who reside in Kāśī; let them always enjoy Kṛtayuga, Uttarāyaṇa and Mahodaya (auspicious Muhūrta).

83. O Three-eyed Lord, O Sadāśiva, let this holy place be far superior to all those holy and sacred things mentioned in the Śrutis.

84. By repeating the Gāyatrī Mantra a hundred thousand times at Kāśī, let everyone have that merit which accrues to one through the study of all the four Vedas.

85. By resorting to Kāśī faithfully, let that merit and more accrue to one, the merit that usually one attains by practising *Aṣṭāṅga Yoga.*

86. Through the observance of fast for one day in Ānandakānana, let that merit be acquired, which one usually acquires through Kṛcchracāndrāyaṇa and other rites.

87. By means of the rite of lying on the bare ground for a year in Kāśī, let there be that benefit and salvation which one gets by performing penance elsewhere for a hundred years.

88. By speaking the truth alone for a fortnight or a day in Kāśī, let there be that benefit known as accruing elsewhere through the rite of silence ever since nativity.

89. By feeding a thousand persons at Kāśī, let one get more than ten thousand times that merit which is spoken as obtained by making a gift of all that one possesses elsewhere.

90. By resorting to Maṇikarṇikā here for only five nights, let there be that benefit which is said to be the result of resorting to all the (other) holy places granting liberation.

91. Merely by visiting Kāśī with faith, let there be that welfare-giving merit one gets through the holy ablution at Prayāga.

92. Let one who has full self-control, get by sleeping for

three nights in Kāśī, that merit which one gets through performing Aśvamedha and Rājasūya.

93. Merely by visiting Kāśī with faith, let that merit accrue, the merit that is duly derived by *Tulā-Puruṣa-Dāna* (making a gift of some object equal in weight to the donor).

94. On hearing these words of Viṣṇu requesting for a boon, the Lord of Devas, the Lord of the universe said with a delighted mind:

Śrī Mahādeva said:

Let it be so, O Madhusūdana.

95. Listen, O Viṣṇu of powerful arms, O origin and goal after death. Create different kinds of beings duly as has been mentioned in the Śruti.

96. Like a father, be the virtuous protector of all living beings. Different kinds of persons who cause destruction of righteousness should be exterminated.

97. Since they have already been killed by means of their own Karmas, O Hari, you shall be the mere instrumental cause in regard to the annihilation of those who stick to paths other than the virtuous.

98. Just as a fully ripe fruit falls itself from the stalk, so also they shall fall with their sins fully matured into fruition.

99. O Hari, I shall become ready for the annihilation of those persons who become arrogant on account of their power of penance and begin to insult you.

100. All the *Upapātakins* (perpetrators of minor sins) and all the *Mahāpātakins* (perpetrators of major sins) shall become free from sins after reaching Kāśī.

101. This holy place extending over an area of five Krośas is dear to me. My command alone is effective here; not the command of anyone else.

102. O Mṛḍānī of splendid eyes, again Viṣṇu was addressed by me, Viṣṇu who was moving about here and there like a mass of brilliance of great and fierce splendour, causing great surprise to all the three worlds.

103. "There is none else chastising the creatures residing in Avimukta and committing sins, O Viṣṇu; I alone chastise them.

104. One may be full of many sins, but if he remembers Avimukta in his heart, even when he is a hundred Yojanas away, he shall not be affected by sins.

105-107. If anyone remembers Avimukta, the holy place that is very dear to me, at the time of his death, though he may be far off and he may be a sinner, he shall drive away all the sins and enjoy heavenly pleasures. After falling from heaven, he shall become a dominant king on the earth, due to the merit of having remembered Kāśī. He will then enjoy various kinds of pleasures. He will then reach Avimukta and due to that meritorious act, attain salvation.

108-109. O lady of pure smiles, if someone stays here for a long time with well-controlled mind and sense-organs, but meets with his death elsewhere as fate would have it, he, too, will enjoy heavenly pleasures and then will be born as a great ruler of the earth. Thereafter, he will come to Kāśī and obtain liberation.

110. O Viṣṇu, continuous residence in Avimukta is capable of uprooting all Karmas, but only in the case of two or three holiest of the holy persons will it be conducive to ultimate salvation.

Viṣṇu said:

111. O Lord of Devas, if a person does not know the greatness of the holy place really, nor does he give credence to it but dies here, what is his goal after death?

Śiva said:

112-113. Take the case of a person who commits elsewhere many great sins. He has no faith nor does he know the real situation. If such a person dies here, O Janārdana of excellent vows, listen to his ultimate goal—the goal of a person ignorant of the greatness of the holy place.

114-116. As he enters Pañcakrośī (the precincts of Kāśī extending to five Krośas), all the multitude of his sins goes out. Nothing penetrates into Kāśī. Due to fear of the Gaṇas who continuously move about at the outskirts with tridents and nooses in their hands the entire multitude (of sins) stays outside. So the man, O sinless one, becomes free from all sins at the time of his very entry. After taking his bath in Maṇikarṇikā he attains excellent merit.

117. By taking a good ablution in Maṇikarṇikā alone, one gets that merit which is usually obtained through elaborate bathing in all the sacred waters.

118-119. The devotee shall take his bath there in accordance with the injunctions, using clay, cowdung, Kuśa grass etc. (for the various rituals), uttering the Varuṇa Mantras in accordance with the branch of the Veda that one owes allegiance to and making use of Dūrvā grass, Apāmārga (*Achyranthes aspera*), Darbha grass etc. (for the requisite rituals). One who takes the holy ablution with perfect faith in Maṇikarṇikā shall obtain the benefit that accrues from all the other holy places and all the merits through all types of gifts.

120. Even if one undertakes the holy ablution in accordance with the injunctions but without faith, he too shall get the merit that enables him to attain heaven.

121. By taking the holy bath with due faith and in accordance with the injunctions and by performing the *Tarpaṇa* rites for the Devas and others by means of gingelly seeds, Darbha grass and barley grains perfectly, one shall obtain the benefit of all the Yajñas.

122. A man with faith, who takes the holy bath in accordance with the injunctions and performs all rites of libation shall obtain the benefit of all the Mantras through the Japa and adoration of the deities.

123. O Śivā, by taking the holy bath with due observance of the vow of silence, and through the visit of Viśveśa, a man who controls all his sense-organs and restrains his speech, shall obtain the welfare brought about by all the holy vows.

124. One should scrupulously observe silence at the time of bathing, worshipping the deities, performing *Japa*, cleaning the teeth, performing *Havana* rites and at the time of passing urine and evacuating the bowels.

125. By adoring Viśveśvara (only) once in accordance with the injunctions, and performing all the Upacāras (ritualistic services), one obtains the benefit of Śiva-worship performed throughout one's life.

126. O Goddess of Devas, one who makes a gift of the wealth legitimately earned, even if it be very little, in my holy place Avimukta, will never become poverty-stricken.

127. A fool who collects together different kinds of riches but does not give it away in Avimukta, dies elsewhere and always grieves over it.

128. All the beautiful things, gems, cows, elephants, horses, garments etc. have been created for the welfare of the residents of Avimukta.

129. One who legitimatley earns wealth or courts death at Kāśī for the purpose of popitiating Viśveśa is really blessed. He is really conversant with righteousness (Dharma).

130. O Umā, Lord Viśveśvara who is stationed in the city of Kāśī assuming the form of a Liṅga is directly the basis of my greatness.

131. Avimukta extending to five Krośas is a great holy place. That alone named Viśveśvara should be known as a Jyotirliṅga ('the Liṅga of refulgence').

132. Just as the disc of the Sun, though stationed in a single place (in a limited space) is seen as present everywhere by everyone, so also is Viśveśvara in Kāśī.

133. The benefit that is obtained elsewhere by means of unimpeded Yogic practice acquired in the course of many births, can be obtained by one casting off his body in Kāśī.

134. The benefit that is obtained elsewhere by persons who have conquered their organs of sense by performing all sorts of penances for a long time, can be obtained at Kāśī in a single night.

135. Even a person who does not know the greatness of the holy place, even one who has no faith, becomes free from sin on entering Kāśī. On death he obtains immortality (salvation).

136. If, after committing heinous sins, one comes to Kāśī in due course and casts off his body, he attains me alone with my favour.

137. Without my favour who attains Kāśī except *Bradhna* (the Sun), O large-eyed lady, who is called here the maker of the day?

138. O Goddess, who can obtain permanent, continuous happiness without coming to Kāśī? For even Brahmā and others are continuously fettered by the nooses of Prakṛti (Māyā).

139. Had it not been for Kāśī, how could the people bound by the neck by means of the twenty-four nooses (i.e., *Tattvas*) and three Guṇas [(1) Strings (2) Attributes] rendered more

firm by means of acts (conducive to *Dharma, Artha* and *Kāma*) be set free?

140-141. Yogic practices are attended with many hindrances. What is known as *Tapas* (penance) has to be acquired (performed successfully) with great difficulties. One who has fallen off from Yoga (i.e., failed in the practice of Yoga), one who has fallen off from penance has to undergo the sufferings of being in the wombs. (But) one who commits sins in Kāśī and dies at Kāśī may become Rudrapiśāca but shall attain salvation.

142. There is no question of fall into hell in the case of those creatures that die in Kāśī by chance, though they might have been perpetrators of sins, because I am their chastiser and controller.

143. After realizing that this physical body is bound to perish, after remembering the painful sufferings undergone within the womb, one should abandon even a flourishing kingdom and permanently resort to Kāśī.

144. Unexpectedly the terrible messengers of Yama may come upon one and strike one after fettering with nooses. So one should resort to Kāśī quickly.

145. Who will not resort to Kāśī where there is no fear from sins, nothing to fear from Yama and where one need not be afraid of staying within the womb again?

146. Death is bound to overtake one today, tomorrow or even the day after. As long as there is some delay or respite from death, one should resort to Kāśī.

147. If death overtakes men, there is a further birth and consequent death. Hence a sensible man should resort to Kāśī, the place of no further rebirth.

148. Setting aside the Vaiṣṇavī Māyā in the form of (attachment to) sons, abode and wives that takes up many forms in the next birth, one should resort to Kāśī that destroys Bhava (birth/Saṁsāra).

Skanda said:

149. One should not think in one's mind like, 'I am now a young man. Death is far off from me.' The sound of the bell round the neck of the buffalo of the god of Death should be definitely heard. Without subjecting oneself to exertion of great magnitude due to the nearness (of the time of death),

a man of sensible mind should quickly abandon his decaying hut (i.e., his house) and go to the city of Dhūrjaṭi.

Vyāsa said:

150. O Sūta, after narrating to Agastya this story that suppresses all sins, Skanda said once again:

CHAPTER TWENTYSEVEN

The Greatness of Gaṅgā

Skanda said:

1. I shall describe how Ānandakānana became well-known as Vārāṇasī as it was narrated by the Lord of Devas.

Īśvara said:

2. Listen, O Viṣṇu of mighty arms, O most handsome one in all the three worlds, how Avimukta got the name Vārāṇasī.

3-5. A highly virtuous and resplendent king of the Solar dynasty,[1] Bhagīratha, had heard about the calamity that befell his ancestors, the sons of Sagara, who were ordered (by Sagara) to protect the horse of the horse-sacrifice and who were burnt down by the fire of Kapila's wrath. He desired to propitiate Gaṅgā and therefore resolved to perform a penance. The king, a storehouse of activities conducive to fame, went to Himavān, the best among mountains, with a desire to redeem his ancestors. He duly vested the burden of the kingdom on his ministers.

6. O Viṣṇu, who can carry to heaven except Gaṅgā flowing in three paths, the living beings who were completely consumed by the fire of a Brāhmaṇa's curse and were conse-

1. The legend how king Bhagīratha brought the heavenly Gaṅgā to the earth for the redemption of his ancestors—the sons of king Sagara—is described in details in VR I.42 & 43 and Mbh, *Vana*, 109-119. This Purāṇa uses it as a background for describing the great sanctity of Gaṅgā in the subsequent verses.

quently reduced to a wretched state?

7. She (the River-Goddess) is another form of mine in a watery form. She is the very soul of welfare. She is the greatest Prakṛti, the mainstay of many Cosmic Eggs.

8. She is the personified form of pure learning and compassion. She possesses three Śaktis, viz. those of will, knowledge and action. She is of the nature of Nectar and bliss. She is the pure form of Dharma.

9. I am sportingly sustaining this support of all the worlds, perfect in form, like the Absolute Brahman for the sake of protecting the universe.

10-12. All the following, O Viṣṇu, are present in subtle form in Gaṅgā: all the sacred rivers and holy places in all the three worlds; all the Dharmas; Yajñas along with the monetary gifts thereof; all the types of penance; the fourfold Vedas along with their Aṅgas; you and I and Brahmā, the creator, and all the groups of Devas; all the Puruṣārthas (aims of life, viz. Dharma, Artha etc.) and the different forms of Śaktis.

13. He who resorts to Gaṅgā is on a par with one who has taken his holy ablutions in all the Tīrthas, who has performed all types of *Kratus* and who has observed all types of vows.

14. He who resorts to Gaṅgā has practised all types of penances, attained all the fruits of Yogic practices and observances and is on a par with a person who makes a liberal gift of everything.

15. A person who bathes in Gaṅgā regularly is superior to everyone in every Varṇa and stage of life, to everyone among Vedic scholars and to everyone who has mastered the sacred scriptures and the topics discussed therein.

16. Even a person defiled by many kinds of evils originating from mind, speech and body, becomes sanctified by seeing Gaṅgā. There is no doubt in this.

17. In Kṛtayuga there are holy Tīrthas everywhere; in Tretāyuga Puṣkara is the greatest of all Tīrthas; in Dvāparayuga, Kurukṣetra (is the best) and in Kaliyuga only Gaṅgā (is the holiest).

18. O Hari, one shall have (the opportunity to) live on the banks of Gaṅgā if there is the *Vāsanā* (impression left after repeated practice) of the previous births, with my great favour.

19. Meditation is the cause of salvation in Kṛtayuga; in

Tretāyuga meditation and penance are the causes of salvation; in Dvāparayuga, meditation, penance and Yajñas are the causes of salvation but in Kaliyuga it is Gaṅgā alone.

20. He who does not leave off the banks of Gaṅgā till his body falls (i.e., death), is always on a par with one conversant with Vedānta, a Yogin and one regularly observing the vow of celibacy.

21. In Kaliyuga there is no other means of salvation than Gaṅgā for persons of defiled minds, enamoured of other people's wealth and performing the rites without due regard for the injunctions (of the scriptural texts).

22. Alakṣmī (lack of wealth), Kālakarṇī (a female ogress), evil dreams and ill thoughts do not have any influence, if the devotee performs Japa like 'Gaṅgā, Gaṅgā.'

23. O Viṣṇu, Gaṅgā contributes to the welfare of all the worlds. She alone bestows benefits here as well as hereafter on all living beings in accordance with their devotional fervour.

24. O Hari, Yajña, Dāna, penance, Yoga, Japa, restraint and observance of holy vows do not merit even a thousandth part of the service rendered to Gaṅgā.

25. Of what avail is Yoga with its eight ancillaries? Of what avail are penances and sacrifices? Mere residence on the banks of Gaṅgā is the cause of the realization of Brahman.

26. O Govinda, Gaṅgā becomes pleased with the devotion of one who understands the greatness of Gaṅgā even if he were to be an undeserving person, even if he stays far off.

27. Faith is the greatest and subtlest Dharma (virtue). Faith is the greatest penance and knowledge; faith is heaven and salvation. She becomes pleased with (one who has) faith (in her).

28. In the case of persons whose minds have been deluded by ignorance, attachment, greed etc. they do not have any faith in Dharma and particularly in Gaṅgā.

29. Just as the external water becomes (sweet) water within a coconut, so also the water of the great Absolute stationed outside the Cosmic Egg becomes Jāhnavī.

30. There is no other acquisition greater than the acquisition of Gaṅgā anywhere. Hence one should resort to Gaṅgā. Gaṅgā itself is the greatest being.

31. O Hari, aimless and purposeless is the birth of one devoid of holy ablution in Gaṅgā even if he happens to be

powerful, learned, virtuous or munificent.

32. If one does not resort to Gaṅgā in Kali Age, (utterly) futile are his family (noble descent), learning, (performance of) sacrifices, penances and all the liberal gifts he has made.

33. In the worship of a deserving virtuous person, one does not attain such a benefit, as one gets from bathing in the waters of Gaṅgā or worshipping it in accordance with the injunctions.

34. This Gaṅgā, the womb whereof consists of the fire of my refulgence, who is well protected by my vigour (and is like me, Comm.) burns down all defects and sins.

35. The cage of the multitude of sins becomes split into a hundred pieces merely by remembering Gaṅgā, like a mountain struck by thunderbolt.

36. One who goes to Gaṅgā and one who rejoices in devotion, both of them, they say, derive the same benefit. Devotion alone is the cause thereof.

37. While walking, standing, repeating the names, meditating, taking food, speaking, walking, awake or sleeping, he who remembers Gaṅgā always, shall become released from bondage.

38-39. If, with the ancestors in view, anyone were to deposit devoutly in the waters of Gaṅgā, milk pudding with honey, along with jaggery, ghee and gingelly seeds, O Hari, his ancestors become gratified for a hundred years. The delighted grandfathers grant him all kinds of cherished desires.

40. Just as the whole universe becomes adored when the Liṅga is propitiated, so also one derives the benefit of all the Tīrthas through ablution in Gaṅgā.

41. A man who takes his holy dip in Gaṅgā everyday and worships the Liṅga, shall certainly get the greatest salvation in a single birth.

42. Agnihotra, Yajñas, Vrataṣ, Dānas and penances are not equal to a ten-millionth part of the adoration of the Liṅga in Gaṅgā.

43. If anyone decides to go to Gaṅgā and (as a preliminary to the pilgrimage) performs Śrāddha etc., at home and remains thus, the ancestors become delighted by his perfect resolve.

44-45. All the sins immediately cry, "Alas, where shall we

go?" Then they have consultation with *Lobha* (Greed), *Moha* (Delusion) etc. again and again and decide: "We shall create obstacles so that he shall not go to Gaṅgā, because once he goes to Gaṅgā, he will eradicate all of us."

46. Being disappointed, sins go away at every step from the body of the person who starts from his house for an ablution in Gaṅgā.

47. O Hari, a meritorious person casts off *Lobha* etc. due to merits performed in previous births, and reaches Gaṅgā after driving away all the obstacles.

48. A man who takes the holy dip in Gaṅgā shall go to heaven even if he does so incidentally, or for a price, or in the course of trading activity or service, even if he is lustful.

49. Just as fire burns even if touched unwillingly, so also Gaṅgā, even if it is bathed in unwillingly, burns sins.

50. A living being wanders in the course of its worldly existence as long as it does not resort to Gaṅgā. After resorting to Gaṅgā, no creature sees the sufferings of worldly existence.

51. He who eschews all doubts and devoutly takes his holy dips in the waters of Gaṅgā, is certainly a Deva covered with human skin.

52. One who undertakes a journey for the sake of taking a holy bath in Gaṅgā, but dies on the way, derives undoubtedly the benefit of a holy ablution in Gaṅgā.

53. Even those who listen to the greatness of Gaṅgā and read about it, become rid of great sins undoubtedly.

54. The evil-minded, wicked, sceptics and rationalists who take Gaṅgā as another ordinary river, O Viṣṇu, are fools.

55. In this birth, men become devoted to Gaṅgā due to the Dānas, penances, holy observances and vows performed in the course of the previous birth.

56. For the sake of those who are devoted to Gaṅga, mansions equipped with charming pleasures have been created by the Self-born Lord (Brahmā) in the cities of Mahendra and others.

57-58. Supernatural powers (Aṇimā etc.), Liṅgas bestowing divine powers, many kinds of *Sparśaliṅgas* (those that turn base metal into gold), gem-built palaces, multitude of Cintāmaṇis (philosopher's stones) etc. lie embedded in the waters of Gaṅgā, because they are afraid of pollution from Kali. Hence in Kali

Yuga, Gaṅgā, the bestower of the achievement of the desired goal, should be resorted to.

59-60. Like patches of darkness at sunrise, like mountains afraid of being smitten with thunderbolt, like serpents on seeing Tārkṣya (Garuḍa), like clouds tossed about by winds, like ignorance and delusion on the realization of Truth, like deer on seeing a lion, all the sins become exterminated at the sight of Gaṅgā.

61-62. Just as ailments perish due to the divine herbal remedies, just as good qualities perish due to greediness, just as the severity of summer heat is dispelled through plunging into a deep whirlpool and just as a heap of cotton perishes instantly by a spark of fire, so also all defects certainly perish by coming into contact with the waters of Gaṅgā.

63-64. Just as the power of penance perishes due to anger, just as good sense is spoiled by lust, just as fortune gets destroyed through defective morals, just as learning gets defiled by conceit, just as Dharma perishes through hypocrisy, crookedness and fraudulence, so also sins perish at the sight of Gaṅgā.

65. After obtaining the rare opportunity of getting human birth which is as inconstant as the fall of lightning, he who resorts to Gaṅgā has reached the height of intellect.

66. Those men who have shaken off all the sins, see Gaṅgā on the earth in the form of the greatest refulgence resembling a thousand suns.

67. Atheists with eyes spoiled by sins see Gaṅgā like an ordinary river filled with ordinary water.

68. Due to compassion for people I, the redeemer from worldly existence, have created a flight of steps unto heaven in the form of the waves of Gaṅgā.

69. On the banks of the glorious Gaṅgā all times are auspicious, all the spots are auspicious and holy, all persons are fit for the receipt of religious gifts.

70-73. Just as a horse-sacrifice is the best among all Yajñas, just as Himavān is the greatest among mountains, just as truthfulness is the greatest among holy vows, just as offering freedom from fear is the best among gifts, just as Prāṇāyāma (restraint of vital breath) is the best among austerities, just as Praṇava (Om) is the best among Mantras, just as abstention from violence is the best among all pious activities, just as Śrī (prosperity and fortune) is the most excellent of all desirable things, just as spiritual learning is the best among all learnings, just as Gaurī is the most excellent one among all women, just as you, O Puruṣottama, are the best among all the Devas, just as a devotee of Śiva is the most excellent one among all deserving persons, so also Gaṅgā Tīrtha is the most excellent one among all the Tīrthas.

74. O Hari, a highly intelligent person who does not make any difference between us both, should be known as a devotee of Śiva. He is a great Pāśupata ('devotee of Paśupati i.e., Śiva').

75. This Gaṅgā of meritorious current is like the great whirlwind unto the dust particles of sin, is like axe unto the tree of sins, and is like forest fire unto the fuel of sins.

76. The Pitṛs (manes) of different forms always sing these songs: "Would that someone in our family takes the holy bath in Gaṅgā."

77. After propitiating Devas and Sages as well as indigent ones, helpless ones and miserable ones, he would take his holy dip faithfully in accordance with the injunctions and offer handfuls of water libation.

78. "Would that he is born in our family, who will impartially look at Śiva and Viṣṇu, who will build temples for both of them and will devoutly clean them and carry out other activities as well."

79. He who dies in Gaṅgā will not see hell whether he cherishes desire or not, even if it is the lower strata of living beings that he belongs to.

80. If those who are staying on the banks of Gaṅgā were to praise another Tīrtha and do not honour Gaṅgā, they are sure to pass on to a hell.

81. A base man who hates me as well as you and Gaṅgā shall go to hell along with members of his family.

82. Sixty-four thousands of Gaṇas always protect Gaṅgā and they create obstacles in the stay of sinners who are no devotees.

83. With the sharp arrows of lust, anger, excessive delusion, convetousness etc., they overwhelm their minds and oust them from there (Gaṅgā).

84. He who resorts to Gaṅgā is a sage. He is a learned

man. He should be known as one blessed with achievement in regard to the four aims of life.

85. One who, just for once, takes his holy dip in Gaṅgā, shall obtain the benefit of a horse-sacrifice. By offering libations of water to the Pitṛs there, he shall redeem them from the ocean of hell.

86. A meritorious man who continuously bathes in Gaṅgā for one month, lives in the world of Indra along with his ancestors, as long as Indra (continues to live).

87. A meritorious man who continuously bathes in Gaṅgā for one year, shall reach the world of Viṣṇu and stay there happily.

88. A man who takes his holy bath in Gaṅgā everyday throughout his life, should be known as *Jīvanmukta* (a living-liberated soul), who with the destruction of the body (after death) becomes completely liberated.

89. Any particular lunar day, asterism or day of special significance need not be taken into consideration in regard to (the holy bath) in the waters of Gaṅgā. Merely through holy dip in Gaṅgā all the hoarded sins perish.

90. He who does not resort to the banks of Gaṅgā worthy of being resorted to very easily, is a fool though learned, is powerless though endowed with Śakti (power).

91. If one does not resort to Gaṅgā, of what use is his longevity free from sickness, of what avail is his ever growing prosperity, of what avail is his blemishless intellect?

92. A man who gets a temple built for an idol of Gaṅgā, enjoys all pleasures. After death he attains the world of Gaṅgā.

93. Those who listen everyday to the greatness of Gaṅgā with respect shall obtain the benefit of a holy dip in Gaṅgā by propitiating with adequate monetary gifts the scholar who reads the text.

94. With Pitṛs in view, if anyone bathes the Liṅga with the waters of Gaṅgā, his ancestors become pleased although they may be in a great hell.

95. Learned men say that far superior to bathing with ghee is bathing with the waters of Gaṅgā, filtered with a cloth, charged eight times with Mantras (pertaining to Śiva or Gaṅgā—Comm.) and rendered fragrant with scents.

96-97. If anyone offers *Argha* at least once to the Sun with the waters of Gaṅgā mixed with the eight Dravyas measured to a *Magadhaprastha* (i.e., 12½ *Palas*) in a copper vessel, he goes to the Solar world in a highly brilliant aerial chariot along with his ancestors and is honoured there.

98-99. The eight *Dravyas* (ingredients) are: water, Kuśa grass, honey, cow's milk, cow's ghee, cow's curd, red sandalpaste and red Karavīra flowers. This *Argha* with eight ingredients is considered extremely propitiatory to the Sun-god. O Viṣṇu, this *Argha* with the waters of Gaṅgā should be known to be ten million times more meritorious than *Argha* with other waters.

100. If a sensible man erects a temple on the banks of Gaṅgā according to his capacity, it has a benefit ten million times more than that of the installation at another Tīrtha.

101-103. Merely by visiting Gaṅgā, one gets that merit which one gets elsewhere by planting Aśvattha, Vaṭa, mango and other trees or by digging wells, tanks and lakes or through watersheds and sacrifices. The very touch of Gaṅgā is superior to the act of making flower gardens etc. By drinking a mouthful of the waters of Gaṅgā, one gets the benefit hundred times more than that of the gift of a virgin in marriage, that of the gift of cows and cooked rice.

104. By drinking the nectar-like waters of Gaṅgā, O Janārdana, one gets more benefit than the benefit derived from a thousand Cāndrāyaṇa observances.

105. What other benefit shall be said as resulting from devout plunge in Gaṅgā, O Hari, than everlasting residence in heaven or ultimate salvation?

106. A man who always worships the pair of sandals of Gaṅgā obtains longevity, merit, wealth, sons, heaven, and salvation.

107. O Hari, for the destruction of the sins and blemishes of Kali, there is no other Tīrtha on a par with Gaṅgā. There is no holy spot on a par with Avimukta in bestowing salvation.

108. On seeing a man regularly engaged in the holy bath in Gaṅgā, the servants of Yama flee in ten directions like deer on seeing a lion.

109. One shall obtain the benefit of a horse-sacrifice by duly worshipping a person staying on the banks of Gaṅgā and regularly worshipping Gaṅgā.

110. By devoutly gifting cows, plots of land and gold on

the splendid banks of Gaṅgā, a man has no rebirth in the miserable world.

111. (On the bank of Gaṅgā) by making gifts of garments, one attains longevity; by gifting books one gets knowledge; by gifting cooked rice one gets wealth; and by gifting a virgin one gets fame.

112. Whatever rite is performed on the banks of Gaṅgā, such as holy vows, *Dāna, Japa* or penance, O Hari, has ten million times more benefit than the ones performed elsewhere.

113-118. One who makes the gifts of a cow along with her calf in accordance with the injunctions on the banks of Gaṅgā, O Viṣṇu, shall have all types of prosperity. By gifting away a Kāmadhenu he will enjoy all desires and pleasures, either in Goloka or in my world for as many Yugas as there are hairs on the body of the cow. Along with his kinsmen, he will enjoy divine pleasure of may kinds, (some of them) not available to even Devas. He will enjoy them along with his ancestors and friends. He will be embellished with all kinds of jewels. Thereafter, he is born in an excellent family possessing good conduct and learning. After enjoying infinite pleasures in the company of sons and grandsons he will come again to Gaṅgā flowing towards the north at Kāśī. After propitiating Viśveśvara, due to the impressions and experiences of the previous births, in due course he may die after which he attains Brahman (i.e., salvation).

119. Listen to the meritorious benefit of the man who devoutly gives away a plot of land on the banks of Gaṅgā extending to two *Nivartanas* (1 Nivartana=30 Daṇḍas).

120-122. After enjoying all delightful pleasures in the worlds of Mahendra and Candra for as many Yugas as there are *Trasareṇus* (particles of dust) in that plot of land, he becomes lord of the seven continents. O Hari, he will be very righteous and he will be able to redeem his Pitṛs from hells and take them to heaven. He will liberate the Pitṛs staying in heaven. He will be highly resplendent. In the end he will chop off Avidyā by means of the sword of knowledge—the Avidyā that has converted itself into the five elements.

123. He may have the greatest Vairāgya (non-attachment) and will practise the excellent Yoga. Or after reaching Avimukta, he will realize the great Absolute Brahman.

124-127. One who, on the banks of Gaṅgā, makes a gift of excellent gold weighing a *Suvarṇa* (i.e., 80 Rattis) to a man of excellent Varṇa, O Hari, will be endowed with all *Aiśvaryas* (supernatural powers) and he will move about in a gold and gemset aerial chariot that can go everywhere. He will be honoured in all the worlds stationed in other Cosmic Eggs and experience all pleasures delighting the mind. O Viṣṇu, he will be adored by all until all the living beings are annihilated. Thereafter, he shall be the sole king in Jaṁbūdvīpa and very powerful and valorous. Then he will come to Avimukta and attain salvation.

128. If anyone takes his holy bath devoutly in Gaṅgā on the day on which the star of his nativity falls, he shall instantly be released from the multitude of sins accumulated in the course of various births.

129. A holy bath in Gaṅgā is very rare (i.e., is of special value) in the months of Vaiśākha, Kārttika and Māgha. The bath is hundred times more beneficial if performed on the new-moon day and a thousand times, on the Saṅkrānti day (transit of the Sun).

130. If the bath is taken on the days of lunar or solar eclipses, it is a hundred thousand times; on the Vyatīpāta day (i.e., if the new-moon day is a Sunday) it is innumerable times; if it is on Viṣuva days (equinox days), it is ten thousand times more beneficial; if it is on the Ayana days, a hundred thousand times.

131. If the lunar eclipse falls on a Monday or the solar eclipse on a Sunday, it is called *Cūḍāmaṇi Parva.* The bath on that day has unlimited benefit.

132. Bathing, *Dāna, Japa* and Homa, whatever is performed on the Cūḍāmaṇi day on the banks of Gaṅgā, O Viṣṇu, is of everlasting benefit.

133. If one takes the holy dip in Gaṅgā in accordance with the injunctions with devotion and faith, one shall become purified even if one is a Brāhmaṇa-slayer. What to say of other sinners!

134. Worms, insects, locusts etc. that die on the banks of Gaṅgā, the trees that fall into Gaṅgā from the bank—all these attain salvation.

135-137. In the bright half of the month of Jyeṣṭha, on the tenth day with asterism Hasta, a man or woman should keep awake at night on the banks of Gaṅgā with great devotional fervour. He (or she) should perform the adoration of Gaṅgā ten times, O Garuḍa-emblemed Hari. There shall be ten kinds of flowers of great fragrance: The Naivedyas shall be of ten fruits on every occasion. There shall be *Daśāṅga Dhūpas* [constituents: Kustha, jaggery, lac, Nakha (?), Harītakī, Sarjarasa, Māṁsī, Śailaja, Ghana (camphor) and bdellium]. A wise devotee shall perform the worship ten times in accordance with the injunctions.

138. He should drop gingelly seeds smeared with ghee into the waters of Gaṅgā. He should then offer ten handfuls of water. Uttering the Mantra he should offer ten balls of fried wheat-flour mixed with jaggery.

139-140. The twenty-syllabled Mantra is to be "*Om namaḥ śivāyai nārāyaṇyai daśaharāyai gaṅgāyai svāhā*" (Om, obeisance to Śivā, Nārāyaṇī, Daśaharā, Gaṅgā). The worship, *Dāna, Japa* and *Homa* are to be performed with the same *Mantra.*

141-145. According to his capacity the devotee should prepare an idol of Gaṅgā with gold or silver. It shall be installed above a Pūrṇakumbha (pot filled with water), the face of which is covered with a cloth. He should then bathe the idol with Pañcāmṛta and adore it.

Thereafter he shall meditate upon Gaṅgā as follows: She is very gentle in form with four arms and three eyes. She is served by Nadīs and Nadas (rivers great and small). She has the frequent application of the nectarine exudation of loveliness all over her physical form. She holds in her four hands a Pūrṇakuṁbha, a white lotus, the gestures of granting boon and freedom from fear. Her lustre is like that of ten thousand moons. She is being fanned with chowries. She shines well with a white umbrella. She has flooded the ground with nectar. She is besmeared with divine scents and unguents. Her feet are adored by all the three worlds. She is eulogized by Devas and the divine sages.

146-147. After meditating and worshipping with the Mantra, he should offer *Dhūpa* and *Dīpa.* In front of the idol of Gaṅgā, he should make small idols of myself, yourself and that of Brahmā, the Sun-god, Himālaya and Bhagīratha with sandalpaste and raw rice-grains and worship them. He should respectfully give ten *Prasthas* of gingelly seeds to ten Brāhmaṇas.

148. These measures of grain are each four times the previous: *Pala, Kuḍava, Prastha, Āḍhaka* and *Droṇa* (Pala: a handful of grain).

149-150. The devotee observing the holy vow should make figures of fish, tortoise, frog, shark and other aquatic beings such as swans, Kāraṇḍavas, Bakas (cranes), Cakra (ruddy geese), Ṭiṭṭibha or Sārasa with pasted flour, copper, silver or gold in accordance with his capacity, worship them with scents and flowers and then cast them into Gaṅgā.

151. By performing this rite thus in accordance with the injunctions, without showing stinginess in spending money, the devotee will be rid of the ten types of sins as mentioned below:

152-155. There are three types of physical sins such as taking away what is not duly offered, indulging in violence without scriptural justification and resorting to other men's wives. There are four types of verbal sins, viz. harsh utterances, untruthful speech, backbiting, indulging in irrelevant and absurd talks. There are three types of mental sins, viz. reflecting constantly on other people's assets, evil thoughts in regard to others and earnest desire for insignificant and unreal things.

That devotee should be rid of all these ten types of sins originating in the course of ten births. There is no doubt about it, O Gadādhara. It is true, it is (definitely) true.

156. He shall redeem from terrible hell ten ancestors and ten successors. He should perform the *Japa* of the prayer presently being recounted with great faith in front of Gaṅgā:

[Prayer to Gangā: (157-174)]

157. "Om, Obeisance to Gaṅgā, identical with Śiva and the bestower of happiness. Obeisance, obeisance, obeisance to you in the form of Viṣṇu. Obeisance to you in the form of Brahmā.

158. Bow to you in the form of Rudra, Śāṅkarī (benefactress); obeisance to you in the form of all gods; obeisance to medicine personified.

159. Obeisance to you, the most excellent physician of all ailments of all people. Obeisance to you, the destroyer of the poisons arising from mobile and immobile beings.

160. Hail to you, the destroyer of the poison of worldly existence; obeisance to the enlivener. Repeated obeisance to

you, the destroyer of the three types of distresses, the goddess of the vital breath.

161. Obeisance to the goddess, the cause of continuous peace; obeisance to you, of pure form; obeisance to the purifier of everything; obeisance to you in the form of the enemy of sins.

162. Repeated salutes to the bestower of worldly pleasures and salvation; obeisance to the bestower of welfare; obeisance to the bestower of pleasures here and hereafter; obeisance to you, the river in the nether worlds.

163. Obeisance to Mandākinī; obeisance, obeisance to the bestower of heavenly pleasures; obeisance to the ornament of the three worlds; obeisance, obeisance to the triple-streamed one.

164. Obeisance to the holy river abiding in the three white ones (pure ones, viz. its source, Prayāga and confluence with the sea); obeisance, obeisance to the one with forbearance; obeisance to the one abiding in the three types of fire; obeisance to the brilliant one.

165. Obeisance to Nandā (Alakanandā); obeisance to one holding the Liṅga; obeisance to the one having nectarine current; obeisance to you, the foremost one in the universe; obeisance, obeisance to Revatī.

166. Obeisance to you, the large one; obeisance to the mother of the worlds; obeisance to the one, the benefactor of the universe; obeisance to the delighter, obeisance.

167. Obeisance to one in the form of the earth; to one with auspicious waters; to the one in the form of the excellent piety; repeated obeisance to you, possessed of hundreds of greater and lesser beings; obeisance, obeisance to you, the redeemer.

168. Obeisance to you, the breaker of the nooses and nets; obeisance to the one devoid of difference (partiality), obeisance to the quiescent one, to the most excellent one; obeisance to the bestower of boons.

169. Obeisance to the fierce one; to the enjoyer of pleasures. Obeisance to you, the enlivener; obeisance to one stationed in Brahman; to the one bestowing Brahman (Vedas); obeisance, obeisance to the destroyer of sins.

170. Obeisance to you, the destroyer of the distress of

those who bow down; obeisance to you, the mother of the universe; obeisance to the one that dispels all adversities; obeisance, obeisance to the auspicious one.

171. O Goddess, well disposed to save the poor and the distressed who seek refuge! O Goddess, O remover of the distress of everyone! Obeisance to the Goddess Nārāyaṇī (the abode of waters).

172. Obeisance, obeisance to the one free from all adhesions and smearings (one without the effects of Avidyā and its products); to the destroyer of the demon Durga; obeisance to you, the efficient one; obeisance to the one beyond the greatest and the least, O Gaṅgā, the bestower of liberation!

173. O Gaṅgā, be in front of me; O Gaṅgā, stand behind me; O Gaṅgā, be at my sides; O Gaṅgā, let me be stationed in you.

174. O auspicious Gaṅgā, you are at the beginning, in the middle and at the end; O auspicious one present in the earth, you are everything; you alone are the original Prakṛti; you are the highest Absolute; O Gaṅgā, you are supreme soul, Śiva; O auspicious one, obeisance to you."

175. He who reads (recites) this prayer, he who listens to it with faith becomes rid of the ten types of sins originating from body, speech and mind.

176. One who is sick becomes rid of ailments; one who is in adversity becomes rid of that adversity; one who is fettered becomes free from bondage; one who is terrified becomes free from that fear.

177. He will obtain all the desires; after his death, he will go to heaven riding a divine aerial chariot and fanned by celestial women.

178. If this prayer is written and kept in the house always or if it is worn always, he will have no cause to fear, fire or thief nor serpents etc.

179. If the tenth lunar day in the bright half of the month of Jyeṣṭha coincides with the asterism Hasta and Wednesday, it destroys all the three types of sins.

180-181. On that tenth day, he who stands in the waters of Gaṅgā and recites this prayer ten times, even if he is poor or (physically) incapable, obtains that benefit which has been mentioned before as accruing from worshipping assiduously

Gaṅgā in accordance with the injunctions.

182. Gaṅgā is on a par with Gaurī. Hence the injunctions laid down for the adoration of Gaurī are also applicable to the worship of Gaṅgā.

183. Just as I am the same as you, O Viṣṇu, so also you are the same as Umā; Gaṅgā is the same as Umā; the forms of the four are not different.

184. He who mentions that there is difference between Viṣṇu and Rudra, between Śrī and Gaurī and between Gaṅgā and Gaurī is silly-minded.

CHAPTER TWENTYEIGHT

The Greatness of Gaṅgā (continued)

Umā said:

1. O Lord, I am thinking of asking something to get rid of my doubts. O Lord, O knower of the three divisions of time, please tell me if you have no difficulty.

2. Where was King Bhagīratha and where was Gaṅgā (Bhāgirathī) then, when Viṣṇu performed austerity on the banks of Cakrapuṣkariṇī?

Śiva said:

3-4. O possessor of large eyes, O ever pure one, no doubt need be entertained in this respect. Three divisions of time are mentioned in the Vedas, Smṛtis and Purāṇas, viz. past, future and present. Do not have any doubt needlessly.

After saying this, Īśa again narrated the excellent greatness of Gaṅgā.

Agastya requested:

5. O son and delighter of Pārvatī, narrate again in full the greatness of the celestial river as was recounted to Hari by the Lord of Devas then.

Skanda said:

6. O son of Mitra and Varuṇa, listen to the sin-eradicating greatness of the triple-streamed river as recounted by the Lord.

7. If on approaching the three-currented river, anyone offers balls of rice, at least once, along with the water libations with gingelly seeds, the Pitṛs are redeemed by him from the ocean of worldly existence.

8. The Pitṛs will stay in heaven as many thousands of years as there are gingelly seeds taken by the men in the course of the pious rite of the Pitṛs.

9. Since the Devas are always stationed in Gaṅgā along with the Pitṛs, neither the ritualistic invocation nor the dismissal-rite need be performed unto them there.

The following types of men go to heaven after being offered libations with the waters of Gaṅgā:

10. those who are dead in the family of father, as well as those in the family of mother; the other kinsmen of the preceptor, father-in-law or other relatives who are dead;

11. those who died before cutting the teeth; those who had become afflicted even while in the womb; those who had been killed by fire, lightning or by thieves or by tigers or other fanged amimals;

12. those who had committed suicide by hanging themselves; those fallen ones; those of self-inflicted death; those who sell themselves; thieves; those who perform the sacrificial rites unto those who are not eligible for them;

13. those who sell *Rasas* (juices); those who suffer from diseases arising from sins (such as leprosy); those who are guilty of arson and administration of poison; those who kill cows; those belonging to one's own family;

14. those who have gone to the following five hells: Asipatravana, Kuṁbhīpāka, Raurava, Andhatāmisra and Kālasūtra;

15-16. those who wander through thousands of other births as a result of their own karmas; those who have been born as birds, animals, worms, trees and creepers of innumerable types; those who are not of very good and auspicious features even among those who can be counted; those who had been taken to the world of Yama by the terrible servants of Yama;

17. those who are not kinsmen; those who are so; those who were kinsmen in the course of other births; those whose names are not known; those of one's own family but without issues;

18. those who died due to poison; those who were struck by horned animals; ungrateful persons; slayers of preceptors and elders; those who had harassed and betrayed friends;

19. those who killed women and children; those who are guilty of treachery; those who were violent and untruthful; those who have always been sinful;

20. those who sell horses; those who take away other people's wealth; helpless ones; the wretched and miserable; those incapable of being born as human beings.

21. If these are offered libations even once with the waters of Gaṅgā in accordance with the injunctions, they go to heaven. After being the dwellers of heaven, they shall attain liberation.

22. He who utters the Mantras and offers the libations of the Pitṛs unto these people and offers Śrāddha and balls of rice, is called as one who is conversant with the procedure.

23. Whatever holy places are there in the three worlds bestowing cherished desires, they resort to Gaṅgā that flows towards the north at Kāśī.

24. O Viṣṇu, the celestial river is sacred everywhere, capable of dispelling the sin of even Brāhmaṇa-slaughter. It is particularly so where its current flows towards the north at Kāśī.

25-26. Devas, sages and groups of Pitṛs sing (i.e., wish): "Will Gaṅgā flowing towards the north at Kāśī be ever seen by us? We can be satiated through the Amṛta (nectarine water) there and be free from the three types of distresses. Presently, with the grace of Viśvanātha we shall attain salvation too."

27. O Hari, Gaṅgā alone is surely conducive to liberation, particularly so in Avimukta, due to the added weight of my presence.

28. After realising that Kali age is excessively terrible, the devotion to Gaṅgā is well-guarded. Ordinary men do not get (the benefit of that holy river) Gaṅgā, the sole bestower of the path of salvation.

29. Without the worship of Jāhnavī who can expect lib-

eration after wandering through various wombs in the course of many thousands of births?

30. O Viṣṇu, Gaṅgā alone is the greatest antidote to men of meagre intelligence, ailing with the ailment of worldly existence, bewildered and distracted on account of sins.

31. If anyone repairs and rebuilds temples on the banks of Gaṅgā, O Hari, he will have never-reducing (everlasting) happiness for a long time in my world.

32. If anyone intends to go to Gaṅgā for his own sake or for other's sake but does not go due to delusion, he will fall (in hell) along with his ancestors.

33. Those embodied human beings who carry out all their (holy) rites by means of the waters of Gaṅgā are immortal ones, O Hari, even though they stay on the earth.

34. He who resorts to Gaṅgā, the celestial river, at least during the last days of his life, shall attain excellent goal even after committing many sins.

35. Men are honoured in the heavenly world for as many thousands of years as their bones rest in the waters of Gaṅgā.

Viṣṇu said:

36-37. O Lord of Devas, O Lord of the universe, O Lord and benefactor of the worlds, if the bone of a wicked, evil-intentioned person were to fall casually in the sinless (sanctifying) waters of the heavenly river, how will he attain the great goal, after his premature accidental death? O Īśa, let this be clearly enunciated.

Maheśvara said:

38. In this regard I shall recount an old ancedote, O Adhokṣaja (Viṣṇu). O Viṣṇu, listen with concentration of mind to the story of the Brāhmaṇa (Vāhīka)[1].

39. Formerly in the land of Kaliṅga, there was a Brāhmaṇa who used to sell salt. He was devoid of even a syllable from the Vedas. He avoided regular ablutions during dusks.

40. His name was Vāhīka. He had only the Yajñasūtra, the sacred thread (to indicate that he was a Brāhmaṇa). The wife

1. The legend of Vāhīka is an illustration of the sanctifying nature of Gaṅgā.

of a weaver who became a widow immediately became his wife.

41. Without a means of sustenance of life, the Śūdra woman accompanied by her husband tormented by famine, left the country and went to another country.

42. In the middle of the Daṇḍaka forest that Vāhīka, emaciated with hunger and devoid of associates, was killed by a tiger fond of human flesh.

43. A certain vulture seized his left leg and flew up. In the sky it had a fight with another flesh-eating vulture.

44. While the two vultures desirous of the meat were fighting together with a desire to vanquish each other, the ankle of the leg fell down from the beak of the vulture.

45. While the vultures were engaged in their duel, the ankle of the Brāhmaṇa Vāhīka who had been killed by a tiger, casually fell into Gaṅgā.

46. As soon as the tiger killed that Vāhīka travelling through the forest, the cruel servants (of Yama) bound him with nooses.

47. He was lashed much with whips; prodded all round with iron rods. He began to shed blood from his mouth. He was thus taken to the presence of Yama.

48. Then, O Consort of Lakṣmī, Citragupta was asked by Dharmarāja: "Tell me after due consideration the merits and demerits of this Brāhmaṇa quickly."

49-50. On being asked by the son of Vivasvān (i.e., Yama) Citragupta of wonderful intellect, who knew all the activities of all the creatures always, told Yamuna's brother (i.e., Yama) all the inauspicious activities of the Brāhmaṇa Vāhīka of foul deeds, ever since the day of his birth.

Citragupta said:

51. The sacred rites[1] of *Garbhādhāna* etc. have not been performed on his behalf before. O Hari (Yama), *Jātakarma* (post-natal rite) was not performed by his ignorant father.

52. On the eleventh day, the *naming* ceremony was not duly performed for him: It is that rite which is the cause for subduing the sins since conception and which bestows happiness throughout the life.

1. VV 51-58 record various Saṁskāras to be performed on every individual since birth.

53-58. On the fourth month, the slow-witted father did not perform the *Nirgama* (going out from the lying-in chamber) rite, the most sacred of all rites whereby he (the son) would have become famous. The father did not perform the *Nirgama* rite on an auspicious lunar day with other auspicious features also. It would have prevented the departure to foreign lands.

On the sixth month, the rite of *Annaprāśana* (feeding with cooked rice) was not performed duly, O son of Bhāskara (i.e., Yama), whereby he (the son) would have always eaten plenty of wholesome food.

On the completion of a year, the rite of *Cūḍākaraṇa* ('making tuft of hair') was not performed befitting the family, through which rite his hairs would have become smooth and glossy and showering flowers.

The rite of *Karṇavedha* (boring the ear) was not performed on an auspicious day by his father, by which rite the ears could have borne gold (earrings) and grasped excellent learning.

O Hari (Yama), it was (only) after the eighth year had passed that the rite of *Mauñjībandha* (binding with the Muñja grass or thread-ceremony) was performed, which rite is intended for learning the Vedas and is conducive to the enhancement of celibacy.

The very mentioning of the rite of *Mauñjī-Mokṣaṇa* (Release from the Mauñjī i.e., *Samāvartana* ceremony) was not performed by his father, after which rite the excellent performance of the duties of a householder would have taken place.

59. Some wife who had discarded the tradition of the family and had become a harlot, was married by this consort of a Śūdra woman, who abducted another man's wife.

60. This fellow had become a pilferer of other men's wealth ever since his fifth year. He was addicted to the game of gambling and he always practised misdeeds.

61. While he was staying in a *Rumā* (salt-producing marsh) a year-old cow was hit by him with a stout stick when it licked salt. And the cow died.

62. He used to kick his mother many times. His father's words were never heeded to by him.

63. He was fond of quarrels. Many times he even ate poison. He habitually **harassed** people, tearing up their stomach.

64. This evil-minded fellow used to swallow on many occasions small poisons such as Dhattūra, Karavīra etc., even at the time of a playful quarrel.

65. O son of Sūrya (i.e., Yama), he was burnt with fire; he was bitten by dogs; hit by horned animals with the tips of their horns.

66. This wicked fellow, despised by all good people, the committer of sins, has been bitten by venomous reptiles. With wooden pieces and lumps of clay, he inflicted injury on himself frequently.

67. His head was struck by himself many times. This evil-minded fellow (violently) shook off his head, the best of all limbs of men which is always revered by good people.

68. Though he was a Brāhmaṇa, this silly fellow did not know even the Gāyatrī. This evil-minded fellow ate fish and flesh as he pleased.

69-70. Many times he got milk pudding cooked for his own sake. This silly fellow used to sell lac, salt, flesh along with milk, ghee and curds, poison, iron (hardware) and weapons, girl-slaves, cows and horses, hair and hides too.

71. His limbs became nourished with the cooked food from Śūdras. He used to indulge in sexual intercourse on festival days and even during the day-time. This wicked-souled fellow was averse to the holy rites pertaining to Devas and Pitṛs.

72. Birds were killed by him and hundreds of animals too. This cruel-minded fellow always cut off trees without any purpose.

73. Untruthful in speech and always engrossed in violence, he caused disgust incessantly even to his kinsmen.

74. O Ravija (son of the Sun i.e., Yama), of what avail is talking too much? He was a slander-monger deeply indulging in the activities pertaining to the stomach and the organ of generation. He never made any monetary gift. He was a living personified form of sins.

75-77. May he be cast into each of the following hells for the period of a Kalpa: Raurava, Andhatāmisra, Kuṁbhīpāka, Atiraurava, Kālasūtra, Kṛmibhuj, Pūyaśoṇitakardama, Asipatravana, the terrible Yantrapīḍa, Sudaṁṣṭraka, Adhomukha, Pūtigandha, Viṣṭhāgarta, Śvabhojana, Sūcībhedya, Sandaṁśa, Lālāpa and Kṣuradhāraka.

* * *

78-79. On hearing those words from the mouth of Citragupta, Dharmarāja rebuked the misbehaving Brāhmaṇa and commanded his servants. With a gesture of Yama's eyebrows he was bound and led to the hell by them. The loud screaming and wailing of the sinners caused horripilation.

Īśvara said:

80-81. In the course of the very severe tortures Vāhīka expired. Since (the ankle) had fallen from the mouth of the vulture into the pure waters of Gaṅgā that yielded benefit at once, there came an aerial chariot from heaven at the same time, O Hari, for the Brāhmaṇa Vāhīka.

82-83. There were many bells hanging down from the aerial chariot. It was divine and full of hundreds of celestial damsels. The Brāhmaṇa who had assumed a divine form and dress climbed on to the divine vehicle. Divine scents and unguents he had applied (to his body) and he was fanned by groups of Apsarās, O Hari, due to the fact that a bone of his had fallen into Gaṅgā.

Skanda said:

84. O Pot-born Sage, the power of certain things is (inexplicably) wonderful. This is a mighty power of Sadāśiva in liquid form.

85. Indeed, it is for the sake of uplifting the worlds that Gaṅgā is made to flow by Śaṁbhu, the Lord of Devas, full of the nectar of kindness.

86. This triple-steamed (*Tripathagāminī*) Gaṅgā should not be considered by good people on a par with thousands of other rivers in the world (though) filled with water.

87. The syllables of Śruti were squeezed out of mercy, O sage, by Śaṁbhu. This Gaṅgā was created by Gaṅgādhara through the liquids arising therefrom (i.e., the water of Gaṅgā is the Brahma-rasa squeezed out of Upaniṣads—Com.)

88. Due to his compassion for all creatures Śaṅkara extracted the essence of Yogic and Upaniṣadic texts and created the most excellent one among rivers.

89. The regions where the celestial river is not present are like nights without the moon and trees bereft of flowers.

90. The regions and quarters devoid of the waters of Gaṅgā are like riches devoid of fairness and sacrifices without monetary gifts.

91. The directions devoid of Gaṅgā are like the courtyard of the sky without the Sun, like a house at night without a lamp and like Brāhmaṇas without Vedic study.

92. Of the two, one of them doing the observance of a thousand *Cāndrāyaṇas* purifying the body and the other drinking the water from Gaṅgā, the one that drinks Gaṅgā water is superior.

93. Of the two, one of them standing on a single foot for a hundred of thousand years and the other drinking the water of Gaṅgā for a year, the one who drinks the water of Gaṅgā is superior.

94. O Hari, a man who lies down on the sandy banks of Bhīṣmasū (Gaṅgā, the mother of Bhīṣma) as on a bed is superior to a man who hangs down with the head downwards for a period of a hundred years.

95. Since Jāhnavī Gaṅgā is the destroyer of the distress resulting from sins of all the living beings suffering from the distress of sins, so there is nothing else like it in Kali age.

96. Just as serpents become rid of their venom by the mere sight of Garuḍa, so also sins become devoid of lustre (power) at the sight of Gaṅgā.

97. A man who keeps on his head the clay from the banks of Gaṅgā certainly bears on his head the solar disc for the purpose of destroying darkness.

98. Gaṅgā alone is spoken as the refuge of that sinner who is devoid of wealth and assailed by many vices. It cannot be otherwise.

99. There is no doubt about this that Gaṅgā shall redeem both the families (father's as well as mother's) of men, if Gaṅgā is heard about, desired, seen, touched, drunk or plunged into.

100. The acts of glorification, seeing, touching, drinking and plunging into with respect to Gaṅgā are successively ten times more effective in increasing merit and destroying demerit.

101. Neither by sons, nor by riches nor by any other excellent activity is obtained that benefit which is derived by men

after resorting to Gaṅgā.

102. Those who never take the holy bath in Gaṅgā that accords liberation even though they are hale and hearty (capable) are cogenitally blind, lame and dead even if they (breathe and) are alive.

103. O Hari, listen to the Śruti that glorifies Gaṅgā. After listening to that Śruti of decisive meaning, an excellent man should resort to Gaṅgā.

104. Those who resort to the heaven-born Gaṅgā go to heaven. She is identical with these five rivers: Irāvatī, Madhumatī, Payasvinī, Amṛtarūpā and Ūrjasvatī.

105. Those who have resorted with all their heart to Jāhnavī rising from the foot of Viṣṇu and reaching the world, having meritorious current, being very ancient and resorted to by sages, go to the abode of Brahmā.

106. Gaṅgā should always be devoutly approached by spiritually inclined if they yearn for the covetable position of Brahmā. Like a mother leading her sons, Gaṅgā always takes the worlds (people) to heaven. She is endowed with all good qualities.

107. One who is desirous of the purity of himself should resort to Gaṅgā that is worthy of being served by good people. She is immortal, and is identical with Sāvitrī Mantra. She is the mother of Guha and is fully equipped with splendid rays. She is desirous (of granting boons), and is Cosmic-formed and possessed of Irā (Earth and Speech).

108. A man who takes his holy dip in Gaṅgā, practises celibacy and remains pure with mental concentration, becomes rid of all sins and he obtains (the benefit of) Vājapeya sacrifice.

109. If they (sinners) resort to her, Gaṅgā shall always redeem those persons who are overwhelmed by inauspicious activities, who sink in the great ocean (of worldly existence) and who are about to fall into hell.

110. Just as the world of Brahmā is the most excellent one among all the worlds, so also Jāhnavī is the most excellent one among rivers and lakes.

111. Within half a Ghaṭikā (i.e., 12 minutes) one gets the benefit that is obtained elsewhere after performing penances for three years with a firm resolve, if one does the same in Gaṅgā.

112. A man staying in heaven and enjoying everlasting pleasure cannot have as much satisfaction as what people get on the banks of Gaṅgā at night when the moon rises.

113. One can assuredly cast like a piece of grass into the waters of Gaṅgā, the dead body of an old person afflicted with sickness. It will enter Amarāvatī (heavenly city).

114. The lunar disc is always washed by the flood of waters of Gaṅgā. Hence at the end of the day it has added lustre.

115. The sin of a person who plunges into the waters of Gaṅgā perishes immediately. At the same moment, he attains the greatest welfare.

116. O Acyuta, the waters of Gaṅgā if faithfully offered to the Pitṛs by their descendants, accord them great satisfaction for three years.

117. She redeems people of the earth, reptiles residing beneath and dwellers of heaven. Hence, O Viṣṇu, she is called *Tripathagā* ('going along the three paths—in three worlds').

118. Gaṅgā is the most excellent Tīrtha of all Tīrthas: she is the most excellent of all rivers. She bestows heavenly goal to all creatures, even to the greatest sinners.

119. O Viṣṇu, in the heaven, on the earth and in the atmosphere there are millions and millions of Tīrthas resorted to by the people everywhere. All of them are present in Jāhnavī entirely.

120. One who regularly takes the holy bath in Gaṅgā and meets with death without committing suicide (i.e., is not a committer of suicide), shall become a heaven-dweller. He never sees hells.

121. Gaṅgā herself is all the Tīrthas. Gaṅgā herself is a penance-grove. Gaṅgā alone is the holy spot of supernatural powers. No doubt need be entertained in this respect.

122. O Pot-born Sage, people taking the holy baths in Jāhnavī dwell where trees bear all desired fruits, where the ground is golden (i.e., in heaven).

123-124. He who adorns with clothes and ornaments a milch cow of excellent behaviour and gives it to a Brāhmaṇa on the banks of Gaṅgā, enjoys heavenly pleasures for as many thousand years as there are hairs on the body of that cow and her calf.

CHAPTER TWENTYNINE

*A Thousand Names of Gaṅgā**
(Gaṅgā-Sahasranāma)

Agastya said:

1. The birth of men is futile without a holy bath in Gaṅgā. Is there any other means whereby one may get the benefit of holy dip?

2. How can the feeble, the lame, those who are overpowered by indolence and those who are in far-off foreign lands, get the benefit of holy bath in Gaṅgā?

3-4. O Six-faced Lord, to me who have bowed down to you, kindly say if there is anything that can yield the benefit of holy ablution in Gaṅgā merely by its performance, be it in the form of monetary gift, *Vrata* (holy vow), *Mantra, Stotra* (hymn), *Japa*, worshipping a deity or holy plunge into another holy river.

5. O Skanda born of the womb of Gaṅgā, O highly intelligent one, none excepting you knows the mighty power of the heavenly river.

Skanda said:

6. O sage, here in different places there are Tīrthas with sacred waters, lakes and rivers occupied by people who have subdued their self.

7. They have mighty power and they give apparent results too. But even a ten-millionth part of the heavenly river is not present there.

8. Gaṅgā is being held on his head by Śaṁbhu, the Lord of Devas. Know (the greatness of Gaṅgā) solely as an inference therefrom, O Pot-born Sage.

---

* It is since the Vedic times that a list of epithets is used as a hymn of prayer, e.g. *Rudrādhyaya* in TS iv.5. The number of epithets in such lists went on increasing to include one thousand "Names" called *Sahasranāma.* Thay are in honour of various deities, great or small, such as Śiva, Viṣṇu, Pārvatī, Śākaṁbharī and even a godlet Malhārī. These epithets are overlapping as these deities came to be regarded as indentical with Supreme Brahman. Hence this Sahasranāma, though only of a river, contains epithets applicable to Brahman.

9. At the time of taking the holy bath in the other Tīrthas, the *Japa* of Jāhnavī is performed by people. Excepting Viṣṇupadī (Gaṅgā) what else is capable of ridding one of sins?

10. O holy Brāhmaṇa, the benefit of the holy bath in Gaṅgā is derived only from Gaṅgā, just as the taste of grapes is only in the grapes, not in anything else.

11. But, O sage, there is one means whereby the entire benefit of the holy bath in the divine river can be obtained. It is a great secret.

12-13. It should be disclosed to one who is a devotee of Śiva, who is quiescent, who has devotion to Viṣṇu also, who has faith, who is an *Āstika* (believer in the existence of God) and who desires release from rebirth. It should not be disclosed to anyone else on any occasion. This is a great secret, destructive of great sins.

14. It is conducive to great welfare and is meritorious. It causes pleasure to the celestial river and continuity of Śiva's pleasure.

15. *A Thousand Names of Gaṅgā* is the most brilliant of all excellent prayers. It is the greatest *Japya* (word worthy of being repeated for holy purposes) of all *Japyas*; it is on a par with the Vedas and Upaniṣads.

16. The japa should be performed carefully by a man who maintains silence. The words are not loudly uttered but the letters should be clearly pronounced. The devotee should be personally pure and sit in a clean place.

17-168. *[A Thousand Names of Gaṅgā alphabetically arranged]*

Om namo gaṅgā-devyai : (Oṁ, obeisance to Goddess Gaṅgā)*

1. Oṁkāra-rūpiṇī (Possessor of the form Oṁ).
2. Ajarā (Immune from old age)
3. Atulā (Incomparable)
4. Anantā (Infinite)
5. Amṛtasravā (Having the current of nectar)

---

* This *Sahasra-nāma* actually contains 997 names or epithets. In enumerating, the epithets in the verses are counted as 1, 2.

The names are alphabetically arranged by the Purāṇa-writer. Some epithets are in masculine and some in neuter gender. The interpretation of these epithets of Gaṅgā follows the commentator Rāmānanda.

6. Atyudārā (Extremely liberal)
7. Abhayā (Fearless)
8. Aśokā (Devoid of sorrow)
9. Alakanandā (A tributary of Gaṅgā)
10. Amṛtā (Nectarine)
11. Amalā (Free from impurities)
12. Anātha-vatsalā (Sympathetic or kind to the helpless)
13. Amoghā (Never futile)
14. Apāṁyoniḥ (Source of waters)
15. Amṛtapradā (Bestower of immortality or Mokṣa)]
16. Avyaktalakṣaṇā (Having the characteristics of the unmanifest or Brahman)
17. Akṣobhyā (Unagitated)
18. Anavacchinnā (Unlimited)
19. Aparā (Having none greater than herself)
20. Ajitā (Unconquered)
21. Anāthanāthā (Protectress of the helpless)
22. Abhīṣṭārthasiddhidā (Bestower of success in what one desires)
23. Anaṅgavardhinī (Increasing love)
24. Aṇimādiguṇā (Having Aṇimā and other guṇas or Siddhis)
25. Ādhārā (Having Viṣṇu as the basis or flowing from Viṣṇu)
26. Agragaṇyā (Worthy of being considered before others)
27. Alīkahāriṇī (Dispeller of the false i.e., ignorance)
28. Acintyaśakti (Of unimaginable power)
29. Anaghā (Sinless)
30. Adbhutarūpā (Of miraculous form or appearance)
31. Aghahāriṇī (Dispeller of sins)
32. Adrirājasutā (Daughter of the king of Mountains)
33. Aṣṭāṅgayogasiddipradā (Bestower of success in the practice of Yoga of eight ancillaries)
34. Acyutā (Never falling from her original form)
35. Akṣuṇṇaśakti (Of unobstructed power)
36. Asudā (Bestower of the vital breaths)
37. Anantatīrthā (Possessor of an infinite number of Tīrthas)
38. Amṛtodakā (Of nectarine waters)
39. Anantamahimā (Of infinite greatness)
40. Aparā (Limitless)

41. Anantasaukhyapradā (Bestower of infinite happiness)
42. Annadā (Bestower of food)
43. Aśeṣadevatāmūrti (Having the forms of the entire host of Devas)
44. Aghorā (Mild in form)
45. Amṛtarūpiṇī (Having a nectarine form)
46. Avidyājālaśamanī (Destroyer of the snare of Avidyā or Dispeller of multitude of illusions)
47. Apratarkyagatipradā (Bestower of a goal beyond imagination)
48. Aśeṣavighnasaṁhartrī (Destroyer of the entire collection of hindrances).
49. Aśeṣaguṇaguṁphitā (Pervaded by all good qualities)
50. Ajñānatimirajyotiḥ (Luminary dispelling the darkness of ignorance)
51. Anugrahaparāyaṇā (Eager to bless)
52. Abhirāmā (One in whom Yogins take delight)
53. Anavadyāṅgī (Of blemishless limbs)
54. Anantasārā (Of infinite power)
55. Akalaṅkinī (Free from stigma)
56. Ārogyadā (Bestower of health)
57. Ānandavallī (A creeper of bliss)
58. Āpannārtivināśinī (Destroyer of the distress of her devotees)
59. Āścarya-mūrti (Miraculous in form)
60. Āyuṣyā (Conducive to longevity)
61. Āḍhyā (Perfect)
62. Ādyā (Primordial one)
63. Āprā (One that fills the surroundings)
64. Āryasevitā (Served by noble ones)
65. Āpyāyinī (Causing fullness)
66. Āptavidyā (One who has attained all lores)
67. Ākhyā (Renowned)
68. Ānandā (Blissful)
69. Āśvāsadāyinī (Consoler)
70. Ālasyaghnī (Destroyer of indolence)
71. Āpadāṁhantrī (Dispeller of adversities)
72. Ānandāmṛta-varṣiṇī (Showerer of nectarine bliss)

73. Irāvatī (Identical with the river Irāvatī or possessor of food, or giver of enjoyments)
74. Iṣṭadātrī (Bestower of what is desired)
75. Iṣṭā (The adored one)
76. Iṣṭāpūrtaphalapradā (Bestower of the benefits of sacrifices—*iṣṭa* and social services—*Pūrta*)
77. Itihāsaśrutīḍyārthā (One whose purpose is praised by Itihāsas and Śrutis)
78. Ihāmutra-śubha-pradā (Bestower of auspiciousness here and hereafter)
79. Ijyāśīla-samijyeṣṭhā (Honoured by those who regularly perform Yajñas and those who realize Brahman)
80. Indrādi-parivanditā (Respectfully bowed to by Indra and others)
81. Ilālaṅkāra-mālā (A necklace adorning the earth)
82. Iddhā (Self-luminous)
83. Indirā-ramya-mandirā (Having Lakṣmī as her abode and resting place)
84. It (One in the form of knowledge)
85. Indirādi-saṁsevyā (Worthy of being served by Lakṣmī and others)
86. Īśvarī (One who controls and rules)
87. Īśvara-vallabhā (Endearing to the Lord)
88. Ītibhītiharā (One who removes the fear due to excess of rain, drought etc.)
89. Īḍyā (Worthy of eulogy)
90. Īḍanīya-caritra-bhṛt (Having adorable conduct)
91. Utkṛṣṭa-śakti (Of excellent power or Viṣṇu's Utkṛṣṭa power
92. Utkṛṣṭā (The excellent one)
93. Uḍupa-maṇḍala-cāriṇī (Moving about in the Lunar Zone)
94. Uditāmbara-mārgā (One by whom the ethereal path is made to rise)
95. Usrā (Brilliant goddess)
96. Uraga-loka-vihāriṇī (One sporting about in the world of serpents)
97. Ukṣā (One who sprinkles fruition)
98. Urvarā (Fertile one)
99. Utpalā (Identical with the lotus)

100. Utkuṁbhā (One who makes pots purified)
101. Upendra-caraṇa-dravā (The water flowing from the feet of Viṣṇu)
102. Udaṇvat-pūrti-hetu (Cause of filling the ocean)
103. Udārā (Liberal)
104. Utsāha-pravardhinī (One who enhances enthusiasm)
105. Udvegaghnī (Destroyer of anguish)
106. Uṣṇa-śamanī (Suppressor of heat and distress)
107. Uṣṇa-raśmi-sutā-priyā (Beloved of Yamunā, the daughter of the Sun-god)
108. Utpatti-sthiti-saṁhāra-kāriṇī (The cause of origin, sustenance and annihilation of the universe)
109. Upari-cāriṇī (Moving above in the sky)
110. Ūrjam-vahantā (Identical with the mantra beginning with "*ūrjaṁ vahantīramṛtam*" etc.—VS 2.34: Or Sustainer of energy and power)
111. Ūrja-dharā (Upholder of strength)
112. Ūrjāvatī (Possessor of energy)
113. Ūrmi-mālinī (Having garland of waves)
114. Ūrdhva-retaḥ-priyā (Beloved of *Ūrdhva-retas* i.e., Sages or god Śiva)
115. Ūrdhvādhvā (Whose path is above in the sky)
116. Ūrmilā (Having waves)
117. Ūrdhva-gati-pradā (Bestower of the goal above viz. Svarga or Mokṣa)
118. Ṛṣi-vṛnda- stutardhī (One whose prosperity is eulogized by groups of sages)
119. Ṛṇatraya-vināśinī (Destroyer of the three types of indebtedness to Devas, Sages and the Pitṛs)
120. Ṛtambharā (Upholder of Truth)
121. Ṛddhi-dātrī (Bestower of prosperity)
122. Ṛk-svarūpā (Of the form of Ṛks)
123. Ṛju-priyā (Beloved of the straightforward)
124. Ṛkṣamārgavahā (Flowing through the path of the Stars)
125. Ṛkṣārciḥ (Having the stellar brilliance)
126. Ṛjumārga-pradarśinī (Guide to the morally straight path i.e., the path to Mokṣa)
127. Edhitākhila-dharmārthā (One who has enhanced the piety

and riches of every one)

128. Ekā (The sole or the important one)
129. Ekāmṛtadāyinī (The bestower of single immortal Brahman)
130. Edhanīya-svabhāvā (One whose nature is to develop continuously)
131. Ejyā (Worthy of being venerated)
132. Ejitāśeṣapātakā (One who has made all sins tremble)
133. Aiśvaryadā (Bestower of prosperity and mastery)
134. Aiśvarya-rūpā (One in the form of prosperity)
135. Aitihyam (Tradition, Mythological truth—regarded as one of the Pramāṇas)
136. Aindavīdyuti (Of Lunar lustre)
137. Ojasvinī (Having energetic power)
138. Oṣadhīkṣetram (Identical with the field of medicinal plants)
139. Ojodā (The bestower of energy)
140. Odana-dāyinī (Bestower of cooked rice)
141. Oṣṭhāmṛtā (Of nectarine lips—sweet in speech)
142. Aunnatya-dātrī (Bestower of a high position)
143. Auṣadhaṁ bhavaroginām (Medicine unto the sufferer from the ailment of worldly existence or Saṁsāra)
144. Audārya-cañcurā (Adept in munificent distribution)]
145. Aupendrī (Identical with Lakṣmī)
146. Augrī (Having the ferocious power of annihilation)
147. Aumeya-rupiṇī (One in the form of Umā)
148. Aṁbarādhvāvahā (Flowing through the celestial path)
149. Aṁbaṣṭhā (Stationed among the devotees of Viṣṇu)
150. Aṁbaramālā (A garland unto the sky)
151. Aṁbujekṣaṇā (Having lotuses for the eyes)
152. Aṁbikā (One in the forms of Durgā; Mother Divine)
153. Aṁbumahāyonī (The primary cause of waters)
154. Andhodā(Bestower of food)
155. Andhaka-hāriṇī (Remover of ignorance)
156. Aṁśumālā (A garland of rays)
157. Aṁśumatī (Endowed with brilliance)
158. Angīkṛta-ṣaḍānanā (One who has adopted the Six-faced Lord as her son)

159. Andhatāmisrahantrī (One that wards off from the hell Andhatāmisra)
160. Andhuḥ (Identical with the *Dharma-Kūpa* well)
161. Añjanā (Identical with Avidyā or Hanumān's mother)
162. Añjanāvatī (Possessing Avidyā)
163. Kalyāṇakāriṇī (The cause of welfare)
164. Kāmyā (Worthy of being desired)
165. Kamalotpalagandhinī (Having the fragrance of lotuses and lilies)
166. Kumudvatī (Having lilies)
167. Kamalinī (Having lotuses)
168. Kānti (Possessing lunar splendour)
169. Kalpitadāyinī (The bestower of cherished desire)
170. Kāñcanākṣī (Golden-eyed)
171. Kāmadhenu (Identical with the divine cow)
172. Kīrtikṛt (One who causes renown)
173. Kleśanāśinī (Destroyer of the five types of *Kleśa*—pain)
174. Kratuśreṣṭhā (Superior to sacrifices)
175. Kratuphalā (Yielding the same benefit as that of a sacrifice)
176. Karmabandha-vibhedinī (Destroyer of the bondage of Karmas)
177. Kamalākṣī (Lotus-eyed)
178. Klama-hārā (One who dispels fatigue)
179. Kṛśānu-tapana-dyuti (Having the lustre of fire and the sun)
180. Karuṇārdrā (Melting i.e., full of compassion)
181. Kalyāṇī (One who is endowed with welfare)
182. Kalikalmaṣa-nāśinī (Destroyer of the sins of the Kali Age)
183. Kāmarūpā (Having the ability to assume any desired form)
184. Kriyāśakti (Having the power of action)
185. Kamalotpalamālinī (Having the garlands of lotuses and lilies)
186. Kūṭasthā (Stationed in Avidyā)
187. Karuṇā (Mercy personified)
188. Kāntā (Dignified and dazzling)
189. Kūrmayānā (Having the tortoise as her vehicle)

190. Kalāvatī (Endowed with Kalās)
191. Kamalā (Of the form of Lakṣmī)
192. Kalpalatikā (Wish-yielding creeper like the divine tree)
193. Kālī (Having the form of Kālī)
194. Kaluṣavairiṇī (Destroyer of sins)
195. Kamanīyajalā (Having desirable or beautiful waters)
196. Kamrā (A lover of Śantanu, the beautiful)
197. Kapardisukapardagā (Stationed in the matted hairs of Kapardin (i.e., Śiva)
198. Kālakūṭa-praśamanī (One who subdues even the Kālakūṭa poison)
199. Kadamba-kusuma-priyā (Fond of the Kadaṁba flowers)
200. Kālindī (Of the form of Kālindī)
201. Kelilalitā (Beautiful in her sports)
202. Kala-kallola-mālikā (Having garlands of waves producing pleasing sounds)
203. Krānta-loka-trayā (One who has transcended the three worlds)
204. Kaṇḍūḥ (One who destroys Avidyā)
205. Kaṇḍu-tanaya-vatsalā (Fond of the son of Kaṇḍu i.e., Mārkaṇḍeya)
206. Khaḍginī (Wielding a sword)
207. Khadga-dhārābhā (Having the lustre of the edge of a sword)
208. Khagā (Flowing through the firmament)
209. Khaṇḍendu-dhāriṇī (Adorned by the crescent moon)
210. Khe-khela-gāminī (One who moves playfully through the sky)
211. Khasthā (One stationed in the firmament or Brahman)
212. Khaṇḍendu-tilaka-priyā (Beloved of the Lord having the crescent moon as Tilaka mark on the forehead)
213. Khecarī (Moving in the firmament)
214. Khecarī-vandyā (Worthy of the salutation of the celestial women)
215. Khyātiḥ (One in the form of renown)
216. Khyāti-pradāyinī (One who bestows renown)
217. Khaṇḍita-praṇatāghaughā (One who splits asunder the multitude of sins of those who bow down to her)

218. Khala-buddhi-vināśinī (One who destroys the evil intention of rogues)
219. Khātainaḥ-kandasandohā (One who has uprooted the multitude of the bulbuous roots of sins)
220. Khaḍga-khaṭvāṅga-kheṭinī (One who plays with swords, Khaṭvāṅgas and Kheṭas as weapons)
221. Khara-santāpaśamanī (One who suppresses fierce heat)
222. Khaniḥ-pīyūṣa-pāthasām (One source of nectar like water)
223. Gaṅgā (One flowing in the sky)
224. Gandhavatī (Sweet-smelling or of the form of the earth)
225. Gaurī (Gaurī i.e., Pārvatī or the wife of the Lord of waters)
226. Gandharva-nagara-priyā (Fond of the cities of Gandharvas)
227. Gambhīrāṅgī (Having majestic limbs)
228. Guṇamayī (Equipped with high qualities)
229. Gatātaṅkā (One who is devoid of extreme fright)
230. Gati-priyā (Fond of the highest goal)
231. Gaṇanāthāmbikā (Mother of Gaṇeśa)
232. Gītā (One who is sung about)
233. Gadya-padya-pariṣṭutā (One who is eulogized in prose and poetry)
234. Gāndhārī (One who supports the earth)
235. Garbha-śamanī (One who suppresses future rebirth)
236. Gati-bhraṣṭa-gati-pradā (One who bestows salvation to those who are fallen from the path of salvation)
237. Gomatī (Identical with the river Gomatī)
238. Guhyavidyā (Identical with the knowledge of Brahman)
239. Gauḥ (Identical with the cow, the earth, the Veda, speech or the heaven)
240. Goptrī (One who protects)
241. Gagana-gāminī (Going through the sky)
242. Gotra-pravardhinī (One who makes the Gotra flourish)
243. Guṇyā (One beneficial to the Guṇas)
244. Guṇātītā (One who transcends the Guṇas)
245. Guṇāgraṇīḥ (One who controls the Guṇas)
246. Guhāmbikā (Mother of Guha or Skanda)
247. Girisutā (The daughter of the Mountain)

248. Govindāṅghri-samudbhavā (Originating from the feet of Govinda)
249. Guṇanīya-caritrā (One whose conduct is to be meditated upon)
250. Gāyatrī (Identical with the Mantra, Gāyatrī *or* one who protects those who sing her glory)
251. Giriśa-priyā (Beloved of Lord Śiva)
252. Gūḍha-rūpā (One whose real form is concealed)
253. Guṇavatī (One possessing Guṇas)
254. Gurvī (The great or mighty one)
255. Gauravavardhinī (One of enhancing majesty)
256. Grahapīḍāharā (One who removes the adverse afflictions from Planets)
257. Gundrā (Identical with the Mustā plant or destroyer of Avidyā)
258. Garaghnī (Destroyer of poisons)
259. Gānavatsalā (One fond of music)
260. Gharma-hantrī (Destroyer of heat)
261. Ghṛtavatī (One having ghee-like waters)
262. Ghṛta-tuṣṭi-pradāyinī (One who bestows the satisfaction through ghee)
263. Ghaṇṭā-rava-priyā (One fond of the jingling sound of bells)
264. Ghorāghaugha-vidhvaṁsa-kāriṇī (One who destroys the terrible mass of sins)
265. Ghṛāṇatuṣṭikarī (One who gives satisfaction to the sense of smell)
266. Ghoṣā (Identical with the majestic sound of the streams *or* one producing the jingling sound of various ornaments)
267. Ghanānandā (One who has excessive bliss)
268. Ghanapriyā (One fond of clouds)
269. Ghātukā (One destroying sins)
270. Ghūrṇita-jalā (One whose waters are whirled up)
271. Ghṛṣṭa-pātaka-santati (One who has crushed series of sins)
272. Ghaṭakoṭi-prapītāpā (One whose waters are drunk through millions of pots)

273. Ghaṭitāśeṣa-maṅgalā (One who has made all the auspicious things happen)
274. Ghṛṇāvatī (One endowed with compassion)
275. Ghṛṇanidhi (Storehouse of mercy)
276. Ghasmarā (Devourer of everything)
277. Ghūkanādinī (Having the sounds produced by owls)
278. Ghusṛṇā-piñjaratanu (One whose form is slightly yellowish in hue due to the unguents)
279. Ghargharā (Identical with the eddy named Gharghara)
280. Gharghara-svanā (Making the sound 'Gharghara' or the sound of the eddy of the name Gharghara)
281. Candrikā (Identical with the moon-light)
282. Candrakāntāmbu (Having the waters like lunar stones)
283. Cañcadāpā (Having flowing waters)
284. Caladyuti (Having glittering and sparkling lustre)
285. Cinmayī (Identical with the Supreme Knowledge)
286. Citirupā (Having the form of blissful consciousness)
287. Candrāyutaśatānanā (Having the face resembling millions of moons)
288. Cāṁpeyalocanā (Having the eyes resembling the Cāmpeya flowers)
289. Cāru (Beautiful)
290. Cārvaṅgī (Having beautiful limbs)
291. Cārugāminī (Flowing beautifully)
292. Cāryā (Worthy of being realized through Upaniṣads)
293. Cāritranilayā (Receptacle of good behaviour)
294. Citrakṛt (Creating the diverse kinds of worlds)
295. Citrarūpiṇī (Having wonderfully variegated form)
296. Campūḥ (In the form of Caṁpū form of literary composition or Caṁpaka flowers)
297. Candana-śucyaṁbu (Having water as sweet-smelling as sandal)
298. Carcanīyā (Worthy of being pondered over)
299. Cirasthirā (Long-standing and firm)
300. Gāru-caṁpaka-mālāḍhyā (Rich with garlands of excellent Caṁpaka flowers)
301. Camitāśeṣa-duṣkṛtā (One who has swallowed sins entirely)

302. Cidākāśavahā (She who takes to the firmament of consciousness)
303. Cintyā (Worthy of being pondered over)
304. Cañcat (That which is sparkling, self-luminous)
305. Coritāśeṣa-vṛjinā (One by whom the entire mass of sins has been stolen away)
306. Caritāśeṣa-maṇḍalā (One by whom the entire range of worlds has been traversed)
307. Cheditākhila-pāpaughā (One by whom all the mass of sins have been chopped off)
308. Chadmaghnī (One who destroys all fraudulent practices or ignorance)
309. Chala-hāriṇī (One who removes the fraudulent ignorance)
310. Channa-triviṣṭa-paṭalā (One by whom the surface of heaven has been pervaded)
311. Choṭitāśeṣa-bandhanā (One by whom the entire range of bondage has been removed)
312. Churitāmṛta-dhāraughā (One by whom the current of ambrosia has been caused to flow)
313. Chinnaināḥ (One by whom sins have been eradicated)
314. Chandagāminī (One who flows at will independently)
315. Chatrīkṛta-marālaughā (One who has made flocks of swans into a big umbrella)
316. Chaṭīkṛta-nijāmṛtā (One by whom her own Amṛta-like water has been displayed together)
317. Jāhnavī (Jahnu's daughter)
318. Jyā (One who resembles bowstring)
319. Jagan-mātā (Mother of the universe)
320. Japyā (Worthy of being eulogized by Japas)
321. Jaṅghāla-vīcikā (Having rapid waves)
322. Jayā (Ever victorious)
323. Janārdanaprītā (Propitiated by Janārdana)
324. Juṣaṇīyā (Worthy of being resorted to)
325. Jagad-hitā (One benevolent to the worlds)
326. Jīvanam (Cause of livelihood)
327. Jīvana-prāṇā (One who is essentially vital to the living beings through water)
328. Jagat (Identical with the universe)

329. Jyeṣṭhā (The primordial one)
330. Jaganmayī (Of the form of the universe)
331. Jīva-jīvātulatikā (The life-giving medicinal creeper unto all living beings)
332. Janmi-janma-nibarhiṇī (One who eradicates rebirth of all living beings destined to be reborn)
333. Jāḍya-vidhvaṁsana-karī (One who destroys sluggishness)
334. Jagadyoni (The cause of origin of the universe)
335. Jalāvilā (Turbid with water)
336. Jagadānanda-jananī (Causing delight to the universe)
337. Jalajā (Born of Viṣṇu)
338. Jalajekṣaṇī (Lotus-eyed one)
339. Janalocanapīyūṣā (Ambrosia unto the eyes of the people)
340. Jaṭātaṭa-vihāriṇī (Sporting about in the matted hairs of Śiva)
341. Jayantī (Victorious)
342. Jañjapūkaghnī (Destroyer of sins)
343. Janita-jñāna-vigrahā (One who creates the figure of knowledge)
344. Jhallarī-vādya-kuśalā (One clever in playing on the musical instrument Jhallarī)
345. Jhalajjhāla-jalāvṛtā (Full of waters producing the sound 'Jhalaj-jhālā')
346. Jhiṇṭīśavandyā (Worthy of being adored by Jhiṇṭīśa—a form of Śiva)
347. Jhaṅkārakāriṇī (Producing the sound of Jhaṅkāra)
348. Jharjharāvatī (Producing the sound Jharjhara)
349. Ṭīkitāśeṣa-pātālā (One who has traversed through the entire region of Pātāla)
350. Ṭaṅkikāinodri-pāṭane (Functioning like a chisel in annihilating the mountain of sins)
351. Ṭaṅkāra-nṛtyat-kallolā (Having waves dancing with the sound of Ṭaṅkāra)
352. Ṭīkanīya-mahātaṭā (Having great banks worthy of being served)
353. Ḍaṁbara-pravāhā (Flowing rapidly)

354. Ḍīna-rājahaṁsa-kulākulā (Occupied by flights of royal swans)
355. Ḍamaḍ-ḍamaru-hastā (Having the Ḍamaru producing "Ḍam" sound, in the hands)
356. Ḍāmarokta-mahāṇḍakā (Having the great Mantra-body Mahāṇḍaka as mentioned in the Ḍāmara scripture)
357. Ḍhaukitāśeṣa-nirvāṇā (One who has brought all types of salvation within the reach of devotees)
358. Ḍhakkā-nādacalajjalā (Having wave of water moving and producing the sound of the drum Ḍhakkā)
359. Ḍhuṇḍhi-vighneśa-jananī (Mother of God Dhuṇḍhi-Vighneśvara)
360. Ḍhaṇaḍ-ḍhuṇita-pātakā (One who removes sins producing the sound "Ḍhaṇat")
361. Tarpaṇī (Causing delight and satisfaction unto all)
362. Tīrtha-tīrthā (Tīrtha of all Tīrthas)
363. Tripathā (Having three worlds as pathways)
364. Tridaśeśvarī (Goddess of Devas)
365. Trilokagoptrī (One who protects the three worlds)
366. Toyeśī (Goddess of waters)
367. Trailokya-parivanditā (Honoured and adored by all the three worlds)
368. Tāpa-tritaya-saṁhartrī (One who eradicates the three types of distress)
369. Tejobala-vivardhinī (One who enhances brilliance and strength)
370. Trilakṣyā (Manifest in three worlds)
371. Tāraṇī (One who redeems all)
372. Tārā (Identical with Oṁkāra *or* with Tārā, one of the five eternal Kanyās)
373. Tārāpati-karārcitā (Worshipped with the rays of the moon)
374. Trailokya-pāvanī-puṇyā (Holiest of the rivers sanctifying the three worlds)
375. Tuṣṭidā (One who bestows satisfaction)
376. Tuṣṭirūpiṇī (One who destroys avidity)
377. Tṛṣṇācchetrī (One who destroys desires)
378. Tīrthamātā (Mother of all the Tīrthas)

379. Trīvikrama-padodbhavā (Arising from the foot of Lord Viṣṇu)
380. Tapomayī (Identical with austerities)
381. Taporūpā (Having the form of austerities)
382. Tapaḥstoma-phalapradā (One who bestows the fruit of penance)
383. Trailokya-vyāpinī (One who pervades the three worlds)
384. Tṛpti (Identical with satisfaction)
385. Tṛptikṛt (One who causes satisfaction)
386. Tattva-rūpiṇī (Identical with reality)
387. Trailokya-sundarī (Charming in the three worlds)
388. Turyā (The fourth state beyond wakefulness, dream and sleep)
389. Turyātīta-padapradā (One who bestows the state beyond the four states)
390. Trailokya-lakṣmī (The glory of the three worlds)
391. Tripadī (Having three different abodes)
392. Tathyā (One who is not affected by the three units of time)
393. Timiracandrikā (Moonlight unto the darkness of ignorance)
394. Tejogarbhā (Having the divine Tejas in the womb)
395. Tapaḥsārā (The essence of penance)
396. Tripurāri-śirogṛhā (Having the head of Lord Śiva as her abode)
397. Trayīsvarūpiṇī (Identical with the three Vedas)
398. Tanvī (Beautiful in form)
399. Tapanāṅgaja-bhīti-hṛt (One who removes the fear from Yama, the son of Sun)
400. Tari (One who takes devotees across the ocean of Saṁsāra)
401. Taraṇijā-mitram (Friendly towards Yamunā)
402. Tarpitāśeṣa-pūrvajā (One who consoled and propitiated all the ancestors)
403. Tulāvirahitā (One without an equal)
404. Tīvrapāpatūla-tanūnapāt (One who functions like fire in the case of sins that resemble cotton)
405. Dāridrya-damanī (One who suppresses poverty)

406. Dakṣā (Very efficient in giving *Bhukti* and *Mukti*)
407. Duṣprekṣyā (Very difficult to be seen)
408. Divyamaṇḍanā (Having divine ornaments)
409. Dīkṣāvatī (Having initiation)
410. Durāvāpyā (Very difficult to obtain)
411. Drākṣā-madhura-vāribhṛt (Having water as sweet as grape-juice)
412. Darśitāneka-kutukā (One who displays various wonderful miracles)
413. Duṣṭadurjaya-duḥkhahṛt (One who removes evil and unsurmountable miseries)
414. Dainyahṛt (One who removes wretchedness)
415. Duritaghnī (One who destroys sins)
416. Dānavāri-padābjā (Born of the lotus-like feet of the enemy of demons i.e., Viṣṇu)
417. Dandaśūkaviṣaghnī (One who removes the venom of serpents)
418. Dāritāghaughasantati (One who removes the series of floods of sins)
419. Drutā (Rapid)
420. Devadrumacchannā (Covered with celestial trees)
421. Durvārāgha-vināśinī (One who destroys even those sins that cannot be warded off)
422. Damagrāhyā (One who can be attained through mental control)
423. Devamātā (Identical with Aditi, mother of Devas)
424. Devaloka-pradarśinī (Guide unto the world of the Devas)
425. Devadevapriyā (Beloved of the Lord of Devas)
426. Devī (Self-refulgent)
427. Dikpāla-padadāyinī (One who bestows guardianship of the quarters)
428. Dīrghāyuḥkāriṇī (One who bestows longevity)
429. Dīrghā (Uninterruptably long)
430. Dogdhrī (One from whom the Puruṣārthas or aims of life can be derived)
431. Dūṣaṇavarjitā (Devoid of blemishes)
432. Dugdhāmbuvāhinī (One in whom milk flows like water)
433. Dohyā (Worthy of being milked)

434. Divyā (Divine)
435. Divyagatipradā (One who bestows divine status)
436. Dyunadī (Celestial river)
437. Dīnaśaraṇam (Refuge unto the wretched)
438. Dehi-deha-nivāriṇī (One who prevents the taking up of a body by the soul i.e., ribirth)
439. Drāghīyasī (Very great)
440. Dāghahantrī (Destroyer of heat of distress)
441. Ditapātaka-santati (One by whom the series of sins has been cut off)
442. Dūradeśāntaracarī (One who traverses far-off countries)
443. Durgamā (Very difficult to be attained)
444. Devavallabhā (Beloved of gods)
445. Durvṛttaghnī (Destroyer of those whose conduct is bad)
446. Durvigāhyā (Very difficult to be entered)
447. Dayādhārā (Receptable of compassion)
448. Dayāvatī (Merciful)
449. Durāsadā (Difficult of access)
450. Dānaśīlā (Habitual bestower)
451. Drāviṇī (Regularly dissolving sins)
452. Druhiṇa-stutā (Eulogized by Brahmā)
453. Daityadānavasaṁśuddhikartrī (Habitually purifying Daityas and Dānavas too)
454. Durbuddhi-hāriṇī (One who removes evil intentions)
455. Dānasārā (One who can be known through the distribution of gifts)
456. Dayāsārā (One who can be known through merciful deeds)
457. Dyāvā-bhūmi-vigāhinī (One who passes through heaven and earth)
458. Dṛṣṭādṛṣṭa-phala-prāpti (One from whom visible and invisible fruits are obtained)
459. Devatā-vṛndavanditā (Revered by groups of Devas)
460. Dīrghavratā (One having rites of long duration)
461. Dīrghadṛṣṭi (One with perception of a long range)
462. Dīptatoyā (One with bright waters)
463. Durālabhā (One who is very difficult to obtain)
464. Daṇḍayitrī (One who metes out punishment)

465. Daṇḍanīti (One who is engrossed in statesmanship)
466. Duṣṭa-daṇḍa-dharārcitā (One who is adored by those who punish evil-doers)
467. Durodaraghnī (One who eradicates the evil of gambling etc.)
468. Dāvarciḥ (Having the splendour like that of forest fire)
469. Dravat (One absorbed in her work and hence perfect)
470. Dravyaika-śevadhi (The principal resort of all objects)
471. Dīnasantāpaśamanī (One who subdues the distress of the wretched)
472. Dātrī (Bestower of bocns)
473. Davathuvairiṇī (Destroyer of the trembling due to the fear of worldly sufferings)
474. Darīvidāraṇaparā (One engaged in splitting i.e., cutting her way through valley)
475. Dāntā (One with perfect control over the senses)
476. Dānta-jana-priyā (Loved by people with self-control)
477. Dāritādritaṭā (One who erodes the ridges of mountains)
478. Durgā (Identical with Goddess Durgā)
479. Durgāraṇya-pracāriṇī (One that regularly flows through impassable forests)
480. Dharmadravā (Having righteousness as the flowing current)
481. Dharmadhurā (Possessing the weightage or responsibility of piety *or* Of the form of excellent Dharma)
482. Dhenu (Idendical with wish-yielding divine cow)
483. Dhīrā (Intelligent, learned; Giver of Advaitic intelligence)
484. Dhṛti (Prop or support)
485. Dhruvā (Permanently stable)
486. Dhenu-dāna-phala-sparśā (One whose contact is the fruit of the gift of cows)
487. Dharma-kāmārthā-mokṣadā (One who bestows righteousness, pleasure, wealth and salvation)
488. Dharmormivāhinī (Having the flowing waves of piety)
489. Dhuryā (The most excellent one)
490. Dhātrī (Nursing mother)
491. Dhātrī-vibhūṣaṇam (Adornment of the earth)

492. Dharmiṇī (Meritorious)
493. Dharmaśīlā (Habitually practising holy rites)
494. Dhanvikoṭi-kṛtāvanā (One who accords protection through millions of bows)
495. Dhyātṛ-pāpaharā (One who eradicates the sins of those who meditate)
496. Dhyeyā (Worthy of being meditated upon)
497. Dhāvanī (One who cleanses)
498. Dhūta-kalmaṣā (One who eradicates sins)
499. Dharmadhārā (Flowing current of piety)
500. Dharmasārā (Essence of piety)
501. Dhanadā (Bestower of wealth)
502. Dhanavardhinī (One who increases wealth)
503. Dharmādharma-guṇa-cchetrī (One who snaps the strings of piety and impiety)
504. Dhattūra-kusuma-priyā (One who is fond of the Dhattūra flowers)
505. Dharmeśī (Goddess of piety)
506. Dharmaśāstrajñā (One conversant with scriptures)
507. Dhanadhānya-samṛddhi-kṛt (One who causes the abundance of wealth and food-grains)
508. Dharmalabhyā (One obtained through piety)
509. Dharmajalā (Having piety for waters)
510. Dharma-prasava-dharmiṇī (One having the function of producing piety)
511. Dhyānagamya-svarūpā (One whose form is understood by means of meditation)
512. Dharaṇī (Identical with earth)
513. Dhātṛpūjitā (Adored by Brahmā)
514. Dhūḥ (One who shakes off sins)
515. Dhūrjaṭijaṭāsaṁsthā (One stationed in the matted hairs of Dhūrjaṭi i.e., Śiva)
516. Dhanyā (Conducive to affluence)
517. Dhīḥ (Intellect)
518. Dhāraṇāvatī (One having the power of retention)
519. Nandā
520. Nirvāṇajananī (Producing liberation)

521. Nandinī (One that causes delight)
522. Nunna-pātakā (One by whom sins have been eradicated)
523. Niṣiddha-vighnanicayā (One who has warded off multitudes of obstacles)
524. Nijānanda-prakāśinī (One who makes the bliss of the absolute manifest)
525. Nabhoṅgaṇacarī (Flowing through the celestial yard)
526. Nuti (In the form of eulogy)
527. Namyā (Worthy of being bowed to)
528. Nārāyaṇī (Identical with the power of Nārāyaṇa)
529. Nutā (Eulogized)
530. Nirmalā (Free from impurities)
531. Nirmalākhyānā (One whose narration is conducive to purification from sins)
532. Nāśinī-tāpasaṁpadām (One who eradicates the series of sins)
533. Niyatā (One at perfect ease)
534. Nitya-sukhadā (One who bestows permanent bliss)
535. Nānāścarya-mahānidhi (The great storehouse of many wonders)
536. Nadī (River)
537. Nadasaromātā (Mother of rivers and lakes)
538. Nāyikā (Controller of everyone)
539. Nākadīrghikā (Heavenly pond)
540. Naṣṭoddharaṇadhīrā (Adept in redeeming those who are lost)
541. Nandanā (One who makes devotees flourish)
542. Nandadāyinī (Habitually bestowing affluence)
543. Nirṇiktāśeṣa-bhuvanā (One who has sanctified the entire universe)
544. Nissaṅgā (Free from contaminating associations)
545. Nirupadravā (Harmless)
546. Nirālaṁbā (Devoid of external support)
547. Niṣprapañcā (One transcending the Saṁsāra)
548. Nirṇāśita-mahāmalā (One who has utterly eradicated great impurities of sins)
549. Nirmala-jñāna-jananī (One that generates knowledge free from blemishes)

550. Niśśeṣa-prāṇitāpahṛt (One who removes the distresses of living being utterly)
551. Nityotsavā (Having permanent festivities)
552. Nityatṛptā (Eternally satisfied)
553. Namaskāryā (One worthy of being bowed to)
554. Nirañjanā (Free from ignorance)
555. Niṣṭhāvatī (One strictly observing restraints)
556. Nirātaṅkā (Free from apprehension)
557. Nirlepā (Free from contamination of sins)
558. Niścalātmikā (One of quiescent soul)
559. Niravadyā (Free from blemishes)
560. Nirīhā (Desirelessly inactive)
561. Nīlalohita-mūrdhagā (Going up i.e., staying on the head of Śiva)
562. Nandibhṛṅgigaṇastutyā (Worthy of being eulogized by the Gaṇas, Nandin and Bhṛṅgi)
563. Nāgā (Identical with Nāgas)
564. Nandā (One who delights or contributes to prosperity)
565. Nagātmajā (Born of the mountain)
566. Niṣpratyūhā (Free from impediments)
567. Nākanadī (Celestial river)
568. Nirayārṇava-dīrghanauḥ (The long boat of redemption from the ocean of hell)
569. Puṇyapradā (One who bestows merit)
570. Puṇyagarbhā (Meritorious in the womb)
571. Puṇyā (Identical with merit)
572. Puṇyataraṅgiṇī (A meritorious river)
573. Pṛthu (Perfect and large)
574. Pṛthuphalā (Yielding great benefits)
575. Pūrṇā (All-pervading *or* Of unobstructed current)
576. Praṇatārti-prabhañjinī (Habitually eradicating the distress of those who bow down)
577. Prāṇadā (One who instils vital airs)
578. Prāṇijananī (Mother of all living beings)
579. Prāṇeśī (Controller of the vital airs)
580. Prāṇarūpiṇī (One identical with the Cosmic Hiraṇyagarbha)
581. Padmālayā (Identical with Lakṣmī)

582. Parāśaktiḥ (The greatest power)
583. Purajitparamapriyā (Highly beloved of the Destroyer of the three Puras i.e., Śiva)
584. Parā (The highest)
585. Paraphala-prāpti (One bestowing the acquisition of the greatest fruit)
586. Pāvanī (One who sanctifies)
587. Payasvinī (Having excellent water)
588. Parānandā (Yielding the highest bliss)
589. Prakṛṣṭārthā (Having excellent objectives)
590. Pratiṣṭhā (Established base of all)
591. Pālanī (One who protects)
592. Parā (One who fills)
593. Purāṇapaṭhitā (Dealt with in the Purāṇas)
594. Prītā (Delighter of all)
595. Praṇavākṣara-rūpiṇī (Identical with the letters of Praṇava)
596. Pārvatī (Identical with Pārvatī)
597. Prema-saṁpannā (Endowed with great love)
598. Paśupāśavimocanī (One who releases the Paśu or individual souls from Pāśas or nooses, fetters)
599. Paramātma-svarūpā (Identical with the Supreme Soul)
600. Parabrahma-prakāśinī (The illuminator of the Supreme Brahman)
601. Paramānanda-niṣpandā (Having the excessive vibratious of the highest bliss)
602. Prāyaścitta-svarūpiṇī (Identical with expiations)
603. Pānīyarūpa-nirvāṇā (With salvation stationed in the form of its waters)
604. Paritrāṇa-parāyaṇā (Ultimate resort in the matter of saving the devotee)
605. Pāpendhana-davajvālā (Functioning like the forest fire amongst the fuels in the form of sins)
606. Pāpāri (Enemy of sins)
607. Pāpanāmanut (Dispeller of sins through the utterance of her names)
608. Paramaiśvarya-jananī (Producer of the greatest powers like aṇimā)
609. Prājñā (Knower of her own refulgence)

610. Prājñā (Extremely intelligent)
611. Parāparā (Identical with the greatest and the smallest)
612. Pratyakṣa-lakṣmīḥ (Lakṣmī incarnate)
613. Padmākṣī (Lotus-eyed)
614. Paravyomāmṛtasravā (Exuding the nectar of the greatest firmament)
615. Prasannarūpā (Having pleasant form)
616. Praṇidhi (Wherein all the objects are deposited in Pralaya)
617. Pūtā (Extremely sacred)
618. Pratyakṣadevatā (Perceptible deity)
619. Pinākiparamaprītā (Great beloved of the Pināka-wielding Śiva)
620. Parameṣṭhi-kamaṇḍalu (Having the water pot of Brahmā as its receptacle)
621. Padmanābha-padārghyeṇa-prasūtā (Originating from the *Arghya* water used for washing the feet of Padmanābha)
622. Padmamālinī (Having garlands of lotuses)
623. Pararddhidā (Bestower of the greatest prosperity)
624. Puṣṭikarī (Nourisher)
625. Pathyā (Having wholesome effect in the case of worldly sufferings)
626. Pūrti (Perfect in form)
627. Prabhāvatī (Having bright splendour)
628. Punānā (Sanctifier)
629. Pītagarbhaghnī (Destroyer of rebirth of those who drink her water)
630. Pāpaparvata-nāśinī (Destroyer of the mountains of sins)
631. Phalinī (Having benefits to be accorded)
632. Phalahastā (Having benefits ready in the hands)
633. Phullāmbuja-vilocanā (Having lotuses in full bloom as eyes)
634. Phālitaino-mahākṣetrā (One who has dug up the great field of sins)
635. Phaṇiloka-vibhūṣaṇam (An ornament unto the world of serpents)
636. Phenacchala-praṇunnaināḥ (One who has eradicated sins and displayed it in the form of foams)

637. Phulla-kairavagandhinī (Having the fragrance of full-blown lilies)
638. Phenilācchāṁbudhārābhā (Having the splendour of clear waters with foams)
639. Phuḍuccāṭitapātakā (One who has eradicated sins by uttering the letters Phuḍ)
640. Phāṇita-svādusalilā (Having the waters as sweet as Phāṇita, a sweetmeat)
641. Phāṇṭa-pathya-jalāvilā (Turbid with water as wholesome as buttermilk)
642. *Viśvamātā (Mother of the universe)
643. Viśveśī (Goddess of the universe)
644. Viśvā (Identical with all)
645. Viśveśvarapriyā (Beloved of the Lord of the universe)
646. Brahmaṇyā (Beneficent unto Brāhmaṇas)
647. Brahmakṛt (One who creates Hiraṇyagarbha etc.)
648. Brāhmī (The Śakti of Brahmā)
649. Brahmiṣṭhā (Stationed in Brahman, Asbolute)
650. Vimalodakā (Having waters free from impurities)
651. Vibhāvarī (Identical with night *or* the consort of King Bhūridyumna)
652. Virajāḥ (Free from Rajas)
653. Vikrāntāneka-vīṣṭapā (By whom many worlds have been pervaded)
654. Viśvamitra (Friendly to the entire universe)
655. Viṣṇupadī (Flowing from Viṣṇu's feet)
656. Vaiṣṇavī (Pertaining to Viṣṇu)
657. Vaiṣṇava-priyā (Beloved of the devotees of Viṣṇu)
658. Virūpākṣa-priyakarī (One that does what is pleasing to Śiva)
659. Vibhūti (Identical with the supernatural powers)
660. Viśvatomukhī (Facing all direction)
661. Vipāśā (Devoid of fetters; Identical with the river Vipāśā)
662. Vaibudhī (Pertaining to Vibudha—Viṣṇu or Devas)
663. Vedyā (Worthy of being known)
664. Vedākṣara-rasasravā (Exuding the sweet nectar of the

---

*Va and Ba are considered to be the same in the following names.

bliss of Brahman)

665. Vidyā (Identical with Supreme Lore)
666. Vegavatī (Of rapid current)
667. Vandyā (Worthy of being venerated)
668. Bṛṁhaṇī (One that evolves the body, sense- organs etc.)
669. Brahmavādinī (Habitually repeating the Brahman)
670. Varadā (Bestower of boons)
671. Viprakṛṣṭā (The most excellent of all)
672. Variṣṭhā (The most exquisite)
673. Viśodhanī (One that specially sanctifies)
674. Vidyādharī (Possessing great lores)
675. Viśokā (Devoid of grief)
676. Vayovṛndaniṣevitā (Served by flocks of birds)
677. Bahūdakā (Having abundance of waters)
678. Balavatī (Possessing power)
679. Vyomasthā (Stationed in the firmament)
680. Vibudhapriyā (Beloved of Devas)
681. Vāṇī (Identical with the Goddess of Speech)
682. Vedavatī (Expounder of the Vedas *or* Identical with the daughter of Kuśadhvaja)
683. Vittā (Knowledge personified)
684. Brahmavidyā-taraṅgiṇī (The river in the form of the knowledge of Absolute Brahman)
685. Brahmāṇḍa-koṭivyāptāṁbu (One whose waters have pervaded crores of Cosmic Eggs)
686. Brahmahatyāpahāriṇī (One who eradicates the sin of Brāhmaṇa-slaughter)
687. Brahmeśa-viṣṇurūpā (Identical with Brahmā, Īśa and Viṣṇu)
688. Buddhi (Intellect)
689. Vibhava-vardhinī (One who makes prosperity flourish)
690. Vilāsisukhadā (One who accords happiness to those who shine exquisitively)
691. Vaiśyā (Identical with the class of merchants)
692. Vyāpinī (Extensive)
693. Vṛṣāraṇī (Cause of the outcome of piety or Dharma)
694. Vṛṣāṅkamauli-nilayā (Having the head of the Bull-emblemed Lord as her abode)

695. Vipannārti-prabhañjinī (One who eradicates the distress of the persons in difficulties)
696. Vinītā (Polite)
697. Vinatā (Excessively humble)
698. Bradhna-tanayā (Identical with Yamunā, the daughter of the Sun)
699. Vinayānvitā (Endowed with humility)
700. Vipañcī (Identical with Vīṇā)
701. Vādyakuśalā (Efficient in instrumental music)
702. Veṇuśruti-vicakṣaṇā (Efficient in the *Śruti* or a quarter tone of Veṇu *or* Expert in knowing the particular *Rāga* while listening to Viṇā —Comm.)
703. Varcaskarī (One who adds to the lustre)
704. Balakarī (One who increases strength)
705. Balonmūlitakalmaṣā (One who has uprooted sins through her strength)
706. Vipāpmā (Devoid of sins)
707. Vigatātaṅkā (Devoid of fear)
708. Vikalpaparivarjitā (One free from *Vikalpas*)
709. Vṛṣṭikartrī (Cause of rains)
710. Vṛṣṭijalā (Having abundance of rain water)
711. Vidhi (Identical with Brahmā)
712. Vicchinna-bandhanā (One who has cut off the bondage of devotees)
713. Vratarūpā (Identical with the holy observances)
714. Vittarūpā (Identical with wealth)
715. Bahuvighna-vināśakṛt (One who causes destruction of many obstacles)
716. Vasudhārā (Having the current of wealth)
717. Vasumatī (Endowed with wealth *or* identical with the earth)
718. Vicitrāṅgī (Having diverse limbs or parts)
719. Vibhāvasu (Identical with the sun or fire)
720. Vijayā (Especially victorious)
721. Viśvabīja (Seed of the universe)
722. Vāmadevī (Identical with Vāmadeva's wife)
723. Varapradā (Bestower of boons)

724. Vṛṣāśritā (Having piety as the basis or the basis of Dharma)
725. Viṣaghnī (Destroyer of poisons)
726. Vijñānormyaṁśumālinī (Having garlands of rays and waves of perfect knowledge)
727. Bhavyā (Conducive to welfare)
728. Bhogavatī (Possessed of enjoyment)
729. Bhadrā (Auspicious)
730. Bhavānī (Bhava's consort)
731. Bhūtabhāvanī (Progenitor of living beings)
732. Bhūtadhātrī (One who protects the living beings)
733. Bhayaharā (One who removes fear)
734. Bhakta-dāridryaghātinī (Destroyer of the poverty of devotees)
735. Bhukti-mukti-pradā (One who bestows worldly pleasures and salvation)
736. Bheśī (The śakti of the lord of the stars, the moon)
737. Bhakta-svargāpavargadā (One who bestows heavenly pleasures and salvation upon the devotees)
738. Bhāgīrathī (Brought down by Bhagīratha)
739. Bhānumatī (Endowed with rays)
740. Bhāgya (Fortune)
741. Bhogavatī (Gaṅgā in the nether worlds)
742. Bhṛti (One who holds or sustains)
743. Bhavapriyā (Beloved of Śiva)
744. Bhavadveṣṭrī (Destroyer of worldly sufferings)
745. Bhūtidā (Bestower of prosperity)
746. Bhūtibhūṣaṇā (One who embellishes prosperity)
747. Bhālalocana-bhāvajñā (One conversant with the views of Lord Śiva who has an eye in the forehead)
748. Bhūtabhavya-bhavatprabhu (One who powerfully rules everything past, present and the future)
749. Bhrānti-jñāna-praśamanī (One who subdues erroneous knowledge)
750. Bhinna-brahmāṇḍa-maṇḍapā (One by whom the structure of the Cosmos has been broken)
751. Bhūridā (One who bestows plenty)
752. Bhakti-sulabhā (Easy of access through devotion)

753. Bhāgyavaddṛṣṭi-gocarī (One who comes within the vision of the fortunate)
754. Bhañjitopaplavakulā (One by whom the series of calamities of devotees has been broken)
755. Bhakṣyabhojya-sukhapradā (One who bestows the pleasure of food and dainties of all kinds)
756. Bhikṣaṇīyā (Worthy of being requested)
757. Bhikṣumātā (Mother unto mendicants)
758. Bhāvā (One who conceives and produces)
759. Bhāva-svarūpiṇī (Identical with objects)
760. Mandākinī (Heavenly Gaṅgā)
761. Mahānandā (Highly blissful)
762. Mātā (Mother)
763. Muktitaraṅgiṇī (One whose waves are conducive to salvation *or* A river bestowing final liberation)
764. Mahodayā (Identical with great prosperity *or* Identical with final beatitude)
765. Madhumatī (Identical with the river Madhumatī)
766. Mahāpuṇyā (Highly meritorious)
767. Mudākarī (Cause of delight)
768. Munistutā (Eulogized by the sages)
769. Mohahantrī (One who removes delusion)
770. Mahā Tirthā (Extremely great sacred river)
771. Madhusravā (Flowing with honey-like water)
772. Mādhavī (Identical with the Śakti of Viṣṇu)
773. Māninī (Having honour)
774. Mānyā (Worthy of being venerated)
775. Manoratha-pathātigā [Going beyond the ken of thought *or* All-pervading (Comm.)]
776. Mokṣadā (One who bestows salvation)
777. Matidā (Bestower of intellect)
778. Mukhyā (Most prominent)
779. Mahābhāgya-janāśritā (Resorted to by those who are fortunate)
780. Mahāvegavatī (Having great rapidity of currents)
781. Medhyā (Sacred)
782. Mahā (Identical with festivities)
783. Mahimabhūṣaṇā (Possessing grandeur as ornaments)

784. Mahāprabhāvā (Extremely powerful)
785. Mahatī (Unlimited)
786. Mīna-cañcala-locanā (Having tremulous eyes in the form of fishes)
787. Mahākāruṇya-sampūrṇā (Filled with great compassion)
788. Maharddhi (Having great prosperity)
789. Mahotpalā (Having big lotuses)
790. Mūrtimat (Possessing actual form)
791. Muktiramaṇī (A beautiful woman in the form of salvation)
792. Maṇimāṇikya-bhūṣaṇā (Possessing jewels and rubies as ornament *or* Who beautifies the ornaments of diamonds and rubies)
793. Muktā-kalāpa-nepathyā (Having clusters of pearls as ornament)
794. Mano-nayana-nandinī (One who causes delight to the mind and the eyes)
795. Mahāpātaka-rāśighnī (One who eradicates heaps of great sins)
796. Mahādevārdha-hāriṇī (One who has taken over a half of the person of Śiva i.e., Gaurīrūpā)
797. Mahormimālinī (Having garland of great waves)
798. Muktā (Identical with the liberated)
799. Mahādevī (Great Goddess)
800. Manonmanī (One who sublimates the mind)
801. Mahāpuṇyodayaprāpyā (Accessible through the outcome of great merits)
802. Māyā-timira-candrikā (Functioning like moonlight in respect to the darkness of Māyā)
803. Mahāvidyā (Identical with the knowledge of Brahman)
804. Mahāmāyā (Great Māyā)
805. Mahāmedhā (Having great intellect)
806. Mahauṣadham (Great medicine)
807. Mālādhārī (Wearing garlands)
808. Mahopāyā (Having the great means of salvation)
809. Mahoraga-vibhūṣaṇā (Having great serpents as ornaments)
810. Mahāmoha-praśamanī (One who suppresses great delusion)

811. Mahāmaṅgala-maṅgalam (Auspicious among all great auspicious things)
812. Mārtaṇḍa-maṇḍalacārī (Moving through the Solar Zone)
813. Mahālakṣmī (The great Lakṣmī)
814. Madojjhitā (Free from haughtiness)
815. Yaśasvinī (The renowned)
816. Yaśodā (Identical with Yaśodā i.e., Kṛṣṇa's mother, *or* Bestower of fame)
817. Yogyā (Conducive to the practice of Yoga)
818. Yuktātmasevitā (Resorted to by those in communion with the Absolute)
819. Yogasiddhipradā (One who bestows the supernatural powers of Yoga)
820. Yājyā (Worthy of being adored)
821. Yajñeśa-paripūritā (Presided over by the Lord of Yajñas)
822. Yajñeśī (Presiding goddess of Yajñas)
823. Yajñaphaladā (Bestower of the benefits of Yajñas)
824. Yajanīyā (Venerable)
825. Yaśaskarī (Causing the renown of devotees)
826. Yamisevyā (Worthy of being resorted to by persons of self-control)
827. Yogayoni (Origin of Yogas)
828. Yoginī (Identical with the attendant Yoginī)
829. Yuktabuddhidā (One who accords the realization of the union of Brahman and Ātman)
830. Yoga-jñāna-pradā (One who bestows the Yogic power and knowledge)
831. Yuktā (Having perfect control)
832. Yamādyaṣṭāṅga-yogayuk (One who puts together the activities of Yoga in the form of the eight ancillaries i.e., *Yama* etc.)
833. Yantritāghaugha-sañcārā (One by whom the movements of multitudes of sins have been checked)
834. Yama-loka-nivāriṇī (One who wards off the world of Yama)
835. Yātāyāta-praśamanī (One who suppresses i.e. stops the arrivals and departures i.e., births and deaths)
836. Yātanā-nāma-kṛntanī (One who exterminates even the names of oppressive tortures)

837. Yāminīśa-himācchodā (Having waters cool and clear like the moon)
838. Yuga-dharma-vivarjitā (One who is free from untruth, violence and other activities of Kali Age)
839. Revatī (Identical with Revatī)
840. Ratikṛt (One who creates pleasure)
841. Ramyā (Beautiful)
842. Ratnagarbhā (Having jewels within)
843. Ramā (Identical with Lakṣmī)
844. Rati (Identical with Kāma's wife)
845. Ratnākara-premapātram (Object of the love of the Ocean)
846. Rasajñā (Conversant with Rasa, the supreme bliss)
847. Rasarūpiṇī (Identical with the bliss of the Absolute)
848. Ratna-prāsāda-garbhā (Having bejewelled palaces within)
849. Ramaṇīya-taraṅgiṇī (Having charming waves)
850. Ratnārciḥ (Having rays like those of jewels)
851. Rudra-ramaṇī (Delighter of Rudra)
852. Rāgadveṣavināśinī (One who eradicates attachment and disgust)
853. Ramā (One who accords pleasure to the eyes and minds)
854. Rāmā (Identical with an excellent woman)
855. Ramyarūpā (Having beautiful form)
856. Rogi-jīvātu-rūpiṇī (Panacea unto people suffering from Saṁsāra)
857. Rucikṛt (Creating interest and brilliance)
858. Rocanī (One who extends appeal) (An appealing Goddess)
859. Ramyā (Conducive to the welfare *or* Lakṣmī)
860. Rucirā (Bestower of splendour or beautiful)
861. Rogahāriṇī (One who removes ailments)
862. Rājahaṁsā (Wherein swans shine)
863. Ratnavatī (Possessing many jewels)
864. Rājat-kallola-rājikā (Having multitudes of waves shining)
865. Rāmaṇīyakarekhā (Possessing beautiful currents)
866. Rujāri (Enemy of ailments)
867. Rogaroṣiṇī (Furious against ailments)

868. Rākā (Identical with moonlight-night)
869. Raṅkārtiśamanī (One who subdues the distress of poor people)
870. Ramyā (Having the support of the beautiful Lord Viṣṇu—Comm.)
871. Rolaṁbarāviṇī (Possessing the humming sound of bees)
872. Ragiṇī (Possessing Rāgas)
873. Rañjita-śivā (One who delights Śiva)
874. Rūpalāvaṇya-śevadhi (Receptacle of beauty and perfection in the structure of limbs)
875. Lokaprasū (Mother of the worlds)
876. Lokavandyā (Venerable unto the worlds)
877. Lolat-kallola-malinī (Possessing surging clusters of waves)
878. Līlāvatī (Possessing sportive movement)
879. Lokabhūmi (Basic support of all the worlds)
880. Loka-locana-candrikā (Moonlight-like delighter of the eyes of the worlds)
881. Lekha-sravantī (Divine river or creator of Śāstras)
882. Laṭabhā (Attractive and comely)
883. Laghuvegā (Flowing slowly)
884. Laghutvahṛt (One who removes weakness)
885. Lāsyattaraṅga-hastā (Having dancing waves resembling hands)
886. Lalitā (Charming)
887. Layabhaṅgigā (Going ahead in a special mode)
888. Lokabandhu (A kinsman unto the worlds)
889. Lokadhātrī (One who nourishes the worlds)
890. Lokottara-guṇorjitā (One who is powerful, possessing most excellent qualities)
891. Lokatrayahitā (Beneficial unto the three worlds)
892. Lokā (One who is pondered over by the world)
893. Lakṣmī (Identical with Goddess Lakṣmī)
894. Lakṣaṇalakṣitā (Possessing excellent characteristics)
895. Līlā (Lord's sports or identical with Līlā, the queen of Padma)
896. Lakṣitanirvāṇā (One who points out the means of salvation)

897. Lāvaṇyāmṛta-varṣiṇī (One who showers jewels of the oceans or one who showers nectar of beauty)
898. Vaiśvānarī (The Śakti of the Fire-god)
899. Vāsaveḍyā (Worthy of being eulogized by Indra)
900. Vandhyatva-parihāriṇī (One who removes barrenness in women)
901. Vāsudevāṅghri-reṇughnī (One who removes the dust particles from the feet of Vāsudeva)
902. Vajrivajra-nivāriṇī (One who thwarts the thunderbolt of Indra).
903. Śubhāvatī (Having auspiciousness all round)
904. Śubhaphalā (Yielding auspiciousness and peace).
905. Śānti (Identical with calmness and peace)
906. Śāntanu-vallabhā (The beloved of Śāntanu)
907. Śūlinī (Wielding the trident)
908. Śaiśavavayāḥ (Possessing the stage of childhood)
909. Śītalāmṛta-vāhinī (Having cool nectar-like waters flowing)
910. Śobhāvatī (Possessing brilliance)
911. Śīlavatī (Having excellent conduct)
912. Śoṣitāśeṣa-kilviṣā (One who has dried up all sins)
913. Śaraṇyā (Worthy of being sought refuge in)
914. Śivadā (One who bestows welfare)
915. Śiṣṭā (Of good conduct)
916. Śarajanma-prasū (Mother of Kārttikeya)
917. Śivā (Identical with Goddess Durgā)
918. Śakti (Divine power)
919. Śaśāṅka-vimalā (Free from impurities like the moon)
920. Śamana-svasṛ-sammatā (Honoured by the river Yamunā, the sister of Yama)
921. Śamā (The suppressor of ignorance)
922. Śamana-mārgaghnī (One who prevents the path of Yama)
923. Śitikaṇṭha-mahāpriyā (Highly beloved of Lord Śiva)
924. Śuci (Holy)
925. Śucikarī (One who makes everyone pure)
926. Śeṣā (One that forms the limit)

927. Śeṣa-śāyi-padodbhavā (Who originates from the foot of Lord Viṣṇu)
928. Śrinivāsa-śruti (One who is heard as identical with Śrinivāsa i.e., Viṣṇu)
929. Śraddhā (Faith)
930. Śrīmatī (Having glory)
931. Śrī (One whom Yogins resort to i.e., Brahmavidyā)
932. Śubhavratā (Having holy vows)
933. Śuddhavidyā (One with pure knowledge)
934. Śubhāvartā (Having auspicious eddies)
935. Śrutānandā (One by whom bliss is heard and realized)
936. Śruti-stuti (One whose eulogy is through Vedic passages)
937. Śivetaraghnī (One who removes everything that is against welfare)
938. Śabarī (One who had assumed the form of a tribal woman i.e., Durgā)
939. Śāṁbarī-rūpa-dhāriṇī (One possessing the form of a female deer)
940. Śmaśāna-śodhanī (One who purifies cremation grounds)
941. Śāntā (Quiescent)
942. Śāśvat (Perennial)
943. Śata-dhṛti-ṣṭutā (Eulogized by Brahmā)
944. Śālinī (One who shines invariably)
945. Śāli-śobhāḍhyā (Having the brilliance of paddy)
946. Śikhi-vāhana-garbha-bhṛ (One who holds the peacock-vehicled Lord Skanda in her womb)
947. Śaṁsanīya-caritrā (One whose conduct is worthy of praise)
948. Śātitāśeṣa-pātakā (One by whom sins have been entirely eradicated)
949. Ṣaḍguṇaiśvarya-saṁpannā (Endowed with the six Guṇas namely, *Aiśvarya* etc.)
950. Ṣaḍaṅga-śruti-rūpiṇī (Identical with Śruti having the six Aṅgas i.e., ancillary topics)
951. Ṣaṇḍhatā-hāri-salilā (One whose waters removes impotence)
952. Ṣṭyāyannada-nadīśatā (Where hundreds of rivers come in a confluence)
953. Saridvarā (The most excellent one among rivers)

954. Surasā (Having excellent taste)
955. Suprabhā (Having excellent splendour)
956. Suradīrghikā (Divine pond)
957. Svaḥsindhu (Celestial river)
958. Sarva-duḥkhaghnī (One who destroys all miseries)
959. Sarva-vyādhi-mahauṣadhā (Great medicine eradicating all ailments)
960. Sevyā (Worthy of being served)
961. Siddhi (Supernatural power)
962. Satī (Identical with Dākṣāyaṇī)
963. Sūkti (Identical with wise saying)
964. Skandasū (Mother of Skanda)
965. Sarasvatī (Presiding deity of speech)
966. Sampat-taranginī (Having riches for waves)
967. Stutyā (Worthy of being eulogized)
968. Sthāṇu-mauli-kṛtālayā (One who has taken up abode on the head of Śiva)
969. Sthairyadā (One who bestows steadiness)
970. Subhagā (Having excellent reputation)
971. Saukhyā (Conducive to happiness)
972. Strīṣu-saubhāgya-dāyinī (One who bestows conjugal bliss unto women)
973. Svarganiḥśreṇikā (The ladder unto heaven)
974. Sūkṣmā (Subtle)
975. Svadhā (Identical with the Mantra of Svadhā)
976. Svāhā (Identical with the wife of god of fire or the Mantra Svāhā)
977. Sudhājalā (Having nectar-like water)
978. Samudra-rūpiṇī (Consort of the Ocean)
979. Svargyā (Conducive to the attainment of heaven)
980. Sarva-pātaka-vairiṇī (Inimical to all sins)
981. Smṛtāgha-hāriṇī (One who removes sins on being remembered)
982. Sītā (Furrow-like)
983. Saṁsārābdhi-taraṇḍikā (The boat that takes one across the ocean of worldly existence)
984. Saubhāgya-sundarī (One having good luck and beauty)

985. Sarvasāra-samanvitā (Equipped with all powers)
986. Harapriyā (Beloved of Śiva)
987. Hṛṣīkeśī (One who controls the sense-organs)
988. Haṁsarūpā (Having pure forms or one assuming the form of a swan)
989. Hiraṇmayī (Golden in hue)
990. Hṛtāgha-saṅghā (One by whom multitudes of sins are eradicated)
991. Hitakṛt (Well-wisher)
992. Helā (Graceful in form)
993. Helāghagarvahṛt (One who removes the arrogance of sins sportively)
994. Kṣemadā (Bestower of happiness)
995. Kṣālitāghaughā (One by whom multitudes of sins have been washed)
996. Kṣudra-vidraviṇī (One who destroys wicked ones)
997. Kṣamā (Having forbearance like the earth)

O Pot-born Sage, this is the list of the thousand names of Gaṅgā. By reciting this a man will obtain the benefit of a holy bath in Gaṅgā.

169. It subdues all the sins. It destroys all the obstacles. It is far better than all other hymns and *Japa*. It makes every sacred thing more sacred.

170. If one has faith, this (hymn) will yield any desired benefit. It gives abundance in all the four great human endeavours. By reciting it once, one obtains the fruit of peforming one sacrifice, O sage.

171. By reciting this three times, one gets the benefit said to accrue to one who takes the holy dip in all sacred rivers or gets initiated into all the Yajñas.

172. One who invariably recites this hymn three times, O Vāḍava (a Brāhmaṇa conversant with the principles of Philosophy) gets that merit which results from all holy vows well-observed.

173. If anyone recites this at the time of taking bath, whatever may be the place of water, Gaṅgā flowing in three streams presents herself there, O sage.

174. A person who seeks welfare, will obtain welfare; one who seeks wealth, obtains wealth; one who seeks love, shall obtain love; and one who seeks salvation, shall obtain salvation.

175. One should faithfully recite this hymn three times a day for a year, keeping his mind pure. A sonless man will then approach his wife at the prescribed period after menstruation. He will thereby become blessed with a son.

176. If anyone recites the *Thousand Names of Gaṅgā* with faith, O sage, he shall not die prematurely. He need not be afraid of fire, thief or serpent.

177. If after reciting the *Thousand Names of Gaṅgā,* one goes to another village for some work, he will attain success therein and will return home without any hindrance.

178. If the man goes to another village after reciting the *Thousand Names,* the defects of the lunar day, the day of the week, the star or the stellar combination with the moon will not be effective.

179. The set of the *Thousand Names of Gaṅgā* is conducive to longevity and freedom from ailments; it is destructive of all harassments and causes the attainment of all powers by the men.

180. By the recitation of the *Thousand Names of Gaṅgā,* the sins that have been acquired during thousands of previous births get destroyed.

181-183. By faithfully reciting the *Thousand Names of Gaṅgā,* all these sinners become free from sins: a slayer of a Brāhmaṇa, a drink-addict, a thief of gold, a defilar of the bed of the preceptor, a man who associates with these sinners, a destroyer of foetus, a slayer of mother, a slayer of father, one who commits breach of trust, one who administers poison, the ungrateful, a betrayer of friends, an arsonist, a slayer of a cow, a thief of the possessions of the preceptor, one guilty of major and minor sins.

184. One who is agitated due to mental anguish or physical ailment, one who is excessively distressed, becomes rid of all miseries by repeating this hymn.

185. With the mind concentrated and controlled, one should recite this for a year with great devotion. He shall obtain the desired benefit. He becomes relieved of all sins.

186. One whose mind is afflicted with doubts, one who hates piety, a hypocrite and one violently ferocious—all these shall become righteous.

187. A man who follows the discipline of the prescribed stage of life and status in the society, one devoid of anger and lust, and a man of spiritual knowledge—whatever benefit these obtain, one obtains by reciting this hymn.

188. By reciting this hymn earnestly once, one shall obtain that benefit which can be acquired by reciting Gāyatrī ten thousands times.

189. By reciting once this *Stavarāja* ('King of hymns'), one shall acquire that merit which a blessed man obtains after making the gift of a cow to a Vedic scholar.

190. A person reciting this hymn thrice a day (after holy dips) and continuing so for one year, shall acquire that merit which an excellent man gets by serving his preceptor throughout his life.

191. By reciting this hymn thrice a day for six months, one obtains that merit laid down here as the result of the study of the Vedas.

192. By practising the recitation of the *Stavarāja* of Gaṅgā everyday, one shall acquire devotion to Śiva or shall become a devotee of Viṣṇu.

193. If anyone recites the *Thousand Names of Gaṅgā* everyday, Goddess Gaṅgā shall always attend to him closely.

194. By reciting the hymn of Gaṅgā, one becomes venerated everywhere, successful on all occasions and happy everywhere.

195. He who recites this hymn should be known as a person of good conduct; he is always clean and pure; he is one who has worshipped all the gods.

196. If he is satisfied, Gaṅgā shall become pleased undoubtedly; hence by all means, one should propitiate the devotee of Gaṅgā.

197-198. He who listens to or recites this *Stavarāja* of Gaṅgā and makes other devotees listen to it without hypocrisy and greed, shall become freed from the three types of sins originating from the mind, speech and body. He shall be devoid of sins in an instant and be the beloved of the Manes.

199-200. He shall be the beloved of all the Devas; he shall be honoured by all the groups of sages; at the end of his life he shall ride in an aerial chariot surrounded by hundreds of celestial damsels. He shall be richly adorned with divine ornaments; he shall enjoy celestial pleasures in Nandana and other parks; he shall rejoice like a Deva.

201. While Brāhmaṇas take their food particularly on the occasion of a Śrāddha, recitation of this hymn causes delight to the Manes.

202. His ancestors rejoice in heaven for as many years as there are boiled rice-grains or drops of water there.

203. By hearing this hymn recited on the occasion of Śrāddha the Manes shall become delighted in the same manner as through the offerings of balls of rice in Gaṅgā.

204. If this hymn is written and worshipped in a house, that house is pure always. There is no fear from sins there.

205. O Agastya, of what avail is much talk? Listen to my firm words. No doubt need be entertained in this respect. No benefit comes to a person who doubts.

206. There are many groups of Mantras and hymns in the mortal world. They are not equal to the *Gāṅgeya-Stavarāja* ('King of Stotras of Gaṅgā').

207. If a person recites this hymn of a thousand names throughout his life, he shall not be reborn even if he were to die in Kīkaṭas (i.e., regions around Gayā).

208. If a man regularly recites this hymn, observing restraints, he shall become like a man dying on the banks of Gaṅgā even if he dies elsewhere.

209. This excellent and exquisite hymn was formerly proclaimed by the Pināka-wielding Lord to Viṣṇu, his devotee. It is a hymn with the syllables—'seeds' of salvation.

210. This Stotra stated by me is a substitute for the holy bath in Gaṅga. Hence, a wise man desirous of getting the benefit of a holy dip in Gaṅgā should recite this hymn.

CHAPTER THIRTY

The Greatness of Vārāṇasī

Skanda said:

1-2. O blessed Agastya, listen. Desirous of redeeming his grandfathers, King Bhagīratha propitiated Śrī Mahādeva with his great penance. That most excellent one among saintly kings wanted to redeem his forefathers who had been reduced to ashes by the curse of a Brāhmaṇa-sage (Kapila) and brought to the earth Gaṅgā which flows in three worlds.

3. For the sake of the great welfare of all the three worlds, the king brought Gaṅgā from there (the heaven) to the place where there was Maṇikarṇikā.

4. Hari's Cakrapuṣkariṇī and Śaṁbhu's Ānandakānana are the same. It is the excellent holy spot of the great Brahman, which bestows salvation without effort.

5. The scion of the family of Dilīpa walked ahead and brought Gaṅgā to the place where the city famous as Kāśī was. It is well-known as Kāśī because is revealed (*kāśanāt*) Nirvāṇa (Liberation).

6-11a. The great holy spot is called Avimukta because it is never left off by Śaṁbhu.

O sage, gold is invaluable by itself and classified as a precious (metal). When it is associated with diamond as sparkling as pure water, it becomes all the more valuable. Similarly, the Tīrtha of Cakrapuṣkariṇī was already the place of all welfare. It became more excellent due to the jewel-set earring of Śaṁbhu. In that Ānandakānana, the shrine of Śiva named Avimukta, the attainment of liberation was already possible. By the contact of Gaṅgā it has become all the more powerful. Ever since the time when Gaṅgā came into contact with Maṇikaraṇikā that holy spot has become difficult of access even to Devas.

After performing different types of act auspicious or otherwise, if a person dies in Kāśī, he shakes them off in an instant and becomes Amṛta (immortal).

11b-17a. One who dies in Kāśī becomes immortal (liberated) without Nididhyāsana (practice of continuous meditation) of Brahman known only from the Vedāntas, without Sāṅkhya (discrimination between Ātman and non-Ātman) and without Yoga (the practice with ancillaries).

O Pot-born Sage, without the knowledge that roots out Karmas, a person who dies in Kāśī becomes immortal, with the favour of the Moon-crested Lord.

With or without effort on one's part, one shall abandon the body and die in Kāśī. Through the imparting of the Tāraka Mantra, he shall become immortal.

Even if one is fettered by the Guṇas of Prakṛti acquired in the course of many births, one who dies in Kāśī becomes immortal through contact with the confluence of Asi.

Casting off of the body here is *Dāna* (religious gift); casting off of the body here is *Tapas* (penance); casting off of the body here is *Yoga*—these in Kāśī accord the happiness of Nirvāṇa (salvation).

Even though a person had committed many evils, he can attain the greatest region of Viṣṇu sportingly, after casting off the body in Kāśī on reaching (Gaṅgā) flowing towards the North.

17b-23. All the Devas including Yama, Indra and Agni observed that all the people were eager to obtain salvation. Hence they accorded protection to the city.

The Devas made Asi river that was like a great sword that cut off the evil intentions of sinners. That *Dhunī* (river) was one that warded off the entry of the wicked ones. The Devas made Varaṇā that prevented all the obstacles and hindrances to that holy spot. Suras created Varaṇā that separated the activities of the wicked and the persons of good deeds. Suras made Asi on the South and Varaṇā on the North, which preserved the holy spot in its power to accord salvation. After making it they attained mental satisfaction.

On the Western side of the holy place, the Moon-crested Lord himself made Dehalivināyaka ('Vighneśvara of the threshold') for the purpose of guarding.[1] All these three grant permissions to enter only to these, whose entry is permitted by the kind Lord Viśveśa and never to anyone else. In this regard I

1. The shrine of this Vināyaka is on the Pañcakrośī Road to the west of Kāśī. It shows the traditional western limit of the city.

shall narrate an old story that causes great wonder and enhances devotion.

Skanda said:

24-25. On the shore of the southern sea, very near Setubandha, there was a certain merchant named Dhanañjaya.[1] He was much devoted to his mother. He earned wealth through meritorious acts and with that wealth he propitiated beggars. These beggars spread his renown. He regularly worshipped the son of Yaśodā i.e., Lord Kṛṣṇa.

26. Though he rose very high due to his affluence, he bowed down due to this humility. Though he was an *Ākara* (mine) of good qualities, he did not loudly proclaim his own good qualities.

27. Though he was highly endowed with handsome features, he was averse to other men's wives. Though he was fully equipped with all Kalā (Arts) he had his rise free from *Kalaṁka* (stigma).

28. Though his profession was commerce, O sage, he was usually fond of truth. Though he was out of the pale of Varṇas, he was praised by men of high castes in the world.

29. Though he was *Sadācaraṇaga* ('always going on foot', 'going along the path of the good'), he was happy moving about in boats. Though he was *Adaridra* ('not poor'), that intelligent man had an intellect poor in sins. (i.e., was pious)

30. Even as he was going about his activities thus once, due to the turn of times, his mother who had become very old and sick, died.

31. In her youth that was as transient as the shadow of a cloud but which she made resemble the flood of a river in rainy season, her own husband had been deceived by her.

32. A woman who out of delusion deceives her husband after attaining the prime of youth that can last but three or four days (i.e., for a brief period), goes to hell of endless duration.

33. Even if he is righteous, the husband shall fall off from heaven acquired with great difficulty if the woman (wife) breaks

1. The story of Dhanañjaya illustrates how even the bones of a sinner are inadmissible in Kāśī.

her chastity. Hence chastity should be preserved by women.

34. The wicked woman herself falls into the hell Viṣṭhāgarta ('Abysmal depth of faeces') and stays there till all living beings are annihilated. Thereafter, she is born as a sow.

35. Then she shall become a flying fox eating its own faeces and hanging suspended from a tree or she will be born an owl, blind during the day and staying in the hollow of a tree.

36. With great effort, this body, the receptacle of meritorious results, should be guarded by a woman from the evil touch of another man that may appear to give pleasure.

37. Did not a chaste woman by her order make the rising sun remain motionless by this every body but surrendered to her husband?

38. Did not Atri's wife, Anasūyā, devoted to the vow of serving her husband, conceive in her womb the three Lords (viz gods Brahmā, Viṣṇu and Śiva) by the power of her own husband?

39. By the fidelity to her husband a woman can acquire extensive renown here (in this world) and perpetual residence in heaven. Also she can get the companionship of the Goddess of Wealth.

40. That woman (mother of Dhanañjaya) forsook her eternal duty towards her husband due to her evil propensities. Having become a wanton, she went to hell after death.

41. As for Dhanañjaya, he became righteous and pious because he associated with a Śivayogin whereby his penance rose up.

42. The pious-souled Dhanañjaya was highly devoted to his mother. He carried the ashes and bones of his mother and took the path leading to Gaṅgā.

43-46. He bathed (the bones) with Pañcagavya (five milk products) and then with Pañcāmṛta (candy, honey etc.). Thereafter he applied Yakṣakardama (special type of unguent) and adored them with flowers. Then he covered them with five different kinds of cloth, viz. *Netravastra, Paṭṭāṁbara, Surasavastra, Mañjiṣṭhavāsas* and *Nepālakaṁbala*. After that he covered them with pure clay. Alas, that merchant put all of them in a copper casket. He carried the entire thing and while on his way he never touched anyone of low caste. With purity he used to lie down on bare ground (during nights). The poor merchant fell down with fever before completing his journey.

47-49. A burden-bearing porter was engaged by him after giving him reasonable wages. O Pot-born Sage, of what avail is much talk? He reached Kāśī. He kept the porter there for guarding his luggage. Dhanañjaya went to the bazar to bring some articles of food etc. After getting an opportunity, the porter took away the copper casket from the bundle thinking it to be a money-chest and went home.

50-51. He returned to the place of rest but did not see him. Thereupon, Dhanañjaya looked into his bundle hurriedly and saw it devoid of the casket. He cried "Alas! Alas!" Beating his chest, he lamented much. Searching for him he went here and there.

52. Without taking his bath in Gaṅgā, without visiting the Lord of the universe, Dhanañjaya went to the abode of that porter.

53. That porter had seen the bones inside the copper casket in the forest. He heaved a sigh, abandoned it there and went to his house.

54-60. With his throat, lips and palate parched, the merchant reached that house. Within the hut he saw that piece of his cloth. He felt a little assured with hope and so asked the porter's wife, "Tell me the truth. Do not be afraid. I shall give you more money certainly. Where has your husband gone? Give me my mother's bones. O gentle lady, we are pilgrims; we will not harm you. Unknowingly but greedily the casket of bones was taken away by him. O fair lady, this is not his fault. Perhaps my mother's fate is such. Or it is not even my mother's fault. I, her son, am an unlucky fellow. O Bhilla woman, I am not destined to fulfil the duty of a son. I have endeavoured but luck being apathetic, I am not successful. Let the forest-wanderer come on the strength of my truthful words. Let him not fear. Let him quickly show me the bones. I shall give you more money." On being told thus the Bhilla woman told her husband (everything).

61. That hunter with his head hanging down in shame told him everything and took Dhanañjaya to the forest.

62. Unfortunately the forest-wanderer (i.e., the porter) had forgotten that spot, O sage. He wandered around in the forest becoming utterly confused as to directions.

63-67. He went from place to place in the forest. Wandering from forest to forest the man became weary and sad. Leaving off the pilgrim in the middle of the forest, he went back to his hut. After wandering here and there for two or three days that excellent pilgrim became lean with hunger. With his throat and lips parched, the merchant lamented "Alas! Alas!" With a faded face he reached the city of Kāśī. From the people he learnt the unfortunate doings (of his mother). O sage, then the pilgrim went to Gayā and Prayāga and thereafter went back to his native place. O Pot-born Sage, even after gaining an entry into Kāśī, her bones were immediately sent out because the permission of Viśveśvara had not been received.

68. A sinner may reach Kāśī, as a result of some little merit; but he does not attain the benefit of that holy place. Instatly he goes out.

69. Hence the behest and permission of Viśveśvara is the giver of a chance to stay in Kāśī where Asi and Varaṇā have been engaged in the work of the protection of the holy place.

70. After getting into contact with Asi and Varaṇā, O great sage, Kāśikā has become well-known as Vārāṇasī ever since[1].

71. Vārāṇasī is, in this world, that merciful divine entity where all living beings can easily abandon the body, enter instantaneously the splendour of the vision of Viśveśvara, and take up the bodiless state of salvation, and experience the identity of Brahman and Ātman.

72. "O creature, you have immersed yourself in many excellent Tīrthas. Though you died there you are reborn and never have you enjoyed peace." So says Vārāṇasī. "Dying here you will attain immortality now; by my power, you shall become (identical with) Smaraśāsana (Śiva)."

73. A twice-born who falls (and dies) in the sacred waters of other places, attains the status of Devas etc. but not so in Kāśī. It is surprising that even a Pulkasa (a low-caste man) who falls here does not rise again (i.e., is not reborn); to say nothing of a high-born one.

74. This is that city where that enemy of Puras (i.e., Śiva) who is *Purahā* (the destroyer of the body—*Pura*—at the time

3. Popular etymology of the name Vārāṇasī.

of salvation), desires to grant the highest aim of life and hence makes all the denizens of this city attain the perfection of attaining the other shore of the ocean of worldly existence.

75. After diving into the waters of other holy places, a man discards the sinfully defiled body and becomes a deity in heaven; but after casting off the body in the precincts of Kāśī he becomes doubtful of having even a body (i.e., rebirth in Saṁsāra).

76. Without recourse to the practice of Yoga and the frequent meditation on the unity of Brahman and Ātman, but making the Tārakamantra heard, Vārāṇasī, the remover of the distress of common people, points out the Absolute Brahman to non-Yogin laymen whereby they cease to be reborn.

77. Alas! after desiring for some desirable region, someone completely forsakes his body, in the precincts of Vārāṇasī that is the abode of Dharma, Artha and Kāma and that grants everything wished for, and becomes more delighted. Let his gain be the cessation of the root (cause of rebirth), since it has been reduced to void.

78. Alas! the laymen inhabiting Kāśī are certainly deceived by the Lord having a female in half of his body and an eye in the forehead, who has seized their desired body, the receptable of good deeds and has granted them only salvation without rebirth.

79. Vārāṇasī is the sole ground of unlimited number of shining merits, all the embodied persons whereof are (like Śiva) stained in their neck by poison, have an eye in the forehead, have a beautiful body of woman in the left half and are bereft of the body in the end (i.e., get salvation).

80. This Ānandakānana is the bestower of happiness even before; there (we have) Maṇikarṇikā, the lake caused by the discus, contact with the celestial river and the most important resort of the Lord of the universe. What is there which is not conducive to liberation?

81. Here, in this world, Vārāṇasī is the most excellent (city) with the two rivers Varaṇā and Asi. It causes grief by the destruction of the sense of separateness. It has shining glory, due to the presence of the celestial river. It is immovable (even at the time of Pralaya) and is the place of rest of the Lakṣmī of salvation (which is) bereft of blemishes. Why does a deluded

creature languish after forsaking this (holy city)?

82. (O deluded one,) why do you go away forsaking Kāśī that can be attained only through the blessings of Śaṁbhu and that holds salvation in her very hands? Alas, have you forgotten the misery arising from stay in womb and the fettering and the hitting inflicted by the messengers of Kṛtānta (god of Death)?

83. The other holy rivers (and spots) remove sins immediately, accord much weal and take (the pilgrim) to heaven. But Vārāṇasī causes utter annihilation of the very root of worldly existence, if one drinks, dives in (the waters of Gaṅgā), performs holy rites and casts off the body (here).

84. By casting off their bodies in Maṇikarṇikā in the precincts of the city of Kāśī, embodied beings obtain without hindrance a body that has an eye in the forehead, that has blue lustre in the neck and that has a beautiful female in the left half (i.e., he attains identity of form with Śiva).

85. After comprehending the power of the holy place, if anyone casts off his impure, stinking body in Maṇikarṇikā, he at once gets merged into the lustre of self-knowledge and does not become separated even in the course of another Kalpa.

86. Those who have their minds and sense-organs filled with too much of passion and other defects and hence consider Kāśī on a par with the other holy places around, despite the fact that the great prowess of Kāśī is unrivalled and divine, are sinners. No one should even talk to them.

87. Why do you, O deluded one, wander in various directions after abandoning Vārāṇasī, the favourite capital city of the destroyer of the god of Love? Even after obtaining the permanent glory and lustre of liberation inaccessible to Brahmā and others, do you covet ordinary worldly wealth fickle by nature?

88. If any man endeavours, it is not difficult for him to acquire learning, wealth, houses, elephants, horses, servants, garlands, sandalpaste, women of exquisite beauty and even heaven; but Vārāṇasī that accords liberation even to locusts and moths, is not easily available.

89. In order to find out the comparative weight the worlds, chief of which is Vaikuṇṭha and Kāśīkā, were held in balance. On account of their lightness they (all the worlds) went up.

On account of the heaviness of all the four aims of life, this city remained low down.

90. A man or a non-man (animals, immobiles) occupying Kāśī city after being established here (by the Lord), is to be revered like the sole Lord Rudra. On account of the weight of miseries caused by nature and various kinds of diseases he shall dispel Karmas and merge into the brilliance of the great Lord.

91. Alas, by casting off the body that is the abode of pains and miseries of birth and death and that is subject to steady misfortunes in Kāśī, how is it that this deluded creature does not take up a brilliant body that is the abode of the greatest bliss and that is steadier, as though accepting a broken bell-metal (for something new)?

92. Alas, it is a pity that this world (people) endures pain. Its intellect is affected by the weight of adversities of great power that destroy all riches but whose end is inevitable. Why should the world be afflicted while Kāśī is present on this earth, where at the time of death Śiva whispers something into the ear whereby the creature does not enter the cave of womb again?

93. Of the two sets of people, one staying in the city of Kāśī taking two or three meals a day and doing everything as one pleases and the other taking in only the air and keeping all the sense-organs under control and remaining a forest-dwelling recluse, there is a speciality in the people dwelling in Kāśī.

94. Of the people meeting with death at Kāśī there is no difference between those who commit sins and those of meritorious deeds, because in this barren spot their seeds of (sins and merits) caused by their Karmas do not germinate, because they have been burned up by the eye of Śiva.

95. O Daughter of the Mountain, all who die at Kāśī become immortal whether they are rabbits, mosquitoes, cranes, parrots, sparrows, wolves, jackals, horses, serpents, monkeys or men.

96. O Daughter of the Lord of Mountain, those who continuously live in Kāśī are considered to be my attendants staying on the earth. They are not dreadful. They are adorned with Rudrākṣas and leading serpents. They hold the Crescent

Moon and are marked with Tripuṇḍra (three parallel lines with holy ash).

97. Whatever their number, all the creatures that stay here in Kāśī, those that move about in water and on the ground, fish, jackals, etc., have the bodies of Rudra, due to my blessings. After the death of the body, they merge into me.

98-102. O goddess, Rudras with rain as their arrows are glorified in heaven; those in the atmosphere are the ones with wind as their arrows; and, O dear lady, those on the earth are the ones with foodgrains as arrows.

Hundred Rudras are stationed in the east, south, west and the north; those who recite the Vedas mention about the Rudras stationed above. Innumerable, thousands of Rudras are on the earth too. In Kāśī there are more creatures in the form of Rudra than all these mentioned in the Śruti. Hence, O Pot-born Sage, Avimukta is mentioned as Rudravāsa ('Abode of Rudras'). Therefore, a man who adores all those stationed in Kāśī belonging to the different castes and the different stages of life with great faith and the belief that they are the Lord himself, attains the benefit of the direct worship of Rudra.

103-104. The word *Śma* means 'dead body'. *Śāna* means 'lying down'. O sage, those who are skilful in the use of words and their meanings explain the derivation of the word *Śmaśāna* thus. Kāśī is called 'Mahāśmaśāna' because the great Bhūtas (elements) lie down here like corpses. Hence it is a great Śmaśāna (cremation ground).

105-107. The earth gets dissolved in water at the time of the ultimate annihilation. The waters get dissolved in the fierce valley of the mouth of fire. The great fire gets dissolved in Mātariśvan (wind) which gets dissolved in *Vyoman* (firmament). Vyoman gets dissolved in Ahaṁkāra. That Ahaṁkāra along with sixteen Vikāras (products) gets dissolved in Mahat otherwise called Buddhi (the Cosmic Intellect). Alas, Mahat gets dissolved in Prakṛti. That Prakṛti consisting of the three Guṇas remains entangled with and embracing Pumān. The great Pumān is the twenty-fifth Principle. He is the lord of the body, his abode. He enlivens the body and the sense-organs.

108. This is called Prākṛtapralaya wherein Brahmā, Hari and Rudra also get dissolved. The great Īśvara, with Time as his form, absorbs sportively that Puruṣa also.

109. He is called Mahāviṣṇu by learned men; they cite him as Mahādeva. He is Śiva devoid of end, beginning and middle. He is the Consort of Śrī. He is the Consort of Pārvatī too.

110. In the course of the *Dainaṁdina Pralaya* (day-to-day annihilation) Hara with many bones of Saṁvarta as his ornament, lifts up his own city at the tip of his trident and holds it aloft. Hence Kāśī is devoid of Kali and Kāla (the ravages of Time and death).

Skanda said:

111. Thus, O Brāhmaṇa, Ānandakānana is mentioned as Vārāṇasī, Kāśī, Rudravāsa and Mahāśmaśāna.

112. It was narrated thus by Śaṁbhu, the Lord of Devas to the goddess. It was heard by me in the same manner as mentioned to Viṣṇu formerly. This is the great secret of Kāśī which has been described to you.

113. By repeating this meritorious chapter that destroys great sins and by narrating this perfectly to Brāhmaṇas, one is honoured in the world of Śiva.

114. Hereafter, O Pot-born Sage, what is it that you wish to hear? Tell me. The story of Kāśī gives me pleasure on being narrated (again and again).

CHAPTER THIRTYONE

The Manifestation of Bhairava[1]

Agastya said:

1. O Skanda, O delight unto the heart of the omniscient Śiva, O destroyer of Demon Tāraka, I am not fully satisfied on hearing the story of Vārāṇasī.

2. If I am worthy of being blessed, if I deserve to hear it, O Lord, tell me the detailed story of Bhairava in Kāśī, O Lord.

3. Who is this (deity) named Bhairava established in the city of Kāśī? Of what form is he? What is his activity? What are his names?

4. How is he to be propitiated so that he will bestow success unto the aspirant devotees? When is he to be worshipped so that Bhairava will be quickly propitiated?

Skanda said:

5. O blessed one, I think no one else has as much love and devotion to Vārāṇasī as you have. Hence I shall narrate everything without omission.

6. The manifestation of Bhairava is destructive of all great sins. One shall obtain the benefit of residence in Kāśī without any hindrance on hearing this.

7. May the great Bhairava who performs the dance of Tāṇḍava in a highly excited manner, protect the three worlds from all adversities. With his pair of hands he squeezes the worlds of the Cosmos all-round as though they were a ripe juicy mango.

8. It is called Prākṛta Pralaya ('the dissolution of Prakṛti') wherein God Brahmā, Viṣṇu and Rudra cease to exist. The all-destroying Supreme Lord understands easily that Supreme Person.

---

1. This chapter deals with the creation and exploits of Kālabhairava. He is known as the Kotwal, the Police Chief, of Kāśī. Though our text locates Kālabhairava on the bank of Kapālamocana Tīrtha (v 138) in the Oṁkāreśvara area north of Maidagin, that side was destroyed during Muslim invasions. Now his temple ("Bhaironath Temple") is located in the maze of lanes between Chaukhamba Lane and Maidāgin Park (BCL 189-193).

9. O Brāhmaṇa, there is nothing mysteriously surprising in this. The Māyā of Lord Śiva is very difficult to cross over. All are deluded by it and hence do not comprehend that great Lord.

10. If that great Īśvara of his own accord makes himself understood, Brahmā and others come to know him. They do not know him by themselves, at their will.

11. Though he is omnipresent, the great Īśvara revelling in himself, is not seen. He is thought as though he is like an ordinary god by deluded persons. He is beyond the pale of mind and speech.

12. Formerly, O Brāhmaṇa, on the peak of Meru, the great sages bowed down to Pitāmaha (Brahmā), the lord of the worlds, and said, "What is that single Principle which is immutable?"

13. Deluded by the Māyā of Maheśa, the progenitor of the worlds, who did not comprehend the great Being, mentioned himself as the most excellent one.

14-15. He said, "I am the source of origin of the universe; I am the only self-born Īśvara (Godhead). I am the Absolute Brahman without a beginning. No one gets liberated without worshipping me. I cause the worlds to function. I am the only one who causes them to recede. It is the truth that no one else among the gods is superior to me, O excellent ones."

16. Even as the Creator was saying thus, Kratu, the deity born of a part of Nārāyaṇa, spoke these words laughingly, his eyes being copper-coloured due to anger:

17-19. "What is this that is propounded without comprehending the Supreme Principle. This ignorance on your part is not proper as you (are reputed to be) one endowed with the practice of Yoga. I am the maker of the worlds. I am Yajña, the great Nārāyaṇa. O unborn Vidhi, the very existence of the worlds is not possible if I am ignored. I am the supreme brilliant lustre. I am the ultimate goal. The activity of creation is carried out by you on being urged by me."

20. In this eagerness to excel each other, these two deluded ones acting antagonistically, asked the four Vedas, the knowers of means of proof or cognition.

Vidhi and Kratu said:

21. O ye Vedas who have gained credence everywhere as the greatest authority undoubtedly, what is it that you accept as the truth?

Śrutis said:

22. If we are to be honoured, O lords who are the cause of creation and sustenance, we shall mention an authority that shall dispel your doubts.

23. On hearing what was declared by the Śrutis they too told them: "What is uttered by you is authority unto us? What is the truth? Let this be clearly stated."

Ṛk said:

24. It is Rudra alone within whom the Bhūtas (elements, living beings) abide; it is from him that everything comes out and functions; it is he whom they call the highest reality.

Yajus said:

25. It is Śiva alone who is all-surveying (omniscient). It is that Īśa who is adored by all Yajñas and through Yoga; we gain authoritativeness through him.

Sāman said:

26. It is the great Tryaṁbaka (Three-eyed Lord) by whose lustre the entire universe shines; it is he who is meditated upon by Yogins and the whole cosmos whirls about due to him.

Atharvan said:

27. They call him Śaṅkara ('Bestower of weal'), the Kaivalya ('Salvation'), the remover of miseries, the only Lord (of Devas) whom blessed people realize through devotion.

28. On hearing what was uttered by the Śrutis, Kratu and Vidhi (Nārāyaṇa and Brahmā) who had been completely overwhelmed by delusion and blindness, O sage, smiled and said:

29-30. "How did that Lord of Pramathas (Goblins) attain the status of Supreme Brahma, the Lord who in a nude state regularly sports about with Śivā (Pārvatī) in a cremation ground, who has become grey with dust, who wears matted hair and despicable dress and serpents as embellishments or ornaments, who moves about on a bull? What a lot of difference between him and Supreme Brahma which is devoid of contacts and association!"

31. On hearing what was spoken by them, the eternal Praṇavātman ('the Soul in the form of Oṁkāra'), though unembodied, took up a form and laughingly said to them:

Praṇava said:

32. Never does this Lord Rudra, Hara, assuming a sportive form divert himself with the Śakti who is not different and distinct from him.

33. This Īśa is the great lord, self-luminous and eternal. Śivā, bliss personified, is his eternal Śakti (and not adventitious).

34. Although this was (clearly) stated, the ignorance of Makhamūrti (Nārāyaṇa, embodiment of Yajña) and Aja (Brahmā) did not perish because of the Māyā of Śrīkaṇṭha (Śiva).

35. Thereafter, in between them a great refulgence appeared filling the space between heaven and earth through its own brilliance.

36. A being in the form of a man was seen in the middle of the luminous orb. Then the fifth head of Brahmā blazed with fury.

37-38. Even as Vidhi was reflecting, 'who can be this that has assumed the form of a man (and stands) in between us both?', the great Puruṣa, Nīlalohita, was seen by the Creator in a moment. The great person had the trident in his hand, an eye in the forehead and was wearing serpents and the Crescent Moon as ornaments.

39-40. Hiraṇyagarbha (Brahmā) said to him, "I know you, the moon-crested one. Formerly you came out as Rudra from the region of my forehead. Since you cried then, you had been named Rudra by me formerly. O son, seek refuge in me alone. I shall accord protection unto you."

41-42. On hearing the arrogant words of the Lotus-born Lord, Īśvara, out of anger, created a Puruṣa of terrifying appearance. He said to him, "O Kālabhairava, this Lotus-born One deserves to be chastised by you. You shine like veritable Kāla. Hence you are *Kālarāja*.

43. You are capable of bearing the universe. You are known as (i.e., called) *Bhairava* through your capability to bear (*Bharaṇa*) the universe.[1] Even Kāla will be afraid of you. Hence you are (called) *Kālabhairava*.

44. Since you, on being enraged[2], will suppress the wicked-minded ones, you will earn reputation everywhere as *Āmardaka*.

45. Since you will be eating up the sins of your devotees within a moment, you will have the name of *Pāpabhakṣaṇa* ('Devourer of sins').

46. O Kālarāja, forever you will have the over-lordship of Kāśī which is mine, the city of liberation, greater than all others.

47. You will be the sole one to admonish and chastise those who commit sins here. Citragupta will not be recording their auspicious or inauspicious activities."

48. After receiving these boons, Kālabhairava plucked off a head of Vidhi in a moment with the tip of the nail of finger of his left hand.

49. Punishment should be meted out only to that limb that has committed the offence. So the fifth head which uttered the words of censure was cut off.

50. Then Viṣṇu, in the form of Yajña, eulogized Śaṅkara. Hiraṇyagarbha (Brahmā) who was terrified recited the Mantra *Śatarudriya*.

51. Mahādeva who is pleased with those who bow down to him, became delighted and so consoled them both. He then told Bhairava having matted hairs, who is another form of his own self:

---

1. As stated commonly, 'Bhairava' is derived from √bhī, 'to fear' and 'Bhairava' means one whose roar (*rava*) is 'terrible'. This Purāṇa writer derives it from √bhṛ, 'to bear, to support'. In order to suit his (Bhairava's) function vv 44-46 give the derivations of other epithets of Kālabhairava.

2. The reading *ruṣṭa,* being more appropriate than *tuṣṭa,* is adopted here.

52-53. "This Adhvara (i.e., Nārāyaṇa) and Śatadhṛti (Brahmā) are worthy of being respected by you. O Nīlalohita, hold the skull of Brahmā and go abegging as a part of holy observance for the purpose of dispelling the sin of Brāhmaṇa-slaughter and thus you personally demonstrate it to laymen." After saying this, Śiva of brilliant form vanished.

54-55. Further (before vanishing) he had created a feminine form (a girl) well-known as Brahmahatyā. She was clad in red and had red garlands, scents and unguents. She also was red in complexion. Her face was hideous with curved fang-like teeth. The lolling tongue made her terrible in appearance. The extremities of her feet were in the firmament. She was drinking up much of blood.

56. She had a knife and a broken pot in her hand. Her tawny-coloured ferocious eyeballs were bright. She was roaring with rapidity. She was terrifying even unto Bhairava.

57-58. "O terrible one, by the time he goes to Vārāṇasī follow Kāla, O lady of hideous form. Excepting the city of Vārāṇasī, you will have easy access everywhere." Saying thus, Śiva employed her on a special task and vanished.

59-60. Due to her close proximity, though he was himself Kālakāla ('Kāla unto Kāla' [death]), Bhairava became black in colour. At the behest of the Lord of Devas, he observed the Kāpālikavrata and travelled the three worlds guiding the common people. The highly terrible Brahmahatyā did not leave off that deity (Bhairava).

61-62. The lord of the three worlds, Ugra, the sole administrator of the three worlds, despite his terrible observance, was never left alone by Brahmahatyā in the course of his wanderings in Satyaloka, Vaikuṇṭha and the cities of Mahendra and others and in every holy spot.

63. O Pot-born Sage, from this alone let the greatness of Kāśī as the dispeller of the sin of Brāhmaṇa-slaughter be known.

64. There are many holy places and divine shrines all over the three worlds. But they do not deserve even a sixteenth part of the greatness of Kāśī.

65. The sins of Brahmahatyā etc. may very well roar but only until they hear the name of Kāśī which acts like a thunderbolt in the destruction of the mountains in the form of sins.

66. Attended upon by his Pramathas, Hara, Kālabhairava

with a skull in his hand, walked all over the three worlds. He then stepped into the abode of Nārāyaṇa.

67-68. On seeing the Three-eyed Lord, Mahākāla with serpents for earrings, who is part of Mahādeva, but was called Bhairava the terrible, coming, the Garuḍa-emblemed Lord fell down on the ground like a log of wood in prostration. So did the Devas, sages and the celestial damsels all round.

69-70. They fell down by way of prostration. With his joined palms kept over the head and eulogizing by means of different kinds of prayers, the Lord of Kamalā (Goddess Lakṣmī), Hari, spoke to Padmā who emerged at the time of the churning of the Ocean of Milk: "O highly blessed, blameless, dear, lotus-eyed one, you are lucky.

71. I too am lucky, O lady of excellent buttocks, because we see the Lord of the universe directly. He is the creator and dispenser of the destiny of all the worlds. He is the lord and ruler of all the worlds.

72. He is beginningless. He is the sole refuge. He is quiescent. He is supreme Absolute, the twenty-sixth principle. He is omniscient. He is the lord of all Yogins. He is the sole lord of all Bhūtas (goblins or beings).

73-78. He is the immanent soul within all living beings. He is the perpetual bestower of everything unto all. Let him be seen now, whom those engaged in meditation, those who are calm and tranquil, those who have cast off their sleep, those who have curbed their breaths, see in their heart by means of their intellect. He who is formless, whom only Yogins of perfectly controlled minds and those who know the principle of the Vedas realize, who is omnipresent, comes here in an embodied form. Oh! Wonderful indeed is the activity of Parameṣṭhin ('Dweller in the Absolute'). He has a body while those who repeat his names become bodiless. Here comes the Lord, the Three-eyed One with the moon as his ornament. On seeing him rebirth on the earth is not got by the men of the world. My eyes large and wide like the petals of a lotus are blessed now. Fie upon the status of Devas, for even after seeing the great Śaṅkara here salvation that puts an end to all miseries, is not obtained!

79. There is nothing more inauspicious in the world of gods than their own god-hood, because even after seeing the

Lord of all the Devas, we do not get salvation."

80. After saying this with joyous horripilation all over his body Hṛṣīkeśa bowed down to Mahādeva. He thus spoke to the Bull-emblemed Lord:

81. "O Lord, the remover of all sins, O immutable one, what is this that is being done by you, the omniscient one, the Lord of Devas, the creator of all the worlds?

82. O Lord of Devas, O three-eyed Lord of great intellect, is this your sport? O odd-eyed (three-eyed) one, O destroyer of Smara, what is the reason of this act of yours?

83. O Lord Śaṁbhu, why do you go abegging? This is my doubt, O Lord of Śakti, O Lord of the worlds, you who bestow the kingdom of the three worlds to those who bow down to you."

84-86a. On being addressed thus, Śaṁbhu spoke thus to Viṣṇu: "Brahmā's head was cut off by me with the nail at the tip of my finger. O Viṣṇu, it is to remove that sin that I am observing this auspicious expiatory holy rite."

On being told thus by Maheśa, the lotus-eyed Lord smiled a little. With head bent down he then spoke:

86b-88. "O Lord of all worlds, sport about as you please. O Mahādeva, it does not behove you to overwhelm me with your Māyā. O mighty Lord, at your behest, I create in every Kalpa crores of lotus-seated ones (Brahmās) out of the lotus from the navel. O Lord, eschew this Māyā very difficult to wade through by those who have not realized their souls.

89-91. O Mahādeva, persons including me are deluded by your Māyā. Hence, O Lord of Śivā, I understand your act as it truly is.

When the time of annihilation comes, when you destroy all the worlds along with the Devas and sages of all castes and in all stages of life, then O Mahādeva, whence unto you is the sin of Brāhmaṇa-slaughter etc.? O Śaṁbhu, you have no dependence on anyone else. Hence you sport about as you please.

92. The garland of the bones of all previous Brahmās shines round your neck. O sinless one, where then had the (sins of) Brahmahatyā gone?

93. If anyone remembers you with emotional fervour, despite the commission of great sins, his sin becomes destroyed

(as) you are the support of all the worlds and the mighty lord thereof.

94. Just as darkness does not stay in the proximity of the sun, so also does the sin of a devotee of Bhava. His sin duly becomes reduced.

95. If anyone of meritorious soul meditates upon the pair of your lotus-like feet, even the sin of Brāhmaṇa-slaughter and the like becomes reduced and destroyed.

96. O Lord of the universe, if the speech of any man is devoutly attached and engrossed in your names, no sin harasses him, even if it be on a par with the peak of great mountain.

97. Where will stay the sin that causes great distress on being immensely increased by means of Rajas and Tamas Guṇas as against your auspicious name of Śiva, the panacea enlivening all, the cure for the ailments of all the worlds?

98. If the names Śiva, Śaṅkara, Candraśekhara etc. of the enemy of Andhaka come out of the lips even casually, one will never have worldly existence again.

99. O supreme soul, O greatest refulgence, O you who have assumed a body out of your own will, this is only a curious whim of yours, O Lord. How can there be dependence on others in the case of a great Lord?

100. Today, I am blessed, O Lord of Devas, for I see that great immutable Lord, the root-cause of the universe whom even the Yogins do not see.

101. I have secured a great acquisition today. I have attained the greatest auspicious achievement. To me who have been satiated by the nectar of your vision, even heavenly pleasures and salvation are like a mere blade of grass."

102. While Govinda was saying thus, certain alms of sacred nature called Manorathavatī ('full of keen desire') were offered unto his bowl by Padmā (Goddess Lakṣmī).

103. With great joy, the Lord too set out from there for begging. On seeing Brahmahatyā following him, Janārdana requested her: "Leave off the Trident-bearing One (Śiva)."

Brahmahatyā said:

104. Under this pretext, I shall attend upon the Bull-emblemed Lord and sanctify myself. Where can I have the vision of Bhava (Lord Śiva or Saṁsāra, the cosmos) once again?

* * *

105. Though addressed (and requested) by Murāri (Viṣṇu), she did not leave his side. Then with his face beaming with smile, Śaṁbhu spoke these excellent words to Hari:

106. "O sinless Govinda, O bestower of honour, I am satisfied by drinking your words resembling nectar. Choose your boon. I am the bestower of boons on you.

107. Mendicants do not get so elated with highly consecrated alms as with nectarine drinks of honour, (because thereby) their pain of wandering for alms becomes eradicated."

Mahāviṣṇu said:

108. This itself is the most esteemed boon that I see you, the Lord of Devas who have gone beyond even the ken of wishful thinking.

109. According to the view of saintly persons, the bliss of seeing you, O Hara, is on a par with a shower of nectar without any cloud, a great festivity without undergoing any strain, the acquisition of a treasure-trove without any effort.

110. O Lord, let me not be separated from the pair of your feet. O Śaṁbhu, this is the boon; I do not choose any other boon.

Īśvara said:

111. O Ananta (the infinite one), let what has been wished by you be so, O highly intelligent one. You will become the bestower of boons to all the Devas.

112. Thus blessing the enemy of the Daityas, he wandered through the worlds of Brahmā, Indra and others and resorted to the city named Vārāṇasī, the mother of liberation.

113. Even the regions of Brahmā and other Devas are not equal to a sixteenth part of Vārāṇasī as the creatures staying there too are subject to adversities.

114. A resident of Vārāṇasī is far better, even if he be a mendicant with matted hair, tonsured head and completely nude, than an emperor of the entire earth with a royal umbrella staying elsewhere.

115. The alms received at Vārāṇasī is far better, (but) not

the state of possessing a hundred thousand (Niṣkas) elsewhere. The lord of a hundred thousand enters the womb (Saṁsāra), but not he who consumes the alms thereof (of Vārāṇasī).

116. The alms there at Kāśī offered to mendicants, even if it be of the size of a fruit of *Emblic Myrobalan*, shall be weightier, if weighed against Sumeru (mountain).

117. A person who gives food for the period of a year to one the members of whose family suffer, is honoured in heaven for as many Yugas.

118. The best among men who gives annuity for food to a man without means of sustenance, never becomes miserable due to thirst and hunger.

119. A person who gives accommodation to others in Vārāṇasī obtains the full merit of those who live in Vārāṇasī.

120. Brāhmaṇa-slaughter and other sins leave off the sinner even when the name of Kāśī is uttered. With what can that Kāśī be compared?

121. The moment the holy place (Vārāṇasī) was entered into (by Śiva), at the sight of Bhairava of terrible form, Brahmahatyā screamed "Alas! Alas!" and entered into the lowest of nether worlds.

122. Even as all the people stood watching, the skull of Brahmā fell down from Rudra's hand. On seeing it fallen, he danced with great joy.

123. While Hara was wandering, the excessively unbearable skull of Brahmā did not leave off his hand at any other place, but at Kāśī it fell instantaneously.

124. The sin of Brahmā-slaughter of the Trident-bearing Lord which was never separated anywhere, became destroyed in a moment at Kāśī. How then is Kāśī not a rare city to be obtained?

125-127. Hence this city should be circumambulated and adored. A creature that repeats this great Mantra "Vārāṇasī", "Kāśī" thrice a day, throughout his life, is never born again. He who casts off his life remembering the great holy shrine Avimukta even while he is very far off is never reborn.

128. He whose mind always remembers Ānandakānana (Kāśī) is never reborn, thanks to the (merit of) hearing the name of that holy spot.

129. A man should always reside in the abode of Rudra with

the mind fully controlled. Even after committing a mass of sins, he gets liberated in due course.

130. After reaching Mahāśmaśāna (i.e., Kāśī) if one dies accidentally, one never meets with the eventuality of lying in a cremation ground again.

131. If men remember the holy spot of Kapālamocana at Kāśī, their sins committed here or elsewhere perish instantaneously.

132. After arriving here and performing ablution in this excellent Tīrtha (called Kapālamocana) and offering libations to the manes and gods, one gets liberated from the sin of Brāhmaṇa-slaughter.

133. If people reside in Vārāṇasī after fully realizing that this (worldly existence) is evanescent, Śaṅkara will bestow the supreme knowledge on them at the time of their death.

134. O Brāhmaṇa, this city of Kāśī is the great physical body of Rudra himself. It is *Anirvācya* ('cannot be adequately expressed in words'). It accords the greatest bliss. It is difficult of access for those who are antagonistic to Īśa.

135. I know the reality of this (city). Or one who is engrossed in devotion to Śiva (also may know it). Creatures get liberated here itself like Yogins by means of Yoga.

136. This Kāśī is the greatest region. This city is the greatest bliss. This itself is the supreme knowledge. This should be resorted to by those who desire salvation.

137. If anyone of crooked intellect stays here and becomes antagonistic to the devotees of Śiva or maliciously and deludedly hates this city, he has no redemption here or elsewhere.

138. Honouring the holy spot Kapālamocana, Bhairava stood there itself eating up the heap of sins of his devotees.

139. Though he might have committed hundreds of sins, why should a devotee of Kālabhairava be afraid of sins after resorting to Pāpabhakṣaṇa ('the devourer of sins').

140. This Kālabhairava became well-known as Āmardaka, because he subdues sins as well as the ambitious desires of the wicked ones.

141. He always puts an end to the influence of Kali on the residents of Kāśī. Hence he became highly famous with the name Kālabhairava.

142. The terrible messengers of Yama are always afraid of

his devotees. Hence he is remembered as Bhairava.

143. On the eighth lunar day of the dark half of Mārgaśīrṣa, one should observe fast and keep awake in the presence of Kālabhairava. He is rid of great sins (committed at Kāśī) as sins committed outside are (already) destroyed while entering Kāśī.

144. What little inauspicious deed was committed due to human weakness of the mind, becomes dissolved at the sight of Kālabhairava.

145. The sin committed by creatures in the course of hundreds of thousands of (previous) birth becomes dissolved quickly on seeing Kālabhairava.

146. By performing different kinds of adoration elaborately with plenty of provisions on the eighth lunar day in the dark half of the month of Mārgaśīrṣa, a man gets rid of (all the) hindrances of a year.

147. By performing the festival of the procession of Bhairava on the eighth and fourteenth lunar days as well as on Sundays and Tuesdays, one gets rid of all the sins committed.

148. A fool who puts obstacles before the devotees of Kālabhairava, the permanent residents of Kāśī, will meet with wretchedness (i.e., hell).

149. Those who are devotees of Viśveśvara but not of Kālabhairava will encounter obstacles at every step at Kāśī.

150. By taking the holy bath in the sacred waters of Kālodaka and performing the libations without haste, and visiting Kālarāja, one will redeem one's Manes from the hell.

151. By circumambulating Pāpabhakṣaṇa eight times everyday, a man prevents getting smeared with sins mental, verbal and physical.

152. By performing the Japa of any of his desired deities seated near the pedestal of Āmardaka for six months, the aspirant achieves supernatural powers (or desired objects)—that is the command of Bhairava.

153. If after staying in the city of Kāśī, a man does not worship Bhairava, his sins go on increasing like the moon in the bright half.

154. By resorting to the service of Pāpabhakṣaṇa with oblations, Pūjā and presents, the devotee obtains whatever he desires.

155. If a person does not worship Kālarāja at Kāśī on every

eighth and fourteenth lunar days and on Tuesdays, his merit declines like the moon in the dark half.

156-157. By listening to this meritorious chapter which is named *Bhairavotpatti* ('Birth of Bhairava') and which dispels the sin of Brāhmaṇa-slaughter, one is freed from all sins. Even a person kept in prison, one in great danger becomes rid of difficulties by listening to the manifestation of Bhairava.

CHAPTER THIRTYTWO

*The Manifestation of Daṇḍapāṇi**

Agastya said:

1. O Lord having peacock as your mount, recount to me the nativity of Harikeśa. Who is he? Whose illustrious son was he? How great is his austerity?

2. How did he happen to be a favourite of the Lord of Devas? How did he become the chief of the citizens of Kāśī? How did he become the holder of a staff (i.e., the chief dispenser of punishment)?

3. How did this highly intelligent one gain the status of the bestower of food? I wish to hear this. O Lord, do me this favour.

4. How did Sambhrama and Vibhrama become his followers? How did they become persons causing confusion to those inimical to the holy spot?

Skanda replied:

5. The question has been put relevantly by you, O Pot-

* Daṇḍapāni is the Sheriff of Kāśī who expels undesirable people out of Kāśī and protects eligible residents of Kāśī. He has Sambhrama and Vibhrama as his assistants. As an assistant of Goddess Annapūrṇā, he feeds the needy at Kāśī. Today, the small shrine of Daṇḍapāṇi is in the Viśvanātha lane to the west of Jñānavāpī Mosque. His Daṇḍa (club) is a pillar-fragment from the Mahāśmaśāna pillar at Laṭ Bhairava in a small shrine near Kālabhairava.

Like Gaṇeśa and Kālabhairava, Daṇḍapāṇi is a major figure in Banaras Pantheon (BCL 198-201).

born One, O Brāhmaṇa-sage. The story of Daṇḍapāṇi is conductive to the good of the citizens of Kāśī.

6. O wise one, by the grace of Viśvabhartṛ (Śiva), a man who hears this story, obtains without hindrance the merit of residing in Kāśī.

7. On the Gandhamādana mountain formerly there was a Yakṣa. He was highly righteous. His prosperity was always directed to the performance of good rites.

8-9. Having obtained a son named Pūrṇabhadra, he considered all his desires fulfilled. Attaining the close of his life after the due enjoyment of many pleasures, he renounced his earthly body by means of Śāṁbhava Yoga (practice of Yoga specially consisting of meditation on Śiva) and attained permanent peace with all the sense-organs and their objects having been rendered quiescent.

10-12. After the death of his father Pūrṇabhadra of great renown enjoyed all the worldly pleasures, the extent of which was acquired through merit. He got everything he desired except a son, the sole cause for the attainment of heaven—a son that embellishes the stage of life of a householder, that functions as contributing much to the good of grandfathers, that acts like a spray of nectar to the limbs scorched by the distress of worldly existence and that is akin to a great boat to those who fall into the great ocean of distress.

13-15. Pūrṇabhadra (who had everything good in plenty) saw his palace that was beautiful to all others, devoid of auspiciousness in view of the fact that it was denied the sweetness of the lisping talk of a child. Without a child he was extremely distressed and saw (his palace) a void like the heart of an indigent person, or a desolate forest. On seeing a lonely path, a traveller becomes distressed. Like that he was also distressed. O Pot-born One, this Yakṣa called his wife Kanakakuṇḍalā, an excellent Yakṣiṇī, and said to her, O Pot-born Sage:

16-25. "O dear wife! I do not consider this palace as pleasing, though it is beautiful with a number of mirror-panels in the interior. The windows are beautifully studded with pearls. The courtyard is paved with lunar crystals. There is pleasing sound all-round. The upper storey is rendered brilliant with the lustres of rubies and sapphires that abound in it. Columns of coral add to its splendour. The walls are covered with shining crystals. A number of fluttering banners adorn it with garlands of jewels and rubies. The fragrance of incense and black agallochum render it very joyous. Very costly seats are placed everywhere. Charming couches embellish it. The doors are fitted with beautiful bolts. The pavilion is covered with silk cloth. There are many beautiful dalliance chambers. The palace shines with a number of horses; it is filled with hundreds of servants and servant-maids; it is resonant with the sound of tinkling bells. The cries of peacocks rendered wistful on account of the sounds of anklets, fill the palace. Many doves chirp. It is lofty and resounds with the cries of Sārikās (MaināS). Pairs of swans sport about. There is the splendour of Cakora birds. The humming sounds of bees attracted by flower garlands are heard everywhere. Winds wafting the sweet scent of camphor and musk blow all-round. Dolls of monkeys kept for sport display jewels and rubies on the top of their curved teeth as though they were seeds of pomegranates. Parrots seize pearls mistaking them to be seeds of pomegranates. It is like another palace of Goddess Lakṣmī and is richly endowed with wealth and foodgrains. It has the sweet scent of lotuses within. But in spite of all these things, O my dear, I do not find it pleasing in the absence of a child in the womb. How can I, O Kanakakuṇḍalā, my dear, see the face of a child?

26 Tell me if there is any means (of getting a son). Fie upon the life of a sonless person! The whole of this house appears to be a void without a child born of my bosom.

27. Fie upon the beauty of this mansion! Fie upon this hoarded wealth! Without a son, my dear beloved, our life too is worthless. Fie upon it!"

28. The chaste Yakṣiṇī, Kanakakuṇḍalā, heaved a deep sigh within herself and spoke to her husband who was lamenting loudly:

Kanakakuṇḍalā said:

29. O my dear, why do you feel aggrieved? You are endowed with knowledge. There is a means of getting a child. Listen with faith.

30. To persons who endeavour (for a goal) what is there difficult to be achieved in this world consisting of the mobile and immobile beings? (The way to achieve one's) desires and

ambition flash before persons who have dedicated their intelligence (mind) to God.

31. O my dear husband, only contemptible fellows speak of fate as the cause of things. That fate is nothing but the Karma that one has done formerly.

32. Hence one should resort to manliness and for the sake of subduing the Karma one should seek refuge in Īśvara, the cause of all causes.

33. Acquisition of child, wealth, wife, necklaces (ornaments), mansions, horses, elephants, all pleasures and even heaven and salvation is not far from devotion to Śiva.

34. There is no doubt in this that all desires and the eight *Siddhis* resort to the doorway of that person who performs devotional rites of Śaṁbhu, O my dear husband.

35. Even Nārāyaṇa, the lord and immanent soul of the universe, became the protector of mobile and immobile beings due to the service rendered to Śrīkaṇṭha.

36. The status of being the creator was given to Brahmā by Śaṁbhu. Indra and others became the guardians of the worlds.

37. Śilāda who had no child got a son who could conquer death. Śvetaketu too regained his life from the noose of the god of Death.

38. Upamanyu acquired mastery over the Ocean of Milk; Andhaka became Bhṛṅgi with the exalted status of the lordship of Gaṇas.

39. Dadhīci conquered Śārṅgin (Viṣṇu) due to the service unto Śaṁbhu. By meditating upon Śaṅkara Dakṣa obtained the status of a Prajāpati.

40. If seen, Mṛḍa (Śiva) shall make (the devotee) realize that region which is beyond the ken of wishful thinking and which cannot be expressed in words.

41. It is certain that no one will get anything anywhere without propitiating Maheśāna, the bestower of everything on all embodied beings.

42. Hence, if you wish for a dear son who is the most excellent of all persons, seek refuge in Śaṅkara by all means, O dear lord.

* * *

43-44. On hearing these words of his wife, Pūrṇabhadra, the king of Yakṣas, who was well-versed in music, propitiated Śrī Mahādeva by means of his musical art. Within a few days his desire was fulfilled. He, of steady vows and observances, acquired the desired son from that wife.

45. By whom have all desired things not obtained by worshipping Nādeśvara (Oṁkāreśvara)? Hence Nādeśvara is to be earnestly served by men at Kāśī.

46. In due course, his pregnant wife delivered a son. The father named him Harikeśa, O Brāhmaṇa.

47. O Agastya, extremely delighted by seeing the face of a son, Pūrṇabhadra and Kanakakuṇḍalā distributed many presents out of pleasure.

48. The child whose countenance was beautiful like the full moon and was like the god of Love (in appearance), went on growing every moment like the moon in the bright half of a month.

49. When the child Harikeśa was about eight years old, he began to love devoutly Śiva alone.

50. Even when he played about in dust, he made Liṅgas out of the dust particles. With all enthusiasm he used to worship (it) with green leaves and tender blades of grass.

51-54. He used to call all his friends by the names of Śiva, such as Candraśekhara, Bhūteśa, Mṛtyuñjaya, Mṛḍa, Īśvara, Dhūrjaṭi, Khaṇḍaparaśu, Mṛḍānīśa, Trilocana, Bharga, Śaṁbhu, Paśupati, Pinākin, Ugra, Śaṅkara, Śrīkaṇṭha, Nīlakaṇṭha, Īśa, Smarāri, Pārvatīpati, Kapālin, Bhālanayana, Śūlapāṇi, Maheśvara, Ajināṁbara, Digvāsas, Svardhunīklinnamaulija, Virūpākṣa, Ahinepathya. Thus he repeated these names.

55. He lovingly called his friends thus. His ears never caught hold of anything except the name of Hara.

56. Except the courtyard of Bhūteśvara, his feet never went anywhere else. His eyes were not capable of seeing any other form.

57. His tongue relished only the nectar of the syllables constituting Hara's name. His nose never desired to smell anything other than the fragrance of the lotus-like feet of Śiva.

58. His hands did only what pleased him. His mind never thought of anything else. All drinks were drunk by him after dedicating them to Śiva with excellent heart.

59. All foodstuffs were eaten by him only after offering them to the Three-eyed Lord. In all conditions everywhere he never saw anything except Śiva.

60. (While) going along, singing, sleeping, standing, lying down, eating or drinking, he saw the Three-eyed Lord alone. He never noticed any other object.

61. During the nights, when asleep, the boy used to wake up frequently saying, "O Three-eyed One, wait for a moment. Where do you go?"

62-70. On seeing thus the clear activities of Harikeśa, his father taught him thus: "Be engaged in domestic activities. O dear child, these horses and colts are yours. These clothes of variegated colours, these silk clothes too are yours. The gems are pure, direct from their very source. They are of diverse kinds. These crystal wares too are yours. (Yours) is the ample wealth of cattle. There are very valuable vessels of silver, brass etc. There are many articles of trade originating from various parts of the land. There are wonderful chowries and many sweet-smelling articles. There are heaps of different kinds of grains. All these articles are your own. O son, learn all the lores helpful in the earning of wealth. Eschew these activities of the indigent people always soiled with dust. Practise all lores and enjoy excellent pleasures. After attaining the closing days of your life, you can adopt this *Bhaktiyoga*."

Though advised thus many times by his father, he disregarded the words of his guardian. Once when he saw his father with eyes blazing angrily, Harikeśa of liberal views and ideas became afraid and went out of his house.

71-73. He then became confounded as to the direction to be taken and began to reflect, 'Alas, puerile in intelligence, the house has been left off by me! Where shall I go? O Śaṁbhu, where shall I stay, so that it will be conducive to my weal? I have been banished by my father. I do not know anything. Formerly the following (didactic utterance) was heard by me lying on the lap of my father, clearly spoken by someone to my father.

Recollected Advice (74—83)

74-75. "Vārāṇasī is their ultimate resort. Those who are forsaken by mothers and fathers, those who are forsaken by their own kinsmen, those who have nowhere else to go, those who are afflicted with old age, those who are crippled or disabled by sickness, those who have nowhere else to go, Vārāṇasī is their ultimate resort.

76. Those who are assailed by adversities day and night, at every step, those who have nowhere else to go, Vārāṇasī is their ultimate resort.

77. Those who are overwhelmed by heaps of sins, those who are beaten down by poverty, those who have nowhere else to go, Vārāṇasī is their ultimate resort.

78. Those who are afraid of the danger of worldly existence, those who are bound by fetters of Karma, those who have nowhere else to go, Vārāṇasī is their ultimate resort.

79. Those who are bereft of Śrutis and Smṛtis, those who have forsaken rules of cleanliness and good conduct, those who have nowhere else to go, Vārāṇasī is their ultimate resort.

80. Those who have slipped down from the practice of Yoga, those who have eschewed austerities and desisted from making monetary gifts, those who have nowhere else to go, Vārāṇasī is their ultimate goal.

81. Those who encounter insult at every step in the midst of their kinsmen, to them the only thing that gives delight is the Ānandakānana of Śaṁbhu.

82. Those good people who take delight in residing in Ānandakānana are blessed by Viśveśa and they have special delight.

83. That Mahāśmaśāna is the greatest resort to those who have nowhere to go, because there the seeds of Karma are roasted by the fire of Viśveśa."

84-85. After reflecting thus, Harikeśa went to the city of Vārāṇasī. In this Avimukta the creatures that eschew their earthly bodies, do not have any further contact with bodies, by the grace of *Tanudveṣin* ('Hater of bodies', Śiva). After reaching Ānandavana he resorted to austerities.

86. After some time, Śaṁbhu entered Ānandakānana and pointed out to Pārvatī his own pleasure grove of sport.

Description of the Pleasure Grove (87-110)

87. There were Mandāra flowers of excessive fragrance. It was adorned by Kovidāras. It was filled with beautiful Caṁpakas

and Cūtas. Fresh Mallikās (jasmine) were in full-bloom.

88. Mālatī was blooming there. It was shining with Karavīra. The groves of Ketakī flowers were in full-bloom. There were plenty of full-blown Kurabaka flowers.

89. The fragrance of blooming Vicakila (a kind of jasmine) spread everywhere. The tender sprouts of Kaṅkelī (Aśoka) over-hung the trees. The grove was echoing with the humming of bees, attracted by the fragrance of Navamallī.

90. There were many Punnāgas putting forth flowers. The grove was rendered fragrant by the sweet scent of Bakulas. All the quarters were sweetened by the scent of succulent Pāṭala flowers.

91. The whole ground appeared to be garlanded by the swarms of bees hanging down in groups. It was pervaded by groups of cuckoos sporting about on the tips of moving Candana branches.

92. There birds of excellent variety were intoxicated as it were by the black Aguru. It was fancifully pleasant with dolls kept on the branches of Nāgakesara.

93. In the shade of Nameru trees as tall as Meru, Kinnaras were sporting about. Pairs of Kinnarīs were singing loudly. Palāśa trees had a number of parrots of sweet voice.

94. Pairs of bees were humming among the clusters of Kadamba trees. The grove shone with Karṇikāra trees whose colour surpassed even the colour of gold.

95. It was covered with Śāla, Tāla, clusters of Tamāla, Hintālī and Lakuca trees. The fragrance of Saptacchada trees spread everywhere. A number of Kharjuri trees made it shine. It was covered with coconut trees. The red colour of Nāraṅgīs gave it a beautiful hue.

96. There were many fruit-bearing Jambīra trees. Bees hovered round Madhūka flowers and hummed loudly. Śālmalī trees had plenty of cool shade. There were great groves of Picumanda (Neem) trees.

97. It was covered with Damana flowers of very sweet scent. It was brilliant with clusters of Marubaka. Gentle wind blew there gracefully shaking the Lavalī creepers.

98. The grove reverberated with the sound of Jhillī's (crickets) that pleasantly accompanied the Hallīsaka dance of the Bhilla (tribal) women. In certain places broods of pigs were playing

about in the lakes.

99. Male swans were eagerly attracted by the lotus stalks round the neck of female swans. The pleasure grove appeared beautiful when the grief-free Koka (Cakravāka) pairs sported about producing Kreṅkāra sounds.

100. Young ones of Bakas (cranes) moved here and there. Sārasa birds were attached to their mates, Lakṣmaṇās (female Sārasas). Intoxicated peacocks cried loudly. Kapiñjala made the grove agitated.

101. The living beings there were happy due to the Jīvañjīva birds; the chirping Karaṇḍava birds spread everywhere. The cool wind blowing over the waters of the lake fanned the entire grove.

102. It was turned reddish yellow due to the pollen dust from the gently moving Kelhāra flowers. The blooming lotuses were its face. The blue lotuses were its eyes.

103. The Tamāla trees constituted its tresses. The shining Dāḍimīs were its teeth. The swarms of bees were its brows. The parrots provided it with splendid nose.

104. The great wells were its ears. It was splendid with Dūrvā grass resembling moustache. The sweet scent of the lotus flowers was its breath. The Biṁbī fruit was its lips.

105. The excellent lotus leaves were its clothe; Karṇikāras were ornaments. The beautiful Kaṁbu tree is its graceful neck. The Śaṅkara tree constitutes the undulating portions of the shoulders.

106. The great serpent ensconced in the sandalwood tree is the staff-like arm, that adorns it. The tender sprouts of Aśoka function as the thumb; and Ketakī is the brilliant nail.

107. The graceful lion constitutes its chest and the boulder the big belly. The whirlpool makes its shining navel and the pair of trees, the pair of calves.

108. The resplendent leaves of the plantain trees function like the Chinese silk-cloth that covers it. The ground lotuses make its feet and the intoxicated elephant accounts for its majestic walk.

109. Various kinds of flowers make it garlanded as it were. It is completely covered with buffaloes and beasts of prey concealed by trees without thorn.

110. The black antelope that was asleep on the lunar cystals

(as if) darkened the moon there. The flowers that were scattered by the trees excelled the stars in the heaven. The Lord entered the grove pointing out the pleasure-garden to the goddess thus.

The Lord of Devas said:

111. O beautiful goddess, (though to a lesser degree than you) just as you are the most beloved of mine, this Ānandakānana is always dear to me.

112. O goddess, the body of those who die here in the Ānandavana becomes immortal through my grace. They are not reborn.

113. The seeds of those who are born and who die in Vārāṇasī become burned through my behest by the fire blazing in the cremation ground.

114. O daughter of the Lord of Mountains, those who sleep the long sleep (i.e. die) in Mahāśmaśāna never again lie and sleep in the womb.

115. Creatures become liberated through the knowledge of Brahma and not otherwise anywhere. Those who cast off their bodies in Prayāga or in the holy spot according realization of Brahma (also become liberated).

116. Towards the end of their life, I give the *Tāraka Mantra,* which is the knowledge of Brahman, to those who die in Kāśī. They become liberated at the very same moment.

117. The people who ridicule those who die at Kāśī take up their sins. Those who praise take up their merit. Those creatures become liberated here.

118. Whence, O goddess, is the realization of Brahman to those who have been overwhelmed by Kali and whose sense-organs are naturally fickle? Hence I give them Brahma (knowledge) here.

119. Yogins who become deluded by their Siddhi-powers fall off from the Yogic exercise. But those who fall (die) in Kāśī do not fall again even in the great annihilation (Mahālaya).

120. Through Yogic practice people do not get the knowledge of Brahman in the course of a single birth; but those people who meet with death in Kāśī become liberated in a single birth.

121. O Girijā, nowhere else is a creature liberated in the

manner as it is liberated in the great holy spot Avimukta with my favour.

122. After practising properly Yoga for many births, a Yogī may or may not become liberated. But the person who dies in Kāśī becomes immediately liberated in a single birth.

123. In Kaliyuga Yoga does not fructify. In Kaliyuga penance does not become effective. But a man gifting away the wealth obtained by legitimate means becomes successful immediately.

124. Neither holy rite, nor austerity, neither sacrifice nor *Japa* nor the worship of the deitites (becomes fruitful). *Dāna* (relgious gift) alone is conducive to liberation and Kāśī is obtained through *Dānas.*

125. In Kaliyuga, Lord Viśveśvara, the city of Vārāṇasī, Gaṅgā Bhāgīrathī and *Dāna* (religious gift) are of special significance.

126. Gaṅgā flowing towards the North at Kāśī and my Liṅga named Viśveśvara in Kāśī, are the two which bestow salvation on men and they are to be attained in Kaliyuga through the power of *Dāna.*

127. A man of meritorious deeds and another even otherwise, becomes liberated, O goddess of Devas, by resorting to my holy spot. No doubt need be entertained in this respect.

128. O goddess, due to the greatness of Avimukta neither *Puṇya* (merit) nor *Pāpa* (sin) become effective though acquired by persons in the course of a hundred births through Karmas.

129. Hence, O goddess, Avimukta should not be left off by a person desirous of salvation, though assailed in diverse ways by hundreds of obstacles.

130. After performing the rite of Kṣetrasannyāsa (permanent residence in a holy place) those men who continue to stay here are Jīvanmuktas ('living-liberated souls'), O goddess; I remove their obstacles.

131. I am not as much interested in staying in the firmament of the heart of Yogins, on Kailāsa or on Mandāra, as I am attached to staying in Kāśī.

132. O goddess, the citizens of Kāśī always stay in my belly. Hence I release them in the end, because this is my promise.

133. Adopting Tāmasī Prakṛti and becoming Kāla (god of Death), I sportingly swallow the mobile and immobile beings, (but) O goddess, I protect Kāśī scrupulously.

134. O Gaurī, there are two recipients of my intense love, viz. you having austere penance as your asset and Kāśī, the place of delight (Ānanda-bhūmikā) and (none) else.

135. Excepting Kāśī, I have no abode; excepting Kāśī I have no attachment for anything else. Without Kāśī there is no salvation (This the truth). I am stating the truth.

136. In this Cosmic Egg, neither through the adoption of Aṣṭāṅga Yoga nor through any other means has liberation been achieved as in a playful way at Kāśī.

137. While saying these things, the Lord of Devas saw Harikeśa performing penance seated at the root of an Aśoka tree.

Description of the Sage (138-144):

138. The collection of his bones was bound together with dried tendons and sinews. He was motionless, while ants, moles and other worms had dried up the blood in his veins.

139. The skeleton of bones that he was, he had no flesh at all. He was steady like a crystal column. The lustre that issued from him was that of a conch, Kunda flower, the moon, snow and a oyster shell.

140. His very vital breath appeared to be sustained through his inner strength and he was kept alive only because he was destined to live for some more time. The fact that he was alive was indicated by the continuity of his breath.

141. The winking of his eyes rendered the animals around aware of his being alive. He had illuminated the quarters through the eyes emitting rays from the tawny eyeballs.

142. The whole forest became faded as it were on being touched by the flames of the forest-fire of penance. All the trees became sprinkled with the shower of nectar from his gentle eyes.

143. He appeared to be directly the rite of penance incarnate in human form, who had adopted an indescribable form of devotion without any specific motive in view, and had begun to perform penance.

144. He was surrounded by fawns of deer wandering in groups. He appeared to be protected by wide-jawed lions of excessively terrible faces.

145-146 On seeing him in such a plight, the goddess submitted to the Lord: "O Lord, fulfil the desire of this devotee of yours by means of the proper boon. He has concentrated his mind in you alone. His very life is under your power. His activities are for your own sake. He considers you as his support and his body is completely dried through very severe austerities. Do bless him through boons granted to this Yakṣa."

147. Accompanied by the goddess, the Lord got down holding the hand proffered by Śailādi (Nandikeśvara). The Lord, with his mind melting with pity, touched the sage who had his eyes closed in the course of his meditation.

148. The Yakṣa opened his eyes and saw in front of him the Three-eyed Lord having the refulgence of a thousand rising suns. He then spoke with the words choked in his excitement due to delight:

149. "Victory unto you, O Īśa, Śaṁbhu, Lord of Girijā, O Śaṅkara, O trident-handed one, O lord with the crescent moon as crest-jewel. O compassionate one, being touched by your lotus-like hand my tender body has become immortal."

150. On hearing the soft-spoken utterance of that intelligent devotee, bearing comparison to a grape fruit, O great sage (Agastya), the great Lord joyously granted a number of boons (to him):

151. "With my blessing, O Yakṣa, be the permanent Daṇḍadhara ('Wielder of the rod of justice') of this holy spot that is dear to me. From today onwards you shall be my favourite one, the punisher of the wicked and the good protector of the meritorious.

152. Now you shall be named Daṇḍapāṇi. At my behest control the ferocious Gaṇas. These two attendants shall always follow you. Their names are true to their meaning, viz. Saṁbhrama and Udbhrama (because they create great and excessive excitement) to men.

153-154. You are to give the final embellishment to the residents of Kāśī, consisting of a blue mark in the neck, snakes for bracelets, a fine eye in the forehead, wearing the hide of an elephant and the left side characterised by (the presence of) a beautiful woman. On the head, the tawny matted hairs shall be had; the meritorious body should be smeared with ash and lo, the whole body should have a fine splendour with the digit of the crescent moon and moving in slow gait like that of a graceful bull.

155. You are always the bestower of cooked food to the residents of Kāśī; you alone infuse them with vital breath; you grant them knowledge; you grant them salvation through the advice from my mouth; you will give them a steady and permanent abode.

156. O Piṅgala ('tawny-complexioned one through penance'), you will harass sinners completely and creating confusion among them, you will drive them out (of Vārāṇasī). In a moment you will bring devotees from afar. You will be the bestower of salvation (on them).

157. Since the excellent holy place has been entrusted to you, who can have salvation without worshipping you? My devotee must at first propitiate you and only then adore me.

158. In my city you will bestow residence (to the devotees). You be the officer-in-charge of justice. Eradicate the evil-minded enemies of Kāśī and guard Kāśī forever joyously.

159. O son of Pūrṇabhadra, O Daṇḍanāyaka, O Yakṣa of the tree-eyed lord, O Harikeśa, O Piṅgala, O bestower of cooked food on all those who stay in Kāśī, be the leader of the Gaṇas, the bestower of knowledge and salvation.

160. Even a person highly devoted to me shall not get an opportunity to stay in Kāśī without devotion to you. Hence, O Daṇḍapāṇi, be the chief recipient of honour among the Gaṇas, Devas and men.

161. Only he who, after performing the rites of libation in the Jñānoda Tīrtha (i.e., Jñānavāpī), propitiates you, the chief of the Gaṇas, shall be fully satisfied as having done his duty. With the unparalleled blessings of mine, he shall be meritorious.

162. O Daṇḍapāṇi, you be here always in the southern direction, just in front of my eyes, punishing living beings of wicked activites and granting freedom from fear to your own men. Stay here."

Skanda said:

163. O Brāhmaṇa, after granting the boons to Daṇḍapāṇi thus, Giriśa mounted his excellent bull and entered Ānandakānana.

164. O Pot-born One, since that time, the king of Yakṣas,

the Daṇḍanāyaka, controls perfectly the city of Vārāṇasī at the behest (of Lord Śiva).

165. I too had to stay here, as he found fault even in my qualities. Though I was staying at Kāśī, he was not (duly) respected by me.

166. O sage, you are such a sage of perfect sense-control, still you left the holy place. Here I suspect that he has acted against you.

167. If, O Brāhmaṇa, Harikeśa were to see even the slightest adverse activity, where is one's stay in Kāśī? Where is happiness? (You will have neither.)

168. Without propitiating Daṇḍapāṇi who can stay happily in Kāśī? Desirous of entering Kāśī, I worship him even from a far distance:

(Prayer of Daṇḍapāṇi)

169. "O excellent son of Pūrṇabhadra born of the limbs of Ratnabhadrā, O Yakṣa, make my stay in Kāśī free from obstacles, for the purpose of acquiring happiness.

170. Yakṣa Pūrṇabhadra is blessed. Kāñcanakuṇḍalā (i.e., Kanakakuṇḍalā) is blessed whose son you were, O wise Daṇḍapāṇi.

171. Be victorious, O lord of Yakṣas. Be victorious, O tawny-eyed lord. Be victorious, O lord with tawny matted hairs. Be victorious, O lord with the staff as your great weapon.

172. O Ugratāpasa, the chief controller of the great holy place Avimukta, O Daṇḍanāyaka of terrible face, be victorious, O beloved one of Viśveśvara.

173. O lord, gentle in face to those who are gentle, O terrible one unto the terrible ones, O lord, you are death unto the sinful-minded ones in the holy place. You are a great favourite of Mahākāla.

174. Be victorious, O giver of life, O eminent Yakṣa, the bestower of cooked food, salvation and stay at Kāśī, O lord whose body is adorned with the shining rays of great jewels!

175. O lord, O generator of great confusion, O instigator of utmost excitement to those who are no devotees! O eradicator of great confusion and utmost excitement of the devotees!

176. O lord, skilful in the final decoration (at the time of death of the devotee)! Be victorious, O bestower of the trea-

sure-trove of knowledge. Be victorious, O lord acting as a bee in the lotus-like feet of Gaurī. O lord clever in finding out and discerning the impending salvation!"

177. O Maitrāvaruṇi, I repeat this meritorious Yakṣarājāṣṭaka ('octave of verses unto the king of Yakṣas) three times everyday. It is conducive to an access to Vārāṇasī.

178. A wise man repeating *Daṇḍapāṇyaṣṭaka* with faith is never assailed by obstacles. He shall get the benefit of stay in Kāśī.

179. One who listens to this manifestation of Daṇḍapāṇi and repeats this prayer is reborn in Kāśī after dying elsewhere.

180. By listening to this chapter of the meritorious origin of Daṇḍapāṇi, by reading and causing this to be read, one prevents the attack of obstacles.

CHAPTER THIRTYTHREE

*Description of Jñānavāpī**

Agastya said:

1. O Skanda, now narrate to me the greatness of Jñānoda Tīrtha. Wherefore do even the heaven-dwellers praise Jñānavāpī very well?

Skanda said:

2. O Pot-born One of great intellect, listen to the origin of Jñānavāpī that removes all sins. It is being narrated now by me.

* Jñānavāpī ("The Wisdom Well"—BCL) is the most famous well in Kāśī, said to be dug by Śiva. It is a deep well, ten feet in diameter and is near the mosque built by Aurangzeb after destroying the grand old temple of Viśveśvara. Now it is set in a spacious columned arcade with iron bars across its top. Pilgrims start their pilgrimages in and about Vārāṇasī after sipping its water (as *Saṅkalpa*) at the beginning and end of their pilgrimage. Śiva dug this well of 'Liquid Wisdom' with his trident long before Gaṅgā came there. (BCL 125-129)

3. O sage, formerly in Satya (Kṛta) Yuga in the primordial universe Īśāna (Rudra, the presiding deity of the North-Eastern direction—Comm.) was wandering here and there.

4-5. Then, even clouds did not rain and rivers (consequently) did not flow (were non-existent). None had any desire for water for drinking or bathing; water could be seen in the oceans of salty or sweet waters. People roamed about over the earth in places here and there.

6-9. Īśāna reached the glorious Ānandakānana ('the forest of bliss'), the holy spot of Nirvāṇaśrī (glory of Mokṣa). It is called Mahāśmaśāna ('the Great Cremation Ground'), a barren spot for all seeds (of worldly existence). It is the place that wakes up creatures lying in deep sleep (of ignorance). It is the boat (that takes out) the people falling into the whirlpool of the ocean of worldly existence. It is a pavilion of rest and recreation for creatures, distressed very much due to the frequent travel (in the course of their transmigration). It functions like a knife cutting off the thread (bonds) of Karmas accumulated in the course of many births. It is the abode of Existence and Bliss; it is the great Elixir of Supreme Brahman; it is the cause of the creation of a series of happiness; it bestows the fruition of all the means of the attainment of salvation.

10-11. Īśāna with matted hairs (covering his head) entered the holy spot. There was a profuse lustre of pure rays from his blazing trident. He espied the Liṅga that manifested itself earlier when there was an intense rivalry between Viṣṇu and Brahmā as to who was the greater of the two.

12. It was surrounded on all sides by garlands of radiant flowers. It was worshipped by multitudes of gods and sages.

13. It was continuously adored by groups of Siddhas and Yogins; it was sung about by Gandharvas and eulogized by Cāraṇas.

14. It was being served in various ways by celestial damsels through their different types of dances. Nāga females served it with the lamps of their luminous jewels through continuous waving with them ceremoniously.

15. It was embellished thrice a day with proper ornaments by Vidyādhara and Kinnara females. Here and there, it was fanned with Chowries by the celestial damsels.

16. On seeing that Liṅga, there arose an idea in the mind

of this Īśāna, 'Let me bathe this great Liṅga with potfuls of cool water.'

17. Īśāna who was identical with Rudra in a terrible physical frame, dug up a deep pit with terrific speed by means of his trident. The place was to the south of Viśveśa and very near him.

18. Then, O sage, columns of waters covering the earth and ten times its size, came out whereby the whole of the world was inundated on all sides.

19. With those waters as cool as snow, but devoid of Jāḍya (i.e. of the nature of knowledge), which removed clusters of sins and which were untouched by other embodied beings, he bathed (the Liṅga).

20. The waters were sparkling in colour like the (pure) minds of good people. They had bluish tinge like the path of the sky. Their lustre was brilliant like moonlight; they were holy and pure like the names of Śaṁbhu.

21. They were excessively sweet like the divine nectar; pleasant to the touch like the limbs of a cow; had grandeur like the intellect of a sinless person and were sparklingly moving to and fro (fickle) like the happiness of the sinners.

22. Their scent excelled the sweet smell of lotuses; they were delightful with the fragrance of the Pāṭalā flowers. They attracted the minds and the eyes of the people in an unprecedented way.

23. They were, as though, the sole protectors of the vital airs of all living beings, distressed through the heat of ignorance. They were capable of yielding more benefit than bathing with potfuls of Pañcāmṛta (curd, milk, ghee, honey and sugar).

24. They were the producers of three Liṅgas(?) in the hearts of those regularly performing the ceremonious rinsing of the mouth with faith ; they functioned like the sun in dispelling the darkness of ignorance; they yielded the benign gifts of wisdom.

25. They caused more happiness to Viśvabhartṛ (Lord Śiva) than even the gentle caress of Umā. They caused more purity than even the excellent bath of *Mahāvabhṛtha* (valedictory bath after the performance of sacrifices).

26. Extremely delighted in his mind, O Pot-born Sage, Īśāna bathed the Liṅga thousand times through pitchers with

thousand streams.

27. Thereby, the holy Lord, the omni-eyed, the omni-souled Śiva, became delighted. He spoke to Īśāna, Rudra of terrible physical frame:

28. "O Īśāna of excellent holy rites, I am pleased with this great rite of yours, never before undertaken by others. It has caused me great delight.

29. Hence, O Īśāna, O great ascetic with matted hairs, engaged in a noble task involving excessive endeavour, tell me what boon (you will have). There is nothing that cannot be given to you today."

Īśāna said:

30. O Śaṅkara, O Lord of Devas, if you are pleased and if I deserve to receive a boon, let this unrivalled holy Tīrtha be named after you.

Viśveśvara said:

31. This Śiva Tīrtha is greater than all those Tīrthas situated in the three worlds, viz., Bhūḥ, Bhuvaḥ and Svaḥ.

32-33. Those who ponder over the meanings of the word, say that *Śiva* means knowledge (wisdom). Here, due to my greatness, that knowledge is liquified (i.e., has taken a watery form). Hence this Tīrtha has become reputed in all the three worlds by the name *Jñānoda.* Merely at the sight of this Liṅga, one is rid of all sins.

34. One shall obtain the benefit of a horse-sacrifice by touching the Jñānoda Tīrtha; and that of a Rājasūya and a horse-sacrifice by touching and rinsing the mouth therewith.

35. By performing Śrāddha rite here, one receives that benefit which is obtained by a man after bathing and offering libations to the grandfathers in Phalgu Tīrtha.

36. The performance of Śrāddha here on a day when there is Vyatīpāta Yoga or the coincidence of Thursday, Puṣya star and the eighth lunar day in the dark half, yields ten million times more benefit than that at Gayā.

37. By offering libations of water with gingelly seeds in Jñāna Tīrtha, one obtains the benefit ten million times more than that obtained by propitiating the Manes at Puṣkara.

38. The benefit that is obtained by offering balls of rice in Sannihatyā (Rāmahrada) in Kurukṣetra, when there is a solar eclipse, is obtained by offering the same everyday in Jñānoda.

39. Those whose sons perform Piṇḍanirvāpaṇa ('offering balls of rice') in Jñāna Tīrtha rejoice in Śivaloka while all the living beings are annihilated (at the end of the Kalpa).

40. An excellent man who takes his holy ablution in the morning and drinks (the holy) water but observes fast otherwise on the eighth and the fourteenth lunar day becomes one full of Liṅgas within.

41. If the devotee observes fast on the eleventh day and drinks three handfuls of water here, undoubtedly three Liṅgas will rise up in his heart.

42-43. The devotee should take his holy ablution in the Īśāna Tīrtha, especially on a Monday, propitiate the gods, the sages and the Manes and make gifts in accordance with his capacity. Thereafter, he would worship Śrī Liṅga elaborately with all the requisites. Here also he should make gifts of various objects. Thereby he shall have accomplished all his duties (or desired objects).

44. By performing *Sandhyā* rites in Jñānoda a Brāhmaṇa shall instantaneously dispel all the sins due to transgression of timely duties. He shall become wise and endowed with knowledge.

45. This has been described as Śiva Tīrtha; this is the splendid Jñāna Tīrtha; this Tīrtha has been called *Tāraka* (that which redeems); this is certainly Mokṣa Tīrtha ('salvation-granting Tīrtha').

46. Certainly multitudes of sins shall perish by remembering Jñānoda. By visiting it, touching it, bathing in it and drinking its water, piousness is engendered.

47-48. Gobiins, ghosts, vampires, ogres, Ḍākinīs, Śākinīs, evil Planets, evil spirits, Jhoṭiṅga, Kālakarṇīs etc., spirits attacking infants, epileptic fits, tertian fevers, fevers recurring every fourth day, swellings—all these subside by seeing the waters of Śiva Tīrtha.

49. If a highly intelligent man bathes the Liṅga with the waters of Jñānodatīrtha, it is certainly on a par with having got it bathed with the waters of all the Tīrthas.

50. I myself, in the form of Jñāna, having assumed the liquid form, shall destroy *Jāḍya* (sluggishness, ignorance) and impart knowledge.

51. After granting boons thus, Śaṁbhu vanished there itself. The trident-bearing Īśāna considered himself one whose desires were fulfilled.

52. Rudra, Īśāna with matted hairs, drank the excellent water and acquired the great knowledge whereby he achieved bliss of Brahman.

Skanda said:

53. Listen, O Pot-born One. I shall recount what took place in Jñānavāpī, the ancient mythological legend of wonderful content.[1]

54. Formerly, in Kāśī, there was a Brāhmaṇa well-known as Harisvāmī. A daughter was born to him. She was unexcelled in beauty in the whole earth.

55. She was clever in all kinds of fine arts. With her (sweet) voice, she vanquished even the cuckoo. No other woman on the earth was equal to her in the excellence of good conduct.

56. There was no other woman like her in this world, either among celestial women or among Kinnara, Vidyādhara, Nāga, Gandharva or Asura women.

57. She was the abode of all beauty; she was an excellent mine (i.e., resort) of all good features. Certainly, out of fear for the Sun, darkness resorts to her tresses of hairs.

58. I suppose, out of fear of the new-moon day, the moon has sought refuge in her face. Even during the day, it does not abandon her because it is afraid of the sun.

59. Her eyebrows appeared like a swarm of bees moving up and down in the spaces between the cheeks, the decorative markings thereon that resemble a creeper (thus appearing) thereby frequently practising flights.

60. The Khañjana birds always passing through the spheres of her eyes, experience the perpetual autumnal pleasure as

1. The legend of Suśīlā, the future queen Kalāvatī, is a contribution of this Purāṇa to extrol the greatn+ess of Jñānavāpī.

they pleased.

61. A golden streak of light has been placed by the Lord of Love in the row of teeth of that beautiful girl. Is there such a fine digit in the moon?

62. Her lips that had the lustre far excelling the coral, are the splendid jewel-set interspaces in the mansion of King Madana (Lord of Love).

63. Lord Smara appears to aver this solemnly through the three lines in her neck, "Neither in heaven nor in the mortal world, nor in the nether region is there a *Rekhā* (line) like this in women."

64. Her two breasts, I believe, constitute the two tent-houses of King Kāma, abounding in valuable jewel treasures.

65. Brahmā made a propped up staff, as it were, as indicated by the line of hairs in the invisible middle of the beautiful girl with arched brows, thanks to the instruction of Anaṅga (Lord of Love).

66. Reaching deep into the cavity of her navel Kandarpa became Anaṅga (bodiless). He performs great penance as if to regain (his) body.

67. By her weighty hips, through the initiation of the Lord of Love, many young men on the earth became unable to be independent in (moving) their eyes (All of them got their eyes riveted to her hips).

68. Whose mind was not arrested and fixed firmly like a pillar by her pillar-like thighs round in shape? Even the minds of sages, despite their disciplined good behaviour, got stuck (like a pillar).

69. Whose lustre of discrimination was not destroyed, O sage, by the lustre of the nail of the big toe of the foot of that fawn-eyed girl?

70. She regularly took her bath in Jñānavāpī everyday and attended to the tasks of sweeping the premises of the temple of Śiva with concentrated mind.

71. The deer-like minds of the youths of Kāśī who grazed, as it were, the grass in the form of the lines (e.g. a lotus, a conch) in the imprints of her soles, did not go to any other place.

72. No other creeper, although it had fragrant flowers was resorted to by the swarm of bees in the form of the eyes of

young men, excepting her lotus-like face.

73. That girl though endowed with beautiful eyes, never looked at the face of anyone. That maiden, though endowed with excellent ears, did not listen to anyone's words.

74. She, of good conduct, endowed with chaste habits, was secretly requested by love-lorn youths of excellent handsome features, but she did not love them in return.

75. Her father too was approached with wealth and requested many times by young men. But he was unable to hand over (in marriage), because she had powerful glory accompanied by good chaste habit.

76. Due to her close worship of Jñānoda Tīrtha, that girl Suśīlā (apparently the name) saw everything within and without pervaded with Liṅgas.

77-79. Once, she was asleep in the courtyard of the house. Enamoured of her excellent beauty, a certain Vidyādhara abducted her then. Along the aerial path he was carrying her off to Malaya mountain. But by that time the demon Vidyunmālī also came there. He had a terrible huge body. Skulls made his ear-rings. His limbs were smeared with suet and blood. He had whiskers and his eyes were tawny.

The Rākṣasa said:

80. O young Vidyādhara, you have come within the range of my vision. I shall despatch you to the abode of Yama along with this woman.

81. On hearing these words, she trembled like a hind attacked by a tiger and like a leaf of a plantain tree again and again in her fright.

82-83. The demon hit that Vidyādhara with his trident. The Vidyādhara youth of sweet form, yet of tremendous power, was attacked and pierced in the chest by his terrible Triśūla. Yet he hit back the demon with his adamantine fist.

84. The Vidyādhara, in the course of the battle, hit Vidyunmālī who was intoxicated with human flesh and suet. Shattered by that blow of the fist, he fell down on the ground.

85. The demon fell a prey to death (on being hit) like a mountain with thunderbolt. The Vidyādhara became crippled by the trident that struck him.

86-87. With rolling eyes, he spoke falteringly, uttering half of her name as *Sus*: "O dear one, you have been brought here in vain." Then that heroic youth gave up his life in battle, remembering his beloved.

88. Experiencing an unprecedented thrill, thanks to his touch, she considered him alone as her husband and consigned her body to the fire of grief.

89. By the close proximity to that girl whose body contained three Liṅgas that demon acquired a divine body and went to heaven.

90. The Vidyādhara youth who had staked his very life in the battle, remembered his beloved at the last moment (of his life). He was reborn as the son of Malayaketu.

91. That girl who forsook her life in the fire of separation meditating on the Vidyādhara youth, was reborn in Karṇāṭa.

92. Mālyaketu, the son of Malayaketu, who had the glory and splendour of Anaṅga, god of Love, married in due course that Kalāvatī who was given away in marriage by her father.

93. Due to the impression of her experiences in the previous birth, that chaste lady excessively interested in the worship of Liṅgas, set aside sandal powder and honoured Vibhūti (holy ash).

94. That lady of natural beauty considered embellishment with Rudrākṣa beads more esteemable than (ornaments of) pearls, lapis lazuli, rubies and topaz.

95. After marrying Mālyaketu, Kalāvatī, the chaste lady, enjoyed divine pleasures and prosperity and gave birth to three sons.

96. Once a certain man from the north, a painter, showed king Mālyaketu a wonderful picture canvas.

97-98. The king presented Kalāvatī with that picture. She became thrilled on seeing the picture again and again in secret. It contained the picture of her revered god and Lord. On looking at the picture, she forget even herself like a Yoginī engrossed in meditation.

99. For a moment she opened her eyes and looked at the picture canvas. Lifting the tip of her index finger, she spoke to herself:

100. "This is the charming confluence of Asi in front, very near Lolārka. This is the excellent river Varaṇā near the shrine

of Keśava (i.e., Ādi Keśava).[1]

101. This is the north-flowing celestial river whose touch is eagerly sought after in heaven and which the heaven-dwellers always desire.

102. This is the glorious Maṇikarṇikā which is conducive to the salvation of good men and is spoken of as the inscrutable Mokṣalakṣmī (glory of salvation).

103. This is the glorious Maṇikarṇikā where death is auspicious and life is frutiful and where heaven is as insignificant as grass.

104. This is Maṇikarṇikā where the meritorious ones desire to die and so giving up their wealth and assets, they stay like ascetics with holy rites, eating only roots and bulbous roots (*mūla-kanda-bhuk*)

105. It is the place where Śaṅkara who holds the crescent moon and Gaṅgā of triple path (on his head) shows the path of salvation to those who die here.

106. It is the place where Śaṁkara annihilates Saṁsāra (worldly existence) though it is difficult to ward off. With Him as helmsman, men, though dead, become immortal (in Mokṣa).

107. It is here where Maheśāna, the ocean of sympathy, whispers (the redeeming Tāraka Mantra) into the (right) ear and hence the steadfast path of salvation in the world does not remain far off.

108. It is through much of the merit accumulated in the course of many births, that men obtain Bhava as the whisperer (of the Mantra) and the dispeller of worldly existence.

109. This is Śrī Maṇikarṇikā where men of great intellect adopt Kṣetrasannyāsa ('renunciation in the form of going away from a fixed holy spot') and by the strength thereof consider god of Death as insignificant as a blade of grass.

110. This is the place where the excellent saintly king Hariścandra, in the company of his wife, considered his body like a blade of grass and sold it off.

111. This is that glorious Maṇikarṇikā, the sandy soft bed whereof even the dwellers of Vaikuṇṭha desire to have.

112. This is that glorious Maṇikarṇikā where (devotees) become liberated after disengaging themselves from the bondage

1. VV 100 ff. describe the various prominent places in Vārāṇasī which Kalāvatī had seen in her previous birth as the Brāhmaṇa girl Suśīlā.

of Karmas arising in the course of many births.

113. This is that glorious Maṇikarṇikā which is desired for ever for the sake of long sleep (i.e., salvation) by those people who dwell even in Satyaloka.

114. This is that Kulastaṁbha (steady pillar) where Śrī Kālabhairava chastises sinners residing within the holy spot, inflicting severe torture.

115. A sin committed elsewhere may perish on seeing Kāśī. But for sins committed at Kāśī the torture administered is extremely terrible.

116. This is the Tīrtha called Kapālamocana. It is also very sacred. It is the place where the skull of Brahmā fell down from the hand of Bhairava.

117. This is the Tīrtha Ṛṇamocana which produces sanctity and purity. Excellent men who take their holy ablution here become liberated from the three types of indebtedness to the Devas, to the Sages and to the Pitṛs.

118. This is the miraculous Oṁkāreśa with five abodes (Āyatana) wherein the absolute Brahman named Praṇava shines forever.

119. The five Āyatanas are A, U, Ma, Nāda and Bindu the fifth one. This is the place where Brahman consisting of the five shines forever.

120. This is that exquisitely beautiful river Matsyodarī.[1] If any excellent man takes his holy ablution here, he will never enter the cavity of a mother's belly—this is the conclusive decision.

121. This Three-eyed Lord endowed with compassion converts his devotee, even if he is in another country, into a three-eyed one (gives *Sarūpatā Mukti* i.e. one having the form similar to that of the Lord).

122. This is Lord Kāmeśvara[2] who fulfils the desires of good people. Even Duravāsas obtained the fulfilment of his desire here.

1. In the 10th cent. CE. Matsyodarī was a small tributary of Varaṇā. It then flowed by the Oṁkāreśvara temple. Today Matsyodarī is a small elliptically shaped park and a pond called Macchodarī at a short distance to the south of Oṁkāra. The great Matsyodarī Tīrtha was drained in 1820s. (BCL 116)

2. Kāmeśvara is just to the east of Macchodarī. It was formerly on the bank of Matsyodarī Tīrtha. It was established by Durvāsas. When Śiva appeared, he vowed to grant all desires of those who worship Kāmeśvara. (BCL 358)

123. For the sake of the fulfilment of the desires of devotees, Maheśa himself became merged here. Hence the name Svarlīna of the Trident-bearing Lord of Devas.

124. This is that wonderful mansion of the Lord who takes pride in his holy spot and who is cited as Mahādeva in Vārāṇasī in the Purāṇas.

125. This is Lord Skandeśvara. If a man visits this Lord with faith, he obtains the benefit of life-long celibacy.

126. This is Vināyakeśvara who bestows all supernatural powers. By serving him all the causes of obstacles of men perish.

127. This is Goddess Vārāṇasī herself, the splendid deity in personified form. By visiting her men are never born again in a womb.

128. This is the great shrine of Pārvatīśvara Liṅga where Maheśāna accompanied by Gaurī is present forever as the bestower of salvation.

129. This is the glorious Lord Bhṛṅgīśvara, the destroyer of great sins. By serving the Liṅga, Bhṛṅgī became a liberated living soul.

130. This is Caturvedeśvara, the creator of all, who upholds the four Vedas. By visiting this Lord, a Brāhmaṇa obtains the benefit of studying the four Vedas.

131. This is the Liṅga named Yajñeśvara installed by Yajñas (Sacrifices). By worshipping it, a man obtains the great benefit of the performance of all Yajñas.

132. This Liṅga named Purāṇeśvara is eighteen Aṅgulas in length and breadth. By visiting this a devotee shall become receptacle of eighteen Vidyās[1] (lores).

133. This is Dharmaśāstreśvara installed by the Smṛtis. By visiting it, one derives the benefit and merit of studying the Smṛtis.

134. This is Sārasvata Liṅga that causes the destruction of all sluggishness and ignorance. This is Sarvatīrtheśvara Liṅga which bestows purity instantaneously.

135. This is the extremely wonderful pavilion of Śaileśvara Liṅga. It has the great splendour of all kinds of jewels.

---

1. The eighteen Vidyās are as follows: Six Aṅgas of the Vedas (e.g. Śikṣā, Kalpa etc.), four Vedas, Mīmāṁsā, Nyāya, Dharmaśāstra, Purāṇa, Āyurveda, Dhanurveda, Gāndharva Veda and Arthaśastra. (SKD. III. p. 389)

136. This is the charming Liṅga named Saptasāgara, on visiting which a man obtains the benefit of taking the holy bath in the seven seas.

137. This is the glorious Mantreśvara who bestows the benefit of reciting Mantras. Formerly in Kṛtayuga this was installed by seven crores of great Mantras.

138. This is the great Kuṇḍa in front of Tripureśa Liṅga which was dug by Tripuras formerly. It is a great favourite of Lord Śiva.

139. This is Bāṇeśvara Liṅga worshipped by Bāṇa who had a thousand arms. It had caused the two-armed Bāṇa to become thousand-armed.

140. This is Vairocaneśvara in front of Prahlādakeśava. This (Lord) is named Balikeśava and this is Nāradakeśava.

141. This is Ādityakeśava to the east of Ādikeśava. This is Bhīṣmakeśava and this one is Dattātreyeśvara.

142. To the east of Dattātreyeśvara, this is Ādigadādhara. This is Bhṛgukeśava and this is Vāmanakeśava.

143. These are Nara and Nārāyaṇa. This is Yajñavārāhakeśava. This is Vidāranārasiṁha and this is the famous Gopīgovinda.

144. This is the palace with a jewel-set flagstaff of Lakṣmīnṛsiṁha by whose grace Prahlāda attained the region of Indra.

145. This is Kharvavināyaka who bestows great spiritual powers on men. This is Śeṣamādhava, formerly installed by Śeṣa.

146. This is Śaṅkhamādhava who stationed himself here after killing Śaṅkha. His devotees do not get themselves burned even by the Saṁvarta fire (of world annihilation).

147. This is the (stream of Sarasvatī), the elixir of the great Absolute. This is the place where the great river Sarasvatī joins Gaṅgā.

148-151a. Men who immerse themselves therein are not reborn on the earth.

This is Śrī Bindumādhava himself, the great Lord of Lakṣmī. A man who bows to him with faith, will not stay in the abode of a womb. He never suffers from poverty. He is never assailed by ailments. Even Yama bows down to the devotee of Bindumādhava. He is the sole Ātman of *Praṇava* assuming the form of *Nāda* and *Bindu*. The unembodied great Brahman is this Bindumādhava.

151b-152a. This is the holy Tīrtha named Pañcabrahmātman. He who takes his holy dip therein, does not take up physical body consisting of the five (gross) elements.

152b-153. This is that Maṅgalāgaurī in Kāśī, the producer of great auspiciousness here and hereafter by means of her grace.

This Lord is termed Mayūkhāditya, the Sun that has garlands of rays and is the dispeller of darkness.

154. This is the great Liṅga Gabhastīśa that bestows divine lustre. Formerly great penance was performed here by the son of Mṛkaṇḍu.

155-156. (Mārkaṇḍeya) had installed a great Liṅga (before performing penance) named after himself. It is the great bestower of longevity.

This Liṅga named Kiraṇeśvara is well-known in all the three worlds. Even if it is bowed to once, it leads one to the region of Kiraṇamālin (Sun).

This Liṅga Dhautapāpeśvara is the purifier of all sins.

157-159a. This is Nirvāṇanarasiṁha, the giver of Nirvāṇa (liberation) unto the devotees. This is Maṇipradīpanāga with great jewels for ornaments. By worshipping it, a man can prevent an attack by serpents. He is never tormented by them.

This is Kapileśa Liṅga installed by Kapila. By visiting this, even monkeys are liberated. Nothing need be said about human beings.

159b-162a. This great Liṅga Priyavrateśvara shines. By worshipping this a creature attains the love and favour of all creatures.

This excellent abode constructed with jewels and rubies belongs to the glorious Kālarāja, the remover of the distress of the Kali Age. He is Pāpabhakṣaṇa ('devourer of sins') who protects his devotees from sins by punishing sinners causing obstacles in the holy spot. He tortures them in hundreds of ways.

162b-166a. This is the beautiful Mandākinī who has come here to perform penance. Having experienced the pleasure of residence in Kāśī, she does not yearn for heaven till today. By taking the holy dip here, propitiating the Pitṛs and performing *Śrāddha* in accordance with the injuctions, even a man committing evil deeds can avoid seeing hells.

This is the Liṅga named Ratneśvara that has become the

crest-jewel of the thousands of Ratnas present in Kāśī. Who has not obtained salvation which is the great crest-jewel of all the aims of human life, after enjoying innumerable Ratnas by the grace of Ratneśvara?

166b-167. This is the loftily erected mansion of Kṛttivāseśvara[1], on seeing which from afar a man may attain even the status of Kṛttivāsas (Lord Śiva).

The Liṅgātmaka Physical Frame of Viśveśvara (167-172)

Of all the Liṅgas, the status of being the head is that of Kṛttivāsas.

168. Oṁkāreśa is to be known as the tuft of hair. Trilocana constitutes the three eyes. Gokarṇa and Bhārabhūteśa are glorified as the ears.

169. The two, Viśveśvara and Avimukta, are the two right hands. The two, Dharmeśa and Maṇikarṇeśa, are the two left hands.

170. The two spotlessly pure feet are Kāleśvara and Kapardīśa. Jyeṣṭheśvara is the waist and Madhyameśvara is the navel.

171. Mahādeva is the Kaparda (matted hairs). Śrutīśvara is the crest-jewel. Candreśa is the heart thereof. The Ātman (Ahaṁkāra—ego) is the great Vīreśvara.

172. Kedāra is its penis (Liṅga). They know that Śukreśvara is the semen virile. Millions and billions of the other Liṅgas should be known as the nails, hairs and the ornaments of the body.

173-175. These two, the right hands (i.e., Viśveśvara and Avimukta), are indeed the perpetual bestowers of salvation on the creatures that fall into the ocean of delusion, after granting them freedom from fear.

This is Goddess Durgā. This is the great Pitṛ Liṅga.

This is Citraghaṇṭeśī. This is the *Hrada* (eddy) of Ghaṇṭākarṇa. This is that famous Lalitāgaurī. This is miraculous Viśālākṣī.

1. Kṛttivāseśvara is to the north-east of Maidagin. It is one of the most ancient Liṅgas in Kāśī. The temple was demolished by Aurangzeb. Now it is a mosque open to Hindus only on the Śivarātri day. (BCL 358)

176. This is Āśāvināyaka. This is the wonderful Dharmakūpa. If a man offers balls of rice here, he will lead his ancestors to the region of Brahmā.

177-180. This is Goddess Viśvabhujā ('Omni-armed'), the great Goddess Bandī, always revered by the three worlds. On being remembered, she frees from bondage even if the persons be in fetters.

This is the Daśāśvamedhika Tīrtha, honoured by the three worlds. Even with three *Āhutis* here, one shall attain the benefit of keeping Agnihotra.

This is the Tīrtha named Prayāga which is the most excellent of all Tīrthas.

This is the Tīrtha named Aśoka. This is Gaṅgākeśava. This is the most excellent gateway to salvation. They know this as the gateway to heaven. (Mokṣadvāra and Svargadvāra are the names of holy shrines.)

CHAPTER THIRTYFOUR

In Praise of Jñānavāpī

Skanda said:

1-2. O Pot-born One, again the slim (slender-limbed) lady saw in the painted canvas, in front of Svargadvāra, the glorious Maṇikarṇikā where Śaṅkara touches with his right hand the ear of the creatures bitten by the serpent of worldly existence and instructs Brahma-knowledge to them.

3. This holy place of salvation shall grant that goal which cannot be attained by men either by Sāṁkhya imparted by Kapila, or by Yoga or by holy rites and observances.

4. Even in Vaikuṇṭha, the abode of Viṣṇu, those engrossed in devotion to Viṣṇu engage themselves in the Japa of the glorious Maṇikarṇikā for the sake of liberation.

5. This is that glorious Maṇikarṇikā which excellent Brāhmaṇas ultimately resort to for attaining salvation, even after performing Agnihotra throughout their life.

6. This is the glorious Maṇikarṇikā which Brāhmaṇas who, after duly reciting the Vedas, engaged themselves in Brahmayajña

in this world, resort to for the sake of liberation.

7. After performing many Kratus with profuse monetary gifts the blessed kings resort to Maṇikarṇikā for the sake of excellence.

8. Chaste women too, always devoted to their husbands, resort to Maṇikarṇikā for salvation, by following (in death) their husbands (here).

9. Vaiśyas too who have accumulated wealth through legitimate means, entrust (by *Dāna*) their riches to holy men in the end and serve the glorious Maṇikarṇikā.

10. Excellent Śūdras treading the path of the moral code, leave off their sons, wives etc., and resort to this Maṇikarṇikā for the attainment of salvation.

11. Those who have conquered the sense-organs and practised celibacy throughout their life, resort to this glorious Maṇikarṇikā for the sake of salvation.

12. Even those persons in the householder's stage of life, who propitiate guests (by due reception) and who are engrossed in the performance of Pañcayajñas do not abandon this Maṇikarṇikā.

13. Those who have adopted the stage of life of the Vānaprastha resort to Maṇikarṇika after controlling all the sense-organs and knowing (it to be) the means of salvation.

14. From the diverse scriptural texts they know that salvation cannot be attained by any other means. Hence Ekadaṇḍa sages who desire salvation resort to Maṇikarṇikā.

15. Tridaṇḍin sages suppress their mind (by Prāṇāyāma), speech (by silence) and body always and resort to Maṇikarṇikā to attain the glory of salvation.

16. Persons observing the holy rite of Ekadaṇḍa, who have forsaken all activites and suppressed the fickle mind, resort to Maṇikarṇikā for attaining salvation.

17. Whether he be *Śikhin* (having tuft), or *Muṇḍin* (shaven-headed), *Jaṭin* (having matted hairs), *Kaupīnin* (having a loin cloth) or nude, which holy man desirous of salvation does not serve (resort to) Maṇikarṇikā?

18. Those who are unable to perform penance, or to make holy monetary gifts, those who do not have the practice of Yoga—to all these this Maṇikarṇikā accords salvation.

19. There are a thousand means of salvation, O sage. But

none of them bestows salvation as easily as this Maṇikarṇikā.

20. Maṇikarṇikā bestows equal salvation in the end on both—on him who has undertaken the vow of fast and on him who takes food thrice a day.

21-22. A person may practise *Pāśupata Vrata* with great steadfastness in accordance with injunction as laid down in scriptures. Another person may continuously remember Maṇikarṇikā in his heart. If the body is cast into the river at Maṇikarṇikā, the goal attained by both is the same. Hence Maṇikarṇikā should be resorted to quickly after forsaking everything else.

23. Those who dive into Maṇikarṇikā and enter Svargadvāra become rid of all sins. Heaven is not far from them.

24. This Maṇikarṇikā is the gateway to heaven. It is the ground leading to both heaven and salvation. Heavenly goal as well as salvation is accessible here itself, neither above nor below.

25. After making many types of gifts and taking a bath in Maṇikarṇikā, people shall enter Svargadvāra. They shall never go to hell.

26. The meaning of the words *Svarga* and *Apavarga* has been settled by learned people: *Svarga* means happiness and *Apavarga*, great happiness (i.e., Mokṣa).

27. Though Indra is seated on a throne, where has he that happiness which one sitting in Maṇikarṇikā attains?

28. In the glorious Maṇikarṇikā, one gets naturally that great happiness which has been indicated in the meditation of those who forget themselves in contemplation.

29. To the east of Svargadvāra and to the west of the celestial river, there is a great territory, the sole storehouse of blessedness and good fortune.

30. As many sand particles shining due to the touch of the Sun (light) (are there, so many) Brahmās (the creators of the universe) passed away, but Maṇikarṇikā did not.

31. Around Maṇikarṇikā there are as many Tīrthas as would leave no space of the size of a gingelly seed vacant.

32. If a person in a certain family is liberated by attaining to Maṇikarṇikā, his descendants become worthy of being respected by even the heaven-dwellers due to his power.

33. Twenty-seven generations of his ancestors are redeemed

by a man who offers libations to the Manes after reaching Maṇikarṇikā.

34. Maṇikarṇikā lies between the middle of the celestial river and Hariścandramaṇḍapa, between Svargadvāra and Gaṅgākeśava.

35. Even the three worlds do not attain equality with even a particle of this Maṇikarṇikā. All the beings stationed in the three worlds endeavour to attain this.

36. Looking the painted canvas thus frequently, Kalāvatī spotted Jñānavāpī to the south of Śrī Viśveśvara.

37. Daṇḍanāyaka, Saṁbhrama and Vibhrama make the evil-minded ones extremely confused and protect the waters of Jñānavāpī from them.

38. This Jñānavāpī, the bestower of knowledge, is the aquatic physical form of the eight-formed Mahādeva cited in the Purāṇas.

39. After viewing Jñānavāpī, Kalāvatī experienced horripilation all over her body like the flowers of a Kadaṁba tree.

40. Her limbs experienced tremor; the region of the forehead was profusely covered with perspiration and her eyes were filled with tears of joy.

41. Her creeper-like body became rigid; the face lost its colour; the voice became choked and the painted canvas fell down from her hands.

42. For a moment she forgot her own self. She did not know "Who am I ?" "Where am I ?" In that state of deep sleep, she was as motionless as the great soul.

43. Her attendants hurriedly moved about here and there and asked one another, "What, what is the matter? What is this?"

44. On seeing her in that plight, those wise and experienced women understood everything through those psychosomatic emotional expresions, and told one another thus:

45. "Some object of her love in a former birth has been seen by her. After coming into contact thereof, she has reached an ecstatic state."

46-47. If it is not so, how did she swoon all of a sudden? While viewing this picture-canvas in secrecy, they carefully pondered over the primary cause of her loss of consciousness and administered pacifying remedies calmly to her.

48. One of them fanned her with plantain leaves. Another

one embellished the blessed lady with circular garlands of lotus fibres.

49. Another attendant sprinkled her with profuse flow of sandal water. A certain attendant removed her sorrow with tender foliage of Aśoka.

50. With the sprays of water from the fountain pavilion, a certain attendant sprinkled the creeper-like tender body of that lady emaciated through separation, in order to get the desired effect.

51. A certain attendant covered her body with a wet cloth. Another smeared it with the paste of camphor powder.

52-58a. A certain attendant arranged a soft bed of lotus petals. Another attendant removed all diamond ornaments from her body and embellished her chest with pearls. Another moon-faced woman made the slim-bodied lady lie down on the ground paved with lunar stone slabs, cool on account of flowing cool water.

A certain attendant named Buddhi-śarīriṇī ('Intellect-bodied') saw the queen being served thus. Distressed very much, she told her companions: "I am aware of a great remedy for the suppression of her excessive distress. Do not delay. Set aside all these modes of remedy. I shall make her immediately rid of all distress. Watch the wonderful feat. It was after seeing the painted canvas that she suddenly became excited. Certainly some object of her love is here itself. Hence she will become rid of her distress at the touch of the painted canvas."

58b-59. At the instance of Buddhiśarīriṇī the other attendants placed that painted canvas in front of Kalāvatī and said: "See here, Kalāvatī. There is your favourite deity here, the cause of your delight."

60. On hearing the name "favourite deity" and on seeing the painted canvas, she appeared to have been sprinkled with nectar. She regained her consciousness and got up quickly.

61. It was like the revival of a herbal plant scorched by drought by means of heavy downpours of shower. Again she began to look at Jñānavāpī, the bestower of knowledge.

62-66. By touching the Vāpī in the picture, Kalāvatī obtained the knowledge of the previous birth and of everything that happened in the previous birth.

Again she pondered over the excellent greatness of the Vāpī: 'How wonderful! This Jñānavāpī in the picture when touched by me has produced in me the knowledge of what happened in the previous birth.' Thereupon, the delighted beautiful lady spoke these words in front of those attendants, regarding the events of her previous life as a result of the power of Jñānavāpī:

Kalāvatī said:

In my previous birth, I was a Brāhmaṇa girl. I rejoiced and sported about in Jñānavāpī near Viśveśvara in Kāśī. My father was Harisvāmī and mother Priyaṁvadā.

67-68. My name was Suśīlā. A Vidyādhara abducted me. While on his way near Malaya mountain, that heroic person was killed by a demon at mid-night. He also killed the demon. Freed from his curse, the demon attained a divine body.

69. This Gandharva was born of Malayaketu. I became the daughter Kalāvatī of the king of Karṇāṭa.

70-71. This knowledge came to me instantaneously on seeing Jñānavāpī.

On hearing these words of hers , the attendant Buddhiśarīriṇī and the other attendants as well, became delighted as was evident from their beaming faces.

They bowed down to that meritorious Kalāvatī and said:

72-75. "How can it be made possible to attain Jñānavāpī whose power is like this? Fie upon the life of those persons in this mortal world, by whom Jñānavāpī is not seen!

Obeissance to you, O Kalāvatī. Carry out our wish too. Make our birth fruitful by requesting the king to take us there. Beginning today, O Kalāvatī, this shall be our main observance. We will experience the delightful pleasures of great magnitude after visiting Jñānavāpī. Necessarily it must be a Jñānavāpī true to its name. It is wonderful that it bestowed on you the knowledge even when painted on a canvas!"

76. She assented to their request. She then got over the excited feelings and controlled them adequately. After carrying out everything pleasing to the king, she, fully conscious of the proposal to make, submitted to the king:

Kalāvatī said:

77. O lord of my life! Nowhere do I have anything more pleasing than you. By having you as my husband, O king, everything desirable and desired has been obtained by me.

78-79. I have a desire to request for, O dear lord. On being pondered over, it will be conducive to your great good too. Since I am dependent on you, it is extremely inaccessible to me. Since you are capable of acting independently, this desire is as good as realized.

80. O dear lord, of what avail is talking too much? If there is any purpose to be served by my being alive, grant me that desire. Otherwise my life will cease to be.

81. On hearing the words of his beloved, dearer to him than his own life, that king spoke as follows pleasing to her as well as to himself:

The king said:

82. O my beloved beautiful lady, I do not see anything that cannot be given to you. Even my very vital breaths have been bought over by you through your decent qualities and skill in arts.

83. Do not delay any longer. Tell me, O Kalāvatī, and know that it is carried out. I think that nothing is inaccessible to chaste ladies like you.

84. Who is the person to be requested? What is it that is sought? Who is the person making the request? My dear Kalāvatī, the relationship between us both is not like that of the commonfolk.

85. O beautiful lady, the whole realm, the entire treasury, the vast army, the fort, and whatever else is here is yours and not mine. I have only a nominal ownership thereof.

86. My ownership extends only to those things other than you. O goddess of my life, O honour-loving lady, I shall consider the kingdom on a par with a blade of grass and cast it off at your instance.

87. On hearing these words of King Mālyaketu, Kalāvatī spoke these sweet words in a voice that was full of gravity:

Kalāvatī said:

88. My lord, formerly different kinds of subjects were created

by Brahmā at the outset and for their good the four aims of life.

89. A life bereft of them is futile. Even one among them shall therefore be achieved for the sake of welfare here and hereafter.

90. What, those conversant with the ancient traditions say, namely that *Trivarga* (the three primary aims of life) prospers there where is affection between husband and wife, has been seen (to be) true.

91. There are hundreds of slaves like me in your palace here. Still my lord's love is prominently seen for me.

92. Even the lowly slave of yours enjoys full pleasures, what then to speak of the lady revelling on your lap! Over and above there is an exclusive possession not available to others, viz. having the husband under one's control.

93. A sensible man shall amass wealth for the purpose of pious rites in the form of *Iṣṭa* and *Pūrta*. He shall keep his life free from hindrances for the sake of austerity and maintain his wife for the sake of progeny.

94. O my beloved lord, all these you have, due to the favour of Viśveśa. If my desire is to be fulfilled I shall mention it, please listen.

95. Send me immediately to the city of Viśvanātha. My vital breaths have already left. I remain behind only in the form of the physical frame.

96. On hearing these specific words of Kalāvatī, King Mālyaketu thought for a moment within himself and said to his beloved:

97-100. "My dear Kalāvatī, if you have to go, of what use is the transitory royal glory unto me when it is bereft of you too?

The mere territory is not the kingdom, they say. Certainly a beloved queen is the glory of the kingdom. The kingdom with all the seven constituents is no better than a blade of grass without her.

The kingdom has been made free from enemies. After enjoying pleasures continuously, the sense-organs having experienced the objects of pleasure have become gratified. An all-round contentment has been realized.

Children are already born. No further task awaits me here. Both of us shall certainly go to the city of Vārāṇasī."

101-102. After consoling his wife thus, King Mālyaketu who decided his course of action called astrologers and honoured representative of the citizens. He entrusted the kingdom to his son. Taking the requisite money and jewels from his son, he proceeded towards Kāśī.

103. After visiting the city of Viśveśvara, the king experienced horripilation (of joy) and considered himself blessed, having reached the other shore of the ocean or worldly existence.

104. Due to the impressions of her previous birth Queen Kalāvatī could recognize the roads of the city like one coming from a village nearby.

105-110. They took their bath in Maṇikarṇikā and offered much wealth as gifts. They propitiated Viśveśvara with diverse kinds of jewels and made gifts of jewels, elephants, horses, herds of cows, silk clothes of various colours, utensils and things of adoration. They gave pots of gold and silver, lamp sticks, mirrors and chowries, flagstaffs and banners and canopies of diverse sizes and designs. After circumambulating the shrine, the king entered the Muktimaṇḍapa. There he listened to the discourse on piety and made monetary gifts there also. After performing the great *Pūjā* in the evening, he kept awake the whole of the night with festivities accompanied by instrumental music. The next day in the morning he got up and performed the routine duties of cleansing. The king went to Jñanavāpī along the path pointed out by the queen.

111-116. The king joyously took his holy ablution along with Kalāvatī there. He offered balls of rice and faithfully propitiated the Pitṛs. To deserving persons there, he offered gold, silver etc. He made poor people, blind persons and miserable and helpless ones, delighted by gifting precious gems. The king then performed the *Pāraṇā* rite. Kalāvatī renovated Jñānavāpī with steps paved with jewels. She took great delight therein in the company of her husband, leading a life of austerity. That sinless lady spent the remaining period of her life like a mere moment by engaging herself in various vows and rites such as fasts on alternate days or some casual fasts. She practised observances by taking meal once in six days or once in a fortnight. She observed fast for a week sometimes. Sometimes she observed fast for even a month. She performed *Cāndrāyaṇa* and *Kṛcchra* rites. All along she continued to serve her husband.

117. Once, both of them had their morning bath in Jñānavāpī. While they were resting, someone with matted hairs came there and handed them holy ash.

118-119a. With a delighted face, he blessed them and said, "Get up and have the Mahānepathya (the great adornment) now itself. Within a moment you will have the Tāraka instruction."

119b-122a. Even as the man with matted hairs spoke these words, an aerial chariot with jingling bells arrived. While people stood watching, the Moon-crested Lord descended from the aerial chariot. He whispered the Mantra of the great brilliance which transcends words, into their ears. The aerial chariot took off immediately illuminating the path of the firmament. The Lord too went to his abode (along with Kalāvatī and Mālyavān—Comm.).

Skanda said:

122b. Ever since then, Jñānavāpī is (considered) unique and superior to all important holy Tīrthas.

123. O sage, it is the bestower of direct knowledge. It is excellent, full of perfect knowledge, identical with all Liṅgas.

124-125. Jñānavāpī is the Cosmic Form of Śiva himself. It generates *Jñāna* (perfect knowledge). There are many Tīrthas that sanctify (devotees) immediately. But they are not equal to even a sixteenth part of Jñānavāpī. If anyone listens to the origin of Jñānavāpī with great attention, his knowledge does not become extinct even on death anywhere.

126. This great narrative is meritorious. It is destructive of great sins. It increases the delight of Mahādeva and Gaurī.

127. By reading or causing to be read or listening to the auspicious narration of Jñānavāpī one is honoured in the world of Śiva.

CHAPTER THIRTYFIVE

*Sadācāra—Conduct of the Good**

The Pot-born Sage (Agastya) said:

1. Avimukta is a great holy spot. It is the best cause of liberation. It is the greatest of all Kṣetras. It is the most auspicious of all auspicious spots.

2. It is the greatest Śmaśāna of all Śmaśānas (where dead bodies are cremated); the greatest Pīṭha (holy seat) of all Pīṭhas; the most arid land of all arid lands (where sins do not grow).

3. It is the greatest cause of bestowing heap of piety on those whose intellect is inclined towards righteousness. O Peacock-vehicled One, to those who seek wealth, it reveals the greatest wealth.

4. It generates love in lovers and bestows salvation on those desirous of salvation. Whichever part of your narrative is heard, it is like the excellent Nectar.

5. O delighter of the heart of Gaurī, after hearing this great tale of Jñānavāpī situated in a part of the holy spot, I think thus:

6. The place wherein Jñānavāpi though speck-like in size is famous in the middle of Kāśī, must be well-known as the honoured one. In its conduciveness to Mokṣa (or fulfilment of one's object), it never fails.

7. How many holy places exist in the whole of the earth? (many) But even out of them, which is equal in comparison even with a small particle of Kāśī? (none)

8. How many rivers in this world flow into the sea? But what river can bear equality (in holiness) with the heavenly river (Gaṅgā) at Kāśī?

9. O Six-faced One, how many Kṣetras capable of (giving) Mokṣa exist on the earth? But there is not even a ten-millionth part of Avimukta in them.

10. What wonder is there in that the glory of salvation

---

* Sadācāra means usages or practices of the good or Śiṣṭas. According to Manu IV. 178, following the path of one's ancestors is Sadācāra.

is achieved where the triad—Gaṅgā, God Viśveśvara and Kāśī, are awake (and watchful)!

11. O Skanda, how can these three be obtained without fail, by men especially in Kali Age, as they are of fickle sense-organs?

12. How can such a penance be (performed) in Kali Age? How in Kali Age, can such a Yoga be practised? Where is such a holy rite or liberal gift? Hence how can men get salvation (in the absence of these)?

13. O Skanda, the six-faced one, it has been stated by you that salvation is possible in Kāśī without penance, without Yoga, without holy rites or without liberal gifts.

14. Tell me, what should be regularly practised to make it possible to attain Kāśī. I think, without good conduct these cherished desires cannot be realized.

15. *Ācāra* (good conduct) is the greatest piety. *Ācāra* is the greatest austerity. Life is lengthened through *Ācāra;* sin is destroyed through *Ācāra.*

16. Hence, O Six-faced One, expound *Ācāra* alone at the outset in the way in which the Lord of Devas has told you.

Skanda said:

17. O son of Mitra and Varuṇa, I shall narrate *Sadācāra* ('rules of good conduct') conducive to the benefit of good men. Practising this always, a man shall attain all his desires and ambitions.

18. Immobile beings (trees etc.), worms, aquatic animals like fishes, birds, animals and human beings are more and more pious in gradation. Suras are more righteous than these.

19. In this graded series the latter ones are a thousand times better than the former ones. All these are highly fortunate ones till the salvation is achieved.

20. Of the four types of living beings, *Prāṇins* (capable of moving about) are very excellent. Of *Prāṇins* all the intelligent ones are the better, O sage.

21. Of all the intelligent ones, human beings are the most excellent, O sage. Among them Vāḍavas (Brāhmaṇas) are the most excellent. Scholars are greater than ordinary Brāhmaṇas. Men of decisive intellect are better than scholars.

22. Those who perform holy rites are better than men

of decisive intellect. Those who are engrossed solely in the Absolute (Brahman) are better than the performers of holy rites. O Pitcher-born One, there is no one to be worshipped by them in the three worlds.

23-24. They make obeisance to one another, thanks to there being no difference in their austerity and acquisition of learning (knowledge of Brahman).

Since he is the lord of all living beings as created by Brahmā, only the Brāhmaṇa deserves everything existing in the world and none else. Indeed a man of good conduct deserves honour by all, not one who has strayed away from good conduct. Hence a Brāhmaṇa shall always be one of good conduct.

25. Sensible men consider that *Sadācāra* is the root of all piety, O sage, which learned men, free from undue attachment and hatred, practise.

26. Though bereft of special (auspicious) characteristics, a faithful person, not maliciously jealous of others, if eagerly engaged in the practice of good conduct, will live for a hundred years.

27. One should resort, without lethargy, to *Sadācāra,* the root cause of piety, as laid down by the Śruti and Smṛti for different persons in the performance of their respective duties.

28. A person of bad conduct shall be despicable in the world. He will be assailed by ailments always. He shall be excessively miserable and short-lived.

29. An act dependent (on the help) of others should be avoided. An act manageable by oneself should always be performed. A person becomes miserable as he is dependent on others. He who is always self-dependent is happy.

30. Only that act in which the conscience is delighted while it is being performed, should be performed and never its opposite.

31. *Yamas* and *Niyamas* have been proclaimed as the essence of the total of righteousness. So effort should be directed only towards them by one who wishes for Dharma.

32. *Yamas* are ten: truthfulness, forbearance, straightforwardness, meditation, absence of ferocity, desisting from violence, control over the sense-organs, cheerfulness, sweetness, and tenderness.

33. *Niyamas* are also ten: internal and external purity (*Śauca*), *Snāna* (holy ablution), *Tapas* (austerity), *Dāna* (liberal gifts), *Mauna* (silence), *Ijyā* (sacrifice), *Adhyayana* (study of the Vedas), *Vrata* (holy vows), *Upoṣaṇa* (fast) and *Upasthadaṇḍa* (avoidance of illegitimate sexual acts).

34. One should be victorious everywhere through the conquest of these six enemies: Lust, Anger, Arrogance, Delusion, Jealousy and Greed.

35. Like ants slowly building up an anthill, one should without causing any injury to others, go on accumulating (performing acts of) piety which will be helpful in the other world.

36. In the life hereafter, it is only Dharma that helps one and not rich possessions, fathers, mothers, sons, brothers, wives, relatives and others.

37. A being is born alone, by itself; it dies alone, by itself; it enjoys merits alone, by itself and it reaps the bitter fruits of evil conduct alone, by itself.

38. (When a person dies his) relatives abandon (his) dead body on the ground as if it is a piece of wood or a lump of clay. They turn their faces away (from him). Only Dharma will follow the soul that passes away.

39. Hence one desirous of accomplishing the requisite deed should amass acts of Dharma that helps one in the life hereafter. Getting Dharma as one's associate, one can transcend the impassable darkness (ignorance or Saṁsāra).

40. A sensible man should be in contact with excellent persons, leaving off the lowly and the base. He shall thus make his family excellent.

41. Getting into touch with excellent persons alone and avoiding base ones, a Brāhmaṇa attains a higher status, but the status of a Śūdra due to a contrary action.

42. The god of Death torments a Brāhmaṇa who does not regularly study the Vedas, who transgresses the *Sadācāra* restrictions, who is idle and eats indiscriminately.

43. Therefore, a Brāhmaṇa should always practise *Sadācāra* assiduously. Even holy Tīrthas yearn for the contact of a man of *Sadācāra.*

44. The *Yāmārdha* (one hour and a half) at the close of the night is called *Brāhma Samaya.* An intelligent man shall

always get up at that hour and meditate upon the (cause of) his weal.

45. At the outset[1], he should meditate on the Elephant-faced Lord (Gaṇeśa), then Īśa along with Aṁbā (Pārvatī); then Lord Viṣṇu accompanied by Śrī and then the Lotus-born One (Brahmā) in the company of Brahmāṇī.

46. He should think of all the Devas beginning with Indra and the sages beginning with Vasiṣṭha; all the rivers beginning with Gaṅgā and all the mountains beginning with Śrī Śaila.

47. He should meditate on the oceans beginning with the Milk Ocean; the lakes beginning with Mānasa; the pleasure groves beginning with Nandana and the cows beginning with Kāmadhenu.

48. He should meditate on the trees beginning with the wish-yielding Kalpa tree; the metals the most important of which is gold; the celestial damsels the chief of whom is Urvaśī; the birds beginning with Garuḍa.

49. He should think of Serpents the chief of whom is Śeṣa; elephants beginning with Airāvata; horses the chief of whom is Uccaiśśravas and the splendid jewels beginning with Kaustubha.

50. He should remember women of note for the vow of chastity, the chief of whom is Arundhatī; sacred forests beginning with Naimiṣa; sacred cities beginning with Kāśī.

51. (He should remember) Liṅgas beginning with Viśveśa; the Vedas beginning with Ṛgveda; Mantras, the chief of which is Gāyatrī; and Yogins beginning with Sanaka.

52. (He should remember) Mahābījas beginning with Praṇava; devotees of Viṣṇu beginning with Nārada; devotees of Śiva beginning with Bāṇa; and persons of steadfast vows beginning with Prahlāda.

53-54. He should then remember liberal-minded sages like Dadhīci etc. and Hariścandra and other kings. Thereafter, he should remember the feet of his mother, the most excellent of all the Tīrthas. With a delighted mind he should meditate on his father and preceptors in the heart. Thereafter, for

1. VV 45-54 give the contents of Prātaḥsmaraṇa ('remembering auspicious things and persons') immediately after getting up.

attending to the calls of nature, he should go towards the southwest direction.[1]

55. If it is a village, he should go to a distance of a hundred bows, but if it is a town, it should be four times that. He should spread grasses on the ground and cover his head with his cloth.

56. Keeping the sacred thread around the ear, he should, by day time or at dawn or dusk face the north at the time of easing himself in silence. He should do the same, facing the south at night.

57. One should not ease oneself standing. He should neither cast faeces into water, O Brāhmaṇa, nor in front of a cow, fire or wind. He should not drop rubbish in the furrows of ploughed ground, nor in the main thoroughfare frequented by people.

58. He should not look at different directions or at luminaries, the sky or the faeces dropped down. Holding the penis with his left hand, he should get up and stand steady.

59-60. He should take up mud free from gravel and worms. He should not take up the mud dug up by rats or mongooses nor the remnants of what has been used by others. He should apply one part on the penis and five parts mixed with water on the anus, ten parts on the left hand and seven on both the hands.

61. He should apply one part of mud on each of the feet and three parts on the palms. Thus the householder should perform *Śauca* (cleansing) till the odour and the stickiness vanishes.

62. In the case of the three stages of a celibate student, a forest hermit and a Sannyāsin twice these in due order are prescribed (i.e., a celibate student should use the above twice the number of times prescribed for a householder, twice that of a celibate student in the case of a Vānaprastha and twice that of a Vānaprastha in the case of a Sannyāsin). At night one should do only half the number of what has been prescribed for day.

---

1. VV 54-87 give the details of performing morning duties upto taking a bath.

63. In case of sickness, half the number and during journeys with dangers from thieves etc., still half that number (is prescribed). In the case of women half that number (is laid down). While one is normal in health, one need not reduce the number.

64. One may cleanse with the waters of all the rivers and heaps of mud and cowdung from foot to head, but if one is mentally defiled, one cannot become pure.

65. The lumps of mud intended for *Śauca* are laid down to be of the size of *Ārdradhātrī* (the green small Indian gooseberry). All Āhutis and mouthfuls of food in Cāndrāyaṇa rite are also so (in size).

66. Facing the east or the north, he should then sit on the pure ground free from husks, ash, bones or smouldering fire and rinse the mouth ceremoniously.

67. The water should not be hot or full of froth. A householder Brāhmaṇa should perform the *Ācamana* rite through the root of the thumb. He should not hurry through the rite. He should see to the purity of the water. The water shall reach the heart.

68. A Kṣatriya becomes pure when the *Ācamana* water reaches the throat and a Vaiśya when it reaches the palate. As for women and Śūdras, they become pure when the water just touches the mouth.

69. One who covers the head or the neck, or keeps the tuft loosened in the water, or does not wash the feet, is considered impure even if he performs the *Ācamana* rite.

70. After sipping water thrice for (internal) purity, he should purify the sense-organs. He should touch the lips twice with the root of the thumb.

71. Thereafter, a sensible man should touch the mouth with three fingers. He should repeatedly touch the nostrils with the tips of the index finger and thumb.

72. He should repeatedly touch the eyes and ears with the tips of the thumb and the ring finger. He should then touch the navel aperture with the combined thumb and the small finger.

73. He should then touch the heart with the palm and the head with all the fingers. Similarly he should touch the shoulders with the tips of the fingers. Everywhere the rite of

touching shall be with water.

74-75. One should perform the *Ācamana* rite twice in the following instances: when the roadway has been approached, after bathing, taking food, drinking water (milk?), at the beginning of auspicious rites, after sleeping, after wearing clothes, after seeing something inauspicious and after touching an unclean thing inadvertently. In these cases, one who performs *Ācamana* rite twice becomes pure.

76. Thereafter, for the sake of the purity of the mouth, the householder should take up the cleansing of the teeth. Without cleansing the teeth even one who performs *Ācamana* rite is impure.

77. On the first lunar day, on the sixth and the ninth, on the new-moon day and on Sundays, the use of a twig against the teeth shall burn the family up to the seventh generation.

78. If a twig is not available or on those days when the use thereof is forbidden, gurgling twelve times with as many mouthfuls of water is enough for the purity of the mouth.

79. The twig should be as thick as the tip of the little finger and twelve *Aṅgulas* or more in length. It should be straight with all the bark unmutilated.

80-82. In the case of the other castes, the length shall gradually be reduced by one Aṅgula each. The following trees are recommended for securing twigs: Āmra, Āmrataka, Dhātrī, Kaṅkola, Khadira, Śamī, Apāmārga, Kharjurī, Śelu, Śrī Parṇī, Pīlu, Rājādana and Nāraṅga. Any tree astringent and bitter in taste or having milky exudation shall be used.

The tongue cleaner should be made excellent in the form of bow.

83-84. These two Mantras are to be uttered at the time of cleansing the teeth:

(a) O Teeth, for the sake of eating of food be clean and of firm rows, as King Soma in the form of the chewing-twig has arrived. He will keep my mouth clean (by washing) and make me famous and fortunate.

(b). O Vanaspati (tree), give us longevity, strength, fame, brilliance, progeny, cattle, wealth, assets, keen perception into Brahman and intellect as well.

85. If anyone performs the cleansing of the teeth after uttering these two Mantras, Soma present in the Vanaspati,

becomes always pleased with him.

86. If the mouth is stale (unwashed) the man becomes impure. Hence one should assiduously perform the rite of Dantadhāvana (cleansing of the teeth).

87. On days of fast Dantadhāvana[1] (i.e., by means of twelve mouthfuls and not with twigs), applying collyrium, scents, ornaments, excellent clothes, unguents and wearing garlands are not faulty and sinful.

88. Beginning with *Dantadhāvana* and after performing morning ablution in sacred water or Tīrthas particularly a householder should perform *Prātaḥsandhyā* (Morning Prayers).

89. This dirty body having nine holes through which dirt flows out day and night, can become (temporarily) pure only through morning bath.[2]

90. Early morning ablution is praised because it generates enthusiasm, intellect, good fortune, handsome features etc.; it is the cause of serenity of the mind.

91. As a man becomes drenched with sweat, saliva etc. while in the grip of sleep, it is only through morning bathe that he becomes fit and eligible for uttering *Mantras, Stotras* (hymns to gods), *Japa* etc.

92. They say that daily bath taken in the morning when there is *Aruṇodaya* (i.e. at dawn before the Sunrise) it is on a par with the observances of the rite Prājāpatya. It is destructive of sins.

93. The morning bath removes sin, misfortune, fatigue, impurity, bad dreams etc., and accords satisfaction and nourishment.

94. Wicked ones do not approach a person who regularly take the morning ablution. Hence it has both visible and invisible benefits. So one should perform the morning ablution.

95. As relevant to the context, O Pot-born One, I shall narrate to you the injunctions regarding morning ablution, since they say that morning bath in accordance with injunctions is hundred times more beneficial than ordinary bath.

---

1. It should be done by (gurgling) twelve mouthfuls of water and not with a twig as tooth-brush.

2. VV 89-109 state the importance of bath in the early morning and the procedure of taking the bath.

96. A householder takes up pure mud, Darbha grass, cowdung and gingelly seeds and places them on a clean spot. Thereafter, he performs *Ācamana* (ritualistic rinsing of the mouth) and takes the holy dip.

97. He should enter the water with the tuft of hair tied up and holding the Darbha grass. Repeating the Mantra beginning with: *uruṁ hi rājā varuṇaś cakāra* (RV I. 24.8), he splashes water.

98. Then he recites the Mantra: *ye te śatam varuṇa, ye sahasram... (Kātyāyana Śr.Sū.,* 25.1.11a.) for the purpose of invoking the waters. He, then offers a handful of water at the outset, reciting the Mantra: (the Purāṇic text of the Mantra is incorrect, the correct one being *sumitrā na āpa oṣadhayaḥ santu: Āpastamba Śr.Sū.* 19.10.5*)* and thereafter offers water with the enemy in view reciting the Mantra: (the correct Text restored) *durmitriyās tasmai santu yo'smān dveṣṭi, yam ca vayam dviṣmaḥ (Vājasaneyī Saṁ.* 6.22).

99-100. After reciting the Mantra: *idaṁ viṣṇur vicakrame,* he should smear the limbs with clay. One lump is used to wash the head, two lumps above the navel and three lumps beneath it. He should then clean the feet with six lumps. Thereafter he should take a dip beneath the water, facing the current and repeating the Mantra: *āpo asmān mātaraḥ śundhayantu (*RV X.17.10).

101. The Mantra *ud id ābhyaḥ śucir ā pūta emi (*RV X.17.10) is to be recited when rising up above water. Thereafter, he should recite the Mantra: *mā nas toke tanaye mā na āyuṣi* (*Vāj. Saṁ* 16.162) and smear the body with cowdung

102-105. The Mantra beginning with: *idam me varuṇa...* is for the sake of the ablution of oneself. The following Mantras too are mentioned as *Abdaivatāḥ (*Pertaining to waters as the deity): Those beginning with:

tattvā yāmi brāhmaṇā vandamānāḥ (RV I.24.11)

tvanna agne varuṇasya vidvān. . . sa tvam na agne avamo (RV IV.1.5)

uduttamam varuṇa pāśam (RV I.24.15)

dhāmno dhāmno rājaṁstato varuṇa no muñca (*Vāj. Saṁ.* 6.22)

mā'po mauṣadhīr hīṁsīḥ (*Vaj. Saṁ.* 6.20)

yad āhur aghnyā varuṇeti śapāmahe tato varuṇa no muñca (*Vāj. Saṁ.* 6.22?)

*muñcantu me śapathyādatho varuṇyaduta (*RV *X.97.16)*

avabhṛtha nicumpuṇa niceruras nicuṁpuṇaḥ (*Vāj. Saṁ.* 3-48) He should recite these Mantras called *Abdaivata,* while taking the ablution.

Then the Brāhmaṇa with great learning should purify himself through Prāṇana and Mahāvyāhṛtis. He should sanctify himself with Gāyatrī and be contented. He should also sanctify himself with the three passages beginning with: *āpo hi ṣṭhā mayobhuvaḥ* etc. Each one of the three Ṛks is purifying.

106-107. The following too are sanctifying Mantras: *idam āpaḥ pravahata* (RV I.23.22); *haviṣmatīḥ imā āpo haviṣmā, ā vivāsati (Vāj.Saṁ.6.23); devīr āpo apām napād ya ūrmir haviṣya indriyāvān madintam (Vāj. Saṁ.6.27); āpo devā madhumatīr agṛbhṇam\ Vāj. Saṁ. 5.12.1*); *drupadā divasaṁjñakāḥ* (AV VI. 115.3); *śanno devīḥ* (RV. I.09.4); *āpo devīḥ; apām rasam*; and *punantu mā.* The nine Mantras beginning with *punantu mā pitaraḥ* (*Vaj. Saṁ.* 19.37) etc. are glorified as *Pāvamānyaḥ* (Sanctifying Mantras).

108. Thereafter he should repeat the *Aghamarṣaṇa* Mantra and then the Mantra beginning with *drupadā* etc. Then he should duly perform *Prāṇāyāma.* Or he should perform *Japa* (standing) in water.

109. Or he may repeat the *Praṇava* three times. A wise man should also remember Viṣṇu. After taking bath thus, he should wash the clothes and wear washed (and dried) clothes.

110-111. Then he should perform *Ācamana* and thereafter perform the morning Sandhyā prayer using Kuśa grass. He who, being a Brāhmaṇa, does not perform Sandhyā prayers becomes a Śūdra even as he continues to live. After death he is certainly reborn as a dog. One devoid of Sandhyā prayers is always unclean and unfit for all holy rites.

112-114. Whatever other work he may do, he will not derive the fruit thereof.

Facing the East, he should remember *Praṇava* and reciting the Mantra beginning with *catuḥ sraktir nābhir ṛtasya (Vaj. Sam. 38.20).* Place the Kuśāsana ('seat made of Kuśa grass') without looking elsewhere or seeing anything else. He should keep the tuft tied and sit facing either the East or the North. Scattering water drops all round him, he should perform *Prāṇāyāma.*

115. Reciting the Gāyatrī along with its Śiras (i.e., *oṁ āpo jyotī rasomṛtaṁ brahma bhūr bhuvaḥ śvarom*) and seven *Vyāhṛtis* (*oṁ bhūḥ, oṁ bhuvaḥ, oṁ svaḥ, oṁ mahaḥ oṁ janaḥ, oṁ tapaḥ,*

om satyam) and he should then utter *oṁ* ten times. This is repeated three times. It is called *Prāṇāyāma*.

116. A Brāhmaṇa with his mind and sense-organs under control repeating the *Prāṇāyāma* regularly, shall be rid of all the sins committed during that day and night instantaneously.

117. If ten or twelve *Prāṇāyāmas* are performed after controlling the mind, it is as though a great penance has been performed by him then.

118. Sixteen *Prāṇāyāmas* duly consisting of the *Vyāhṛtis* and the *Praṇava* should be performed everyday. Within a month, even the slayer of a foetus becomes purified.

119. Just as the impurities of metals and metallic ores are burned off by the process of furnace combustion, so also all the ills brought about by the sense-organs are burned off through the *Prāṇāyāma* rite.

120. Through twelve *Prāṇāyāmas* performed with faith, one gets the benefit of feeding a Brāhmaṇa duly.

121. The entire Vedic literature is established on *Praṇava.* Hence (the devotee) desirous of reciting Vedic hymns, should practise *Praṇava,* the initial Mantra in the Vedas.

122. To one who is permanently connected with *Praṇava,* the seven *Vyāhṛtis* and the *Gāyatrī* Mantra of three feet, there is no cause of fear anywhere.

123. The single-syllabled *Praṇava* is the Supreme Absolute. *Prāṇāyāma* is the greatest penance. O Pot-born One, there is nothing more sacred than Gāyatrī.

124. After getting up early in the morning, one can, by means of *Prāṇāyāmas,* dispel whatever sin he may have committed the previous night mentally, verbally and physically.

125. Performing the evening *Sandhyā* rites, one should, by means of *Prāṇāyāma,* remove the sin committed during the day mentally, verbally and physically.

126. (The devotee) should recite the *Sāvitrī* Mantra in the morning till the Sun becomes visible; during the evening prayers (he should recite it) till the stars are clearly visible.

127. One who recites the Mantra in the morning eradicates nocturnal sin and one who recites the Mantra in the evening destroys sins committed during the day.

128. One who does not perform the *Sandhyā* Prayer in the morning and one who does not pray in the evening should

be excluded from all Brāhmaṇical holy rites as though he is a Śūdra.

129. One should perform the daily routine rite after reaching the water-front. One should recite the *Gāyatrī* with mental attention and purity even after going to the forest.

130. The *Sandhyā* Prayer performed outside in the open air has many times the benefit of the prayer performed at home. If a Brāhmaṇa is of controlled sense-organs but practices the *Japa* of *Gāyatrī* (and is not learned in the Vedic lore) he is excellent.

131a. A Brāhmaṇa who has mastery over the three Vedas is not to be honoured, if he eats everything (i.e., is indiscriminate in eating) and sells everything (including the Veda).

131b-132a. The *Gāyatrī* Mantra whose deity is Savitā (the Sun-god) and mouth is the Fire-god, has three (metrical) feet. Her seer is Viśvāmitra and the metre is Gāyatrī. (Such *Gāyatrī* Mantra is of a special significance.)

132b-134. In the morning, one should meditate upon *Gāyatrī* as of red complexion with God Brahmā as her Deity and the Swan as her mount. She is eight years old. She has decorated herself with a red garland and unguents. She is of the nature of the Ṛgveda. She holds a rosary of beads hanging loosely and grants freedom from fear.

She is of *Anuṣṭubh* metre. She is being eulogized by Vyāsa. By meditating on the morning deity, sin committed at night disappears.

135. The excellent *Ācamana* is with the Mantra beginning with *sūryaśca mā manyuś ca (Tait. Āraṇyaka* 10.25.1) etc. Then the devotee performs the *Mārjana* rites with the three Mantras beginning with *āpo hiṣṭhā.* etc. (RV X.9.1-3).

136. He should sprinkle water in nine ways—on the ground, on the head, in the sky, in the sky, on the ground, on the head, on the head, in the sky and on the ground.

137. The word 'ground' denotes the feet; 'sky' denotes the heart; 'on the head' has literal meaning. This (explanation) is cited by the people conversant with the rite of *Mārjana.*

138. This *Brāhma (Mānasa) Snāna* is the greatest, greater than *Vāruṇa Snāna, Āgneya Snāna, Vāyavya Snāna, Aindra Snāna* and even *Mantra Snāna.*

139. He who has performed the bath of the *Brāhma* type

is pure externally and internally. He becomes qualified and deserving in all the rites such as adoration of the deity.

140. Boatmen and fishermen are immersed in water day and night. But are they holy and pure? Those who are emotionally defiled and disturbed are not pure though they might have had hundreds of baths.

141. The holy ash can sanctify only those who are pure mentally. Are the donkeys grey with ash glorified as sacred?

142. He whose mind is free from impurities is considered to have taken his holy ablution in all the Tīrthas; he is devoid of all impurities; it is as though he has performed hundreds of sacrifices.

143. O sage, listen, how that mind can be free from impurities. If Viśveśa (Lord Śiva) is pleased, only then can it be so, and not otherwise anywhere.

144. Hence for the sake of the purity of mind, one should resort to the Lord of Kāśī. By resorting to him, the impurities of mind definitely become reduced.

145. One whose mental impurities have become reduced completely due to the great blessings of Viśveśa, attains the great Absolute after casting off this body.

146. Good conduct of men has been regarded as the cause of the blessings of Viśveśa. Hence one should resort to that good conduct cited by the Śruti and the Smṛti.

147. Thereafter, the devotee recites the Mantra beginning with *drupadā* and holds water in the hand. Then the devotee conversant with the injunctions performs the rite of *Aghamarṣaṇa* through the Mantra *ṛtaṁ ca* etc.

148. A scholarly devotee who immerses himself in water and recites *Aghamarṣaṇa* Mantra three times, certainly attains the benefit of one who has performed *Avabhṛtha* (valedictory ablution) of *Aśvamedha.*

149. Just as darkness perishes at the rising of the Sun, so also does the flood of sins of that person who performs *Aghamarṣaṇa* on a bank or in water.

150. The Brāhmaṇa then performs the *Ācamana* rite reciting the Mantra beginning with *imaṁ me varuṇa* etc. (*RV* I.25.29). Some Ācāryas belonging to other Śākhās desire that the Mantra shall be as follows:

151. The Mantra is *antaścarasi* etc. (*Tait. Āraṇyaka* 10.31.1),

"You move about within living beings in their cave-like heart with faces directed all-round. You are Yajña. You are Vaṣaṭkāra. You are waters and fire. You are bliss. You are the immortal one."

152. Then the devotee drops three handfuls of water reciting the *Gāyatrī* Mantra without its *Śiras* (see verse 115) but with the *Mahāvyāhṛti* in the beginning and *Praṇava* at the outset. He should recite the Mantra while standing.

153. Like mountains struck by thunderbolt, the enemies of the Sun, the demons named Mandehas, become perished, due to that adamantine water-libation.

154. If a Brāhmaṇa does not offer three handfuls of water to assist Vivasvān and to destroy Mandehas, he will also become a Mandeha himself.

155. At dawn the person should stand reciting the Mantra till the Sun becomes visible. In the evening he should sit and recite the Mantra till the stars become visible.

156. Time should not be wasted by a Brāhmaṇa desirous of his welfare. Hence he should drop the adamantine water libation at the time of the semi-setting and semi-rising (of the Sun).

157. *Sandhyā* Prayer though duly performed shall be fruitless if it is delayed. The example cited is the sexual intercourse with a barren woman.

158. If *Sandhyā* is performed after keeping the water (vessel) in the left hand, it should be regarded as a Śūdra woman causing delight to groups of demons.

159. The *Upasthāna* Mantras (Mantras for adoration) of Bradhna (the Sun) that bestow Siddhis are those beginning with *udvayaṁ tamasas pari* (RV I.50.10), *udutyaṁ jātavedasam* (RV I.50.1), *citraṁ devānām* (*Vāj. Saṁ.* 17.69?), *taccakṣur devahitam* (RV VII.66.16) etc.

160. The devotee should perform adoration of the Sun by means of the *Devī Gāyatrī* repeated a thousand times, a hundred times or ten times.

161. A Brāhmaṇa who repeats the *Gāyatrī* a maximum of a thousand times, a middling number of a hundred times or a minimum number of ten times is never smeared with sins.

162. He should also recite either the *Anuvāka* beginning with *vibhrāḍ bṛhat pibatu* (RV X.170 etc.) or the *Puruṣa Sūkta*

or the *Śivasaṅkalpa* Mantra or the *Brāhmaṇa Maṇḍala.*

163-166. These Mantras of *Upasthāna* (adoration) are pleasing to the Sun. The devotee should offer *Arghya* with water mixed with raw rice grains, flowers, Kuśa grass etc. and also mixed with red sandalpaste while reciting Vedic or Āgamic Mantras.

All the three worlds become worshipped by one who has adored Savitṛ. Savitṛ, propitiated duly, bestows sons, cattle, wealth and monetary boons. He removes ailments, bestows longevity and fulfils all desires.

This Āditya is Rudra. This Divākara is Hari. This Ravi is Hiraṇyagarbha. This Aryaman is in the form of the three Vedas.

167. Through the propitiation of Ravi (the Sun-god) Brahmā, Viṣṇu and Maheśvara become delighted. So also all the Devas including Indra and the great sages including Marīci.

168. Similarly human beings, the chief of whom is Manu, and the grandfathers including Somapās become propitiated.

After adoring Ravi thus, the devotee should begin *Tarpaṇa* (water libation).

169-170. He should take five, seven or nine blades of Darbha grass having hollow tips and roots and uncut with his right hand. Then along with his left hand he should perform *Tarpaṇa* of the six Vināyakas (viz. Caṇḍa, Pracaṇḍa, Dharma, Vināyaka, Vighnarāja and Mahāgaṇapati), the Devas including Brahmā and the sages including Marīci.

171. Uttering "Let them be pleased", he should offer libations with pure water mixed with sandal, agallochum, musk and fragrant flowers.

172. While offering libations to human beings beginning with Sanaka, the Brāhmaṇa should keep the straight Darbhas between the two thumbs using Yava (barley) and keeping the sacred thread like a garland.

173. He should offer libations to the Pitṛs such as Kavyavāṭ, Anala etc. of divine nature with double the number of Darbhas mixed with gingelly seeds. He should keep the sacred thread as *prācīnāvīti* (on the right shoulder proceeding towards the left side).

174. A Brāhmaṇa, desirous of welfare, should never use gingelly seeds for libation on Sundays, Fridays, on the seventh and thirteenth lunar days, during nights or twilight hours.

175-176. If at all he offers libations, he should make use

of white gingelly seeds. Thereafter, he should offer libations to the fourteen Yamas, viz. Yama, Dharmarāja, Mṛtyu, Antaka, Vaivasvata, Kāla, Sarvabhūtakṣaya, Audumbara, Dadhna, Nīla, Parameṣṭhin, Vṛkodara, Citra and Citragupta uttering *namaḥ*. Then he should utter the name of his *Gotra* and offer libations to his own Pitṛs joyously while resting on the left knee and dropping the water between the thumb and the index finger. He should exert restraint on speech.

177. Devas desire one handful each; Sanaka and others two each; Pitṛs three and women one handful each.

178-179. Daiva Tīrtha is at the tip of the finger; Ārṣa (belonging to the sages) is at the root of the finger; Brāhma Tīrtha is at the root of the thumb; that of Prajāpati is in the middle of the hand; the Tīrtha of Pitṛs is between the thumb and the index finger. The learned devotee should utter the nine *Ṛks* and perform the libation of the Pitṛs.

180-184. Those Mantras are those beginning with *udīratām, aṅgirasaḥ, āyāntu naḥ pitaraḥ, ūrjam vahantī, pitṛbhyaḥ svadhāyibhyaḥ, ye ceha* and the three beginning with *madhuvātā*.

After saying "Obeisance to ye, O Pitṛs" he should utter the Mantra *ā brahma stambaparyantaṁ* and pour water on the ground.

"May the Devas, Pitṛs, Sages, human beings etc. beginning with Brahman and ending with a blade of grass be pleased. May the maternal grandfather and other Pitṛs be pleased.

May this water libation with gingelly seeds pass on to the crores of members of our family residing in the seven continents upto the world of Brahmā.

Thanks to the waters squeezed out from the cloth, may those persons of our *Gotra* born in our family but dead without issues be propitiated."

185-187. After performing the rites in fire he should proceed on to *Vedābhyāsa* (i.e., practice recitation of Vedas). The Vedic (recitation) practice should be of five types: (a) *Svīkāra* (acceptance), (b) *Arthavicāraṇam* (pondering over the meaning), (c) *Abhyāsa* (repetition), (d) *Japa* (muttering) and (e) *śiṣyebhyaḥ pratipādanam* (imparting to the disciples).

In order to retain what is acquired and to acquire what has not been acquired, the devotee should approach a donor and increase his own status as preceptor. O excellent Brāhmaṇa, thus the daily morning routine of the twice-born has been described.

188. Or (in the case of those persons incapable of taking early morning bath) after getting up in the morning and performing *Śauca* and *Ācamana* rites the devotee should cleanse the teeth with a brush twig.

189. After cleansing all the limbs, he should perform the morning *Sandhyā*. He should then understand the meanings of the Vedic passages and learn different kinds of lore.

190. He should teach good disciples possessing intelligence and favourably disposed for the purpose of the achievement of *Yogakṣema* (acquiring what is not acquired and retaining what has been acquired) etc.

191. Thereafter for performing the necessaries of midday, he should perform *Snāna* as mentioned before. A wise devotee should perform the midday *Sandhyā* prayers after the bath.

192-194. "Sāvitrī Devī (the description of Sāvitrī at midday) has Rudra for her deity, the metre is *Triṣṭup*. She is as pure as pure crystal and is endowed with the prime of youth blooming all over her body. The sage thereof is Kaśyapa and she is in the form of Yajurveda. She has three *Akṣaras* (syllables A, U, M, and is mounted on a bull. She is the great bestower of freedom from fear."

The devotee should worship her and then perform the *Naityika* rites (daily). The *Pacana* fire should be kindled and *Vaiśvadeva* rite should be performed.

195-196. One should eschew all these in *Vaiśvadeva:* Niṣpāva, Kodrava, Māṣa, Kalāya and Caṇaka (various kinds of grains and lentils). Sweets prepared in oil and all eatables saltish in nature, Āḍhakī, Masūra and circular Varaṭas should be avoided. So also leavings of food and stale foodstuffs should be eschewed.

197. After *Ācamana,* he should perform *Prāṇāyāma* with the Darbha grass in the hand. He should perform *Paryukṣaṇa* (sprinkling water all-round the sacred fire) rite reciting the Mantra beginning with *pṛṣṭhodivi* etc. (RV I.98.2).

198. After the rite of *Paryukṣaṇa* performed clockwise, he should spread the Darbha grass in three rows. Reciting the Mantra beginning with *eṣo ha deva* etc. (*Vāj. Saṁ.* 32.4), he should make the fire face-to-face with himself.

199. He should worship Vaiśvānara with flowers mixed with ghee and raw rice-grains. He should then offer three *Āhutis*

beginning with *bhūḥ,* ending with *svāhā* and having the *Praṇava* initially.

200. Then the Brāhmaṇa should offer another *Āhuti* uttering *oṁ bhūrbhuvaḥ svaḥ svāhā.* Then he makes six *Āhutis* uttering *devakṛtasya enaso vayajanamasi svāhā* etc. (*Vāj. Saṁ.* 8.13) (offerings expiatory of sins committed by the Devas etc.).

201. One *Āhuti* is offered silently to Yama. Then two Ahutis are offered uttering *agnaye sviṣṭakṛte svāhā.* Then he offers oblations on the ground to Viśvedevas.

202. To the north thereof *namaḥ* (obeisance) is offered to all the living beings. To the south thereof he should offer the oblations to the Pitṛs with the sacred thread turned left.

203. The water of *Nirṇejana* (washing) and the cooked rice should be offered to *Yakṣman* in the north-east. Thereafter to the north thereof *namaḥ* is offered to the Devas beginning with Brahmā.

204. Offerings are made to Sanaka etc. in the *Nivītī* position (i.e., with the sacred thread like a garland) and to the Pitṛs in *Apsavya* (the sacred thread turned to the left) position. Sixteen (handfuls) make one *Grāsa* and four handfuls make one *Puṣkala.*

205-210. Alms given to the extent of a *Grāsa* bestows merit on the householder.

Adhvaga (traveller), *Kṣīṇavṛtti* (one who has no means of livelihood), *Vidyārthī* (student), *Gurupoṣaka* (one who maintains the preceptor), *Yati*(ascetic) and *Brahmacārī* (celebate student)—these six are *Dharmabhikṣukas* ('mendicants of piety').

Atithi (guest) is a pedestrian traveller. *Anūcāna* is one who has mastered the Vedas. These two are to be honoured by householders who wish to attain the world of Brahmā.

Neither to a Cāṇḍāla nor unto a dog can the cooked rice offered be futile. When a person seeking food arrives, one should not begin to reflect whether he is one who deserves or not.

Cooked rice should be scattered on the ground outside for dogs, fallen ones, Cāṇḍālas, persons suffering from sinful foul diseases, crows and insects.

The Mantra for oblations to crows: "May the crows of the quarters of east, west, northwest, northeast and southwest accept this ball of rice offered by me on the ground."

The Mantra for oblations to dogs: "There are two dogs *Śyāma*" (dark in colour) and *Śabala* (variegated in colour). They are born in the family of Yama. I shall offer a ball of rice unto them. May they be non-violent."

211-213. The Mantras for *Bhūtabali* (oblation unto the living beings):

"Devas, men, animals, Rākṣasas, Yakṣas, serpents, birds, Daityas, Siddhas, Piśācas, Pretas (ghosts), Bhūtas (spirits), Dānavas, the grasses, the trees,—all these are desirous of the food offered by me. Worms, insects, locusts etc. are hungry and they are bound by Karmas. For their satisfaction food has been offered by me. May that be for their joy."

214. After offering the Bhūta-oblation thus the householder shall wait for as much time as is required to milk a cow, for any guest who may come. Thereafter he should enter the dining room.

215-220. Without offering oblations to crows, one should perform *Nityaśrāddha*. In the *Nityaśrāddha* the householder shall feed three, two or one (Brāhmaṇa) according to his capacity.

A weak man (poor man) should take something from all the items of food prepared and offer *Pitṛyajña* (one oblation for all together).

This *Nityaśrāddha* has no deity in particular. It has no guiding injunctions. There is no Dakṣiṇā to be offered. It has no Vrata binding the donor and the receiver.

After performing *Pitṛyajña* thus, the householder should sit on an undefiled seat with his mind calm and normal. He will not be overanxious. He should then take food along with the children. His mind should be in excellent mood. He should apply sweet scent (over his body) and wear a flower garland. He should be clad in two clean clothes. He should take food seated facing the east or the north. The cooked food should be made for and enjoyed by his Pitṛs (It should not be naked i.e., ghee or something should be poured over and beneath too). In accordance with the injunctions regarding food and drink, a wise Brāhmaṇa should do everything and then take food.

221. The injunctions referred to are as follows: Uttering *bhuvaḥ pataye svāhā* (to the Lord of the Earth), *bhuvanapataye svāhā* (to the Lord of the Universe), *bhūtānām pataye svāhā* (to

the Lord of the living beings) he should offer three oblations on the ground.

222. Sipping water once (uttering the conventional Mantra i.e., *amṛtopastaraṇamasi)* the householder should offer five *Āhutis* into the *Jaṭhara* fire (fire in the stomach). At that time he should hold Darbha in his hand and should be of pleasant mood mentally.

223. If anyone holds Darbha in his hand while taking food, he meets with no harm arising from hair, worms etc. So one should take food holding Darbha.

224. While one is eating delicious food, one should not mention its merits or demerits. The Pitṛs shall partake of the food only when the merits and demerits are not mentioned.

225-226 Hence he who takes food silently enjoys the pure Amṛta. After concluding the meal, the householder should drinks as Anupāna (liquid to wash down the meal) milk, buttermilk or water uttering the Mantra *amṛtāpidhānamasi.* He should drink water once. The water that is left after drinking should be poured down on the ground uttering the following Mantra:

227-228. "May the water of *Ucchiṣṭa* (remnant after taking food) from the root of the thumb of the right hand not yet washed, reach the people who stay in Raurava, the abode of demerit, for millions of years (*Padma* and *Arbuda* are high numbers) without any redemption, since they are desirous of the *Ucchiṣṭa* water.

229. The highly intelligent householder then performs another *Ācamana* and becomes pure. He should then, with effort, take water in the hand and utter this Mantra:

230. "The Puruṣa (Being) of the size of the thumb has resorted to the thumb. He is the lord and master of the entire universe. He becomes pleased as *Viśvabhuk* ('the consumer of everything')."

231. After considering (all the aspects) of the food thus, he should wash his hands and feet. Thereafter, he should utter these Mantras for the digestion of the food:

232. "Induced by wind and provided with room by ether, may the fire digest all the bodily constituents of earthy character. Let there be happiness unto me."

233. "May the food be nutritious unto Prāṇa, Apāna, Samāna,

Udāna and Vyāna. Let there be unobstructed happiness unto me."

234. "May these, viz. the sea, the submarine fire, the Sun and the son of the Sun (i.e., Yama) completely digest whatever has been consumed by me."

235. He should then get his mouth purified (by chewing betel etc.). He should spend the remaining part of the day by listening to the Purāṇas etc. Then he should begin the performance of Sandhyā.

236. *Sandhyā* performed in a cowpen has ten times more benefit than that performed in the house; that performed on the banks of a river has ten times more benefit than that performed in a cowpen; that performed at the confluence of two rivers shall have hundred times more benefit and that performed in the presence of Śiva has infinite benefit.

237. *Sandhyā* performed outside subdues the sin of sexual intercourse indulged in during day-time, the sin of uttering a lie, and that of inhaling the odour of liquors.

238-239. The *Gāyatrī* Mantra is in the form of Sarasvatī. Viṣṇu is the deity thereof. Tārkṣya (Garuḍa) is the vehicle. She destroys all obstacles. She is in the form of Sāmaveda and is accompanied by Sage Vasiṣṭha. The *Aṅgas* (limbs) are dark in colour. The cloth is black in colour. Her youth has passed off a little. She has *Jagatī* as the Metre. The householder should meditate on her, the great one of single syllable.

240. The intelligent householder should perform the rite of *Ācamana* uttering the Mantra beginning with *Agniśca* etc. He should sit facing the west and repeat the Mantra of *Gāyatrī* till the stars become visible.

241-242. The householder should duly honour the guest who pays visit in the evening even with verbal utterance, offering of ground (to sit) and water (to drink). The first *Yāma* of the night should thus be spent by the intelligent householder. Thus the householder performs the rites of the day time by reading and teaching *Śruti*. Not satisfied too much, he should go to bed on a cot consisting of a single wood (i.e., wood of the same kind or full-length wood without joints).

243. The rules regarding the daily rites have thus been narrated in a general way. A Brāhmaṇa who acts according to these, never experiences difficulty at all.

CHAPTER THIRTYSIX

The Rites and Duties of a Religious Student

Skanda said:

1. O Pot-born One, I shall again mention a special type of good conduct on hearing which an intelligent man never enters the darkness of ignorance.

2. The three *Varṇas,* Brāhmaṇas, Kṣatriyas and Vaiśyas, are known as twice-born; they are born of their mothers first and then for a second time when *Upanayana* (investing with the sacred thread) is performed.

3. The holy rites beginning with *Niṣeka* (impregnation) and ending with *Śmaśāna* (Funeral rites) are prescribed by Vedic injunctions. A wise man should perform the rite of impregnation at the menstrual period avoiding the stars Maghā and Mūla.

4. The rite of *Puṁsavana* is performed before the quickening of the child in the womb and thereafter the rite of *Sīmantonnayana* (parting of the hair) which is performed in the sixth or the eighth month. The rite of *Jātakarma* is performed after birth.

5. On the eleventh day the rite of naming is to be performed. The rite of *Niṣkrama* ('coming out') from the lying-in-chamber is performed in the fourth month. The rite of *Annaprāśana* ('feeding with food') is in the sixth month. The *Cūḍā* rite is performed when a year is completed or as is the practice in the family.

6. In this manner the sin born of the seed or the womb is subdued. In regard to women, these rites are silent (i.e., without Mantra) ones, but the rite of *Pāṇigraha* (marriage) is with Mantras.

7. A Brāhmaṇa (child) deserves (imparting of) Sāvitrī (the Gāyatrī Mantra) in the seventh or eighth year, a royal (i.e., Kṣatriya) child in the eleventh year and a Vaiśya child in the twelfth year or as is the practice in the family.

8. In order to get the spiritual lustre (*Brahmatejas*) increased, a Brāhmaṇa deserves (this rite) in the fifth year, a king (Kṣatriya) desirous of power should get it performed in the sixth year and a Vaiśya should wear the *Mauñjī* (girdle made of Muñja grass) in the sixth year.

9. The preceptor should teach Veda along with the *Mahāvyāhṛti.* After performing the rite of *Upanayana,* he should initiate him in the practice of *Śauca* (purity—external and internal) and *Ācāra* (Rules of good conduct).

10-12. The rites of *Śauca* and *Ācamana* should be performed in accordance with the injunctions mentioned before. After defecation, the tongue and the teeth should be cleansed. Uttering the Mantras with water as the deity, he should perform the rite of *Snāna;* he should then duly perform *Prāṇāyāma* rite and he should perform the *Upasthāna* (adoration) of the Sun in both the *Sadhyās* (dawn and dusk). After performing the rite of Fire-worship, he should make obeisance unto the Brāhmaṇa saying, "I belong to such and such a *Gotra.* I bow down (to you)."

13. Day-by-day longevity, fame, strength and intellect of one who habitually makes obeisance and who is engaged in serving elderly people get increased.

14. He engages in the study of the Vedas. On being summoned by the Guru he should recount to him what has been acquired (learnt). He shall always perform mentally, verbally and physically what is conducive to his benefit.

15. They should be taught righteously and not for monetary consideration. Those who have acquired knowledge perfectly should give money if they are competent. Those should be grateful, pure, non-harassing and free from malice.

16. They should wear girdles, staff, sacred thread and *Ajina* (deerskin). For their sustenance they should take alms from non-censurable Brāhmaṇas.

17. The mode of begging for alms among the Brāhmaṇas, Kṣatriyas and the Vaiśyas is by using the word *Bhavatī* in this order: at the beginning, in the middle or in the end. Thus a Brāhmaṇa should say: *"bhavatī, bhikṣām dehi"*; a Kṣatriya should say: *"bhikṣām, bhavatī, dehi"*; a Vaiśya should say: *"bhikṣām dehi, bhavatī."*

18. On being permitted by the Guru, he should take food silently without depreciating the food. During Śrāddha he should not take food at the place of the same man (twice); but in exceptional cases, e.g. of emergency, he may take food.

19. Excessive intake of food is against one's health and longevity. It is not meritorious or conducive to heavenly plea-

sure. It is hated by people. Hence it should be avoided.

20. An excellent Brāhmaṇa should not take food twice on the same day (during day-time) on any account. A Brāhmaṇa conversant with the injunctions of *Agnihotra* rite should take food in the morning and in the evening

21. (A Brāhmaṇa) should avoid liquor, meat, injuring living beings, looking at the Sun, applying collyrium, women, stale food, leavings of other's food and slandering.

22. The maximum limit of age for the rite of *Upanayana* in the cases of Brāhmaṇas, Kṣatriyas and Vaiśyas is respectively sixteenth, twenty-second and twenty-fourth.

23. Beyond these years, they are not worthy of consecration. They are devoid of piety; they are fallen. But their fallen state shall be eradicated by means of the *Yajña* named *Vrātyastoma.*

24. No one should have any social intercourse with people fallen from the Sāvitrī Mantra (i.e., whose thread ceremony is not performed). The skin to be used by the three *Varṇas* should be respectively from Eṇa deer, Ruru deer and goat.

25. They shall wear respectively garments made of jute, silk and wool. The girdle of a Brāhmaṇa is made of Muñja grass; Maurvī in the case of a Kṣatriya and that of a Vaiśya is made of jute fibres. The girdle shall have three strands equal in length and very glossy.

26. In the absence of Muñja grass, the girdle should be made of Kuśa grass, Aśmantaka and Balva. There shall be one, three or five knots as is the practice in the family.

27. The sacred thread should be made of cotton, jute or wool. It should be with three strands and shall be twisted rightwards for the purpose of longevity.

28. The staff of a Brāhmaṇa should be made of Bilva or Palāśa; in the case of a Kṣatriya, of Nyagrodha or Khadira; and in that of a Vaiśya, of Pīlu or Udumbara.

29. The staffs shall respectively come up to the head, forehead and nose of a Brāhmaṇa, Kṣatriya and Vaiśya. The bark shall be intact and shall not be defiled by fire.

30. A Baṭu (i.e., boy whose *Upanayana* is performed) should circumambulate the Fire and adore the Sun and should be equipped with a staff, deerskin and the sacred thread. He should beg for alms in the manner mentioned before.

31. The mother, mother's sister, sister and father's sister—

these are to be approached at the outset for begging for alms. Those should not say "No" to him.

32. As long as he performs the Vedic rites and studies the Vedas, he will be called *Brahmacārin*. Afterwards, on taking the requisite concluding ablution he would become a householder.

33. A Brāhmaṇa in the state of pupilage is called *Upakurvāṇa*. Another one is called *Naiṣṭhika* who continues to stay in the hermitage of his Guru till the end of his life.

34. A Brāhmaṇa who enters the stage of a householder and takes up the stage of celibacy once again is neither a Yati nor a Vanastha. He shall not belong to any of the Āśramas (stages of life).

35. No Brāhmaṇa shall remain devoid of any Āśrama even for a day, because, remaining without an Āśrama makes him subject to expiatory rites.

36. A person who has fallen off the Āśrama but performs any of these rites: *Japa, Homa, Vrata, Dāna, Svādhyāya* or *Pitṛtarpaṇa*, shall not derive the benefit thereof.

37-38. The girdle, deerskin and staff shall be the characteristic marks of a religious student; the Vedas, *Yajñas* etc. are the characteristic marks of a householder; long hairs and nails are those of a Vānaprastha; Tridaṇḍa etc. are the characteristic marks of an ascetic. One who has none of these marks is subject to expiatory rites everyday.

39. If the Kamaṇḍalu (waterpot), staff, sacred thread or deerskin becomes spoiled or broken, it has to be cast off into water and fresh one taken like a new Mantra.

40. The *Keśānta* (*Samāvartana*) rite should be duly performed in the sixteenth year so that the stage of a householder can be entered into in the twenty-second or twenty-fourth year.

41. In the case of (twice-born ones) *Śruti* alone is the means of acquiring the glory of liberation (*Mokṣa*) rather than doing auspicious Karmas (actions) like penance, performance of sacrifices or pious observances.

42. The *Praṇava* should be uttered when the recitation of the Veda begins or is concluded. What is not attended with *Om* is fruitless. What is read so (without *Om*) is not conducive to fulfilment (of the fruit thereof).

43. The great Gāyatrī consisting of three metrical feet is

spoken of as the face of the Vedas. (It is recited) with the three *Mahāvyāhṛtis* with *Praṇava* in the beginning.

44. A man with restraint repeating these three a thousand times or a little more everyday for a month outside (on a river bank etc.) becomes rid of great sins.

45. With the mind not turned towards anything else, a man should practice repeating thus everyday for a period of a little more than a year. He shall become Vyomamūrti (pure in body or perfect in form) and pure in soul. He attains the great Brahman.

46. The set of three, viz. *Bhūḥ, Bhuvaḥ,* and *Svaḥ,* Oṁkāra consisting of three syllables and the three feet of Sāvitrī—these have been milked by the three Vedas.

47. This imperishable Oṁkāra, the Gāyatrī should be uttered along with the Vyāhṛtis at the time of dawn and dusk by a Brāhmaṇa conversant with the Vedas. He becomes possessed of the Vedic merit

48. He attains the fruit of Japa which is ten times more than *Vidhikratu* (like Darśa and Paurṇamāsa sacrifices). *Japakratu* is spoken of as ten times more effective than *Vidhikratu.*

49. *Upāṁśu* (a *Japa* done in low voice) is hundred times more effective and *Mānasa* (mental one) is a thousand times more effective.

50. By studying all the Vedas, two Vedas or one, in accordance with one's competence, a Brāhmaṇa attains the benefit of gifting away the earth filled with gold.

51. In order to perform penance, an excellent Brāhmaṇa should always study the Śruti. The study of Śruti alone is praised as the greatest penance of a Brāhmaṇa.

52. One who abandons the study of Śruti and wishes to study something else is (no better than) one who sends away a milch cow and desires to milk a rural pig.

53. A Brāhmaṇa should perform the *Upanayana* rite of his disciple and teach him the Vedas along with all its esoteric secrets and the *Kalpa.* Scholars consider such a Brāhmaṇa an *Ācārya.*

54. A person who teaches a part of the Śruti or the Aṅgas (ancillary subjects) for the sake of maintenance of his livelihood is considered an *Upādhyāya* by scholars.

55. A Brāhmaṇa who duly performs the rites of *Niṣeka*

etc. and maintains (disciples) with cooked food is glorified as a *Guru.*

56. On being invited (by a householder), if any learned Paṇḍita performs the rite of *Agnyādheya* (the rite of kindling holy fires), *Pākayajñas (Aṣṭaka* etc.) and the sacrifices of *Agniṣṭoma* etc., he is called his *Ṛtivk.*

57. From the point of venerability, an *Ācārya* is ten times greater than an *Upādhyāya;* father is a hundred times venerable than an *Ācārya* and mother a thousand times more venerable than father.

58. Superiority among Brāhmaṇas is based on knowledge, that among Kṣatriyas is based on valour, that among Vaiśyas on wealth and grain storage and that among Śūdras on priority of birth.

59. A Brāhmaṇa who has not studied the Vedas is like a wooden elephant or stuffed deer. These three are merely bearers of the names like 'Brāhmaṇa' etc.

60. A religious student of the three Varṇas who, without lust, gets the emission of semen during sleep, shall take bath, worship the Sun and repeat the Ṛk beginning with *punar mām aitvindriyam* (AV 7.67.1).

61. A religious student should go for alms everyday to the house of persons regularly performing the rites of Vedic *Yajñas,* strictly adhering to their own religious obligations. He should be pure (in word, mind and deed).

62. If a religious student (even if) being well, fails to beg for alms and to kindle the holy fire, he should perform expiatory rites for seven nights.

63. When he is within the sight of his Guru, a religious student should not indulge in wilful movements of the limbs as he pleases. He should not mention his (Guru's) name without appellations even in his absence.

64. Where the Guru is being censured, where there is slandering (of his Guru), he will close both his ears if he stays there, or shall go elsewhere.

65. One who reproves the Guru will become a mule (or an ass) and one who censures the Guru will be born as a dog. One who is jealous of the Guru shall be born as a worm of no worth and one who takes food before the Guru shall become an insect.

66. If a religious student is of twenty years and so is able to discriminate between good and bad, he should not pay respects to the youthful wife of the Guru by touching her feet.

67. The nature of women is fickle-mindedness. Hence (if anything goes wrong), the fault is that of men. Learned men never err in regard to youthful maidens.

68. They make learned or illiterate ones agitated or bring them under control, like a bird tied with a string.

69. One should not stay isolated alone with his mother, daughter or sister. The sense-organs are powerful and they delude even the learned ones.

70. Just as a person who assiduously digs the ground obtains water, so also by the service of the Guru, the disciple obtains learning.

71. If the Sun rises or sets even as a Brahmacārin is asleep, he should fast for a day (performing the Japa of Gāyatrī).

72-73. Since parents undergo various pains and distress ever since the son's birth, that (indebtedness) cannot be adequately repaid even in a hundred years. Hence, a son should always do what is pleasing to them and to the Guru. When those three are fully pleased, all the (fruit of) penance is obtained.

74. Service rendered to those three is called the greatest penance. If anyone does anything transgressing them, he will never be successful in any venture.

75. By propitiating these three, the sensible one conquers all the three worlds. By increasing their satisfaction and pleasure, he shines in heaven like the Devas.

76. One who fulfils one's duties, wins over Bhūloka through devotion to mother, Bhuvarloka through service unto father, and Svarloka through service to Guru.

77. If their satisfaction is brought about, it is the accomplishment of the four great aims of life by men.

(Another Upadharma is being described:)

78. After studying all the Vedas, two Vedas or one Veda duly, a Brāhmaṇa who has not swerved from celibacy, should resort to Gṛhāśrama (the stage of a householder).

79. One should be a person of undefiled celibacy through the blessing of Viśveśa. The blessing of Viśveśa is also one that brings about the attainment of Kāśī.

80. Knowledge is derived by reaching Kāśī. From knowledge one obtains salvation. Indeed the effort for practising good conduct maintained by sensible ones, leads to salvation.

81. Abidance by (the prescribed canons of) good conduct in the other stages of life is not as important as it is in Gṛhāśrama. After acquiring all the lores, one should resort to Gṛhasthāśrama.

82. If wife is favourable, there is nothing greater than Gṛhāśrama. Harmonious relation between husband and wife is conducive to the accomplishment of *Trivarga* (the three *Puruṣārthas*).

83. If there is concordance of wife, of what value is heaven? If there is discord of the wife, of what avail is hell?

84. The householder's life is for the achievement of happiness. That happiness has its source in wife. She who is modest, is the real wife. *Trivarga* is humility and modesty certainly.

85. Young women are compared to leeches only by those who are slow-witted. If we ponder, there is great difference between the fawn-eyed ladies and leeches.

86. The poor, scorched leech takes up only the blood. But a young woman always takes away the mind, wealth, strength and happiness.

87. A woman endowed with following qualities is Goddess Lakṣmī herself who has assumed the form of a woman. She is clever and efficient. She has children. She is chaste. She speaks pleasing words. She is under one's control.

88. With the permission of the preceptor, the religious student should take the customary bath and conclude the *Vrata* (of celibacy) and formal Vedic study. Then he should take unto him a wife having all excellent characteristics and belonging to his own *Varṇa*.

89. A girl who is not of the Gotra of his father and not a *Sapiṇḍaka* of his mother is worthy of being the bride of a Brāhmaṇa. She is conducive to the increase of piety.

90. In contracting a marital alliance, one should leave out a family of epileptics, consumptives and lepers. He should also leave off one who is exorcised and one who is likely to give birth only to a girl.

91. A Brāhmaṇa should take unto him a wife of gentle facial features, gentle in speech, free from illness, having a

brother and slightly younger to him.

92. A sensible man does not marry a girl having the name of a mountain, star, tree, river, serpent or bird or one whose name smacks of slavery. Her name shall be gentle.

93. There shall not be any extra limb nor should there be deficiency in limbs. She should not be too tall or too lean. She should neither be hairy nor hairless. The hairs on the head should not be rough or thick.

94. Out of delusion, he should not marry a girl of low family. By marrying a low and base girl, one makes the progeny too very lowly and base.

95. After carefully examining the characteristics at the outset, a girl should be taken as bride. A girl of excellent characteristics and good conduct enhances the longevity of her husband.

96. O Pot-born One, the activities and characteristics of a religious student have been mentioned to you. Incidentally, I shall now recount the characteristics of women.

CHAPTER THIRTYSEVEN

The Characteristics of Women

Skanda said:

1. If wife is endowed with good characteristics, a householder always enjoys happiness. Hence, for the sake of happiness and prosperity, a man should look for the characteristic features.[1]

2. The bases of characteristics have been mentioned by scholars as eight: (1) *Vapus* (limbs), (2) *Āvarta* (curls), (3) *Gandha* (odour), (4) *Chāyā* (splendour), (5) *Sattva* (mental stability), (6) *Svara* (modulation of voice), (7) *Gati* (gait) and (8) *Varṇa* (complexion).

3. Beginning with the sole of the foot and ending with the

1. Ancient Indians believed in prognosis by external bodily characteristics. Jainas called it Aṅga Vidyā. The present chapter gives a list of auspicious and inauspicious characteristics found on the 66 parts of women's body.

hair, O sage, I shall state the auspicious and inauspicious characteristics. Listen.

4-9. The following sixty-six are the parts of the body of a woman, the base of characteristics: The sole of the foot is the first, then the lines thereon, big toe, other toes, nails, the instep, two heels, two ankles, calves, hairs, knees, thighs, lips, buttocks, front of the loins, vagina, portion beneath the navel, navel, two sections of the stomach, sides, side of the belly, three curls of hair in the middle, row of hairs, heart, chest, two breasts, nipples, *Jatru* (joint of the shoulders), shoulders, root of the arms, hand, two wrists, back of the hand, palm, lines in the palm, thumb, fingers, nails, back, nape of the neck, chin, lower part of lips, two parts of the chin, cheeks, mouth, lower lip, upper lip, teeth, tongue, lower part of the tongue, palate, laughter, nose, sneeze, eyes, eyelashes, eyebrows, ears, forehead, head, middle part of the head and tresses of hair.

10. The sole of the foot of women should be glossy, fleshy, soft and even. It should not perspire but be warm and it should be pink in colour. These characteristics are fit to give much enjoyment.

11. If the sole is hard, rough, discoloured, dried up, having the imprint broken up (here and there) and is of the form of a winnowing basket it indicates misfortune.

12. If the lines on the sole are in the form of a wheel, Svastika (a trianqular figure—Comm.), conchshell, banner, fish or umbrella, the girl shall become wife of a king.

13. If a line moves up and joins the middle toe, it is conducive to unbroken enjoyment. A line resembling a mouse, a serpent or a crow indicates misery and poverty.

14. If the big toe is lifted up, fleshy and round, it accords incomparable enjoyment. If it is crooked, short and flattened, it destroys happiness and good fortune.

15. One with a wide big toe shall become a widow and with a long, big toe full of misfortune. Soft, close-set, round and lifted up toes are praiseworthy.

16. If a girl has long toes, she will become a wanton woman; if she has lean toes, she will be utterly penniless; if the toes are very short, she will be short-lived; if the toes are curved, she will be crooked in her behaviour.

17-22. If the toes are flattened, she will become a slave girl. If the toes leave spaces in between them, she will become poor.

If the toes, as it were, are riding on one another, the woman will kill many husbands and then become one dependent on others.

If dust particles are raised up when a woman walks on the road, she will become a whore destructive of the three families (of father, mother and husband).

If the small toe does not touch the ground when the woman walks, she will kill her husband and take another man as her husband.

If the *Anāmikā* (i.e., one between middle toe and small toe like the ring finger of the hand) and the middle toe do not touch the ground, two husbands will be killed by the former and three husbands by the latter.

If these two toes are missing or defective, they cause the absence of a husband (i.e., widowhood or spinsterhood).

If the *Pradeśinī* (the toe between the big toe and the middle toe like the index finger of the hand) is inseparable from the big toe, it is certain that she will become wanton and remain unmarried.

23. The nails of the foot are auspicious, if they are glossy, lifted up, round and copper-coloured (otherwise inauspicious).

24. If the instep of a woman is upraised or elevated, does not perspire, has no sinews (visible), is fleshy, soft and glossy, it indicates queenship.

25. If the instep is depressed in the middle the woman becomes poor; if it is sinewy, she will be incessant traveller; if it is full of hairs she will become a slave; if it is devoid of flesh, she will be unfortunate.

26. Hidden ankles are said to be conducive to welfare if they are not sinewy and are perfectly round. If they are visible, loose and uneven, they indicate misfortune.

27. A level-heeled woman is auspicious; a woman with broad heels is unfortunate. If the heels are lifted up (raised), the woman becomes a whore; one with long heels experiences misery.

28. If the calves are devoid of hair, similar, glossy, gradually circular in shape, devoid of sinews and very pleasing, she

will become wife of a king.

29. One with a single hair in the hair cavity becomes wife of a king; one with two hairs becomes happy; and one with three hairs in the cavities of the hair will experience the misery of widowhood.

30. The pair of knees are praiseworthy, if they are fleshy and round in shape; if they are devoid of flesh, the woman will become a wanton; if they are not firm, the woman will become a destitute.*

31. With thighs resembling the trunk of an elephant, glossy, dense, perfectly round and devoid of hairs, a woman will become beloved of kings.

32. Widowhood is indicated by thighs full of hairs; if they are flattened, it indicates misfortune; if there are depressions in the middle, there is great misery; if the skin is rough and hard, it indicates poverty.

33. The hips of a fawn-eyed woman are praiseworthy if they are rectangular, lifted up and possessing fleshy back portion. A perfect hip measures twenty-four Aṅgulas.

34. If the hip is bent down, flattened, large, devoid of flesh, contracted, short and full of hairs, it indicates misery and widowhood.

35. If the *Nitaṁba* (back of the hip) of a woman is raised up, fleshy and large, it is conducive to great enjoyment of pleasures. The reverse thereof is considered to be conducive to misery.

36. If the *Sphiks* (buttocks) are round like wood-apple, soft, fleshy, dense and free from curls, they cause increase in the happiness of love-play.

37. If the vulva is like the back of a tortoise (dense and firm) or elevated like the shoulders of an elephant, it is auspicious. If its elevation is tilted to the left, it indicates that the woman will give birth to daughters; if it is tilted above to the right, it indicates that a son will be born to her.

38. An auspicious vulva has also the following characteristics: It has tawny hairs like those of a mouse. The clitoris is hidden. It is very dense, firm and large. It is lifted up. It is like a lotus leaf or like a leaf of the holy fig tree.

* So far twelve limbs have been described—Comm.

39. That vulva which is in the form of the hoof of a deer, that which resembles the inner part of an oven, that which is hairy, that which has open mouth and that the *Nāsā* (central portion of the hymen that is intact) of which is visible—the vulva of these characteristics indicates misery and misfortune.

40. She whose vulva is curled like a conch-shell does not wish to conceive (i.e, is barren). The vulva that has the shape of a potsherd, and is flattened, accords the position of a servant maid.

41. So also the vulva of these characteristics is inauspicious: if it resembles a leaf of bamboo or reed; if it has hairs like those of an elephant; if the Nāsā is elevated and long; if it is hideous and ugly and if it is crooked in shape. If the lower part of its opening is long, it is inauspicious.

42. *Jaghana* (front part of body above the vulva) is the forehead, as it were of the vulva. If it is wide and ample, if it is elevated and fleshy, if it is soft with soft hairs curling to the right, then it is auspicious.

43. If the *Jaghana* has hairs curling to the left, if it is devoid of flesh or if it is crooked, it is an indication of widowhood. If it is contracted, if it is unevenly elevated and depressed and if it is rough, it always brings misery.

44. The lower belly below the navel (*Basti* or *Vasti*) is praiseworthy, if it is ample, soft, a bit raised. If it is hairy, sinewy or marked with lines, it is not good.

45. The navel shall be conducive to happiness and prosperity, if it is deep and curling to the right with the lines or hairs. If the curling is towards the left, if it is raised a little or if the central spot is prominent, then it does not forebode good.*

46. A woman with a large belly experiences happiness. She gives birth to many sons. A woman with a belly resembling that of a frog, gives birth to a son who will become a king.

47. If the belly is raised up or elevated, the woman will become barren. If it has folds, she will become a recluse woman. If it has curls due to looseness of skin, she will become a servant maid.

* Twenty limbs covered—Comm.

48. Undoubtedly a woman shall have good fortune and happiness, if she has fleshy level sides of great softness with bones well-ensconced.

49. If the sinews are visible in the sides, if they are lifted up and hairy, the woman shall bear no child. She will have bad manners. She will be a storehouse of misery.

50. If the lower belly or the side of the belly is very small, free from sinews and the skin is soft, the woman becomes one enjoying all pleasures and consuming delicacies of food everyday.

51. The side of the belly in the form of a pot or Mṛdaṅga (drum) indicates that the woman will be extremely poor. So also if it is like ash-gourd, or barley, it is difficult to be filled.

52. A woman of very ample side belly has no issues and becomes unfortunate. If the same is hanging loose, the woman is sure to slay her father-in-law and brother-in-law.

53. A woman of slender waist is very fortunate. One having three *Valis* (folds) enjoys pleasures. If the cluster of hairs is straight and slender, the woman enjoys pleasure and is jovial in temperament.

54. If the cluster of hairs is tawny in colour, crooked, stout and broken in the middle, the woman will take to theft, become widowed or become unfortunate.

55. If the bosom is devoid of hairs, level and free from depressed state, the woman will have prosperity and enjoy the love of her husband. She will not become a widow.

56. A woman of wide bosom becomes a lustful wanton without kindness. A woman with hairs growing on the front of bosom, certainly kills her husband.

57. A bosom elevated and stout, extending to eighteen *Aṅgulas*, is conducive to happiness. If it is hairy, uneven and large it is conducive to misery.

58. If the two breasts are equal, supple, round, firm and stout, they are praiseworthy. If the tips are stout and the breasts are not close together but leave space in the middle and if they are dry, they are not conducive to happiness.

59. If the right breast is (more) lifted up, the woman gives birth to sons. She stands at the head of women. A woman with the left side breast lifted up, gives birth to a girl who will be beautiful and enjoy conjugal bliss.

60. Breasts resembling a pot in the water-raising wheel

indicate evil habits. Breasts with mouths stout and the sides very large are not splendid. If there is space between the breasts, it is not beautiful.

61. If the breasts are plump at the root and gradually become thinner with the tips pointed, they are conducive to happiness initially but later they accord misery.

62. Dark, circular and firm nipples are praiseworthy. If they are depressed within, long and lean they are conducive to distress.*

63. With stout clavicles a woman becomes a storehouse of grain and wealth. If they are depressed, uneven and loose-boned, the woman becomes poverty-stricken.

64. The shoulders are splendid if they are unbound, bent and neither long nor lean. If they are crooked, stout and hairy, they indicate slavery and widowhood.

65. If the upper part of the shoulders keeps the joint hidden and the tips are loose, if the upper portion of the shoulders is well knit, it indicates good. If the tips are lifted up, the woman shall become a widow; if they are devoid of flesh, they cause great misery.

66. If the armpits are high with fine delicate hairs, if they are glossy and fleshy, they are praiseworthy. If they are deep, sinewy, with profuse perspiration, they bode no good.

67. The arms are completely devoid of faults if the bones and the joints are hidden and the arms are hence tender. The arms of fawn-eyed women should not be sinewy and hairy.

68. If the arms are hairy, they indicate widowhood. If short, they indicate misfortune. If the sinews are visible in the arms, they tend to the distress of women.

69. If the pair of hands of fawn-eyed women has the shape of a lotus-bud and if the thumb and the fingers face each other, it indicates enjoyment of much pleasure.

70. If the palm is red and soft with the centre raised up, if it is devoid of holes, it is praiseworthy. It shall have praiseworthy lines. Very few lines indicate splendid glory.

71. With the palm having many lines, a woman becomes a widow; if the palm has no lines, she becomes destitute and

* Thirty limbs described—Comm.

if the palm is sinewy, she becomes a Bhikṣukī (female mendicant).

72. The back of the hand that is devoid of hairs and sinews and that is raised up is praiseworthy. That which is full of hairs and sinews and devoid of flesh should be abandoned (i.e., not good).

73. If the lines in the hand of a woman are red, clear, deep, glossy, full and circular, they are splendid and they favour good fortune.

74. If the lines form a fish-like figure, the woman enjoys conjungal bliss; if a Svastika figure, the woman bestows wealth on others; if a lotus-like figure, she becomes wife of a king and gives birth to a son destined to be a king.

75. In the palm of the wife of an emperor, there shall be the figure of *Nandyāvarta* (a kind of building where rich men live) in clockwise form. The figures of conch, umbrella and tortoise indicate mothership of a king.

76-77. Two lines in the form of a balance indicate status of the wife of a merchant. The lines in the form of elephant, horse, bull, palace or thunderbolt in the left hand, point out that the son shall be a Tīrthakara (a pilgrim or a writer of philosophical treatises—Comm.). If there are lines making the figure of a cart or a yoke, she will be the wife of a farmer.

78-79. If the lines form figures of chowries, goad and bow, the woman shall certainly become wife of a king. If a line starts from the root of the thumb and goes to the small finger, the woman will be murderess of her husband. A sensible man should abandon her outright. With the lines forming the figures of a trident, sword, mace, Śakti, spear and war, drum the woman shall become famous all over the earth for her renunciation.

80. Lines forming the figures of a heron, jackal, frog, wolf, scorpion or serpent, donkey, camel and cat on the palm, accord misery to the woman.

81. A thumb that is straight and round with circular nail bestows auspiciousness.

82. Fingers with excellent joints, long, round, and gradually tapering are auspicious.

Flattened, unevenly elevated and depressed and rough fingers with hairs on the back are inauspicious.

83. Very short, lean, crooked fingers leaving spaces in between cause sickness. Fingers of women with large joints are conducive to misery.

84. High, pink-coloured finger-nails with crests are auspicious to women. Depressed ones, yellow or discoloured ones resembling oyster shells accord poverty.

85. In the nails of wanton-like women, there will be white dots. Even men become miserable with such dotted nails.

86. The back of the hand with bone in the shape of bamboo, depressed and sunk beneath, and fleshy too, is auspicious. If the back of the hand is hairy, the woman certainly becomes a widow.

87. If the back of the hand is bent and depressed and is also sinewy, the woman becomes miserable.

If the back of the neck is straight, fleshy and lifted up, it is excellent.

88. If it is dry, sinewy, hairy, wide and crooked, it is inauspicious. A neck that measures four *Aṅgulas* and that is circular and fleshy is excellent.

89-90. A neck that is marked with three lines and that is compact is praiseworthy. The bone shall not be prominently visible. A neck without flesh, that is flattened, long and unevenly elevated does not accord auspiciousness.

A woman with a stout neck becomes a widow; with a crooked neck becomes a servant maid; one with flattened neck is a barren woman and one with a short neck does not give birth to a son.

91. A chin measuring two *Aṅgulas* is praiseworthy. It shall be round, thick and tender.

That which is very stout, long, hairy and divided into two should be abandoned (i.e., that woman is not worthy of marriage).

92. A *Hanu* (lower part of the lips) adhering to the chin and very compact is praiseworthy. It should be without hairs. If it is crooked, very stout or lean and short with hairs, it is not auspicious.

93. The cheeks of a woman are praiseworthy, if they are plump and fleshy, round and raised up.

One should avoid hairy, rough, depressed, fleshless cheeks. A woman with such cheeks is not fit for marriage.

94. A face fleshy, glossy, fragrant, round and level is praiseworthy. Only blessed people have such face resembling that of the father.

95. The lower lip of a woman becomes endearing to a king if it has the colour of a Pāṭala flower, if it is round and glossy and has the central part adorned with lines.

96. A lean, suspended, rough and cloven lip indicates misfortune. The lip that is dark brown in colour and very stout accords widowhood and quarrelsomeness.

97. The upper lip of a woman if glossy, has its central (part) raised a little and free from hairs bestows enjoyment of pleasures.

98. All the thirty-two teeth shall be glossy and have the colour of cow's milk. They should be equally set in the upper and the lower rows. They should be slightly raised. Such teeth, thus, forebode good.

99. If the teeth are yellow or dark, brown, big, long and have two rows, if they are like oyster shells with spaces in between, they cause misery and misfortune.

100. If there are more teeth in the lower row, the woman will eat up her mother. If the teeth are hideous, she will be bereft of her husband. If there are teeth deficient in number, the woman shall become a wanton.

101. If the tongue is red in colour and soft, the woman shall enjoy what is pleasing and delicious. If it is dark, narrow in the middle and wide in front, it is conducive to misery.

102. If the tongue is white, it indicates watery grave; if it is black, the woman will be fond of quarrels. If it is fleshy, the woman will be poor; if it is hanging down, the woman will eat what should not be eaten.

103. With a wide tongue, the woman becomes one who (habitually) commits mistakes.

The palate that is glossy and tender, having the lustre of a red lotus is praiseworthy.

104. If the palate is white, it indicates widowhood; if it is yellow, the woman will renounce the world and become a recluse; if it is black, she will be separated from her children and be distressed; if it is rough and hard, she will have a large family.

105. The *Ghaṇṭī* (lower part of the tongue) should be

thick at its neck; it shall be perfectly round, very red and sharper towards the end. It should not hang down. Then it is splendid. If it is very thick and black in colour, it accords misery.

106. The smile of splendid-eyed women is praiseworthy when the teeth are slightly not visible and slightly the cheeks become blown up and the eyes are not closed.

107. If the nostrils are symmetrical and round and the hollow portion is small, then it is splendid. If the tip is thick and the nose is lifted up and the middle is depressed it is inauspicious.

108. If the tip (of the nose) is bent and pink in colour, it accords widowhood and distress. If it is flattened, the woman becomes a slave unto others. If it is very short or very long, the woman becomes fond of quarrel.

109. If the sneeze is long and is repeated twice or thrice at the same time, it accords long life.

The eyes of women are praiseworthy if the extremities are red and the pupils are dark in colour.

110. If a woman has bulging eyes with dark eyelashes, very glossy, clear, and coloured like cow's milk, she does not live long. A woman with circular eyes shall be a wanton.

111. A sheep-eyed, buffalo-eyed and squint-eyed woman is not good. One with tawny eyes like those of a cow is greedy and lustful. She is also ill-behaved.

112. The conduct of a woman with eyes like those of a dove is not good; a red-eyed woman kills her husband. A woman with eyes like the hollow in a tree is wicked. A woman with eyes like those of an elephant is no good.

113. A woman blind in the left eye is libidinous and one blind in the right eye is barren. A woman with honey-tawny eyes enjoys plenty of wealth and grains.

114. If the eyelashes are well-knit, glossy, dark-coloured and subtle, the woman is fortunate. If they are brown-coloured, thick and sparse, the woman is worthy of censure.*

115. If the eyebrows are circular, glossy, dark and not closely knit, they are praiseworthy. The hairs should be soft and the eyebrows should have the shape of a bow.

* Sixty limbs covered—Comm.

116. They are not praise-worthy, if the hairs are rough, large, scattered or straight, if they group together or if the hairs are long and tawny-coloured.

117. Long ears with splendid circular curls bestow happiness and auspiciousness. Those without curls, those that are sinewy, crooked and thin are worthy of censure.

118. The forehead should be three Aṅgulas broad in a woman. There should not be sinews or hairs. It should resemble the crescent moon. It should not be depressed. Such a forehead is the cause of good health.

119. If the lines like Svastika are clear in the forehead, the woman will enjoy the prosperity of a kingdom. If the forehead is prominent, the woman certainly kills her husband's brother.

120. If it is hairy and sinewy and very high the woman is sickly.

121. The middle part of the head should be straight. It is praiseworthy then.

The head lifted up is praiseworthy. If a woman has a head resembling the forehead of an elephant, it indicates conjugal bliss and prosperity as evidenced by her behaviour.

122. A woman with very big head becomes a widow. One with a long head becomes a whore. One with a broad and big head becomes the victim of misfortune.

123. Hairs having the lustre of a swarm of bees, subtle, glossy and tender, curled and bent slightly at the tips are very splendid.

124. Rough hairs, hairs split at the tips, sparesly grown hairs, tawny-coloured, light and rough hairs cause misery, poverty and bondage*.

125. A mosquito-like freckle between the eyebrows or on the forehead indicates acquisition of a kingdom. Such a freckle on the left check, red in colour insures delicious food to the woman.

126-129. A mole or a spot on the bosom is the cause of conjugal bliss.

If there are red moles or spots on the right breast of a woman, she gives birth to four girls and three sons.

* Sixty-six limbs described—Comm.

If there is a red mole or spot on the left breast of a woman, she gives birth to a son and then becomes a widow.

If there is a mole on the right side of the private parts of a woman she will become wife of a king or she will give birth to a son who will become a king.

A mosquito-like red freckle at the tip of the nose occurs only in a queen.

130. The same, black in colour, occurs in an unchaste woman who kills her husband. A mole, freckle or spot beneath the navel is auspicious.

131-134. A freckle, mole or spot around the ankle causes poverty.

If one of these three occurs on the hand, ear, cheek or neck on the left side, it bestows a son in the womb.

Due to a trident-like mark on the forehead caused by the creator himself, a woman shall be the leader of thousands of women.

If a woman in sleep gnashes her teeth noisily, she is not praiseworthy even if she has all good features. A woman who babbles something in sleep is also like that.

A clockwise curl on the hand is righteous. An anticlockwise one is not splendid.

135. A clockwise curl of hairs round the navel, ear, or chest is praised. A clockwise curl to the right of the backbone is conducive to happiness.

136. A clockwise circular curl like that in the navel, in the middle of the back, causes increase in long-lived sons. A clockwise curl can be seen above the vulva of the wife of a king.

137. If the curl resembles a cart, it accords many children and happiness.

If that curl goes up to the tip skirting the private parts, it causes death of children.

138. Two clockwise curls on the back skirting the side of the belly, are not splendid. With one of them the woman kills her husband, with the other she becomes a libidinous wanton.

139. A clockwise curl on the neck is the cause of misery and widowhood. The same on the parting of the hair or on the forehead should be cautiously avoided.

140. If there is a curl of hairs, clockwise or anticlockwise, in the middle of the back of the neck, the woman will kill the

husband within a year.

141. If there is one anticlockwise curl on the head or two on the left side, the woman will kill the husband within ten days. That is to be avoided by sensible persons.

142. A woman with a curl of hair on the hip becomes a whore. A woman with a curl of hair in the navel is very chaste. One with a curl on the back becomes the murderess of her husband or a prostitute.

Skanda said:

143. A woman of bad conduct is the worst of persons of evil characteristics, even if she may possess good marks.

A chaste woman is one with all good marks, even if she has none (on her person).

144. It is only due to the blessings of Viśveśa, that one gets a wife of excellent characteristics, good manners and conduct and one who is under one's control or one who considers her husband as her deity.

145. Those women by whom *Suvāsinīs* (women with husbands alive) were adorned in the previous birth with various ornaments, become beautiful (in this birth).

146. Those by whom (their) bodies were destroyed or abandoned in excellent Tīrthas are reborn with excellent marks and perfect beauty.

147. Those by whom the Mother of the worlds was adored, become good-conducted women with husbands under control like the wife of Mṛḍa (i.e., Goddess Umā).

148. To the fawn-eyed women of good conduct, having their husbands under their control, heaven and salvation are here alone. It is the result of the excellent characteristics.

149. Young women, through their good conduct and excellent characteristics, make their husbands long-lived and cause of delight, even if they were originally destined to be short-lived.

150. Hence wise people should marry only women of excellent characteristics after carefully examining all the characteristics at the outset, after rejecting women of evil characteristics.

151. Characteristics have been described by me for the happiness of householders. O Pot-born One, I shall describe the various types of marriages also.

CHAPTER THIRTYEIGHT

The Characteristics of Women (continued)

Skanda said:

1. Marriages are of eight types, viz. (1) Brāhma, (2) Daiva, (3) Ārṣa, (4) Prājāpatya, (5) Āsura, (6) Gāndharva, (7) Rākṣasa and (8) Paiśāca which is said to be the eighth.

2. A groom is invited and a bride well-adorned is given over to him. This is called *Brāhma*. The son born of them sanctifies twenty-one generations.

3. A bride is given to a Ṛtvik presiding over a Yajña. It is called *Daiva*. The son born to them redeems fourteen generations. The bride is given over after taking two cows from the bridegroom. This is *Ārṣa*. The son born to them redeems six generations.

4. The bride is given to the seeker after saying "Both of you together carry on the performance of pious acts." This is *Prājāpatya* form of marriage. The son born of them sanctifies six generations.

5. These four types of marriage are sacred in the case of Brāhmaṇas. In *Āsura* marriage a bride is bought through money. The *Gāndharva* type is based on mutual love.

6. Marriage involving forcible kidnapping of the bride is called *Rākṣasa*. This is censured by good people. Abduction of a girl through fraud is called *Paiśāca*. This eighth type of marriage is also censured.

7. Generally speaking, the marriages of the types of Gāndharva, Āsura and Rākṣasa are in vogue among Kṣatriyas and Vaiśyas. The eighth one is the most heinous one. It is adopted by sinful persons.

8. At the time of marriage, a bride of the same caste as that of bridegroom should hold the hand (of the groom). An arrow held by the groom is caught by a Kṣatriya girl, if the groom is not of the same caste. A goad is similarly caught by a Vaiśya girl and the tip of the cloth is caught by a Śūdra girl.

9. This injunction regarding couples of different castes occurs in the Smṛtis and is followed during marriages. All the couples of the same caste hold the hands. This is the rule.

10. Righteous and pious children living upto a hundred years are born of righteous marriages. Unfortunate, poor and short-lived children are born of unrighteous wedlock.

11. This is a greatest pious act on the part of householders that they should indulge in sexual intercourse on specific days after menstruation, or in view of the boon received by women, he should approach her whenever desire overpowers (her).

12. Intercourse during day time very much curtails the extent of the life of men. A day of Śrāddha and all the Parvan days (i.e., new-moon, full-moon, Saṅkrānti etc.) should be avoided by a sensible man.

13. One who indulges in co-habitation during those days due to delusion falls from the highest piety.

14. A person who approaches his wife only on the specific days after menstruation and who is attached only to his wife, should be known as a perpetual Brahmacārī (celibate) and a good householder.

15. There are sixteen nights in the menstrual period. Four of them are prohibited ones. Of the rest the even ones cause the conception of sons and the odd ones that of daughters.

16. Avoiding a lunar eclipse day, Maghā star and the star of which Pūṣan is the deity, a householder should remain pure in mind and enjoy his wife on the days of the stars with masculine names (Śravaṇa, Hasta, Punarvasu, Mūla, Puṣya and Mṛgaśīrṣa). The woman shall give birth to a pure son who will get all the aims of the man fulfilled.

17. Offer of a pair of cows in the Ārṣa type of marriage is not something praiseworthy. Even the least amount of money offered to the parents of the bride causes the sin of selling the bride.

18. One who sells his children (i.e., raises money by that act) will go to the hell Viṭkṛmibhojana. (Persons in this hell feed on faeces and worms) for the period of a Kalpa. Hence the father should not make use of even the minutest of the money of his daughter.

19. Those kinsmen who make use of the wealth of the bride out of delusion, do fall into the hell. So also do their ancestors.

20. The delighted Mahālakṣmī shall stay along with Dānavāri (the foe of demons i.e., Lord Viṣṇu) in the place where woman becomes delighted and satisfied with her husband and where husband is satisfied with wife.

21. The following are the causes of downfall in the family (of a Brāhmaṇa): practicc of trade, service to the king, not teaching the Vedas, omissions in the sacred rites and wrong marriage.

22. A householder should perform everyday the Gṛhya Karmas, the Pañcayajña rites and the daily cooking work in the Vaivāhika (pertaining to the marriage rite) fire.

23. Everyday the householder has to perform five Sūnākarmas (acts involving violence). The Sūnās or things involving violence are: (1) Kaṇḍanī (pounding with wooden mortar and pestle), (2) Peṣaṇī (use of the grinding stone), (3) Cullī (oven), (4) Udakuṁbha (water pot), and (5) Mārjanī (act of sweeping with a broom).

24. The five Yajñas prescribed are the means of eradication of the five Sūnās. They are conducive to increase in the welfare of the householder.

25. The five Yajñas are: (1) *Brahmayajña* or teaching of the Vedas, (2) *Pitṛyajña* i.e., the offering of oblation to the Pitṛs, (3) *Daivayajña* i.e., *Homa,* (4) *Bhūtayajña* or oblation to the spirits and living beings, and (5) *Nṛyajña* or worship of guests.

26. A householder with a desire to propitiate the Pitṛs should perform Śrāddha everyday with cooked food, water, milk, bulbous roots or fruits.

27. After honouring duly a deserving mendicant by giving him alms in accordance with the injunctions, one gets the benefit resulting from the gift of cows.

28. Offering cast into fire kindled with penance, learning and sacrificial twigs, redeems one from clusters of obstacles and the ocean of sins very difficult to cross.

29. If a guest not duly honoured goes away disappointed, the householder instantly comes out of, i.e. loses, all his merits accumulated ever since his birth.

30. To the satisfaction of a guest, these should be offered: consoling words, ground for resting down, grass and water.

31. A householder regularly eating another man's cooked food shall become a pet animal of that man after death, because the man who makes gift of cooked food takes away the *Śreyas* (everything that is good) of one who nourishes himself on another man's food.

32. A guest who visits in the evening, at the time of sunset, should be assiduously honoured. If he goes away elsewhere on not being duly honoured, he transfers to him (the householder) much of his sins and demerits.

33. One who partakes of the food remaining after the guest has been fed, enjoys longevity and wealth. A householder who eats discarding a guest, becomes a sinner.

34. One who arrives at the conclusion of the Vaiśvadeva rite or at sunset, is said to be (the true) guest and not one who comes before time or one who has been seen before.

35. When a Brāhmaṇa householder holds the vessel of oblation, if another guest arrives, that oblation need not be given. He should offer cooked rice in accordance with his capacity.

36. Small boys, married women staying in their household, pregnant women, and persons acutely sick are to be fed even before guests. There is nothing to hesitate in this matter.

37. A householder consumes *Amṛta* (nectar) if he takes food after feeding Pitṛs, Devas and human beings. One who cooks merely for oneself incurs sins. He fills his own belly.

38. A householder himself should perform the midday Vaiśvadeva. His wife should offer the evening oblation with ready-cooked food without uttering the Mantras.

39. In a householder's life, this is called *Sāyantana Vaiśvadeva*. In this manner Vaiśvadeva should be performed both in the morning and in the evening assiduously.

40. All those Brāhmaṇas should be known as Śūdras, even if they have learned the Vedas, if they are devoid of Vaiśvadeva and do not practise hospitality.

41. Those base Brāhmaṇas who take food without performing Vaiśvadeva rite, will become deprived of food in this world. Then they are reborn as crows.

42. A householder should always perform his duty as laid down in the Vedas. If he assiduously performs them as his capacity allows, he shall attain the greatest goal of the good.

43. In oil, sin resides during the sixth and eighth lunar days (i.e., no oil should be used on these days). In flesh (meat) it resides always. In the vulva and the razor, it resides on the fourteenth and fifteenth days (i.e., on these days one should not shave oneself or indulge in sexual intercourse).

44. One should not see the Sun as he rises or as he sets, when he blazes in the middle of the sky, when he is eclipsed or when he is reflected in water.

45. One should not look at one's own reflection (in the mirror etc.) frequently; one shall not run quickly when it rains; one should not transgress the rope with which a calf is tethered; one should not enter water in nude state.

46-47. While passing by these, one should go clockwise: a temple, a Brāhmaṇa, a cow, honey, ghee, Gopīcandana etc., the eldest in the community, an old man, learned men, a sage, a holy fig tree, a tree that is usually worshipped, the preceptor, a pot full of water, cooked food, curd and white mustard.

48. One should not indulge in love-play with a woman in her monthly course; one should not take food in the company of one's own wife; one should not take food wearing a single cloth nor should one be seated in an excessively elevated seat etc. while taking food.

49. An excellent Brāhmaṇa desirous of brilliance should not watch a woman (wife) taking food. One should not eat cooked food (from new harvest) without propitiating Pitṛs or Devas.

50-54. One who is desirous of long life should not eat sweets and meat. One should not pass urine near a cowpen, or on an anthill or on ash, nor in pits where there are living beings. One should not pass urine walking or standing.

One shall neither pass urine nor evacuate the bowels facing cows, Brāhmaṇas, the sun, wind, fire, the moon, stars, water or elderly persons.

One should be silent when passing urine or evacuating the bowels. The head should be covered with a cloth. The ground should be covered with clods of earth, twigs, leaves, grass etc.

During night in a shady place or dark corner, during day when there is panic or danger to life, one should face and sit as is convenient to one and evacuate the bowels.

One should not blow against a fire. One should not stare

at a naked women.

55. One should not warm the feet over fire nor cast impure things into it. One should not injure living beings. One should not take food during dawn or dusk.

56. One should not sleep during dusk nor should keep the head towards the west or north. One desirous of living for a long time should not spit, pass urine or evacuate the bowels, into waters.

57. One should not make a mention of suckling cow; one should not point out the rainbow; one should not sleep anywhere alone; one should not waken (an elderly person) lying down.

58. One should not travel along the road alone; one should not drink water with joined palms. One should not eat oil cake etc. after the essence has been taken out during day time; one should not eat curd during night.

59. One should not be in conversation with a woman in her monthly course; one should not eat till complete satisfaction (i.e., bellyful) during nights; one should not be too fond of music and musical instruments; one should not get the feet washed in a bell-metal vessel.

60. If a man devoid of wisdom partakes of a Śrāddha, he does not gain the benefit; the partaker shall become a sinner.

61. One should not wear the cloth worn by others or their shoes; one should not sit in a place destroyed by fire.

62. One desirous of living for a long time should avoid riding on cows (bulls), the smoke from (a buring) dead body, crossing a river by swimming, the morning sunshine and sleeping during day time.

63. After taking bath, one should not scrub the body with the hand or the cloth worn at the time of taking bath; one should not unloose the tuft (of hair) on the path; one should not shake the hand or the hands; one should not drag a seat by means of the foot.

64. One should never pare or uproot hair or nail with one's teeth. One should avoid cutting of the nails, or grass with one's nails.

65. One should assiduously avoid that activity which is not conducive to auspiciousness whether to one's own house or another's. One should not enter otherwise than through

the regular door.

66. One should not play with dice; one should not sit together with sick persons or with violaters of piety; one should not lie down anywhere naked; no householder should take food on the palm of the hand.

67. If one takes food after washing the hands and feet and rinsing the mouth, one shall live for a long time; one should not go to sleep with wet feet; one shall not go anywhere in an *Ucchiṣṭa* state (i.e., without washing, after taking food).

68. No Brāhmaṇa should take food, drink any beverage or perform Japa while lying on bed; one should not perform *Ācamana* rite with shoes on, nor should one drink water flowing in currents.

69. No one desirous of welfare should eat in evening edibles made of gingelly seeds. One should not look at faeces or urine; no one should touch the head in an *Ucchiṣṭa* state.

70. One should not step on husks, burning coal, ash, hair or potsherd. Association with fallen people is conducive only to downfall.

71. A Brāhmaṇa should not at all recite a Vedic Mantra to a Śūdra. (If it is recited) the Brāhmaṇa loses his Brāhmaṇahood and the Śūdra loses his piety.

72. If a Śūdra begins imparting instruction in righteousness, it acts contrary to his own welfare. Serving the twice-born is considered as the greatest duty of Śūdras.

73. Scratching the head with both the hands is not considered auspicious; so also is the beating (the breast while) lamenting as well as plucking the hairs.

74. Accepting monetary gifts from a greedy king not following the injunctions of the sacred scriptures, a Brāhmaṇa falls into hell along with the members of his family up to twenty-one generations.

75. *Anadhyāya* (prohibition of Vedic study) has been proclaimed when there is untimely thunder, when there is a dust storm, during rainy season, when there is a loud report of violent gust of wind, and during nights.

76. When there occurs fall of meteors, earthquake, preternatural red glow in the horizons, at dead of night, during dusk and dawn, in the vicinity of a Śūdra or an irreligious

person, impurity due to birth and death to a king and during eclipse (there shall be no Vedic study).

77-79. During the new moon, the Aṣṭakas (7th, 8th, and 9th, lunar days), Caturdaśī (14th lunar day), after having partaken of Śrāddha, during the first lunar day, during the full-moon, when an elephant or camel crosses the path, when asses, camels or jackals cry, when they make noise together, Upākarama day, Utsarga day, while taking a voyage in a boat or raft in water, after learning the Āraṇyaka and on hearing the sound of an arrow or Sāman hymn (and piteous cry—Comm.)—in the course of these *Anadhyāya* days a Brāhmaṇa should never study the Vedas.

80. A Brāhmaṇa should not study the Vedas when there are disturbances created by frogs, mice, dogs, serpents and ichneumons. A householder shall remain celibate (i.e., avoid sex) on eighth, fourteenth and fifteenth lunar days.

81. Approaching another man's wife affects longevity. Hence it should be abstained at all costs. So also doing service to enemies.

82. One should not under-estimate oneself when the early fortunes leave one, because neither prosperity nor learning can be difficult of acquiring to those who always endeavour.

83. O Pot-born Sage, one should speak the truth; one should speak pleasing words but should not speak the truth if it is unpleasant. One should never speak agreeable untruths. This is the Dharma.

84. One should always speak auspicious things; one should always think about auspicious things; here in this world, one should always associate with auspicious ones and not with inauspicious ones.

85. An intelligent man should never offend those deficient in physical charm, wealth and nobility of birth. A man physically defiled, should not stare at the moon, the sun or luminaries.

86. One should control and avoid impetuosity of words, harshness of the tongue and agitation of the mind. One should keep off from a long distance the wealth acquired through bribery, gaming, carrying messages or extortion.

87. One should never touch a cow, a Brāhmaṇa and fire with hands unwashed after eating, unless one is ill. One should

never touch one's sense-organs without any adequate reason.

88. One becomes impure by touching the hairs of the private parts, waste water with which feet are washed, urine, (the remnant of) food and water eaten or drunk by another person.

89. One should cast away to a long distance spittings and phlegm.

By muttering (reciting) the Vedas day and night and by repeating Vedic passages day and night and by resorting to rules of cleanliness and good habit and through an intellect that is never harmful to others, a Brāhmaṇa shall be able to remember the previous birth.

90. One should promptly make obeisance to old men and give up one's own seat for their sake. He should keep the neck (Comm.) bent down. He should thus follow them.

91. One should never speak disparagingly of Śrutis, Brāhmaṇas, Devas, kings, saints, ascetics, and chaste women.

92. One should not eulogize human beings. One should not under-value oneself; one should not discard what is given unsolicited (*or* one should not drive away a person who is ready to exert himself) nor should one utter words divulging the secrets of others.

93. A person may prosper in the beginning through impiety and may even conquer enemies. But after gaining welfare all-round, he will perish along with his family.

94. One should take bath in a pond etc. dug by others after taking out (at least) five lumps of clay therefrom. If he does not do so, he shall have to incur a fourth of the sins of the person who has dug it up.

95. After obtaining a deserving person if any amount of wealth is given away with great faith, with due care for the place, time and the injunctions, that (good act) will be conducive to infinite benefit.

96. A person who gifts away plots of land shall become an emperor; persons who gift away cooked food will be happy everywhere; a donor of water will be always satisfied; and one who gifts away silver shall become handsome.

97. One who gifts away lamps shall become clear-visioned; one who presents cows (as *dāna*) attains the world of Aryaman; a person who makes gift of gold shall be long-lived; and one

who makes a gift of gingelly seeds shall have good progeny.

98. One who offers houses as a gift becomes the owner of a very lofty mansion; one who makes a gift of garments attains the lunar world; one who makes a gift of horses gets divine vehicles; and one who gives away, as *dāna*, bulls becomes prosperous.

99. A person who offers a palanquin (as a gift) gets a good wife; a person who makes a gift of excellent bedsteads becomes prosperous always with plenty of grain; and a person offering freedom from fear becomes a lord.

100. A person who makes a gift of Brahma (i.e., Veda) is one who performs a sacrifice, the goal of which is Brahmā's world; a person who makes the gift of Brahma is considered one who donates everything. A person who finds out some means of handing over (imparting) Brahma is also one like him.

101. He who receives gifts with faith and he who gives away with faith, both of them will get heaven. (But) if bereft of faith, one falls very low.

102. Yajña perishes due to falsehood; the power of penance perishes due to arrogance. Munificence in gifts perishes due to self-glorification about the same; span of life becomes reduced by slandering a Brāhmaṇa.

103. All these things offered to one without being requested should be accepted even from a base person: scents, flowers, Kuśa grass, bed, greens, meat, milk, curd, jewels, fish, house, and grain.

104. Honey, water, fruit, root, fuel, freedom from fear, monetary gifts—all these things offered unsolicited should be accepted even from a lowly one.

105. Servants, barbers, cowherds, family friends, Ardhasīrins (ploughmen receiving half the crops for their labour)—all these belonging to the caste of Śūdras can be fed with cooked food. So also one who dedicates himself (a devotee).

106. A householder should get himself freed from indebtedness to the Devas, sages and Pitṛs in this manner. Thereafter, he should entrust his sons with everything connected with the house and himself be indifferent to them.

107. Or he should pursue knowledge in the house itself; or resort to Kāśī. Salvation is through perfect knowledge or

in the shrine of Viśveśa.

108. Whence can a person gain perfect knowledge in a single life? In Vārāṇasī liberation is assured only through the renunciation of the body there.

109. The body is sure to go away quickly today, or tomorrow or the day after or after more than a hundred years. If that happens in Kāśī, the man becomes immortal.

110. Vārāṇasī can be obtained always by one who strictly follows rules of good conduct. Hence a learned man should never transgress injunctions regarding good conduct.

111. On hearing this, Agastya said to the Six-faced Lord again: "Tell about Kāśī further, which one gets through good conduct.

112. O Skanda, what are those Liṅgas which bestow perfect knowledge at Kāśī. Describe this to me as I ask.

113. Without Kāśī I have no pleasure. With Kāśī I have no other things of interest. O Six-faced Lord, I am a puppet painted in picture without Kāśī.

114. I do not sleep. I am not keeping awake. I do not eat. I do not drink water. I drink the two-lettered nectar alone, named Kāśī."

115. On hearing these words uttered by Agastya, Skanda began to narrate the greatness of Kāśī (Avimukta).

CHAPTER THIRTYNINE

*Manifestation of the Lord of Avimukta**

Skanda said:

1. Listen, O glorious Agastya, to the sin-destroying narrative pertaining to Avimukta. It is the means of attaining the glory of permanent salvation and welfare.

2-3. The Supreme Brahman that has been revealed in the Vedas, which is devoid of Prapañca, indeterminate, has no diversity or fixed shape, is unmanifest and has both gross and subtle forms, has permeated this whole region, though it is omnipresent.

What else is there anywhere (beyond and outside it)? This is capable of liberating beings from bondage to the transmigratory world.

4-9. Listen to how Bhava (Lord Śiva) liberates (beings) here itself.

Śiva may liberate (beings) elsewhere with the help of great Yogic practice, great gifts made without any ulterior desire or by means of great austerities.

But in the process of liberation in the Kāśī shrine, Śiva does not seek the assistance of great Yogic practice, great liberal gifts, nor of long continuance of austerities. That is because he does not dissociates himself from Kāśī even during the greatest of calamities.

This alone is the great Yoga. There is another thing utilized here. The flower, fruit, leaf and water regularly offered unto the Lord of the Viśva with a good mental attitude, is the greatest of gifts, in this connection.

After taking bath in the nectar-like waters of Gaṅgā, if the

---

*Lakṣmīdhara, on the authority of the *Liṅga Purāṇa,* locates Avimukteśvara just to the north of Jñānavāpī, precisely where the mosque stands today and where Viśveśvara was previously located. Purāṇas and modern tradition in Vārāṇaśī regard Avimukteśvara as the *Guru* of Viśveśvara, whom the latter worshipped. 'Today, however, a trace of that Liṅga—an ancient fragment of stone hidden amidst three Muslim graves on the north side of Jñānavāpī, is there. On Māgha Śivarātri day, some flowers are sprinkled on it. Recently a Liṅga 'Avimukteśvara' has been established to the south-east corner of the present Viśvanātha Temple". (BCL, pp. 130-131)

devotee sits for a while steadily in the Muktimaṇḍapikā ('the pavilion of salvation'), this alone is the most excellent penance.

After duly honouring a Bhikṣu (mendicant, recluse) in Kāśī, if alms are given to him, it is a great meritorious act. *Tulāpuruṣa* (the gift of anything weighing as much as the donor-devotee) does not deserve even the sixteenth part of this.

10. If one closes one's eyes for a moment after thinking about Viśveśa in his heart on the right side of the Lord, this is most excellent Mahāyoga.

11. This alone is the fiercest penance if one subdues the fickleness of the sense-organs and disregards utterly hunger and thirst and stays in Kāśī.

12. If one takes food only at night on the fourteenth lunar day here, one obtains the benefit that one obtains elsewhere by performing *Cāndrāyaṇa Vrata* every month.

13. If one observes a single *Upavāsa* (fast) with great faith at Kāśī, one certainly gets the benefit of a month-long fast elsewhere.

14. Undoubtedly, by means of the fast on the eleventh lunar day at Kāśī one gets the great benefit mentioned as the result of *Cāturmāsya Vrata* elsewhere.

15. By performing fast on the Śivarātri day at Kāśī, one certainly gets the benefit through the avoidance of cooked food for six months elsewhere.

16. O sage, if one observes fast for three days at Kāśī one gets entirely the benefit an observer of holy vows gets by observing fasts for a year.

17. By drinking the water (of Gaṅgā) flowing in the northern direction at Kāśī, even if it be a mouthful, one obtains the benefit one gets elsewhere by drinking the water from the tips of Kuśa every month.

18. Who is competent enough to describe the unlimited greatness of Kāśī where Śiva whispers (a Mantra) into the ears of a creature about to die there?

19. Into the ear of the living being about to die, Śaṁbhu whispers that syllable on hearing which even the dead one becomes immortal.

20. Having gone to Mandara, Lord Śaṅkara frequently remembered the city of the enemy of Cupid, like you and yearned much to regain it and grieved over it.

Agastya said:

21. I was compelled to leave the city of Kāśī, O Lord, by the terrible Devas clever in achieving their own ends. Wherefore did Lord Hara leave it?

22. Is the Lord of Devas, wielding the Pināka bow, dependent upon others like me? Why did he leave Kāśikā, the heap of jewels of salvation?

Skanda said:

23. O sage born of Mitra and Varuṇa, I shall narrate the story how at the importunity of Brahmā, Sthāṇu abandoned Kāśī.

24. O sage, just as you were requested by the Devas for the sake of helping others, so also Rudra who is competent to protect his people was requested by Brahmā.

Agastya said:

25. O Six-faced One, how did Lord Rudra, the ocean of mercy, come to be requested by Druhiṇa (Brahmā)? What for was he requested? Tell me.

Skanda said:

26. Formerly, in Svāyaṁbhuva Manvantara, at the time of Padma Kalpa (when the world was conceived and created in the navel lotus of Lord Viṣṇu), O Brāhmaṇa, there was a drought that shook all the worlds and living beings.

27-28. This drought lasted sixty years. All the living beings were tormented by it. People took the way of life of sages, consuming fruits, roots etc., some staying near seashores, some staying near water-sheds on mountains and some staying in deep mountain gorges. The whole earth turned into wilderness without villages and *Kharvaṭas* (i.e., where villages and towns are settled at the foot of and on mountains).

29. There were only flesh-eaters in all the towns and cities. In the entire world, there were lofty trees licking the clouds (but were dry—*Comm.*).

30. Thieves were robbed by more powerful thieves here and there. All living beings saved their lives by sustaining themselves on meat.

31. When there was anarchy and chaos all over the world indicating great calamity, the endeavour at creation of the Creator became futile.

32. Due to the destruction of the created beings, the Creator of the universe (i.e., Brahmā) was greatly worried. When the population became depleted, Yajña and other rites got reduced.

33-39. When the rites were not in vogue, all the Yajñabhuks (Devas) became deficient in strength. Creator Brahmā became worried and began to ponder. Then he saw the excellent saintly king, the destroyer of enemies' cities, well-known by the name Ripuñjaya. With all sense-organs steady, he was performing penance in the great religious spot Avimukta. He was a scion of the family of Manu and seemed like the rising spirit of the Kṣatriyas. Then God Brahmā came to him and said with great respect, "O King Ripuñjaya of great intellect, you are the protector of the earth. Protect the earth along with the oceans, mountains and forests.

Vāsuki, the king of serpents, will give you as wife, the Nāga girl named Anaṅgamohinī whose ornaments are virtue and decency.

O great king, being satisfied with the way in which you govern the subjects, the Devas of heaven *(Divo Devāḥ)* will give (*dāsyanti*) you every now and then jewels and flowers.

Hence you will get the well-known epithet Divodāsa. O king, may you be endowed with divine power by my power."

40. On hearing the words of Brahmā, the excellent king eulogized him in diverse ways and spoke these words:

The King said:

41. O Grandfather of great intellect, the whole surface of the earth is full of people. How is it that the other kings are not asked? Why do you ask me alone?

Brahmā said:

42. When you justly govern the kingdom, the Lord will cause (adequate) rainfall. When a king becomes a sinner and indulges in vices, the Lord does not shower any rain.

The King said:

43. O Grandfather worthy of great esteem, you are capable of creating the three worlds. With my head bowed down, I receive your behest as a great favour from you.

44. I am desirous of submitting something. If you kindly do it for my sake, I shall govern the kingdom of the earth without a rival.

Brahmā said:

45. Out with it without delay, O king; regard it as carried out. Speak out what is in your mind, O king of powerful arms. There is nothing which cannot be given to you.

The King said:

46 If I am to be the lord of the earth, O Grandfather of all the worlds, let the Devas who are called Divisads ('residents of heaven') stay in heaven and not on the earth.

47. With the Devas staying in heaven and I remaining on the earth, the subjects will get happiness as the kingdom will be without rivals.

48-49. On being told "Let it be so" by the Creator of the world, Divodāsa announced with beating of wardrum: "Let the Devas proceed to heaven. Let not the Serpents come here. Let the men be peaceful and calm. Even as I govern the earth, let the Suras remain in their own places."

50. In the meantime, even as Brahmā bowed down to Viśveśa and was about to submit something, the Lord said to him:

51-52a. "O Lord of the worlds, do come. The Mountain named Mandara has come here from Kuśadvīpa. He is performing a very difficult penance. We both shall go to grant a boon to him who has been performing penance for a long time."

52b-53. After saying this, the Lord of Pārvatī got on to his bull and went to the place where Mandara was. He was accompanied by Nandi and Bhṛṅgi. The Bull-emblemed Lord, the god of Devas who was pleased within himself said thus:

54a. "Get up, Oh, get up, O excellent Mountain; welfare unto you. Speak out the boon you choose."

54b-59. On hearing (the words of) Maheśāna, the three-eyed lord of the Devas, the Mountain bowed down on the ground many times and submitted: "O Śaṁbhu, O sole storehouse of mercy unto those who bow down, O lord asssuming various bodies playfully, though you are omniscient, how is it that you do not know my desire. O saviour of those who seek refuge in you, O lord conversant with all the events, O delighter of the hearts of everyone, O omnipresent Śarva, O creator of everything! If a boon is to be given to me, a stone by nature, who am a suppliant and am highly pitiable, O lord, O annihilator of the distress of those who bow down, I then desire to have parity with Avimukta Kṣetra. Accompanied by Umā, O Lord, be pleased to stay on my head along with all your attendants and proceed to Kuśadvīpa. This is the boon I seek."

60. When Śaṁbhu, the bestower of everything to everyone tarried while pondering over (the grant of the boon), God Brahmā keeping his palms to his head out of reverence, came forward. Bowing down, he submitted to Śaṁbhu:

Brahmā said:

61. O Viśveśa, O Lord of the worlds, I have been engaged by your lordship who were pleased, (with the task) to create the four kinds of living beings.

62. With your permission I accomplished that task of creation with great effort. But due to the drought lasting over a period of sixty years, all the subjects of the earth perished.

63-64. There was a great chaos and anarchy. The universe experienced miserable plight. Thereupon, the saintly king named Ripuñjaya, born of the race of Manu, was crowned by me as the king to govern the subjects. That king of great penance and supreme power put forth a condition.

65. "If all the heaven-dwellers stay in heaven at your bidding and all the Serpents in the region of the Nāgas, then I shall rule the kingdom."

66. I too said "Let it be so." Let my words be made truthful. Thus, O storehouse of mercy, a boon too can be granted to Mandara.

67-73. Let that king have this desire fulfilled in order to protect the subjects.

After all, my suzerainty is only for two Ghaṭikās (of your reckoning). The same is the case with Śatakratu (Indra). Where do the men come under this reckoning since they wink (exist) but half a moment (of mine)?

Lord Hara who considered that Mandara was free from impurities and had beautiful caves, consented to it, thereby upholding the dignity of Brahmā.

Just as Kāśī bestows salvation always in the Jaṁbūdvīpa, so also for a long time that Mandara in Kuśadvīpa also became the bestower of salvation.

When the Lord was about to go to Mandara having diverse wonderful caves, he had established without the knowledge of Brahmā, his own Liṅga that constitutes one of his cosmic bodies in order to bestow all *Siddhis* on those who instal, to give the glory of salvation to all the creatures that die and to protect the shrine of all who steadfastly stay here.

This pilgrimage centre was not entirely abandoned by the Pināka—bearing Lord who had repaired to the Mandara Mountain. He had not abandoned it in the form of the Liṅga. Hence it is remembered as *Avimukta.*

74. This holy spot was glorified by the name *Ānandavana* formerly. But since this time it became well-known over the world by the name *Avimukta.*

75. The name *Avimukta* was of both the holy spot as well as of the Liṅga. By attaining these two, no one enters the womb again.

76. By visiting Avimukteśvara Liṅga in the holy spot of Avimukta, one shall certainly be liberated from all bondages of Karma.

77. All adore Viśveśa. Viśveśa, the creator of the universe, worships Avimukteśvara Liṅga that bestows salvation and worldly enjoyment.

78. Before this, no Liṅga of anyone was installed anywhere by anyone. Nor did anyone know what the shape of a Liṅga was.

79. Brahmā, Acyuta and others as well as the sages including Vasiṣṭha installed Liṅgas after seeing the shape and form of Avimukta.

80. The great Avimukteśvara is proclaimed as the primordial Liṅga. It was only afterwards that other Liṅgas came into existence in the world.

81. Even by hearing the name of Avimukteśa a mortal being becomes instantly rid of all sins acquired throughout the life. In this matter no reflection or pondering is necessary.

82. From far away if one just remembers the Liṅga Avimukteśvara, he becomes instantly rid of the sins committed in two births.

83. By visiting Avimukta (Liṅga) in the great holy spot Avimukta, one sheds off the sins of three births and becomes meritorious.

84. By touching Lord Avimukteśa, the sin committed in five births due to ignorance or the swerving from perfect knowledge, perishes, not otherwise.

85. By adoring the great Avimukteśvara Liṅga a man becomes blessed and contented. Thereafter he shall not take birth again.

86. One who eulogizes, bows down to and adores Avimukteśvara in the holy spot of Avimukta in accordance with his intellect and capacity, himself is eulogized, bowed to and adored.

87. This Liṅga is one without beginning. It is adored by Viśveśa himself. This Avimukteśvara Liṅga in Kāśī should be assiduously resorted to for the purpose of salvation.

88. There are many Liṅgas in the holy shrines (elsewhere). They come (here) on the fourteenth day in the dark half of the month of Māgha.

89. If one keeps awake in the presence of Avimukteśa on the fourteenth day in the dark half of Māgha, one attains the goal of a Yogin who is devoid of sleep perpetually.

90. The Liṅgas of different shrines that bestow all the four aims of human life serve Avimukteśa on the fourteenth day in the dark half of Māgha.

91. If a man holds the Vajra (thunderbolt) of devotion to Avimukta Liṅga, why should he be afraid of the mountain of sins committed by him. He should be bold and self-possessed.

92. Where is the great Liṅga Avimukta from which the four aims of human life come up? Where is the mountain of sins which is insignificant and which perishes the moment it is conceived?

93. They are deluded ones by whom the excellent Liṅga Avimukta has not been seen in the great holy spot Avimukta presided over by Viśveśa.

94. On seeing from afar a person who has visited Avimukta, Yama, the bearer of a baton, joins his palms in reverence and makes obeisance to him.

95. (*Defective verse*) Blessed is that eye wherewith Avimukta has been seen. Blessed are those hands that touch Avimukteśvara.

96. If one keeps himself pure and regularly performs Japa three times everyday, he shall obtain the benefit of one who dies in Kāśī though he may have actually died in a far-off place.

97. After seeing the great Avimukteśvara Liṅga one may go to another village (for some purpose). He shall fulfil his purpose quickly and return home safe and sound.

CHAPTER FORTY

Duties of a Householder

Skanda said:

1. The greatness of Avimukteśa has been described by me to you. What are you desirous of hearing further? I shall narrate it now.

Agastya said:

2. On repeatedly listening to the greatness of Avimukteśa my ears have become excellent. Yet I do not feel satiated.

3. Recount to me, O Ṣaṇmukha, how one will attain these two: Avimukteśvara Liṅga and the holy place Avimuktaka.

Skanda said:

4. Listen, O Pot-born One of great intelligence, I shall tell you how the attainment of Avimukta, the bestower of eternal bliss is possible.

5. A desired object is obtained through the power of meritorious acts. That meritoriousness shall be obtained by resorting to the Vedic path, O Brāhmaṇa.

6. Kali and Kāla are ready to strike, on seeing a loophole. O sage, they perish at the very contact of a person who resorts to the Vedic path.

7. In one doing what is prohibited and not doing what is prescribed, Kali and Kāla see a loophole and strike down that Brāhmaṇa.

8. Hence I shall tell you what things are prohibited. By avoiding them from afar, a man can prevent his fall in hell.

9. Onion, shit-thriving pigs, Śelu, garlic, carrot, Gopīyūṣa (milk of a cow before the lapse of ten days from calving), Taṇḍulīya (a grain growing in faecal rubbish) and mushrooms—all these are to be avoided.

10. One shall avoid *Vraścanas* (greens etc. growing even after being cut), exudations from trees, puddings, pies, fried Śaṣkuli and meat never consecrated to deities or Manes and the milk of a cow without a calf.

11. The milk of *Ekaśapha* (animals having no cloven hoofs), camel and sheep is to be avoided. One should not eat curds during the night nor butter during the day.

12. The following should not be eaten: birds like Ṭiṭṭibha, sparrow, swan, ruddygoose, stork and all flesh-eating birds, Sārasa, crane, cock and parrot.

13. One should not eat Jālapāda-swans, Khañjariṭas and those birds which sink down into the water and eat fishes. One who eats fish is no better than a flesh-eater. So one should avoid fishes in every respect.

14. Fishes like Pāṭhīna and Rohita have been recommended for *Havya* (food of gods) and *Kavya* (food of Manes). They can be taken in by regular meat-eaters. They can eat rabbit, porcupine and tortoise.

15. Śvāvit (porcupine) and Godhā (alligator) are good; so also all well-known animals and birds. Meat should be avoided assiduously by those who wish for longevity and heavenly bliss.

16. Killing of animals for the sake of Yajña is conducive to heavenly bliss. Not the other one. One should abandon all stale things utterly devoid of oiliness or ghee.

17. One who eats meat when threatened with danger to life, during Yajña, in Śrāddha, as a medicine, for pleasing a Brāhmaṇa without being over-tempted, cannot be blamed.

18. One who desires hunting as a means of sustenance

does not incur such a sin after death, as one who eats flesh after being over-tempted.

19. Animals, trees, deer and herbs have been created by Brahmā for the sake of Yajñas. A Brāhmaṇa who kills them is really *Ahimsaka* (non-killer). They too will attain splendid goal (after death).

20. Causing injury for the sake of Pitṛs, Devas and Yajñas and also for *Madhuparka* is no injury. Injury in other cases cannot be overcome (i.e., is a sin without remedy).

21. He who kills animals for self-nourishment is weak in knowledge and of evil conduct. He will never have happiness here or hereafter.

22. *Himsakas* (perpetrators of violence) are of eight kinds: (1) one who eats flesh, (2) one who permits it, (3) one who prepares it, (4) the buyer, (5) the seller, (6) the actual killer, (7) one who make a present of it, and (8) one who persuades others to kill.

23. A person may perform yearly horse-sacrifices for a hundred years. Another person may abstain from eating meat. Of these two, the latter is superior.

24. Another man should be seen in the same way as oneself by one who wishes for happiness. Happiness and misery are equally present in oneself and in others.

25. If happiness or the other one (to the contrary), is caused unto others, it will recoil on oneself afterwards.

26. Without pains or exertions money cannot be earned. How can one carry out holy rites without money? How can one have piety without holy rites? How can one get happiness without piety?

27. Happiness is desirable by all. That originates from Dharma. Hence Dharma should be performed assiduously by persons of all the four castes.

28. All rites for benefits in the other world should be performed by means of wealth acquired by legitimate means. Religious gifts must be duly made with devotion and faith to deserving persons at the proper time.

29. If one makes a gift to an undeserving person and does not follow the relevant injunction in this regard, then not only that (merit accruing from the) gift vanishes but also does his remaining Puṇya (merit).

30. What is given to relieve distress, to sustain the family and to repay debts, becomes *Akṣaya* (having everlasting benefit) both here and hereafter.

31. If one consecrates an orphan through Mauñjī, Pāṇigraha etc. (investing with sacred thread, celebrating the marriage etc.) by spending one's own money, his *Puṇya* is infinite indeed.

32. Neither through Agnihotra nor through Agniṣṭoma and other Makhas (sacrifices) can that merit be obtained by men that is acquired when a Brāhmaṇa is honoured.

33. He who gets the marriage of a helpless Brāhmaṇa celebrated and has accomplished his purpose, enjoys happiness here and he shall attain everlasting heavenly bliss.

34. If a virgin girl has her first menstruation in her father's house without her marriage being solemnised, her father should be known as a *Bhrūṇahā* ('destroyer of a foetus') and that girl a Vṛṣalī (Śūdra girl).

35. He who, out of delusion, marries her will be the husband of a Śūdra girl. He is an *Apāṅkteya* (not fit to sit in the same row as the others at the time of meals). The very conversation with him should be abandoned forever.

36. After knowing the fault of both, i.e., that of the girl and the groom, the father should perform their marriage (once again) afterwards. Otherwise the father is blameworthy.

37. Women are always pure. They do not get defiled by anything whatsoever. The monthly menstrual flow drives away their sins.

38. Women are enjoyed first by Suras, Soma, Gandharva and Vahni. Men enjoy them afterwards. They are not defiled by anything.

39. Soma gave women cleanliness; Pāvaka (Fire-god), purity above all. Gandharvas gave them auspicious speech. Therefore, women are always pure.

40. Agni enjoys a virgin at the time of the menstruation, the Moon when the (pubic) hair begin to grow and Gandharvas when the breasts begin to develop. Hence a girl is to be given in marriage before this.

41. A girl with hairs visible (before marriage is consecrated) kills her children; she with the breasts in developed form destroys the family; she who has menstruated destroys the father. Hence one should avoid all (such girls).

42. Hence one who is desirous of the benefit of gift of a virgin should give her in marriage before Agni and others enjoy her. If not, the giver does not enjoy any benefit; one who receives her in marriage falls down (incurs sin).

43. One who gives away a girl not enjoyed by Soma and others, attains the benefit of the religious gift. Giving her who has been enjoyed by Devas, the donor does not attain heavenly pleasures.

44. The wise do not condemn (as defiled) beds, seats, vehicles, Kuṇapa (a sword, or a blanket from Nepal—Comm.), the mouth of a woman, *Darbha* grass, sacrificial utensils.

45. A calf is pure at the time of the discharge of milk from the udder of the cow, a bird at the time when it causes a fruit to fall, women during sexual intercourse, and a dog when it catches a deer.

46. The mouth of goats and horses is pure; cows are pure at their backs; Brāhmaṇas are pure in their feet; and women are pure (in all parts of their person).

47. A beloved wife should not be abandoned even if she is raped or if she falls into the clutches of robbers. Abandoning her is not laid down (anywhere).

48. Copper becomes pure when sour (acidic) things are applied; brass becomes pure by using Bhasma (ash). A woman becomes pure through her menstruation and a river through the flow (of water).

49. A woman who does not even mentally think of another men enjoys pleasures with Umā and enjoys renown here in the world too.

50. The order of the guardians of a girl is: father, grandfather, brother, a member of the same family, mother, the man who formally gives her in marriage. If the preceding one is not available the succeeding one (is the guardian) naturally.

51. If the guardian does not give her in marriage, he incurs sin of slaughter of a foetus in every menstural cycle. If there is no one to give her in marriage, a girl should choose her own husband.

52. If a woman strays from the path of sexual purity, she shall be divested of all her rights and kept dirty and discarded from the bed. Of course, she should be given a morsel of food for sustenance.

53. If the lapse in morality is only mental, the woman becomes pure after menstruation. She is abandoned if she conceives, or kills the foetus or the husband or commits any other great sin.

54. A Śūdra takes a Śūdra girl for wife; a Vaiśya takes a Śūdra girl as well as a Vaiśya girl for wife; a Kṣatriya takes a Śūdra, a Vaiśya as well as a Kṣatriya girl for wife; and a Brāhmaṇa takes all the other three girls as well as a Brāhmaṇa girl.

55. By allowing a Śūdra woman to lie on his bed (i.e., marrying a Śūdra woman — Comm.) a Brāhmaṇa incurs downfall; by procreating a son of her, he swerves from the status of a Brāhmaṇa.

56. If the rites performed by him in connection with Yajñas, Śrāddhas or hospitality to guests are presided over by the Śūdra wife, Devas, etc. do not partake of it. He too shall not attain Svarga.

57. Close female relatives curse the household wherein they are not properly honoured (which takes place in such a Brāhmaṇā-Śūdra household). Thereby these households certainly perish as if struck down by Kṛtyās (female deities of destructive powers).

58. Hence Suvāsinīs (women with husbands living) should be propitiated through jewels, raiments and food by men desirous of prosperity and by welcoming them in the course of festivities.

59. Where women are happy due to ornaments, clothes and foodstuffs offered to them, deities rejoice there. All the holy rites become fruitful there.

60. At every step, there shall be prosperity in that household where the wife (woman) is fully satisfied with the husband and the husband is completely satisfied with the wife.

61. These five Yajñas are auspicious and splendid: *Āhuta*, *Huta*, *Prahuta*, *Prāśita* and *Brāhmahuta*.

62. Japa (Repetition of Mantras) is *Āhuta*; performance of Homa is *Huta*; oblations given to the Bhūtas constitute *Prahuta*; propitiation of Manes is *Prāśita*, and the adoration of Brāhmaṇas is *Brāhmahuta*.

63. A Brāhmaṇa regularly performing these five Yajñas is never faced with a disaster. By not performing these, he shall incur the sin of the five Sūnās (murders).

64. On meeting a Brāhmaṇa, one should enquire about his *Kuśala* (welfare); on meeting a Kṣatriya one should enquire about his *Anāmaya* (health, freedom from illness); on meeting a Vaiśya one should enquire about his *Sukha* (happiness); and on meeting a Śūdra one shall enquire about his *Santoṣa* (satisfaction).

65. Till the eighth year is completed a child is no better than a new-born baby. Till the *Upanayana* ceremony is performed, the child does not become defiled due to indiscriminate eating (prohibited food).

66. The proper sustenance of those people of the *Poṣya* group (i.e., worthy of being brought up and nourished) has both visible and invisible benefits. In case they are not maintained there shall be disaster. Hence they are to be assiduously sustained.

67. *Poṣyas* are nine: mother, father, wife of preceptor, one's own children, dependents, (preceptor), a casual visitor, regular guests and the sacred fire.

68. A man who is depended upon for subsistence by many people, lives in the real sense (of life). A man who fills his own belly should be regarded as dead though alive.

69. One with a desire for prosperity should make gifts unto the wretched, the helpless and the distinguished (scholars). Those who do not make liberal gifts are born as persons living upon other men's fortune.

70. A householder of good conduct, sharing what he has with others, one having kindness and perfect forbearance and a devotee of deities and guests is said to be pious and righteous.

71. A Brāhmaṇa who sleeps in the two middle Yāmas of the night (i.e., between 9.00 a.m. and 3.00 a.m.) and drinks the ghee that remains after Homa has been performed, never faces difficulties.

72-73. The following nine should always be practised at the visit of a guest by a householder: Enquiry after welfare (*Kuśala*) in speech, eyes, mind and face; standing up for wel-coming; greeting affectionately at the outset by words like "Welcome here"; *Upāsana* (making him sit near oneself or massaging his feet — Comm.), *Anuvrajyā* (following a few steps behind the guest at the time of departure). These acts which involve no expenditure are conducive to prosperity of a householder.

74-75a. Similarly the following nine should be practised involving a little expense: offering of seats, water for washing the feet, feeding within one's capacity, ground as bed (grass underneath the bed — Comm.), water for drinking, oil for bath and lights. These nine give *Siddhis* (powers) in the life of a householder.

75b-76. Similarly the following nine *Vikarmas* (ill actions) should be avoided by a householder: Backbiting, approaching other men's wives, injury, ruthlessness, falsehood, displeasing behaviour, hatred, arrogance and deceitfulness. These nine are obstacles in the path of heaven.

77-79. There are nine essential daily duties to be performed. They are: bath, Sandhyā prayers, *Japa, Homa,* study of the Vedas, worship of deities, Vaiśvadeva (oblation into fire before meal), receiving guests and the ninth one, libations to the Pitṛs.

O sage, listen to the nine things to be kept as secret and guarded: The star of nativity, sexual intercourse, Mantras (spells, secret counsels), interfamily feud, deception, span of life, monetary position, insult to prestige, and wife. These are not to be revealed at all.

80. These nine things can be revealed: secret sin, undespised thing or person, everything conducive to practical application, repayment of debts, one with the family, sale, purchase, giving away daughter (in marriage), perfection of good qualities. Nothing else should be revealed by anyone anywhere.

81. What is given to the following nine yields inexhaustible benefit: deserving persons, friends, humble ones, poor people, helpless ones, those who help others, mother, father and preceptors.

82. Futile indeed are these if given over to these nine: a garrulous one, a flatterer, a thief, a bad physician, a cheat, an outrageous one, a rogue, a wrestler, and a prisoner.

83-84. Even during emergency these nine things should never be given away: entire property if one has progeny, wife, those who seek refuge, short-term deposits, long-term deposits, pledged things, traditional avocation, dowry amount and a son. One who gives away these is a deluded soul. He can become pure only through expiatory rites.

85-86. By realizing these nine sets of nine, one shall achieve what is pleasing. I shall mention another set of nine that accords the pathway to heaven unto everyone: truthfulness, cleanliness, abstention from violence, forbearance, liberal-mindedness, mercy, mental control, non-stealing and control over the sense-organs. All these are means of piety (*Dharma*).

87. A householder who adopts these ninety things that illuminate the pathway to heaven and that are approved by good persons and so are holy, is never faced with difficulties.

88. Everywhere one will get high estimation if he has the following: humility, a wife, a son, a brother, a friend, a servant, dependents and (his) tongue (sweet speech).

89. The following six things defile women: drinking (wine), association with wicked persons, separation from the husband, wandering, over-sleeping and staying in another's house.

90. He who collects (purchases) foodgrains cheap and sells dearly (with high rates), is a usurer. No one should partake of his food.

91. On seeing a buffalo-keeper (*Māhiṣika*)* in the beginning, husband of a Śūdra woman (Vṛṣalī)* in the middle and a usurer at the end (at the time of the Śrāddha), Manes are disappointed and they go away.

92. (Explanation of the above two words in another way) The woman devoid of chastity is called *Mahiṣī*. He who loves that wicked woman is called *Māhiṣika*.

93. She who casts off her Vṛṣa (husband) and loves another *Vṛṣa*, should be known as *Vṛṣalī* and not a Śūdra woman (alone).

94. The Manes partake of the food offerings as long as the cooked rice is hot, people eat silently and the good qualities of the *Havis* (food offering) are not (boastfully) described.

95. When a man well-versed in the Vedas and possessing learning and humility comes to the house (as a guest), all the medicinal herbs sport about (saying) "We will attain the highest state."

96. If the food is offered to a man who is ignorant of the Vedas, who is unclean, who does not practise good conduct or holy vows and who is fallen, the food begins to lament,

* These are apparent meanings; for the real meanings see the next two verses.

"What sin has been committed by me?"

97. If a man (guest) is able to digest the food going into his belly due to the Vedic study and practice, he redeems ten previous generations and ten succeeding generations (of the donor).

98. Women are not to be shaven completely. One should not follow cows (as an avocation). One should not stay in a cowpen during the night. One should not utter Vedic passages (at night, or in a cowpen).

99. *Muṇḍana* (shaving the head) of women shall be done thus: Lifting up the whole of the tress cut off to a length of two *Aṅgulas* (an Aṅgula is a little less than two centimeters).

100. A king, or a prince or a Brāhmaṇa of much learning should not be subjected to tonsure. Some other expiatory rite should be fixed.

101. For the preservation of the hairs, twice the usual Vrata should be prescribed and twice the ordinary *Dakṣiṇā* should be given to a Brāhmaṇa who has mastered the Vedas.

102. If a man considers himself a Gṛhastha (householder) without taking up the marital fire, his food should not be eaten. He is called a *Vṛthāpāka* ('one with futile cooking').

103. If the younger brother takes up a wife and gets initiated on Agnihotra even as the elder brother is awaiting it, he should be known as *Parivettṛ* and the elder brother becomes *Parivitti*.

104. In such a case all the five, namely *Parivitti, Parivettṛ*, the bride acting as instrumental (in this sinful act), the person who gave her in marriage and the priest who presided over the rite shall go to hell.

105. (If the elder brother happens to be) impotent, in exile, dumb, a sluggish one, one who has renounced the world, humpback, dwarf or a fallen one, there is no harm in *Parivedana* ('supersession in marriage etc.').

106. The Brāhmaṇa who sells the Vedas incurs as many Bhrūṇahatyā ('killing a foetus') sins as the Vedic syllables he has utilized for monetary gain.

107. If a person who has become a recluse has sexual intercourse thereafter, he is born as a worm in faeces for sixty thousand years.

108. The following sins make even the most brilliant one fall:

the food of a Śūdra, association with Śūdras, occupying the same seat as a Śūdra and the acquisition of learning from a Śūdra.

109. Ignorant Brāhmaṇas who fetch donations from a Śūdra and cook that for Brāhmaṇas, being deprived of the lustre of Brāhmaṇahood, go to a terrible hell.

110. If Honey, Phāṇita (raw sugar), greens, milk products, salt and ghee are offered into the hand and taken in, (the expiatory rite is) fasting for a day.

111. Hand-to-hand offering of oils, salt, pickles etc. does not benefit the donor and one who eats them incurs sin.

112. If cooked food is offered in an iron vessel, the giver shall go to hell and the person who eats it eats it like faeces.

113. Cleaning the teeth with finger (i.e., index finger), (handling) only salt and eating clay are on a par with eating cow's flesh.

114. Water, milk pudding, alms, ghee and salt should not be accepted if offered hand-to-hand because it is on a par with eating cow's flesh.

115. If a foolish one sits in front and the meritorious one sit far off, the gift is to be made to the meritorious one. There is no (harm) due to non-observance of precedence in the case of a fool.

116. If a Brāhmaṇa is bereft of the study of the Vedas, there is no harm in transgressing the rule of precedence in favour of Brāhmaṇas. An oblation is not offered in ash, leaving off blazing (fire).

117. In the matter of taking food and offering of monetary gifts, if anyone disregards the precedence in favour of a Brāhmaṇa well-versed in the Vedas and seated nearby, it shall burn the family till the seventh generation.

118. One should treat these Brāhmaṇas on a par with Śūdras: those who tend cows, traders, craftsmen, actors, messengers and usurers.

119. Families come to ruin quickly by sharing the money of gods (i.e., in a temple), by misappropriating a Brāhmaṇa's property and by disregarding the precedence in favour of a Brāhmaṇa.

120. If anyone says "Do not give", in regard to cows, fires and Brāhmaṇas, he shall be born in a hundred species of brutes and then is born among Cāṇḍālas.

121. If what (e.g. a gift) is promised orally but is not carried out in practice, it should be deemed a debt whose repayment becomes a duty in this world and in the other world.

122. One will be Vighasāśin ('one who eats leavings of food') always or Amṛtabhojana ('having nectar for food'). Remnants of Yajña are Amṛta and remnants of what is eaten is *Vighasa.*

123. If the cloth has fallen down from the left shoulder and has come to rest near the navel, the man becomes *Ekavāsāḥ* ('wearer of one cloth'). One should exclude him from the rites of gods and Manes.

124. If an excellent Brāhmaṇa, after taking bath, performs *Tarpaṇa* (water libation) with water, he obtains the entire benefit of the rites of Pitṛyajña thereby.

125. If anyone, after taking food, washes his hands and then swallows the mouthful of water, he injures and destroys all the three, viz. the divine rite, the rite of the Manes and his own soul.

126. One should perform *Cāndrāyaṇa* rite by way of expiation, after partaking of food in the following cases: group feeding, food cooked or offered by courtezans, food at the place of village priest and food at the celebration (of *Sīmanta*) at the time of the first confinement of women.

127. One should perform the expiatory rite of *Cāndrāyaṇa* after taking food at the place of a wicked man, where no Brāhmaṇa has taken food in the course of a fortnight or a month.

128. No *Sūtaka* (i.e., pollution due to births and deaths of relatives) need be observed in the case of Sattrins (those who take part in long-drawn Yajñas), Dīkṣitas (who have become initiated), ascetics, religious students and those who perform the rites of Ṛtviks.

129. Bath is prescribed in the case of indigestion, vomiting, getting shaved, indulgence in sexual intercourse, seeing a bad dream and touching a wicked person.

130. One should take bath along with one's clothes after touching a Caitya-vṛkṣa (tree worshipped by villagers), a funeral pyre, a sacrificial post, one who partakes of *Śivanirmālya* (leavings of the food offerings to Śiva) and one who sells the Vedas.

131. One should leave footwear out of the chamber of sacrificial

fire, cowpens, in the presence of the Devas and Brāhmaṇas, while reciting Vedic Mantras, while drinking and while eating.

132. The grain on a threshing floor and field, the water in wells and tanks and the water in a cowpen can be accepted from a prohibited one.

133. It is the way of eating of demons, if one covers the head while taking food, if one takes food facing south and if one takes food with shoes on.

134. Yātudhānas, Piśācas, Rākṣasas and men of ruthless activities take away the essence of the food not encircled by Maṇḍala (mystic drawing).

135. All the Suras including Brahmā, all the great sages including Vasiṣṭha, derive livelihood from Maṇḍala. Hence one should make the Maṇḍala.

136. The Maṇḍala to be made by a Brāhmaṇa is square. That by a Kṣatriya is a triangle and that by a Vaiśya is a circle. It is laid down that sprinkling of water should be done in the case of a Śūdra.

137. One should not take food (placing the plate) on the lap, nor in hand, nor in soiled garment, nor on seat, nor on bed. One should not take food when got muddy.

138. The Brāhmaṇas are seated in the chariots of Dharmaśāstras. They hold the sword of the Vedas. Even that which they utter playfully is remembered as the greatest Dharma.

139. One desirous of piety and virtue should not eat food mixed with parched grain and curds at night. If one eats so, one shall become impious and is also afflicted with ailments.

140. A Brāhmaṇa should perform *Kṛcchra Cāndrāyaṇa* (expiatory rite) after giving (in case he gives) with bare hands Phāṇita, milk, water, salt, and gruel.

141. A person conversant with Dharma who makes gifts of scents, ornaments and garlands shall always be delighted and fragrant, wherever he happens to be.

142. One should cast away a cloth dyed in indigo. It is not harmful in a bed intended for sexual intercourse with women.

143. By growing Nīlī plants, by selling them and by sustaining himself thereby, a Brāhmaṇa becomes impure. He shall become pure by observing three Kṛcchra rites.

144. He who wears a cloth dyed with Nīlī does not attain the benefit of holy ablution, gifts, penance, homas, study of

Vedas, libation to the Manes and the great Yajñas.

145. If a Brāhmaṇa wears a cloth dyed in Nīlī, he shall certainly reside in hell for as many (years) as there are threads in the cloth.

146. After fasting for a day and a night, he becomes pure by taking in *Pañcagavya*.

147. If food is offered on a cloth dyed in Nīlī, the person who eats it, eats faeces, as it were, and the person who offers it shall fall into hell.

148. The food of a Brāhmaṇa is Amṛta; the food of a Kṣatriya is remembered as milk; the food of a Vaiśya is the real food and that of a Śūdra is remembered as blood.

149. The food of a Brāhmaṇa is consecrated through Ṛk, Yajus and Sāman, by Vaiśvadeva rite, Homa, adoration of the deities and Japas. Hence it is Amṛta.

150. The food of a Kṣatriya is acquired through the meting out of justice befitting the cases and the due protection of the subjects. Hence it becomes milk.

151. The food which a Vaiśya offers is produced by means of bullocks yoked for hours to a plough, and is consecrated by performance of Sītā-yajña (a holy sacrifice offered to the plough).

152. A Śūdra is blind due to the darkness of ignorance and is addicted to liquor. The food of a Śūdra is devoid of Vedic Mantras. Therefore it is blood.

153. A good man should not make futile affidavit for the sake of small sums of money. One who makes it comes to ruin here and hereafter.

154. There is no sin in swearing for the sake of beautiful loving women, marriage, fodder for cows, when money has been lost and in protecting a Brāhmaṇa.

155. A Brāhmaṇa must be made to swear by truth, a Kṣatriya by vehicles and weapons, a Vaiśya by cows, seeds and gold and a Śūdra by all sorts of sins.

156. A Śūdra may be asked to carry fire; he may be sunk in water or he may be asked to touch the heads of his sons and wife severally.

157. They do not call only Yama by the name *Yama*. It is the self that is called Yama. If the self is controlled, what can Yama do (to him)?

158. A sword cannot be as sharp, a serpent as intractable or an enemy as perpetually angry, as the self out of control.

159. There is only one fault in those possessing forbearance; there is nothing else as the second. That is, people may consider a patient man to be weak.

160. There is no salvation to one engrossed in the science of words (Grammar); nor to one fond of beautiful residence; nor to one who is fond of food and raiment (dress); nor to one engaged in taking away the wealth of the (other) people.

161. Salvation is certain to one who always habitually remains alone, one who makes all desires for sensual pleasures recede, and one whose mind is directed towards Yoga and Svādhyāya (student of Vedas) and who is always nonviolent.

162. There is salvation in Kāśī naturally even without a man living an isolated life, without ceasing to enjoy sensual pleasures, without practising Yoga and without worshipping deities.

163. Meditation on Viśveśa alone is Yoga; residence in the city of Viśveśa alone is penance; the ablution alone in the celestial river that flows north constitutes *Vratas, Dānas, Niyamas* and *Yamas.*

Skanda said:

164. A householder who acquires wealth by legitimate means, who is engaged in acquiring the knowledge of reality, who is fond of guests, who performs Śrāddhas and who habitually speaks the truth becomes liberated here itself.

165. By giving food particularly to the poor, the blind and the miserable suppliants and by performing those rites that are praise-worthy, a householder shall obtain welfare (salvation).

166. The Lord of Kāśī becomes pleased with men who practise these. It is through the favour of the Lord of Kāśī that one attains Kāśī that accords salvation.

167. One by whom Kāśī is resorted to is one who has taken excellent baths in all the Tīrthas, who is initiated into all the Kratus and who has given all the Dānas.

CHAPTER FORTYONE

The Path of Yoga

1. After staying in the house in the second stage of life thus, a Brāhmaṇa should proceed on to the third stage of life, when he becomes grey-haired and wrinkled.[1]

2. After seeing the progeny of his progeny, after eschewing all foodstuffs prepared in his village, the Brāhmaṇa should enter the forest along with his wife (if she is ready to go) or after entrusting her to the care of his sons.

3. He should wear bark-garments or leather (e.g. deer-hide) ones. He should maintain the sacrificial fires and sustain himself with the foodstuffs befitting sages. He should grow matted hairs and beard and make the hairs and nails grow long. He should take bath in the morning and evening (and also at midday).

4. He should not discontinue the five Yajñas even if he has to make use of greens, roots and fruits. He should propitiate mendicants and guests through the alms consisting of water, roots and fruits.

5. He should not accept anything from anyone. He should give others (whatever he can). He should control his mind and be engaged in the study of the Vedas. He should duly perform Agnihotra in the Vaitānīya fire (i.e., in Āhavanīya and Dakṣiṇāgni eschewing Gārhapatyāgni).

6. He should prepare Puroḍāśa with *Munyanna* (foodgrains grown without cultivation like Nīvāra rice) brought by himself. He should eat the salt prepared by himself. Only things derived from fruits (are to be used).

7. He should eschew the plants of Śelu, Śigru and Kavaka and also honey and meat. In the month of Āśvina, he should avoid using the Nīvāra rice hoarded earlier.

8. He should forego fruits and roots grown in village or *Phālaja anna* (foodgrains grown by ploughing i.e., cultivation, even though the owner of the field neglected to collect it—Comm.). He should use his teeth as mortar and pestle (i.e., chew the paddy with teeth) or he should use two stones to

1. VV 1-13 describe Vānaprastha or Vaikhānasa (Forest-hermit) stage of life.

separate the grain from the chaff.

9. He may collect grains, fruits, roots etc. required for a single day, or one month, three months, six months or even twelve months.

10. He may be (the adopter of any of these *Vratas*): one who eats only at night; one who takes food on alternate days, or once in three days, or one who follows *Cāndrāyaṇa Vrata* or takes food once in a fortnight or once in a month.

11. He should follow the Vaikhānasa mode of life or solely live on fruits and roots. He should cause emaciation of the body through austerities. He should perform *Tarpaṇas* unto Pitṛs and Devas.

12. (If he is too weak to follow the above mode) he should consign the sacred fire into himself (by drinking in ash dissolved in water) and wander without any permanent abode. To keep his life going, he should resort to begging of alms from ascetics dwelling in forest.

13. (In case this is not available) he may also bring in food from the village and take eight morsels while living in the forest. A Vanāśramī (forest-dweller) Brāhmaṇa practising thus, is honoured in the world of Brahmā.

14. After spending the third stage of his life thus in the forest, one should eschew all contacts in the fourth stage and lead the life of a wandering recluse.[1]

15. Without repaying the three debts of life, i.e., without studying the Vedas, without procreating sons, and without performing Yajñas, if one wishes for salvation one faces downfall.

16. All the living beings always accord fearlessness to him from whom there is not even an iota of fear to the living beings.

17. He should wander alone forever without any abode and fire. For the purpose of Siddhi (achievement of aim), he should remain aidless. He should resort to a village only for food.

18. The ascetic should crave neither for life nor for death. He should bide his time like a salaried worker waiting for (further) instruction (from the master).

1. VV 14-37 describe the discipline of the fourth (Sannyāsa) stage of life. This Purāṇa prescribes Sannyāsa after the householder's stage of life and not otherwise (v 15).

19. A (recluse) desirous of salvation should be devoid of *Mamatā* (sense of mineness or possession) everywhere; he should have equanimity everywhere. He should stay even at the root of a tree. Such a one is praised here.

20. An ascetic has only four activities: meditation, (maintaining internal and external) purity, begging for alms and remaining isolated always. There is no other fifth activity.

21. An ascetic should not move out anywhere for the four rainy months, because thereby he may injure germinating shoots and creatures.

22. He should move on avoiding creatures. He should drink water filtered with a cloth. He should speak words without excitement. He should not be angry with anyone anywhere.

23. He should move about with his soul alone for aid and support. He should be free from desire and eagerness for support. He should always be engrossed in contemplating the Absolute (Brahman). He should have perfect control over the senses. He should neither trim nor clip the nails and hairs.

24. He should wear saffron-coloured cloth, hold a staff and eat what is received as alms. He should not boast of his excellence. A vessel made of any of these four things, namely potgourd, wood, clay or hollow bamboo, is recommended, not a fifth one.

25-27. No metallic vessel should ever be taken by a mendicant. Even if a Varāṭaka (cowrie) is hoarded everyday the sin incurred is that of killing a thousand cows. (So says) the eternal Śruti. If a recluse looks even for once at any woman with the feeling of love in his heart, he shall certainly remain in Kumbhīpāka hell for two crores of Brahmakalpas.

A recluse should beg for alms only once in a day and should not make it elaborate.

28. An ascetic should beg for alms in houses where the smoke (from the kitchen) has subsided, where the threshing pestle has come to a stop, where there is no burning charcoal, where the people have taken their food and where the platters have been kept down.

29. Only that Bhikṣu mendicant is eligible for salvation who takes very little food, who remains isolated, who is not enamoured of sensual objects and who is free from passionate attachment and hatred.

30. A person in whose hermitage an ascetic takes rest even for a short while, becomes blessed and has his objectives accomplished having done his duty. Of what avail are to him the injunctions laid down in many religious tracts?

31. An ascetic who spends even a night in the house of a householder completely burns down the sins (of the householder) accumulated by him in the course of his life till death.

32-35. Whatever be the stage of life one may be in, one should endeavour for salvation on having seen or in view of the following: the onslaught of old age, the unendurable affliction of sickness, death, being born once again, the terrible sufferings in the womb, birth in various species of living beings, separation from the beloved ones, contact with undesirable persons, the outcome of misery due to impiety, falling again into hell, the sufferings and tortures in various hells and the diverse forms of human plights originating from defective Karmas, non-permanence of bodies and permanence of the Soul Supreme.

36. (There are ascetics) who have no alms-bowl. They are well-known as *Karapātrins* ('users of hands as bowl'). Everyday their merit increases hundred times.

37. A wise one who maintains all these four stages of life thus and then frees himself from the pairs of opposites (e.g. pleasure-pain) and eschews attachment, becomes qualified to get merged in the Absolute.

38. The uncontrolled Ātman of those with crooked intellects can only remain in bondage. The same Ātman controlled by the wise accords the status free from ailments.

39-41. These are the means of acquiring the knowledge of Self: Śrutis, Smṛtis, Purāṇas, Vidyās, Upaniṣads, Ślokas, Sūtras, Bhāṣyas and other similar literature. After knowing the Vedic passages (containing instructions) the devotee should practise celibacy, austerities, control of the mind, faith, observance of fasts etc., that are also independent means of the knowledge. That self-same Ātman should be known by persons in all the stages of life. It should be known though the Vedas pondered over and assiduously realized.[1]

42. Liberation is possible through the knowledge of Ātman. That cannot happen without Yoga. That Yoga can be acquired only through a practice extending over a long period.

1. See *Bṛhadāraṇyaka* 4.5.6.

43. Yoga cannot be acquired merely by resorting to forest, nor by reflecting on the various texts, neither through *Dānas* nor through *Vratas*, neither through austerities nor through sacrifices.

44. Yoga is not acquired through the lotus-posture nor by looking at the tip of the nose; neither by scrupulous cleanliness nor by observing silence nor by repeating Mantras and resorting to other means of adoration.

45. By perseverance and everlasting practice, by steadfast adherence thereto and by desisting from despondency, Yoga can be accomplished and not otherwise.

46. To one who always sports with the self, to one who is ever in communication with the Supreme Self, to one who is always contented with the self, perfection in Yoga is not far off.

47. He who does not see anything else as different and distinct from the Ātman is a great (perfect) Yogī. He takes complete delight in his Ātman. He becomes identified with Brahman here itself.

48. The union of Ātman (soul) and Manas (mind) is called Yoga by wise men. The union of *Prāṇa* and *Apāna* is also called Yoga by some.

49. The unwise and the not very learned say that the contact of the sense-organs with the objects of pleasure is Yoga. Knowledge and salvation are far away from those whose minds are attached to worldly pleasures.

50. The functioning of the mind is difficult to prevent. As long as it does not stop, how can even the talk about Yoga be possible?

51. The mind should be made free from all functions and the individual soul should be united with the Supreme Soul. He (such a person) gets liberated and is called a *Yogayukta* (one endowed with Yoga).

52. All the external and the internal sense-organs should be merged in the mind and then all the senses and mind should be made to remain in communion with the soul.

53. One should dissolve the individual soul free from all *Bhāvas* (inclinations) unto the Supreme Brahman. This is Dhyāna and Yoga. Everything else is mere verbosity.

54. That which is not present in all the worlds cannot be

said to exist. It is contradictory. On being asserted so (by the philosopher) it does not enter the heart of the other (the layman).

55. That Brahman is to be realized by the self. Hence an *Ayogī* ('non-yogī') does not understand Brahman just as a virgin cannot understand the felicity of a married woman or the born-blind cannot see the flame of a burning wick.

56. It can be made an object of direct experience by one who regularly practises (Yoga). Because of its subtlety, the eternal Brahman cannot be pointed out (to others).

57. Just as water wafted by wind does not remain steady even for a moment, so also (does) the mind (that is shaken by the internal wind *Prāṇa*). It may not have credence in Brahman.

58. Hence, in order to steady the mind, the aspirant should control the *Prāṇa* (wind). For the purpose of controlling the wind he must practise Yoga having six Aṅgas[1] (ancillaries).

59. These are the six Aṅgas: *Āsana* (posture), *Prāṇasaṁrodha* (restraint of breath), *Pratyāhāra* (withdrawal of the senses), *Dhāraṇā* (retention), *Dhyāna* (meditation) and *Samādhi* (absorption).

60. There are as many Āsanas as there are living species of creatures. The following is said to be *Siddhāsana* because it gives success in the practice of Yoga to a Yogī.

61-63. The right foot is placed over the left thigh and the left one over the right thigh. This they know as *Padmāsana*. By practising this continuously one shall attain firmness of physical body. Thereafter, the aspirant knowing how to get a firm grasp should hold the big toes with the hands. By repeated practice of this *Padmāsana*, he attains firmness of physical form.

64. Or the aspirant can be seated in any other posture such as *Svastika* etc. wherein he is comfortable. The aspirant conversant with Yoga should be in communion with that Brahman.

65-66. He should not practise Yoga near water and fire, in a dilapidated cowpen, in a forest, in a place infested with

1. VV 58 ff. describe the path of Yoga as based on Patañjali's *Yoga Sūtra*. It is called *Ṣaḍaṅga* (of six stages) instead of *Aṣṭāṅga* (of eight stages) as in Patañjali, because the first two stages, Yama and Niyama, are deleted in this Text.

flies and mosquitoes, in a Caitya (rustic temple overhung by trees) nor in quadrangle. He should not practise in a place defiled by fallen hair, ash, husk, coals, bones etc., nor in a stinking place with putrefying matter, nor in a crowded spot.

67. Yogic exercises should be practised in a place pleasing to all the sense-organs, where the mind is elated and where there is fragrance of garlands and incense. It must not have any obstacles.

68. The aspirant should neither be hungry nor overfed, nor one in a hurry to ease himself of urine and faeces. He should not be exhausted after a walk, nor worried with thoughts when practising Yoga.

69-71. Then the aspirant begins his Prāṇāyāma thus.[1] The feet turned up shall be placed on the thighs; the hand is placed on the thigh. The face is slightly turned upwards and pressed with the chest. The eyes are closed and the mind is calm. The teeth should not touch one another. The tongue is kept steady touching the palate and the mouth is kept shut. He should remain motionless. He should control all the sense-organs. He should be seated neither too high nor too low. Thereafter he begins the *Madhyama* and *Uttama* Prāṇayāmas (as well as the *Laghu* or *Manda*— see 76th verse).

72. When the wind is moving, everything moves. When it is steady, everything is steady. By controlling the wind (breath) a Yogin attains the status of Sthāṇu (Śiva or steadiness).

73. As long as Prāṇa is stationed in the body there is life. If that goes out, it is death. Hence one should control Prāṇa (the breath).

74. How can there be any fear from death as long as the wind (vital breath) is restrained within the body and the mind is devoid of (unconcerned with) external objects and the eyesight is fixed in between the eyebrows?

75. Even Brahmā always practises Prāṇāyāma due to the fear of Kāla (god of Death). Yogīs have attained *Siddhi* (spiritual glory) by perfect control of *Prāṇa.*

76. What is called *Mātrā* is the time for a *Laghu Akṣara* (such *a, i, u*). The *Manda* (type of Prāṇāyāma) has twelve *Mātrās. Madhyama* one is twice the previous one and *Uttama* is twice that.

1. VV 69-92 deal with Prāṇāyāma (Breath-control) (See vv 97-100).

77. This will generate sweat, tremor and exhaustion in due succession. One should control the sweat by means of the first and the tremor through the second.

78. Exhaustion should be removed by the third. Thus Prāṇa when completely mastered by a Yogī (shall control all these). Duly checked and mastered by the Yogī and duly resorted to, Prāṇa takes him wherever he wishes to go.

79. When checked forcibly, Prāṇa escapes through the pores of hairs on the body. It may split the body or produce leprosy etc.

80. Hence Prāṇa should be tenderly tackled like a wild elephant. A wild elephant and a lion shall become softened and tamed when tackled gradually.

81. That elephant carries out the directions of the driver. It does not transgress it. Similarly, Prāṇa mastered gradually by a Yogī and resorted to, calms down.

82. The Prāṇa called *Haṁsa* is thirty-six Aṅgulas as it goes out. It is called *Prāṇa* as it (the breath) goes out through the *Savya* and *Apasavya* path (or *Iḍā* and *Piṅgalā nāḍīs* i.e., through left and right nostrils).

83. When the entire *Nāḍīcakra* (system of tubular organs like veins and arteries) becomes purified without being agitated a Yogī becomes capable of restraining Prāṇa.

84. Seated firmly in a posture, the aspirant inhales Prāṇa through Candra (i.e., through the left nostril, tubular vessel called *Iḍā,* the deity of which is Candra) and exhales through Sūrya (i.e., through the right nostril, the tubular vessel called *Piṅgalā* , the deity whereof is Sūrya). This is called Prāṇāyāma.

85. Meditating on the flowing currents of nectar accompanied by Candra an eminent Yogī performs Prāṇāyāma and instantly obtains joy thereby.

86. The Yogī inhales through Ravi (i.e., Piṅgalā or right nostril) and fills the cavity inside. After *Kuṁbhaka* (i.e., retaining the breath) he gradually exhales through Candra (i.e., Iḍā, the left nostril).

87. While performing Prāṇāyāma, the Yogī meditates in his heart on the hot-rayed Sun having the brilliance of a column of blazing fire. By means of this Yamyāyāma (i.e., Prāṇāyāma) the excellent Yogī attains happiness i.e., the bliss of Brahman.

88. Practising thus for three months the two types of

Prāṇāyāma, the Yogī gets all his Nāḍīs purified. He is then called *Siddhaprāṇa* ('one who has mastered Prāṇa').

89. Due to the purification of Nāḍīs, the following results are achieved: control of breath within as long as one pleases, stimulation of the (gastric) fire, *Nādābhivyakti* (ability to hear the sound of the *Parāvāk* in the *Ādhāracakra*), and freedom from ailments.

90. Prāṇa is the air within the body. *Āyāma* is the restraining thereof. The time thereof is the Mātrā of one breath. Thus is the word *Prāṇāyāma* derived.

91. In the lowest Prāṇāyāma there will be sweat; tremor takes place in the middle one. In the Uttama (highest) the aspirant seated in Padmāsana often goes up levitating.

92. One should burn down one's faults through Prāṇāyāma, sins through Pratyāhāra, get mental courage through Dhāraṇā and the vision of God through Samādhi.

93. One attains salvation through Samādhi after eschewing both Dharma and Adharma, yielding auspiciousness and otherwise. Firmness of the physical form is attained through Āsana. Thus all the six Aṅgas have been explained.

94. Pratyāhāra has been cited (as achieved) through twelve Prāṇāyāmas; Dhāraṇā is proclaimed (to have been achieved) through twelve Pratyāhāras (i.e., one hundred and forty-four Prāṇāyāmas).

95. Dhyāna is conducive to the attainment of God and it consists of twelve Dhāraṇās (or one thousand seven hundred and twenty-eight Prāṇāyāmas). Samādhi is constituted by twelve Dhyānas (or twenty thousand seven hundred and thirty-six Prāṇāyāmas).

96. After Samādhi, the endless refulgence, the self-luminous brilliance (comes into view). When it is seen, all the groups of activities, the cycle of death and birth, cease.

97. When the wind (Prāṇa) reaches the firmament (i.e., when Prāṇa reaches the cerebral aperture), a loud sound of bells and other excellent musical instruments (is heard). Thereafter the attainment of spiritual power is not far off.

98. Prāṇāyāma properly practised brings about destruction of all ailments. If it is improperly performed and repeated, it brings about all sorts of ailments.

99. Impropriety in the practice of Prāṇāyāma results in

several diseases like hiccups, gasping for breath, coughing and pains in head, ear and eyes.

100. While exhaling, the wind should be released slowly, little by little; while inhaling the wind shall be taken in slowly; and while retaining it shall be properly and sparingly kept checked. A wise Yogī accomplishes his purpose thus.

101. The withdrawal of sense-organs that move about among the sense-objects as they please, is called *Pratyāhāra.* This shall be effected through *Yukti* (i.e., by realizing the defects in the sense-objects).

102. Like a tortoise that withdraws all its limbs, he who withdraws the sense-organs through the proper procedure of Pratyāhāra shall become free from sins.

103. The Sun is stationed in the navel region and the Moon in the palatal region. The Moon facing down showers (nectar). The Sun with face lifted up swallows it.

104. The *Karaṇa* (function) should be carried out whereby that nectar is obtained (by keeping) the navel above and the palate down below (so that) the Sun is placed above and the Moon is placed below. This function or activity called *Viparīta* is achieved through practice.

105. With the mouth resembling the beak of a crow, the Yogī conversant with the arrangement of Prāṇa can drink the extremely cool Prāṇa. He becomes free from old age.

106. The Yogī should place the tongue in the hollow of the palate keeping the face looking up. By drinking the nectar he shall certainly be a *Nirjara* ('free from old age') within a period of six months.

107. The aspirant conversant with Yoga, who steadies himself and imbibes (the nectar of) the Moon with the tongue raised conquers death within half a month.

108. Prodding the great shining inner cavity (at the root of the tongue) with the tip of his tongue and meditating on the goddess of nectar, he becomes a poet within six months.

109. Within two or three years, the body of the Yogī is filled with Amṛta (nectar). His semen virile has upward flow. It gives rise to spiritual powers like Aṇimā and others.

110. If the Yogī gets his body filled with Somakalā (nectar) forever, no poison has any affect on him even if he were to be bitten by Takṣaka.

111. After practising and mastering Āsana, Prāṇāyāma and Pratyāhāra he should begin to practise Dhāraṇā.

112. Keeping the mind motionless and retaining severally the five Bhūtas in the heart is called Dhāraṇā.[1]

113. The aspirant meditates and retains in his heart the element called earth. It resembles Haritāla (Yellow orpiment) in colour and has four corners (rectangular?). It has God Brahmā as its deity and the letter *LA* as its Bīja. This is called *Kṣitidhāraṇā*.

114. In the neck, Aṁbu (water) principle which resembles (in whiteness) the crescent moon and a Kunda flower is meditated upon along with Viṣṇu as its deity and *VA*-kāra as its Bīja. Thus he should win over the water element.

115. Tejas (fire) element which is stationed in the palate, is triangular in shape and resembles a glowworm and is presided over by Rudra, should be meditated along with *Repha* (*RA*) and thus he should conquer the fire-element.

116. The Vāyu principle should be meditated upon in the middle of the eyebrows. It is circular in form and resembles collyrium. The Bīja is *YA* and the deity is Īśa. Thus he should win over the element wind.

117. The Ākāśa element resembles mirage-water (the sun—Comm.). It is stationed in the cerebral aperture. It should be meditated upon along with Lord Sadāśiva and letter *HA* (as the Bīja). It is calm. In that Ākāśa, Prāṇa of fivefold form should be retained for five Ghaṭikās along with the mind in the contemplation of the Ātman. This is called *Nabhodhāraṇā* (Dhāraṇā of the firmament). It is capable of opening the portals of salvation.

118. These Dhāraṇās of the five Bhūtas are to be (called) *Staṁbhanī* (Paralysing), *Plāvanī* (flowing), *Dahanī* (burning), *Bhrāmaṇī* (whirling) and *Śamanī* (subduing).

119. The root *Dhyai* means 'to think' (*Cintā*)[2]. Thinking connotes steadiness on a particular object. This is called Dhyāna. It is of two types *Saguṇa* and *Nirguṇa* (with and without object).

120. *Saguṇa* (type of contemplation) is when there are different forms (or objects). The objectless one is considered *Nirguṇa*. Know that *Saguṇa* is attended with Mantras and the *Nirguṇa*

---

1. VV 112-118 deal with the esoteric technique of Dhāraṇā on five Bhūtas (Elements).

2. VV 119-123 deal with the Dhyāna stage.

is without Mantras.

121. The aspirant is resting in a comfortable sitting (posture) with the mind turned inwards and the eyes kept outside. There is calmness in the bodily position. This *Dhyānamudrā* bestows excellent *Siddhis*.

122. That *Puṇya* (merit) which a Yogī of steady posture obtains with a single *Dhyāna* is not attained either through a horse-sacrifice or through a Rājasūya.

123. Dhyāna is limited to that state where the *Tanmātras* of *Śabda* (sound) etc. remain in the ear etc. Thereafter it is (the state of) Samādhi (absorption).

124. Dhāraṇā has the duration of five Ghaṭis (i.e., about 2 hours); Dhyāna, of sixty Ghaṭis (i.e., 24 hours). It is called Samādhi when its duration is twelve days.

125. Just as there is identity after the mixing together of water and salt, so also the identity (merger) of the Ātman and the mind is called Samādhi in this[1] Yoga Śāstra.

126. When the vital breath becomes extinct and the mind is dissolved, there comes an excellent bliss. This is called Samādhi.

127. The identity of the two, the *Jīva* (individual soul) and the Supreme Soul, when all Saṁkalpas (thought processes) become lost, is called Samādhi.

128. The excellent Yogī in the Samādhi state of Yoga does not know himself nor others, neither cold nor heat, neither happiness nor its opposite (misery).

129. The Yogī in the state of Samādhi is not carried away (or influenced) by Kāla (death or time), is not affected by Karmas, nor is he pierced by missiles and weapons.

130. The Yogī sees (realizes) the *Tattva* (Reality) with moderation in food and recreation and limited activity in Karmas, and also limited (properly controlled) sleep and wakeful state.

131. The *Tattva* referred to is called Brahma by the knowers of Brahma, which is of the nature of *Vijñāna* (perfect knowledge) and bliss. It has neither reason nor an example (i.e., it can't be known by inference). It is beyond the ken of speech and mind.

132. Through the practice of the Ṣaḍaṅga (having six ancillaries) Yoga, the Yogī becomes merged into the Supreme Brahma

---

1. VV 125-129 explain the Samādhi stage.

which is free from fear and ailments and does not require any support.

133. When clarified butter is put into clarified butter it too becomes clarified butter; if milk is poured into milk, it becomes milk; so also the Yogī merging into Brahman becomes identical with Brahman.

134. The Yogī should smear his body with Bhasma etc. not mixed with water. He should eschew things too hot or not at all hot. He should forego salt. He should always subsist on milk.

135. He should practise celibacy; subdue anger and covetousness. He should be free from jealousy. If he practises continuously thus for a year, he is called a Yogī.

136. The Yogī who perfectly understands (and practises) Mahāmudrā, Nabhomudrā, Uḍḍīyāna, Jālandhara and Mūlabandha[1] possesses all the Yogic Siddhis.

137. Purification of the system of *Nāḍīs* (blood vessels), coupling of Candra and Sūrya (Nāḍīs) and perfect drying up of the Rasas is called *Mahāmudrā*.

138-139. (*Another explanation)* The genital organ is covered (supported) with the left foot; the chin is placed on the chest and the right leg is stretched and held by both the hands for a long time. The inside is filled with Prāṇa and *Recana* (exhaling) is carried out slowly. This is called *Mahāmudrā* and it dispels great sins.

140. This Mudrā is to be practised at the outset in *Candrāṅga* (Iḍā). Then the practice is transferred to Sūryāṅga (Piṅgalā) till the numbers (of Pūraka, Kuṁbhaka and Recaka) become equal. Then the Mudrā is abandoned.

141-142. To a person who practises Mahāmudrā, nothing is unwholesome food. He has no prescribed regimen in regard to diet. All (poisonous) juices are devoid of their poisonous nature. Even if terrific poison is imbibed it can be digested like nectar. All ailments like consumption, leprosy, piles, swelling, indigestion etc. are removed.

143. The tongue is turned backward and enters the cerebral hollow of the skull. Vision is fixed in between the eyebrows. This is the *Khecarīmudrā* (*Nabhomudrā*).

144. He who understands Khecarīmudrā is never afflicted

1. These terms are explained in vv 137-152.

by volleys of arrows; is never affected by Karma. He is not tormented by Kāla (Death, time).

145. Since the mind traverses the firmament and the tongue too moves therein, this Mudrā resorted to by Siddhas is named *Khecarī*.

146. As long as the semen virile is retained there is no fear of death. As long as the *Nabhomudrā* (*Khecarī*) is practised the semen virile does not go away (from the body).

147. Since the Mahākhaga (Great Bird —the principal vital air) makes its upward flight day and night, this Yogic activity is called Uḍḍīyāna. The same Bandha is being laid down (explained).

148. The *Paścima Tāna* is to be placed on the belly above the navel (on the middle part of the extended feet —Comm.). This is the *Uḍḍīyāna Bandha.* (Hereby) one should eschew the fear of even death. (? *Obscure*)

149. The network of *Śirās* (tubular vessels) checks the water of the firmament (i.e., the juice from the Moon within the body) at the neck. This *Jālandhara Bandha* is destructive of clusters of miseries.

150. When the Jālandhara Bandha which is characterised by drawing in of the neck and placing it (the chin) on the chest (Comm.) is practised the nectar (trickling down from the "moon" in the forehead) does not fall down into the (gastric) fire, nor is the wind provoked.

151. The aspirant should press the privy parts with the heel and make the anus shrink after dragging up the wind Apāna. It is thus that *Mūlabandha* is practised.

152. When Apāna and Prāṇa get mixed together faeces and urine become reduced. By practising Mūlabandha constantly, even an old man becomes young.

153. The Jīva (individual soul) is under the control of Prāṇa and Apāna and it moves up and down through the left and right paths (i.e., through Iḍā and Piṅgalā). Hence it is unsteady.

154. If a bird is tied with a string, it can be pulled back even if it goes away. Similarly the Jīva fettered by Guṇas (strings, the three qualities of Sattva etc.) can be pulled back by means of Prāṇāyāma.

155. Apāna pulls Prāṇa and Prāṇa pulls Apāna. The aspirant conversant with Yoga joins together these two, stationed

above and below.

156. The breath goes out with the *HA* sound and comes with the sound of *SA*. Hence Jīva always recites the Mantra *Haṁsa, Haṁsa.*

157. Jīva always recites this Mantra, twenty-one thousand six hundred time, in the course of everyday and night (i.e., 900 times per hour).

158. This Mantra is called *Ajapā Gāyatrī*. It bestows salvation unto the Yogī. By mere thought of this Mantra, a man gets rid of all sins.

159-163. The following spiritual powers indicating perfect mastery of Yoga become obstacles to the Yogī bringing in loss of Yogic power. News of far-off events is heard. Objects existing far away are seen in front. There comes the ability to travel a hundred Yojanas in half a moment. Sacred treatises are learnt by heart even without being pondered over. The power of retention in memory becomes excessive. Even great burdens becomes light. The Yogī can become lean in a moment; stout in another; tiny in a moment and huge in another. He can enter the physical body of another and understand the speech of animals. He can emit divine fragrance from his body and utter divine speech. He is even sought by celestial maidens and acquires celestial body.

164. If the mind of the Yogī is not distracted by these obstacles here, he attains the rare status of Brahman etc.

165. O Pot-born One, by means of the Yogic practice with the six ancillaries, one attains that form which one does not lose nor repents or regrets after the attainment.

166. How can such a Yoga be mastered in a single birth? Without the Yogic perfection, how can salvation be obtained?

167. There are only two ways for the acquisition of salvation, O Pot-born One; either one casts off the body at Kāśī or acquires such a Yoga as this.

168. How can there be Yogic achievement for men of short span of life, in view of the unsteadiness of sense-organs and the expansion of the sins of Kali Age?

169. Hence , for all creatures, Viśveśvara, the ocean of mercy, stationed in Kāśi, is the bestower of the highly elevated status.

170. Salvation is attained easily by living beings at Kāsī, but not so easily elsewhere even through Yogic and other means.

171. The union with the body itself (i.e., living) at Kāsī is cited as perfect Yoga. Here no one is liberated by any other means of Yoga so quickly.[1]

172. Viśveśvara, Viśālākṣī, the celestial river, Kālabhairava, the glorious Ḍhunḍhi (i.e., Gaṇeśa) and Daṇḍapāṇi (Kārttikeya?)—these constitute the Yoga of six limbs.

173. If anyone practises this Yoga of six Aṅgas at Kāśī constantly, he attains the prolonged Yogic slumber and imbibes Amṛta (Nectar).

174. Another set of six-limbs includes (the Liṅgas) Oṁkāra, Kṛttivāsāḥ (Elephant-hide-clad), Kedāra, Triviṣṭapa (heaven or lord of heaven), Vīreśvara and Viśveśa.

175. The confluences of Pādodaka (i.e., Varaṇā) and Asi (with Gaṅgā), Jñānavāpī, Maṇikarṇikā, Brahmahrada, Dharmahrada constitute another great Yoga of six Aṅgas.

176. If a creature practises this Ṣaḍaṅga Yoga at Vārāṇasī, O excellent one among men, it never gets birth in the mother's womb.

177. Ablution in Gaṅgā is the Mahāmudrā that destroys great sins. One who practises this Mudrā attains immortality.

178. Wandering around in the streets of Kāśī is *Khecarī Mudrā*. As a result of this Mudrā the devotee becomes *Khecara* ('moving in the firmament' i.e., Brahman itself).

179. Fleeing towards Vārāṇasī from the regions all-around is the great Bandha named *Uḍḍīyāna*. This is conducive to salvation.

180. Keeping the water arising from the ablution of Viśveśa on the head is the Bandha named *Jālandhara* which is inaccessible even to the entire host of Suras.

181. If a sensible man does not forsake Kāśī though surrounded by a hundred difficulties, that itself is remembered as *Mūlabandha* that destroys the root of miseries.

182. Thus, O sage, two types of Yoga have been explained to you, one with the six Aṅgas and the other with Mudrā. It has been propounded by Śaṁbhu for the attainment of salvation.

183. One should be engaged in the practice of Yoga as long as the sense-organs do not become feeble, as long as one is

1. VV 171-184 to explain how life of Kāśī itself is a Yoga and it is called Kāśī Yoga.

not afflicted with ailments and there is some delay for the arrival of god of Death.

184. Between the two types of Yoga, this Yoga of Kāśī is the best one. By practising Kāśīyoga one shall attain the excellent Yoga i.e., the identity of the soul and the Absolute.

185. One should realize that the god of Death is nearby when old age attended with mental and physical illness comes indicating death. Then one should resort to the Lord of Kāśī.

186. Where is the fear of Kāla for men after resorting to Kāśīnātha. Even the taking away of life by angry Kāla in Kāśī is very auspicious.

187. Just as a righteous man awaits a guest at the time of hospitality, so also the fortunate one at Kāsī awaits the arrival of Kāla (death).

188. Kali Age, Kāla and the Karma performed by one—these are called Trikaṇṭakas ('three thorns'). These three are ineffective in the case of the inhabitants of Ānandavana.

189. In places other than Kāśī, unexpected death undoubtedly afflicts one. If one wishes freedom from fear of death, one should resort to Kāśī.

CHAPTER FORTYTWO

Means of Dodging Kāla

Agasti said:

1. How is it known that Kāla (death) is nearby, O son of Hara? Tell me a few of those indications as I ask.

Kumāra said:

2. I shall tell those signs which appear in men when death is imminent, O sage.[1] Listen to them.

3. If one breathes in and out through the right nostril alone day and night, his life, even though unbroken, comes to an end within three years.

4. If the air blows constantly for two or three days and

1. VV 2-40 give the indications prognosticating death within a particular time-limit. These are pseudo-scientific superstitions.

nights through Ravi (the right tubular vessel) it is said that his life limit is a year.

5. If the wind (breath) blows through both the nostrils continuously for ten days, along with its egression, the person lives only for three days.

6. Leaving off its two-fold path through the nostrils if the breath blows through the mouth, the person's departure along the path of death before the end of two days can be foretold.

7. The time when death shall come all of a sudden, should be well-thought of by a person afraid of death.

8. If the Sun is in the seventh house in the Zodiac and the Moon is in the star of nativity and the breath flows through the right (nostril), that time should be seen as Pauṣṇakāla (time of which the Sun is the deity).

9. At that time (of Pauṣṇakāla) if anyone were to see a black and tawny person and immediately some other form, he will live for two years.

10. If semen, faeces and urine or sneeze, urine and faeces were to fall out simultaneously, his life extends but to a year.

11. If anyone sees in the sky groups of Nāgas (serpents, elephants) resembling sapphire and moving about, he shall not live for six months.

12. On a day when there is no cloud, a person should stand with the sun behind him and fill his mouth with water. He shall then spit it out forcibly and quickly. If he does not see a rainbow, then his life will extend to only six months.

13-14. One whose death is imminent does not see Arundhatī, Dhruva, the three footsteps of Viṣṇu and the fourth one, the region of Mātṛs (Mothers). Arundhatī means the tongue; the tip of the nose is mentioned as Dhruva; the steps of Viṣṇu are in the middle of the brows; and the region of the Mātṛs is the middle of the eyes.

15. If anyone perceives blue and other colours or bitter, sour and other tastes otherwise (not in the proper colour or taste without any proper reason such as eye-ailment or fever), he faces death within six months.

16. If a man is sure to die within six months, his throat, lips, tongue, teeth and, the fifth one, palate—all these become parched and lustreless.

17. If the semen, fingers and extremities of the eyes turn

blue, the man goes to the city of Yama in the sixth month.

18. If a man engaged in sexual intercourse sneezes in the middle or at the end, it is certain that he will become the guest of Dharmarāja (god of Death) in the fifth month.

19. If a three-coloured (namely of blue, red and yellow colour) chameleon suddenly climbs on to the head and goes away, his life becomes extinct within six months.

20. If after taking excellent bath, the heart (chest) feet or hands become immediately dried up, his life limit is the period of three months.

21. If the imprint on dust or mud of the foot of anyone has the shape of a broken foot. he lives but five more months.

22. If the shadow of anyone trembles even when the physical form is steady, the messengers of Yama will bind that man in the fourth month.

23. If anyone does not see the head of his own reflection in water, ghee, mirror etc., he perishes in a month.

24-26. These are the indicators of death. If the mind swerves, gets confused, if the speech falters, if he sees rainbow-like form (when there is no rainbow), two moons in the nights, two suns in the day, galaxy of stars by the day, the extensive sky, rainbows all-round simultaneously, Gandharva city (imaginary city) on the top of a tree or mountain and the dance of ghosts and devils by the day (he will die soon).

27. Even if he sees anyone of these signs, death shall await only the period of a month and not more.

28. If by closing the ears with the hands, a man does not hear any sound, if a stout man (suddenly becomes) lean or a lean one stout, he returns (i.e., dies) within a month.

29. If anyone sees his shadow resting in the southern direction, he lives for five days and meets with death.

30-31. If in his dream anyone sees himself carried on the back or devoured by Piśācas, Asuras, crows, goblins, ghosts, dogs, vultures, jackals, camels, pigs, donkeys, monkeys, herons, mules and cranes, he ceases to live by the end of a year and comes face to face with Yama.

32. If during dream any man sees his own body adorned with fragrant red flowers, red perfumes or red clothes, Alas, he lives only for eight months.

33. If anyone mounts an anthill, sacrificial post or heap

of dust in dream, he perishes in six months.

34-35. If, in dream, a man sees himself mounted on a donkey with the body smeared with oil or the head shaved, if he sees his ancestors in dream being taken to the southern direction, or if a man sees grasses or dry twigs on his head or body, he does not live in the sixth month.

36. If a man sees a black man wearing black clothes and holding an iron rod standing in front, he cannot live beyond three months.

37. If anyone is embraced by a dark-complexioned virgin in dream, he sees the city of Yama within a month.

38. If in dream a man goes towards the east riding a monkey, he sees Saṁyaminī (city of Yama) within five days.

39. If a miserly person becomes munificent and if a munificent one becomes miserly, if the nature undergoes aberration, then he faces death.

40. The significant indications of (the advent of) Kāla (god of Death) are many. After knowing them a man should resort to Yoga.

41. O sage, I am not aware of any other means of deceiving Kāla except Mṛtyuñjaya ('Conqueror of Death'—Śiva), the Lord of Kāśī who prevents future births.[1]

42. Sins roar and King Yama roars only as long as a devotee does not resort to Viśveśvara.

43. Who does not become respectable (even to gods) if he has reached the residence of Viśveśvara, drunk the waters of Gaṅgā flowing towards the North and touched the excellent Liṅga of Viśveśa?

44. Even if angry, what will Kāla do to the men dwelling in Kāśī where Śiva himself whispers the Mantra of redemption into the ears at the proper time.

45. Just as infancy passes off, just as childhood goes off the way it comes, so also the period of youth and old age is what vanishes quickly.

46. As long as there is no onslaught of old age, as long as there is no feebleness in the sense-organs, a sensible man should eschew everything insignificant and seek refuge in Kāśī.

1. VV 41 ff. emphasize that Kāśī and its presiding deity are sure means of dodging Kāla.

47. May other signs of the advent of Kāla stand aside, O Pot-born One. Old age itself is the first sign. It is surprising that none is much afraid of that even.

48. When overcome with old age, one is insulted by all like a man devoid of wealth, when the ruby of the prime of youth is taken away.

49. Sons do not carry out his behest, wife gives up love and kinsmen do not mind him when the man is in the embrace of old age.

50. Even a loving wife turns her face away on seeing (the husband) embraced by old age, naturally suspicious as if of another (rival) woman.

51. There is no sickness on a par with old age; there is no misery on a par with old age; old age itself is death unto men because it causes loss of respect.

52. Neither by penance nor through Yogic practice, can Kāla be so conquered as he is conquered through stay in Kāśī without any delay.

53. Who feels a keen desire to attain Kāśī without excessive store of *Puṇya* (merit), without *Yajñas,* without *Dānas* (gifts) and without *Vratas, Japas,* etc.?

54. Attainment of Kāśī is *Yoga*; attainment of Kāśī is penance; attainment of Kāśī is *Dāna;* and attainment of Kāśī is identity with Śiva.

55. If Vārāṇasī is resorted to, what is Kali Age, who is Kāla, what is old age, what is evil, sin, what is pain and ailment, what are obstacles? (All these are insignificant and ignorable.)

56-57. Kali Age afflicts them, Kāla desires to kill them and sins afflict and torment them who have not resorted to Kāśī. Those who have resorted to Kāśī and worshipped Viśveśvara, get rid of the bondage of Karmas by attaining the *Tāraka Jñāna.*

58. Rich men do not get as much happiness as is obtained inexhaustibly by meeting with death at Kāśī.

59. Blessed is one who duly resides in Kāśī and not one who occupies the region of heaven-dwellers. The former acquires the end of misery and the latter the end of happiness.

60. Though Lord Īśa was stationed on Mandara abounding in lovely caves, he did not feel pleased without Kāśī where King Divodāsa was staying.

CHAPTER FORTYTHREE

King Divodāsa's Valour

Agasti said:

1. How did the Three-eyed Lord make King Divodāsa abandon Kāśī and how did he come from Mandara? O lord, relate this anecdote for the joy of the listeners.

Skanda said:

2. Due to the importance (given) to Brahmā's request and becoming pleased with the penance of that mountain Mandara, the Lord went to Mandara.

3. When Lord Viśveśvara went to Mandara, a beautiful mountain, all the heaven-dwellers too went along with Giriśa (Lord Śiva).

4. Abandoning the Vaiṣṇava shrines hereof on the earth, Lord Viṣṇu too went to Mandara where the Lord of the Devas, the consort of Umā, resided.

5. Abandoning all the holy places pertaining to Gaṇapati Gaṇeśa went there. I too, O eminent Brāhmaṇa, went towards Mandara.

6. Abandoning all the places sacred to Sun-god, Sun too quickly went away from his abode. All the other Devas too went after leaving their respective sacred places (on the earth).

7. When all the groups of Devas had gone away from the earth, the valorous King Divodāsa ruled the unrivalled kingdom.

8. Making the eternal city of Vārāṇasī his capital, that highly intelligent king righteously protected the subjects and made them prosperous.

9.* He became scorcher of the hearts and eyes of wicked-hearted ones like the sun, and to all the friends of good hearts he was like the moon to their eyes and minds.

10. By the armies of the enemies fleeing like clouds he was seen wielding with ease his unbroken bow which was like that

---

*The king's similarity with Lokapālas (Protectors of the World like the Sun, Indra etc.) is described in vv 9-15.

of Indra and twanging it on the battlefield.

11. Like Dharmarāja (Yama), he became the discriminator of piety and impiety, honouring those who should not be punished and punishing those who deserved punishment.

12. He destroyed the enemies like fire burning down numerous forests. Even from far-off he fettered the group of enemies like Varuṇa.

13. He became the lord (protector) of meritorious persons like Nirṛti, the lord of Puṇyajanas (Rākṣasas). He cut off the demon-like enemies like Nirṛti who made his friends, the Rākṣasas, prosperous. Like wind, he was eagerly engaged in making the universe breathe and live.

14. He was Rājarāja ('king of kings', Kubera) bestowing wealth on all good people. He was seen like Rudra in physical form by the enemies in battle.

15. Since by means of his austerities he assumed the forms of all the Devas, they all eulogized and worshipped him.

16. He could not be conquered by Sādhyas (a class of Devas). He was superior to Vasus in wealth. He had the physical form of Planets and he prevented them from being malignant. He had more beauty than Dasras (Aśvins).

17. He did not mind the group of Maruts. He pleased Tuṣitas through his good qualities. Among all the Vidyādharas, he was the greatest of *Vidyādharas* ('possessor of learning').

18. He made Gandharvas bereft of pride by his singing. Yakṣas and Rākṣasas protected his fortress that was on a par with heaven.

19. Nāgas (serpents) did not perpetrate anything evil unto him who was more powerful than the Nāgas (serpents, elephants). Danujas (Demon) assumed human form and served him.

20-21. Guhyakas became his secret spies all-round among men. (To him Asuras said,) "O king, we shall serve you through our wealth and power, because in your territory residence is impossible even for Suras. *Āśuga* (Wind-god) taught his horses the ability to run fast, because he was in the path of *Pāvamāna* ('the treatise on training horses').

22. On seeing his elephants whose origin was the mountainous region and whose bodies were on a par with the mountains and who were incessantly exuding ichor (*Dāna*) others also became givers of (religious) gifts (*Dāna*).

23. In his assemblies the scholarly propounders were not conquered by anyone at any place in scriptural lores. In his battlefield the warriors were not conquered by anyone at any place by means of weapons.

24. In the realm of that king the enemies were never seen *Anaṣṭapadāḥ* ('those whose position was not lost'); in his realm the subjects were never seen *Naṣṭapadāḥ* ('those whose positions were lost').

25. Even in heaven there is only one *Kalāvān* ('Master of arts', the Moon) among the heaven-dwellers; but in the realm of that king, all were *Kalālayas* ('abodes of arts').

26. There is only one Kāma in heaven and he is devoid of limbs; but in his realm the Kāmas (Kāma = 1. god of love 2. desire) of everyone were complete in their limbs and parts of limbs (had their desires fulfilled in all respects).

27. In his realm, no one was anywhere heard to be *Gotrabhid* ('breaker of family tradition'). In heaven the lord of the heaven-dwellers is glorified as Gotrabhid. *(Gotrabhid*—'who chopped off the wings of mountains').

28. No one was heard in his realm by anyone to be a *Kṣayī* ('suffering from consumptive disease'). In heaven the lord of the night (Moon) is expected to wane in the different fortnights (Kṣayī).

29-31. In heaven there are *Nava Grahas* ('Nine Planets'). His lands are *Anavagrahas* ('have no drought').

Even in heaven there is only one Hiraṇyagarbha (Brahmā). The abodes of all the inhabitants of his realm have gold within (i.e. are *Hiraṇyagarbhas)*.

There is only one *Aṁśumān* ('the Sun, having rays or raiments') blazing in heaven with but seven horses. But his citizens have many good silk clothes and many horses everyday.

32. Just as the heavenly region is *Sadapsarāḥ* ('having excellent celestial damsels'), so also his city is *Sadapsarāḥ* ('having lakes with excellent water'). In the world of Vaikuṇṭha, there is only one Padmā (Goddess Lakṣmī) but he has a hundred *Padmākaras* ('abodes of Padmā', 'lotus ponds').

33. His villages are *Anītis* ('having no divine calamities' and 'having no justice') but there are no *Arājapuruṣas* ('men spreading anarchy' or 'men with no royal glory'). In heaven there is only one *Dhanada* i.e. Kubera, the lord of Alakā, here

in every house there are *Dhanadas* (Kuberas, donors of wealth).

34. Even as that Divodāsa was ruling Kāśī thus, every year passed off like a day and thus eighty thousand years elapsed.

35. Even as he followed the path of righteousness, the Devas who were desirous of taking malafide action against him took counsel with Guru (Jupiter).

36. O sage, the Devas usually bring about great disasters to persons of righteous activities like you.

37. Although this king very much propitiated those partakers of the offerings (gods) in the fire by means of sacrifices very difficult to be performed, yet they were not friendly towards him.

38. Inability to bear the prosperity of others is but the nature of these heaven-dwellers. In what way was offence committed by Bali, Bāṇa, Dadhīci and others against them?

39. Obstacles do indeed happen at every step in the performance of piety. Still their own duty is never forsaken by pious-minded ones.

40. Unrighteous ones do flourish with abundance of wealth and grain; but due to the same unrighteousness they face downfall along with their roots (completely).

41. Not even an iota of unrighteousness was incurred by that king who protected his subjects like his own bosom-born progeny and who conquered the enemies.

42. The Suras did not come to know of any vulnerable point in that king who was aware of the six *Guṇas* (expedients of political success). His mind was very powerful on account of the three Śaktis, viz. intellect, army (or physical prowess) and brilliance, and he was perfectly conversant with clever strategic means.

43. Although they were intelligent and they endeavoured to harm him, the Devas did not succeed in doing the least harm to that king.

44. All the men in his realm were steadfast in their vow of having only one wife each. Among women there was no one who was not chaste.

45. No Brāhmaṇa remained without learning. No Kṣatriya was unheroic and no Vaiśya was without an adequate knowledge of the means of earning wealth.

46. In the realm of that King Divodāsa, Śūdras had unswerving

devotion to the service unto the twice-born.

47. In his kingdom religious students maintained their celibacy unaffected. They were always obedient to their preceptor's family and desirous of learning the Vedas.

48. The householders everywhere were keen in the observance of their duties of entertaining guests, masters of the scriptures and always behaved honourably and decently.

49. Those who were in the third stage of their life, scrupulously abided by the conduct prescribed for hermits without any desire for the activities of the village and followed the Vedic path.

50. The ascetics therein eschewed all desires and were free from attachments of every sort. They maintained the three Daṇḍas (signifying mastery over) speech, mind and physical action.

51. Persons of mixed castes (whether born of the regular order, i.e. husband of a superior caste and wife of an inferior one, or vice versa and of the irregular order, i.e. husband of an inferior caste and wife of a superior one) never swerved in the least from the path traditionally inherited by them.

52. In that realm there were no men without children, no one devoid of wealth, no one who did not serve the elders and no one who met with death prematurely and unaccountably.

53. There were no garrulous persons or fickle ones, no cheats or persons of violent nature, no heretics and no imbeciles, none dying childless and no liquor-sellers.

54. Everywhere there was heard the loud sound of Vedic chanting; at every place there debate on scriptural literature was held; everywhere there were pleasing melodious auspicious songs.

55. There were heard the sounds of lutes and flutes and drums of sweet melody. Excepting the intake of the Soma juice, no other sort of drinking was heard of.

56. Therein meat-eating was practised only with respect to the sacrificial Puroḍāśa (oblation) and never elsewhere. There were no gamesters there; no one in debts and no thieves.

57. Adoration of the feet of his parents (was considered by a son as) worship of gods, holy fasts, vow and observance, holy spot and the greatest worship of the deities.

58. To women worship of the feet of the husband was the

worship of the lord; his word is (as authoritative as) the Vedas. All men always worshipped their elder brothers.

59. Servants joyously worshipped the lotus-like feet of their masters. The persons of superior caste were extolled by those of inferior caste on account of deference for good qualities.

60. They worshipped the deities of Kāśī thrice a day. Everywhere all the learned men were worshipped by laymen with great zeal.

61. Persons steadfast in austerities were worshipped by scholars. Those who had conquered the sense-organs were adored by those who were steadfast in penance. Those who were well-established in knowledge were adored by those who had mastered the sense-organs and Śiva Yogins were adored by those who were well-established in knowledge.

62. Day and night sacrificial offerings well-consecrated, sanctified by Mantras and of great worth were duly made in the fire constituting the mouth of the Brāhmaṇas.

63. In that realm, at every step, there were many persons who dug wells, tanks and lakes and planted parks utilizing (their) wealth acquired by legitimate means.

64. In his realm people of all castes were seen delighted and well-nourished. Excepting hunters and animal killers, all were richly endowed with a desire to be engaged in uncensurable services.

65. Thus that king was pure in every respect. The Devas who were given to find fault could not find even the least weak point in that king.

66. The preceptor of Devas said thus to the Devas who were desirous of harming that virtuous king who was the foremost among those who were conversant with Mantras.

Guru said:

67. Here no one knows (the six expedients in politics viz.) Sandhi, Vigraha, Yāna, Āsana, Saṁśraya and Dvaidhībhāvana (i.e. peace, war, marching against, halting, seeking shelter and duplicity) as that king.

68. O heaven-dwellers, among the four *Upāyas* (means of strategy) there is only one, namely *Bheda* (sowing dissensions) which perhaps may be successful in regard to that king who is very powerful due to his austerities.

69. Devas have been banished from the earth by that king. Yet there are many there who are partial and sympathetic towards us.

70. They are honourd by him too as well as by us. Even for a moment he will not be happy without them.

71. They keep moving in and out constantly. They are objects of trust unto everyone. If once they come here, all that we desire can be achieved.

72. On hearing the words uttered by Gīṣpati (i.e. Bṛhaspati) all the Devas understood the implications thereof. Hence they duly honoured those spies who moved within and without and said, "It shall be so."

73. Thereafter Śakra (Indra) called Vītihotra (god Fire) standing in front and spoke to him sweetly with great reverence.

74. "O Havyavāhana, withdraw immediately your form established there in the realm of that king.

75. When that form comes back, all the subjects with their sacred fires having extinguished, shall become deprived of the rites of *Havya* and *Kavya* and so will be averse to the king.

76. Bereft of the attachment of the subjects—the wish-yielding divine cow of the kingdom, the title *Rājā* (a king, a delighter of the subjects) acquired with very great difficulty, shall become meaningless.

77. A king is called so (*Rājā*) because he makes the people delighted. This is the conventional meaning acquired (by the word). If that convention gets spoilt and lost the very kingdom shall perish.

78. The king alienated from the subjects will before long perish, though he may be richly endowed with treasury, fortress, army etc., like a tree on the bank (of a river).

79. The means of achieving the three aims of life for a king is his subjects at the very outset. If the subjects become weak, the threefold objective gets weakened.

80. When the three-fold aim gets weakened the attainment (of the pleasures) of the two worlds too becomes very weak."

81. At these words of Indra, god Fire endowed with Yogic Māyā quickly withdrew his form from the region of the earth.

82. At the instance of the Thunderbolt-wielding Lord, god

Fire withdraw not only the *Tretāgnis* (the three types of sacrificial fires) but also the gastric fire having the power of digesting foodstuffs.

83-84. When god Fire had gone back to the heavenly region, at midday, the king concluded the midday rites and quickly entered the dining hall. The trembling officials in charge of the kitchen submitted as follows to the hungry king.

The Cooks said:

85-86. O king, you have excelled the Sun by means of your brilliance and god Fire by means of your exploits. Though it is untimely, we are desirous of submitting something, O king skilled in fighting battles. If you accord to us freedom from fear, we shall intimate to you with palms joined in reverence.

87. When the command was given with an indication from his eyebrows by the king of esteemed countenance, the officials incharge of the Royal Kitchen submitted softly:

88. "O lord, we are not fully aware by what mischievous means Vaiśvānara (god Fire), terrified much at your exploits and fully conscious* (of the consequences), vanished from the city.

89. How can there go regular cooking acitivity when fire has vanished? Still some cooking has been completed by us with solar power.

90. On getting your lordship's command we shall bring it here. O king, we think that today's cooking is good."

91. On hearing the words of the cooks that highly intelligent king of noble temperament thought that it was the mischief done by Devas.

92-96. Presently he meditated and visualized by means of the power of his penance that god Fire abandoned not only the kitchen but also the cavities of belly and went away to the abode of the gods, away from the earth.

'Let it be so. What harm has been done to us when god Fire has left? The harm is that of the gods thanks to the disorderly

*If taken as *avidvān* instead of *vidvān*, it means "The fool, that he is etc."

activity (i.e. cessation of sacrifices etc.). Has the kingdom been taken over by me on the strength of their power? It has been assigned to me by the Creator, Brahmā, with due weightage.'

While that king who ruled the middle world (Earth) like Indra was thinking thus, the citizens came to the royal threshold along with the people of the surrounding countryside. At the king's behest they were allowed to enter by the doorkeeper.

97-98. They were given due precedence and approach and they bowed down to the king (the Indra on the Earth). Some of them were addressed by the king in a voice indicating reverence. Some were welcomed with eyes beaming with delight. Some were received with gestures of the hands. They left their seats and were received by the king with due deference.

99. All of them resorted to the courtyard. It was served (lighted) with the rays of precious stones. The fragrance thereof surpassed that of celestial trees (in sweetness). It was auspicious and splendid due to the shade of the royal umbrellas of a hundred ribs.

100-111. Then the king, having come to know their purpose as evinced by their facial colour (expression), began to speak:

"O citizens, do not be afraid. If fire is taken away from the earth by the Devas committing mischief, does it by itself amount to an attack on me by them?

O citizens, I myself had a desire of doing this but did not bring it into effect. Fortunately it has been recalled after a long time.

Fire has gone away. That is good. Let god Wind too go away from here. Let Varuṇa too along with the Sun and the Moon, go away without delay.

By means of the power of my penance I myself shall be Indra, the bestower of the abundance of all vegetation to the delight of the realm all-round.

Thanks to the power of penance and Yoga, I shall divide myself into the three forms of fire for carrying out the activities of cooking, sacrificial rites and warming (those affected by chillness).

I shall adopt the duty of Wind within (the body) and outside (in the world) and become capable of knowing the internal activities of everyone.

I shall assume the form of water, the sole enlivener of all

creatures, and resuscitate all the subjects. Of what use are the waters in my realm?

When the Moon and the Sun are overwhelmed by Tamas (Rāhu at the time of eclipse), O citizens, do we not keep alive without them in the world?

I shall make the subjects delighted by assuming the splendour of the Moon. Of what avail is the night-stalking Moon that wastes away and is defiled by a stigma?

Bhāskara (the Sun) is the founder of our dynasty. He is decidedly worthy of our respect. Let him remain happily and carry on his movements to and fro.

He alone is the very soul of all the worlds. Particularly he is our family deity. He does not stoop to commit any harm. That is his excellent vow."

112. After imbibing these nectar-like words of the king through the cups of their ears, the citizens with their faces beaming with delight went away to their respective abodes without any worry in their minds.

113. The king too did accordingly. What is it that cannot be achieved by penance in the three worlds? Adopting the refulgence far excelling that of fire and the Sun, he became, as it were, a great thorn in the heart of the heaven-dwellers.

CHAPTER FORTYFOUR

Description of Kāśī

Skanda said:

1-2. Hara, the Lord of the universe, beautified with the digit of the crescent moon, was staying in his palace studded with precious stones and shining with the splendour of jewels within the caves of Mandara. The place was very high in the firmament, surrounded by the peaks of the mountain and the Devas were occupying the seats all-around. Yet Śaṅkara did not feel delighted because of the rising fever born of the separation from Kāśī.

3. In order to calm down the scorching fire of separation, sandalpaste from Malaya was smeared on his body by the

Lord, the enemy of the three Puras. That had dried up and assumed the form of the ash (on his body).

4. Tender stalks of lotus were tied round his hands like bracelets for the removal of the scorching heat. The Lord then shouted out that they were serpents (so stinging and scorching). That turned out to be a fact. Alas! The wish of the Great Lord (prevails).

5. The cool full-moon that had been drawn out by the Devas after churning the Ocean of Milk became lean and thin with its body wasting away due to the heat of the head of the Lord scorched by the fire of separation.

6. On being scorched (with the heat of separation from Kāśī) Hara does not let go even today the heat-quelling celestial river which he had held up in a corner of his extensive matted hair.

7. Śaṅkara of habitual, perfect self-control had become a victim of a great (fire of) separation, but since he covered it up perfectly, he was not known to be so by the Suras present in his assembly.

8. This is very surprising that the pure Lord of the three worlds should be scorched by the fire arising from the separation from his own city, even though the fire is his own form.

9. The Lord always adorns his forehead with a digit of the moon. Still that moon scorched the Lord. When one is in misery who is not against one?

10. The poison is shining in the throat but he is not scorched thereby. It is surprising that he is scorched by the clusters of cool, nectar-like rays of the moon.

11. He was afflicted with the mass of Haricandana (sandalpaste) water applied over the chest for the removal of the heat of separation but not with the poison issuing from the spreading hoods of the serpents.

12. This Lord Hara is capable of destroying all the erroneous conceptions such as those of serpents in garlands. It is surprising that he too had the misconception of a serpent in a distinctly visible garland.

13. That unborn Lord (Śiva) is capable of destroying the three *Tāpas* (distresses) merely on being remembered. But he too was distressed due to the separation from Kāśī. He then began to prattle thus:

14. 'Even if the wind blowing from Kāśī were to embrace my limbs, the heat therein may subside but not by diving into a vast expanse of snow.

15. The distress of mine was heightened by the separation of the daughter of Dakṣa. How could it have subsided if the daughter of Himālaya, the creeper that enlivens me, had not manifested immediately?

16. When Dakṣa's daughter cast off her body, my mind was distressed, but it was not as much as the present distress due to the great heat arising from the separation from Avimukta.

17. O Kāśī, when will I have the joyous pleasure of coming into contact with you whereby all my limbs shall cool down instantaneously and surprisingly?

18. O Kāśī, you have destroyed all sins. The fire due to the separation from you gets increased through the cool drops of the digits of the nectar-rayed moon as though through the offerings of ghee. It is really surprising.

19. Formerly my fever (heat) due to the separation from Dakṣa's daughter vanished due to the remedy in the form of Himavān's daughter. Indeed now I will not attain peace unless I see Kāśī quickly.'

20. Śiva had perfectly concealed the aberration due to distress. But when he began to lament mentally, he was somehow understood by the mother of the universe and of all the intellects, as lamenting for separation from something.

21. Even by that beloved who was a half part of his body, the cause of Śiva's grief of separation was not understood. She, therefore, addressed the following probing words to the Lord who dispels the distress of all living beings that bow unto him.

Śrī Pārvatī said:

22. O omnipresent one, everything is within the grasp of your hand. What separation do you have, O Lord endowed with Yogic power? Sacred ash besmeared by you bestows prosperity (on the devotees). (By your grace) the entire earth is rid all of adversities.

23. O Lord, in the absence of your supervision in a moment all the worlds become annihilated and undergo miserable plight. O Lord, if anyone is not favoured by you with the least of

mercy, he undergoes downfall as an alien.

24. The moon the sun and fire do not cause distress unto you, O Three-eyed One, because they are your eyes. Your beloved with refulgent water i.e. Gaṅgā is on your head itself.

25. These serpents always resort to your arms (as ornaments). O Blue-throated One, no poison affects you. O Vāmadeva, I am the splendid woman constituting your left side here and acting favourably to your mental predilection.

26. When this was uttered in a way conducive to welfare by the mother of the seed of the worldly existence, with a selected collection of words, Giriśa (Śiva) began to speak (in reply).

Īśvara said:

27. O Kāśī, the Lord having eight cosmic forms*, Bhava, Hara, has been certainly captivated by you, Kāśī.

This is understood by Śivā (Pārvatī) quickly.

28. Thereupon Śivā (Pārvatī) described Avimukta, the city that bestows salvation, the sylvan creepers whereof had been her childhood friends.

Pārvatī said:

29. O Smarahara (Śiva), we shall go to Kāśī, the city that is held on the trident by Bhava at the time of deluge, when the water reached upto the sky, where it assumed the splendour of a lotus.

30. O Dhūrjaṭi, even the realm of (my father) the Lord of mountains does not delight me so much as your Kāśikā, the foremost city which is no part of the earth though it is on the earth (as it is held aloft by the Lord on his trident).

31. O Lord, how will that city of Kāśī become the object of our vision, the city where there is no fear arising from Kali Age, the city wherein (if) one dies, he is not reborn, the city where there is no fear arising from sins.

---

*The eight forms of Śiva are five elements, the Sun, the Moon and the self.

32. Don't we have thousands of cities everywhere abounding in all types of prosperities? But I swear by you, none like Kāśī has come within the range of my vision, O Śiva.

33. Aren't there hundred cities in Heaven, the source of origin of all fanciful things? But, O Purāri (Śiva), in comparison with the city of thine, the destroyer of worldly sufferings, they are all worthless.

34. The fever due to the separation from Kāśī does not effect you as much as it affects me. For the quiescence of the distress, the only remedy is that city or my native land.

35. O Lord, after attaining Kāśī, the bestower of peace all round, the cause of the destruction of all sorts of distress, the distress due to the separation from my native land has not been thought of by me.

36. The Lakṣmīs of salvation have not been directly perceived by any embodied being anywhere. I am aware, O Lord, O bestower of happiness, indeed Kāśikā is the salvation akin in form to the bestower of all happiness and welfare.

37. Neither by performing meditation on the Absolute (Brahma), avoiding unsteadiness of sense-organs, nor by (performance of) *Kratu* (sacrifice) and other rites, nor by Vedic knowledge and lore, is salvation attainable as easily as by casting off the body at Kāśī.

38. Nowhere is such happiness possible as is found in Kāśī. It is neither in heaven nor elsewhere in the world. How can it be found even in Pātāla which is so very beautiful. Where can be even a talk of happiness in the mortal world?

39. O trident -bearing Lord! Your holy place Avimukta is never bereft of the Lakṣmī (glory) of salvation. If a meritorious creature were to exercise (control over) his mind there, he will always be practising the Yoga with the six ancillaries.

40. Through the Yoga with six ancillaries, men cannot achieve that bodily Yoga-Siddhi instantaneously which one attains very easily, O Śiva, by fixing the eyes on you for a moment after reaching Kāśī.

41. Better indeed is a brute without the gift of intellect and not a human possessing the power of intellect, which refuses to be benefited by failing to visit Kāśī (by postponing to go there) as life is transient resembling a bubble of water on a lotus leaf.

42. The two eyes that have seen Kāśī are blessed; O Śiva, the body that resides in Kāśī is blessed; the mind that has resorted to Kāśī is blessed; the face is blessed that has been turned towards Kāśī.

43. Even a dust particle of Kāśī is excessively sacred and always destroys Rajas and Tamas qualities. It is as brilliant as the splendour of the moon. It is held in great esteem by the Suras when it sticks to their forehead touching in making obeisance to the region around Maṇikarṇikā.

44. Neither the world of Devas, nor Satyaloka, nor the world of serpents can be on a par with Maṇikarṇikā, because the ear of a person who dies at that place becomes fit to receive *Brahmarasāyana* (Praṇava or Rāmamantrarāja).

45. The region of Maṇikarṇikā is the source of excellent refulgence, where the expanse of darkness (i.e. ignorance) which is accumulated and increased in the course of hundreds of births and which cannot be quelled by fire or the rays of the sun and the moon, gets destroyed.

46. Is (It is as if) the region of Maṇikarṇikā, the throne of ultimate salvation or the soft bed of the Lakṣmī of salvation, or the source of origin of the great bulbous root (i.e. the prime cause) of the highest bliss?

47. By means of minute particles of refulgent pebbles persons who are happily seated (in Maṇikarṇikā) count the number of those creatures who have previously attained salvation there. They themselves eagerly await the destruction of their bodies, which constitutes a great festival unto them.

Skanda said:

48. After describing the city of Vārāṇasī thus, O sage, Aparṇā (Pārvatī) once again urged the Pināka-wielding Lord to proceed to Kāśī.

Śrī Pārvatī said:

49. O Lord of Pramathas, O Lord of all, O bestower of boons, you are ever independent in your existence. Kindly see that I am enabled to go to Ānandavana.

Skanda said:

50. On hearing this Giriśa became pleased. He spoke unto Girijā whose words had excelled even nectar in sweetness and who was brilliant in the exposition of Kāśī.

Śrī Devadeva said:

51. O my beloved Gaurī, I have been thrilled and refreshed by the sprays of nectar in the form of your words. Now I shall endeavour to reach Kāśī.

52. O great goddess, you are aware that I enjoy only that thing which is not enjoyed by others and not other things.

53. As, at the behest of the Grandfather (Brahmā) King Divodāsa is administering the city righteously what remedy should be employed?

54. How can that righteous King Divodāsa who is eager to protect the subjects, be dislodged from that city of Kāśī?

55. Since there can be obstacles only on the path of the unrighteous and not that of others, O goddess, whom should I send there who will dislodge him from Kāśī?

56. If anyone puts in obstacles to those who follow the righteous path, he himself will face obstacles on the other hand, O enhancer of love.

57. Without any fault (on his part), I am not enthusiastic enough to assail him. Indeed, O dear one, those who strictly adhere to righteousness should be protected by me.

58. Old age will not afflict him. Death will not desire to take away his life. Ailments do not torment him who sticks to the path of righteousness here.

59. Even as the Lord was thinking thus, he saw in front of him a group of Yoginīs of great maturity, capable of accomplishing hard tasks.

60. After discussing the matter with the goddess, O great sage Vyomakeśa, Hara called the group of Yoginīs and spoke these words:

61-63. "O Yoginīs, hasten to my city Vārāṇasī where King Divodāsa rules the kingdom with adequate adherence to righteousness. O intelligent Yoginīs equipped with the power of Yoga and Māyā, proceed in that manner which will make the king swerve from his duty and abandon Kāśī. O Yoginīs, quickly carry out such means as will enable me to go to Vārāṇasī after renovating it."

64. Having accepted with bowing heads this behest considering it as a divine favour, the group of Yoginīs bowed down again and departed therefrom.

65. Those Yoginīs were highly delighted. With a speed far exceeding that of the mind, they passed through the sky talking to one another.

66-67. "Today we are further blessed because the Lord of Devas himself bestowed his favour and sent us to the glorious Ānandakānana. Today all of a sudden we had two rare advantages, the honour conferred by the Three-eyed Lord and the opportunity to visit Kāśī."

68. Thus, the delighted group of Yoginīs departed from the pleasure-grove in the Mandara mountain, travelled through the sky quickly and espied that city.

CHAPTER FORTYFIVE

The Arrival of Sixty-four Yoginīs

Skanda said:

1. Then that group of Yoginīs extended their visions from afar and praised the length of their vision which had become fruitful.

2. They praised also the festoons and banners of the groups of divine places, the tips of which were fluttering as though they were inviting respectfully the wayfarers on the paths far away.

3. They also praised the blue sky that appeared to be bright due to the glittering rubies in the places with increased rays.

4.* They concealed their divinity by means of their Māyā and assumed the guise befitting Karpaṭikās (an order of ascetics

*VV. 4-17 describe the various professions of women of that period.

wearing red garments). Thus the group of Yoginīs entered Kāśī in an irregular order (not simultaneously in a group).

5. One of them adopted the form of a woman Yoginī or a Kāpālikā, another became a woman ascetic, one of them became a *Sairandhrī* (a female attendant) and another (assumed the form of) one fasting for a month.

6. One of them became wife of a gardener, another a beautiful maiden of a barber conversant with the activities connected with cases of delivery and another an adept in science of medicine.

7. A certain Yoginī became a Vaiśya woman—very clever in buying and selling. One of them became a serpent-charmer and another a governess and another a slave girl.

8. One of them became a woman expert in dancing and another an adept in singing. Another became a flute player and still another a lute player.

9. One Yoginī became one conversant with playing on the Mṛdaṅga drum and a certain one an expert in the art of beating time. One of them was a specialist in the art of seduction and another a maker of pearl-necklaces.

10. One became expert in the art of apportioning scents; one was a specialist in the game of dice; another was an adept conversationalist and a certain one became a *Catvāracāriṇī* (a mendicant woman roaming in quadrangles).

11. One of them became a clever woman climbing a bamboo pole and another a rope-walker. One became a lunatic with curious pranks and another clothed herself with rags picked from the highway.

12. One lived in that city as one capable of blessing the childless with children. Another was an expert in palmistry.

13. A certain (Yoginī) captivated the minds of the common people through her skill in drawing pictures. A certain one roamed there proclaiming herself an expert in the spells of captivating persons.

14. One of them was bestower of supernatural powers through *Guṭikās* (pills); one of them was able to bestow *Añjana Siddhi* (supernatural power through use of collyrium); another was an expert in *Dhātuvāda* (Alchemy) and another bestowed *Pādukā Siddhi* (transport to a desired place by touching the sandals).

15. One of them taught the arts of *Agnistambha* ('arresting

fire'), *Jalastaṁbha* ('preventing the movement of water') and *Vākstaṁbha* ('arresting the power of speech'); one of them offered *Khecaritva* ('the ability to walk in the sky') and another one offered the power of being invisible.

16. One of them offered the *Ākarṣiṇī Siddhi* ('the power to drag to oneself woman or man desired); another offered *Uccāṭana* (upsetting and unsettling persons of stability); a certain one enamoured the minds of young men through the beauty of her limbs.

17-19. One of them could bestow anything thought of; one of them was an expert in astrology.

In such disguises and professions, the group of Yoginīs entered every house and every yard around. Thus they spent a year roaming about in the city day and night. They were desirous of creating obstacles unto the king, but could not find any inlet or loophole. Their desired missions were not fulfilled. All these Yoginīs gathered together and stayed there taking counsel together. They never went back to Mandara.

20. "If one had been honoured in the open assembly (by being entrusted with a task) but could not carry out the task and if the one is not even wounded, can that one stand in front of the lord and master?"

21-23. Further, the following steps were thought of by the Yoginīs, O sage. 'We can very well live without the Lord but not without Kāśī. Even if the master is angry with the servant, he can only take away the means of livelihood. But, if Kāśī slips out from the grasp, it may take away all the four aims of life.'

O great sage, ever since then, till today the Yoginīs never left Kāśī and stayed elsewhere, though they wander through all the three worlds.

24-28. (The Yoginīs thought further:) 'Even after coming to Kāśī, the glorious city, if any wretched-minded man were to think of leaving it, it is he who will be, on the other hand, abandoned by the four *Puruṣārthas,* viz. Dharma, Artha, Kāma and Mukti. After coming to Kāśī which man of wretched intellect desires to go elsewhere with his mind dwelling on insignificant glory? Kāśī is, as it were, the treasure-chest of salvation. Even if the master turns away his face from us (to express his displeasure), he will see us face to face (to express his pleasure) due to the merit of resorting to Kāśī.

The Lord will be our own merit personified. Hence we shall be contented that we have done our duty.

The Lord, omniscient Śiva, will be coming here in a few days, because the Three-eyed Lord does not feel happy elsewhere except at Kāśī.

This Kāśī is the Śakti (power) of Śaṁbhu. It is not perceptible to all. Śaṁbhu alone knows its greatest happiness.'

29. Having concluded thus in their minds, the group of Yoginīs stayed back in the Ānandakānana of Śaṁbhu, enveloping themselves with an indescribable Māyā.

Vyāsa said:

30-31. On hearing this, the sage asked the Six-faced Lord again: "O Lord, what are their names? Enumerate them. What benefit accrues by worshipping the Yoginīs at Kāśī? What is the holy occasion on which they are to be worshipped? How are they to be worshipped? Mention that."

32 On hearing these questions concerning the Yoginīs, the son of Umā replied: "O sage, I shall mention. May Your Holiness listen attentively."

Skanda said:

33. O Pot-born One, I shall mention the names of the Yoginīs, on hearing which all the sins of the persons of worldly existence perish instantaneously.

34-41. The sixty-four names of the Yoginīs*:

(1) Gajānanā, (2) Siṁhamukhī, (3) Gṛdhrāsyā, (4) Kākatuṇḍikā, (5) Uṣṭragrīvā, (6) Hayagrīvā, (7) Vārāhī, (8) Śarabhānanā, (9) Ulūkikā, (10) Śivārāvā, (11) Mayūrī, (12) Vikaṭānanā, (13)Aṣṭavakrā, (14) Koṭarākṣī, (15)Kubjā, (16) Vikaṭalocanā, (17) Śuṣkodarī, (18) Lalajjihvā, (19) Śvadaṁṣṭrā, (20) Vānarānanā, (21) Ṛkṣākṣī, (22) Kekarākṣī, (23) Bṛhattuṇḍa, (24) Surāpriyā,

* Though there might have been separate temples for the Yoginīs formerly, now they are worshipped in one temple called 'Chauṁsaṭhī Devī Temple'. The temple is small, located in a tiny lane in the Bengali Tola area, high above the Chauṁsaṭhī (or Rana Mahal) Ghāṭ. (BCL 158)

(25) Kapālahastā, (26) Raktākṣī, (27) Śukī, (28) Śyenī, (29) Kapotikā, (30) Pāśahastā, (31) Daṇḍahastā, (32) Pracaṇḍā Caṇḍavikramā, (33) Śiśughnī, (34) Pāpahantrī, (35) Kālī, (36) Rudhirapāyinī, (37) Vasādhayā, (38) Garbhabhakṣā, (39) Śavahastā, (40) Āntramālinī, (41) Sthūlakeśī, (42) Bṛhatkukṣī, (43) Sarpāsyā, (44) Pretavāhanā, (45) Dandaśūkakarā, (46) Krauñcī, (47) Mṛgaśīrṣā, (48) Vṛṣānanā, (49) Vyāttāsyā, (50) Dhūmaniḥśvāsā, (51) Vyomaikacaraṇā, (52) Ūrdhvadṛk, (53) Tāpanīdṛṣṭi, (54) Śoṣanīdṛṣti, (55) Koṭarī, (56) Sthūlanāsikā, (57) Vidyutprabhā, (58) Balākāsyā, (59) Mārjārī, (60) Kaṭapūtanā, (61) Aṭṭāṭṭahāsā, (62) Kāmākṣī, (63) Mṛgākṣī, (64) Mṛgalocanā.*

42. If any man repeats these sixty-four names everyday at dawn, midday and dusk, all his sufferings due to evil spirits become subsided.

43. Neither Ḍākinīs nor Śākinīs, neither Kūṣmāṇḍas nor Rākṣasas afflict him who recites these names.

44. They give peace to infants and the unborn. They accord victory in battle, royal household and debates.

45. He who serves Yoginī Pīṭhas (pedestals) shall obtain desired powers. One who repeats other Mantras in front of their pedestals shall also achieve powers.

46. The Yoginīs become quickly pleased with oblations, adorations and offerings and dedications of incense and lamps and they shall fulfil all desires.

47. In autumnal season a devotee conversant with Mantras, should perform a great Pūjā in accordance with the injunctions and make ghee offerings. He shall attain great benefit.

48. In the month of *Aśvayuj* (October-November), beginning with the first lunar day of the bright half and ending with the ninth day, a man should worship (the Yoginīs). He shall obtain whatever is desired.

49. The excellent man should observe fast on the fourteenth day in the dark half and keep awake during the night. He shall obtain great benefit.

50-51. The devotee should repeat all the names affixing the Praṇava in the beginning and using them in the Dative

---

*The names in this list show that these so-called Yoginīs must be ogresses worshipped by the masses before their Brāhmaṇīsation. They came to be called "Yoginīs" after their absorption in the Śaiva cult.

case and perform one hundred and eight *Havanas* for each name at night with Guggulu (aromatic gum resin) mixed with ghee, making each lump of the size of a small *Badarī* fruit. He shall obtain great benefit and whatever power he may desire, the man shall obtain it.

52-54. On the first day in the dark half of Caitra a Pilgrimage (Yātrā) should be performed assiduously for the purpose of quelling obstacles to the holy spot by meritorious persons. If anyone staying in Kāśī, out of contempt or indifference, does not perform the annual pilgrimage, the Yoginīs create obstacles unto him. Keeping all of them ahead at Kāśī in Maṇikarṇikā, a devout man should perform obeisance. Merely on account of this he can ward off all obstacles.

CHAPTER FORTYSIX

*Description of Lolārka**

Skanda said:

1. After the group of Yoginīs had departed, O Pot-born One, the Lord of Devas who was desirous of knowing the situation in Kāśī sent the Sun-god.

The Lord of Devas said:

2. O Seven-horsed One, go quickly to the splendid city of Vārāṇasī where Divodāsa, a Dharma incarnate, is the ruler.

3. Do something quickly so that the holy spot gets ruined due to the king's transgression of the path of piety. But do not think lightly of that king.

4. If insult or disrespect is shown towards anyone treading the path of piety, that will surely recoil on oneself. Great sin too will befall.

5. If due to your intellectual skill he swerves from the

*There are twelve Āditya (Sun-god) temples at Banaras. Lolarka is the most important and famous. It is located in the extreme south of Vārāṇasī, near the confluence of Asi and Gaṅgā. The two copper-plate grants of Gāhadwal kings (after their baths here) show its ancient importance (BCL **177**).

path of virtue, O Sun, you can devastate that city with your fierce rays.

6. The notorious bad qualities of lust and anger, greed and delusion, rivalry and arrogance have no place in him. Hence even the god of Death cannot conquer him.

7. As long as the intellect is well-established in piety, as long as the mind is steadfast in piety, O Sun-god, whence can be the rise of obstacles in the case of men even in adversities?

8. O Bradhna (Sun-god), you are aware of the activities of all creatures. Hence you are called *Jagaccakṣuḥ* ('The eye of the universe'). Go, then for the accomplishment of the task.

9. The Sun took the order of the Lord, and assumed another form capable of going along the sky both day and night. He then proceeded towards Kāśī.

10. The Sun was very much eager to see Kāśī. Though he had a thousand feet (rays), he still yearned for more feet (rays).

11. The state of being *Haṁsa* ('one who goes continuously') of the Sun became meaningful and fruitful because he was desirous of going towards Kāśī and so was proceeding along the sky continuously.

12. After reaching Kāśī, the Sun moved within and without (Kāśī) but could not see even the least of an instance of deviation from piety in the case of the king.

13. The Sun stayed in Kāśī for a year in various guises, but could not find any loophole in that righteous king.

14. The Sun sometimes became a guest seeking something very difficult to get; but he did not see anything rare to be got in the realm of that king.

15. Sometimes he became a beggar; sometimes he became a bestower of many things. Sometimes he became one in a wretched state and sometimes he became an astrologer.

16. Sometimes he performed rites beyond the pale of Vedas. Sometimes he established the philosophy of this-worldliness believing in only what is perceived.

17. Sometimes he became one with matted hair. Sometimes he remained a nude mendicant. He sometimes became a snake-doctor, and expert in antidotes against poisons.

18. Sometimes he became one well-versed in all heretical

doctrines; sometimes an expounder of Brahma (Absolute). He became a juggler sometimes making people perplexed by creating illusions.

19. Sometimes he made chaste ladies much agitated through instructions in different kinds of vows and observances with many narratives as illustration.

20. Sometimes he became a Brāhmaṇa engaged in the vow of a Kāpālika; sometimes a Vijñānin (follower of Buddhist Vijñānavāda; sometimes a Dhātuvādin, alchemist—MW & Com.)

21. At some places he became a Brāhmaṇa; somewhere a royal prince, a Vaiśya or a Śūdra; somewhere he became a religious student observing celibacy; somewhere a householder and somewhere a forest-dweller.

22. Sometimes he became a recluse. Thus he tried to make the people confused. In some places, he became (posed to be) omniscient, an expert in all lores.

23. Thus the Lord of Planets wandered in Kāśī in different forms. But, nowhere did he find at any time any vulnerable point in the people.

24. The son of Kaśyapa (i.e. Sun-god) became very worried with thoughts and censured himself. "Fie upon being one who runs an errand for others, wherein no fame is obtained."

Mārtaṇḍa said:

25. If I want to go back to Mandara now, the Lord will get angry immediately with me, because I have not fulfilled the task. He will become angry as though I am an ordinary servant.

26. If somehow I go there, how shall I stand in front of him like a foolish servant?

27. If I somehow go there accepting (pocketing) the insult, the Three-eyed Lord may stare at me angrily. Poison should be drunk by me then.

28. If I became a victim to the fire of wrath of Lord Hara like a moth, even the Grandfather (Brahmā) will not be able to save me.

29. Hence I shall stay here forever. I will never leave this. I shall establish my hermitage in Vārāṇasī in accordance with the injunctions regarding (permanent stay) in a holy spot.

30. If I stay back here without intimating the non-fulfilment of the task to Purāri (Śiva), I may incur sin; but Kāśī itself shall be the means of redemption from that sin.

31. Other sins too, whether great or small, of the good people who have entered Kāśī, become reduced entirely.

32. This sin has not been incurred by me knowingly. At the outset, it was ordained by Purāri himself: "May Dharma be protected."

33. While the body is of quickly vanishing nature, if Dharma is protected by anyone, it is as though the three worlds have been protected by him. Of what avail are love and wealth, even if protected well.

34. If *Kāma* (love) is to be protected, why then was he made *Anaṅga* (bodiless), though he had been the bestower of happiness on many?

35. If it has been asserted by many that *Artha* (Wealth) should be always protected, then how did Hariścandra not protect it in the case of Viśvāmitra?

36. Dharma has been safeguarded by all, even at the cost of the body by Śibi and other kings as well as by Dadhīci and other Brāhmaṇas.

37. This Dharma itself arising from rendering service to Kāśī will certainly protect me even from the infuriated Rudra.

38. After attaining Kāśī very difficult to be attained, which sensible being forsakes it? Who will desire to collect worthless pieces of glass after giving up a jewel in one's hand.

39. He who desires to go elsewhere leaving Kāśī, kicks off a treasure with his foot and wishes to get wealth through begging for alms.

40. Sons, friends, wives, fields and riches are obtained in every birth but Kāśī alone is not attained.

41. A great happiness that is very difficult to achieve even with the riches of all the three worlds has been acquired by that man by whom the city of Kāśī capable of redeeming the three worlds, has been attained.

42. Indeed the angry Rudra may cause some reduction in my splendour. But in Kāśī, I will achieve that splendour arising from the realization of the self.

43. Other luminaries shine with a modicum of light of a glowworm only as long as the splendour arising from Kāśī

does not flourish.

44. Thus the dispeller of darkness, the eye of the universe, conversant with the power of Kāśī divided himself into twelve and established himself in the city of Kāśī.

45-47. O Pot-born One, the following are the twelve Ādityas (Suns): (1) Lolārka, (2) Uttarārka, (3) Sāṁbāditya, (4) Drupadāditya, the fourth, (5) Mayūkhāditya, (6) Khakholka, (7) Aruṇāditya, (8) Vṛddhāditya, (9) Keśavāditya, (10) Vimalāditya, (11) Gaṅgāditya, and (12) Yamāditya, the twelfth one, in the city of Kāśī. They always protect the holy spot from evil ones with dominant Tāmasa quality.

48. Since the mind of the Sun became very eager (*Lola*) to see Kāśī, the Sun in Kāśī acquired the name *Lolārka.*

49. Lolārka is established in the southern direction (of Kāśī) at the confluence of Asi (with Gaṅgā). He shall always make the inhabitants of Kāśī achieve and preserve the good.

50. By performing the annual pilgrimage on the seventh lunar day in Mārgaśīrṣa or on the sixth day falling on a Sunday*, a man is rid of all sins.

51. Whatever sins have been committed by men during the year, are destroyed the very moment. One sees Lolārka on the sixth lunar day falling on Sunday.

52. By taking the holy bath at the confluence of Asi (and Gaṅgā), by propitiating the Pitṛs and the deities and by duly performing Śrāddha, one gets free from the indebtedness to the Pitṛs.

53. Whatever sacred rite is performed, like *Dāna*, *Homa* and *Arcanā* of the deities, at the confluence (of Asi and Gaṅgā) known as 'Lolārka-Saṅgama' is capable of according never-ending benefit.

54. The rites of holy ablution, *Dāna* etc. at Lolārka at the time of a solar eclipse shall undoubtedly be ten times more efficacious than that at Kurukṣetra.

55. On the Rathasaptamī day (i.e. seventh day in the bright half of Māgha) a devotee should take his holy dip at the confluence of Gaṅgā and Asi. Immediately he becomes free from the sins

---

*BCL p. 279 notes that the annual pilgrimage of Lolārka Ṣaṣṭhī is in Bhādrapada.

incurred in the course of seven births.

56. If anyone pays a visit to Lolārka on every Sunday, observing the vows of cleanliness, he will never have any misery in this world

57. He who visits Lolārka on Sundays or imbibes the water washing the god's feet, will never have any misery, nor such skin-diseases as *Pāma, Dadru* or *Vicarcikā* (itches, scabs etc.).

58. If anyone even after staying in Vārāṇasī does not serve Lolārka, pains and miseries arising from hunger and sickness will certainly afflict him.

59. Lolārka is the first and foremost of all holy Tīrthas in Kāśī. Other Tīrthas are only subsidiaries. They are watered by its holy waters.

60. All the other Tīrthas existing in the entire range of the earth do not deserve even a fraction of one-sixteenth of the holy Tīrtha, of the confluence of Asi (and Gaṅgā).

61. From the holy ablution, at the confluence of Asi and Gaṅgā one gets the entire benefit that is acquired by the holy ablution in all the Tīrthas.

62. O sage, this is not a mere eulogical utterance, nor is it flattery. This is truly a statement of facts. It should be respectfully believed by all good people.

63. Where Viśveśvara is directly present, where there is the celestial river, there only sophists and jealous ones regard it as untrue.

64. All those foolish ones, arrogant of their power, who indulge in sophistical reasoning and say that this is a mere eulogical utterance, become worms in faeces in every Yuga.

65. O sage, indeed even all the three worlds will never be on a par with the greatness of anyone of the holy Tīrthas in Kāśī.

66. Kāśī should not be extolled before these atheists, those who are outside the ken of the Vedas, those who value the penis and the belly and the low-born ones.

67. Being scorched by the rays of Lolārka and being cut (obstructed) by the current of the river Asi, persons of great sins cannot enter Kāśī.

Being heated by the hands of brave persons brilliant like Lolārka and cut down by the edge of their swords, Kāśī-haters, the great sinners, cannot enter Kāśī.

68. On hearing the greatness of Lolārka, an excellent man never experiences misery in the ocean of sorrow in the worldly existence.

CHAPTER FORTYSEVEN

*Description of Uttarārka**

Skanda said:

1. There is an excellent Kuṇḍa (holy pool) in the northern side, named *Arka.* The Sun established himself there with the name of Uttarārka.

2. Scorching (dispelling) the cluster of miseries and making good people flourish, Uttarārka, the Sun of great splendour, ever protects Kāśī.

3. O holy sage of excellent vows, please listen to the historical event that happened there. There was a certain Brāhmaṇa named Priyavrata born of the family of Atri.

4. He was in Kāśī, ever devoted to guests and doing only what is splendid. His wife named Śubhavratā was extremely charming.

5. She was ever engaged in serving her husband. She was skilful in domestic works. He begot of her a daughter of excellent features.

6. She was born in the first quarter of the constellation Mūla while Bṛhaspati (Jupiter) was in the Kendra (fourth, seventh or tenth zodiacal position from the Lagna). Like the Moon in the bright half, she grew up day by day.

7. She was beautiful in form. Her behaviour was modest. She delighted her parents by doing what was pleasing to them. She was very clever in keeping household articles and utensils clean.

---

*The site of Uttarārka is near Bakaria Kuṇḍa ('Uttarārka Kuṇḍa' in the Text), just south of today's Grand Trunk Road. The original temple was destroyed by Muslims and its ruins were transformed into Muslim structures. M.A. Sherring discovered here a Sun disc with relief carvings of the Sun, thus confirming the site of this Sun-god. (BCL 179)

8. As the girl was growing up in the parental abode, the worry of her father too increased day by day.

9-10. He began to think thus: 'To whom is this beautiful girl of excellent features to be given? Where is that excellent bridegroom befitting her to be obtained by me? He should be endowed with nobility of faith, youth, good habits, learning, comely features and adequate wealth. To whom should she be given so that she may be happy?'

11. As he worried thus his fever became excessively terrible. The fever named worry in the case of men does not subside through medicines.

12 As a result of that constellation Mūla and that of the fever called worry, the Brāhmaṇa met with his death forsaking everything such as the house etc.

13. When the father of the girl died, the mother too named Śubhavratā followed her husband leaving behind her virgin daughter.

14. This is the eternal duty of a chaste wife who is expected to follow righteous conduct, that she should remain with her husband living or not living.

15. Neither the progeny nor her own mother nor father nor other kinsmen accord protection to a woman. It is the service alone rendered to the feet of her husband that protects a woman.

16-21. The girl though endowed with excellent features became highly miserable, when her parents died. All the funeral rites were completed and the tenth day ceremonies too were concluded. Bereft of a gurdian and meeting with wretchedness, she became extremely worried: 'I am alone without my father and mother. How can I cross the ocean of worldly existence that is excessively difficult to cross? Womanhood comes into clash with everything. I have not been given over to anyone by my parents. Having not been handed over by them, how can I woo another bridegroom? What if he is neither meritorious nor of good habits, despite being wooed by me? Though he may be independent, what will happen when he is wooed?' That girl richly endowed with the qualities of beauty, munificence etc., was pressingly approached frequently by many young men. Yet the girl did not give to anyone free access to her mind.

22. She had witnessed the death of her parents. Remembering their excessive fondness, she cursed her own self and cursed the entire world.

23-24a. "Where have my parents gone, the parents who gave birth to me and protected me? Fie upon the transience of the embodied ones! Alas! Even my body is only a part of my parents. Just as my parents have gone, this too may go away."

24b-25. On deciding thus that girl performed a very severe penance sustaining steadfast celibacy in close vicinity of Lord Uttarārka. She conquered the sense-organs and the mind and stabilised the mind.

26. While she was performing penance, a very tiny kid used to come there everyday and stand still in front of her.

27. In the evening it used to eat some grass or leaves and drink the water from that pool. Then it used to go back to the abode of its master.

28. Thus five or six years passed off. Once the Lord, sportingly wandering about, along with the Goddess came there.

29. Sthāṇu saw Sulakṣaṇā performing penance near Uttarārka, steady like a pillar and grown emaciated due to the penance.

30. Thereupon Lord Śaṁbhu was requested by the Daughter of the Mountain moved with pity, "Kindly bless this beautiful girl devoid of kinsmen by bestowing on her a boon."

31. On hearing the words of Śarvāṇī, Śarva, the storehouse of mercy, Hara, the bestower of boons, spoke to her, as she remained in her state of meditation with closed eyes.

32. "O Sulakṣaṇā! I am pleased. O girl of excellent vows, choose your boon. You are fatigued due to the penance of long duration. What is your desire?"

33. On hearing the words of Śaṁbhu shedding nectar from the mouth that suppressed excessive distress, she opened her eyes.

34. On directly perceiving in front of her the Three-eyed Lord eager to bestow boons and the Goddess stationed to his left side, she joined her palms in reverence and bowed down.

35. Even as that girl of charming waist thought thus, 'What shall I choose?' the tiny goat kid was seen in front by her.

36-37. 'Which man does not live in this world of creatures for his own sake? But he who lives for the sake of rendering help to others, lives really. For many years I have been attended to by this (kid) who is a witness of my penance and holy rites. Hence I shall request the Lord of the universe for some boon on its behalf.'

38-39. After considering this in her mind Sulakṣaṇā said to the Three-eyed Lord: "O Mahādeva, O storehouse of mercy, if a boon is to be given to me, then at the outset may this poor insignificant kid of a goat be blessed. She has the same lovely devotion to me but does not know how to speak it out, being an animal itself."

40. On hearing these words of Sulakṣaṇā, showing (eagerness for) helping others, Īśa, the destroyer of the distress of those who bow down to him, became all the more pleased.

41. Then the Lord of the Devas said: "O Goddess, O Daughter of the Lord of mountains, see this. The intellect of good persons is of this nature—it is all the more powerful with (the readiness of) helping others.

42. Those who endeavour for helping others in all earnestness are the blessed ones, in all the worlds. They are the supports of all kinds of piety.

43. The gathering together of all the worldly objects does not last long. O my beloved, ony one thing—rendering help to others, lasts for a long time.

44. This Sulakṣaṇā is blessed and capable of obliging others. O my beloved Goddess, tell me, what boon should be given to her? What should be given to this kid?"

The Goddess said:

45. O Creator of all creators! O omniscient one! O destroyer of the distress of those who bow down to you! May this Sulakṣaṇā of excellent conduct and splendid effort be my companion.

46-52. May this Sulakṣaṇā be one of my companions like Jayā, Vijayā, Jayantikā, Śubhā, Nandā, Sunandā, Kaumudī, Ūrmilā, Caṁpakamālā, Malayavāsinī, Karpūralatikā, the splendid Gandhadharā, Aśokā, Viśokā, Malayagandhinī, Candananiḥśvāsā, the excellent Mṛgamadā, Kokilālāpā, Madhurabhāṣiṇī, Gadyapadyanidhi, Anuktajñā, Dṛgañcalā, Iṅgitajñā, Kṛtamanorathā and Gānacittaharā. Since she is a celibate ever since childhood, she will become my greatest favourite. Let her be so in this same body with divine limbs and ornaments, divine garments, divine unguents and endowed with divine knowledge. Let her be near me forever, holding the moving chowries.

53. Let this kid be born as the princess of the king of Kāśī. After enjoying the pleasures here, she will attain the excellent salvation.

54. This kid has bathed in this Arkakuṇḍa on the Sunday in the Puṣya month (December-January) before sunrise without being afflicted in the mind by chillness.

55. O Lord Viśveśvara, by your power of besotwing boons, let this (kid) be a princess of splendid vision due to merit.

56. Let this Arkakuṇḍa be also known by another name Barkari Kuṇḍa*. Its idol (image) should be worshipped by men here.

57. The annual pilgrimage of Lord Uttarārka should be performed on a Sunday in the month of Puṣya by devotees desirous of the benefit of Kāśī.

58. After carrrying out everything mentioned by Mṛḍānī, the all-powerful omnipresent Lord Viśvanātha unexpectedly entered his own palace.

Skanda said:

59. O Brāhmaṇa of great fortune, the greatness of Lolārka and Uttarārka has been described to you. Now listen to the legend of Sāṁbāditya.

60. On hearing the excellent meritorious narrative of Lolārka and Uttarārka, no man will be afflicted with diseases or poverty.

---

*The name indicates Muslim influence. These verses are probably later additions to explain how the ancient Arka-Kuṇḍa came to be designated as Bakariā-Kuṇḍa.

CHAPTER FORTYEIGHT

*The Greatness of Sāṁbāditya**

Skanda said:

1-2. Listen, O Maitrāvaruṇi, Vāsudeva, the abode of the universe, manifested himsef as Kṛṣṇa with fiery brilliance in Devakī through Vasudeva in Dvārakā. He was the greatest among Yādavas. (He manifested himself) for reducing the burden of the earth by slaying demons.

3. A hundred thousand and eighty sons of solar refulgence were born to him. O Pot-born One, even in heaven, there are no such boys of excellent behaviour.

4. They were richly endowed with supreme handsomeness. They were extremely powerful. They were highly conversant with scriptures and the art of wielding weapons. They had highly splendid characteristics.

5-8. Once Nārada came to see the city of Dvārakā built by Viśvakarman, which surpassed even the celestial city in excellence. Nārada was a mental son of Brahmā and a storehouse of penance. He had a bark garment as loin cloth and a deer hide as the (upper) garment. He held a Brahmadaṇḍa (staff held by a religious student). He had a girdle of three-stringed Muñja grass. A Tulasī garland embellished his chest. Liquid paste of Gopīcandana was the unguent shining on his body. All his limbs were emaciated due to austerities. He shone like a personified form of fire. He came by the aerial path.

9. On seeing Nārada all the Vṛṣṇi folk bent down their necks in humility. With joined palms held over the head they bowed down to him.

10. Sāṁba who was deluded by everything that he possessed such as comely features and charm, did not bow down to the sage. He was laughing at the excellence(?) of the form (of the sage).

---

*Now, a small shrine of Sāṁbāditya is near Suraj Kuṇḍa (Sūrya Kuṇḍa; near Godaulia crossing in the heart of the city). But the plinth of the destroyed temple shows that it was an extensive temple. BCL 180-181 notes: Two Sun-discs lying under a tree in a rubble near the ruins, are witness to the ancient impressive temple.

11. After knowing perfectly well what Sāṁba thought, the great sage Nārada entered the extremely beautiful palace of Kṛṣṇa.

12. On seeing Nārada coming, Kṛṣṇa rose up to welcome him, honoured him with *Madhuparka* and made him share his own seat.

13. After conversing with him on a variety of topics Nārada whispered into Kṛṣṇa's ears the misbehaviour of Sāṁba when Kṛṣṇa was alone.

14. "O delighter of Yaśodā, here there is something (unusual). Generally it does not happen but perhaps there is nothing that is impossible in the case of women.

15. Sāṁba is the most handsome of all young men in the three worlds. Fickle indeed is the mind of women whose eyes are by nature tremulous.

16. These beautiful-eyed damsels, when deluded by the god of Love, do not care to follow the norms of noble birth, good conduct, learning or riches. They see only charming features.

17. Or perhaps there is nothing not known to you in regard to the activities of the cowherd lasses. Excepting your eight crowned queens, all the other ladies are enamoured of him."

18. Kṛṣṇa knowing as he did the natural inclinations of beautiful women and relying on Nārada's words, believed what Nārada had reported as true.

19. 'Ladies of tremulous eyes have fortitude and discretion only as long as the seeker of love is not in a secluded spot. If he is in a secluded spot, their fortitude and discretion become inoperative. They become otherwise.'

20. Thinking thus in his mind, Kṛṣṇa checked the current of the river of his fury by means of the dam of discretion. The wise Kṛṣṇa bade goodbye to Nārada.

21. After the departure of the celestial sage, though Kṛṣṇa watchfully observed day and night, he could not perceive any misbehaviour on the part of Sāṁba.

22-23. After the lapse of some time, the sage came again. On coming to know that Kṛṣṇa was in the midst of the sporting women, Nārada called Sāṁba who was playing outside and said thus: "Go immediately to Kṛṣṇa and inform him that I have come."

24-28. Sāṁba hesitated for a while, thinking: 'Should I go? Should I not go? How can I go to my father who is in a lonely spot in the company of women? How can I disobey this Brahmacārin who is like a blazing charcoal? There is dazzling brilliance all over his body. Once I had ridiculed him while all the other boys were bowing down. If now too I refuse to go, disobeying thereby this great sage, there shall be greater danger in view of the two sins and defaults. A father's anger towards me is better than that of a Brāhmaṇa towards me. Those who are burnt down by the fire of the wrath of a Brāhmaṇa never flourish. Those who ae burnt down by other (kinds of) fires do grow again like things reduced to ash by a forest fire.'

29-30. After reflecting thus for a short while, Sāṁba, the son of Jāṁbavatī, entered the apartment of his father. Even as he hesitatingly bowed down to Kṛṣṇa in the midst of the assembly of ladies from fear and reported to him Nārada too followed him to accomplish what he intended.

31. On seeing Sāṁba and Nārada, Kṛṣṇa stood up in a flurry and put on the yellow silk cloth.

32. When the son of Devakī got up, all those cowherdesses bashfully stood up tucking up their respective clothes.

33. Kṛṣṇa grasped the hands of the great sage and made him sit on the couch of great value. Sāṁba went away to play.

34. Due to Kṛṣṇa's dalliance with them, all those ladies had experienced orgasm with drenched vaginal apertures. On seeing them dripping even as they stood in front of him, the sage said to Kṛṣṇa:

35. "O my dear intelligent fellow! Lo and behold. On seeing the son of Jāṁbavatī these ladies are dripping because their minds are agitated by his comely features."

36. Though Sāṁba looked upon everyone like (his mother) Jāṁbavatī, Kṛṣṇa called his son and cursed him due to the adverse action of fate:

37. "Be a leper because it was on seeing your handsome features that these lasses experienced this drenching of their organs. Further you had intruded untimely."

38. Trembling on account of the terrible fear of the great disease, Sāṁba pleaded in many ways for the purpose of quelling the sin.

39. By this time Kṛṣṇa realized (his mistake) and told his

bosom-born son Sāṁba: "To get the cure from leprosy, go to the city of Viśveśvara.

40. By propitiating the Sun-god there, you will regain your normal state. Excepting in Vārāṇasī there is no quelling of great sins elsewhere.

41. After reaching the city of Vārāṇasī where Viśveśvara is directly present and where there is the celestial river, there is surely redemption and purity, removing those great sins for which no remedy has been seen even by sages.

42. At Vārāṇasī, not only from (self-incurred) sins is one liberated, but also from Prākṛta sins (sins foisted on one by Prakṛti), at the behest of Śaṅkara.

43. Formerly, due to his great mercy, Avimukta was created by Purāri for the liberation of all creatures that give up their bodies in the end.

44. O Sāṁba, the curse on you will be exonerated there in the Ānandavana of Śaṁbhu. Hence listen. There is no redemption from the curse otherwise."

45. Nārada, the living-liberated soul, free from of all binding Karmas, became happy on having concluded his mission. He took leave of Kṛṣṇa and went away by the aerial path.

46. After going to Vārāṇasī and propitiating the Sun-god, Sāṁba left the Kuṇḍa. He regained normalcy.

47. Ever since then, the Sun-god Sāṁbāditya has become dispeller of all ailments. On all his devotees he bestows all riches free from evil and illness.

48. If anyone takes his holy dip in Sāṁbakuṇḍa early at dawn on a Sunday and worships the deity Sāṁbāditya, he is never afflicted by diseases.

49. No woman meets with widowhood after the worship of Sāṁbāditya. Even a barren woman will give birth to a son endowed with pure handsome features.

50. O Brāhmaṇa, the seventh lunar day in the bright half of the month of Māgha, especially if it falls on a Sunday, is called a day of great festival. It is as auspicious as solar eclipse.

51. By taking the holy bath early at dawn, one is rid of even great diseases. By worshipping Sāṁbāditya, one acquires inexhaustible piety.

52. There is no doubt in this that on Ravisaptamī day in Māgha at Kāśī one gets the same merit (*Puṇya*) as one acquires

at the time of the Solar (or Lunar) eclipse by being present in Kurukṣetra.

53-54. On a Sunday, in the month of Madhu (Caitra) the annual pilgrimage and festivities take place. The devotee should worship Sāṁbāditya with Aśoka flowers after taking the holy bath in accordance with the injunctions. The devotee will never be afflicted with grief. Instantaneously he becomes freed from the sins incurred throughout the year.

55. In the western quarter of Viśveśa, the splendid idol of the Sun-god bestowing auspiciousness was perfectly propitiated by the noble-souled Sāṁba.

56. This future image thereof has been told to you, O Agasti. By circumambulating it eight times and by worshipping and bowing to it, a man becomes free of sins. He shall attain the benefit of stay in Kāśī.

57. O highly intelligent one, the greatness of the deity Sāṁbāditya has been narrated to you, on hearing which no man will ever see the world of Yama.

58. Now, O sinless one, I shall describe Draupadāditya. This Draupada Āditya should be served. He is the bestower of supernatural powers on his devotees.

CHAPTER FORTYNINE

*Description of Draupadāditya and Mayūkhāditya**

Sūta said:

1. O Sage Vyāsa, O son of Parāśara, there was no daughter of Drupada when Kumāra (Skanda) narrated this story to the Pot-born Sage.

Vyāsa said:

2. The Purāṇasaṁhitā is proclaimed as the story of all the three aspects of time (past, present, future). No doubt is

*Draupadāditya is in the west of Viśvanātha Temple and is under a tree. Mayūkhāditya is inside Maṅgalā Devī Temple.

to be entertained in this regard, because everything is comprised therein.

Skanda said:

3. Listen, O sage. Formerly, the five-faced Hara divided himself in five forms and manifested on the earth for the sake of the welfare of the universe.

4. Umā, the mother of the universe, also manifested herself as a very beautiful lady from the sacrificial fire pit of king Drupada.

5. The five sons of Pāṇḍu were the embodied forms of Rudra taking incarnations on the earth from heaven for the destruction of the wicked ones.

6. Lord Nārāyaṇa attained the form of Kṛṣṇa and accompanied them as the suppressor of the activities of the evildoers and the sustainer of the good.

7. Those sons of Pṛthā shone brilliantly and secured great prosperity and extinction of adversities.

8. Once those great warriors encountered great danger brought about by adversaries and they had to live in forests.

9. Pāñcālī, their wife, was distressed on account of the misery of her husbands. The lady of tender limbs, given to virtuous conduct, went to Kāśī to the Sun-god and assiduously propitiated him.

10. On being propitiated by the daughter of Drupada, the Sun-god gave her an inexhaustible vessel with a lid and a ladle.

11-13. Delighted in his mind the Sun-god said to the daughter of Drupada, who had propitiated him devoutly and whose mind was pure in every respect:

"O blessed lady, as long as you do not take food, all those who seek food, irrespective of their number, will become satisfied. This vessel, full of cooked food, the storehouse of delicious side dishes and the bestower of all the desired foodstuffs will become empty when you have taken food."

14. This boon was attained by her at Kāśī. Another boon was also given to her by the lord, Sun-god.

Ravi said:

15. If a man propitiates me while standing on the right

side of Viśveśvara and keeping you in front, he will never have distress due to hunger.

16. O chaste lady, another boon has been granted to me by Viśveśa who was pleased with my penance. Listen, I shall narrate it to you.

17. "O Ravi, if any man visits me after worshipping you at the outset, you will remove the darkness of his misery with your own rays."

18. Hence, O righteous lady, after attaining this boon from Viśveśvara, I am dispelling forever the collection of sins of the creatures stationed at Kāśī.

19. To these people endowed with faith, who worship me with hands raised aloft to grant boon unto you, I will grant whatever they wish.

20-21. If men or women with great fervour worship you, the chaste wife of Yudhiṣṭhira, stationed near me in the vicinity of Daṇḍapāṇi towards the right (south) of Viśveśa, they will never experience the fear due to separation from the near and dear ones.

22. They will nowhere have fear of illness or that arising from the faults of hunger and thirst, O Draupadī, O sinless beloved of Dharmaputra, after visiting you.

23. After granting these boons, the Sun-god, the bestower of everything on the good, began to propitiate Śaṁbhu and Draupadī went back to Yudhiṣṭhira.

24. If any man listens with devotion to the story of Āditya propitiated by Draupadī, his sins will become dispelled.

Skanda said:

25. O Pot-born One, the greatness of Draupadāditya has been narrated succinctly by me. Listen to the greatness of Mayūkhāditya now.

26. Formerly, the thousand-rayed Sun-god performed a fierce penance in the holy spot of Pañcanada renowned in all the three worlds.

27-29. He installed the great Liṅga named Gabhastīśvara and Gaurī, the perpetual bestower of auspiciousness on the devotees, named Maṅgalā. He propitiated Lord Śiva who has made the crescent moon his crest jewel, along with Umā, O sage, for a period of a thousand celestial years multiplied by a hundred. By means of his natural refulgence the Sun is capable of scorching the three worlds. Hence he shone all the more brilliantly, O sage, due to his severe austerities.

30. At that time the entire space between heaven and earth was overspread by the rays of the Sun, capable of burning the three worlds.

31. All movements (travel to and fro) through the firmament were abandoned by Devas moving about in aerial chariots, as if they were afraid of being reduced to the state of locust in the fierce heat of the Sun.

32. Above, below and obliquely too, only the rays of the Sun were seen and not the Sun himself as in the case of the Kadaṁba bud where the pericarp is not seen but only the petals.

33. The three worlds including the mobile and immobile beings trembled due to the fear of the flames of penance of the Sun, a mass of refulgence.

34. "The Sun is the very soul of this universe, mobile and immobile." So it is said in the Vedas. If he himself were to be one who burns who can be our protector?

35. This Sun is the eye of the universe. This Bhāskara is the soul of the universe. He wakens up and enlivens the universe, almost dead (during night), every morning.

36. Rising up everyday, spreading his hands (rays) all-round, he lifts up the entire living beings that have fallen in the blinding well of darkness.

37. When the Sun rises, we rise up. When he sets, we lie down and rest. Hence Ravi is the cause of our rising and taking rest.

38. Viśveśvara, the protector of the universe, saw the entire universe agitated thus. So he went (there) to grant boons to the Sun.

39. On seeing the Sun with the full complement of rays remaining very steady, forgetting himself in mental absorption, he became wonder-struck in regard to his penance.

40. Śrīkaṇṭha, the destroyer of the distress of those who bow down, became pleased in his mind and said: "O Dyumaṇi (Crest-jewel of the firmament i.e. the Sun), O storehouse of refulgence, enough of your penance. Tell me the boon you

wish to have."

41. Since the Sun had controlled the activities of all the sense-organs through mental absorption and meditation he did not grasp the words of Śaṁbhu though repeated two or three times as though he had no ears.

42. Realizing that he had become a log of wood as it were, Śiva touched him with his hands shedding nectar, dispelling the distress due to the great penance.

43. Then the Sun (*Viśvalocana*—'the eye of the universe') opened his eyes like a cluster of lotuses (that open up their petals) in the morning when he himself rises.

44. With all his distress dispelled by the touch of the Lord, the Sun became glad like vegetation, the glory of which was tarnished by drought, becoming flourishing once again due to the clouds.

45. The Sun directly looked at the Three-eyed Lord who was visible in front, prostrated in front of him like a log of wood, and eulogized the Pināka-wielding Lord loudly:

Ravi said: (Prayer to Śiva: vv 46—53)

46. I bow unto you, O Lord of Devas, O Lord of the worlds, O all-powerful one, O Bharga (the bestower of happiness), O Bhīma (terrible), O Bhava (the place of origin), O lord having the moon as ornament, O lord of goblins, O destroyer of the fear of worldly existence, O bestower of the desired things on those who bow down!

47. O Candracūḍa, O Mṛḍa, O Dhūrjaṭi, O Hara, O Tryakṣa, O destroyer of the sacrifice of Dakṣa, O quiescent one, O everlasting Lord, O Śivā's consort, O Śiva, I bow unto you, the giver of the desired things to those who bow down.

48. O Nīlalohita, O bestower of desired objects, O three-eyed one, O Virūpalocana, O Vyomakeśa, O destroyer of the bondage of living beings, I bow down unto you, the giver of the desired things to those who bow down.

49. O Vāmadeva, O Śrīkaṇṭha, O trident-bearing Lord with moon for crest-jewel, O Lord with serpents for ornaments, O Lord of souls bringing about the desired things, O Maheśvara, I bow unto you, the fulfiller of the desires of those who bow down.

50. O Tryaṁbaka, O Tripurasūdana, O Īśvara, O Trāṇakṛt (Saviour), O Trinayana, O Trayīmaya, O Kālakūṭadalana ('one who rendered the poison ineffective'), O destroyer of the god of Death, I bow unto you, the bestower of the desires of those who bow down.

51. O Śarva, devoid of Māyā, O omnipresent one, O bestower of the happiness of the path of heaven, O enemy of the demon Andhaka, O Lord with matted hairs, I bow down unto you, the bestower of the desires of those who bow down.

52. O Śaṅkara, O Ugra, O Lord, O Lord of the Daughter of Mountain, O Viśvanātha, O Lord eulogized by Brahmā and Viṣṇu, O Lord capable of being known only through the Vedas, O Lord who have understood the internal thoughts and wishes of everyone, I bow unto you, the bestower of the desire of those who bow down.

53. O Viśvarūpa (omniformed god), O great one, O Lord devoid of forms, O Brahman, devoid of deception, O bestower of Amṛta (Nectar, freedom from death), O Lord beyond the ken of the mind and words, O Dūraga ('one who has gone far'), I bow unto you, the bestower of the desires of those who bow down.

54. After praying to Lord Mṛḍa thus, Mārtaṇḍa (the Sun) who was delighted in his mind eulogized Mṛḍānikā who appropriated half the body of Śiva.

Ravi said: (Prayer to the goddess: vv 55—62)

55. O goddess, if anyone efficient in the activity of bowing down, renders his forehead grey by means of the dust particles of thy lotus-like feet, the beautiful digit of the moon makes his forehead all the more bright.

56. O Śrī Maṅgalā, the source of origin of every auspicious features, O Śrī Maṅgalā, the fire that burns all sins like cotton, O Śrī Maṅgalā, the dispeller of the arrogance of all the Dānavas, O Śrī Maṅgalā, protect this entire universe.

57. O Viśveśvarī (goddess of the universe), you are the creator of the people of all the worlds; you are the protectress and the destroyer at the time of the ultimate annihilation. The river of great pure merit arising out of the repetition of thy names dispels all the sins as though they were the trees on its banks.

58. O mother Bhavānī, O destroyer of the entire collection of the fierce miseries of worldly existence, you alone are the refuge. There is no one else. Only they are blessed in all the worlds, only they are worthy of honour, they, in whom your splendid glance of mercy falls and shines.

59. Those who remember you always, you who have the innate brilliance, who are stationed in Kāśī, who constitute the glory of salvation unto those who bow down, are remembered by Lord Smarahara ('Destroyer of the god of Love') as the people of pure intellect and clever and deserving to have salvation and protection.

60. O mother, if anyone retains in his heart the pair of your feet free from impurities, the entire universe is within the grasp of his hands. If, O Maṅgalā-Gaurī, anyone repeats your name everyday, the eight Siddhis never leave his house.

61. O goddess, you are of the form of Praṇava, the mother of Vedas; you are Gāyatrī; you are the wish-yielding cow of the twice-borns. You are the three *Vyāhṛtis* (*Bhūḥ, Bhuvaḥ* and *Svaḥ*) here for the fulfilment of all Karmas. You are Svāhā, the giver of the satisfaction to Devas, and Svadhā, the giver of satisfaction to Pitṛs.

62. O Goddess, O mother, you are Gaurī in respect to the Moon-crested Lord; you are Sāvitrī in respect to Vedhas (Brahmā); you are the charming Lakṣmī in respect to the Discus-bearing Lord Viṣṇu. O fine-featured goddess, you, the glory of salvation in Kāśī, O Maṅgalā-Gaurī, you are my refuge.

63. After eulogizing the goddess who is the splendour of half of Śiva's body, through the great prayer called *Śrī Maṅgalāṣṭaka*, the Sun circumambulated the goddess and the Lord many times, bowed down and stood silent in front of Śiva and Śivā.

The Lord of Devas said:

64. Rise up, rise up. Welfare unto you, O highly intelligent one, O Mitra, I am delighted. You are always present in my eye. I see the mobile and immobile beings (through you).

65. O Sūrya, you are my cosmic form. Be omniscient and omnipresent, the mass of all splendours, the knower of all the activities of everyone.

66-69a. You will dispel all the miseries of all the devotees. With my sixty-four names, you have uttered a prayer of eight verses. Any man will attain excellent devotion unto me by eulogizing me with this prayer. The eight verses of the prayer of Maṅgalāgaurī will be known as *Maṅgalāṣṭaka.* By eulogizing Maṅgalāgaurī with this prayer, one will acquire auspiciousness. The octave containing sixty-four names and this *Maṅgalāṣṭaka* are holy excellent prayers destructive of all sins.

69b-74a. Any excellent man in exile in far-off lands should repeat this thrice everyday. He shall become purified in soul and will attain Kāśī very rarely obtained. If these two prayers are repeated everyday by men, all their sins incurred everyday will be washed. There is no doubt about this. In the body of that embodied one no sin can stay, the one who repeats this splendid pair of hymns thrice a day always. Of what avail are the many prayers that could only grant transient glories to the men on being repeated? This pair of prayers shall accord the glory of salvation in Kāśī. Hence these two prayers should be assiduously repeated by men desirous of salvation by eschewing many other hymns.

74b-76. All this *Prapañca* (world) consisting of mobile and immobile beings, has evolved from us both. Hence by means of this eulogy of ours, people can be rid of the *Prapañca.* After attaining great prosperity along with sons and grandsons, the man who repeats this prayer acquires salvation in the end, O Saptāśva ('one having seven horses'). O Divākara, the king of Planets, listen to something more.

77-80a. The Liṅga named Gabhastīśvara has been installed by you and served with devotional fervour. It will yield all Siddhis. The Liṅga will get the name Gabhastīśvara, O Sun, because the Liṅga of the Lord has been devoutly worshipped by you through clusters of rays having the lustre of Campaka and lotuses. If a man takes his holy bath in Pañcanada and adores Gabhastīśvara, he becomes rid of all sins. He is never born in any mother's womb.

80b-86. Any devotee, man or woman, should worship Maṅgalāgaurī in the following manner. Fast is observed on the third lunar day in the bright half of Caitra. The deity is worshipped with all great means of services, silk clothes, ornaments etc. The devotee keeps awake in the night through dances, songs and holy discourses and the like. The next morning, twelve virgins are to be honoured with coverings (clothes) etc. They must be fed with excellent, sweet, cooked food. Others should be one given monetary gifts, accompanied by recitation of the Mantra beginning with *Jātavedas* (TA I.18.1). In the dawn, there should be one hundred and eight *Tila-Ājya Āhutis* (offerings of gingelly seed and ghee into the fire). To a Brāhmaṇa burdened with a family, a pair of cows (or bulls) should be offered. A Brāhmaṇa couple should be embellished with ornaments faithfully and fed with rich, cooked foodstuffs accompained by uttering the recitation of the Mantra "May Maṅgalā and Īśvara be pleased". The devotee breaks fast in the morning. This devotee never incurs wretchedness or poverty.

87. He never meets with break in the line of progeny. He never faces cessation of pleasures and enjoyments. The woman never attains widowhood. Nor does the man become separated from his wife.

88. All the sins become extinct. Heaps of Merits are acquired. Even a barren lady begets child after performing this Maṅgalāvrata.

89. Ugliness in form can always be warded off by performing this Vrata. A virgin gets a husband equipped with excellent qualities and handsome features.

90-93. A bachelor gets an excellent wife after performing this Vrata. There are many Vratas according riches and desires. But they will never be on a par with Maṅgalāvrata. The annual pilgrimage should be performed on that lunar day (third day in the bright half) in the month of Madhu by the men residing in Kāśī for the sake of subduing all obstacles. O Dyumaṇi (Sun-god), I shall mention another thing. While you were performing penance only the rays were seen and not your body. Hence, O son of Aditi, your name shall be Mayūkhāditya.

94. If you are adored, no sickness can afflict men. If you are visited on Sundays no one will incur poverty.

95. After granting many boons to Mayūkhāditya thus, Śiva vanished there and the Sun stood there itself.

96. If a man listens to this meritorious narrative of Mayūkhāditya along with that of Draupadāditya, he shall never go to hell.

CHAPTER FIFTY

*Description of Khakholkāditya**

Skanda said:

1. O Pot-born One, there are other Ādityas also in Vārāṇasī. Henceforth, I shall gladly describe them to you. All of them are destroyers of all sins.

2. The Āditya deity to the north Triviṣṭapa (the shrine of Śiva) is glorified by the name Khakholka (or Khaṣolka). He is the destroyer of all ailments.

3-4. Listen how the name Khakholka was attained by that Āditya. Two splendid daughters of Dakṣa, Kadrū and Vinatā, became wives of Kaśyapa, son of Marīci and a fromer Prajāpati (Patriarch). Once, while they were playing together, O sage, they said thus:

Kadrū said:

5. O Vinatā, if you know, tell it to me as you have unobstructed movement in the firmament.

6. We hear that there is a horse named Uccaiśśravā in the chariot of Savitṛ (Sun). Tell me quickly whether it is white in colour or variegated.

7. O auspicious lady, O sinless one, bet a wager on this, whatever you like. Time cannot pass this way alone without some pastime.

Vinatā said:

8. O my sister, what is the necessity of betting in this regard? I shall speak simply (without bet). What pleasure can I have, if you win? What joy will you have, in case I win?

9. Knowingly no one should bet a wager, if mutual friendship is desired. Certainly, at the victory of one, the other will get infuriated.

---

*The story of rivalry between Kadrū and Vinatā and Garuḍa's exploit is based on Mbh, *Ādi*, Chs. 20-34.

The deity Khakholkāditya is now in Kāmeśvara Temple. (BCL 362)

Kadrū said:

10. O dear sister, this is only a play. There is no cause for anger in this. This is only a playful transaction and something is mentioned in regard to the wager.

Vinatā said:

11. O serpentess! Do as you please.

Therupon Kadrū of a crooked mind, said to Vinatā:

12. "She who is defeated shall become the slave of her by whom she is defeated. In this matter of wager all these friends of ours are the witnesses."

13. When the serpentess and the bird betted the wager thus, Kadrū said that the horse was variegated in colour and the winged one (Vinatā) told that it was white.

14. They both fixed the time when they should go. Thereafter, they stopped their play and went to their respective bodes.

15-18. When Vintatā had gone away, Kadrū called her sons and said: "My sons, at my behest all of you go quickly. Go quickly to the horse Uccaiśśravas that had come out of the Milk Ocean that was being churned and being agitated by Mandara hitting it.

An effect gets the features similar to those of the cause. Hence it has the colour of milk. Dear sons, make it dark in colour. Occupy its tail and assume the form of dark hairs. Make the hairs too on its body dark by means of poisonous puffs of air. "

19. On hearing these words of their mother, the sons of Kadrū consulted one another. Becoming furious, they told their mother:

The Serpents said:

20. Mother, when you called us, we left our games and came here delighted that our mother will give us sweets to eat.

21. Far from giving sweets, you have uttered what is more caustic than even poison. This is not going to be subdued either by Mantras or by medicines.

22. We are not going. Let anything befall us.

This was uttered by those poison-mouthed, crooked-gaited ones.

Skanda said:

23-24. There are others too with crooked gaits and cruel hearts who make their parents ashamed. They resort to (take advantage of) the loopholes of others. They don't pay heed. They set at nought the words of their parents and remain highly arrogant. Such ones will court great danger here and ere long will perish.

25. On hearing the words (of her sons), "We are not going", the serpentess became angry and cursed them—the serpents who had committed an offence (of disobedience).

26. "Because you have transgressed my words, you will become prey unto Tārkṣya. Let all female serpents eat their young ones immediately after the birth."

27. The nether worlds were resorted to by some of them who were afraid of the fire of curse. The behest of the mother was carried out by a few who were eager to be alive.

28. Those extremely sensible ones got on to the tail of Uccaiśśravas and made it resemble one with very dark hairs. They made its body variegated in colour.

29. It was brought about by the columns of smoke of their poisonous fire augmented by puffs and sighs issuing forth. They were not burnt by the rays of the Sun because of the merit of carrying out the behest of their mother.

30. Then out of affection, Kadrū got on to the back of Vinatā and went by the path of the sky. She saw then the solar disc.

31-34. Kadrū then became excessively agitated in her mind due to the ferocity of the Sun. She told the bird: "O Vinatā, proceed gingerly. My body is extremly scorched by the hot rays of the Sun. I am cautious by nature and you are wholly hopeful (*sāpekṣā?*). You are Pataṅgī in form and the Sun is also Pataṅga (a flier). Hence you do not have any affliction in the sky arising from scorching heat. This Sun is a Haṁsa (Swan) in the lake of the sky. You are one with the gait of a Swan. Hence the fierce fire of the hot-rayed Sun does not harm you."

35-37. Again the serpentess said to the bird about to fly high in the sky, "Sister, save me, save me. We shall go away from the path of the sky. O Vinatā, why don't you protect me, humble that I am? You are a bird. I shall be your slave taking in what you leave off after eating. I shall drink the water washing your feet as long as I live."

38. The serpentess then went into a swoon taking hold of the wings (of Vinatā). Where she ought to have said "O friend, a firebrand is about to fall", she became agitated and very falteringly said, "Khakholka may fall".

39. Since the word *Khakholka* was uttered by Kadrū whose mind was extremely agitated, the Sun was diversely eulogized by Vinatā in the name of *Khakholka*.

40. While the Sun proceeded along the sky, he became slightly cool. Then the horse fitted to the chariot was seen slightly dark in colour.

41. The cruel serpentess whose eyes were bedevilled by the heat, was then told by Vinatā who was worthy of being honoured by the world and who spoke the truth:

42-43. "O gentle Kadrū, you have won. Though the horse Uccaiśśravas has the lustre of the rays of the moon, it appears as though it is dark-complexioned.

It is wonderful, O serpentess, that fate is all-powerful in regard to the matters of victory and defeat. The cruel one becomes victorious somewhere and the mild one too becomes the vanquished."

44. Vinatā, the receptacle of humility, said thus as they proceeded ahead. After reaching the abode of Kadrū, she became her slave.

45. Once Vinatā was seen with her eyes filled with tears by Suparṇa (Garuḍa). She was in a wretched condition without the facial colour and purity. She was sighing deeply.

46-50. "Alas, my mother, where do you go in the morning everyday and return in the evening, pale and afflicted in mind?

Wherefor do you sigh deeply with the eyes full of tears like a woman whose sons are impotent and who has been discarded by her husband.

O mother, O winged one, tell me quickly why you are very vexed even as I, your child, am alive, I who have terrified even Kāla (god of Death).

O lady in a pitiable codition! What is the cause of your shedding tears? Nothing inauspicious is expected in a woman of excellent conduct.

Fie upon those sons whose mother is miserable even as they are alive! It would rather be better that she whose sons are ineffective in their ambitions, remain barren and childless."

51. On hearing these forceful words of Garuḍa, her son, Vinatā spoke to the son who was full of devotion to his mother:

52-54. "O my son, I am the slave of Kadrū of cruel mentality. O my son, everyday I bear her and her sons too on my back. Sometimes I go to Mandara, sometimes to Malaya mountain and sometimes to an island with lakes in the famous oceans. Wherever the haughty sons of Kadrū take me I too go, O son, because I am a slave unto them."

Garuḍa said:

55. Oh daughter of Dakṣaprajāpati! O sinless beloved of Kaśyapa! O mother of excellent features, what is the cause of your slavery?

56. Vinatā related to Garuḍa all those previous events that brought about her slavery, along with the fact of seeing the horse of the Sun.

57-58. On hearing this, Garuḍa told his mother: "Go quickly, dear mother, and ask those wicked sons of Kadrū in these words: 'Whatever be the thing for which you have any great desire, even if it be very rare and difficult to be got, you can ask for it in lieu of redeeming me from slavery. I shall give it to you.' "

59. Vinatā did so. On hearing what was uttered by her, the serpents were delighted in their minds. They consulted one another and spoke to her:

60. "If, in order to remove the curse of our mother, he gives us heavenly nectar, you can have what you desire. If he does not give, you continue to be a slave."

61. Accepting that offer and taking leave of Kadrū, the bird of quick motion (Vinatā) saw Garuḍa who was glad in his mind and told him (everything).

62. The enemy of serpents then said to his mother who was excessively worried: "Mother, know that the heavenly nectar

is already brought. Give me my food."

63-67. Vinatā experienced horripilation due to joy and said to her son: "O Suparṇa, go to the ocean quickly. Good luck to you! There are many Niṣāda fishermen with their houses at the seashore. Eat those wicked-souled ones. Those evil-minded ones who live on others' lives, should be chastised assiduously. Their chastisement is very much conducive to welfare. Violence done unto those who indulge in great violence shall be a means to the attainment of heaven, for people are protected when the wicked ones are killed. But, O son, if there is any Brāhmaṇa among those fish-killing Niṣādas, he should be assiduously protected. He is never to be eaten."

Garuḍa said:

68. How can a Brāhmaṇa residing among the fish-eating ones be known and recognized by me? Tell me some significant things about that person who is said by you as one who should not be eaten.

Vinatā said:

69-71. There is a sacred thread free from impurities round his neck along with the upper cloth. The clothes are washed everyday. The forehead is marked by a Tilaka. His hands have the Pavitra. The knot of his cloth keeps Kuśa grass within. His hairs do have a tuft. He is to be known as a Brāhmaṇa by you. He who recites at least one verse from Ṛk, Yajus and Sāman or he who recites the Gāyatrī Mantra should be known by you as a Brāhmaṇa.

Garuḍa said:

72-73. O mother, I do not consider anyone of these things as a significant feature of a Brāhmaṇa who may be living for ever in the midst of the Niṣādas.

Dear mother, tell me another characteristic feature making him known as a Brāhmaṇa, whereby realizing him as a Brāhmaṇa I can free him, should he be caught in my throat.

74-75. On hearing it, Vinatā said: "O my son, cast him off, the person who may scorch you like a burning Khadira charcoal when he is caught up in your throat.

The injury to any Brāhmaṇa is never conducive to welfare. In due course it annihilates the land, the family, the glory and the wealth."

76. On hearing this, the lord of the birds, the son of Kaśyapa, bowed down to the feet of his mother. After taking her blessings he quickly went by the aerial path.

77-78. He saw from a distance the Niṣādas who live on fish. The lord of the birds shook his wings, filled heaven and earth with dust particles. He blinded the various regions of the quarters and finally sat on the seashore opening his mouth widely like a huge cave.

79-81. The Niṣādas who ran helter-skelter due to fear entered his mouth themselves. While they were entering the throat considering it to be their own path, a certain Brāhmaṇa burned his cave-like throat with a scalding touch, like that of a burning charcoal. Thereupon Tārkṣya made those who had previously entered go into the cavity of his belly and realizing the person stationed in the throat and the palate to be a Brāhmaṇa quickly vomited him out, as he was checked by the words of his mother.

82. On seeing the man vomited out, the king of birds spoke, "Who are you by caste? You are burning my throat. Tell me."

83. On being asked, he spoke thus to Garuḍa: "I am a Brāhmaṇa. I live among these Niṣādas making use of my caste alone as sustenance."

84. After sending him away and eating most of the others, Garuḍa, blowing like a violent gust of wind at the time of deluge, made the sky agitated.

85. On seeing him fiery with brilliance, enveloping the quarters with flames and appearing like a mountain with blazing forest fires, heaven-dwellers became afraid.

86. Making the armies and the weapons ready, mounting their respective vehicles and wearing the coats of mail, the Suras got ready for battle.

87-89. The Devas well-versed in polity began to think: 'This person is proceeding obliquely. Hence he is not the Sun. He is not fire which emits smoke (This person does not). He is not lightning (which is momentary). Who is this person who has come in front of us? Such a splendour is not to be found among Daityas. Such a form is not among Dānavas. Who is this that creates terror in us? He is making our heart tremble.' Even as the Devas were puzzled thus, the king of birds of excessive strength shook his wings.

90. Due to the gust of wind raised by his wings (those Suras) fell down along with their weapons and vehicles. It was not known where they were thrown like things made of leaves and grasses.

91. When they had been destroyed, the king of birds pursued intelligently and found out the treasure house of nectar and also the guards thereof.

92. He made those Suras with raised weapons and missiles in their hands, scattered around. Thereafter he saw a mechanical device in the form of scissors placed above the nectar (-receptacle).

93. It was moving rapidly with the speed of mind and wind. Even if a mosquito was to come into contact with it, it would be cut into millions of pieces.

94-100. The lord of birds sat fearlessly near that machine and thought for a moment:

'Oh! what shall I do here? It is not possible to touch this. Even the wind is not powerful enough in this regard. What means is to be employed? Alas, my effort has become fruitless.

Force cannot be effective here nor manliness. Wonderful indeed is the care and effort of Devas in regard to the security of the heavenly nectar.

If my devotion to Śaṅkara is undisputed and steady, may that Lord of Devas bless me with great presence of mind.

If I am devoted to my mother even more than to Śaṅkara. Let my keen intellect be capable of taking away the heavenly nectar.

This effort on my part is not for my own selfish ends. This that omnipresent Lord knows. I am endeavouring for the heavenly nectar to redeem my mother from slavery.

If one's parents are pretty old, if one's children are very young and if one's wife is chaste and loyal, there is no harm even in one's improper act for their sustenance.'

101-104. Even as he thought thus, the noble-souled one had an idea. He made his form minuter than the minutest. He assumed a highly miraculous form, a thousandth of the size of an atom and entered the mechanical device of the scissors below, due to the minuteness of his body. He was afraid of the machine and saved his body from being cut even by the wind therefrom. He uprooted it quickly and seized the receptacle of the heavenly nectar. Even as the heaven-dwellers were shouting, he came out along the path of the wind.

105. The nectar-imbibers (Devas) went to the Lord of Vaikuṇṭha and said, "O Discus-bearing Lord, we are defeated and the nectar, our own very life, is being carried away."

106-107. On hearing this Hari granted them freedom from fear. Hurriedly he fought with him (Garuḍa) a battle on a par with that of the demon Śuṁbha and the Goddess, O Sūta. The great battle lasted for sixty-four Ghaṭikās. Garuḍa was superior therein. The Lord, the bestower of everything, became pleased with the great battle.

108. He went to Garuḍa and said, "O lord of birds, I am delighted. Welfare unto you, the conqueror of the group of Devas. Choose a boon."

109. Garuḍa laughed and said to the omniformed Lord Janārdana, "I too am delighted. You can choose two boons."

110. Thereupon the conqueror of Kaiṭabha delightfully said to the son of Vinatā, "O liberal-minded one, chosen, chosen. Grant me, grant me the two boons."

111-112. On hearing these words utterd by Viṣṇu, the lord of birds laughingly said: "Of what avail is the delay? Hence tell me. The two boons are given, are given. Even if there is no acquisition of profit in a game of dice etc. attended with success and prosperity, a fair-minded one should give (the due) to the deserving one. How can one expect profit and successs always?"

Śrī Viṣṇu said:

113. O lord of birds, you are strong. Hence be my vehicle. O granter of boons, this is one of the boons. O son of Kaśyapa, listen to the second one.

114-115. O wise one, just show to the serpents the nectar brought for the redemption of your mother from slavery. Manage it in such a way that they do not eat it immediately. The heavenly nectar should be given to the Devas. Let this be my second boon.

The lord of birds promised, "So be it" and departed from heaven.

116-119. That son of Kaśyapa released his mother from slavery. He placed the great pot of the heavenly nectar in front of the serpents. The extremely intelligent one spoke to them as they were desirous of drinking the nectar: "O serpents, this splendid nectar should be swallowed after making yourselves clean (after bathing). If not, this nectar, well-preserved by the winkless ones (Devas), is likely to vanish when touched by unclean people devoid of bath etc. If, even an ordinary foodstuff is touched anywhere by unclean people the Devas take away its essential juice and it remains insipid."

120. After saying this and placing the pot of nectar on a mat of Kuśa grass at their request, Garuḍa went out with his mother.

121-122. While the serpents had gone for their bath the pot of nectar was taken away by Viṣṇu and given to Devas as if it were their very life. After their bath, the serpents returned. Not seeing the pot of nectar they shouted: "Alas! We have been cheated. The nectar has been taken away."

123. Thereafter, desirous of contact with the nectar, they licked the Darbha grass. Far from getting the nectar, they got their tongues split into two.

124. In the case of others too, if they are desirous of enjoying something got through illegitimate means, they do not get any chance to enjoy. Their effort does not become fruitful.

125. The very rare Sudhā was obtained by Garuḍa who was ready to abide by just means. Though acquired by the serpents, it disappeared in a moment after being seen, because they had obtained it by unjust means.

126. Then, released from the state of slavery, Vinatā told the sky-walker (Garuḍa): "O son, I will go to Kāśī for eradicating the sin of slavery.

127. Even all those sins incurred in the course of many births, appear to be very great as long as Kāśī, the destroyer of rebirth, is not retained in the heart.

128. What wonder is there that sins disappear merely by thinking of Kāśī? Due to the great blessings of Viśveśvara, even the possibility of rebirth disappears.

129. Where Viśveśvara is directly present, the Lord with

the Moon for an ornament shall redeem the devotees from the ocean of worldly existence through the raft of the Tāraka Mantra.

130. The idea of going to Kāśī shall occur only in the minds of those who are blessed by Viśveśa and whose Karmas have been destroyed. Never does it occur to the minds of the others.

131. Only they are human beings, whose mind is attracted to Kāśī and whose sins have been washed off. It is true that others are beasts in human form.

132. Those alone who have attained Vārāṇasī, have defeated Kāla; only they are free from sins and they have no further birth.

133. One should not waste this human life, the means to the highest good. Without a visit to Kāśī that good is inaccessible even to Devas.

134. If the holy place Avimukta is visited, Kali has no power. What can Kāla do or the different types of Karmas do?

135. Those who do not resort to Varaṇā and Asi capable of striking the forest of frequent births, remain in the womb; they continue to be born in a womb."

136. On hearing these words, Garuḍa said after bowing down to his mother, "I shall also come to visit Kāśī honoured by Śiva."

137. Getting the permission of his mother, the lord of birds, accompanied by his mother, instantaneously reached Vārāṇasī, the place ensuring salvation.

138-140. Both the higly intelligent ones performed very severe penance. The lord of birds with steady sense-organs, installed Śaṁbhu's Liṅga and Vinatā installed the splendid one named Khakholka Āditya. Ere long due to their great penance Lord Śaṅkara and Bhāskara became pleased. Umāpati came out of the Liṅga installed by Garuḍa.

141-146. He granted many rare boons to Garuḍa: "O lord of birds, you are my devotee. You will acquire knowledge. All my secrets not known to the Suras will be understood by you. This Liṅga installed by you is named Garuḍeśvara. If seen, touched and worshipped, it bestows perfect knowledge on men. Listen to one thing more, O lord of birds. I shall tell you something beneficial. You should not see me and Viṣṇu as different. O lord of birds, becoming the vehicle of the Lord, the destroyer of the power of lords of Daityas, you will also be worthy of adoration."

After granting this boon to Garuḍa, his devotee, Śaṁbhu vanished there itself. Garuḍa went to Lord Viṣṇu. Becoming the vehicle of Hari, he became worthy of adoration on the earth.

147-149. Lord Bhāskara, the greatest cosmic form of Śiva and named Khakholka, once saw Vinatā performing penance. He granted her the boon of destruction of sins along with the knowledge of Śiva. He remained there in Kāśī and was named Vinatāditya (also). He destroyed the various sins of the residents of Kāśī. Thus is Khakholka Āditya, the destroyer of darkness and obstacles in Kāśī.

150-151. In Kāśī, in the holy Tīrtha named Paiśaṅgila (Pilipilā Tīrtha), a devotee should visit Khakholka. Merely by the sight thereof, he is freed from all sins. The man attains whatever he thinks of. Instantaneously he becomes free from illness. By listening to this narrative of Khakholka Āditya along with that of Garuḍeśa one is freed from all sins.

: : End of Kāśīkhaṇḍa Pūrvārdha : :

the left corner of the power of lord of Dharma you will also [illegible] worthy of adoration.

After granting this boon to Gaṇeśa, [illegible] ... [illegible] ... the vehicle of [illegible] he became worthy of adoration on the earth.

[illegible] ... [illegible] ... [illegible] ... of Śiva [illegible] ... [illegible] ...

[illegible] ... [illegible] ... [illegible] ...

End of [illegible]

INDEX

ANCIENT INDIAN TRADITION & MYTHOLOGY

Translated by

A BOARD OF SCHOLARS

And Edited by

Dr. G.P. BHATT

VOLUME 58

ANCIENT INDIAN TRADITION AND MYTHOLOGY SERIES

[PURĀṆAS IN TRANSLATION]

VOLUMES

ŚIVA 1-4
LIṄGA 5-6
BHĀGAVATA 7-11
GARUḌA 12-14
NĀRADA 15-19
KŪRMA 20-21
BRAHMĀṆḌA 22-26
AGNI 27-30
VARĀHA 31-32
BRAHMA 33-36
VĀYU 37-38
PADMA 39-48
SKANDA, PARTS I-X, 49-58

VOLUMES UNDER PREPARATION

SKANDA, PARTS XI-XXIV
BHAVIṢYA
BRAHMAVAIVARTA
DEVĪBHĀGAVATA
KĀLIKĀ
MĀRKAṆḌEYA
MATSYA
VĀMANA
VIṢṆU
VIṢṆUDHARMOTTARA